Beards, Azymes, and Purgatory

OXFORD STUDIES IN HISTORICAL THEOLOGY

Series Editor
Richard A. Muller, Calvin Theological Seminary

Founding Editor
David C. Steinmetz†

Editorial Board
Robert C. Gregg, Stanford University
George M. Marsden, University of Notre Dame
Wayne A. Meeks, Yale University
Gerhard Sauter, Rheinische Friedrich-Wilhelms-Universität Bonn
Susan E. Schreiner, University of Chicago
John Van Engen, University of Notre Dame
Robert L. Wilken, University of Virginia

THE SYNOD OF PISTORIA AND VATICAN II
Jansenism and the Struggle for Catholic Reform
Shaun Blanchard

CATHOLICITY AND THE COVENANT OF WORKS
James Ussher and the Reformed Tradition
Harrison Perkins

THE COVENANT OF WORKS
The Origins, Development, and Reception of the Doctrine
J. V. Fesko

RINGLEADERS OF REDEMPTION
How Medieval Dance Became Sacred
Kathryn Dickason

REFUSING TO KISS THE SLIPPER
Opposition to Calvinism in the Francophone Reformation
Michael W. Bruening

FONT OF PARDON AND NEW LIFE
John Calvin and the Efficacy of Baptism
Lyle D. Bierma

THE FLESH OF THE WORD
The extra Calvinisticum *from Zwingli to Early Orthodoxy*
K.J. Drake

JOHN DAVENANT'S HYPOTHETICAL UNIVERSALISM
A Defense of Catholic and Reformed Orthodoxy
Michael J. Lynch

RHETORICAL ECONOMY IN AUGUSTINE'S THEOLOGY
Brian Gronewoller

GRACE AND CONFORMITY
The Reformed Conformist Tradition and the Early Stuart Church of England
Stephen Hampton

MAKING ITALY ANGLICAN
Why the Book of Common Prayer Was Translated into Italian
Stefano Villani

AUGUSTINE ON MEMORY
Kevin G. Grove

UNITY AND CATHOLICITY IN CHRIST
The Ecclesiology of Francisco Suarez, S.J.
Eric J. DeMeuse

RETAINING THE OLD EPISCOPAL DIVINITY
John Edwards of Cambridge and Reformed Orthodoxy in the Later Stuart Church
Jake Griesel

CALVINIST CONFORMITY IN POST-REFORMATION ENGLAND
The Theology and Career of Daniel Featley
Gregory A. Salazar

BEARDS, AZYMES, AND PURGATORY
The Other Issues That Divided East and West
A. Edward Siecienski

Beards, Azymes, and Purgatory

The Other Issues That Divided East and West

A. EDWARD SIECIENSKI

OXFORD
UNIVERSITY PRESS

Oxford University Press is a department of the University of Oxford. It furthers
the University's objective of excellence in research, scholarship, and education
by publishing worldwide. Oxford is a registered trade mark of Oxford University
Press in the UK and certain other countries.

Published in the United States of America by Oxford University Press
198 Madison Avenue, New York, NY 10016, United States of America.

© Oxford University Press 2023

All rights reserved. No part of this publication may be reproduced, stored in
a retrieval system, or transmitted, in any form or by any means, without the
prior permission in writing of Oxford University Press, or as expressly permitted
by law, by license, or under terms agreed with the appropriate reproduction
rights organization. Inquiries concerning reproduction outside the scope of the
above should be sent to the Rights Department, Oxford University Press, at the
address above.

You must not circulate this work in any other form
and you must impose this same condition on any acquirer.

Library of Congress Control Number: 2022018899
ISBN 978-0-19-006506-5

DOI: 10.1093/oso/9780190065065.001.0001

1 3 5 7 9 8 6 4 2

Printed by Integrated Books International, United States of America

*To all those throughout the centuries who worked to
bridge the gap between Christian East and West*

Contents

Preface   ix
Abbreviations   xvii

Introduction   1

I. BEARDS

1. Beards in the Biblical and Patristic Tradition   15
2. Beards in the East-West Polemic   38

II. AZYMES

3. Bread and Leaven in the Biblical and Patristic Tradition   79
4. The Azyme Debate: The Eleventh and Twelfth Centuries   116
5. The Azyme Debate: The Fourth Crusade to the Modern Era   151

III. PURGATORY

6. Purgatory in the Biblical and Patristic Tradition   189
7. Purgatory in the Thirteenth and Fourteenth Centuries   233
8. Purgatory from Ferrara-Florence to Modern Times   275

Bibliography   313
Index   367

Preface

In 2008, while working on *The Filioque: History of a Doctrinal Controversy*, I gave a paper at the annual meeting of the Byzantine Studies Conference (BSC) called "Damn Those Beardless Azymites: Rhetoric and Reality behind the Byzantine Critiques of Latin Christianity." A few years later I presented another paper, "Holy Hair: Beards in the Patristic Tradition," at the 2012 meeting of the North American Patristics Society that, like the earlier talk at the BSC, was greeted with the occasional giggle.[1] This was not an unwelcome response, for both papers were written and presented with tongue firmly in cheek.[2] You see, by this time I had spent several years dealing with the Filioque debates and I thought it might be a fun distraction to speak about the "other issues" that once divided Christendom—the beardlessness of the Western clergy and the Latins' use of unleavened bread (*azymes*) in the mass. These questions, once thought so central to the genesis and maintenance of the East-West schism, were now regarded by most scholars as nothing more than relics of a bygone age—that is, as tools used by medieval polemicists to vilify the religious "other" that, even then, had little or no theological significance. To the twenty-first-century mind it seemed ridiculous that a church-dividing schism should occur on account of beards or different types of Eucharistic bread, and I used that fact in order to elicit a few laughs. As time passed I realized I was probably wrong to do so.

The more I worked through the material, especially as I was researching my second book (*The Papacy and the Orthodox: Sources and History of a Debate*), the more I came to regret the lighthearted way I treated the "other issues" that came to divide Christian East and West. It is true that today the Filioque and the papacy are the two (and perhaps only) significant barriers to restored communion between the Catholic and Orthodox Churches. Yet in working through these questions and examining the literature, it was impossible to escape the conclusion that for centuries the Filioque and papacy were not the only issues at stake, and indeed, for many of the participants in the medieval debates they were not even issues at all. For example, while the Roman primacy was never mentioned during the events of 1054, included in Cardinal Humbert's anathema against Patriarch Michael Keroularios was the charge that "preserving their hair and beards [the Greeks] do not receive into communion those who, according to the custom of the Roman church, cut their hair and shave their beards."[3]

---

[1] An expanded version of this paper was later published as "Holy Hair: Beards in the Patristic Tradition," *St. Vladimir's Theological Quarterly* 58 (2014): 41–67.

[2] Because of its humorous tone one friend continues to regard the "Beards" paper as the best I have ever given, and on several occasions has expressed disappointment that none of my subsequent talks have been as funny.

[3] *Excommunicatio qua feriuntur Michael Caerularius atque ejus sectatores*; Cornelius Will, ed., *Acta et Scripta quae de controversiis ecclesiae graecae et latinae saeculo undecimo composite extant* (Leipzig, 1861), 153–54; Eng. trans.: Deno John Geanakoplos, *Byzantium: Church, Society and Civilization Seen through Contemporary Eyes* (Chicago: University of Chicago Press, 1984), 208–9.

For others the schism was not about the Filioque, but rather caused by the "heresy of the *fermentacei*, which poured scorn on the holy Roman see, or rather the whole Latin and western church, for offering a living sacrifice to God in unleavened bread."[4] Today the schism persists because of the Filioque and the papacy, but it did not begin that way.

By the Council of Ferrara-Florence (1438–39) another issue had raised its head and become an obstacle toward reunion—the Western doctrine of Purgatory. First raised during a thirteenth-century debate between the metropolitan of Corfu, George Bardanes, and a Franciscan friar named Bartholomew, the Latin teaching was viewed with great suspicion by the Greeks, who thought it advocated the sort of universalism once taught by Origen.[5] In fact, of all the issues discussed during the council (among which were the Filioque, *azymes*, and the primacy) it is interesting to note that both sides decided that "the fires of Purgatory" (*ignis purgatorium*) should be discussed first.[6] Purgatory, although introduced rather late as a reason for the schism, had by the fifteenth century taken its place among its chief causes.

Purgatory, beards, and *azymes*—these were the "other issues" that separated East and West that few spoke of anymore. Today there are (quite literally) hundreds of books on the Roman primacy, and over the last fifteen years more than a few on the Filioque, but one has to look very hard for recent books or articles on *azymes*, or clerical beards, or the East-West debates on Purgatory.[7] Even those who have written about these issues tended to view them as historical curiosities rather than as genuine theological problems, or as Tia Kolbaba put it, as cultural differences that only gained "religious significance as the conflict between East and West heated up."[8] Having played so central a role in the genesis of the schism, they had simply receded into the background, not even considered worthy topics for modern-day dialogues between the two churches.

However, if ecumenical dialogue truly aims to heal the millennium-old schism between the Catholic and Orthodox Churches, it will certainly be necessary to retrace the steps that separated them in the first place. Of course, when one asks what actually "caused" the Great Schism, there are a variety of possible answers—divergent theological methodologies and ecclesiological approaches, differences in language and culture, different political systems and ways of reading history—all of which are, to a certain degree, valid. Yet there is another level where one is forced to admit that the immediate cause of the schism was the simple fact that half the church used leavened

---

[4] *The Life of Pope Leo IX* in Ian Robinson, ed. and trans., *The Papal Reform of the Eleventh Century: Lives of Pope Leo IX and Pope Gregory VII*, Manchester Medieval Sources (Manchester: Manchester University Press, 2004), 146.

[5] Martiniano Roncaglia, ed., *Georges Bardanès, métropolite de Corfou et Barthélémy de l'ordre franciscain*, Studi e Testi Francescani 4 (Rome: Scuola tipografica italo-orientale, 1953).

[6] Joseph Gill, ed., *Quae supersunt Actorum Graecorum Concilii Florentini: Res Ferrariae gestae*, CF 5.1.1 (Rome: Pontifical Oriental Institute, 1953), 19.

[7] There are, of course, notable exceptions, many of which I utilized in the writing of this book. These include, but are not limited to, the works of Yury Avvakumov and Chris Schabel on *azymes*, Christopher Oldstone-Moore on beards, and Jerry Walls, Vasileios Marinis, and Demetrios Bathrellos on Purgatory. Older works, such as Jacques Le Goff's *The Birth of Purgatory*, Mahlon Smith's *And Taking Bread . . .* , and Giles Constable's "Introduction on Beards in the Middle Ages" were also invaluable.

[8] Tia Kolbaba, *The Byzantine Lists: Errors of the Latins* (Chicago: University of Illinois Press, 2000), 57.

bread and the other unleavened bread. One is forced to admit that beards (or their lack) among the clergy was seen as reason for breaking Eucharistic communion. One is forced to admit that divergent understandings of the soul's fate after death helped poison the last attempt at repairing the breach at Ferrara-Florence. The "other issues" cannot, and should not, be laughed off.

It was for this reason that I decided to write the present book, essentially completing the trilogy I began over a decade ago with *The Filioque*. The idea was simple—three books that would cover all of the issues that had separated Christian East and West, allowing the reader to trace the history of these debates from their beginning to the present. The big difference was that the third book would deal with issues that, unlike the Filioque and the papacy, did not appear very often in ecumenical dialogues or internet discussion forums. To put it simply, I did not have to convince anyone familiar with the history of Catholic-Orthodox relations that the papacy was still an important ecumenical issue. Beards were going to be a tougher sell.

In choosing only three topics—Purgatory, clerical beards, and *azymes*—I was consciously avoiding a host of other issues raised in the millennium-old debate between East and West. In fact, when one studies the Byzantine lists of Latin errors drawn up between the eleventh and fifteenth centuries, one discovers dozens of other differences cited as reasons for breaking communion with the West—Konstantinos Stilbes's "On the Faults of the Latin Church" found no fewer than seventy-five! For over a thousand years polemicists on both sides had kept busy cataloguing the errors of their Latin or Greek counterparts, and they did their job remarkably well. According to the Byzantines the Latins fasted improperly (especially during Lent), ate unclean foods, stood and sat at the wrong time during the liturgy, and crossed themselves incorrectly. Their bishops wore rings and silken vestments, and because they forbade their clergy to marry, many priests engaged in secret fornication under the bedcovers, allowing them to pretend that ejaculation was caused by "a dream and a sleeping fantasy which they [then] hold blameless."[9] According to some of the lists, the Latins did not properly revere the *Theotokos* (calling her instead simply "Mary ... [like] the Nestorians and the Jacobites"), the Greek fathers, or the icons, a charge given legitimacy by their behavior inside Byzantine churches during the sack of Constantinople in 1204.[10]

Naturally the Latins had their own grievances—aside from their refusal to acknowledge the orthodoxy of the *filioque* and the primacy of the Roman pontiff, they complained that the Greeks "castrate their guests and promote them not only to the priesthood but even to the episcopate, ... permit and defend [carnal] marriage for ministers of the holy altar ... [and deny] communion to menstruating women or those about to give birth."[11] Greek priests did not consecrate wine mixed with water, but rather (incorrectly) added water to the wine only after the consecration, rebaptized Latin Christians as if they were pagans, and administered the holy chrism as if they were bishops.

---

[9] Jean Darrouzès, ed., "Le mémoire de Constantin Stilbès contre les Latins," *Revue des études byzantines* 2 (1963): 70; Eng. trans.: Kolbaba, *The Byzantine Lists*, 40.

[10] Kolbaba, *The Byzantine Lists*, 51–53.

[11] *Excommunicatio qua feriuntur Michael Caerularius atque ejus sectatores*; Will, *Acta et Scripta*, 153–54; Eng. trans.: Geanakoplos, *Byzantium*, 208–9.

Any one of these charges, to the degree that they were factually true, could be included in a volume like this. One could also add those issues that arose only much later in Catholic-Orthodox relations, including the debate about the precise moment of consecration (i.e., the *epiclesis* debate)[12] and the two Marian dogmas of the Catholic Church: the Immaculate Conception (1854) and the Bodily Assumption of Mary (1950).[13] In fact, there are no shortage of issues one could explore if one went searching for them—for example, the Gregorian versus Julian calendar, the allegedly diverse metaphysical/philosophical approaches of the East and West[14]—any of which could be cited as a genuinely church-dividing difference.

Among the reasons I limited myself to these particular three issues was, first of all, the time period involved. I wanted to deal only with those questions that were part of the eleventh- to fifteenth-century debates leading up to the Council of Ferrara-Florence, the last great encounter between East and West prior to the twentieth century. This time frame naturally precluded the Marian dogmas, while the *epiclesis* debate was just beginning in the fifteenth century and had not yet ripened into a genuinely church-dividing issue by the Council of Florence. The question of Purgatory was still relatively "new" in 1438, but its presence among the five key topics discussed at the council, and its subsequent importance in both Eastern and Western theology, both argue for its inclusion.

The second reason was relevance. Even a cursory examination of the literature is enough to convince the reader that for the medievals the Latins' use of unleavened bread was the immediate cause of the schism and remained for centuries the chief difference between the two halves of Christendom. For the Greeks, "azymite" became (along with "Frank") the chief referent for the Latins and their unionist allies. For example, when the Florentine delegates arrived back in Constantinople in February 1440, already regretting their signatures on the union decree, they allegedly cried out: "We have betrayed our faith. We have exchanged piety for impiety. We have renounced the pure sacrifice and become azymites."[15] The people's response was equally revealing: "We need neither the aid of the Latins nor Union. Keep the worship of the azymites far from us."[16]

---

[12] We see this clearly in the *Commentary on the Divine Liturgy* of Nicholas Cabasilas (d. 1392): "Certain Latins attack us thus: they claim that, after the words of the Lord 'Take and eat' and what follows, there is no need of any further prayer to consecrate the offerings, since they are already consecrated by the Lord's word. They maintain that to pronounce these words of Christ and then to speak of bread and wine and to pray for their consecration as if they had not already been hallowed, is not only impious but also futile and unnecessary." Nicholas Cabasilas, *Commentary on the Divine Liturgy*, trans. J. M. Hussey and P. A. McNulty (London: SPCK, 1960), 71–72. There is evidence from Cyprus that this was already a matter of contention by the 1310s.

[13] See, for example, the works of Christiaan Kappes, *The Immaculate Conception: Why Thomas Aquinas Denied, While John Duns Scotus, Gregory Palamas, & Mark Eugenicus Professed the Absolute Immaculate Existence of Mary* (New Bedford, MA: Academy of the Immaculate, 2014).

[14] See David Bradshaw, *Aristotle East and West: Metaphysics and the Division of Christendom* (Cambridge: Cambridge University Press, 2007).

[15] Doukas, *Decline and Fall of Byzantium to the Ottoman Turks (Historia Turco-Byzantina)*, trans. Harry Magoulias (Detroit: Wayne State University Press, 1975), 181. See George Demacopoulos, "The Popular Reception of the Council of Florence in Constantinople (1439–1453)," *St. Vladimir's Theological Quarterly* 43 (1999): 37–53.

[16] Doukas, *Decline and Fall of Byzantium*, 204–05.

I will admit that clerical beardlessness does not so easily fit into this last category despite the fact that it was featured in Humbert's *Anathema*, Michael Keroularios's *Letter to Peter of Antioch*, and over half the lists of Latin errors.[17] Yet what is fascinating about the beard debate is how this seemingly inconsequential cultural difference—Greeks had beards while the Latins did not—became endowed with such deep theological significance. For the Byzantines beardlessness manifested a clear "Judaizing" tendency within Latin Christianity, as well as a willingness to violate the "apostolic institutions" and the "ancient canons" of the undivided church. Whether any of this was true, and whether clerical beards actually carried theological significance, will be explored in subsequent chapters, but it cannot be denied that many of those involved in the debate genuinely believed it was.

The third reason was personal. Over the last decade I have plowed through a great deal of primary and secondary literature concerning the East-West schism and its causes. Although focusing my attention on the Filioque and the papacy, I have read a great deal on these other subjects and increasingly wanted to learn more about how these debates affected the course of events. Simply put, having spent so much time in my peripheral vision, I wanted to give beards, *azymes*, and Purgatory the focus and attention I thought they deserved. Lest this sound like simple self-indulgence, let me say that I also became convinced that these debates still had something to contribute to East-West ecumenical dialogue. For in the midst of all the heated exchanges, many of which manifested an appalling lack of Christian charity, there were those who were able to distinguish genuinely problematic issues (like the Filioque) from those other questions (like beards and the *azymes*) that so occupied the polemicists. Even Photios, revered today in the East as a great defender of the Orthodox faith, knew that "a definition issued by a local church can be followed by some and ignored by others. Thus some people customarily shave their beards while others reject this practice through local conciliar decree."[18] Patriarch Peter III of Antioch (1052–56) and Theophylact of Ohrid (d. 1107) likewise condemned those who "through unmeasured zeal ... and lack of humility" accused the Latins of all sorts of heresies, despite the fact that many of their charges were either laughably erroneous or based on nothing but differences in custom.[19] Moderation and charity, while rare qualities in the age of polemics, did exist, allowing figures on both sides to recognize the fundamental truth that not every difference in theology or practice need be church-dividing.

---

[17] In a private email to the author, Yury P. Avvakumov suggested that beards might better be handled "as one issue among many other questions of this type, i.e., controversial questions about ritual (including but not limited to: baptismal formula, zeon, Sabbath fasting, singing of alleluia, blood consumption, time and minister of chrismation, administering the Eucharist to infants, clerical marriage, etc., etc.—practically all those numerous issues that are mentioned in the lists of Latin errors) ... I think these issues constitute a special type of controversial questions—the 'ritual type' which deserve further discussion and interpretation." For Dr. Avvakumov's own treatment of ritual studies as it relates to the schism see his "Die Fragen des Ritus als Streit- und Kontroversgegenstand. Zur Typologie der Kulturkonflikte zwischen dem lateinischen Westen und dem byzantinisch-slawischen Osten im Mittelalter und in der Neuzeit," in Rainer Bendel, ed., *Kirchen- und Kulturgeschichtsschreibung in Nordost- und Ostmitteleuropa. Initiativen, Methoden, Theorien* (Münster: LIT Verlag, 2006), 191–233.

[18] Photios of Constantinople, *Letter to Pope Nicholas I of Rome* (*Epistle* 2) (PG 102: 604–5); Eng. trans.: John Meyendorff, *Living Tradition* (Crestwood, NY: St. Vladimir's Seminary Press, 1978), 24. See also Jack Turner, "Was Photios an Anti-Latin? Heresy and Liturgical Variation in the Encyclical to the Eastern Patriarchs," *Journal of Religious History* 40 (2016): 475–89.

[19] Theophylact of Ohrid, *De Iis in quibus Latini Accusantur* (PG 126: 224).

Today two of these debates, concerning *azymes* and beards, are thought by most to be over. Even the more fervent anti-ecumenists among the Orthodox find it hard to make the case that these are still reasons for refusing communion with the Catholic Church, perhaps explaining their absence from modern-day dialogues and debates. Purgatory is a different matter, as it remains at issue in the (extremely interesting) intra-Orthodox debates about the state of souls after death, especially the legitimacy of the τελώνια, or "toll-house," tradition,[20] and David Bentley Hart's call to re-examine the possibility of universal salvation.[21] Nevertheless, while maintaining its historic objections to the Latin doctrine of Purgatory as defined and explained at Ferrara-Florence, contemporary Orthodox thinking on the afterlife is not that dissimilar from the modern Catholic position, which today "understands purgatory in terms often more similar to those of Mark [of Ephesus] and the Greeks than to their Latin predecessors."[22] The debate over Purgatory is not over, but it certainly does not generate the "heat" it did centuries ago.

As with its predecessors, this book attempts to trace the history of these three debates—Purgatory, clerical beards, *azymes*—from their beginnings to the present day, chronicling not only their development as doctrines or practices, but also the context in which the Latin or Greek response was framed. Context, as always, is key. For example, the first Greek critiques of the *azymes*, inspired in part by Byzantine interaction with the Armenians, came at a time when the pope was becoming increasingly self-aware of his universal role as "pastor and teacher of all Christians." Cardinal Humbert's subsequent attacks upon the Byzantines as "impudent" and "bold" can only be understood in this light, as he thought it the height of presumption to teach the Roman church how to celebrate the Lord's Supper, "as if the Heavenly Father has hidden from Peter, the Prince of apostles, the proper rite of the visible sacrifice."[23] This is primarily a work of dogmatic history, but the political, cultural, and ecclesiological background of the East-West "estrangement" cannot and will not be forgotten.

For the biblical and patristic material, I was able to avail myself of resources that the participants in these debates did not always have on hand. Medieval authors arguing over the fate of souls did not have critical editions of the fathers to consult, which is why so much effort was wasted debating the authenticity of texts, many of which were indeed spurious.[24] In this book I have tried to utilize the most recent critical editions and translations when I could, although many of the works cited can still only be found in the *Patrologia Graeca* (PG) or *Patrologia Latina* (PL). Where there are English-language

---

[20] See, for example, Michael Azkoul, *Aerial Toll-House Myth: The Neo-Gnosticism of Fr Seraphim Rose* (Dewdney, BC: Synaxis Press, 2005); Lazar Puhalo, *The Soul, the Body and Death* (Dewdney, BC: Synaxis Press, 2013); Lazar Puhalo, *The Tale of Elder Basil "The New" and the Theodora Myth: Study of a Gnostic Document and a General Survey of Gnosticism* (Dewdney, BC: Synaxis Press, 1999); Seraphim Rose, *The Soul after Death* (Platina, CA: St. Herman of Alaska Brotherhood, 2009); St Anthony's Greek Orthodox Monastery, *The Departure of the Soul According to the Teaching of the Orthodox Church* (Florence, AZ: St Anthony's Greek Orthodox Monastery, 2017).

[21] David Bentley Hart, *That All Shall Be Saved: Heaven, Hell, and Universal Salvation* (New Haven: Yale University Press, 2019).

[22] Demetrios Bathrellos, "Love, Purification, and Forgiveness versus Justice, Punishment, and Satisfaction: The Debates on Purgatory and the Forgiveness of Sins at the Council of Ferrara-Florence," *Journal of Theological Studies*, NS 65 (2014): 120–21.

[23] Leo IX, *Epistola ad Michaelem Constantinopolitanum Archiepiscoporum* in Will, *Acta et Scripta*, 68.

[24] The patristic quotations employed by Thomas Aquinas to defend Purgatory in his *Contra Errores Graecorum*, most of which were taken verbatim from the *Libellus de fide ss. Trinitatis* of Nicholas of Cotrone,

translations I have utilized them, occasionally adding the original Greek or Latin when clarity demanded it. Through an email exchange with Dr. Christopher Oldstone-Moore, who kindly put me in contact with Katie Derrig, I was fortunate enough to gain access to her unpublished translations of Ratramnus and Aeneas of Paris that she had done for the book *Of Beards and Men*. Dr. Jeff Brubaker provided advance copies of his translation of the 1234 debates, soon to be published by Liverpool University Press. All other translations are my own unless otherwise noted.

I would like to thank the library staff at Stockton University for their assistance in obtaining many of these primary and secondary sources that I used while writing, many of which were only obtainable through the Interlibrary Loan system. Much of this book was written in 2020 and 2021, when the Covid-19 pandemic made access to materials quite difficult, making their job even harder. Several authors were kind enough to send their books or articles directly to me during this time, including Drs. Alessandra Bucossi, Angel Nikolov, and Nicholas Zola, all of whom have earned my enduring gratitude. Drs. Andrea Riedl and Matt Briel answered several questions about particular texts, helping me to understand and handle the material better. Dr. Tia Kolbaba along with Dr. Jeff Brubaker read draft chapters of the book, providing insights that were key in improving the final product. Drs. Yury P. Avvakumov, Christopher Schabel, and Demetrios Bathrellos not only sent me books and articles during lockdown, but also graciously read and commented upon the azyme and Purgatory material, areas in which they are quite rightly regarded as experts. I would also like to thank my dear friend, Dr. Allan Austin at Misericordia University, who, as he did with my other books, read through the manuscript and made invaluable suggestions in order to make the work more accessible to a wider readership. My colleagues in the Philosophy/Religion Program at Stockton University—Drs. Rodger Jackson, Anne Pomeroy, Lucio Privitello, and Jongbok Yi—have always been supportive of my work and have, through their kindnesses to me, made it possible to devote time to the necessary research.

My parents, Edward and Terri Siecienski, have continued to be a source of support and inspiration, and my mother-in-law, Martha Matwijcow, can always be counted upon when help is needed with the children. Of course, my children, Alex and Alana, are getting older now and no longer need "babysitting"—they are in high school and have even begun to ask questions about my work. While the questions about the afterlife were occasionally perspective-changing, our dinner table conversations about beards were (quite frankly) more fun. Last, I want to thank my wife, Kiev, whose strength and love provide the foundations for everything I have been able to accomplish, both at home and at work.

> A capable wife who can find? She is far more precious than jewels.
> The heart of her husband trusts in her, and he will have no lack of gain.
> (Proverbs 31:10–11)

---

were either corrupted or completely spurious. See Antoine Dondaine, "Nicolas de Cotrone et la sources du *Contra errores Graecorum* de Saint Thomas," *Divus Thomas* 29 (1950): 313–40; Mark Jordan, "Theological Exegesis and Aquinas' Treatise 'Against the Greeks,'" *Church History* 56 (1987): 445–56.

Abbreviations

ACW	Ancient Christian Writers
ANF	Ante-Nicene Fathers
CCCM	Corpus Christianorum Continuatio Mediaevalis
CCG	Corpus Christianorum Series Graeca
CCL	Corpus Christianorum Series Latina
CF	Concilium Florentinum: Documenta et Scriptores
CSCO	Corpus of Oriental Christian Writers
FC	Fathers of the Church
MGH	Monumenta Germaniae Historica
NPNF	Nicene and Post-Nicene Fathers
PG	Patrologia Graeca
PL	Patrologia Latina
SC	Sources chrétiennes

Introduction

In 1576, as the Protestant Reformation continued to sweep across Western Europe and Catholic prelates tried to stem the tide through diligent application of Trent's reforming agenda,[1] the cardinal archbishop of Milan, Charles Borromeo (1538–1584) penned a letter to his clergy. In order to restore the church to its former glory, he enjoined his "beloved brethren" to "bring back good observances and holy customs which have grown cold and been abandoned over the course of time."[2] Chief among them, he wrote, was a custom that, although ancient, had been "practically lost nearly everywhere in Italy.... I mean the practice that ecclesiastical persons not grow, but rather shave the beard.... a custom of our Fathers, almost perpetually retained in the Church" that was "replete with mystical meanings."[3] Yet Borromeo knew that a clean-shaven face was of little good unless "accompanied by a true resolution to execute and put into practice the things that are signified by this custom," for it would be a "source of shame to us to have an external appearance different from laymen if we are going to be no different in our habits from worldly people.... With our disdain for this common decoration of the face, let us renounce all vain human adornments and glories."[4]

Borromeo was certainly right to worry that this practice had largely been lost, for since the pontificate of Julius II (1503–13), who had vowed to grow his beard as a response to the loss of Bologna, beards had begun to reappear among the Western clergy after an absence of almost 140 years.[5] Martin Luther, while disguised as "Junker Jörg" in 1521, grew out his beard (although he later chose to remain clean-shaven), and subsequent Protestants came to see facial hair as a sign of both manliness and resistance to Rome.[6] By the time of Clement VII (1523–34), whose own beard of mourning was a response to the 1527 sack of Rome by imperial troops, a new, hairier era was dawning in Western Europe. In 1531 Pope Clement gave permission for all priests to grow beards, a policy defended by Pierio Valeriano, whose now famous *Pro sacerdotum*

---

[1] The Council of Trent, which met intermittently between 1545 and 1563, tried to rid the Catholic Church of many of the abuses (e.g., concubinage, sale of indulgences) that had occasioned such fierce Protestant attacks.

[2] Charles Borromeo, *Selected Orations, Homilies, and Writings*, ed. and trans. John Clark and Ansgar Santogrossi (London: Bloomsbury T&T Clark, 2017), 97.

[3] Ibid., 96.

[4] Ibid., 99, 101.

[5] Christopher Oldstone-Moore, *Of Beards and Men: The Revealing History of Facial Hair* (Chicago: University of Chicago Press, 2017), 108.

[6] Luther later said: "The original sin in a man is like his beard, which, though shaved off today so that a man is very smooth around his mouth, yet grows again by tomorrow morning. As long as a man lives, such growth of the hair and the beard does not stop. But when the shovel beats the ground on his grave, it stops. Just so original sin remains in us and bestirs itself as long as we live, but we must resist it and always cut off its hair." Martin Luther, *What Luther Says: An Anthology*, ed. Ewald M. Plass (St. Louis: Concordia Publishing House, 1959), 1302–3.

barbis apologia (*An Apology in Favor of Priestly Beards*) provided justification for the new practice.[7] By Borromeo's time beards, not the clean-shaven face, were the norm among the clergy although some (unsuccessfully) tried to stem the tide. In France the universities and law courts required professors and judges to shave, while King Francis I placed a special tax on clerics who grew out their beards. The French bishops could easily afford the tax and kept their beards, but many of the priests could not, causing a great deal of resentment among the lower clergy. According to one (possibly spurious) story, when Guillaume Duprat (1507–1560), bishop-elect of Clermont and allegedly owner of the finest beard in the kingdom, went to take possession of his cathedral, he found the doors of the church barred against him. He was then confronted by the dean and canons of the cathedral, who showed him a razor, scissors, soap, and a shaving bowl, telling him that he would not be allowed in the church until he had been properly shaved. Duprat, grieved at the possible loss of so fine a beard, gave up his bishopric and retreated to his family's estate where, two days later, he allegedly died of "vexation."[8]

What is astounding about all of these shifts for and against bearded clergy is that they occurred only a few decades after the Council of Ferrara-Florence (1438/39), when bearded Greeks and beardless Latins sat across from one another in order to heal the centuries-old rift between East and West. Although beards were not on the agenda at Florence, the beardlessness of the Latin clergy had long been one of the chief differences between the two churches, often cited by both sides as one of the original reasons for the schism. At the top of that council's agenda were the theology of the procession and the addition of the Filioque to the creed, thought by most to be the weightiest issues at stake.[9] Days and weeks were spent haggling over the authenticity of a few disputed texts, each side hoping to persuade the other that their position was the more orthodox. When the Byzantines, worn down by the mounting patristic evidence, eventually came to accept the orthodoxy of the Latin position, it did not usher in a new golden age of unity. The teachings of *Laetentur Caeli* on the procession, imposed upon a weary Greek delegation with little consideration ever given to its reception by the Byzantine population, were too "foreign" ever to be accepted in the East. The Greeks' eventual rejection of the council was a foregone conclusion, for the Latins, in their desire for complete victory, had sowed the seeds of their ultimate failure.

Interestingly, the role of the papacy, considered today to be "the only seriously debated theological issue"[10] between East and West, was treated almost as an afterthought at Florence.[11] As early as Pope Leo I (440–61) there had been questions about

---

[7] The work was soon translated into English as *A treatise vvriten by Iohan Valerian a greatte clerke of Italie, which is intitled in latin Pro sacerdotum barbis translated in to Englysshe* (1533).

[8] Reginald Reynolds, *Beards: An Omnium Gatherum* (London: George Allen & Unwin, 1950), 193. Reynolds himself doubts the veracity of the story, since Duprat was appointed bishop of Clermont in 1529 and did not die until 1560.

[9] For the history of the Filioque debates see A. Edward Siecienski, *The Filioque: History of a Doctrinal Controversy* (Oxford: Oxford University Press, 2010); Bernd Oberdorfer, *Filioque: Geschichte und Theologie eines ökumenischen Problems* (Göttingen: Vandenhoeck & Rupert, 2001).

[10] Walter Kasper, *That They May All Be One: The Call to Unity Today* (London: Burns and Oates, 2004), 19.

[11] For more on the papacy as an issue in East-West relations see A. Edward Siecienski, *The Papacy and the Orthodox: Sources and History of a Debate* (Oxford: Oxford University Press, 2017).

the primacy of Rome, the reasons for it, and the limits (if any) on the powers attached to it. By the time of Leo IX (1049–54) the popes had become conscious of a unique universal mission demanding an authority without geographical boundaries, while the East held on to the idea that the bishop of Rome was simply first among the patriarchs and not, in any way, "head of the church." These two ecclesiological visions collided following the Fourth Crusade (1204), as the Byzantines came face to face with the realities of the reformed papacy and rejected it in increasingly strident terms. As with the Filioque, at Florence the Greeks reluctantly came to accept the Latins' understanding (albeit with small concessions made to the pentarchy), but this too was an illusory unity. For many in the Orthodox world, even to the present day, rejection of the papacy has become the shibboleth of the "correct" faith.

There were two other issues on the agenda at Ferrara-Florence, issues that today are rarely discussed or debated—the West's use of unleavened bread (*azymes*) in the Eucharist and the Latin doctrine of Purgatory. The first of these, the use of unleavened bread, had always been a much bigger issue for the East, as almost all Latins were happy to admit that the type of bread used in the Eucharist was a matter of some indifference. For centuries the Greeks had argued that unleavened bread "differ[ed] not from a lifeless stone or a brick of clay" and symbolized the "misery and grief" of the Jews, whereas the leavened bread of the Byzantines was "joy and mirth entire ... elevat[ing] us from the earth through joy to heaven, as even the leaven does to the bread through its own heat."[12] For them the Latins' mass was a "dead sacrifice" that proved "that they were under the shadow of the ancient Torah and eat a Jewish meal rather than the Logos-filled and living flesh of God."[13] Aside from this, the Byzantines maintained that the use of leavened bread had been the long-standing practice of the universal church, and thus the West's decision to change to unleavened bread was a "novelty"—one of the most damning criticisms they could offer—signaling the Latins' embrace of some sort of Judaizing tendency or heterodox teaching—the most common being monophysitism (i.e., the belief that Christ had only one nature), since the Armenians, who also used unleavened bread, were accused of the same heresy.[14]

Of the five issues under discussion at Ferrara-Florence, Purgatory was the most recent, having only been raised in 1231 or 1236 during a debate between the metropolitan of Corfu, George Bardanes, and a Franciscan friar named Bartholomew.[15] The Latin teaching sounded strange to Byzantine ears, especially the notion of a "purgatorial fire" (*ignis purgatorius* or πῦρ ποργατόριον) that seemed to raise the specter

---

[12] Leo of Ohrid, *Epistula ad Ioannem Episcopum Tranensem*, in *Erzbischof Leon von Ohrid (1037–1056): Leben und Werk (mit den Texten seiner bisher unedierten asketischen Schrift und seiner drei Briefe an den Papst)*, ed. Elmar Büttner (Bamberg: Elmar Büttner, 2007), 180–93; Eng. trans.: Joseph Ahmad, *Epistle of the Bishop of Bulgaria Sent to a Certain Bishop under Rome regarding Matzos (Azymes) and Sabbaths*, https://www.academia.edu/39045414/Leo_of_Ochrid_1st_Epistle_to_John_of_Trani_on_azymes_1054_DRAFT, accessed March 20, 2022.

[13] Peter III of Antioch, *Epistola ad Dominicum Gradensem*, in Will, *Acta et Scripta*, 208–28; Eng. trans.: Mahlon Smith, *And Taking Bread ... Cerularius and the Azymite Controversy of 1054*, Théologie Historique 47 (Paris: Beauchesne, 1978), 56 n. 72.

[14] For more on this charge see Tia Kolbaba, "Byzantines, Armenians, and Latins: Unleavened Bread and Heresy in the Tenth Century," in George Demacopoulos and Aristotle Papanikolaou, eds., *Orthodox Constructions of the West* (New York: Fordham University Press, 2013), 45–57.

[15] For questions about dating this encounter see Dragaş-Gabriel Mîrşanu, "Dawning Awareness of the Theology of Purgatory in the East: A Review of the Thirteenth Century," *Studii Teologice* 4 (2008): 181.

of Origenism—that is, if everyone could be cleansed after death, then it was possible for all to be saved. The problem, of course, is that while the Latins had spent centuries refining their beliefs about the world to come, the Byzantines had not, which explains why in debate the Greeks often had problems articulating their own position regarding the afterlife.[16] In fact, one of the real achievements of Florence was that it gave Mark of Ephesus (1392–1445), making "his most significant contribution to the Florentine Council," the opportunity to present a positive Byzantine statement on the fate of souls after death.[17] Although there remains some intra-Orthodox debate about certain aspects of the afterlife (e.g., the τελώνια, or "tollhouse," tradition), Mark's writings on the subject remain very much an important part of the Orthodox tradition.

These "other issues"—clerical beards, *azymes*, Purgatory—do not get the attention that the Filioque and the papacy have gotten, mostly because hierarchs and scholars have (perhaps rightly) decided that they do not have the same theological significance.[18] After all, the Filioque concerns "God's mode of subsistence as Trinity, so central a Christian doctrine that to deny the orthodox position (whatever that may be) placed one outside community of faith."[19] While the debate about the primacy is about power and authority, it is also a theological debate about "a vision of the Church willed by Christ himself, hardly an issue one can simply ignore."[20] Conversely these medieval battles about beards and bread strike the modern Christian as theologically and ecumenically insignificant, and therefore as issues best left to historians. In short, if we have forgotten them it is because they are forgettable.

Yet to write off these other issues completely just because they are not on the same level as the Filioque and the papacy would be to ignore an inescapable historical truth—for the Christians who first began to identify their Latin or Greek counterparts as the religious "other," these issues were just as important as, if not more important than, the ones we currently regard as church-dividing. This was especially true of the *azymes*, for as John Erickson once observed, "For most Byzantine churchmen of the eleventh and twelfth century, the principal point of disagreement with the Latins was not papal primacy or even the *filioque*, but rather the use of unleavened bread in the Eucharist."[21] Even during the crusades, as increased contact allowed the Byzantines to see all of the "horrible infirmities" of the Latin Church, Patriarch John the Oxite of Antioch wrote that "the chief and primary cause of the division between them and

---

[16] This same dynamic had been operative in the Filioque debate, namely, "that the East found itself consistently *reacting* to the West, addressing themselves to positions centuries after they had first been articulated and long after they had become established teaching. This delay put the Byzantines at a distinct tactical disadvantage, since their Latin counterparts almost always came to the table better prepared and with the benefit of doctrinal unanimity." Siecienski, *The Filioque*, 9–10.

[17] Constantine Tsirpanlis, *Mark Eugenicus and the Council of Florence: An Historical Re-evaluation of His Personality* (New York: Kentron Buzantinwn Ereunwn, 1979), 77.

[18] Concerning azymes it has long been noted that "despite the issue's obvious historical significance in the Middle Ages ... most modern scholars have paid little attention to the details of the medieval disputes." Chris Schabel, "The Quarrel over Unleavened Bread in Western Theology, 1234–1439," in Martin Hinterberger and Chris Schabel, eds., *Greeks, Latins, and Intellectual History, 1204–1500* (Leuven: Peeters, 2011), 87.

[19] Siecienski, *The Filioque*, 5.

[20] Siecienski, *The Papacy*, xi.

[21] John Erickson, "Leavened and Unleavened: Some Theological Implications of the Schism of 1054," in *The Challenge of Our Past* (Crestwood: St. Vladimir's Seminary Press, 1991), 134.

us [remains] the matter of the *azymes* ... [for] it involves in summary form the whole question of true piety."[22] As late as the fifteenth century, after union was (briefly) achieved at Florence, it is interesting to note that when the Latins celebrated a solemn liturgy of thanksgiving, not one member of the Byzantine delegation received the sacrament confected with unleavened bread. Recognizing the legitimacy of *azymes* was bad enough, but receiving the unleavened host was unthinkable.[23]

Thus if one wants to understand the schism between East and West, or (going even further) to try to heal it, one is forced to deal not only with the reasons it remains, but also with the reasons it began. These disagreements about bread, beards, and the state of souls after death may not appear to be church-dividing issues today, but they are nevertheless among the reasons the church is divided. This was a schism over *azymes* long before it was a schism over the primacy, and the beardlessness of the Latin clergy was cited as a reason for breaking communion with Rome prior to all the subsequent arguments about the orthodoxy and liceity of the Filioque in the creed.[24] If today we can differentiate the properly theological reasons for the schism (Filioque, papacy) from issues based on cultural or practical differences, it is only because over the centuries we have (for the most part) learned how to distinguish polemics from theology. During the centuries that the East-West schism developed and hardened, there were very few figures who could, which explains in large part how we got where we are today.

Clerical Beards

Surprising as it may sound, early Christian literature addressed the issue of men's beards, both as a positive and as a negative, quite often, usually in conjunction with the biblical prohibition against long or styled hair. In their writings the fathers cited such passages as Leviticus 19:27 ("Do not cut the hair at the sides of your head or clip off the edges of your beard") and 1 Corinthians 11:14 ("Does not nature itself teach you that if a man has long hair it is a disgrace to him"), both of which spoke directly to the subject. Naturally there were cultural and regional differences that affected how the fathers viewed beards. For many (perhaps most) of the early church fathers beards were a positive thing, associated with manliness and its associated virtues. To shave the beard, and appear like a young boy or a woman, often carried with it the implication that one wanted to play this role in some sort of "unnatural" sexual act. One sees this especially in the writings of Clement of Alexandria, who wrote that men who

---

[22] John IV Oxita, *De azymis* 2; Bernard Leib, *Deux inédits byzantins sur les azymes au début du XIIe siècle*, Contribution à l'histoire des discussions theologiques entre grecs et latins (Rome: Pontificio Instituto Orientale, 1924), 113; Eng. trans.: Kallistos Ware, *Eustratios Argenti: A Study of the Greek Church under Turkish Rule* (Oxford: Clarendon Press, 1964), 113.

[23] Mark of Ephesus later chided the Greek unionists for this, writing, "And they say together with them [i.e., the Latins] that unleavened bread is the Body of Christ, and yet together with us do not dare to accept it." Mark of Ephesus, *Encyclical Letter to All Orthodox Christians on the Mainland and in the Islands* (Boston, MA: Romiosyne, 2013), 3.

[24] Although the Filioque had been an issue during the so-called Photian Schism (863–67), it was only after Cardinal Humbert accused the Greeks of *omitting* it from their creed that it became for the East the chief theological difference between the churches.

shaved or adorned their hair only did so for one of two reasons, both of which were to be equally condemned—"if it is to attract men, is the act of an effeminate person, if to attract women, is the act of an adulterer."[25]

There are other places, however, where the fathers poured scorn upon the beard, especially when it was employed as a prop to snare women. Both Jerome and John Chrysostom derided those who used their outward appearance, especially their "philosopher's beard," to convince others that they were seekers of wisdom but were "in character no wise better than those who are engaged on the stage, and in the sports of actors; and they have nothing to show beyond the threadbare cloak, the beard, and the long robe!"[26]

By the ninth century the vagaries of fashion had led Christian East and West to develop diverse attitudes toward facial hair. In the East, "It is commonly accepted that one of the defining cultural characteristics of Byzantine civilization from the seventh to the fifteenth centuries is the wearing of beards by adult males."[27] Scholars differ on the reasons why this occurred, some speculating that the role of eunuchs in the empire may have strengthened the link between beardlessness and effeminacy. In the West, for very different cultural and theological reasons, beardlessness became associated with the virtue of humility, viewed as one of the necessary traits for priestly ministry. Although attitudes in the West shifted depending on time and place, with regional church councils codifying current local practice, by the ninth century the fact was that Latin priests tended to be beardless while Greek priests almost always had beards. This largely cultural difference was obvious for all to see, so that when people began pointing out the differences between the two halves of Christianity during the so-called Photian Schism, it was among the easiest to notice, even if Photios himself did not necessarily attach any theological significance to it.

By the eleventh century Photios's irenicism had long been forgotten, and the beardlessness of the Latin clergy was given a nefarious theological significance by the Byzantine polemicists. Beginning with Michael Keroularios, writings from the eleventh century onward began to maintain not only that a beardless clergy was a clear "Judaizing" tendency within Latin Christianity, but that it violated the "apostolic institutions" and the "ancient canons."[28] This was a serious charge, for despite their different readings and interpretations of the patristic witness, both Latins and Greeks believed themselves bound to it. The Latins had no choice but to respond, and the battle over beards had begun.

What is interesting is that after a brief flurry of polemical exchanges about clerical beards during the eleventh through the thirteenth centuries, the subject largely disappeared from the literature, and for reasons that remain unclear it became a nonissue during the fourteenth century. We know that many Latins in the East (e.g., the

---

[25] Clement of Alexandria, *Paidogogus* 3.3; Eng. trans.: ANF 2: 275–77.
[26] John Chrysostom, *Homilies on the Statutes* 19; Eng. trans.: NPNF 1.9.465.
[27] Shaun Tougher, "Bearding Byzantium: Masculinity, Eunuchs and the Byzantine Life Course," in Bronwen Neil and Lynda Garland, eds., *Questions of Gender in Byzantine Society* (London: Routledge, 2013), 153.
[28] For example, the twelfth-century *Opusculum contra Francos* claimed that "the [Latin] priests shaved their beards in the manner of soldiers and against the apostolic institutions." Joseph Hergenröther, ed., *Monumenta graeca ad Photium eiusque Historiam Pertinentia* (Ratisbon, 1869), 71.

Knights Templar) adopted beards in keeping with the Eastern custom, and practice in the West was never completely uniform—for "while canonical rules prohibiting beards and requiring shaving remained in force ... they were widely disregarded, especially by the higher clergy."[29] Perhaps it was difficult to maintain the polemic when Latin practice itself was in flux, or perhaps it was simply that by this time other, more pressing, issues began to appear on the scene.

Azymes

If any one issue could claim to be the immediate cause of the Great Schism between East and West, it is the Latin use of unleavened bread (ἄζυμος, or *azymes*) for the Eucharist. When in 1089 Pope Urban II (1088–99) asked Alexios I (1081–1118) why his name was not included in the Constantinopolitan diptychs, the emperor's response made no mention of the primacy or the theology of the procession, but rather spoke of "that schism whereby the Greeks sacrifice with leavened bread while the Latins use unleavened."[30] Among the Byzantines' complaints was that the Latin practice was a novelty and thus counter to the long-standing practice of the universal church. In this they were probably correct, as it seems that the use of leavened bread throughout the West was normative until the ninth or tenth century. As far back as the seventeenth century Catholic scholars like the Jesuit Jacques Sirmond in his work *Disquisitio de azymo* had admitted as much, and today it is almost universally accepted that "during the first millennium of church history it was the general custom in both East and West to use normal 'daily bread,' that is, leavened bread, for the Eucharist."[31] The famed twentieth-century liturgical historian Joseph Jungmann wrote that it was only from the ninth century on that "various ordinances appeared [in the West] ... all demanding the exclusive use of unleavened bread for the Eucharist" and that this "new custom did not come into exclusive vogue [in Rome] until the middle of the eleventh century" and then only under certain northern influences.[32]

The Roman justification for this new practice was largely based on a biblical argument—according to the Synoptic Gospels (Matthew, Mark, Luke) Jesus had celebrated the Last Supper as a Passover meal and thus he would have used unleavened bread for the institution of the Eucharist. The church (or at least the Roman church) was simply acting in imitation of its savior. The Byzantine response was also based on biblical evidence—according to the Gospel of John (whose chronology of Jesus's last days differs from the Synoptics), the Last Supper was not a Passover meal, which is why the gospels and Paul (1 Cor 11:23–26) talk about the bread used that night as

---

[29] Giles Constable, "Introduction on Beards in the Middle Ages," in R. B. C. Huygens, ed., *Apologiae duae*, Corpus Christianorum: Continuatio mediaeualis, 62 (Turnhout: Brepols, 1985), 114.

[30] Goffredo Malaterra, *Historia Sicula* 4.13; Eng. trans: Geoffrey Malaterra, *The Deeds of Count Roger of Calabria and Sicily and of His Brother Duke Robert Guiscard*, trans. Kenneth Baxter Wolf (Ann Arbor: University of Michigan Press, 2005), 188–89.

[31] Johannes Emminghaus, *The Eucharist: Essence, Form, Celebration*, trans. Matthew O'Connell (Collegeville, MN: Liturgical Press, 1978), 161.

[32] Joseph Jungmann, *The Mass of the Roman Rite*, vol. 2 (Westminster, MD: Christian Classics, 1986), 33–34.

ἄρτος ("bread" or "loaf") rather than ἄζυμος ("unleavened"). Because so much depended on their respective readings of the Scripture, examining the biblical and historical data surrounding the Last Supper, and how Latins and Greeks each read it, will be necessary to understanding the whole *azyme* debate.

Naturally there were other arguments against the Latin practice aside from its relative novelty. According to the Byzantines there was an intimate connection between leaven and life, so that just as "the body without breath is dead ... matzo—which does not have leaven—is dead, and not a living loaf. For the leaven gives life and oneness to the dough, just as the spirit does to the body."[33] What is interesting about this Byzantine argument is the generally positive interpretation given to leaven, which elsewhere in the Bible (e.g., Mt 16:5–12) is spoken of quite negatively, a fact often noted by the Latins. Did not Scripture itself tell Christians to "celebrate the festival, not with the old yeast, the yeast of malice and evil, but with the unleavened bread of sincerity and truth" (1 Cor 5:8)? What the Bible and the church fathers said about leaven became for both Latins and Greeks remarkably important, especially when there was doubt as to translation or meaning. This was especially the case with Galatians 5:9 ("A little yeast (ζύμη) leavens (ζυμοῖ) the whole batch of dough"), which appeared in Jerome's Vulgate as "A little leaven (*fermentum*) corrupts (*corrumpit*) the whole loaf," an interpretation that caused no end of problems.

Another interesting feature of the azymite debate was how remarkably one-sided it was. For while the Byzantines objected, often quite strenuously, to the Western practice of using unleavened bread, Latin theologians rarely questioned the Eastern tradition and "*universally* accept[ed] the validity of the Greek sacrament using leavened bread."[34] It is true that the Latins thought the Greeks presumptuous for denying the validity of their Eucharist, and they were genuinely outraged at the charges of heresy leveled against them, yet they did not respond by attacking the use of leavened bread or demanding that the Greeks adopt *azymes*. Instead they simply demanded that the Greek attacks stop, and that the validity of the Latin practice be accepted by the Byzantines just as the Greek practice was accepted by the West. If the pope demanded the East's submission when it came to the Filioque and the primacy, he was certainly not seeking it as it concerned the use of *azymes*.

From the eleventh century, when the debate began, to the Council of Ferrara-Florence in 1438/39, the Latins' use of *azymes* appeared on almost every list of Latin errors and was considered by most to be the chief cause of the schism until later replaced by the Filioque and the primacy. It is true that at Florence Mark of Ephesus hoped the pope would ban the use of *azymes*, but by the end of the council most of the Greeks willingly conceded the legitimacy of the Latin practice without much debate. In fact, more time was devoted at the council to the (relatively) new debate about the moment of consecration than to the type of bread used. *Azymes*, after centuries of prominence, had receded into the background, but it had not gone away.

---

[33] Pseudo-Athanasius, *De Azymis* (PG 26: 1327–32); Eng. trans.: Smith, *And Taking Bread*, 137 n. 181.
[34] Schabel, "Quarrel over Unleavened Bread," 92.

Purgatory

The Latin doctrine of Purgatory has a history that goes back, at least from the Catholic perspective, to the Scriptures, and particularly to 2 Maccabees 12:41–46, which became the chief proof text for the doctrine. Later, as the Western church began clarifying its teaching on the "purgatorial fire" (*ignis purgatorius*), Matthew 12:31–32, Luke 16:19–26, and 1 Corinthians 3:11–15 were also read as biblical warrants for the teaching, each in their own way supporting efficacious prayers for the dead, the possibility of forgiveness of sins after death, and the idea of a cleansing fire. Church fathers of both the West and the East allegedly taught the doctrine, including Augustine of Hippo and Gregory of Nyssa, providing not only patristic support but also a sure defense against the charge that the teaching was novel.

Of course, for the Byzantines the teaching *was* novel, in that they were only introduced to it in the middle of the thirteenth century. It is not that the Greek theological tradition had been uninterested in the question of a soul's fate after death, since (as Nicholas Constas has noted) there were already a variety of views on the subject prior to the East's first encounter with the doctrine of Purgatory.[35] Yet when presented with the Latin teaching of a "place" with "fire," the Byzantines balked, unable to reconcile this teaching with the Greek tradition yet concurrently unprepared to fully articulate their own teaching on the afterlife. The Latins pressed them: Where then do souls go after death? Do they receive judgment and reward/punishment immediately? What is the purpose of prayers for the dead if these prayers can in no way aid them? The Greeks were (temporarily) at a loss.

Interestingly, despite having "percolated" in the West for several centuries, and having long become part of the Catholic consciousness, it was not until the encounter with the East that the Latin church began to give Purgatory its formal dogmatic framework. According to Jacques Le Goff, it was Innocent IV who provided the doctrine's "birth certificate" in a 1254 letter to his legate on Cyprus,[36] demanding that since the "Greeks themselves, it is said, believe and profess truly and without hesitation that the souls of those who die after receiving penance but without having had the time to complete it, or who die without mortal sin but guilty of venial [sins] or minor faults, are purged after death and may be helped by the suffrages of the Church," they should give the place where it happens its proper name, "calling it Purgatory according to the traditions and authority (*auctoritates*) of the Holy Fathers."[37]

It was not really until the Council of Ferrara-Florence that the Greeks finally started to flesh out a response, although even here unanimity was hard to achieve. For example, the "tollhouse" tradition was deliberately avoided by Mark of Ephesus, despite George Scholarios viewing it was "the Byzantine equivalent of Purgatory, minus the fireworks."[38] Yet it would be in the writings of Mark that the Greek tradition found their answer to the Latins, essentially becoming the de facto official position of the

---

[35] Nicholas Constas, "To Sleep, Perchance to Dream: The Middle State of Souls in Patristic and Byzantine Literature," *Dumbarton Oaks Papers* 55 (2001): 91–124.
[36] Jacques Le Goff, *The Birth of Purgatory*, trans. Arthur Goldhammer (Chicago: University of Chicago Press, 1984), 284.
[37] Innocent IV, *Sub Catholicae*; Eng. trans.: Le Goff, *The Birth of Purgatory*, 283–84.
[38] Constas, "To Sleep, Perchance to Dream," 109.

Orthodox Church on the afterlife. Despite many common beliefs about the world to come, Purgatory, as a place of fire and punishment, had to be rejected.

The conciliar debates on Purgatory, which began on June 4, 1438, have been described as "a theological goldmine" providing two contrasting visions of the afterlife and the church's tradition vis-à-vis judgment, mercy, justice, and forgiveness.[39] Essentially it demonstrated a "radical difference of perspective, [for] while the Latins took for granted their legalistic approach to divine justice—which, according to them, requires a retribution for every sinful act—the Greeks interpreted sin less in terms of the acts committed than in terms of a moral and spiritual disease which was to be healed by divine forbearance and love."[40] The irony is that while Greeks and Latins never came to a genuine agreement about the doctrine, in finally bringing their opposing views into focus they actually achieved something positive, a rarity for any of the Florentine debates.

Ferrara-Florence and Beyond

In 1438, when Christian East and West came together to discuss the restoration of full ecclesial communion, they were fulfilling a long-standing demand of the Greeks that union could only be achieved at a genuinely ecumenical council.[41] For the Latins, however, the gathering was never intended to be a genuine dialogue, but merely a concession to Greek sensibilities allowing the Byzantines to be reincorporated into the Roman church on terms dictated by the pope and his supporters. The simple truth was that after centuries of estrangement the two halves of Christendom knew very little about the theological ethos of the other, and neither was particularly eager to change the situation.[42] There was a woeful ignorance of the Western fathers among the Byzantines, despite efforts made in the fourteenth century to translate the works of Augustine and Aquinas into Greek.[43] The Latins, however, were hardly guiltless in this matter, for while they had made an effort to translate the Greek fathers, enabling

---

[39] Bathrellos, "Love, Purification, and Forgiveness," 82.

[40] John Meyendorff, *Byzantine Theology: Historical Trends and Doctrinal Themes* (New York: Fordham University Press, 1975), 220.

[41] Donald Nicol, "Byzantine Requests for an Oecumenical Council in the Fourteenth Century," *Annuarium Historiae Conciliorum* 1 (1969): 69–95; Marcel Viller, "La question de l'union des Eglises entre Grecs et Latins depuis le Concile de Lyon jusqu'à celui de Florence (1274-1438)," *Revue d' histoire ecclésiastique* 17–18 (1921–22): 260–305; 20–60; John Boojamra, "The Byzantine Notion of the 'Ecumenical Council' in the Fourteenth Century," *Byzantinische Zeitschrift* 80 (1987): 59–76; John Meyendorff, "Projet de concile oecuménique en 1367: Un dialogue inédit entre Jean Cantacuzène et le légat Paul," *Dumbarton Oaks Papers* 14 (1960): 147–77.

[42] As Yves Congar wrote: "In substance it (i.e., the schism) consisted in the acceptance of the situation of non-rapport.... Not that the schism is of itself the estrangement ... it was the acceptance of the estrangement." Yves Congar, *After Nine Hundred Years: The Background of the Schism between the Eastern and Western Churches* (New York: Fordham University Press, 1959), 88–89.

[43] At several points during the council the Greek delegates admitted their total ignorance of the Latin tradition: "If we cannot discern in certain of our own manuscripts of Chrysostom, which we read from infancy to old age, the false or true, what will it be regarding the Western saints, of which we have never known or read the writings?" Syropoulos, *Memoirs*, 9.7 in Vitalien Laurent, ed., *Les mémoires du Grand Ecclésiarque de l'Église de Constantinople Sylvestre Syropoulos sur le Concile de Florence (1438-1439)*, CF 9 (Rome: Pontifical Oriental Institute, 1971), 440.

them to be placed in florilegia as proof texts, the West had long since lost the ability to understand them on their own terms.[44]

The union decree, *Laetentur Caeli*, signed amid great pomp and pageantry on July 6, 1439, gave the Latins everything they wanted. The Filioque, papal primacy, the use of *azymes*, and Purgatory were all defined and defended in terms dictated by the Roman church with little thought given to the council's reception in the East. After the union was formally repudiated in 1454, its teachings on the Filioque and the primacy were rejected in increasingly strident terms by those who blamed Constantinople's fall on the betrayal at Florence.[45] Interestingly, the polemics against *azymes* now started to disappear, and little mention was made of the Latins' beardlessness. The "other issues" had finally receded into the background, and for Catholic-Orthodox writers of subsequent centuries the schism became all about the procession and the primacy.

Purgatory, however, re-emerged as a theological issue in 1517 when Martin Luther wrote and posted his famous Ninety-Five Theses, challenging the pope's authority to release souls from Purgatory by the granting of indulgences.[46] Soon even suffrages for the dead were attacked as unscriptural and superstitious, "a perverse mode of prayer in the church" introduced by an "ill-advised diligence" and allowed to continue "because of public custom and common ignorance."[47] At the Council of Trent (1545–63) the Roman Catholic Church reaffirmed that the "sound teaching on Purgatory, handed down by the holy fathers and the sacred councils, is [to be] believed and held by the Christian by the faithful."[48] When the Orthodox of Ukraine entered into the Union of Brest in 1595, they claimed they would "not enter into dispute about Purgatory" but instead expressed that they were "ready to be instructed [concerning it] by the Holy Church."[49]

The Orthodox, despite having a common enemy in Rome and objections to certain Catholic doctrines, were, for the most part, unsympathetic to the Protestant cause. Aside from their defense of the Filioque, the Protestants continued the use

---

[44] According to John Erickson, "The Latins were oblivious to the basic intuitions and concerns of the Greek patristic tradition.... Misjudging the weight and consistency of their sometimes questionable sources, they sought to fit the theology of others into their own narrow system." John Erickson, "*Filioque* and the Fathers at the Council of Florence," in *Challenge of Our Past*, 163.

[45] George Scholarios, the same author who had berated his fellow delegates at Florence for their ignorance and implored them to union in order to save the Great City, now wrote: "Wretched Romans, how you have been deceived! Trusting in the might of the Franks you have removed yourselves from the hope of God. Together with the City which will soon be destroyed, you have lost your piety.... Know, O wretched citizens, what you do! Captivity is about to befall you because you have lost the piety handed down to you by your fathers and you have confessed your impiety. Woe unto you in the judgment." Doukas, *Decline and Fall*, 204.

[46] Included among Martin Luther's Ninety-Five Theses are the propositions "22. As a matter of fact, the pope remits to souls in purgatory no penalty which, according to canon law, they should have paid in this life" and "26. The pope does very well when he grants remission to souls in purgatory, not by the power of the keys, which he does not have, but by way of intercession for them." Timothy Lull, ed., *Martin Luther's Basic Theological Writings* (Minneapolis: Fortress Press, 1989), 23.

[47] John Calvin, *Institutes of the Christian Religion* 5.10, ed. John T. McNeill (Louisville, KY: Westminster John Knox Press, 1960), 682.

[48] Norman Tanner, *Decrees of the Ecumenical Councils*, vol. 2 (Washington, DC: Georgetown University Press, 1990), 774.

[49] Articles of Union 5, quoted in Borys Gudziak, *Crisis and Reform: The Kyivan Metropolitanate, the Patriarchate of Constantinople, and the Genesis of the Union of Brest* (Cambridge, MA: Harvard University Press, 1998), 265.

of unleavened bread in the Eucharist, even if, "not for any reason whatever, would [they] wish to quarrel with anyone over this."⁵⁰ In order to ward off the teachings of Protestant and Catholic missionaries, Orthodox confessions of faith composed in the sixteenth and seventieth centuries maintained the traditional stand on most of the disputed issues, including Purgatory and *azymes*, although neither was given center stage. Clerical beardlessness was still occasionally mentioned, as when Nicodemus of the Holy Mountain (1749–1809) condemned the priests of the Latins, "who shaved off their mustache and their beard and who look like very young men and handsome bridegrooms and have the face of women."⁵¹

By the twentieth century, as the Catholic and Orthodox Churches entered an era of rapprochement, little thought was given to the "other issues" that had once divided the churches. It is true that as late as the eighteenth century Eustratios Argenti (c. 1687–c. 1758) was still writing the treatise *Against Unleavened Bread*, but by the 1950s–1960s only historians of dogma were interested in such things. Ecumenists and theologians concentrated on the Filioque and the primacy, which even today remain the key sticking points in the efforts to reunite the two churches. Aside from Purgatory, which the Orthodox continued to reject despite their own internal debate about the fate of souls after death, few of the old complaints about Latin practices raise their head. Even among modern-day polemicists, writing blogs rather than treatises, more space is given to newer issues like the Immaculate Conception and the alleged heresies of the *Novus Ordo* than to the *azymes*. Ironically, the blogosphere *has* found room for the lovers of beards, as hipsters have mined the patristic texts to laud the virtues of facial hair and the manly strength of "bearded gospel men."⁵²

Formal ecumenical dialogue between the Catholic and Orthodox Churches has not concerned itself much with "the other issues," and by and large this is probably a good thing, as untangling the problems that do persist will take a great deal of time and effort. That said, it would be a shame to forget them, as they constitute so great a part of the churches' shared history. Simply put, they *were* the things that once divided East and West but now divide them no longer. Catholics and Orthodox have learned together how to forget, how to move beyond the polemics of the past, and these are not insignificant lessons. The story of how they came to be church-dividing issues is fascinating. What they have to teach us may be more important.

---

⁵⁰ *Second Exchange between Tübingen Theologians and Patriarch Jeremiah II*, in George Mastrantonis, ed., *Augsburg and Constantinople: The Correspondence between the Tübingen Theologians and Patriarch Jeremiah II of Constantinople on the Augsburg Confession* (Brookline, MA: Holy Cross Orthodox Press, 1982), 263.

⁵¹ Nicodemus the Hagorite, *The Rudder or Pedalion* (Chicago: Orthodox Christian Educational Society, New York: Luna Printing Co., 1957), 403–5.

⁵² Jared Brock and Aaron Alford, *Bearded Gospel Men: The Epic Quest for Manliness and Godliness* (Nashville, TN: W Publishing Group, 2017).

PART I
BEARDS

1
Beards in the Biblical and Patristic Tradition

It needs to be recognized at the outset that "beards came into the Christian world with a heavy baggage of pre-historic and classical symbolism of which the Church fathers were not unaware."[1] Of course, the symbolism was often dependent upon time and place, for while in some cultures shaving the beard was a sign of grief,[2] in others it was the growing of facial hair that indicated a period of mourning.[3] As a sign of maturity the growth of the beard was an important marker, and in some societies a man's first shave was done ritually, with offerings made to the gods.[4] "In Greek society [the beard] marked the end of the stage when a boy might legitimately be the object of sexual advances from an older man."[5] Others spoke of the "philosopher's beard" that conveyed one's search for, and acquisition of, wisdom.[6] Simply put, growing or shaving the beard had a variety of meanings in the ancient world, and this lack of consistency is sometimes reflected in the writings of the fathers on the subject.[7]

---

[1] Constable, "Introduction on Beards in the Middle Ages," 59.

[2] Isaiah 15:2: "Over Nebo and over Medeba Moab wails. On every head is baldness, every beard is shorn."

[3] "Such was Caesar's love for them [i.e., his soldiers] that when he heard of the disaster to Titurius, he let his hair and beard grow long, and would not cut them until he had taken vengeance." Suetonius, *The Lives of the Caesars*. Eng. trans.: J. C. Rolfe, *The Lives of the Caesars I* (Cambridge, MA: Harvard University. Press, 1979), 89.

[4] "At the gymnastic contest, which he [i.e., Nero] gave in the Saepta, he shaved his first beard to the accompaniment of a splendid sacrifice of bullocks, put it in a golden box adorned with pearls of great price, and dedicated it in the Capitol." Suetonius, *The Lives of the Caesars*. Eng. trans.: J. C. Rolfe, *The Lives of the Caesars II* (Cambridge, MA: Harvard University Press, 1979), 107. This practice of a ritualized first shave (*barbatoria*) seems to have survived well into the Christian period, and can be seen in the works of Paulinus of Nola (*Carmina* 21) and Gregory of Tours (*Historia Francorum* 10.16).

[5] Constable, "Introduction on Beards in the Middle Ages," 59.

[6] The Stoic philosopher Epictetus famously defended his philosopher's beard even when threatened with death: " 'Come, then, Epictetus, shave off your beard.' 'If I am a philosopher,' I answer, 'I will not shave it off.' 'But I will take off your neck.' 'If that will do you any good, take it off.' " Epictetus, *Discourses* I.2.29. Eng. trans.: W. A. Oldfather, *Discourses I* (Cambridge, MA: Harvard University Press, 1967), 23.

[7] See Peter Brown, *The Body and Society: Men, Women and Sexual Renunciation in Early Christianity* (New York: Columbia University Press, 1988). For the topic of hair in particular see Kristi Upson-Saia, "Hairiness and Holiness in the Early Christian Desert," in Alicia Batten, Carly Daniel-Hughes, and Kristi Upson-Saia, eds., *Dressing Jews and Christians in Antiquity* (Aldershot: Ashgate, 2014), 155–72. Among the recent studies she cites are Anthony Synnott, "Shame and Glory: A Sociology of Hair," *British Journal of Sociology* 38.3 (1987): 381–413; Gananath Obeyesekere, *Medusa's Hair: An Essay on Personal Symbols and Religious Experience* (Chicago: University of Chicago Press, 1981); Pauline Stafford, "The Meaning of Hair in the Anglo-Norman World: Masculinity, Reform, and National Identity," in Mathilde van Dijk and Renee Nip, eds., *Saints, Scholars, and Politicians: Gender as a Tool in Medieval Studies* (Turnhout: Brepols, 2005), 153–71; Molly Myerowitz Levine, "The Gendered Grammar of Ancient Mediterranean Hair," in Howard Eilberg-Schwartz and Wendy Doniger, eds., *Off with Her Head! The Denial of Women's Identity in Myth, Religion, and Culture* (Berkeley: University of California Press, 1995), 76–130; Elizabeth Bartman, "Hair and the Artifice of Roman Female Adornment," *American Journal of Archaeology* 105 (2001): 1–25; Christian Bromberger, "Hair: From the West to the Middle East through the Mediterranean," *Journal of American Folklore* 121.482 (2008): 387; Robert Bartlett, "Symbolic Meanings of Hair in the Middle Ages," *Transactions of the Royal Historical Society* 4 (1994): 43–60; Robert Mills, "The Signification of

On one hand the church fathers did not spend a great deal of time writing about facial hair—after all, there were far more important dogmatic and pastoral questions to be answered. When they did, they brought with them not only an entire set of cultural assumptions about its meaning, but also the teaching of the Scriptures, which, in fact, contain a good deal about the growing and shaving of beards. The first generation of Christians were themselves Jews, bound by the law of Moses and its precepts concerning facial hair, which means it is likely that Jesus and the apostles were themselves bearded men. As Christianity spread beyond its Jewish origins into the Greco-Roman world, the church fathers' assumptions about masculinity, sexual morality, and the natural distinction between the sexes all affected how they spoke about the beard, positively and negatively.

When the fathers did have cause to speak of beards, they were, with few exceptions, extremely laudatory. Beards were manly, a sign of virtue and strength, man's natural adornment akin to the lion's mane. Conversely, shaving the beard was a sign of effeminacy, associated with unnatural behaviors, the loss of comeliness, or sinful self-adornment. While the practice of the early church was not always uniform, and depended often enough on changing cultural norms, the patristic corpus points to the view that the ancient church generally encouraged its members, clergy and lay, to be bearded rather than beardless. Yet beards were never the real issue, as if they believed them to be holy or imbued by God with an inherent theological significance. The real issue was always morality (particularly sexual morality) and the desire that Christian men should avoid the sins of vanity and lust, especially those deemed *contra natura*. When certain fathers came to believe that growing the beard also led to these sins (e.g., by trying to lure women with the "philosopher's beard"), they would condemn the beard as vociferously as others defended it.

It is only with this in mind that the canonical legislation of the ancient church, which in East and West sometimes mandated, and sometimes outlawed, the growing of facial hair, makes any sense. These canons were never about hair, but about Christian morality, and what is particularly interesting about them is the fact that they were usually aimed at both priests and laity alike. When specific mention was made of priests, the logic underlying the canons was the same—if all Christian men are discouraged from sins involving effeminacy, vanity, and lust, how much more should priests and monks avoid these traps. Later the growing or shaving of hair would be used to distinguish the clergy from the laity, but this was not the case in the early church. Bearded or beardless, what was important was not how hairy a man was, but how holy he should be.

The Scriptures

The Hebrew word *zaqan*, or "beard," appears nineteen times in the Old Testament, as distinguished from *sapham*, or "mustache," which appears five times, and *se ar* ("hair"

---

the Tonsure," in Patricia Cullum and Katherine Lewis, eds., *Holiness and Masculinity in the Middle Ages* (Toronto: University of Toronto Press, 2005), 109–26.

or "hairy covering"), which appears over twenty-five times.[8] The word *glḥ* ("to shave") and its variants *gazaz* ("to shear"), *gara* ("to shave the beard"), *hiqqiph* ("to shave around" or "to cut around"), *qarach* ("to make bald"), and *kasam* ("to cut the hair") appear throughout the Scriptures, usually associated with periods of mourning (e.g., Job 1:20, Is 15:2, Jer 48:37) or shame/humiliation (2 Sam 10:4, Ez 27:31).[9] Although there are exceptions, the norm throughout the Old Testament was for men to have long, styled hair and a beard, which were considered not only adornments (2 Sam 14:26), but also signs of manliness and power.[10]

This was certainly true for Samson, famed for his prodigious strength. According to the Scriptures, his barren mother was told by an angel that she would "conceive and bear a son. No razor is to come on his head, for the boy shall be a *nazirite* ("consecrated") to God from birth. It is he who shall begin to deliver Israel from the hand of the Philistines" (Jgs 13:5). When he grew Samson was indeed able to accomplish great feats in the Lord's name, yet he told Delilah that this was only because "a razor has never come upon my head; for I have been a *nazirite* to God from my mother's womb. If my head were shaved, then my strength would leave me; I would become weak and be like anyone else" (Jgs 16:17). When she called a barber and had him "shave off the seven locks of his head," Samson did become like other men, for "the LORD had left him" (Jgs 16:19).

This Nazirite vow was also made by the mother of Samuel, who promised the Lord that if she should be given a male child she would "set him before you as a *nazirite* until the day of his death. He shall drink neither wine nor intoxicants, and no razor shall touch his head" (1 Sam 1:11). The connection between consecration to God and the prohibition against cutting the hair, seen throughout the Old Testament, may stem from "the primitive manaistic ideas which believed that divine power resides in a person's hair" or the belief that "long hair could have been the external symbol of a lifelong commitment to the service of Yahweh."[11] In Numbers 6:1–21 rules for the Nazirites repeat the idea that "no razor shall come upon the head; until the time is completed for which they separate themselves to the Lord, they shall be holy; they shall let the locks of the head grow long" (Num 6:5). However, here the vow was not permanent but only for a defined period, for at the end of his service it was commanded that "the *nazirites* shall shave the consecrated head at the entrance of the tent of meeting and shall take the hair from the consecrated head and put it on the fire under the sacrifice of well-being" (Num 6:18).[12] According to G. B. Gray, the logic

---

[8] See James Strong, *The New Strong's Expanded Exhaustive Concordance of the Bible* (Peabody, MA: Hendrickson, 1996). The Strong's reference numbers are H2206, H8222, H8181 respectively.

[9] G. Johannes Botterweck, "*gillach*," in G. Johannes Botterweck and Helmer Ringgren, eds., *Theological Dictionary of the Old Testament*, vol. 3 (Grand Rapids, MI: Eerdmans, 1978), 5–20. For example, Isaiah warned the people of their upcoming humiliation by telling them, "On that day the Lord will shave with a razor hired beyond the River—with the king of Assyria—the head and the hair of the feet, and it will take off the beard as well" (Is 7:20).

[10] "The Talmud calls the beard 'the adornment of a man's face' (Baba Metzia, 84a) and disparagingly refers to a male over twenty years of age who doesn't sport one as a eunuch (Yevamot, 80b)." Ze'ev Maghen, *After Hardship Cometh Ease: The Jews as Backdrop for Muslim Moderation* (Berlin: de Gruyter, 2012), 219.

[11] Botterweck, "*gillach*," 13.

[12] What has apparently happened is that the "charismatic dimension to the nazirite's activity" has now been institutionalized and extended "to the laity at large." The vow, exercised under the jurisdiction of the priesthood" has been transformed "into a commitment which is normally of limited duration" even if 'it could still be for a substantial period." The purpose of the legislation is "not [to] devalue the commitment

behind the Nazirite practice, both the growing and the offering of hair, stems from the same belief—that "hair is part of a man's vital being ... [thus when] the main object [of growing the hair] is to keep the man's power of vitality to the full, the hair is never shaven," but when "the object is to present the deity with part of a man's life, the hair is a suitable means of achieving this."[13]

Numbers also mandated that in order to purify the priests of the temple Aaron should "sprinkle the water of purification on them, have them shave their whole body with a razor and wash their clothes, and so cleanse themselves" (Num 8:7). This sort of ceremonial shaving/purification was a common practice for priests of the Near East, yet for the Israelites "it seems that this ritual was a one-time transformation, after which the new, sanctified hair was not to be shaved off again."[14] In fact, God later told the priests through Ezekiel that they should "not shave their heads or let their locks grow long; they shall only trim the hair of their heads" (Ez 44:20). The priests of Israel would not, like their neighbors, go about hairless, but neither would they be permitted Samson's locks.

The most important, and by far the most influential, passages concerning shaving and beards are found in the Holiness Code of Leviticus. Leviticus 19:27 ("You shall not round off the hair on your temples or mar the edges of your beard)" applies "to all the congregation of the people of Israel," while Leviticus 21:5 ("They shall not make bald spots upon their heads, or shave off the edges of their beards or make any gashes in their flesh") speaks only to the "sons of Aaron" (i.e., the priests).[15] Susan Niditch interprets Leviticus 21:5 in terms of ritual purity—that is, because "the priest is 'holy,' set apart" he must be ritually pure, and this "holiness is related symbolically to bodily wholeness. Thus the priest needs to maintain bodily boundaries demarcated by intact hair and body."[16] She assumes, as most have, that the prohibition in Leviticus 19 is simply a "democratization" of the priestly holiness code—that is, the rules for priests were extended to the rest of the people—although others point to the very different language of Leviticus 21.[17] In either case the Levitical legislation seems to be specifically aimed at certain mourning rituals that involved "the making of a bald spot on the hair above the forehead" and the diminishment of the beard, although from the

---

of the nazirite, but [rather] to control and regulate it." Philip Budd, *Numbers*, Word Biblical Commentary 5 (Waco, TX: Word Books, 1984), 73–74.

[13] George Buchanan Gray, *A Critical and Exegetical Commentary of Numbers*, International Critical Commentary (New York: Charles Scribner's Sons, 1906), 69. See also the discussion in Baruch Levine, *Numbers 1–20*, Anchor Bible 4A (New York: Doubleday, 1993), 229–34. Levine, examining certain Phoenician inscriptions that dealt with hair offerings, contextualized the Nazirite practice of shaving/burning hair "within the larger regional system of votive dedication." Ibid., 234.

[14] Oldstone-Moore, *Of Beards and Men*, 36.

[15] "Leviticus 21:5 has been interpreted in various Jewish circles as a command to grow *peyes*, or side-locks still worn today among certain Hasidic groups." It is clear from the biblical context, however, that the verse applies only to priests and in the context of mourning." Susan Niditch, *"My Brother Esau Is a Hairy Man": Hair and Identity in Ancient Israel* (Oxford: Oxford University Press, 2008), 106.

[16] Ibid., 106–7.

[17] The argument is that "round off the hair on your temples" is not the same as "make bald spots on the head," nor is "mar the edges of your beard" the same as "shave off the edges of their beards"). Ibid., 15. Jacob Milgrom, however, regards the two as "functionally equivalent." Jacob Milgrom, *Leviticus 17–22*, Anchor Bible 3A (New York: Doubleday, 2000), 1802.

context it is difficult to know whether it refers to trimming one's facial hair or cutting it off completely.[18]

It is possible, even probable, that these prohibitions have their foundation in the practices of the Israelites' pagan neighbors, many of whom had unique hairstyles and/or cut their flesh, especially during worship or periods of mourning.[19] "Determined to restore their identity as the chosen people, [and] set apart from all others by their covenant with God," it is likely that the law aimed at "distinguish[ing] the ways of Jews from those of non-Jews" by enforcement of certain "hair codes."[20] The Jews' neighbors, according to Herodotus (c. 425 BC), included those who "deem none other to be gods save Dionysus and the Heavenly Aphrodite ... cropping their hair like ... the hair of Dionysus, cutting it round the head and shaving the temples."[21] Lucian (c. AD 180) and Apuleius (c. AD 170) also spoke, albeit much later, about how in the temples of Syria "priests, eunuchs without beards, offered sacrifice and cut their own flesh with knives whilst the sacrifice was going on."[22]

Accounts such as these help explain why laws about shaving and the cutting of the flesh are so often placed together in the Old Testament, whether it is in the context of worship or mourning. It also throws light on other passages (e.g., Dt 14:1), where the Israelites are told not to imitate the pagans because "You are children of the Lord your God. You must not lacerate yourselves or shave your forelocks for the dead."[23] Yet there may be more than simply a question of identity—some have interpreted the law against scarring the body as a command "not to disfigure the divine likeness

---

[18] John Hartley, *Leviticus, Word Biblical Commentary 4* (Dallas, TX: Word Books, 1992), 348. See also the discussion in Milgrom, *Leviticus 17–22*, 1690–94. It is interesting to note how the *halakhah* (Jewish law) handles this question today. According to the *halakhah*, "It is forbidden for a man to shave off the hair of his temples or to shave off the corners of his beard. Both of these rules apply only to shaving with a razor. Using a depilating cream, a waxing process, or just pulling the hair out by hand would not be forbidden. Trimming with scissors and most forms of electric shavers (where the razor does not touch the face) are not forbidden either." Retrieved from https://thetorah.com/the-prohibition-of-shaving/#4.

[19] Since the publication of Edmund Leach, "Magical Hair," *Journal of the Royal Anthropological Institute* 88 (1958): 147–68 there have been attempts to probe the deeper meanings of hair/shaving in religious practice, and in particular the Judeo-Christian tradition. Leach argued that whenever hair appears in a ritual context there is a clear sexual/phallic significance, with long hair signaling unrestrained sexuality, a close-shaven head signaling celibacy. This view was challenged by C. R. Hallpike in "Social Hair," *Man*, NS 4 (1969): 256–64, who saw hair more in societal terms—i.e., "that long hair is associated with being outside society and that the cutting of hair symbolizes re-entering society, or living under a particular disciplinary regime within society." Saul M. Olyan, "What Do Shaving Rites Accomplish and What Do They Signal in Biblical Ritual Contexts?," *Journal of Biblical Literature* 117 (1998): 611–22, maintained that all shaving rituals "effect a change in the individual's status and serve as a public temporary marker of this status change" (621). See also Charles Berg, *The Unconscious Significance of Hair* (London: Allen & Unwin, 1951); P. Hershman, "Hair, Sex, and Dirt," *Man*, NS 9 (1974): 274–98.

[20] Oldstone-Moore, *Of Beards and Men*, 36. In Jeremiah, for example, God threatened "all those who are circumcised only in the foreskin: Egypt, Judah, Edom, the Ammonites, Moab, and all those with shaven temples who live in the desert" (Jer 9:25–26).

[21] Herodotus, *Histories*, Books 3–4, trans. A. D. Godley (New York: G.P. Putnam's Sons, 1928), 11.

[22] Lucian, *On the Syrian Goddess*, trans. J. L. Lightfoot (Oxford: Oxford University Press, 2003). The cutting of the flesh is also attested to in 1 Kings 18:28: "Then they (i.e., the priests of Baal) cried aloud and, as was their custom, they cut themselves with swords and lances until the blood gushed out over them."

[23] Milgrom suggested that many of the mourning rites of Israel's neighbors were "dedicated to underworld deities" and were thus deemed inappropriate for worshipers of Yahweh since "he was the God only of life and of the living, and not of the deceased" (PS 6:6, 88:6). Milgrom, *Leviticus 17–22*, 1694.

implanted in us" since "the external appearance of the people should reflect their internal status as the chosen people of God."[24]

For Jesus and the first generation of Jewish-Christians the Law of Moses retained its binding force, and there is no reason to suppose that any of them would have deviated from the legislation concerning hair and beards.[25] This cannot necessarily be proven, since the New Testament itself is completely silent about beards—the word itself (πώγων) never appears—although there are several passages dealing with hair. Acts 18:18 mentions that "at Cenchreae [Paul] had his hair cut, for he was under a vow [εὐχήν]," and Acts 21:23–26 relates how James instructed Paul to subsidize a group of men who were going through the rite of purification following a Nazirite vow.[26] James told Paul that paying for their ritual shaving would quell rumors that he was an enemy of the law, for by taking part in the rite "all will know that ... you yourself observe and guard the law." As for James, later tradition held that "the Brother of the Lord" was himself a Nazirite, "holy from his mother's womb; he drank no wine nor strong drink, nor did he eat flesh [and] no razor came upon his head."[27]

Perhaps the New Testament passage that most influenced later debate about hair and beards is 1 Corinthians 11:2–16, where Paul addressed the proper head-coverings for both men and women.[28] Paul believed that "any man who prays or prophesies with

---

[24] Gordon Wenham, *The Book of Leviticus* (Grand Rapids, MI: Eerdmans, 1979), 272.

[25] In Matthew 5:17–18 Jesus explicitly said: "Do not think that I have come to abolish the law or the prophets; I have come not to abolish but to fulfill. For truly I tell you, until heaven and earth pass away, not one letter, not one stroke of a letter, will pass from the law until all is accomplished."

[26] Paul's vow and the resulting hair-cutting raise a number of questions, including whether it was a Nazirite vow or simply a private one. Arguing against the view it was a Nazirite vow is the fact that the hair-cutting took place in Cenchreae rather than Jerusalem, where he could offer the hair in the Temple as a burnt sacrifice. This led Ernst Haechen and others to argue that "there can be no question of a nazirite vow in this instance" and this passage is merely meant to communicate to the reader that Paul, as a "Jew of exemplary devotion to the law," has taken upon himself a vow for the successful completion of his missionary journey and that this was not "diametrically opposed to the Pauline doctrine of grace." Ernst Haenchen, *Acts of the Apostles: A Commentary*, trans. Bernard Noble and Gerald Shinn (Philadelphia, PA: Westminster Press, 1971), 546. Both Luke Timothy Johnson and Joseph Fitzmyer held that this passage "clearly" refers to the Nazirite vow, and that he is either cutting his hair at the beginning of the vow, "In which case the translation of the imperfect as 'he was making a vow' would probably be better" (Luke Timothy Johnson, *The Acts of the Apostles*, Sacra Pagina 5 [Collegeville, MN: Liturgical Press], 330) or that Luke is simply uninterested in the details of the ritual, emphasizing only that "Paul carries out the requirements of a Jewish vow" because "he is again a model Jew in his conduct" (Joseph Fitzmyer, *Acts of the Apostles*, Anchor Bible 31 [New York: Doubleday, 1998], 634).

[27] Eusebius, *Ecclesiastical History* 2.23; NPNF 2.1.125.

[28] Scholarly debate persists as to what Paul is really addressing in 1 Corinthians 11:2–16—i.e., head coverings or hair length. See, for example, Benjamin A. Edsall, "Greco-Roman Costume and Paul's Fraught Argument in 1 Corinthians 11.2–16," *Journal of Greco-Roman Christianity and Judaism* 9 (2013): 132–46; Preston T. Massey, "Long Hair as a Glory and as a Covering: Removing an Ambiguity from 1 Cor 11:15," *Novum Testamentum* 53 (2011): 52–72; Preston T. Massey, "The Meaning of κατακαλύπτω and κατὰ κεφαλῆς ἔχων in 1 Corinthians 11.2–16," *New Testament Studies* 53 (2007): 502–23; Preston T. Massey, "Veiling among Men in Roman Corinth: 1 Corinthians 11:4 and the Potential Problem of East Meeting West," *Journal of Biblical Literature* 137 (2018): 501–17; Cynthia L. Thompson, "Hairstyles, Head-Coverings, and St. Paul: Portraits from Roman Corinth," *Biblical Archaeologist* 51 (1988): 99–115; Troy W. Martin, "Paul's Argument from Nature for the Veil in 1 Corinthians 11:13–15: A Testicle Instead of a Head Covering," *Journal of Biblical Literature* 123 (2004): 75–84; Mark Goodacre, "Does Περιβόλαιον Mean 'Testicle' in 1 Corinthians 11:15?," *Journal of Biblical Literature* 130 (2011): 391–96; David W. J. Gill, "The Importance of Roman Portraiture for Head-Coverings in 1 Corinthians 11:2–16," *Tyndale Bulletin* 41 (1990): 245–60; Mark Finney, "Honour, Head-Coverings and Headship: 1 Corinthians 11:2–16 in its Social Context," *Journal for the Study of the New Testament* 33 (2010): 31–58.

something on his head disgraces his head, but any woman who prays or prophesies with her head unveiled disgraces her head" (1 Cor 11:4–5). After giving the theological reasons for this position, he then went on to ground the practice in nature itself, since women had a "natural covering" of long hair while men should not. "Does not nature itself teach you that if a man wears long hair, it is degrading to him (οὐδὲ ἡ φύσις αὐτὴ διδάσκει ὑμᾶς ὅτι ἀνὴρ μὲν ἐὰν κομᾷ, ἀτιμία αὐτῷ ἐστιν), but if a woman has long hair, it is her glory?" (1 Cor 11:14–15). According to Hans Conzelmann, this "reference to the shortness of a man's hair and the length of a woman's" assumes that "nature gives directions for conduct.... He presupposes not only the naturally given facts, but also the prevailing custom, which is held to be in harmony with nature."[29] Most exegetes agree that in this context "'nature' is probably best understood here as 'convention'" rather than "'nature' as moderns usually understand the term."[30] For Paul men or women who wanted to look like the other violated the natural (i.e., conventional) order of things and by their "flouting of these established customs" brought shame "before the church and God."[31] According to scholars, on this matter Paul was merely echoing the view of the Stoic philosophers, who believed "that men should be men and women should be women, and all should look like what they are."[32]

The unspoken assumption behind this injunction is that during Paul's lifetime "men did not wear long hair ... and [that] long hair was effeminate and shameful."[33] It is true that in the first century according to "Roman custom ... short-cropped male hair was usual, but Greek custom was not so uniform or well-established."[34] Spartan men, for example, were known for their longer hair, and yet "it was true, then as now, that most cultures maintained a relative difference in hair length between men and women."[35] There were, of course, exceptions like the Nazirites, but according to J. D. M. Derrett it was the prevalence of shorter hair that made the "vow to wear your hair long a vow of significance."[36] Others have commented that what Paul addressed in this passage is not necessarily the length of a man's hair (θρίξ), but the way it was styled (κομάω), for when hair was worn as an "adornment" (like that of a woman) it was both unmanly

---

[29] Hans Conzelmann, *1 Corinthians: A Commentary on the First Epistle to the Corinthians* (Philadelphia: Fortress Press, 1975), 190–91.

[30] Joseph Fitzmyer, *First Corinthians*, Yale Anchor Bible 32 (New Haven, CT: Yale University Press, 2008), 420. Nature in this context is "that which is almost instinctive because of long habit." Craig Blomberg, *1 Corinthians*, NIV Application Commentary (Grand Rapids: Zondervan, 1994), 213.

[31] Paul Gardner, *1 Corinthians*, Zondervan Exegetical Commentary on the New Testament (Grand Rapids, MI: Zondervan, 2018), 496.

[32] Raymond Collins, *First Corinthians*, Sacra Pagina 7 (Collegeville, MN: Liturgical Press, 1999), 399. Although Paul does not mention the beard in the context of maintaining these distinctions, the philosopher Epictetus (c. AD 135) did, writing: "Is there anything less useful than the hair on the chin? What then? Has not nature used this also in the most fitting way possible? Has she not by means of it distinguished male from female? Has not the nature of each one of us immediately cried out from afar, I am a man; on this understanding approach me, speak to me, seek nothing else; here are the signs? ... For this reason we ought to keep the signs God has given, we ought not to throw them away, nor to confound, so far as we can, the distinction of the sexes." Epictetus I.16.9–14.

[33] J. Duncan M. Derrett, "Religious Hair," *Man* NS 8 (1973): 101.

[34] Fitzmyer, *First Corinthians*, 420.

[35] Blomberg, *1 Corinthians*, 213.

[36] Derrett, "Religious Hair," 101. See also Stuart Douglas Chepey, *Nazirites in Late Second Temple Judaism: A Survey of Ancient Jewish Writings, the New Testament, Archaeological Evidence, and Other Writings from Late Antiquity* (Leiden: Brill, 2005).

and immodest.³⁷ The first-century Stoic philosopher Musonius Rufus scolded men who "trim and arrange their hair to attract the attention of women and boys whose praise they seek.... Clearly, such men have been broken by luxurious living and have become completely emasculated: they don't mind looking androgynous and woman-like, something real men would never tolerate."³⁸

The question, to which scholars have given a variety of answers over the years, is whether Paul's condemnation of long hair occurs precisely because of this link to effeminacy and/or homosexual behavior. Many scholars, including Hans Conzelmann, Hans Lietzmann, and Joseph Fitzmyer, believe it is "questionable ... [that] Paul is alluding to long-haired μαλακοί, ('effeminates')" in this verse.³⁹ Yet there are a similar number of authors, citing the myriad of quotations from the ancient world linking effeminacy to hair length,⁴⁰ who hold that the earlier condemnation of sodomy in 1 Corinthians 6:9⁴¹ and the activity of the Dionysian cult in Corinth make it likely that Paul knew "that some males in the church had engaged in passive or active homosexual acts prior to their conversion," and thus he "was deliberately addressing it in this letter."⁴² Jerome Murphy-O'Connor, among the chief advocates of this position, was unambiguous—for Paul long hair was closely associated with male homosexuality and as such was to be condemned.⁴³ It is likely, he argued, that Paul simply shared the views of the Jewish philosopher Philo (c. AD 50), who scorned pederasts "who habituate themselves to endure the disease of effemination ... and leave no ember of their male sex-nature to smoulder."⁴⁴ Such men, wrote Philo, "conspicuously ... braid[ing] and adorn[ing] the hair of their heads," transforming "the male nature to the female"

---

³⁷ "The real issue was the way hair was dressed. The slightest exaggeration was interpreted as a sign of effeminacy; it hinted at sexual ambiguity." Jerome Murphy-O'Connor, "Sex and Logic in 1 Corinthians 11:2–16," *Catholic Biblical Quarterly* 42 (1980): 487. The *Sentences* of Pseudo-Phocylides (210–12) also bear out this point: "Do not grow locks in the hair of a male child. Braid not his crown or the cross-knots on the top of his head. For men to wear long hair is not seemly, just for sensual women." Walter Wilson, *The Sentences of Pseudo-Phocylides* (Berlin: de Gruyter, 2005), 200.

³⁸ Musonius Rufus also directly addressed facial hair, writing, "The beard should not be shaved, since it is a protection provided to us by nature. Furthermore, the beard is the emblem of manhood—the human equivalent of the cock's crest and the lion's mane. Therefore, a man ought to remove hair that is bothersome, but not his beard." Musonius Rufus, *Lectures & Sayings*, trans. Cynthia King (Scotts Valley, CA: CreateSpace Independent Publishing, 2011), 81.

³⁹ Conzelmann, *1 Corinthians*, 190–91; Hans Lietzmann, *An die Korinther I/II* (Tübingen: Mohr Siebeck, 1949), 55; Fitzmyer, *First Corinthians*, 421. See also Kirk MacGregor, "Is 1 Corinthians 11:2–16 a Prohibition of Homosexuality?," *Bibliotheca Sacra* 166 (2009): 201–16.

⁴⁰ See especially the collection of Hans Herter, "Effeminatus," *Reallexikon für Antike und Christentum* 4 (1959): 620–50.

⁴¹ "Do you not know that wrongdoers will not inherit the kingdom of God? Do not be deceived! Fornicators, idolaters, adulterers, male prostitutes, sodomites."

⁴² Philip Barton Payne, *Man and Woman, One in Christ: An Exegetical and Theological Study of Paul's Letters* (Grand Rapids, MI: Zondervan, 2015), 143. In this he is also followed by Paul Gardner, who also thinks this verse "has to do with conventions that long hair on a man, as in many contemporary societies, indicates effeminacy or that men are trying to look like women." Gardner, *1 Corinthians*, 496. See also C. K. Barrett who thinks "the horror of homosexualism is behind a good deal of Paul's argument in this paragraph." *The First Epistle to the Corinthians* (New York: Harper and Row Publishers, 1968), 257.

⁴³ Murphy-O'Connor, "Sex and Logic," 482–500; see also Murphy-O'Connor, "1 Corinthians 11:2–16 Once Again," *Catholic Biblical Quarterly* 50 (1988): 265–74; for a different view see J. Delobel, "1 Cor 11:2–16: Towards a Coherent Explanation," in Albert Vanhoye, ed., *L'apôtre Paul: Personalité, style et conception du ministère* (Leuven: Leuven University Press, 1986), 369–89.

⁴⁴ Philo of Alexandria, *On the Special Laws*, 3: 37–38; *Philo Works*, vol. 7: *On the Decalogue. On the Special Laws, Books 1–3*, trans. F. H. Colson (Cambridge, MA: Harvard University Press, 1937), 499.

without "rais[ing] a blush," are "rightly judged worthy of death by those who obey the law, which ordains that the man-woman who debases the sterling coin of nature should perish unavenged."[45]

If Jews and Greeks shared similar attitudes about hair length, the same cannot be said about beards, for while the Jews continued to grow facial hair in observance of the law, most of their contemporaries did not, for "the practice of shaving, or at least trimming the beard, prevailed in the Greco-Roman world, with occasional vagaries of fashion, from the time of Alexander the Great."[46] Ticinius Mena, a Sicilian, is reputed to have been the first to bring barbers to Rome shortly after the death of Alexander, while Scipio Aemilianus (d. 129 BC), adoptive grandson of Scipio Africanus (d. 183 BC), introduced the practice of daily shaving.[47] By the time of Christ, and for several centuries afterward, Roman men were, by and large, beardless, portraying their heroes, emperors, and gods in similar fashion.

It is this last fact that best explains why, throughout the first five centuries of the Christian era, most images of Christ portrayed him as clean-shaven despite the historical likelihood that, as a Jew, he would have been bearded.[48] "Early Christians worked from what they knew, and this was representations of the pagan gods such as Apollo, Hermes, or *Sol Invictus* (i.e., Invincible Sun). In classical art these gods were depicted with long, loose locks and smooth, ageless faces," which is why the earliest images of Christ (e.g., the Good Shepherd) tend to show a youthful, beardless Jesus.[49] Robin Jensen, citing the sixth-century mosaics of Saint Appollinaire Nuovo in Ravenna (alongside other depictions), notes that this was especially true of the "healing and wonder-working" Jesus, who was often pictured as an ageless and beautiful youth, while Christ the "philosopher, teacher, ruler" tended to be older and bearded.[50]

---

[45] Ibid.

[46] Constable, "Introduction on Beards in the Middle Ages," 86. "Before Alexander's time, a respectable Greek man was fully bearded. Afterward he was shaved." Oldstone-Moore, *Of Beards and Men*, 38. The Greeks did not let go of the beard so easily. Dio Chrysostom (c. AD 155) told a story of a gathering of Greeks: "A philosopher would have been vastly pleased at the sight, because all were like the ancient Greeks described by Homer, long-haired and with flowing beards, and only one among them was shaven, and he was subjected to the ridicule and resentment of them all. And it was said that he practiced shaving, not as an idle fancy, but out of flattery of the Romans and to show his friendship toward them. And so one could have seen illustrated in his case how disgraceful the practice is and how unseemly for real men." Dio Chrysostom, *Discourses*, vol. 3, trans. J. W. Cohoon (Cambridge, MA: Harvard University Press, 1995), 437.

[47] "The next agreement between nations was in the matter of shaving the beard, but with the Romans this was later. Barbers came to Rome from Sicily in 300 B.C., according to Varro, being brought there by Publius Titinius Mena; before then the Romans had been unshaved. The second Africanus first introduced a daily shave. His late Majesty Augustus never neglected the razor." Pliny the Elder, *The Natural History* 7.59, trans. H. Rackham (Cambridge, MA: Harvard University Press, 1942), 649.

[48] The bibliography for early Christian art is vast, but some recent works in English include Robin M. Jensen, *Face to Face: Portraits of the Divine in Early Christianity* (Minneapolis, MN: Augsburg Fortress, 2004); Robin M. Jensen, *Understanding Early Christian Art* (London: Routledge, 2000); Jeffrey Spier, ed., *Picturing the Bible: The Earliest Christian Art* (New Haven, CT: Yale University Press, 2009); Jaś Elsner, *Imperial Rome and Christian Triumph: The Art of the Roman Empire, AD 100–450* (Oxford: Oxford University Press, 1998); John Lowden, *Early Christian and Byzantine Art* (London: Phaidon, 1997); Thomas Matthews, *The Clash of Gods: A Reinterpretation of Early Christian Art* (Princeton, NJ: Princeton University Press, 1993).

[49] Oldstone-Moore, *Of Beards and Men*, 65–66. For the Christian appropriation of Greek mythology see the classic work of Hugo Rahner, *Greek Myths and Christian Mystery*, trans. B. Battershaw (New York: Harper & Row, Publishers; 1963).

[50] Jensen, *Face to Face*, 146–65; Robin M. Jensen, "The Two Faces of Jesus," *Bible Review* 18 (2002): 42–50.

Sometimes artists portrayed the Jesus of earthly ministry as youthful, while the Jesus of the passion and resurrection was older—"the mature god who is entering his inheritance and becoming both King and Lord."[51] In many depictions what stands out is how Jesus's facial hair or lack of it "contrasts with those around him, reinforcing his uniqueness. On earth the smooth-faced Christ is the divine man among bearded mortals. In the world above, he is the bearded Son of Man, in striking contrast to the smooth-faced angels who populate heaven."[52] Only later (sixth to seventh centuries) would images of the bearded, more iconic, Jesus come to predominate, although the beardless Christ appears in the West as late as the sixteenth century, most famously in Michelangelo's *Last Judgment*.[53]

Imperial whim sometimes affected how beardlessness was perceived during Christianity's early centuries, for while the majority of emperors were clean-shaven, occasionally emperors did allow their beards to grow. For example, facial hair briefly came back into fashion during the reign of the emperor Hadrian (d. 138), who allegedly "wore a full beard to cover up the natural blemishes on his face."[54] Marcus Aurelius (d. 180) was bearded, perhaps inspired by the writings of his personal physician Galen, who maintained that men's hairiness confirmed not only their manliness but also their natural superiority and strength.[55] Julian the Apostate (361–63) composed his famous work *The Beardhater* (*Misopogon*) after a stay in Antioch when locals made sport of his unkempt beard.[56] Julian contrasted his own bearded masculinity with the effeminacy of the Antiochenes, whom he deemed girlish and morally corrupt. Writing about his beard, he told them:

> You say that I ought to twist ropes from it! Well I am willing to provide you with ropes if only you have the strength to pull them and their roughness does not do dreadful damage to your "unworn and tender hands." But you, since even in your old age you emulate your own sons and daughters by your soft and delicate way of living, or perhaps by your effeminate dispositions, carefully make your chins smooth, and your manhood you barely reveal and slightly indicate by your foreheads, not by your jaws as I do.[57]

---

[51] Jensen, *Face to Face*, 162.

[52] Oldstone-Moore, *Of Beards and Men*, 72.

[53] A rare example of the beardless Christ in the East is found at Thessaloniki in the apse of Hosios David (the Latomou Monastery). This fifth- to sixth-century mosaic of the Theophany, which has the beardless Christ seated on a rainbow, may be an anti-Arian effort to portray Jesus as divine (Thomas Mathews and Eugenio Russo, *Scontro di dei: Una reinterptretazione dell'arte paleocristiana* [Milan: Jaca Books, 2018]) or simply a depiction of Jesus as a new kind of emperor (Andre Graber, *Christian Iconography: A Study of Its Origins* [Princeton: Princeton University Press, 1968]). Many thanks to my dear friend Prof. Evangelia Amoiridou of the University of Thessaloniki for giving me a tour of the site during my visit there.

[54] *Scriptores Historiae Augustae I*, 26, trans. David Magie (Cambridge, MA: Harvard University Press, 1921), 79.

[55] See Margaret Tallmadge, ed. and trans., *Galen on the Usefulness of the Parts of the Body: De usu partium*, 2 vols. (Ithaca, NY: Cornell University Press, 1968).

[56] "And let no one suppose that I am offended by your satire. For I myself furnish you with an excuse for it by wearing my chin as goats do, when I might, I suppose, make it smooth and bare as handsome youths wear theirs, and all women, who are endowed by nature with loveliness." Julian, *Misopogon*, trans. Wilmer Cave Wright in *The Works of the Emperor Julian II* (Cambridge, MA: Harvard University Press, 1913), 425. For more on this work see Nicholas Baker-Brian, "The Politics of Virtue in Julian's *Misopogon*," in Nicholas Baker-Brian and Shaun Tougher, eds., *Emperor and Author: The Writings of Julian the Apostate* (Swansea: Classical Press of Wales, 2012), 263–80.

[57] Julian, *Misopogon*, 425.

The Church Fathers

Among the Greek-speaking fathers the one who spoke most directly to the topic of facial hair was Clement of Alexandria (c. 215), who on several occasions spoke to the majesty and manliness of the beard. Clement, like many writers before him, equated beardlessness and long, styled hair with either youthful beauty or effeminacy,[58] which meant that men who shaved or adorned themselves were thought to have done so for one of two reasons, which were to be equally condemned—"if it is to attract men, is the act of an effeminate person, if to attract women, is the act of an adulterer."[59] For this reason he condemned all those who cut "their hair in an ungentlemanlike and meretricious way," divining them to be "adulterers and effeminate ... living for unholy acts of audacity ... and nefarious deeds."[60] For the sake of these men the cities were now "full of those who ... shave and pluck out hairs from these womanish creatures," places where men "give their hair to be pulled out in all ways by those who make it their trade, feeling no shame before the onlookers or those who approach, nor before themselves, being men."[61]

Although Clement denounced the clientele of such places as both shameless and vain,[62] he focused his attacks on the issue of effeminacy and the sexual sins to which it led. "How womanly," he argued, "for one who is a man to comb himself and shave himself with a razor, for the sake of fine effect, to arrange his hair at the looking-glass, to shave his cheeks, pluck hairs out of them, and smooth them.... And, in truth, unless you saw them naked, you would suppose them to be women."[63] Those who behaved in this manner "we ought not to call ... men, but lewd wretches, and effeminate, whose voices are feeble, and whose clothes are womanish both in feel and dye."[64] Clement concluded (and in this he was not alone) that these men had acted thus because they had chosen to play the role of a woman, or a young boy, in the sexual sphere, for "he who in the light of day denies his manhood, will prove himself manifestly a woman by night."[65] He believed that this kind of activity had been rightly condemned by the

---

[58] A later Greek saying captures this attitude perfectly: "There are two kinds of people in this world that go around beardless—boys and women, and I am neither one." See also Christina Thérèse Rooijakkers, "The Luscious Locks of Lust: Hair and the Construction of Gender in Egypt from Clement to the Fāṭimids," *Al-Masāq* 30 (2018): 26–55.

[59] Clement of Alexandria, *Paidogogus* 3.3; Eng. trans.: ANF 2:275–77.

[60] Ibid.

[61] Ibid. Even the very process of having the hair removed was to Clement a sign of the deviancy it led to, for "the using of pitch to pluck out hair" necessitated acts whereby "violence [was] done to nature's modesty," such as "the act of bending back, bending down ... and bending backwards in shameful postures. Yet the doers [are] not ashamed of themselves, but conduct themselves without shame in the midst of the youth, and in the gymnasium, where the prowess of man is tried. [Is not] the following of this unnatural practice ... the extreme of licentiousness? For those who engage in such practices in public will scarcely behave with modesty to any at home. Their want of shame in public attests their unbridled licentiousness in private." Ibid.

[62] Clement reserved particular scorn for the vanity of the elderly, who by the "dyeing of hair and anointing of grey locks ... think, that like serpents, they divest themselves of the old age of their head by painting and renovating themselves. But though they do doctor the hair cleverly, they will not escape wrinkles, nor will they elude death by tricking time." Ibid.

[63] Ibid. According to Giles Constable, Clement's writings were "probably directed against the smooth skin achieved by daily shaving or by depilation and did not mean that men were expected to have long or full beards." Constable, "Introduction on Beards in the Middle Ages," 86.

[64] Clement of Alexandria, *Paidogogus* 3.3; Eng. trans.: ANF 2:275–77.

[65] Ibid.

ancient Romans, who "detested effeminacy of conduct; and the giving of the body to feminine purposes, contrary to the law of nature, they judged worthy of the extremest penalty, according to the righteousness of the law."[66] Yet Alexandrian society had become so decadent that it had come to accept this unnatural state of affairs as natural, where "men play the part of women, and women that of men, contrary to nature; women are at once wives and husbands: no passage is closed against libidinousness; and their promiscuous lechery is a public institution."[67] This decadence had permitted, and even sanctioned, pederasty, where young boys are "taught to deny their sex [and] act the part of women," compelled to practice things "they would, if they were men, die rather than do."[68]

In order to correct this unnatural state of affairs, Clement urged Christian men to follow the "natural" way—that is, that they should behave and look like men, which included growing the very "mark of the man," the beard. The beard, he wrote,

> by which he is seen to be a man, is older than Eve, and is the token of the superior nature. In this God deemed it right that he should excel, and dispersed hair over man's whole body. Whatever smoothness and softness was in him He abstracted from his side when He formed the woman Eve.... It is therefore impious to desecrate the symbol of manhood, hairiness. "But the very hairs of your head are all numbered," says the Lord; those on the chin, too, are numbered, and those on the whole body.[69]

In the same section he wrote:

> God wished women to be smooth, and rejoice in their locks alone growing spontaneously, as a horse in his mane; but has adorned man, like the lions, with a beard, and endowed him, as an attribute of manhood, with shaggy breasts, a sign this of strength and rule. So also cocks, which fight in defense of the hens, he has decked with combs, as it were helmets; and so high a value does God set on these locks, that He orders them to make their appearance on men simultaneously with discretion, and delighted with a venerable look, has honored gravity of countenance with grey hairs.[70]

Since this was the way of nature, and thus God's own will, Clement argued that "it is not lawful to pluck out the beard, man's natural and noble ornament," for just as "lions glory in their shaggy hair ... and boars even are made imposing by their mane," men are called to glory in their hair.[71] It is the beard by which "he is anointed ... on which descended the prophetic ointment with which Aaron was honoured."[72] Rather than be sheered like sheep, it is better if we imitate the barbarians (like the Celts and Scythians) whose bushy hair "has something fearful in it and its auburn color threatens war, the

---

[66] Ibid.
[67] Ibid.
[68] Ibid.
[69] Ibid.
[70] Ibid.
[71] Ibid.
[72] Ibid.

hue being somewhat akin to blood."[73] Like them we should abandon the luxury that inculcates immoral behavior, and obtain the true beauty to which we are called—the beauty of the mind and the soul.[74]

This equating of beardlessness with effeminacy, and with the moral implications of confusing sexual roles, appears also in *The Panarion* of Epiphanius. In treating the Messalians Epiphanius related that because they "have supposedly come to faith in Christ, they see fit to gather [in mixed companies] of men and women [and] in the summertime they sleep in the public squares, all together in a mixed crowd, men with women and women with men."[75] Although Epiphanius had no concrete knowledge that this led to sexual misconduct, "they can have no lack of this especially with their custom of sleeping all together in the same place."[76] This disregard for sexual differentiation had led the Messalian men not only let their hair grow long (in violation of the biblical injunction of 1 Cor 11:14) but to commit "the opposite error"—that is, to cut off their beards, "the mark of manhood."[77] This, he argued, was contrary to "the sacred instruction and teaching of the Ordinance of the Apostles [which] says not to 'spoil,' that is, not to cut the beard."[78]

The "Ordinance of the Apostles" mentioned here refers to the *Apostolic Constitutions*, with which Epiphanius was familiar, and which had provided (among other things) rules to govern relations between the sexes.[79] After enjoining Christian men not to become a scandal to women by making themselves too beautiful (and thus an occasion of sin), the *Constitutions* provided a list of prohibitions that served to keep men from ensnaring women. Prohibited were gold rings; fine shoes, stockings, and garments; and, of course, long hair.

> Thus, do not thou permit the hair of thy head to grow too long, but rather cut it short; lest by a nice combing thy hair, and wearing it long, and anointing thyself, thou draw upon thyself such ensnared or ensnaring women.... for it is not lawful for thee, a believer and a man of God, to permit the hair of thy head to grow long, and to brush it up together, nor to suffer it to spread abroad, nor to puff it up, nor by nice combing and platting to make it curl and shine; since that is contrary to the law, which says thus, in its additional precepts: "You shall not make to yourselves curls and round rasures."[80]

---

[73] Ibid.
[74] "The man, who would be beautiful, must adorn that which is the most beautiful thing in man, his mind, which every day he ought to exhibit in greater comeliness; and should pluck out not hairs, but lusts." Ibid.
[75] Epiphanius of Salamis, *Panarion*, 80; Eng. trans.: Epiphanius of Salamis, *Panarion of Epiphanius of Salamis, Book II and III (Sects 47–80, De Fide)*, 2nd ed., trans. Frank Williams (Leiden: Brill, 2013), 646.
[76] Ibid., 648.
[77] Ibid., 651.
[78] Ibid.
[79] Modern scholarly opinion suggests the *Apostolic Constitutions* were composed in Syria around 350–380, although it was long believed to be from an earlier period (i.e., from the time of Clement of Rome). Sections I–VI are a reworking of the earlier *Didascalia Apostolorum*. For more on the *Constitutions* the recent critical edition in Marcel Metzger, *Les Constitutions Apostoliques 1–3*, SC 320, 329, 336 (Paris: Les éditions du Cerf, 1985–87).
[80] *Apostolic Constitutions* I.2; ANF 7:392.

As was often the case, the prohibition against long, luxurious hair was joined with the injunction:

> Nor may men destroy the hair of their beards, and unnaturally change the form of a man. For the law says: "Ye shall not mar your beards." For God the Creator has made this decent for women, but has determined that it is unsuitable for men. But if thou do these things to please men, in contradiction to the law, thou wilt be abominable with God, who created thee after His own image.[81]

What is interesting here is the reference to Leviticus 19:27, for since the time of Paul the church had made it abundantly clear that the Law was unnecessary for salvation and for this reason had since abandoned most of its precepts. Why then was the Levitical legislation concerning hair apparently still binding? The answer is perhaps provided later in the *Constitutions*, where Christians were asked "to distinguish what rules [in the Law] were from the law of nature, and what were added afterwards ... in the wilderness ... after the making of the calf."[82] Christians were not "bound to observe the additional precepts ... which were further laid upon them after they had sinned ... for our Savior came for no other reason but that He might deliver from wrath that which was reserved for them."[83] However, the Levitical legislation concerning beards was apparently part of the "law of nature" governing the relationships between men and women—that is, ensuring each sex maintained its own distinct characteristics—and as such it had *not* been abrogated by the coming of Christ.

Because the Law's precepts regarding hair and beards remained valid as reflections of the natural law, many fathers continued to cite them when writing on the subject. Ambrosiaster, in his commentary on Corinthians, grounded Paul's prohibition against long hair on Leviticus 19:27,[84] and in giving advice to Quirinus on how the God-fearing must act, Cyprian of Carthage included the injunction that "the beard must not be plucked," citing Leviticus as biblical warrant.[85] The idea that church teaching on hair and beards was related to the natural law also governed several fathers' commentaries on 1 Corinthians 11:14, as Augustine and others argued that when people ignored the tradition of the church (perhaps, he speculated, because "they were trying to furnish greater leisure to the barbers"), one could, like Paul, still appeal to the law of nature.[86] According to John Chrysostom, Paul here was "betaking himself of common custom," in order to show that the prohibition against long hair was "written in the law of nature," so that the law of God was merely ratifying an idea "which even from men's

---

[81] Ibid.
[82] Ibid.
[83] *Apostolic Constitutions* I.6; ANF 7:393.
[84] "This is in line with Leviticus which prohibits a man from having long hair." Ambrosiaster, *Commentary on Romans and 1–2 Corinthians*, trans. Gerald Bray (Downers Grove, IL: IVP Academic, 2009), 173.
[85] Cyprian of Carthage, *Three Books of Testimonies Against the Jews* 3.84; ANF 5:553.
[86] Augustine asked whether those with long hair "wish to imitate the birds of the gospel? Maybe they fear being plucked so that they might be unable to fly?" Augustine of Hippo, *De opere monachorum* 39; Eng. trans.: Augustine of Hippo, *Treatises on Various Subjects*, trans. Sister Mary Sarah Muldowney, FC 16 (Washington, DC: Catholic University of America Press, 1952), 389. Ambrosiaster too wrote: "Since the Corinthians were ignoring [church tradition], Paul made his appeal not to the authority of tradition, which they had disregarded, but to the argument from nature, and what he says is right." Ambrosiaster, *Commentary on Romans and 1–2 Corinthians*, 173.

ordinary practice they might have learned. For such things are not unknown even to Barbarians."[87] Ambrose wrote that "nature lays down definite instruction" in this matter, for it was both a "falsification of nature" and "unsightly ... for a man to act like a woman," assuming "women's clothing and female gestures ... [and] curl[ing] their hair like women.... For this reason the Law declares that every man who puts on a woman's garment is an abomination to the Lord."[88]

Although not as concerned with shaving's association with effeminacy and certain proscribed sexual activities, the Western fathers, like their contemporaries in the East, lionized the beard as a sign of both manliness and manly virtues. For Lactantius, beards "contribute in an incredible degree to distinguish the maturity of bodies, or to distinguish the sex, or to contribute to the beauty of manliness and strength."[89] However, Augustine maintained that the beard is an essentially useless item, since it served no real purpose—it was simply for the adornment of man.[90] He argued that this fact "is made clear by the smooth faces of women who, as weaker, are obviously the ones who ought to be better protected."[91]

It was Augustine who, in his *Exposition on the Psalms*, provided one of the most detailed explanations of the meaning of the beard, both societally and theologically. Commenting on Psalm 132(3):2 ("It is like precious oil poured on the head, running down on the beard, running down on Aaron's beard, down upon the collar of his robes"), Augustine wrote that just as the oil poured from Aaron's head onto his beard, so too the grace of the Holy Spirit poured from Christ, the head, onto the beard, the apostles, for "the beard is a sign of strong men; a beard is typical of young, vigorous, energetic eager people. That's why we say, 'He's a bearded fellow' when we describe someone of this character."[92] The apostles and martyrs, fortified against persecution like a beard anointed with oil, "suffered but were not overcome," allowing the oil to flow down upon the tunic, the church.[93] Cassiodorus followed Augustine's exegesis

---

[87] John Chrysostom, *Homilies on First Corinthians* 26; NPNF 1.12.154.

[88] "If you investigate the matter well, what nature herself abhors must be unsuitable, for why do you want to seem not a man when you were born one? Why do you assume an appearance not yours? Why play the woman, or you, woman, the man? Nature clothes each sex in its proper raiment." Ambrose could understand why some women preferred to dress as men and "imitate the nature of the better sex, but why should men want to assume the appearance of the inferior sex?" Ambrose of Milan, *Letter 78 to Irenaeus*; Eng. trans.: Ambrose of Milan, *Letters*, trans. Sister Mary Melchior Beyenka, O.P., FC 26 (Washington, DC: Catholic University of America Press, 1954), 435–37.

[89] Lactantius, *On the Workmanship of God* 7; ANF 7:288.

[90] "There are some things that are positioned in the body in such a way that they have only beauty but no use. A man's chest has nipples, for example, and his face has a beard." Augustine of Hippo, *City of God* 22.24; Eng. trans.: Saint Augustine, *The City of God Books 11–22*, trans. William Babcock (Hyde Park, NY: New City Press, 2013), 540.

[91] Ibid., 540–41.

[92] Augustine of Hippo, *Commentary on Psalm 132.7*; St. Augustine, *Exposition on the Psalms*, vol. 5, trans. Maria Boulding (Hyde Park, NY: New City Press, 2004), 182. The Venerable Bede continued along these lines, arguing, "A beard too, which is a sign of male sex and maturity, is customarily taken to mean virtue." Bede, *On Ezra and Nehemiah*, trans. Scott DeGregorio (Liverpool: Liverpool University Press, 2006), 140.

[93] Augustine of Hippo, *Exposition on the Psalms*, vol. 5, 182. Ambrose included not only the apostles but also "priests ... [who] are as the cheeks of the Church, on which is the beard of Aaron, that is, the beard of the priesthood (*barba Aaron, hoc est barba sacerdotalis*) upon which the ointment descends from the head." Ambrose, *De obitu Valentiniani* 7; Eng. trans.: St Gregory Nazianzen and St Ambrose, *Funeral Orations*, trans. Leo McCauley, John Sullivan, Martin McGuire, and Roy Deferrari, FC 22 (Washington, DC: Catholic University of America Press, 1953), 268.

of this passage, writing that "we do well to interpret beard as apostles here, for a beard is the mark of the most forceful manliness, remaining immovable below its head."[94] Elsewhere, describing how to recognize a good man, Cassiodorus described him as someone "made reverend by a long beard," associating facial hair not only with strength, but also with the Christian's contemplation of wisdom and truth.[95]

Other passages in the Old Testament that dealt with beards (e.g., 1 Kgs 21:13, 2 Kgs 10:4–5 and 19:24, Is 7:20 and 15:2) did not elicit much comment, although several fathers spoke to the Nazirite vow as found in Numbers 6:1–21. The idea that the Nazirite should grow his hair and then, at the conclusion of his vow, shave his head and present the hairs to the Lord as a sacrifice, was interpreted by Isidore of Seville and others as a precursor of the clerical tonsure.[96] Isidore wrote that tonsure was the symbol of something "performed in the soul" whereby we "cast off crimes of our flesh just like our hairs."[97] Gregory the Great—whose own beard was described as "somewhat tawny and sparse" (*subfulva et modica*)[98]—likened the Nazirite practice to the cutting off of "superfluous thoughts" and the "overcom[ing] of evil habits," two things to which every priest should aspire.[99] Gregory's view, it should be noted, eventually became the chief argument for both tonsure and clerical beardlessness in the Latin West.

The one mention of beards in the Old Testament that did generate interest was Ezekiel 5:1–4, which described the Lord's command to Ezekiel that he completely shave his head, divide the hairs, and burn them in a fire.[100] The cutting of the prophet's hair and beard were interpreted by Theodoret of Cyrus as a "loss of comeliness"[101] and by Jerome as the "shameful nakedness" associated with the removal of one's "beauty and virility."[102] Jerome, later commenting upon the rules for the Levitical priesthood,[103] encouraged those who served the Lord to wear their hair short "to show forth the modesty that should characterize a priest's outward appearance."[104]

---

[94] Cassiodorus, *Explanation of Psalm 132*; Eng. trans.: Cassiodorus, *Explanations of the Psalms*, vol. 3, trans. P. G. Walsh, ACW 53 (New York: Paulist Press, 1991), 334.

[95] Cassiodorus, *De Anima* 2.13; Eng. trans.: Cassiodorus, *Institutions of Divine and Secular Learning and On the Soul*, trans. James W. Halporn and Mark Vessey (Liverpool: Liverpool University Press, 2004), 273.

[96] Isidore of Seville, *De Ecclesiasticis Officiis*, 2.4.3–5; Eng. trans.: Isidore of Seville, *De Ecclesiasticis Officiis*, trans. Thomas Knoebel, ACW 61 (New York, Paulist Press, 2008), 70–71.

[97] Ibid.

[98] John the Deacon, *Vita Gregorii* 4.48; Eng. trans.: Constant Mews and Claire Renkin, "The Legacy of Gregory the Great in the Latin West," in Bronwen Neil and Matthew Dal Santo, eds., *A Companion to Gregory the Great* (Leiden: Brill, 2013), 326.

[99] Gregory the Great, *Moralia in Iob* 2.82; Eng. trans.: Gregory the Great, *Morals on the Book of Job*, vol. 1, trans. Edward Pusey, John Keble, and John Henry Newman (Jackson, MI: Ex Fontibus, 2012), 117–18.

[100] "And you, O mortal, take a sharp sword; use it as a barber's razor and run it over your head and your beard; then take balances for weighing, and divide the hair. One third of the hair you shall burn in the fire inside the city, when the days of the siege are completed; one third you shall take and strike with the sword all around the city; … and one third you shall scatter to the wind, and I will unsheathe the sword after them. Then you shall take from these a small number, and bind them in the skirts of your robe. From these, again, you shall take some, throw them into the fire and burn them up; from there a fire will come out against all the house of Israel."

[101] Theodoret of Cyrus, *Commentaries on Ezekiel* 5; Theodoret of Cyrus, *Commentaries on Ezekiel*, trans. Robert Charles Hill (Brookline, MA: Holy Cross Orthodox Press, 2006), 59.

[102] Jerome, *Commentarii in Ezechielem* 2.5; Eng. trans.: Jerome, *Commentary on Ezekiel*, trans. Thomas Scheck, ACW 71 (New York: Newman Press, 2017). Jerome writes that this prophetic gesture was a sign that just as the hairs are removed from the body and thus dead, "so Jerusalem and its people are dead and separated from the living body of God."

[103] "They shall not shave their heads or let their locks grow long; they shall only trim the hair of their heads" (Ez 44:20).

[104] Jerome, *Commentarii in Ezechielem* 13.44; Eng. trans.: Jerome, *Commentary on Ezekiel*.

It was this preoccupation with Christian modesty that governed much of the fathers' thinking concerning both hair and beards, especially in the West.[105] Tertullian was among the many fathers who equated shaving with the excessive (and sinful) desire to adorn the body in order to lure the opposite sex. In his work *On the Apparel of Women*, having first addressed women on the virtue of modesty, he then turned to men.

> This sex of ours acknowledges its own deceptive trickeries, peculiarly its own—(such as) to cut the beard too sharply; to pluck it out here and there; to shave round about (the mouth); to arrange the hair, and disguise its hoariness by dyes; to remove all the incipient down all over the body; to fix (each particular hair) in its place with (some) womanly pigment; to smooth all the rest of the body by the aid of some rough powder or other.[106]

Cyprian of Carthage pursued the same logic, criticizing those who had lapsed from the faith and begun to adorn themselves without shame, with men plucking their beards and women going about with "their faces painted, their eyes ... daubed other than God made them [and] their hair stained a color not their own."[107]

Of course, it was also quite possible that men might *grow* their beards in order to lure the opposite sex, explaining Jerome's warning in his *Letter to Eustochium* against those who claimed to "minister" to women with their "hair contrary to the apostle's admonition, worn long like a woman's, with beards like goats.... All these things are the devil's tricks."[108] Elsewhere he protested against allegedly holy men who go about "with girded loins, sombre tunics, and long beards, who yet can never leave women's society. They live with them under one roof ... and, save that they are not called husbands, they enjoy all the privileges of marriage."[109] John Chrysostom also recognized the dangers posed by these alleged purveyors of wisdom who went about "clad in tattered robes displaying a long beard ... making themselves more vile than dogs under the table yet doing everything for the sake of the belly."[110] Having forsaken the search for true wisdom, they used their outward appearance (including their "philosopher's beard") to deceive and were "in character no wise better than those who are engaged on the stage, and in the sports of actors; and they have nothing to show beyond the threadbare cloak, the beard, and the long robe!"[111] Christian philosophers, true lovers

---

[105] A key text in this regard was 1 Peter 3:3–4: "Do not adorn yourselves outwardly by braiding your hair, and by wearing gold ornaments or fine clothing; rather, let your adornment be your inner self with lasting beauty of a gentle and quiet spirit, which is very precious in God's sight."

[106] Tertullian, *On the Apparel of Women* 2.8; ANF 4:22. For more on this subject see Carly Daniel-Hughes, *The Salvation of the Flesh in Tertullian of Carthage: Dressing for the Resurrection* (New York: Palgrave Macmillan, 2011).

[107] Cyprian of Carthage, *On the Lapsed* 6; Eng. trans.: Cyprian of Carthage, *The Lapsed: The Unity of the Catholic Church*, trans. Maurice Bévenot, ACW 25 (New York: Paulist Press, 1956), 17.

[108] Jerome, *Letter to Eustochium* 22.28; Jerome, *The Letters of Jerome*, vol. 1, trans. Charles Christopher Mierow, ACW 33 (New York: Newman Press, 1963), 162.

[109] Jerome, *Letter to Rusticus* 125.6; Jerome, *Select Letters of Saint Jerome*, trans. F. A. Wright (New York: G.P. Putnam's Sons, 1933), 407.

[110] John Chrysostom, *Homilies on the Statutes* 17 (NPNF 1.9.454). Chrysostom often attacked the external trappings of the philosophers, including their beards, staffs, and robes.

[111] John Chrysostom, *Homilies on the Statutes* 19 (NPNF 1.9.465).

of wisdom, "on the contrary, bidding farewell to staff and beard, and the other accoutrements, have their souls adorned with the doctrines of the true philosophy, and not only with the doctrines, but also with the real practice."[112]

Interestingly, the thinking behind Chrysostom and Jerome's anti-beard stance and the pro-beard stance of the other fathers is remarkably similar. For all concerned the issue was not the beard itself, but the message it sent both spiritually and, perhaps more importantly, sexually. Aside from the sinful preoccupation with the beauty of the body, there was always the fear that one would use facial hair, or the lack of it, to lure men and women into illicit sexual activity. For Clement, Tertullian, and Cyprian beardlessness meant that men were trying to attract others by looking younger or more feminine, while for Jerome and Chrysostom the beard was a prop used to ensnare innocent women. The real issue for everyone involved was not facial hair, but chastity.

This same logic also seems to be behind the ninety-sixth canon of the Quinisext Council, (also known as the Council in Trullo), which had echoed the *Constitutions* by condemning "those who adorn and arrange their hair to the detriment of those who see them ... and by this means put a bait in the way of unstable souls."[113] Centuries later, long after the beardlessness of the Latin clergy became an issue, Nicodemus the Hagorite interpreted this canon as a prohibition against both long hair *and* beardlessness, applying the excommunication associated with it to

> those who shave off their beard in order to make their face smooth and handsome after such treatment, and not to have it curly, or in order to appear at all times like beardless young men; and those who singe the hair of their beard with a red-hot tile so as to remove any that is longer than the rest, or more crooked; or who use tweezers to pluck out the superfluous hairs on their face, in order to become tender and appear handsome; or who dye their beard, in order not to appear to be old men.[114]

Monastic legislation in both East and West often demanded that no one could enter the community "with a female (i.e., beardless) face"—the idea being that one had to be a mature man rather than a beardless youth in order to be a monk.[115] Although Macarius

---

[112] Ibid.

[113] "Those who by baptism have put on Christ have professed that they will copy his manner of life which he led in the flesh. Those therefore who adorn and arrange their hair to the detriment of those who see them, that is by cunningly devised intertwinings, and by this means put a bait in the way of unstable souls, we take in hand to cure paternally with a suitable punishment ... [so that they] may thus come as near as possible to God through their purity of life; and adorn the inner man rather than the outer, and that with virtues, and good and blameless manners, so that they leave in themselves no remains of the left-handedness of the adversary. But if any shall act contrary to the present canon let him be cut off." *Canons of the Council in Trullo* 96; NPNF 2.14.406. For more on the council see Demetrios Constantelos, *Renewing the Church: The Significance of the Council in Trullo* (Brookline, MA: Holy Cross Orthodox Press, 2006); George Nedungatt and Michael Featherstone, eds., *The Council in Trullo Revisited* (Rome: Pontifical Oriental Institute, 1995); O. H. Ohgme, "Das Concilium Quinisextum. Neue Einsichten zu einem umstrittenen Konzil," *Orientalia Christiana Periodica* 56 (1992): 367–400.

[114] Nicodemus the Hagorite, *The Rudder (Pedalion) of the Metaphorical Ship of the One Holy Catholic and Apostolic Church of the Orthodox Christians*, trans. Denver Cummings (Chicago: Orthodox Christian Educational Society, 1957), 403–5.

[115] André-Jean Festugière, *Vie de Théodore de Sykéon, Subsidia hagiographica 48* (Brussels: Société des Bollandistes, 1970), 202.

related how he accepted two young men, "one [of whom] had a beard, the other was beginning to grow one,"[116] others (e.g., Euthemius and Sabas) rejected youths who had not yet begun to shave. In the desert, where monastics were, and in many cases still are, marked by the length of their beards, biographers took pains to note this distinctive feature. Abba Or was described as angelic in appearance, "with a snowy white beard down to his chest,"[117] while Daniel the Stylite allegedly had a beard "divided into two and each plait was three cubits in length."[118] The hermit's beard was interpreted as a sign of renunciation, and in many cases the beard itself was seen to be one of the very marks of the monastic life.[119] At the same time, the severe ascetic practices of some saints was actually blamed for their inability to grow a proper beard, Palladius writing in the *Lausiac History* that Macarius of Alexandria went about "without a beard, having hair only about the lips and at the end of his chin, for the asceticism he practiced did not allow hair to sprout on him."[120] This tradition of "holy hairlessness" also manifested itself in the life of John of Lycopolis, who "in his ninetieth year [had] a body so worn out by *ascesis* that even his beard no longer grew on his face."[121]

Yet there were those who did not necessarily equate the beard (or its lack) with holiness. According to Grimlaicus's *Rules for Solitaries*, the desert father Apollo[nius] "scolded severely those who let their beard and hair grow long. He used to say: 'It is certain that these people are seeking praise from human beings and they are letting their beard and hair grow long to show off, even though we are commanded to celebrate even our fasts in private.'"[122] Quoting some advice given by Gregory the Great to a Roman laymen, Grimlaicus added: "If holiness were in a beard then no one would be holier than a goat."[123]

While the Council in Trullo never achieved great recognition in the West for a variety of ecclesiastical and political reasons, and Eastern monastic practice did not necessarily translate into the Latin world, that did not mean that Western canons were silent concerning hair and beards, especially when it came to the clergy. Already in

---

[116] *The Sayings of the Desert Fathers*, Macarius the Great, 33; Eng. trans.: *The Sayings of the Desert Fathers: The Alphabetical Collection*, trans. Benedicta Ward, CS 59 (Kalamazoo, MI: Cistercian Publications, 1975), 134.

[117] *Historia Monachorum in Aegypto*; Eng. trans.: *The Lives of the Desert Fathers*, trans. Norman Russell, CS 34 (Trappist, KY: Cistercian Publications, 1980), 63.

[118] *Life of Daniel the Stylite*, 98; Elizabeth Dawes and Norman H. Baynes. *Three Byzantine Saints: Contemporary Biographies of St. Daniel the Stylite, St. Theodore of Sykeon, and St. John the Almsgiver* (Oxford: Blackwell, 1948), 69.

[119] Some modern scholars even associate the abnormal growth of hair among the ascetics with the "protagonists' spiritual state … that the increased hairiness of desert hermits—a phenomena [sic] that resulted from their rigorous ascetic regimes—could have been read as already other-worldly.... [For] Christian ascetics were routinely figured as having progressed beyond the confines of their corporeality and—to some degree—to have achieved an 'angelic' state already in the here-and-now" (156). Upson-Saia, "Hairiness and Holiness in the Early Christian Desert."

[120] Palladius, *Lausiac History*, trans. Robert Meyer, ACW 34 (New York: Newman Press, 1964), 67.

[121] *Historia Monachorum in Aegypto*; Eng. trans.: *The Lives of the Desert Fathers*, 54.

[122] Grimlaicus, *Rules for Solitaries*, trans. Andrew Thornton, CS 200 (Kalamazoo, MI: Cistercian Publications, 2011), 136–37. The English translation of Rufinius's *Historia Monachorum* does not mention beards, only saying that Apollo "censured those who grow their hair long, wear iron around their neck, or perform any gesture which is done ostentatiously to attract attention." Rufinius, *Inquiry about the Monks in Egypt*, trans. Andrew Cain, FC 139 (Washington, DC: Catholic University of America Press, 2019), 122.

[123] Grimlaicus, *Rules for Solitaries*, 136–37. See also the earlier work of Eugene of Toledo, *Carmen* 89; MGH Auctores antiquissimi XIV, 266.

the second century Pope Anicetus had decreed that clerics "should not groom [their] hair ... as the apostle had instructed,"[124] and Augustine condemned long hair for monks in his *De opere monachorum*.[125] Among the earliest canons dealing specifically with beards was the fifth-century *Statuta ecclesiae antiqua* (c. 475), which mandated that "*clericus nec comam nutriat, nec barbam radat*" ("the cleric shall not let his hair grow, neither shall he shave his beard").[126] Ironically, this canon actually became the basis for later Western legislation *against* beards, as the *radat* at some point went missing from later manuscripts, so that it read "*clericus nec comam nutriat, nec barbam*" ("the cleric shall not let his hair grow nor his beard"). According to Giles Constable, how and when this happened remains a mystery, although the evidence suggests that the medieval copyists removed, or perhaps one should say "shaved off," the *radat* in order to conform with later Western practice.[127]

The same apparently happened to the third canon of the First Council of Barcelona (c. 540), which repeated the *Statuta ecclesiae antiqua*'s prohibition against shaving and long hair almost verbatim ("*Ut nullus clericorum comam nutriat aut barbam radat*").[128] This was probably done because Spain was then "being overrun by Visigoths and other barbarians wearing long beards," and because assimilation often helped priests in their "duty to convert and Christianize" them, it is "no wonder that bishops ordered the clergy to adopt, as far as possible, their way of living."[129] However, by the ninth century the canon was changed to read "*nullus clericorum comas nutriat vel barbam sed radat*" ("no cleric shall grow his hair or beard, but instead shall shave"), and it was in this form that it entered later canonical collections.[130]

Although these early canons seem to support a bearded clergy, "Neither *Statuta* 25 nor 1 Barcelona 3 is known to have had any influence in its original form."[131] Instead there is ample evidence that beardlessness was the general rule among the Latin clergy, who simply adopted the norms of Roman society and thus shaved their

---

[124] *Liber Pontificalis*; *The Book of Pontiffs*, trans. Raymond Davis (Liverpool: Liverpool University Press, 1989), 5. This is how the English translation rendered "*ut clerus comam non nutriet secundum praeceptum apostoli.*"

[125] Although he did not want to be too condemnatory "out of respect for certain long-haired brethren, ... whom, in almost all other respects, we hold in high esteem." Augustine of Hippo, *De opere monachorum* 39; Eng. trans.: Augustine. Of Hippo, *Treatises on Various Subjects*, 389.

[126] Charles Munier, *Le Statuta ecclesiae antiqua*, Bibliothèque de l'Institut de droit canonique de l'Université de Strasbourg, 5 (Paris: Presses universitaires de France, 1960), 85. Often wrongly cited as the forty-fourth canon of the Fourth Council at Carthage.

[127] See Constable, "Introduction on Beards in the Middle Ages," 103–5. Despite the efforts of some throughout the centuries to argue against this interpretation, Reginald Reynolds argued that it was more probable that "if any ruling was ever laid down about the year 500 or earlier it would have been in order to insist upon clerical beards rather than prohibit their growth." Reynolds, *Beards: An Omnium Gatherum*, 104.

[128] *Concilium Barcinonense Primum*, Canon 3 (PL 84:607).

[129] Charles Seghers, "The Practice of Shaving in the Latin Church," *American Catholic Quarterly Review* 7 (1882): 292.

[130] The 1234 Decretals of Pope Gregory IX, in the section dealing with the "Life and Character of the Clergy" (*Decretalium D. Gregorii Papae IX, Liber Tertius, Titulus I*), cited the amended Council of Carthage (*Clericus neque comam nutriat, neque barbam*) in support of clerical beardlessness. When Renaissance scholars like Giovan Pietro Pierio Valeriano first realized that the ancient canons had been altered in this way, it became a powerful weapon in their battle to reintroduce clerical beards in the West. See next chapter.

[131] Constable, "Introduction on Beards in the Middle Ages," 106.

beards.¹³² Later canons merely enforced a practice that had already become accepted custom, using the corrupted versions of the *Statuta ecclesiae antiqua* and the Council of Barcelona to give them the veneer of antiquity and authority. In support of this practice, canons originally forbidding only long hair (e.g., Canon 20 of the First Council of Agde [506]; Canon 17 of the Council of Rome [721]; Canon 8 of the Council of Rome [743]) were then interpreted to prohibit both long hair *and* beards, the growth of either usually punishable by anathema.¹³³ Sometimes the canons themselves were altered to reflect this change, so that by the time they entered the medieval collections they *explicitly* anathematized "any cleric or monk [who] lets down the hair *or presumes not to cut his beard*."¹³⁴ Beardlessness, especially among the clergy, was now well established both in practice and in law.

The justification for this practice came from two sources. The first was the ongoing concern that priests and those in orders should comport themselves in a manner consistent with the religious life. Modesty and chastity, especially for the clergy, remained paramount. The second reason was theological and concerned the legend of St. Peter's tonsure, a tradition known in both East and West.¹³⁵ According to the story, attested to as early as Gregory of Tours (d. 594), St. Peter, in order "to teach humility" (*ob humilitatem docendam*),¹³⁶ had "his head shaved by those who did not believe his word, as if in mockery."¹³⁷ Although the beard was not explicitly mentioned, its removal was soon assumed,¹³⁸ explaining why Peter was often portrayed in Western art as both tonsured and beardless.¹³⁹ At times St. Peter's tonsure, which was a circle cut away in the midst of the hair and interpreted as "a crown not made of precious stones [but rather with] the stone and rock of faith,"¹⁴⁰ was differentiated from the "total

---

¹³² "Beards were an unusual thing among the Romans, with the exception of philosophers; it is, therefore, more than likely that the early Roman Christians complied with that national custom." Seghers, "The Practice of Shaving in the Latin Church," 288.

¹³³ Canon 20 of the First Council of Agde (506) read, "*Clerici qui comam nutrient, ab archidiacono, etiam si noluerint, invite detundantur*"; Canon 17 of the Council of Rome (721) "*Si quis ex clericis relaxaverit comam, anathema sit*"; while canon 8 of the 743 council stated, "*Si quis clericus aut monachus comam laxare praesumpserit, anathema sit.*" According to Constable, all of these "were extended to apply to beards as well as hair already by the eleventh century." Constable, "Introduction on Beards in the Middle Ages," 107.

¹³⁴ Ibid. See Massimo Fornasari, ed., *Collectio Canonum in V Libris*, CCCM 6 (Turnholt: Brepols, 1970), 411. Canons from sixth-century Ireland mandated that priests should cut their hair and shave in the Roman fashion (*more Romano*) or else be excluded from "the company of Christians and the church." Ibid.

¹³⁵ In later centuries both Ratramnus of Corbie and Peter III of Antioch would cite the legend as a justification for tonsure/beardlessness. See next chapter.

¹³⁶ Gregory of Tours, *De Gloria Martyri* 1.28; Eng. trans.: Gregory of Tours, *The Glory of the Martyrs*, trans. Raymond Van Dam (Liverpool: Liverpool University Press, 1988), 45.

¹³⁷ Germanus of Constantinople, *On the Divine Liturgy*, trans. Paul Meyendorff (Crestwood, NY: St. Vladimir's Seminary Press, 1984), 65.

¹³⁸ Bede mentions a vision in which Peter and Paul appeared to a young boy, with Peter appearing "tonsured, like a cleric," which many have taken to indicate that by the eighth century Peter's tonsure was already understood to have included the beard. Bede, *The Ecclesiastical History of the English People*, trans. Judith McClure and Roger Collins (Oxford: Oxford University Press, 1969), 196. The seventeenth-century historian Christianus Lupus (d. 1681) quoted an allegedly ancient chronology that wrote how the pagans captured and shaved both Peter's beard and head (*barba rasus et capite*), thus instituting this practice in the church. See Seghers, "The Practice of Shaving in the Latin Church," 289.

¹³⁹ See John Higgitt, "The Iconography of St Peter in Anglo-Saxon England and St Cuthbert's Coffin," in Gerald Bonner, D. W. Rollason, and Clare Stancliffe, eds., *St. Cuthbert, His Cult and His Community: To AD 1200* (Woodbridge, Suffolk: Boydell Press, 1989), 267–86.

¹⁴⁰ Germanus of Constantinople, *On the Divine Liturgy*, 65.

tonsuring of the head in imitation of the holy Apostle James, brother of the Lord, and the Apostle Paul."[141] By the time legislation in the West began to mandate tonsure (understood as the cutting of both the hair and beard), specific reference was often made to Peter's example.[142] As far as the West was concerned, clerical beardlessness was now part of the apostolic tradition.

Conclusion

Having examined the subject of beards in Scripture and the fathers, it can be seen that there was indeed a biblical/patristic consensus on the matter of facial hair, and that it did, with some qualifications, favor the beard. It is, of course, true that beards were not one of the subjects upon which the fathers wrote a great deal, yet when they did have cause to speak of beards, the fathers, with few exceptions, spoke about them in a positive light. Beards were manly, a sign of virtue and strength, man's natural adornment akin to the lion's mane. Conversely, shaving the beard was a sign of effeminacy, associated with unnatural behaviors, the loss of comeliness, or sinful self-adornment. While the practice of the early church was not always uniform, and depended often enough on changing cultural norms, the patristic corpus as it has come down to us points to the view that the ancient church generally encouraged its members, clergy and lay, to be bearded rather than beardless.

This occurs, from what we have seen, for a number of reasons. The first is that, for the fathers, beards were part of the natural order—that is, grown men had beards, while boys and women did not. This led several of the fathers, most noticeably Clement and Epiphanius, to the conclusion that the beardless male was trying to play a sexual role contrary to his nature, shamelessly confusing the natural order of things as established by God himself. When Clement and the other fathers condemned the removal of the beard, it was not because they believed it to be holy or imbued by God with an inherent theological significance. On the contrary, the evidence suggests that beardlessness is condemned only to the extent that it had implications for Christian morality, especially as it concerned sexual behavior. Sexual immorality is condemned, and beardlessness only condemned insomuch as it was a sign of this lifestyle.

The second reason for the fathers' exaltation of the beard is closely related to the first and revolves around the sin of vanity. When a man spent his time curling his golden locks or making his face clean and beautiful, he demonstrated a vanity unseemly for a Christian, making his body attractive at the expense of his soul. Worse yet, if he did all this to lure members of the opposite sex into sins of the flesh, he became a danger to the moral health of the Christian community. Again, here it is not the beard, for its own sake, that is encouraged. In fact, Jerome and Chrysostom attest that the opposite

---

[141] Ibid., 69. According to Bede, the Greek monk Theodore, who had come to England to serve as Archbishop, had been given St. Paul's tonsure ("after the manner of the Easterns") and had to wait four months for his hair to grow so that "it could be shorn in the shape of a crown." Bede, *Ecclesiastical History of the English Nation*, 7. For more on the different forms of tonsure and their significance see Louis Trichet, *La Tonsure* (Paris: Les éditions du Cerf, 1990), 69–95.

[142] Among the first occurrences of this was at the Council of Limoges (1031).

is also true—that is, if the beard is grown in order to lure women, then it is the beard, rather than the clean-shaven face, that is to be condemned. Condemned are vanity and lust, and beardlessness only condemned as it led to these sins.

It is only with this in mind that the canonical legislation of the *Apostolic Constitutions* and the *Council in Trullo* make sense. These canons were never about hair, but about Christian morality. And what is particularly interesting about them is the fact that they were aimed at both priests and laity alike, and that it was only in the local Western councils that specific mention was made of clergy. Even here the logic was the same—if Christian men are discouraged from sins involving effeminacy, vanity, and lust, how much more should priests and monks avoid these traps. Interestingly, in the Latin West these canons originally encouraged the growth of the beard, despite later alterations as practice shifted in the post-patristic period. That said, what should be remembered is that both subsequent Latin practice and the long-standing Byzantine custom were ultimately grounded on the same underlying principles—that is, that Christian and clerical appearance should encourage the virtues of modesty and chastity, never giving rise to scandal or temptation. This was the true message of the fathers when it came beards—for Christian men, and especially for the clergy, the question whether to grow or to shave the beard was completely secondary to the primary goal of maintaining one's holiness, modesty, and virtue. For the fathers, East and West alike, a holy priest was far more pleasing to God than a hairy one.

2
Beards in the East-West Polemic

By the beginning of the ninth century the various linguistic, cultural, and political differences between East and West were already on display for all to see. This was especially true of the theological differences that had begun to emerge—for example, the growing awareness of the change the Franks had made to their creed—creating a perception that Greek Christianity and Latin Christianity were now becoming distinct entities. Charlemagne's imperial coronation on Christmas Day in the year 800, creating a rival to the empire centered in Constantinople, motivated both sides to highlight and weaponize these dissimilarities in their respective quests for legitimacy. The argument was simple: the true Christian Empire professed the orthodox faith, and the heterodox practices/belief of the other side clearly demonstrated why they had lost God's favor.[1]

It was in this atmosphere that the Byzantines first took note of the Latin clergy's habit of shaving, distinguishing it from the (relatively) long-standing Eastern practice of men wearing beards. At first not much was made of the difference, and exchanges in the ninth century rightly regarded it as a matter of custom rather than theology. Unfortunately, the rising tensions between East and West, coupled with the increased significance Latin authors gave to tonsure as a mark of the clerical state, meant the end of such toleration. By the mid-eleventh century beards, or the lack of them, became a casus belli in the conflict between Cardinal Humbert and Patriarch Michael Keroularios, and a firm fixture in subsequent polemical exchanges for the next two hundred years.

As with the azymes, the polemical heat generated by clerical shaving came largely from the Byzantine side, since for most Western authors facial hair, or its lack, seemed like a matter of little consequence. Even the rabidly anti-Byzantine Ratramnus of Corbie regarded the matter as "trivial" (*levis*), although he did not fail to remind the Greeks of the superiority of the Latin tradition. Although the theologians and canonists in the West had actually spent a great deal of time dealing with hair and beards, and on occasion even criticized the "long, ... ugly, and unclean" beards of the Greeks, for the West the real issue was not the growing or shaving of beards, but rather the presumption of the Byzantines in accusing the Latin church of heresy. Whatever their

---

[1] In a letter from Western Emperor Louis II (d. 875) to Byzantine Emperor Basil I (d. 886) the logic of the argument was set forth: "As we, through our faith in Christ, are the seed of Abraham, and as the Jews for their treachery have ceased to be the sons of Abraham, we have received the government of the Roman Empire for our right thinking or orthodoxy. The Greeks for their cacodoxy, that is, wrong thinking, have ceased to be Emperors of the Romans—not only have they deserted the city and capital of the Empire, but they have also abandoned Roman nationality and even the Latin language. They have migrated to another capital city [i.e., Byzantium] and taken up a completely different nationality and language." Quoted in Peter Rietbergen, *Europe: A Cultural History* (New York: Routledge, 1998), 89.

thoughts about facial hair, they could not let these attacks against the orthodoxy of the Western church go unchallenged.

Byzantine polemicists, always more apt to ascribe theological significance to cultural and liturgical variations, charged the Latins not only with effeminacy (and the presumed sexual sins that surrounded it), but also of violating the mandates of Leviticus and the canons. Yet alongside the polemicists there were still those, like Patriarch Peter III of Antioch (1052–56) and Archbishop Theophylact of Ohrid (d. 1107), who were able to distinguish between minor cultural differences and the important theological issues (e.g., the Filioque) that required real attention. Beards, they believed, were not a genuinely church-dividing issue.

Following the Fourth Crusade (1204) the irenicism of Peter and Theophylact was largely forgotten as lists of Latin errors began to proliferate in the East. Such lists were hardly new, but now the number of charges increased exponentially, focusing not only on the two most contested issues of the period (the Filioque and the azymes), but also a host of liturgical and cultural differences that allegedly demonstrated the heretical nature of Western Christianity. Some were minor ("They mix the wine of the Eucharist with cold water instead of warm"),[2] others were laughably erroneous ("They do not revere the Virgin Mary"), and still others were probably based on a misinterpretation of then-current Latin practices ("Upon entering a church, [the Latins] fall on their faces on the ground, trace a cross in the dust, kiss the cross, and then, when they stand up to leave, trample upon that very cross").[3] Clerical shaving appears among the charges in many of these lists, perhaps because, as differences go, it was among the most immediate and striking. That such a practice had some nefarious purpose or manifested some deeper error was beyond a doubt, serving as a potent reminder that despite the claims of the Greek unionists, one could not maintain that Latins and Greeks shared the same faith.

It is a curious fact of history that after centuries of featuring prominently in both Greek and Latin polemical literature the issue of clerical beardlessness all but disappeared at some point in the fourteenth century. Why this happened remains shrouded in mystery, but it is very possible that both sides simply realized there were far more substantive matters to discuss, and deeper theological questions that needed to be explored. Whether or not priests should or should not shave, long cited as a reason for the schism between East and West, was simply not judged to be one of them. And yet even today there are Christians, both East and West, who still wax lyrically about the

---

[2] Taken from the *Dialogue of Panagiotes with an Azymite* in Kolbaba, *The Byzantine Lists*, 202. For the significance of the *Zeon* see Hans-Joachim Schultz, *The Byzantine Liturgy: Symbolic Structure and Faith Expression*, trans. Matthew O'Connell (New York: Pueblo, 1980), 30–31, 40–43.

[3] Kolbaba believes this is a description, albeit garbled, of "a local variant of genuflection or prostration." The issue was not the prostration itself, a practice "hardly foreign to the Byzantine church," but to the drawing of the cross on the ground, something prohibited by the Council in Trullo, canon 73 ("Since the life-giving cross has shown to us Salvation, we should be careful that we render due honour to that by which we were saved from the ancient fall. Wherefore, in mind, in word, in feeling giving veneration [προσκύνησιν] to it, we command that the figure of the cross, which some have placed on the floor, be entirely removed therefrom, lest the trophy of the victory won for us be desecrated by the trampling under foot of those who walk over it. Therefore those who from this present represent on the pavement the sign of the cross, we decree are to be cut off"). Kolbaba, *The Byzantine Lists*, 54.

majesty of the beard, believing it to have some deep theological meaning, reminding us just how "hairy" the whole subject can be.

The Ninth Century

In the years prior to his imperial coronation, Charles the Great, or Charlemagne, was urged by his advisers to adopt a more "Roman" style and dress, which explains why, unlike his heavily bearded Frankish forebearers, the emperor wore his hair short with only a bushy mustache. It was, scholars have noted, a sort of compromise, for "It was German, but not too far from the Roman preference for modesty in hair."[4] Most of the Frankish nobility continued to wear their hair and beards long, unlike priests who sported short hair in the *more Romano*, thus easily distinguishing them from pagans.[5] Several Roman councils had already anathematized clerics who wore their hair long,[6] and by 816 the Synod of Aachen went so far as to mandate that monks should shave at least twenty-four times a year, or approximately once every fifteen days.[7] Short hair and beardlessness were so common in Rome that Arab visitors noted how all the males of the city, "young and old, shave off their beards entirely, not leaving a single hair," allegedly being told that this was "the Christian thing to do."[8]

However there were many Christians, especially in the East, who did not feel the same way, and beginning in the mid-ninth century they began to comment negatively upon the Roman practice. Early Byzantine emperors, including Justinian (d. 565), had continued to shave following the Roman custom ("*Justinianus erat mento rasus, ritu Romanorum*"), but by the time of Phokas (602–10) beards became standard, at least if portraiture on imperial coinage is to be believed.[9] By the reign of Constans II (d. 668), known as "Constantine the Bearded" (Κωνσταντῖνος ὁ Πωγωνάτος), the "Byzantine beard" was well ensconced, considered de rigueur in a society where it became "a vital means of distinguishing non-eunuch adult males from eunuch native males."[10] This

---

[4] Oldstone-Moore, *Of Beards and Men*, 82. See also Paul Edward Dutton, "Charlemagne's Mustache," in *Charlemagne's Mustache and Other Cultural Clusters of a Dark Age* (New York: Palgrave Macmillan, 2004), 3–42.

[5] The earlier Synod of Braga (563) had prohibited lectors from having long hair like pagans, and other legislation mandated that any cleric who served at the altar should have his hair cut so that his ears were not covered. Trichet, *La Tonsure*, 45.

[6] See chapter 1 n. 133. Constable pointed out that these canons "may have been designed to require clerics and later monks who had long hair to wear it tied up, in a bun, like Greek Orthodox clerics today, rather than to cut it off." Constable, "Introduction on Beards in the Middle Ages," 107.

[7] Ibid., 116.

[8] Oldstone-Moore, *Of Beards and Men*, 84.

[9] Constance Head, "Physical Descriptions of the Emperors in Byzantine Historical Writing," *Byzantion* 50 (1980): 226–40; Barry Baldwin, "Physical Descriptions of Byzantine Emperors," *Byzantion* 51 (1981): 8–21.

[10] Tougher, "Bearding Byzantium," 166. Among the rare exceptions to this rule was Germanos I, who is portrayed iconographically "as an eunuch, namely beardless ... [and] is the only beardless hierarch of the Eastern Orthodox Church. According to the established iconographic canons, beardlessness was quite common among some of the warrior-saints and also among some of the other saints, among the fathers and doctors of the Church, however, it was generally despised." Otto Meinardus, "The Beardless Patriarch: St. Germanos," Μακεδονικά 13 (1973): 179. See also Shaun Tougher, "Byzantine Eunuchs with Special Reference to Their Creation and Origin," in Liz James, ed., *Women, Men, and Eunuchs: Gender in Byzantium* (New York: Routledge, 1997), 168–84.

was especially the case once the Byzantines began to employ more native Greeks, and not just captive foreigners, as eunuchs, since the beard allowed non-eunuch males to be easily differentiated while concurrently asserting the masculinity and manliness of its owner.[11] Court manuals, for example, used the term "'bearded' to designate those officials who were male but not eunuchs."[12] *Real* men wore beards, eunuchs did not.

The Byzantine bias against beardlessness, linked as it was with both a lack of manliness and the fathers' warnings against effeminacy and its associated sexual sins, probably explains why the earliest Eastern comments on the Latins' lack of facial hair were largely negative.[13] The first to raise the issue was Patriarch Photios of Constantinople (d. 893), whose role in the Filioque and the papacy debates have been covered in detail elsewhere.[14] In 861 he wrote to Pope Nicholas I about many of the differences already existing between the Greek and Latin churches, distinguishing between those practices that were "prescribed by common ecumenical decision [and] must be held by all" and those that arise because they were "ordained by some local council" or because "one of the fathers prescribe[d] something for himself."[15] Practices in this latter category must be held only "by those who have accepted it, and it is not a grave matter if it is not held by those who have not received it."[16] As an example Photios specifically cited the fact that "some have the custom of cutting their hair and shaving, while to others this is prohibited by certain conciliar decrees."[17] Thus he recognized that "different customs and rules exist in different places" and that one should condemn "neither those who hold such rules themselves, nor those who have not accepted them."[18] That said, Photios reminded Nicholas that many of the other practices cited "are not without fault, or above reproach since some of them can be considered incorrect and, therefore, must be rejected," mentioning the marriage of clergy as a specific example.[19]

---

[11] "Eunuchs were ... recognized as holding a somewhat ambiguous masculinity in that they did not possess the traditional attributes of the male gender, lacking, for instance, 'masculine musculature, body hair and beards' or a thundering, deep voice. That possession of a beard appeared to have been recognized as an attribute of the gendered body, relating to sex but also to socially constructed perceptions of masculinity, is suggested in Byzantine writing. The term used to identify bearded men (*barbatos*) notably possessed additional connotations of reproductive potency, which ... was often regarded as the measure of masculinity in Byzantium." Myrto Hatzaki, *Beauty and the Male Body in Byzantium Perceptions and Representations in Art and Text* (New York: Palgrave Macmillan, 2009), 99.

[12] Tougher, "Bearding Byzantium," 154–55.

[13] The *Oneirocriticon of Daniel*, a Byzantine book dealing with the interpretation of dreams, stated that "'shaving off your beard or having it fall out is a bitter sign for anyone' ... [since the] beard was indicative of manliness, and the loss of it constituted a severe punishment." Steven Oberhelman, *Dreambooks in Byzantium: Six Oneirocritica in Translation, with Commentary and Introduction* (Aldershot: Ashgate, 2008), 31. The *Oneirocriticon of Manuel II Palaiologos* "identified the beard as a symbol of family and friends" which meant that in dreams "beardlessness signif[ied] the loss of both." Ibid., 206.

[14] Siecienski, *The Filioque*, 100–104; Siecienski, *The Papacy and the Orthodox*, 219–32.

[15] Photios to Nicholas of Rome; Joseph Hergenröther, *Photius, Patriarch von Constantinopel: Sein Leben, seine Schriften und das griechische Schisma* 1 (Regensburg: Manz, 1867), 407–11; Eng. trans.: Photius of Constantinople, *The Mystagogy of the Holy Spirit*, trans. Holy Transfiguration Monastery (Astoria: Studion Publishers, 1983), 44–47.

[16] Ibid.

[17] Ibid.

[18] Ibid.

[19] Ibid. "How, for instance, can some observe Sabbath rights although they are Christians and not Jews? Or who would be bold enough to shutter at lawful marriage, which the goodness of the Creator made and established, unless he follows the teaching of shameless and godless men?"

Interesting to note here is that while Photios noted the difference in East-West shaving practices, he immediately wrote it off as a minor variance in custom rather than as a genuinely church-dividing issue. The question, still unanswered, is whether Photios's view changed as the relationship between Rome and Constantinople became more contentious, and whether the Constantinopolitan Synod of 867, at which Nicholas was condemned, also censured the shaving practices of the Latin church. Unfortunately our knowledge of the proceedings is scant, for "little of what occurred there has reached us, the meagre information we happen to possess coming exclusively from anti-Photianist sources."[20] The belief that clerical beardlessness was condemned stems largely from Nicholas's 867 letter to Hincmar of Reims (d. 882), where the pope listed the accusations then being made against the West, including the fact that "they reprove us because our clerics shave their beards and theirs do not."[21]

However, Francis Dvornik noted long ago that Nicholas's list, given to him by his legates in Bulgaria, was probably gleaned, not from the conciliar proceedings, but rather from a pamphlet "which the Greek missionaries had tried before their expulsion to disseminate among some half-civilized Boyars."[22] In fact, Dvornik maintained that the council deliberately avoided general criticisms of the Western church—Photios was at the time seeking support among Nicholas's enemies in Europe—intending only to be "the Eastern Church's reply to the attacks the Frankish missionaries in Bulgaria."[23] That it was later interpreted as a general "declaration of war between the two churches and a rupture between the Latins and the Greeks" is solely the work of Nicholas, whose letter to Hincmar framed it in those terms.[24]

A second reason for doubting the council's condemnation of beardlessness is Photios's earlier *Encyclical to the Eastern Patriarchs*, in which he listed the errors that needed to be addressed at the upcoming council.[25] It is significant that nowhere in

---

[20] Francis Dvornik, *The Photian Schism: History and Legend* (Cambridge: Cambridge University Press, 1948), 120–21.

[21] Among the other accusations noted by the pope were "that we fast on Saturdays ... we say that the Holy Spirit proceeds from the Father and from the Son ... we abhor marriage because we prohibit priests from choosing wives ... we prevent priests from anointing the foreheads of the baptized with chrism ... we do not stop eating meat eight weeks before Easter ... at Easter we offer and bless a lamb, in the manner of the Jews, on the altar besides the Lord's body ... because a deacon can be ordained a bishop without having ever held the office of priest." Nicholas, *Epistula 100 ad Hincmarum et caertos episcopos in regno Caroli constitutos* (MGH Epistolae VI, 601–9). Eng. trans.: Tia Kolbaba, *Inventing Latin Heretics: Byzantines and the Filioque in the Ninth Century* (Kalamazoo: Medieval Institute Publications, 2008), 135. See also *Annals of St-Bertin*, trans. Janet Nelson (Manchester: Manchester University Press, 1991), 141–42.

[22] Dvornik, *The Photian Schism*, 118.

[23] Ibid., 122.

[24] Ibid., 123. Nicholas regarded it as a "ridiculous and utterly abominable disgrace" that "the Holy Church of God" should be accused of "heretical crimes" by that "fornicator and invader of the Church" Photios. He asked both Hincmar of Reims and Liutbert of Mainz (d. 889), to call together the bishops of Germany so that, "advancing together in concerted battle," the West could issue a conciliar response to the "madness" of the Greeks. Nicholas, *Epistula 100 ad Hincmarum*; MGH Epistolae VI, 601–9.

[25] Although there were several charges—that "they compel the faithful to fast on Saturdays, ... convinced the faithful to despise the marriage of priests, ... persuaded them that all who had been chrismated by priests had to be anointed again by bishops"—the West's chief sin was that "they attempted by their false opinions and distorted words to ruin the holy and sacred Nicene Symbol of Faith ... by adding to it that the Holy Spirit proceeds not only from the Father, as the Symbol declares, but from the Son also." Photius, *Epistula 2: Encyclica ad sedes orientales*, in Vasileios Laourdas and Leendert Gerrit Westerink, eds., *Epistulae et amphilochia*, vol. 1 (Leipzig: Teubner, 1983), 39–53. Eng. trans.: Photius of Constantinople, *The*

the letter was the topic of beards raised, although Photios listed several other minor complaints against the Latins, believing that even "the least departure from Tradition can lead to a scorning of every dogma of our faith."[26] It seems unlikely that Photios, who had cited shaving as a matter of some indifference in his earlier letter to Pope Nicholas, and who had omitted it from his criticisms here, would have added clerical beardlessness to the council's condemnations. Thus despite the claims of later Latin polemicists, the war over beards probably did not begin with Photios.[27]

Nevertheless, the fact that Nicholas and his allies interpreted the synod of 867 as an attack upon "the whole Church that uses the Latin language" meant that it required a coordinated response, which Hincmar was charged with leading.[28] The most grievous charge, of course, had concerned the Filioque, explaining why the Latins focused their energies on answering the Eastern critique.[29] Yet the criticism of clerical beardlessness was not forgotten, and was addressed in many of the works produced in the years that followed.

Among the first responses was that of Aeneas of Paris (d. 870), author of the rabidly anti-Byzantine *Liber adversus Graecos*.[30] After an extended quotation from Isidore of Seville's *De Ecclesiasticis Officiis* on the nature of priestly tonsure, Aeneas complained that "the Greeks reproach the Latins and the Romans for shaving their beards," despite the fact that in matters of style and dress "different nations observe their own customs ... and this happens without any offence so long as it does not depart from the Catholic faith."[31] If challenged on their appearance the Latins could well ask "why the laity of the Greeks grow out their hair in a feminine manner against the thunderous command of Paul" in 1 Corinthians 11:14–16.[32] The Latins, he wrote, "think it unworthy to grow out their hair" because they want "to avoid resembling women in their appearance," while "the Greeks consider [it] more holy ... [to] wear heads that look like those of women."[33] If they think that sanctity is found in hair, "perhaps more

---

Mystagogy of the Holy Spirit, 49–54. See also Jack Turner, "Was Photios an Anti-Latin? Heresy and Liturgical Variation in the Encyclical to the Eastern Patriarchs," *Journal of Religious History* 40.4 (2016): 475–89.

[26] Photius of Constantinople, *The Mystagogy of the Holy Spirit*, 49–54.

[27] The long-standing but far from accurate Western appraisal of Photios as "father of schism" had little trouble believing him responsible for the whole debate, as can be seen in the work of Charles Seghers, who wrote that "the foul work of sowing cockle was ... consummated by ... the ambitious hypocrite ... Photios ... [for] among the many accusations he brought against the Latins, [he] made a grievous matter of their practice of shaving, though he was himself a glabrous, smooth faced eunuch." Seghers, "The Practice of Shaving in the Latin Church," 282. This last charge is based on the work of Cardinal Baronius (d. 1607), who had described Photios as a beardless eunuch (*cum alioquin ipse esset eunuchus glaber*) without providing any basis for the claim. According to Reginald Reynolds, it seems incredible "in a Church where so much was made of beards in general, and the beard clerical and patriarchal in particular, any *eunuchus glaber* could have held priestly office, still less attained the distinction among his bearded fellows which Photius achieved." Reynolds, *Beards: An Omnium Gatherum*, 98.

[28] *Annals of St-Bertin*, 141.

[29] Siecienski, *The Filioque*, 104–8.

[30] Aeneas of Paris, *Liber adversus Graecos* (PL 121:683–721). The unpublished translation of this text was done by Katie Derrig, who prepared it for Christopher Oldstone-Moore during the writing of his book *Of Beards and Men*. My thanks to both for allowing me to use it here.

[31] Ibid.

[32] Ibid.

[33] Ibid.

could be found in the beards of he-goats!"[34] It is the Greeks who "reject the Apostle by growing out their hair," and thus they should in no way think less of the ministers of Christ "because they shave their beards."[35]

The most detailed refutation of the Greek argument came from Ratramnus of Corbie in his *Contra Graecorum Opposita Romanam Ecclesiam Infamantium*.[36] Ratramnus, like Aeneas, wrote off the Greeks' charge as trivial (*levis*), especially since none of "the writings of the apostles or the foundational documents of the church ... made a decision on such a matter."[37] For this subject—that is, whether priests grew out their hair or cut it—"like many others, was left to the customs of individual churches to decide," which is why "clerical custom is not uniform across all churches."[38] Thus it was silly for the subject to become a matter of contention, for "how is the shaving or the keeping of a beard (*barbae detonsio, vel conservatio*) relevant to the beginning of justice, much less its fulfillment?[39] However, if the Greeks and their emperors wanted to dispute the matter, the West was prepared to respond.[40]

Like Aeneas, a key text for Ratramnus was Paul's injunction against long hair in 1 Corinthians 11:14–16, which was interpreted here to include beards. "Clerics who grow beards," he wrote, "should therefore consider ... whether they are not going against the apostolic precept."[41] Ratramnus then cited the example of the Nazirites, who cut their hair and placed it "in the sacrificial fire, showing by this, and not only in their actions, that they were consecrating also all their thoughts to the Lord."[42] Ezekiel too had been instructed to "take a sharp sword; use it as a barber's razor and run it over your head and your beard" (Ezekiel 5:1).[43] Ratramnus, citing Acts 18:18 ("At Cenchreae he had his hair cut, for he was under a vow")[44] and Acts 21:23–26 (where Paul was instructed by James to subsidize four Nazirites), spoke about the enduring nature of this practice, which is why "the clerics of the Romans, and of almost all the Western churches, following this custom, shave their beards and trim the hair on their heads,"[45] imitating both those in the Old Testament who were called Nazirites and those in the New Testament who were said to have done the same.

---

[34] Ibid.
[35] Ibid.
[36] Ratramnus of Corbie, *Contra Graecorum Opposita Romanam Ecclesiam Infamantium* (PL 121:225–346). As with the *Liber adversus Graecos*, the translation here, with but a few exceptions, is that of Katie Derrig. My thanks to her and Dr. Oldstone-Moore for permitting me to use it.
[37] Ibid.
[38] Ibid. "For among some it is the custom to cut their hair or beards; among others, not to cut the beard, but to shave the head completely free of hair; others are pleased to rob their face of all hair, to strip the tops of their hairs of hair, and sometimes to leave a remaining section surrounding the bald part of the top of the head." Ibid.
[39] Ibid.
[40] Ratramnus's text took aim chiefly at the emperors, Michael III ("the Drunkard") and Basil I, who were accused in the work of heresy, blasphemy, and outright stupidity ("*vel falsa, vel haeretica, vel superstitiosa, vel irreligiosa*"). Ratramnus of Corbie, *Contra Graecorum* (PL 121:226).
[41] Constable, "Introduction on Beards in the Middle Ages," 111.
[42] Derrig translation.
[43] Ibid.
[44] Ratramnus, like Aeneas, attributed this act not to Paul but to "Priscilla and Aquila. Jews who believed in Christ, who cut their hair in Cenchreae, for they had made a vow." Ibid.
[45] Ibid.

Ratramnus then went on to discuss the significance of priestly tonsure, like Aeneas using many of the images and examples found in Isidore. He wrote that by leaving an unshaven ring of hair around their head Latin clerics "signify both a king's glory and a priestly sign. For it is a source of glory for kings to wear crowns on their heads, while priests used to wear tiaras on their heads in the temple, and the tiara bears a likeness to a hemisphere, while a crown, in the shape of a circle, generally surrounds the head."[46] Peter had called Christians "a chosen race, a royal priesthood" (1 Pt 2:9), and "this is what the Roman (or Latin) clerics wish to signify by shaping the hair atop their heads like a tiara ... representing a kind of crown that shows their royal dignity. In this way, they mark out the royal priesthood."[47]

Following Gregory the Great and Isidore by interpreting hair as "superfluous thoughts" and the cutting of hair as "the conquering of exterior vices," Ratramnus argued that "in the shaving of their faces [priests] show the purity of their hearts," just as Paul had written in 2 Corinthians 3:18.[48] "For the appearance of the head makes known the appearance of the heart," and just as shaving removed hair from the face of the head, "the face of the heart ought to continually be stripped of earthly thoughts, in order that it may be able to look upon the glory of the Lord with a pure and sincere expression, and to be transformed into it through the grace of that contemplation."[49]

The example of "Peter's tonsure" was then brought forward, for "the blessed apostle Peter, as well as many others of the apostles and other disciples of Christ, is said to have shaved his beard and head" and this fact has been confirmed "by the skill of painters" [i.e., existing pictures of Peter].[50] If "the Apostle and the other disciples of Christ did not find it displeasing to present such an appearance," why should the Greeks accuse us?[51] "For if it is a sin to trim the beard, or some transgression of divine law, let them explain why the prophet shaved his beard when the Lord commanded it, why this custom existed among the Nazarenes, why, finally, the apostles did not abhor this practice."[52] Ratramnus concluded: "Let us desist from this controversy, since we observe that it is neither strengthened by any virtuous reason, nor supported by any serious dignity. Unless we think we can be overtaken by the less thoughtful, nothing more can come from this line of argument."[53]

---

[46] Ibid.
[47] Ibid.
[48] Ibid. "And all of us, with unveiled faces, seeing the glory of the Lord as though reflected in a mirror, are being transformed into the same image" (2 Cor 3:18).
[49] Oldstone-Moore, *Of Beards and Men*, 85. Grimlaicus, "playing with the similar sounds of *criminibus* (sins) and *crinibus* (hairs)," made the same argument in his *Rules for Solitaries*: "Consequently, I regard it as reasonable and fitting that solitaries, and especially those who handle the sacred mysteries, shave and trim their hair every forty days as the Apostle says: let us 'scour off the old human being with its deeds and put on the one who is renewed unto knowledge of God' (Colossians 3:9–10) that is, let us strip off the sins of our flesh like the hairs of our head and so let us shine with our senses renewed. This renewal ought to take place in our mind, but it ought also to be shown on our head, where the mind is thought to dwell." Grimlaicus, *Rules for Solitaries*, 137.
[50] Derrig translation.
[51] Ibid.
[52] Ibid. *Si enim barbam tondere peccatum est aliquod, vel divinae legis ulla transgressio, dicant cur propheta Domino jubente barbam raserit; cur Nazaraeis iste mos exstiterit; cur denique apostoli hanc consuetudinem non exhorruerint.*
[53] Ibid.

The Eleventh Century

For most of the tenth century and into the eleventh a "mute schism" (*stummes Schisma*)[54] existed between East and West, as neither side seemed eager to continue the theological debates raised during the time of Photios. The Byzantines, enjoying a cultural, intellectual, and military renaissance under a series of successful emperors, appeared to put the whole affair behind them, while the Latin church, suffering through a "dark age" (*saeculum obscurum*) led by a series of notoriously bad popes,[55] had neither the incentive nor strength to attack the Greeks.[56] In this atmosphere it is easy to understand why disputes about beards were given scant attention.[57]

Yet events in the West soon disrupted this relative peace, as a succession of reforming popes attempted to arrest the rot and instill some discipline back into church life. Much of their energy was focused on the lives and morals of the clergy, many of whom were thought to have fallen prey to various sins of the flesh (e.g., sodomy, concubinage).[58] This is why during the eleventh century there arose a renewed concern for priests' dress and deportment, with particular emphasis placed on how they should model the virtues of modesty and simplicity. For the reformers, many of whom were from monastic communities like Cluny, Brogne, and Gorze, the monk became the model, which explains the increased monasticization of the secular clergy that took place in the years that followed.[59] They believed that priests, like monks, needed to become a "distinct order with a lifestyle totally different from that of the layman," and this should be manifest not only in how they acted, but also in how they presented

---

[54] Anton Michel, ed., *Humbert und Keroularios: Quellen und Studien zum Schisma des XI. Jahrhunderts* (Paderborn: Schöningh, 1924), 23.

[55] "The new age (*saeculum*) which was beginning, for its harshness and barrenness of good could well be called iron, for its baseness and abounding evil, leaden, and moreover for its lack of writers, dark (*obscurum*)." Caesar Baronius, *Annales Ecclesiastici*, vol. 10.

[56] For this period see George Ostrogorsky, *History of the Byzantine State* (New Brunswick, NJ: Rutgers University Press, 1969), 283; Warren Treadgood, *A History of Byzantine State and Society* (Stanford, CA: Stanford University Press, 1997), 488–533; Whittow, *The Making of Byzantium, 600–1025*, 310–57. John Julius Norwich, in the second volume in his three-volume history of Byzantium, described this period as "the apogee."

[57] There were exceptions. Ian Wood observed that "following the death of the German missionary Bruno of Querfurt on the borders of Russia in 1009, a Greek bishop arrived, and, according to Ademar of Chabannes, encouraged the growing of beards (*morem grecum in barba crescenda et ceteris exemplis eos suscipere fecit*: "he made them follow the Greek tradition in growing a beard and in other ways"). Ian Wood, "Hair and Beards in the Early Medieval West," *Al-Masāq Journal of the Medieval Mediterranean* 30 (2018): 108.

[58] Peter Damien's *Liber Gomorrhianus*, which condemned (in graphic detail) homosexual practices among the clergy, was an example of the reformers' efforts along these lines. See Peter Damien, *Book of Gomorrah: An Eleventh-Century Treatise against Clerical Homosexual Practices*, trans. Pierre J. Payer (Waterloo, ON: Wilfrid Laurier University Press, 1982).

[59] It was during this period that celibacy became an "absolute prerequisite" for ordination to the priesthood, inculcating both a "monastic discipline" and a "sense of solidarity and corporate identity.... Behind the campaign for celibacy, in sum, aside from the moral and canonical issues involved, was the desire to set all churchmen apart from and above the laity; the need to create a spiritual elite by the separation of the priest from the ordinary layman was an urgent priority." Aristeides Papadakis, *The Christian East and the Rise of the Papacy* (Crestwood, NY: St. Vladimir's Seminary Press, 1994), 37. See also Jennifer D. Thibodeaux, *The Manly Priest: Clerical Celibacy, Masculinity, and Reform in England and Normandy, 1066-1300* (Philadelphia: University of Pennsylvania Press, 2015).

themselves.⁶⁰ With this renewed emphasis on the clergy's distinctiveness, especially vis-à-vis the laity, hair and beards became more important because "clerics did not as a rule wear a distinctive dress except when celebrating the sacraments," meaning that "the tonsure and shaving were often the only signs of their clerical status."⁶¹

Outside of clerical circles, by the beginning of the eleventh century the beard was enjoying a renaissance, especially in Germany, where "the emperors after Otto III are all depicted with beards."⁶² Liudprand of Cremona related how during his journey to Constantinople courtiers commented on his "shaggy hair" and "unkempt" beard, which they thought unusual "by your standards" (*prolixa contra morem barba*).⁶³ When fashion started to change later in the century, and men began to shave, more conservative churchmen protested. In 1043 Abbot Siegfried of Gorze (protégé of William of Volpiano) wrote to Abbot Poppo of Stavelot about the "shameful custom ... execrable to modern eyes" now practiced by "the vulgar French in cutting their beards."⁶⁴ Otloh of St. Emmeram related a story of a man criticized by his priest for shaving, since "you are a layman and should not shave your beard at all (*minime rasa*) as is the custom of laymen ... [instead] you, spurning the law of God, shave your beard like a cleric."⁶⁵

This last statement witnesses to the fact that even before the Gregorian Reform, clerical beardlessness in the West was already well established. Ratherius of Verona (d. 974) wrote that one could easily tell a layman from a priest by his beard, and St. Adalbert of Prague (d. 997) grew a beard when he disguised himself as a layman in order to do missionary work.⁶⁶ Clerical beardlessness was also the norm in Saxon England, where King Harold's spies originally thought the invading Normans in 1066 were an army of priests, since "they had their entire face with both lips, shaved."⁶⁷ As early as 1005, Canon 47 of the Canons of Edgar in England had mandated that the priest should neither "conceal his tonsure, nor let his hair be trimmed, nor retain his beard for any time," while Canon 34 of the Northumbrian Priests Law of 1008/23 held that "if a priest neglects the shaving of beard or hair, he is to compensate for it."⁶⁸ In France the 1031 Council of Bourges mandated tonsure for "all who minister in the Holy Church," clarifying that tonsure included "both a shaven beard and a circle on the head."⁶⁹

---

⁶⁰ I. S. Robinson, *Authority and Resistance in the Investiture Contest: The Polemical Literature of the Late Eleventh-Century* (Manchester: Manchester University Press, 1978), 2–3.
⁶¹ Giles Constable, *The Reformation of the Twelfth Century* (Cambridge: Cambridge University Press, 1997), 194.
⁶² Constable, "Introduction on Beards in the Middle Ages," 93.
⁶³ Liudprand of Cremona, *The Complete Works of Liudprand of Cremona*, trans. Paolo Squatriti (Washington, DC: Catholic University of America Press, 2007), 269. They assumed that he must be suffering some "immense distress," but Liudprand assured him that he was fine and had only grown his beard in order to make the Greeks more comfortable with his appearance.
⁶⁴ Constable, "Introduction on Beards in the Middle Ages," 94.
⁶⁵ Ibid., 94–95. When the man broke his promise not to shave, saying he had promised never to use a razor rather than a knife, Otloh related how divine justice prevailed and the man was attacked and blinded by his enemies.
⁶⁶ Ibid., 92.
⁶⁷ Ibid., 95.
⁶⁸ Ibid., 108.
⁶⁹ Ibid. Similar provisions were enacted at the Councils of Coyac (1050), and Toulouse (1119).

That same year the Council of Limoges issued similar rulings, citing the legend of St. Peter's tonsure as basis for the practice. Yet while mandating clerical shaving, the council recognized that the Greeks had a different tradition, since they "have chosen the custom of not shaving. They ground their choice upon the example of the apostles Paul and James, the brother of the Lord, saying with reason (for nothing should be concealed) that the clergy, like the laity, ought to preserve on their faces this ornament of virility, as a dignity of the human condition, a dignity created by God himself, and with which he has been pleased to honor man alone.... the Greeks add likewise that Our Lord of Nazareth always wore his beard."[70] Since the different practices existed for different reasons, the council maintained that it was not possible for the Greeks to reproach the Latins, nor the Latins the Greeks (*et hac in re neque illi nos, neque nos possumus reprehendere illos*).[71] Very soon, however, events conspired to bring the broad-mindedness of Limoges to an end, with beards becoming a central issue in the schism to come.

The events leading up July 16, 1054, especially as it concerns the so-called heresy of the *fermentacei* that led to Cardinal Humbert's journey to Constantinople, will be discussed elsewhere in the book. Important to note, however, is that in both excommunications—that of Humbert against Keroularios and Keroularios against Humbert—the beardlessness of the Latin clergy is listed among the reasons for the breech. For Humbert the Greeks behaved like Nazarenes, who "maintain the bodily cleanness of the Jews to such a point that they deny baptism to infants who die before the eighth day ... [and] communion to menstruating women or those about to give birth."[72] Not only that, but "preserving their hair and beards, [they] do not receive into communion those who, according to the custom of the Roman church, cut their hair and shave their beards" (*et secundum institutionem Romanae ecclesiae barbas radunt, in communione non recipiant*).[73]

Patriarch Michael Keroularios, in the *Synodal Edict* against Humbert that followed, also cited the West's shaving practice as cause for the division, although he made the claim that it was the Latins who were trying to foist their customs upon the Greeks, because "we refuse to shave our beards as they do and to alter the natural human appearance."[74] The Byzantines, Keroularios argued, rightly refused to "contravene the Scripture when it says 'You shall not mar the edges of your beard.'"[75] The question, difficult (if not impossible) to answer, is whose version of the debate is historically

---

[70] Reynolds, *Beards: An Omnium Gatherum*, 118–19. "A further explanation they add is that the Lord wanted to be an untrimmed nazirite and that no razor came upon his head until he accepted to bear the crown of thorns on his head. On this model the crown of clerics is shaped by a razor on the head top, so that Christ's kingship and priesthood may be visualized even on the heads of clerics." Michele Bacci, *The Many Faces of Christ: Portraying the Holy in the East and West, 300 to 1300* (London: Reaktion Books, 2014), 119. See also Philipp Hofmeister, "Der Streit um des Priesters Bart," *Zeitschrift für Kirchengeschichte*, ser. 3.42 (1943–44): 72–94.

[71] Reynolds, *Beards: An Omnium Gatherum*, 118–19.

[72] Humbert, *Excommunicatio*, in Will, *Acta et Scripta*, 153; Eng. trans.: Geanakoplos, *Byzantium*, 209.

[73] Humbert, *Excommunicatio*, in Will, *Acta et Scripta*, 153–54; Eng. trans.: Geanakoplos, *Byzantium*, 209.

[74] Keroularios, *Edictum Pseudosynodi Constantinopolitanae*, in Will, *Acta et Scripta*, 157–58; Eng. trans.: Bryn Geffert and Theofanis Stavrou, eds., *Eastern Orthodox Christianity: The Essential Texts* (New Haven, CT: Yale University Press, 2016), 247.

[75] Keroularios, *Edictum Pseudosynodi Constantinopolitanae*, in Will, *Acta et Scripta*, 158; Eng. trans.: Geffert and Stavrou, *Eastern Orthodox Christianity*, 247.

correct—that is, were the Byzantines denying Eucharistic communion to the Latin clergy because they were beardless, or were the Latins trying to enforce Roman practices in the Constantinopolitan church?

Soon after Humbert's departure, Keroularios wrote to the other Eastern patriarchs to enlist their support, telling them that "the Romans are not spitted on only one pike ... but on many and various ones."[76] Shaving was listed among their "Judaizing practices" along with "azymes, observing the Sabbath, eating unclean meats, monks eating pork fat, [and] eating meat on Wednesday and cheese and eggs on Friday."[77] Alongside these many sins, "They do also other things which it would be a great work to enumerate one by one. Therefore, if they live in such a way and, enfeebled by such customs, dare these things which are obviously lawless, forbidden, and abominable, then will any right-thinking person consider that they are at all to be included in the category of the orthodox? I think not!"[78]

Among the recipients of this letter was the irenic Peter III of Antioch, who quickly realized that many items on Keroularios's list of Latin "errors" were either manifestly untrue ("Who could consider this accusation admissible—that the Romans neither revere the holy and reverend images nor honor the relics of the saints?"), or concerned trivial matters that should not affect the maintenance of ecclesial communion.[79] Referencing the legend of St. Peter's tonsure he wrote:

> We have surveyed the Roman errors which you enumerated. Some of them seem abominable and should be fled; others are curable; still others can be overlooked. For what does it matter to us if their bishops shave their beards and wear rings.... For we also make a *garara*[80] on our heads wholly in honor of the Prince of the Apostles, Peter, on whom the great church of God was founded. For that which some impious men have made into an insult to the saint, we who are pious have made in his honor

---

[76] Michael Keroularios, *Epistula I ad Petrum Patriarcham Antiochenum*, in Will, *Acta et Scripta*, 179; all translations of this letter are from Tia Kolbaba, Medieval Sourcebook, https://sourcebooks.fordham.edu/source/1054michael-kerularious-to-peter-of-antioch1.asp.

[77] Ibid., 180. Judaizing was associated with several other Latin practices, including the purifications and aspersions of priests and fasting on the Sabbath. See Gilbert Dagron, "Judaïser," *Travaux et Mémoires* 11 (1991): 359–80.

[78] Michael Keroularios, *Epistula I ad Petrum Patriarcham Antiochenum*, 183. In addition to their chief error, which was undoubtedly the addition to the creed, were things such as clerical celibacy, the wearing of rings by bishops, bishops going forth to battle, baptizing with only one immersion, failure to adore the relics of the saints or icons, and their refusal to accept the Eastern fathers.

[79] Peter of Antioch, *Epistola ad Michaelem Cerularium*, in Will, *Acta et Scripta*, 201. All translations of this letter are from Tia Kolbaba, Medieval Sourcebook, https://sourcebooks.fordham.edu/source/1054peter-of-antioch-to-michael-kerularious1.asp. Peter "was ashamed of these claims contained in the letter," especially those aspects of it he personally knew to be false. This was particularly true of Keroularios's statement that "from the sixth holy and ecumenical council to the present the commemoration of the pope has been excised from the sacred diptychs because the pope at that time, Vigilius, did not want to come to the council." Peter knew this to be false, as he had personally heard the pope's name commemorated at Constantinople in 1009. Ibid., 190–91.

[80] According to Kolbaba, "In the Migne edition, this is identified as a word of Syriac origin meaning clerical tonsure. That it is something on the head, surely, is clear from context, but I question the identification of this word with tonsure because Peter mentions tonsure by its normal name in the next sentence: *papalethra*." Kolbaba, https://sourcebooks.fordham.edu/source/1054peter-of-antioch-to-michael-kerularious1.asp.

and for his glory: Romans, on the one hand, shaving their beards and we, on the other, practicing the tonsure on our heads.[81]

Diverse shaving practices were thus a matter of great indifference to Peter, and while certain accusations (like the addition to the creed) were indeed serious and had to be resisted, most of "the other things should be overlooked, since the word of truth is not at all harmed by them. For we should not readily be persuaded by vain accusations, nor believe in our own suspicions."[82] Keroularios might break communion with Rome over these issues, but Peter would not. "As for me, I will make my opinion clear: if ever they would correct the addition to the holy creed, I would demand nothing else, leaving as a matter of indifference, along with all the other matters, even their fault regarding the unleavened bread."[83]

Although later remembered as the beginning of the "Great Schism," the events of 1054 were soon forgotten, written off by almost everyone as a minor dust-up between two hot-headed clerics. In fact, in southern Italy, where relations between Greeks and Latins were often complex, the two traditions coexisted side by side in relative peace for decades.[84] Yet occasional tensions did occur when a territory shifted between Latin and Byzantine rule, as change in ecclesiastical leadership often resulted in clashes of ecclesial culture.[85]

One example of this occurred in 1080, during the pontificate of Pope Gregory VII (1073–85). Gregory, long an advocate of the Reform, had always been eager to see the canons on tonsure and shaving enforced throughout the church, so that the entire clergy might better raise themselves to the "high standard" of monks and "give themselves wholly to the service of God."[86] This was especially true of those territories closer to home, like the island of Sardinia, which only recently (under Alexander II [1061–73]) had renewed relations with the Roman church. Latin monks soon arrived on the island, followed by two new archbishops ordained and given the pallium by Gregory himself.[87] Up to this time the Sardinian Church had largely been influenced

---

[81] Peter of Antioch, *Epistola ad Michaelem Cerularium*, in Will, *Acta et Scripta*, 193.

[82] Ibid., 201.

[83] Ibid., 203.

[84] On one hand, "The ancient cultural feud between Latins and Greeks provided Southern Italy with a smoldering cinder-bed of misunderstanding and distrust." Smith, *And Taking Bread*, 117. On the other, "The long-lived cooperation and coexistence of Latins and Greeks [also] provided Southern Italy with reserves of understanding, tolerance, and trust that could hold Rome and Constantinople together." Tia Kolbaba, "The Virtues and Faults of the Latin Christians," in Paul Stephenson, ed., *The Byzantine World* (New York: Routledge, 2010), 119. See also Jules Gay, *D'Italie méridionale et l'empire Byzantin 867–1071* (Paris: Frontemoing, 1904); G. A. Loud, *The Latin Church in Norman Italy* (Cambridge: Cambridge University Press, 2007); *La chiesa greca in Italia dall'viii al xvi secolo. Atti del convegno storico interecclesiale (Bari, 30 Apr.–4. Magg. 1969)*, 3 vols. (Padua: Editrice Antenore, 1972–73).

[85] For example, despite Pope Urban II's claims for jurisdictional control of southern Italy, he often "left the Greek monasteries and many of the Greek churches unmolested." When Reggio in Calabria was contested by both a Byzantine and a Norman candidate, Urban clearly asserted his jurisdictional claims to the area, telling the Greek candidate, Basil, that his ordination at the hands of the Constantinopolitan patriarch did not entitle him to a see within papal jurisdiction. Yet Urban did offer Basil and several other Greek bishops sees in southern Italy as long as they acknowledged papal jurisdiction there." Kolbaba, "The Virtues and Faults of the Latin Christians," 119.

[86] Oldstone-Moore, *Of Beards and Men*, 87.

[87] Michelle Hobart, ed., *Companion to Sardinian History, 500–1500* (Leiden: Brill, 2017), 187–88. The pallium is a vestment, worn over the shoulders, given by the pope to metropolitan bishops as a sign of their authority.

by Byzantine Christianity, although the extent of that influence remains under debate.[88] Nevertheless, Gregory worked hard to inculcate a greater "devotion to St Peter" and used every weapon in his arsenal to make it happen, including threats.[89] In this vein he wrote to Judge (*Judex*) Orzocco of Cagliari about enforcing Latin shaving practices, threatening any cleric who refused to shave with confiscation of his property. He wrote:

> We trust that Your Prudence has not taken it amiss that we have forced your Archbishop James to obey the custom of the holy Roman Church, the mother of all churches, and especially of yours, in effect, that as the clergy of the whole western church have had the custom of shaving the beard from the very origins of the Christian faith (*ab ipsis fidei Christianae primordiis*) so he, our brother, your Archbishop, should also shave. Therefore, we also instruct Your Eminence to receive and listen to him as a pastor and spiritual father and with his advice to make and compel all the clergy under your authority to shave their beards.[90]

One on level Gregory's claim that he "was enforcing a practice of the church 'from the beginning' ... was pure fiction."[91] Yet canonical collections of the period had by this time altered earlier decrees (e.g., the c. 475 *Statuta ecclesiae antiqua*) to give the prohibition against beards the veneer of antiquity.[92] By the end of the century clerical beardlessness in the West was almost universal, seemingly ancient, and (thanks to Aeneas and Ratramnus) well grounded in the Latin theological tradition.[93] In many parts of Europe beardlessness even became popular among the laity, with the archbishop of Rouen in 1096 threatening to excommunicate anyone, clergy or layman, with a beard. Thus when, that same year, these shaved Latins descended upon the East by the thousands, called there by the pleas of Emperor Alexios I Komnenos (d. 1118), the difference between them and their bearded Byzantine brethren could not have been starker.[94]

---

[88] "Even in the medieval period, from the eleventh to the fifteenth centuries, the monastic and penitent saints of the Greek Menologium remained highly venerated and had more churches dedicated to them than did the monastic saints of the West." Ibid., 186. See also Giulio Paulis, *Lingua e cultura nella Sardegna bizantina: Testimonianze linguistiche dell'influsso Greco* (Sassari: Asfodelo, 1983).
[89] Hobart, *Companion to Sardinian History*, 189.
[90] Gregory VII, *Letter to Orzocco, Judex of Cagliari*; Eng. trans.: Ephraim Emerton, ed., *The Correspondence of Pope Gregory VII: Selected Letters from the Registrum* (New York: Columbia University Press, 1990), 164.
[91] Oldstone-Moore, *Of Beards and Men*, 87.
[92] See pages 34.
[93] Nine years later the bishop of Amiens denied communion to any male who refused to shave.
[94] What exactly Alexios asked for remains the subject of debate. Most scholars today consider it unlikely that Alexios actually suggested a Frankish-Byzantine crusade for Jerusalem and believe what he really wanted was simply some "foreign auxiliary troops" to assist in Asia Minor (Papadakis, *The Christian East and the Rise of the Papacy*, 85). For various views on Alexios's motives and the nature of his request see Dana Munro, "Did the Emperor Alexius I Ask for Aid to the Council of Piacenza, 1095?," *American Historical Review* 27 (1922): 731–33; Peter Charanis, "Byzantium, the West, and the Origin of the First Crusade," *Byzantion* 19 (1949): 17–36; Jonathan Shepard, "Aspects of Byzantine Attitudes and Policy towards the West in the Tenth and Eleventh Centuries," *Byzantinische Forshungen* 13 (1988): 67–118; Jonathan Shepard, "Cross Purposes: Alexios Comnenus and the First Crusade," in Jonathan Phillips, ed., *The First Crusade: Origin and Impact* (Manchester: Manchester University Press, 1997), 107–29; Jonathan Harris, *Byzantium and the Crusades* (New York: Palgrave, 2003); Laiou and Mottahedeh, eds., *The Crusades from the Perspective of Byzantium and the Muslim World*.

The Twelfth Century

There is a sad irony in the fact that the Crusades, inspired in large part by Pope Urban's desire for better relations with the Eastern church, are responsible for consummating the schism that had grown up between them.[95] Urban had hoped that a joint campaign against a common foe would draw the Eastern and Western churches closer together, which explains why in 1095 he issued his call for a pilgrimage to recapture Jerusalem and assist the Greeks. Despite early signs that Latins and Byzantines could coexist peacefully, increased contact soon proved these hopes illusory. It was a clear example of familiarity breeding contempt.

Immediately upon the Franks' arrival in the East, their lack of facial hair was cause for comment, as beards often served as a marker of one's ecclesial allegiance, especially in areas where there was dispute. As early as 1060, at the Synod of Split, Croatian and Dalmatian bishops had accepted the demands of the Roman legate Majnard that "all priests shave their beards and trim their hair in order to distinguish them from Orthodox priests."[96] The Coptic patriarch, criticized by other Christians for permitting circumcision, noted that there was no difference between this custom and the beardlessness of the Franks, since "some sects have approved customs that are disapproved by other sects, such as ... the shaving of beard by the Faranj [and] the shaving of the crown of the head by the priests of the Rûm."[97]

It was not long before these cultural differences came to be seen as manifestations of the Latins' various heresies and listed among their many sins. Writings of the period testify to this phenomenon (e.g., "The things which are done and taught by the Franks contrary to the orthodox faith"),[98] although not everyone was caught up in the polemical fervor. In 1090 Theophylact of Ohrid (d. 1107), wrote a letter to a Constantinopolitan deacon, *On the Errors of the Latins*, listing twelve Western practices that some in the East considered to be heretical (e.g., fasting practices, bishops wearing rings, wearing of colored silken vestments), including the fact that Latin priests "cut their hair and shaved their beards."[99] Theophylact criticized all those who "through unmeasured zeal ... and lack of humility" attacked the Latins in this way,

---

[95] According to Aristeides Papadakis, "Before 1095, in both East and West, Christians still believed in a single undivided Christendom, whereas afterward very few did so." Papadakis, *The Christian East and the Rise of the Papacy*, 105.

[96] Mitja Velikonja, *Religious Separation and Political Intolerance in Bosnia-Herzegovina*, trans. Rang'ichi Ng'inja (College Station, TX: Texas A&M University Press, 2003), 42. The other mandate was that all priests had to speak Latin.

[97] al-Safi ibn al-'Assal, *Al-Majmo'a Al-Safawi*, vol. 2, ed., Guiguis Filotheus Awad, 420–21; Eng. trans.: https://coptliterature.wordpress.com/2013/12/17/coptic-evidence-that-the-copts-of-the-middle-ages-did-not-brand-their-children-with-hot-iron-to-make-crosses-on-their-faces/.

[98] Text in Andrei Pavlov, *Kriticheskie opyty po istorii drevneishei greko-russkoi polemiki protiv latinian* (Saint Petersburg: Imperatorskaia akademiia nauk, 1878), 151–57.

[99] Theophylact of Ohrid, Προσλαλιά τινι τῶν αὐτοῦ ὁμιλητῶν περὶ ὧν ἐγκαλοῦνται Λατῖνοι, in Paul Gautier, ed., *Théophylacte d'Achrida: Discours, traités, poésies. Introduction, texte, traduction et notes* (Thessaloniki: Association de Recherches Byzantines, 1980), 249 (also PG 126:224). For more on the letter see Margaret Mullett, *Theophylact of Ochrid: Reading the Letters of a Byzantine Archbishop*, Birmingham Byzantine and Ottoman Monographs 2 (London: Variorum, 1997), 239–40.

insisting, as had Peter III of Antioch, that only their use of the Filioque truly mattered, all the other issues being either insignificant or easily resolvable.[100]

Beardlessness not only distinguished the Franks from the Greeks, but also from the Muslims, for whom beards were de rigueur.[101] For decades Christians in Spain had forced Muslims to wear longer beards "so that they could easily be distinguished from their short-bearded Christian superiors."[102] Giles Constable noted that using beards this way sometimes became a problem, as when crusaders who had stopped shaving were mistaken for Muslims "owing to the likeness of their beards" and accidentally killed during the Siege of Antioch in 1098.[103] At the Siege of Acre (1189–91) a boatload of Muslims successfully resupplied the city by masquerading as Franks, deceiving the Latin blockaders by shaving, placing a cross on the flag, and letting pigs roam freely on deck. A similar problem occurred in 1290 when a group of drunken Italian knights in Acre began rioting, killing anyone with a beard, assuming they must be Muslims, despite the fact that many Christian Syrians also sported beards.[104] Yet notwithstanding these occasional mix-ups, as it concerned religious identity beards remained "a generally reliable sign of whose side you were on."[105]

It is true, however, that some Latins in the East did allow their beards to grow. In his *Historia orientalis* the bishop of Acre, Jacques de Vitry, bemoaned the fact that many crusaders adopted oriental vices like long hair and beards.[106] William of Tyre wrote that in 1109 Baldwin of Edessa tricked his father-in-law, Gabriel of Malatia, into giving him money by confiding that he had sworn to shave his beard should his debts go unpaid. According to William, "Gabriel was astounded at this novel

---

[100] "Any man who is versed in ecclesiastical history has learned that it is not every custom which can sever from the Church, but that only which leads to a difference of dogma. And these things, which our wonderfully wise judges will have to be such great errors, are most certainly nothing more than customs ... none of which can separate us from them ... at least not if the case [is to] be judged by those who are willing to follow the rules of the Fathers." Theophylact of Ohrid, Προσλαλιά τινι τῶν αὐτοῦ ὁμιλητῶν περὶ ὧν ἐγκαλοῦνται Λατῖνοι, in Gautier, *Théophylacte d'Achrida: Discours, traités, poésies*, 279; Eng. trans.: William Palmer, *Dissertations on Subjects Relating to the "Orthodox" or "Eastern Catholic" Communion* (London: Joseph Masters, 1853), 27.

[101] In one particular Hadith (sayings of the prophet) Mohammad stipulated, "Be different from the mushrikeen: let your beards grow and trim your moustaches." For these and other relevant Hadith see Faegheh Shirazi, "Men's Facial Hair in Islam: A Matter of Interpretation," in Geraldine Biddle-Perry and Sarah Cheang, eds., *Hair: Styling, Culture and Fashion* (Oxford: Berg, 2008), 111–22.

[102] Oldstone-Moore, *Of Beards and Men*, 99.

[103] Giles Constable, *Crusades and Crusading in the Twelfth Century* (London: Routledge, 2008), 333. "A terrible neglect covered the thinnest of the weary cheeks of our men who, continually prepared for battle, worn out by continual traveling, had stopped shaving their beards in the Franks' manner. The Bishop of Puy noticed this, and to prevent mutual slaughter in case they confronted each other in battle (each thinking the other a Turk because of the beard) ordered them to shave often, and to hang on their necks crosses made of silver or of some other material so that no one, mistaken for a foreigner, would be struck down by a comrade." Guibert of Nogent, *The Deeds of God through the Franks: A Translation of Guibert de Nogent's Gesta Dei per Francos*, trans. Robert Levine (Woodbridge, Suffolk: Boydell Press, 1997), 93.

[104] "Poor Saracen peasants came into Acre carrying goods to sell, as they were accustomed to do. It happened one day, ... that the crusaders, who had come to do good and to arm themselves for the succor of the city of Acre, brought about its destruction, for one day they rushed through Acre, putting all the poor peasants who had brought goods to sell in Acre to the sword. They also slew a number of bearded Syrians ... because of their beards, mistaking them for Saracens." Paul Crawford, trans. *The Templar of Tyre: Part III of The Deeds of the Cypriote Crusade, Texts in Translation 6* (Aldershot: Ashgate, 2003), 101–2.

[105] Oldstone-Moore, *Of Beards and Men*, 99.

[106] Jessalynn Bird, ed., *Jacques de Vitry's History of the East* (London: Routledge, 2021).

agreement ... and began to pant and boil with excessive rage. For Orientals, both Greeks and other nationalities, cherish the beard with most earnest care, and if perchance even one hair be pulled from it, this insult is regarded as the highest dishonor and ignominy."[107] There is also an account of the 1113 Council of Benevento, when two representatives of Bernard of Valence traveled West to make appeals to the pope. These men, according to the report, "whose hair and beards were matted and waved not, as it would seem, by design but through neglect, threw themselves at the pope's feet."[108] According to Bernard Hamilton, "This comment suggests that already by the early years of the twelfth century the Franks in Syria were adopting different fashions from those prevalent in the West."[109]

Back in the West, facial hair for laymen went in and out of style in different regions for various reasons. In Germany and Anglo-Saxon England laws were actually enacted to protect beards, with those desecrating another man's beard punished by fine (e.g., twenty shillings in the Law Code of Alfred the Great)[110] or other means.[111] Sources indicate that men frequently took oaths while holding their beards "as if out of reverence in order that whatever they affirm by swearing on their beards may be held not only believable, but also holy."[112]

Yet Constable notes that by the "second half of the eleventh century" things had changed, and that "many, if not most, men in Northern Europe, and especially in France and England, shaved their beards."[113] Unshaven laymen now came in for censure, as when Serlo of Séez (d. 1123) berated the long-bearded Normans for looking like "billy-goats, whose filthy viciousness is shamefully imitated by the degradations of fornicators and sodomites."[114] He speculated that they had stopped shaving "for fear that the short bristles [of their beards] should prick their mistresses when they kiss them, and in their hairiness look more like Saracens than Christians."[115] Serlo did make an exception for penitents and pilgrims, who sported long beards "so that those who in the sight of God inwardly are bristling with sins and are unkempt may walk

---

[107] William of Tyre, *History of Deeds Done beyond the Sea*, vol. 1, trans. Emily Atwater Babcock and A. C. Krey (New York: Columbia University Press, 1943), 480. The beard, Gabriel argued, "ought to be guarded with the greatest care," for it was "the characteristic feature of a man, the glory of the face, [and] the chief dignity of man," and should not be pledged "as if it were a thing of no consequence that might be lost without dishonor." Ibid.

[108] Bernard Hamilton, *The Latin Church in the Crusader States: The Secular Church* (London: Routledge, 2016), 27.

[109] Ibid.

[110] Martin Brett, Christopher Robert Cheney, Dorothy Whitelock, Frederick Maurice Powicke, Christopher Brooke, and Arthur West Hadden, eds., *Councils and Synods with Other Documents Relating to the English Church I (871–1204)* (Oxford: Clarendon Press, 1964), 31. "If a man shave off another's beard let him make amends with twenty shillings. If he bind him first and then shave him like a priest (*hine to preoste bescire*) let him make amends with sixty shillings."

[111] "In Frederick Barbarossa's *Landfried* of 1152, it was forbidden either to seize a man by the beard or to tear any hairs from his head or beard. In the Frankish *Pactus Legis Salicae*, if a *puer crinitus* (long-haired boy) was shorn without the consent of his parents, the heavy fine of forty-five solidi was imposed." Simon Coates, "Scissors or Sword? The Symbolism of a Medieval Haircut," *History Today* 49 (May 1999): 7–13.

[112] "A man of this type says 'By this beard, it is so' ... [or] 'May the evil flame devour this beard if it is otherwise.'" Constable, "Introduction on Beards in the Middle Ages," 64.

[113] Ibid., 95.

[114] Serlo of Séez, cited in Orderic Vitalis, *The Ecclesiastical History of Orderic Vitalis*, vol. 6: Books 11, 12, and 13, trans. Marjorie Chibnall (Oxford: Clarendon Press, 1978), 63–67.

[115] Ibid.

outwardly bristling and unshorn and proclaim by their outward disgrace the baseness of the inner man."[116] For John of Beleth, penitents "let their hair and beard grow in order to show the abundance of crimes with which the head, that is, the mind of the sinner, is burdened."[117] This was also true of pilgrims, whose "captivity" to pilgrimage was symbolized by their beard.

Yet while styles changed for laymen, clerical beardlessness remained the norm throughout the Latin West, supported by the argument used by earlier authors (e.g., Gregory the Great, Isidore, Ratramnus) that the removal of hair symbolized the renunciation of vice. For example, Amalarius of Metz wrote that ministers should shave off all "superfluous thoughts in order that the eye of the intellect can look at eternal things."[118] John of Beleth held that even when the practice of shaving was suspended during Lent, monks were required to shave before the Easter vigil to signify that "we must cut off the vices and sins which are superfluous in us" before properly celebrating the resurrection.[119]

Sicard of Cremona (d. 1215), who later participated in the Fourth Crusade, summarized the spiritual arguments in favor of clerical shaving in his nine-volume *Mitralea*, a commentary on the liturgy.[120] He maintained that the practice was rooted in St. Peter's tonsure, for since Peter had his beard cut and head shaved by his captors, shaving had become "a memory of the Lord's passion and the morality that ought to be in us."[121] We remove the "superfluous thoughts by the razor of the fear of God so that [the mind] may contemplate celestial things with the naked face of the heart."[122] The circle of hairs that remain after tonsure "is the adornment of the virtues," for the harmony of its shape (i.e., the perfect circle) symbolized "the concord of love."[123] Sicard also claimed that "we shave our beards in order to look like boys" who by

---

[116] Ibid., vol. 4: Books 7–8, p. 118.

[117] John Beleth, *Summa de ecclesiasticis officiis*, cited in Constable, "Introduction on Beards in the Middle Ages," 67.

[118] Amalarius of Metz, *Liber officialis* II, 5, 1–7, cited in Constable, "Introduction on Beards in the Middle Ages," 71.

[119] John Beleth, *Summa de ecclesiasticis officiis*, cited in Constable, "Introduction on Beards in the Middle Ages," 71–72. Echoing earlier authors, Guglielmus Durandus (d. 1296) also wrote: "The Lord said to Ezekiel, 'Take the sharp knife, take the barbers razor and cause it to pass upon thine head and upon thy beard for the length of the hair signifies the multitude of sins.' This passage teaches the clerics that they must shave their beards. For the reason given for the hair of the beard, which is said to have come from the superfluous humours of the stomach, indicates that we must cut off the vices and sins which are superfluous in us." Guillaume Durandus, *Rationale Divinorum Officiorum*, vol, 2: Books 2 and 3, trans. Janet Gentles (Bedford: Paschal Light, 2019), 15–16.

[120] Gábor Sarbak and Lorenz Weinrich, eds., *Sicardi Cremonensis episcopi Mitralis de officiis Corpus Christianorum, Continuatio Mediaevalis 228* (Turnhout: Brepols, 2008).

[121] English translation in Constable, "Introduction on Beards in the Middle Ages," 72. Other commentators (e.g., Bede) would talk about tonsure and the passion of Christ by relating the remaining hairs of the monk's head to the crown of thorns or shaving to the wounds of Christ. In the canons of Springiersbach and Rolduc, compiled in the 1120s, the tonsure of hair and beard was numbered among the stigmata of Christ. "Those who want to be glorified with Christ must therefore conform to his passion and bear the signs of his splendor. 'For who, when he is ready to give his soul to Christ, loves the hair of his body more than Christ?'" Ibid., 75.

[122] Ibid., 72. For Sicard, even when clerics let their beards grow during Lent "in order that we may look like penitents," this was to demonstrate that certain worldly actions "which are not opposed to God, such as building churches and the like," should not be rejected. Ibid.

[123] Ibid., 72, These remaining hairs remind us that "it is necessary sometimes to think about temporal things" and this must be done by harmonizing reason with "the sensual nature" Ibid., 72–73.

"their humility and innocence ... dine with the Lord and enter into the Kingdom of Heaven ... equal to the angels, who forever flourish in a youthful age."[124] Finally, he argued that shaving was supported both by reason and by custom, so that "even if the present church does not know the originators," one could not dispense with so ancient a practice without good cause.[125]

Bruno of Segni (d. 1123) added another dimension to the argument for clerical beardlessness by distinguishing between those who were "interiorly bearded" (i.e., spiritual strong) and those only "exteriorly bearded."[126] Although the beard was normally a good thing because it distinguished the sexes and manifested strength, Bruno held that it was more important to be strong rather than simply appearing so.[127] Thus in order to show forth "the strength of men rather than the softness of women," priests should let their "interior beard grow just as the exterior is shaved; for the former grows without impediment while the latter, unless it is shaved, creates many inconveniences and is only nurtured and made beautiful by men who are truly idol and vain."[128] The holy women of old, "who frequently surpassed men in strength of spirit," knew this truth, which is why, according to Bruno, despite their natural lack of facial hair they could be referred to "as bearded (*barbatas*)."[129]

However, despite all of these theological arguments in favor of beardlessness, it has long been noted that many of the canons regarding shaving were "widely disregarded, especially by the higher clergy."[130] "Almost all the popes and many bishops and abbots in the eleventh and twelfth centuries had some sort of beard," and "Lucius III (1181–84) is the first pope of this period known to have been clean shaven."[131] Matters became so serious that Pope Alexander III, writing to the archbishop of Canterbury, allegedly mandated that any priest who refused to shave should be forcibly shorn by their archdeacon (*Clerici qui comam nutriunt et barbam etiam inviti a suis archdiaconis tondeantur*).[132] Even among monks, for whom shaving was the general rule, there were important exceptions (hermits, anchorites, recluses), and many hermit-saints became famous for their long beards.[133] Another important exception

---

[124] Ibid., 73. Durandus followed Sicard in writing: "We therefore shave our beard so that, by innocence and humility, we should appear pure, and become the equals of the angels, who are always in the flower of youth. However, in fasting we sometimes let our hair grow because the thoughts which are not against God, such as building a church, cultivating a field, and the like, which are customarily done during the time of abstinence, should not be forbidden." Guillaume Durandus, *Rationale Divinorum Officiorum*, 16.

[125] Constable, "Introduction on Beards in the Middle Ages," 73.

[126] Bruno of Segni, *In Leviticum* 19.26–27 (PL 164:444).

[127] "Men who are strong are superior to those who only wish to seem so." Eng. trans.: Oldstone-Moore, *Of Beards and Men*, 93.

[128] Constable, "Introduction on Beards in the Middle Ages," 70.

[129] Ibid., 69–70.

[130] Ibid., 114.

[131] Ibid., 113. There is some room for questioning this, for although some claim that "Anastasius IV (Pope from 1153 to 1154) was the first shaven pontiff in the twelfth century ... two of his predecessors (Celestine II and Lucius II) are represented as shaven in Papenbroeck's *Propylaeum*—both twelfth-century popes. Pascal II, who occupied the Holy See from the end of the eleventh century until 1118[,] denounced long hair. And although his omission of any mention of beards might be considered significant, the engraving in the *Propylaeum* shows him as shaven." Reynolds, *Beards: An Omnium Gatherum*, 111–12.

[132] Reynolds, *Beards: An Omnium Gatherum*, 120. This letter was cited in this form by the 1234 Decretals of Gregory IX, although "*et barbam*" is most likely an interpolation. Seghers, "Practice of Shaving in the Latin Church," 292.

[133] Constable, "Introduction on Beards in the Middle Ages," 119.

were lay brothers (*conversi*), who were "recruited from the peasant class" in order "to labor in the monastery's fields and workshops rather than pray in the choir stalls."[134] Distinguished from the (unshaven) monks by their beards, they were often referred to as the "bearded brothers" (*fratres barbati*) and treated as the inferiors of their beardless confreres.

In 1160 this distinction caused a great controversy at the Cistercian Abbey of Rosières, after the lay brothers complained to Buchard of Bellevaux about his recent comments concerning their beards. Buchard had allegedly heard reports of bad behavior among them and threatened to have their beards (metaphorically) burned if they did not mend their ways.[135] The lay brothers, already sensitive about their "beards and lack of tonsure," which often served as "a mark of ignominy, setting them apart from the clerical monks,"[136] "felt threatened rather than moved by Buchard's words: Why did he scorn their beards?"[137] To clarify his position and mollify those who felt slighted by his earlier missive, Buchard wrote the *Apologia de Barbis*, which addressed the subject of beards at great length.[138]

Buchard began the work by assuring the brothers that "so barbaric a thought as the desire to burn their beards" had never entered his mind (*Absit a me ut venerit in mentem meam tam barbara cogitatio, barbas vestras optare comburi*).[139] Rather, he praised the beard as

> appropriate to a man as a sign of his comeliness, as a sign of his strength, as a sign of his wisdom, as a sign of his maturity, and as a sign of his piety. And when these things are equally present in a man he can justly be called "full-bearded," full since his beard shows him to be, not a half-man or a womanly man, but a complete man with a beard that is plentiful on his chin, and along the jaw, and under his chin.[140]

Beards were therefore fine as long as they did not become manifestations of vanity, which is why he argued that the beards of lay brothers should instead look "neglected in rustic lack of fashion rather than shaped with excessive care into a lustful composition."[141] Clergy, however, needed to shave "in order to aim for perfection in mind and spirit ... strip[ping] away all that is superfluous and this-worldly from [their] feelings and desires," and working on their "interior beard" (an argument he borrowed from Bruno of Segni).[142] Lay brothers, who in their "simplicity" could not "penetrate these

---

[134] Oldstone-Moore, *Of Beards and Men*, 90.
[135] He was equating their behavior with bloody clothing, echoing Isaiah's warning that "all the boots of the tramping warriors and all the garments rolled in blood shall be burned as fuel for the fire" (Is 9:5). This image of burning beards reappears in certain jokes made about the lay brothers' beards, which included the line "Woe to those dirty and lousy beards; let the fire burn those that deserve to be burned! Woe to those beards full of vermin; woe to the beards fouled by saliva flowing down, worthy of spitting and execrations and justly condemned to the fire." Constable, "Introduction on Beards in the Middle Ages," 100.
[136] Ibid., 129.
[137] Oldstone-Moore, *Of Beards and Men*, 90.
[138] Buchard of Bellevaux, *Apologia de Barbis* in R. B. C. Huygens, ed., *Apologiae duae*, Corpus Christianorum: Continuatio mediaeualis, 62 (Turnholt: Brepols, 1985).
[139] Ibid., 151.
[140] Oldstone-Moore, *Of Beards and Men*, 92.
[141] Ibid.
[142] Ibid.

spiritual matters" in the same way, spent their time "occupied by earthly labor" and for this reason remained appropriately bearded.[143] In one of the last chapters of the work *De claritate et Gloria barbarum post hanc vitam*, Buchard even affirmed that come the resurrection, all men—clergy and laity—would be bearded, their hairs "white as wool, white as snow" as it says in Scripture.[144]

Back in the Levant, once the Franks began to establish themselves as permanent residents in the East, the shaving practices of men, both clerical and lay, began to change. The most famous example of this new style were the Knights Templar, whose long beards became "important symbols of [their] corporate identity and vocation."[145] The Templar Rule itself neither mandated nor prohibited facial hair, saying only that superiors "should ensure that the brothers are so well tonsured ... and we command you to firmly adhere to this same conduct with respect to beards and moustaches, so that no excess may be noted on their bodies."[146] Soon, however, this demand for trimmed hair and beards seemed forgotten, as long beards worn "in the Templar style" became "major components of Templar identity."[147] There is no record of when or why they did this, but it did serve to distinguish them from both "choir-monks" and "knights errant who served temporary terms of duty."[148] Of course, these long beards were only for the non-ordained, since "the few ordained chaplain brothers in the Templar Order were explicitly commanded to shave their beards."[149]

As tensions between Latins and Greeks continued to mount throughout the twelfth century, Byzantine lists of Latin errors once again appeared, with the shaving practices of the Latins a regular feature.[150] For example, the *Opusculum contra Francos*, written between the mid-eleventh and mid-twelfth century and among the best known of the anti-Latin lists, included among its thirty-four (or thirty-six) complaints the charge that Western "priests shave their beards in the manner of soldiers and against the apostolic institutions."[151] From the West we also have the witness of Joachim of Fiore (d. 1202), the apocalyptic writer who saw the schism between East and West as prefigured in the discord between the bearded Esau (the Greeks) and the beardless Jacob

---

[143] Ibid.

[144] "His head and his hair were white as white wool, white as snow; his eyes were like a flame of fire" (Rv 1:14).

[145] "A key component of a Templar's appearance—the projected identity making him recognizable as a Templar instantly and nonverbally, even to non-Christians—was his possession of a clerical tonsure in spite of his lay status, which in turn was indicated by his beard." Kevin James Lewis, "A Templar's Belt: The Oral and Satorial Transmission of Memory and Myth in the Order of the Temple," in *Crusades* 13 (London: Routledge, 2014), 204.

[146] Judith M. Upton-Ward, ed., *The Rule of the Templars: The French Text of the Rule of the Order of the Knights Templar* (Woodbridge, Suffolk: Boydell Press, 2005), 25.

[147] Alain Demurger, "The Beard and the Habit in the Templars' Trial: Membership, Rupture, Resistance," in Helen Nicholson and Jochen Burgtorf, eds., *Templars, the Hospitallers and the Crusades: Essays in Homage to Alan J. Forey* (London: Routledge, 2020), 129–37.

[148] Oldstone-Moore, *Of Beards and Men*, 101.

[149] Lewis, "Transmission of Memory and Myth," 204.

[150] Niketas Seides's *Adversus Latinos* listed twelve errors, and while he did not include shaving among them, the accusation that the Latins did not address Mary as *Theotokos* was now ranked alongside the Filioque and azymes as their chief shortcomings. Kolbaba, *The Byzantine Lists*, 177. Text in Reinhard Gahbauer, ed., *Gegen den Primat des Papstes: Studien zu Niketas Seides* (Munich: Verlag Uni-Druck, 1975).

[151] Joseph Hergenröther, *Monumenta graeca ad Photium ejusque historiam pertinentia* (Regensburg: Manz, 1869), 71. Eng. trans.: Kolbaba, *The Byzantine Lists*, 56–57.

(the Latins).¹⁵² The Greeks had, like Esau, lost their inheritance and in doing so had surrendered their previous privileged position to the Latins.¹⁵³ As a chastisement for their sins the Greeks were now being overrun by the Saracens, but God would eventually bring them back into the fold following a series of trials and tribulations.

Relations between East and West continued to deteriorate as the century closed. During the brief but turbulent reigns of Emperors Alexios II (1180–83) and Andronicus I (1183–85), a wave of anti-Latin sentiment swept through Constantinople, culminating in the 1182 riots in the city's Latin quarter. The Latin chronicler William of Tyre described how "the perfidious Greek nation ... this brood of vipers" returned the Latins' longtime friendship by indiscriminately slaughtering thousands, decapitating the papal legate, and tying his head to the tail of a dog to be dragged in the street.¹⁵⁴ Three years later the Normans matched brutality for brutality as they sacked the city of Thessaloniki as if they were "making war on God Himself,"¹⁵⁵ entering the churches and "then uncover[ing] their privy parts to let the *membrum virile* pour forth the contents of the bladder, urinating round the sacred floor."¹⁵⁶

Eustathios of Thessaloniki (d. 1195), who chronicled the sack, had earlier noted the difference in shaving practices and how "those who follow the Latin customs... try artificially to look as if they are just getting a beard. They therefore torture their beard by constant close shaving and feel dishonored if the beard appears to grow."¹⁵⁷ Now he took particular care to detail how the Normans, "even when leaving us alone in other respects," showed their "dislike both for our long hair and for our long beards ... us[ing] at one moment of a razor, at another a knife, and the more hasty among them the sword" to cut them off."¹⁵⁸ Eustathios wrote that "it became a rarity to see in any place a Greek whose head was still untampered with.... And if any man's beard escaped and hung down in an orderly manner in accordance with nature then

---

¹⁵² "The exegesis of Jacob and Esau fighting in Rebecca's womb as a type for the Latins and Greeks [had] featured in the [Joachim's] *Commentary on Jeremiah*." Brett Whalen, *Dominion of God: Christendom and Apocalypse in the Middle Ages* (Cambridge, MA: Harvard University Press, 2009), 197. See also Marjorie Reeves, "The Originality and Influence of Joachim of Fiore," *Traditio* 36 (1980): 269–316.

¹⁵³ "The schism between the Latins and Greeks, Joachim realized, was just as much a part of God's plan as the division between the Synagogue and the Church. Much like the Jews before them, the Greeks had failed to transcend fully their carnal understandings of God's word. They had rejected the decrees and guidance of the Roman Church, refusing to acknowledge the apostolic authority granted to the papacy by Peter. Their priests took wives, not realizing that the Church was a cleric's true bride. They believed that Latins hated them, as much as they hated Latins." Whalen, *Dominion of God*, 110–11. For Joachim's defense of the Filioque see Peter Gemeinhardt, "Joachim the Theologian: Trinitarian Speculation and Doctrinal Debate," in Matthias Riedl, ed., *A Companion to Joachim of Fiore* (Leiden: Brill, 2018), 41–87.

¹⁵⁴ William of Tyre, *History of Deeds Done beyond the Sea*, vol. 2, trans. Emily Atwater Babcock and A. C. Krey (New York: Columbia University Press, 1943), 464–65.

¹⁵⁵ Eustathios of Thessaloniki, *The Capture of Thessaloniki: A Translation with Introduction and Commentary*, trans. John R. Melville-Jones (Canberra: Australian Association for Byzantine Studies, 1988), 115.

¹⁵⁶ Niketas Choniates, *O City of Byzantium, Annals of Niketas Choniates*, trans. Harry Magoulias (Detroit: Wayne State University Press, 1984), 166.

¹⁵⁷ Eustathios of Thessaloniki, *Commentarii ad Homeri Odysseam*, ed. G. Stallnaum (Leipzig: Weigel, 1825), 382. Eng. trans.: Constable, "Introduction to Beards in the Middle Ages," 97. Anna Komnene took note of this Latin custom in her description of Bohemond of Taranto: "Whether his beard was red or of any other colour I cannot say, for the razor had passed over it closely, leaving his chin smoother than any marble." Anna Komnene, *Alexiad*, trans. E. R. A. Sewter (London: Penguin Classics, 2003), 384.

¹⁵⁸ Eustathios of Thessaloniki, *The Capture of Thessaloniki*, 131–33.

these wretched barbers grabbed it with one hand, and the hair of his head with the other, and said that all was well with the latter hair but not with the former, jesting over matters which were not fit for mirth."[159]

The Thirteenth Century

The story of the Fourth Crusade and the subsequent sack of Constantinople in April 1204 is an oft-told and tragic tale, which need not be recounted in full here.[160] Pope Innocent III (1198–1216) was appalled by the reports, especially as it concerned the treatment of churches and people consecrated to God, and told the crusaders so in no uncertain terms.[161] Yet the pope soon reconciled himself to the new situation, since the election of Thomas Morosini (1204–11) as patriarch theoretically meant an end to the schism and the return of the Constantinopolitan church to papal obedience.[162]

---

[159] Ibid. Choniates, who used Eustasthias as a source, wrote how the Latins "would grab their beards with both hands and pull the hair on their heads, contending that these were unbefitting; they ridiculed the shagginess and length of the beard and insisted that the hair be clipped round about according to their own style.... These utterly shameless buffoons, having no fear of God whatsoever, would bend over and pull up their garments, baring their buttocks and all that men keep covered; turning their anus on the poor wretches, close upon their food, the fools would break wind louder than a polecat. Sometimes they discharged the urine in their bellies through the spouts of their groins and contaminated the cooked food, even urinating in the faces of some." Niketas Choniates, *O City of Byzantium*, 169.

[160] Primary Latin accounts include Robert of Clari, *The Conquest of Constantinople*, trans. Edgar Holmes McNeal (New York: Columbia University Press, 2005); Gunther of Pairis, *The Capture of Constantinople: The Hystoria Constantinopolitana of Gunther of Pairis*, trans. Alfred Andrea (Philadelphia: University of Pennsylvania Press, 1997), 112. See also Geoffrey de Villehardouin, "Chronicles of the Fourth Crusade and the Conquest of Constantinople," in Margaret Shaw, ed., *Chronicles of the Crusades* (New York: Penguin, 1972), 1–136. Recent histories of the crusade include Donald Queller and Thomas Madden, *The Fourth Crusade: The Conquest of Constantinople* (Philadelphia: University of Pennsylvania Press, 1997); Thomas Madden, *The Fourth Crusade: Event, Aftermath, and Perceptions* (London: Ashgate, 2008); Michael Angold, *The Fourth Crusade: Event and Context* (Harlow: Longman, 2003); Jonathan Phillips, *The Fourth Crusade and the Sack of Constantinople* (New York: Penguin, 2005).

[161] "For although you vowed, in obedience to the crucified one, to liberate the Holy Land from the hands of the pagans, and although you were forbidden under threat of excommunication to attempt to invade or violate the lands of Christians ... [you] appear to have rashly turned away from the purity of your vow when you took up arms not against Saracens but Christians, not aiming to recover Jerusalem but to occupy Constantinople, and, more seriously, it is reputed far and wide that some showed no mercy for reasons of religion, age, or sex but committed acts of fornication, adultery, and lewdness in the sight of all, and they exposed not only married women and widows but even matrons and virgins dedicated to God to the filth of the lowborn. It was not enough to empty the imperial treasuries and to plunder alike the spoils of princes and lesser folk, but rather you extended your hands to church treasuries and, what was more serious, to their possessions, ripping away silver tablets from altars and violating sacristies, carrying away crosses, icons, and relics. The result is that the Greek church, afflicted to some degree by persecutions, disdains returning to obedience to the Apostolic See. It has seen in the Latins nothing other than the example of affliction and the works of Hell, so that now it rightly detests them more than dogs." Innocent III to Baldwin of Flanders; Eng. trans.: Alfred Andrea, *Contemporary Sources for the Fourth Crusade*, Medieval Mediterranean 29 (London: Brill, 2000), 173–74.

[162] Innocent was initially torn about Morosini's election, for although a Latin patriarch technically meant a united church under papal control, the irregular manner of the election carried out without Innocent's permission gave him pause. To solve this conflict Innocent wrote to the crusaders informing them that that the election was clearly uncanonical and had been "declared null in open consistory." However, he immediately added that "since a transgression by people ought not to flood over to the injury of churches, out of the plentitude of power conferred on us, we have elected and confirmed this same man, our subdeacon, a member of the Apostolic See, so to speak, as patriarch to that very church," making the office a de facto papal appointment. Innocent III, *Register* 7.203; Eng. trans.: Andrea, *Contemporary Sources for the Fourth*

Unfortunately for Innocent, the fact that Morosini recognized Rome's authority did not guarantee the obedience of Constantinople's clergy, most of whom continued to recognize John X Kamateros, living in exile at Nicaea, as their rightful bishop.

The Byzantine chronicler Niketas Choniates, who had little love for Morosini, took particular pains to note the new patriarch's foreignness, describing him as "fatter than a hog" and "clean-shaven, as is the case with the rest of his race, and his chest plucked smoother than pitchplaster."[163] Elsewhere Niketas remarked that Morosini's "beard was shaved smoother than if removed by a depilatory, so that the surface of his cheeks gave no indication whatsoever of the first appearance of hair but looked like a field stripped of crops."[164] His "clerical assistants and attendants at the holy altar were seen to be identical in everything with their primate, in dress and regimen and in the cropping of the beard."[165]

Angered by the pretensions of the Latin clergy and the pope's efforts to enforce their obedience, "Byzantine xenophobia, [and] anti-Latin sentiment" reached new heights in the years after the Fourth Crusade.[166] Lists of Latin errors, which had long circulated in the East, increased in length exponentially as further practices allegedly demonstrating the heretical nature of Western Christianity were added.[167] Konstantinos Stilbes, author of one of the longest such lists, included among his seventy-five accusations that "their bishops shave not only their beards but also the hair on the rest of their body, for they consider this, which is a Judaic practice, to be purificatory"[168] and that "by their appearance, one cannot tell a consecrated person from an unconsecrated one, for they all shave their beards and look like women."[169]

It is interesting to note that in addition to shaving somehow being a Judaizing practice, Stilbes added that it made Latin priests "look like women."[170] Effeminacy had long been associated with beardlessness in Byzantium, where eunuchs (whose most distinguishing physical feature is their lack of beard) were seen as a sort of "feminized male."[171] The fact that Latin priests, like eunuchs, were both beardless *and* unmarried

---

Crusade, 139. For more on Innocent's motives and reactions see Kenneth Setton, *The Papacy and the Levant 1204–1571*, vol. 1 (Philadelphia: American Philosophical Society, 1976), 1–26.

[163] Niketas Choniates, *O City of Byzantium*, 357.

[164] Ibid., 342.

[165] Ibid., 357.

[166] Aristeides Papadakis, "Byzantine Perceptions of the Latin West," *Greek Orthodox Theological Review* 36 (1991): 234.

[167] "Unlike theological treatises on points of difference between the churches, lists of Latin errors simply enumerate said errors without discussion or refutation. They present a catalog of Latin beliefs and practices in a form which implies that the abhorrent nature of those beliefs and practices is self-evident." Tia Kolbaba, "Meletios Homologetes: On the Customs of the Italians," *Revue des études byzantines* 55 (1997): 140. See also Tia Kolbaba, "Byzantine Perceptions of Latin Religious 'Errors': Themes and Changes from 850 to 1350," in Angeliki Laiou and Roy Parviz Mottahedeh, eds., *The Crusades from the Perspective of Byzantium and the Muslim World* (Washington, DC: Dumbarton Oaks, 2001), 117–43.

[168] Jean Darrouzès, "Le mémoire de Constantin Stilbès contre les Latins," *Revue des Études Byzantines* 21 (1963): 71. Eng. trans.: Kolbaba, *The Byzantine Lists*, 57.

[169] Jean Darrouzès, "Le mémoire," 78. Eng. trans.: Kolbaba, *The Byzantine Lists*, 57.

[170] Conversely the charge of effeminacy had also long been hurled by the West against the Greeks, Odo of Deuil writing that the Byzantines had long since "degenerated entirely into women; putting aside all manly vigor, both of words and spirit." Odo of Deuil, *De Profectione Ludovici VII in Orientem. The Journey of Louis VII to the East*, trans. Virginia Gingerick Berry (New York: Norton, 1948), 57.

[171] Tougher, "Bearding Byzantium," 163.

probably increased the association between them in the Byzantine mind, leading many Greeks to perceive Western clergy as "feminized" or unmanly.[172] For example, Michael Choniates, bishop of Athens, battled against the Latinization of his flock by berating any who dared shave. He told them:

> O what disfigurement of the divine icon.... Whoever puts off the manly hair of his chin has unconsciously transformed himself from a man into a woman. Well may many of you present cover your faces in shame as you look into this sermon as into a mirror and see how you have altered yourselves. Shame indeed it is, shame, to don a unisex appearance like the hermaphrodites of ancient Greece, who lay supine for men no less than they mounted women.[173]

Sometime between 1220 and 1225 Nicholas of Otranto (aka Nektarios of Casole), a bilingual monk who served as translator for the papal envoys in Constantinople despite his rejection of several Latin teachings, wrote Περὶ Γενείων (*On the Beard*), which he appended to his Τρία Συντάγματα, on the issues that divided East and West.[174] In it he called the Latins "ignorant" because they "boast especially in shaving" while simultaneously "despis[ing] those who heed the [true] form of man."[175] Nicholas held that "the faithful must not shave ... for God the Creator made this seemly for women [but] ordained it unfit for men."[176] If one shaved, one "opposed the law of God and become abominable in the eyes of God who created you in his own image."[177] He then took aim at "the Church of Rome [which] has adopted this" practice because of "what the impious did in violence against the apostle Peter plucking out his beard."[178] For this reason they not only shave but also cut "in a circle the heads of the Latin and Greek priests" because they believe it representative of the crown of thorns."[179] This practice, according to Nicholas, was "asserted against the apostolic tradition" and "entirely

---

[172] Some scholars have concluded that there is "a fairly strong argument for connecting the hairlessness of the Latin clergy with the celibacy that was at least prescribed for them and viewing the hairiness of the Greek clergy as an appropriate badge for a married clergy." Robert Bartlett, "Symbolic Meanings of Hair in the Middle Ages," *Transactions of the Royal Historical Society* 4 (1994): 57.

[173] Spyridon Lambros, ed., *Michaēl Akominatou tou Chōniatou Ta sōzomena*, vol. 1 (Athens, 1879), 43. Eng. trans.: Paul Magdalino, *The Empire of Manuel I Komnenos, 1142–1180* (Cambridge: Cambridge University Press, 1993), 385. See also Mario Gallina, "La reazione antiromana nell'epistolario di Michele Coniata, metropolita d'Atene," in Gherardo Ortalli, Giorgio Ravegnani, and Peter Schreiner, eds., *Quarta crociata. Venezia-Bisanzio Impero Latino: Relazioni presentate alle giornate di studio organizzate per l'ottavo centenario della Quarta crociata, Venezia, 4–8 maggio 2004* (Venice: Istituto veneto di scienze, lettere ed arti, 2006), 423–46.

[174] English translation in Linda Safran, *The Medieval Salento: Art and Identity in Southern Italy* (Philadelphia: University of Pennsylvania Press, 2014), 77–78. For Nicholas see Johannes M. Hoeck and Raimund J. Loenertz, *Nikolaos-Nektarios von Otranto Abt von Casole. Beiträge zur Geschichte der ostwestlichen Beziehungen unter Innozenz III. und Friedrich II* (Ettal: Buch-Kunstverlag, 1965); Claudio Schiano, "Omnes civitates nostre obedient venerationi: Nicola di Otranto e le fonti latine," *Rudiae. Ricerche sul mondo classico*, NS 3 (2017): 151–90; Claudio Schiano, "Nicholas-Nektarios of Otranto: A Greek Monk under Roman Obedience," in Barbara Crostini and Ines Angeli Murzaku, eds., *Greek Monasticism in Southern Italy: The Life of Neilos in Context* (London: Routledge, 2018), 208–25.

[175] Safran, *The Medieval Salento*, 77.
[176] Ibid.
[177] Ibid.
[178] Ibid.
[179] Ibid.

without a council" based on the spurious story of Pope Anacletus, a Greek who allegedly "ordered tonsure and beards to be shaved."[180]

As the polemical battle became more intense, the Latin religious orders in Constantinople—especially the Dominicans and Franciscans who had been charged by the pope with the *reductio Graecorum*—felt duty-bound to take up the pen in defense of the Roman church.[181] The 1252 work *Tractatus contra Graecos* by an anonymous Dominican, among the most influential and widely used of the genre, contained a list of charges then being made against the Latins (most taken directly from the 1178 translation of the *Opusculum contra Francos* done by Hugh Eteriano [d. 1182]), including the fact that their priests shaved like soldiers against the apostolic institutions (*Radunt barbas presbyteri more suorum militum preter apostolicam institutionem*).[182] In response the *Tractatus* quoted the 1177 *De haeresibus et praevaricationibus Graecorum* of Hugo's brother Leo Tuscus (d. 1182), which accused Greek priests of growing their beards in the manner of Jews (*Sacerdotes eorum more Iudiaco barbas nutriunt*), causing them to drench their beards in the Lord's blood when they drank from the chalice (*que semper Dominico sanguine, cum ab illis bibitur, madent*).[183]

Bonacursius of Bologna's (d. late thirteenth century) *De erroribus Graecorum* addressed the Greek accusation that the Latin monks and priests "are like women" (*sunt*

---

[180] Ibid., 78.
[181] For the work of these orders in Byzantium see Raymond-Joseph Loenertz, "Les établissements dominicains de Péra-Constantinople," *Échos d'Orient* 34 (1935): 332–49; Robert Lee Wolff, "The Latin Empire of Constantinople and the Franciscans," *Traditio* 2 (1944): 213–37; Martiniano Roncaglia, *Les frères mineurs et l'église grecque orthodoxe au XIII siècle (1231–1274)* (Le Caire: Centre d'Etudes Orientales de la Custodie Franciscaine de Terre-Sainte, 1954); Marie-Hélène Congourdeau, "Notes sur les Dominicains de Constantinople au début du 14 siècle," *Revue des études byzantines* 45 (1987): 175–81; Claudine Delacroix-Besnier, *Les dominicains et la chrétienté grecque aux XIVe et XVe siècle* (Rome: Ecole française de Rome, 1997), 277–90; Claudine Delacroix-Besnier, "Les Prêcheurs, du dialogue à la polémique (XIIIe–XIVe siècle)," in Hinterberger and Schabel, *Greeks, Latins, and Intellectual History 1204–1500*, 151–68; Claudine Delacroix-Besnier, "Mendicant Friars between Byzantium and Rome—Legates, Missionaries and Polemists (XIIIth–XVth Centuries)," in Falko Daim, Christian Gastgeber, Dominik Heher, and Claudia Rapp, eds., *Menschen, Bilder, Sprache, Dinge Wege der Kommunikation zwischen Byzanz und dem Westen 2: Menschen und Worte* (Mainz: Verlag des Römisch-Germanischen Zentralmuseums, 2018).
[182] Many thanks go to Dr. Andrea Riedl for her invaluable assistance with this material. Her recent critical edition of the work—Andrea Riedl, ed., *Tractatus contra Graecos (1252)*, CCCM 303 (Turnhout: Brepols Publishers, 2020)—and her monograph on the *Tractatus*—Andrea Riedl, *Kirchenbild und Kircheneinheit: Der dominikanische "Tractatus contra Graecos" (1252) in seinem theologischen und historischen Kontext* (Berlin: De Gruyter, 2020)—should help draw attention to this long-ignored but very important text. The *Tractatus* has been called "the basis for [all] future Dominican polemics against 'the Greeks'" and the work that essentially set the agenda for Ferrara-Florence two centuries later. Antōnios Kaldellēs, *Hellenism in Byzantium: The Transformations of Greek Identity and the Reception of the Classical Tradition* (Cambridge: Cambridge University Press, 2011), 359. See also Andrea Riedl, "Polemik im Kontext literarisch-theologischer Auseinandersetzung zwischen Ost- und Westkirche im 13. Jahrhundert," in Svorad Zavarský, Lucy Nicholas, and Andrea Riedl, eds., *Themes of Polemical Theology across Early Modern Literary Genres* (Newcastle upon Tyne: Cambridge Scholars, 2016), 129–42; Antoine Dondaine, "'Contra Graecos': Premiers ecrits polemiques des dominicains d'Orient," *Archivum Fratrum Praedicatorum* 21 (1951): 320–446.
[183] Riedl, *Tractatus contra Graecos*, 183. See also Leo "Tuscus", "De haeresibus et praevaricationibus Graecorum," in Antoine Dondaine, "Hugues Éthérien et Léon Toscan," *Archives d'histoire doctrinale et littéraire du Moyen Âge* 19 (1952): 67–134; Charles Haskins, "Leo Tuscus," *English Historical Review* 33 (1918): 492–96; Krijnie N. Ciggaar, *Western Travellers to Constantinople: The West and Byzantium, 962–1204: Cultural and Political Relations* (Leiden: Brill, 1996).

sicut mulieres) because they did not nourish their beards.[184] In response Bonacursius answered that Western priests were only following the example of the apostle Peter, who accepted tonsure because he "suffer[ed] dishonor for the sake of the name" (Acts 5:41). Everyone knew that it was unpleasant to find hairs in one's drinking cup, so how much worse was it that those dedicated to the service of God should dip their "long, ... ugly, and unclean" (*prolixas ... turpia et immunda*) beards in the blood of Jesus Christ, which is why Pope Anacletus, himself a Greek, had ruled that all priests shave their heads and beards, a rule repeated at the general council held at Carthage.[185] Besides, Bonacursius wrote, our struggle against evil is like that of the wrestler who shaves his head and beard lest his opponent have something to grab.[186] If some objected to the practice because Christ himself had a beard, it should be remembered that he was also circumcised to fulfill the old Law, a law to which we are no longer bound.[187]

Almost immediately following the recapture of Constantinople by Michael VIII Palaeologos (1258–82) in 1261, the new emperor reached out to the pope about the possibility of ecclesiastical reunion.[188] It was clear, both then and now, that the emperor's desire for church unity stemmed almost exclusively from his political need for security rather than from any great love of the Latins. In preparation for the reunion council that would eventually meet at Lyons in 1274, Pope Gregory X commissioned Humbert of Romans (d. 1277) to write the *Opusculum tripartitum*, a generally irenic work whose second part detailed both the history and the nature of the separation as he perceived it.[189] Among its causes, Humbert believed, were such

---

[184] Friedrich Stegmüller, "*Bonacursius contra Graecos*: Ein Beitrag zur Kontroverstheologie," in *Vitae et Veritati: Festgabe für Karl Adam* (Düsseldorf: Patmos-Verlag, 1958), 81.

[185] Ibid., 82.

[186] Ibid. Here he referenced Gregory the Great: "We who are naked have to struggle with other naked beings. If someone who is clothed begins to struggle with one who is naked he is quickly thrown to the ground, since there is something by which he can be held." Gregory the Great, *Homily 32*; Eng. trans.: Gregory the Great, *Forty Gospel Homilies*, trans. Dom David Hurst, Cistercian Studies 123 (Kalamazoo, MI: Cistercian Publications, 1990), 258.

[187] Stegmüller, "*Bonacursius Contra Graecos*," 82. This argument would later be employed by the Greeks regarding the use of azymes—i.e., even if Christ celebrated the Passover with unleavened bread, he also accepted circumcision in keeping with the old Law.

[188] Michael's "position was precarious.... He faced the ambitious Balkan kingdoms, the Latin principalities by now firmly rooted in Greek soil, the new Western claimants to the Latin Empire of Baldwin II ... in addition to the disquieting uncertainties in the Asian world caused by Mongol turmoils and rising Turkish powers. Like his Lascari predecessors, Michael VIII saw his best hope in coming to terms with the papacy." J. M. Hussey, *The Orthodox Church in the Byzantine Empire* (Oxford: Clarendon Press, 1986), 222. See also Deno Geanakopolos, *Emperor Michael Palaeologus and the West* (Cambridge, MA: Harvard University Press, 1959); Deno Geanakopolos, "The Byzantine Recovery of Constantinople from the Latins in 1261: A Chrysobull of Michael VIII Palaeologus in Favor of Hagia Sophia," in *Constantinople and the West* (Madison: University of Wisconsin Press, 1989), 173–88; Alexander Alexakis, "Official and Unofficial Contacts between Rome and Constantinople before the Second Council of Lyons (1274)," *Annuarium Historiae Conciliorum* 39 (2007): 99–124.

[189] See Charles Elliott, "The Schism and Its Elimination in Humbert of Rome's *Opusculum Tripartitum*," *Greek Orthodox Theological Review* 34 (1989): 71–83;; Edward Tracy Brett, *Humbert of Romans: His Life and Views of Thirteenth Century Society* (Toronto: Pontifical Institute for Medieval Studies, 1984); Karl Michel, *Das Opus Tripartitum des Humbertus de Romanis, o.p.: Ein Beitrag zur Geschichte der Kreuzzugsidee und der kirchlichen Unionsbewegungen* (Graz: Styria, 1926); A. Burguière, *Humbert de Romans et le II° Concile de Lyon à travers l'Opusculum Tripartitum: Une étude des problèmes de la chrétienté à la fin du XIII° siècle* (Paris: Université de Paris, 1961) Humbert saw the division of the Latins and Greeks among the three great trials the church had to undergo: "First, the persecution of infidels from without, ... second, the division

things as "the wearing of the beard" and "the matter of the sacrament of the eucharist."[190] Yet while there were faults on both sides, the Greeks were chiefly to blame for the schism despite the fact that many of their practices were closer to those of the primitive church.[191] For example, unlike the Latins "they had adhered to the ancient ways of the apostles by still wearing beards and abstaining from the use of bells in rituals."[192]

When the Byzantine delegation left Lyons in July 1274, they knew, despite all the pomp and ceremony that had surrounded the council, that while church union was easy to proclaim, its unpopularity in the East would make it far more difficult to enforce. The efforts of the new patriarch of Constantinople, John XI Bekkos (1275–82) to convince the Byzantines of the Latins' orthodoxy fell flat, for while he might argue that the Spirit's procession "through the Son" and procession "from the Son" were equivalent, there were too many other differences proving them heretics.[193] *The Heresies of the Franks and Their Neighbors* (c. 1281), written during this period, listed thirty-eight such charges, including the fact that their priests were beardless.[194] The highly polemical *Dialogue of Panagiotes with an Azymite*, written around the same time,[195] went so far as to give the "true" reason behind the practice.[196] In the dialogue

---

between Greeks and Latins, who wrestled in the womb of Rebecca (that is, of the Church), on account of which the kingdom of the Church, divided within itself, ... [and] third, the church of the Latins, having kept the faith, as far as practices are concerned, [was] caught up in great foulness." Eng. trans.: Whalen, *Dominion of God*, 196.

[190] Elliott, "The Schism and Its Elimination in Humbert," 72.

[191] "There are many Latins, who, although they do not give occasion for the previously mentioned scandal, nevertheless care little or not at all about the sad state of the Greeks. The Greeks are Christians like themselves, and, therefore, the Latins are like the priest and the Levite, who, meeting a wounded brother on the road, passed by caring nothing for him.... Those Latins, therefore, sin against nature who do not care that the Greeks, who are members of the same body as themselves, are in a sad state. The Greeks are less healthy in the faith than the Latins. Concerning such infirmity the apostle said, 'Assist those infirm in faith.' But where are the doctors?" Brett, *Humbert of Romans*, 189.

[192] Ibid., 188. Humbert also mentioned the cruelty of the Latin occupation, where the Latins "treated the Greeks to misery, the dragging by the beard and multiple affronts." Elliott, "The Schism and Its Elimination in Humbert," 72.

[193] For more on Bekkos see Peter Gilbert, "Not an Anthologist: John Bekkos as a Reader of the Fathers," *Communio* 36 (2009): 259–304; Joseph Gill, "John Beccus, Patriarch of Constantinople," *Byzantina* 7 (1975): 251–66; Romulad Souarn, "Tentatives d'union avec Rome: Un patriarche grec catholique au XIIIe siècle," *Echos d'Orient* 3 (1899–1900): 229–37, 351–70; V. Grumel, "Un ouvrage recent sur Jean Beccos, patriarche de Constantinople," *Echos d'Orient* 24 (1925): 229–37; Jean Gouillard, "Michel VIII et Jean Beccos devant l'Union," in *1274: Année charnière. Mutations et continuities* (Paris: CNRS, 1977), 179–90; Alexandra Riebe, *Rom in Gemeinschaft mit Konstantinopel: Patriarch Johannes XI. Bekkos als Verteidiger der Kirchenunion von Lyon (1274)* (Wiesbaden: Harrassowitz Verlag, 2005). For a discussion of his theology of the procession see Siecienski, *The Filioque*, 138–40.

[194] Kolbaba notes that the list itself (found in Juliette Davreux, "Le Codex Bruxellensis [Graecus] II 4836 [*De Haeresibus*]," *Byzantion* 10 [1935]: 91–106) is highly derivative, essentially repeating many of the charges made either by Keroularios or the *Opusculum contra Francos*. Kolbaba, *The Byzantine Lists*, 180.

[195] Kolbaba (ibid., 183 n. 33) gives a date between 1274 and 1277, based largely on the work of M. Concasty, "La fin d'un dialogue contre les Latins azymites d'après le Paris Suppl gr. 1191," in *Akten des xi. Internationalen Byzantinistenkongresses München, 1958* (Munich: C.H. Beck, 1060), 86–89.

[196] See Deno John Geanakoplos, "A Greek Libellus against Religious Union with Rome after the Council of Lyons (1274)," in *Interaction of the Sibling Byzantine and Western Cultures in the Middle Ages and Italian Renaissance (330–1600)* (New Haven, CT: Yale University Press, 1976), 156–70.

Panagiotes asks Azymite why the Pope shaves. Azymite explains that during the night an angel visited the Pope and ordered him to cut his beard. What follows is Panagiotes' vehement refutation: "This is not true, now you have lied! Listen, Azymite, let me tell you the truth.... The Pope wanted a certain woman. So he sent the woman [a letter] to come and lie with him. Then the woman sent him [a letter] saying: 'If you want me to come and lie with you, shave off your beard.' And the Pope cut his beard and sent [a letter] to the woman. The woman said, 'Because you cut your beard and shamed your honor for the sake of my female sex... I don't want to come to you!'" ... The pope [then] convened an ecclesiastical council and announced that an angel sent by God had told him that he and his bishops should cut their beards to become worthy of an angelic order. "This is what you have been doing ever since... [for] a woman shamed you and you shaved your beards for the sake of the female sex."[197]

Among the Latins' other faults in the *Dialogue* is that in their icons they portray Christ "like a Frank" (i.e., without a beard),[198] which is significant because among the charges then being leveled at the Greek unionists (e.g., George Metochites) was ethnic betrayal ("Instead of refutative proof, instead of arguments from the Scriptures, what we ... constantly hear is 'You have become a Frank!'").[199] To commune with, or even to look like, a Frank was to be "a supporter of a foreign nation and not a Byzantine patriot," solidifying the beard as a marker not only of orthodoxy, but also of national identity.[200] The issue of identity was crucial, notes Kolbaba, because in all these debates "it was not a simple matter of 'us' versus 'them' but a debate about the very definition of 'us.'"[201]

The Fourteenth and Fifteenth Centuries

The issue of clerical beards, which had been among the most prominent features of East-West polemical exchanges since the time of Photios, largely disappeared by

---

[197] Eng. trans.: Angel Nikolov, "Mediaeval Slavonic Anti-Catholic Texts from the Manuscript Collection of the Romanian Academy," in Irina Vainovski-Mihai, ed., *New Europe College Regional Program 2003–2004, 2004–2005* (Bucharest: New Europe College, 2007), 275–76. Nikolov notes that "the Greek copies published so far, as well as the first redaction of the Slavonic translation, do not include this motif." Ibid., 288 n. 86. He also notes that a version of this story also circulated in *A Story about How Rome Fell from the Orthodox Faith*, written by a Serb or Bulgarian some time later. In it, "A maiden ... sent a letter to the Pope; she wrote, 'Holy Pope, send me your golden hair, and your beard and moustaches, if you want to make love to me.' ... The Pope fulfilled the maiden's wish. The maiden saw the Pope's golden beard and moustaches and cried bitterly, cut her golden hair, and hit her head into the stones." Firmly resolved to expose the pope, she composes a letter, which is read aloud all around Rome: "Let it be known to you, rulers and Roman lords, this is how Rome fell. The Pope shaved off his beard and his moustaches for the sake of a woman's eyes." The pope is on the verge of suicide, but then Peter the Mutterer comes to him, consoles him, and writes his first false heretical book in which it says, "Let it be known to the East, and the West, and the South, and the North! Know, brothers, that this night Archangel Michael came and brought this letter from heaven, and told us to follow Saint Peter the Apostle's rule—everyone must shave their beard and moustache." Ibid., 277.
[198] Kolbaba, *The Byzantine Lists*, 204.
[199] George Metochites, *De Processione Spiritus Sancti* (PG 141:1405–17); Eng. trans.: Geanakoplos, *Byzantium*, 219.
[200] Ibid.
[201] Kolbaba, "Byzantine Perceptions of Latin Religious 'Errors,'" 126.

the middle of the fourteenth century, although there were some notable exceptions. Matthew Blastares, in an *Epistolary Discourse on the Procession of the Holy Spirit* addressed to Guy de Lusignan in 1341, appended a list of other Latin customs he found objectionable, and among them was still found the fact that Latin priests shaved their beard.[202] On the other side, the Greek unionist Manuel Kalekas (d. 1410), employing an argument used earlier in the *Tractatus* and in Bonacursius, defended the Latin custom by maintaining that despite the claim that shaving violated the form of God in man, beardlessness was more fitting since it prevented the Savior's blood from being contaminated by the priest's hair when he drank from the chalice at mass.[203]

Among the last notable attacks on Latin beardlessness was made by Symeon of Thessalonike (d. 1429), who in his *Dialogus contra Omnes Haereses* (also known as the *Dialogue in Christ*)[204] berated the Latins for their dramatic portrayals of religious events. When it was necessary to depict God in these plays, an act that was in itself blasphemous, the Latins compounded their error by having the man playing God put on a fake beard. According to Symeon, they did this because

> the Latins don't hold shaving them to be effeminate and contrary to natural law [and thus] they put on fake ones, hence showing they contrive things as they see fit. For if the prophets saw that God has a beard, iconically speaking, we too have beards in honor of nature and according to what God intended. So they act contrary to what God intended, shaving to the disgrace of nature, especially priests and monks, who defend this bodily vanity.[205]

It is unclear exactly why references to clerical shaving began to decline during this period. On one hand "Shaving in the West became almost universal by the late 1300s," so much so that "facial hair no longer distinguished different orders of men" (clergy and lay), as it had years earlier.[206] If almost everyone in the West was beardless, it should have made the difference between them and the bearded Greeks even more apparent. However, there is reason to suspect that the Greeks would not have met a lot of shaved Latins, since many Westerners traveling East let their beards grow, either because of "a pilgrimage vow or ... a calculated attempt to adopt the styles of Eastern

---

[202] "At the end of his epistolary discourse Blastares added a small section with additional concise arguments concerning the azymes and certain Latin customs (fasting, celibacy and shaving of the beard by Latin priests) which he had not incorporated in his [earlier] *Refutation of the Errors of the Latins*." Konstantinos Palaiologos, "An Annotated Edition of the *Refutation of the Errors of the Latins* by Matthaios Blastares" (PhD thesis, University of London, 2011), 110. See Matthew Blastares, *Epistolary Discourse*, in Archimandrite Arsenij, ed., *Pis'mo Matfeja Vlastarja, ieromonacha Solunskago i pisatelja XIV věka, k princu Kirpskomu, Gju de Luzin'janu s obličeniem Latinskago nepravolmyslija* (Moscow, 1891), 1–86.

[203] Manuel Kalekas, *Contra graecorum errores libri quatuor* (PG 152:213).

[204] Symeon of Thessalonica, *Dialogue in Christ against All Heresies* (PG 155:33–176).

[205] Symeon of Thessalonica, *Dialogue in Christ against All Heresies* (PG 155:112). Eng. trans.: Andrew Walker White, "The Artifice of Eternity: A Study of Liturgical and Theatrical Practices in Byzantium" (PhD thesis, University of Maryland, 2006), 249.

[206] Oldstone-Moore, *Of Beards and Men*, 101. Reynolds questioned the universality of beardlessness in the fourteenth century, arguing that the clergy's opposition to shaving, which he likened to their opposition to enforced celibacy, forced the church to repeat its prohibitions against *barbas prolixas* (long beards) at several local councils (Orleans [1323], Avignon [1337], London [1342], Paris [1333] Rouen [1370]) throughout the 1300s. He maintains that shaving in the West became universal the following century. Reynolds, *Beards: An Omnium Gatherum*, 123.

Mediterranean courts."²⁰⁷ For example, Francesco Balducci Pegolotti told merchants traveling to the East that "you must let your beard grow long and not shave" in order to better assimilate to local fashion.²⁰⁸ Pero Tafur, a Spanish knight who sported a beard while living in Constantinople, later went to visit Emperor John VIII during his 1438 stay in Ferrara. According to Tafur's account, when he arrived for the audience shaved and dressed in Western-style clothes, the emperor balked.²⁰⁹

> As he saw me, he said it pained him greatly that I had shaved off my beard, which he said was the greatest source of pride and the best thing that men have. I responded to him, "Lord, we believe the contrary, and only in the case of a very grave injury do we wear a beard." And so on this theme we conversed a goodly amount of time.²¹⁰

This seemingly widespread practice of Westerners growing beards while in the East may have decreased the immediate association of beardlessness and Latin-ness, but this is only speculation. Against this there is also evidence that while no longer considered by most a theological *point de division*, beards still remained a conspicuous marker of East-West cultural differences. The *Travels of Sir John Mandeville* (c. 1360) related that Greeks in Constantinople continued to criticize Latin grooming practices, believing it was a "deadly sin" to shave the beard, "For they say that the beard is a symbol of manhood and the gift from God. And they who shave their beards do it only to appear well to the world and to please their wives."²¹¹ Petrarch (d. 1374), in arguing against a Greek colleague, wrote that his arguments "were longer and more unkempt than his beard and hair (*barba et crinibus suis horridior maiorque*)."²¹²

Another potential cause for the growing silence about clerical shaving is the possibility that religious communities in the East may have actually adopted beards in order to better evangelize the Greeks.²¹³ Francis of Assisi was described as having a beard,²¹⁴

---

²⁰⁷ Shayne Legassie, *The Medieval Invention of Travel* (Chicago: University of Chicago Press, 2017), 218.
²⁰⁸ Francesco Balducci Pegolotti, "Notices of the Land Route to Cathay," in Henry Yule, ed., *Cathay and the Way Thither: Being a Collection of Medieval Notices of China*, vol. 2 (Cambridge: Cambridge University Press, 2009), 291.
²⁰⁹ See A. Vasiliev, "Pero Tafur: A Spanish Traveler of the Fifteenth Century and His Visit to Constantinople, Trebizond, and Italy," *Byzantion* 7 (1932): 75–122; Barry Taylor, "Late Medieval Travellers in the East: Clavijo, Tafur, Encina, and Tarifa," in Rosamund Allen, ed., *Eastward Bound: Travel and Travellers, 1050–1550* (Manchester: Manchester University Press, 2004), 221–34.
²¹⁰ Legassie, *The Medieval Invention of Travel*, 218. For Tafur's complete account see Pero Tafur, *Travels and Adventures (1435–1439)*, trans. Malcolm Letts (New York: George Routledge and Sons, 1926).
²¹¹ John Mandeville, *The Travels of Sir John Mandeville*, trans. C. W. R. D. Moseley (London: Penguin Books, 1983), 51.
²¹² Legassie, *The Medieval Invention of Travel*, 284. Petrarch's *Letter 3.6* in Francis Petrarch, *Res seniles*, vol. 1, ed. Silvia Rizzo with Monica Berté (Florence: Casa Editrice Le lettere, 2006), 232.
²¹³ See Girolamo Golubovich, "Cenni storici su Fra Giovanni Parastron," *Bessarione* 10 (1906): 295–304.
²¹⁴ Francis's first biographer, Thomas of Celano, described him as "medium height, closer to short, his head was of medium size and round. His face was somewhat long and drawn, his forehead small and smooth, with medium eyes black and clear. His hair was dark; his eyebrows were straight, and his nose even and thin; his ears small and upright, and his temples smooth.... His teeth were white, well set and even; his lips are small and thin; his beard was black and sparse; his neck was slender, his shoulders straight; his arms were short, his hands slight, his fingers long and his nails tapered. He had thin legs, small feet, fine skin and little flesh." Thomas of Celano, *Life of Saint Francis*, in Regis J. Armstrong, J. A. Wayne Hellmann, and William J. Short, eds., *Francis Trilogy: Life of Saint Francis, The Remembrance of the Desire of a Soul, The Treatise on the Miracles of Saint Francis* (Hyde Park, NY: New City Press, 2004), 93.

and it is possible that his followers in the East did the same.[215] This becomes even more likely if they adhered to the practice, often followed by missionaries, of changing their appearance in order to blend in with the local inhabitants. Dominic himself had grown a beard in preparation for ministering to the Muslims,[216] and there are reports from circa 1230 of Dominicans setting out for missionary work in Hungary with their "hair and beards [already] grown out in the manner of the barbarians."[217] Thus it is not unreasonable to assume that religious communities in Constantinople, explicitly charged with helping the Greeks come to terms with the Roman church, deliberately grew their beards in order to make themselves more acceptable to the Orthodox.

A third option, and it to my mind remains the most likely, is that as debates about more substantive matters (Filioque, primacy, azymes) became more heated, joined in the thirteenth century by the dispute over Purgatory, the subject of clerical beards was increasingly recognized as the nonissue it really was. By the time negotiations began for another reunion, clerical beards, like most of the other "errors" on the Byzantine lists, were simply no longer regarded as essential.[218] The council, which eventually began meeting in Ferrara in 1438, discussed only the issues that both sides believed to be genuinely church-dividing—the interpolation of the Filioque, the theology of the procession, the papacy, azymes, and Purgatory.[219] Just as the moderates like Peter III of Antioch and Theophylact of Ohrid had urged centuries earlier, the presence or absence of facial hair was considered a difference in custom that need not divide, and thus need not be contested. Ferrara-Florence would debate many things, but it would not debate the beard.

Epilogue

Although beards would not be discussed at Ferrara-Florence, it remained a distinctive marker of cultural/religious identity, so much so that in the subsequent Eastern

---

[215] "Paulus Walther, for instance, tells the story of a Greek on the island of Rhodes who allegedly grabbed a Franciscan friar by the beard and started taunting him about the *filioque* (Paulus Walther, *Itinerarium*, 87)." See Nickiphoros Tsougarakis, "Perceptions of the Greek Clergy and Rite in Late Medieval Pilgrimage Accounts to the Holy Land," in Nikolaos G. Chrissis, Athina Kolia-Dermitzaki, and Angeliki Papageorgiou, eds., *Byzantium and the West: Perception and Reality (11th–15th C.)* (London: Routledge, 2019), 236.

[216] "Peter [of Ferrand] takes the time to tell us, Dominic himself had desire to go to the *terra Saracenorum* to preach, and was even preparing for departure by growing a beard 'for a certain time'—*aliquanto tempore* ... [but] Dominic abandoned that venture entirely, Peter describing him almost immediately afterwards as wending his way to Bologna—his scratchy new beard apparently shaved off." Thomas Burman and Lydia Walker, "Spain, Islam, and Thirteenth-Century Dominican Memory," in Mark T. Abate, ed., *Convivencia and Medieval Spain: Essays in Honor of Thomas F. Glick* (Cham, Switzerland: Palgrave Macmillan, 2019), 320.

[217] Mary Dienes, "Eastern Missions of the Hungarian Dominicans in the First Half of the Thirteenth Century," in James Ryan, ed., *The Spiritual Expansion of Medieval Latin Christendom: The Asian Missions* (London: Routledge, 2016), 71.

[218] In addition to the works already cited see Marcel Viller, "La question de l'union des Eglises entre Grecs et Latins depuis le Concile de Lyon jusqu'à celui de Florence (1274--1438)," *Revue d' histoire ecclésiastique* 17 and 18 (1921 and 1922): 260–305, 20–60; J. Loenertz, "Les dominicains byzantins Théodore et André Chrysobergès et les négociations pour l'union des Eglises grecque et latine de 1415–1430," *Archivum Fratrum Praedicatorum* 9 (1939): 5–61.

[219] These were the issues first laid out in the *Tractatus contra Graecos* two centuries earlier. Although it was not on the council's agenda, Pero Tafur took time to note that the emperor's retinue at Ferrara contained "a great company of people, all of whom went about in long robes and with great beards, showing themselves to be grave and serious persons." Pero Tafur, *Travels and Adventures (1435–1439)*, 176.

debates about the council's reception Mark of Ephesus could write, "Whoever commemorates the pope as an orthodox hierarch takes upon himself the whole of Latinism, even to the shaving of the beard."[220] The unionist Plousiadenos chided Mark and his compatriots for their stubbornness, since they refused to obey the pope "not because he is a sinner, but because he is a Latin, and because of the shaving of the beard."[221] At the papal conclave of 1455, when Bessarion of Nicaea (an advocate for union at Florence and later a cardinal of the Roman church) was suggested as a candidate, his Greek beard got in the way, for "a bearded cardinal was bad enough, a bearded pontiff still unthinkable."[222] According to reports, Cardinal Alain of Avignon stood up and asked those assembled, "Shall we elect for a Pope, for head of the Latin Church, a Greek, a mere interloper? Bessarion still wears his beard and forsooth, he is to be our Lord?!? (*Nondum barbam rasit Bessarion et nostrum caput erit*?)."[223]

Attitudes toward beards changed radically in the West during the sixteenth century, beginning with the pontificate of Julius II (1503–13), who grew his now-famous beard in mourning for the loss of Bologna. A few years later, the Fifth Lateran (1512–17) commanded that those "clerics holding benefices and those in holy orders are not to pay special attention to their hair and beards" (*nec comam neque barbam non nutrient*), which seemingly would have permitted the short beards then in fashion.[224] Clement VII (1523–34), the unfortunate Medici pope, followed Julius's example and grew a beard of mourning as a response to the 1527 sack of Rome by imperial troops. The big difference: while Julius only wore his beard for a short time and shaved it off before his death, Clement kept his.[225] It was he who in 1531 gave permission for all priests to grow beards,[226] a policy defended by Pierio Valeriano (d. 1558), whose work *Pro sacerdotum barbis apologia* (*An Apology in Favor of Priestly Beards*) provided justification for the new practice.[227]

---

[220] Mark of Ephesus, *Letter to Theophanes of Euboea*; Ludovico Petit, ed., *Marci Eugenici, metropolitae Ephesi, opera antiunionistica*, CF 10.2 (Rome: Pontifical Oriental Institute, 1977), 173–74.

[221] He continued in this vein: "You shun him ... because he is a Latin, and you hold him as heterodox; for you consider the Latins as aliens to the faith; and you teach the more simple to flee from them as from the face of a serpent." John Plousiadnenos, *Expositio pro sancta et oecumenica synodo florentina quod legitime congregata est, et defensio quinque capitum quae in decreto ejus continentur* (PG 159:1357). Eng. trans.: Charles Yost, "Neither Greek nor Latin, but Catholic: Aspects of the Theology of Union of John Plousiadenos," *Journal of Orthodox Christian Studies* 1 (2018): 54–55.

[222] Reynolds, *Beards: An Omnium Gatherum*, 182.

[223] Quoted in Mark Zucker, "Raphael and the Beard of Pope Julius II," *Art Bulletin* 59 (1977): 524–33. Another story tells how King Louis XI of France grabbed Bessarion's beard during an embassy in 1471, upsetting the cardinal so much that "his death a year later must be attributed to it." Reynolds, *Beards: An Omnium Gatherum*, 182.

[224] Norman Tanner, *Decrees of the Ecumenical Councils 1* (Washington, DC: Georgetown University Press, 1990), 619. "The prohibition against nourishing the beard ... clearly cannot be taken to mean that he must shave ... and has been interpreted as not inconsistent with a short beard." Reynolds, *Beards: An Omnium Gatherum*, 185.

[225] Although Raphael's portraits of Julius give the impression that he was bearded throughout his pontificate, the reality is that he wore the beard for a short period and shaved it off almost a year before his death. Clement's beard was only the first of many, and for next 170 years all the Bishops of Rome—from Paul III to Innocent XII—were bearded. See Zucker, "Raphael and the Beard of Pope Julius II," 524.

[226] Ibid., 532.

[227] Pierio Valeriano, *A treatise vvriten by Iohan Valerian a greatte clerke of Italie, which is intitled in latin Pro sacerdotum barbis translated in to Englysshe* (1533). A similar work is Johannes Barbatus's *Barbae Maiestas hoc est, De Barbis Elegans, Brevis Et Accvrata Descriptio* (1614).

Valeriano's work essentially upended the centuries-old Latin defense of beardlessness by appealing to the very arguments that the Greeks had long employed. Importantly, he proved that the manuscripts of Barcelona and the *Statuta ecclesiae antiqua* had been altered in order to condemn, rather than promote, the beard, thus removing the canonical barriers. Beards, he argued, were natural and healthy, "expelling bad humours from the body, preventing tooth decay and other ailments (*dentes diutius a putredine conservat*), and protecting the skin from extremes of hot and cold."[228] The patriarchs of the Old Testament, Christ, and the apostles were all bearded men, setting an example of manliness and moral strength.[229] Gone was the theology of the "inner beard," replaced by the argument that shaving manifested "excessive refinement ... easy living, and effeminate ways."[230] Bearded priests, he argued, would avoid

> the suspicions of effeminacy and calumny and finally appear as men rather than woman. For why should we be ashamed of our beards if it has been revealed to us what exactly the beard is and how it adorns the dignified and honorable man and how much it contributes to the status and reputation of the priest.[231]

Valeriano's conclusions were largely echoed by the Gentian Hervert (d. 1584), whose 1536 lectures on beards argued that neither beards nor the lack of them manifested any special virtues, especially as it pertained to the clergy.[232] He maintained that we should not condemn nor condone those who shave or grow their beards, exercising the same moderation and tolerance in such matters as the ancients. Some, like Charles Borromeo in Milan, resisted the new practice and remained firmly committed to the "ancient usage" of "shav[ing] the beard ... a custom replete with mystical meanings, for the purpose of making us realize both the excellence of our state ... and the unique way of life ... which our vocation requires."[233] Yet Borromeo was clearly swimming against the tide. By 1536 the Constitution of the Order of Friars Minor (the Capuchins), a Franciscan reform movement, required that "the beard be worn because it is something manly and natural, rough, worthless and austere," following "after the example of Christ most holy and all our early saints."[234]

---

[228] Oldstone-Moore, *Of Beards and Men*, 111. "What filthiness is in a beard? For truly I can find in it nothing filthy nor dishonest." Reynolds, *Beards: An Omnium Gatherum*, 199.

[229] "Certain men, who describe the face of Christ from knowledge [gained] from their forefathers, affirm that he had a long and yellow beard." St. James, he goes on, was much praised "because he never used shaving nor anointing." Reynolds, *Beards: An Omnium Gatherum*, 199–200.

[230] Ibid.

[231] Oldstone-Moore, *Of Beards and Men*, 112.

[232] "Nature takes both sides of the argument, by both spontaneously producing the beard and being willing to allow it to be shaved." Gentian Hervert, *Orationes* (Veneunt Aureliae apud Franciscum Gueiardum Bibliopolam, 1536). Eng. trans.: Oldstone-Moore, *Of Beards and Men*, 113.

[233] Charles Borromeo, *Selected Orations, Homilies, and Writings*, 96. Borromeo was not alone. In 1550 in France The Bishop of Avranches, Robert Cenalis, threatened fines against any clergyman who "failed to present themselves freshly shaved at a council." Reynolds, *Beards: An Omnium Gatherum*, 195. Robert Bellarmine spoke negatively about beards, ironic since "he chose to damn ... a fashion in which he himself, the whole College of Cardinals, and the popes of his time conformed." Ibid., 211.

[234] Paul Hanbridge, ed. and trans., *The Capuchin Constitutions of 1536* (Rome: Collegio San Lorenzo da Brindisi, 2009), 10.

During the Reformation many Protestant clergymen came to see the beard not only as a sign of "patriarchal masculinity" but also of the "priesthood of all believers" that (unlike the papists) did not distinguish between the clerical "caste" and the laity.[235] A century earlier the bearded proto-reformer John Wycliffe (d. 1384) had described how the priests of the anti-Christ can be known by their "shaved crowns and beards," a mocking reference to the Roman practice.[236] According to Diarmaid MacCulloch, beards also helped Protestant preachers "look like everyone's picture of an Old Testament prophet," thus giving them a certain gravitas in the pulpit.[237] This explains why by the 1540s "most reformers were bearded ... led by the majestically bushy Heinrich Bullinger in Zurich" and (later) Archbishop Thomas Cranmer in England.[238] According to the reformer Johan Eberlin von Günzburg (1533), in the coming Christian utopia "All men are to wear long beards. Men with smooth faces like women should be held an outrage."[239]

Things changed by the end of the seventeenth century as beardlessness once again became the fashion in the West. According to Oldstone-Moore, despite impassioned defenses of the beard by figures such as John Bulwer and Johann Pagenstecher, by the eighteenth century "Facial hair was nowhere to be found outside enclaves that deliberately cut themselves off from the mainstream."[240] The French court had abandoned the beard under Louis XIV (d. 1715), giving Europe a new model of masculinity defined more by "refinement and education" than by hairiness.[241] Popes, who had been bearded since the time of Clement VII, now shaved, the last bearded pope being Innocent XII, who died in 1700.

Among the Orthodox, beards for both clergy and laity remained the norm, although Russian hierarchs did occasionally have to fight the nobility's temptations to Westernize. In 1460 the archbishop of Rostov told those who shaved that they were "abandoning the image of God," and the Stoglav Council of 1551 forbade shaving since it was "not an Orthodox, but a Catholic tradition."[242] Ivan the Terrible (d. 1584) allegedly claimed that "shaving the beard is a sin the blood of all martyrs will not wash away."[243] In 1690 Patriarch Adrian of Moscow decried those who adopted the customs

---

[235] Diarmaid MacCulloch, *The Reformation: A History* (New York: Viking, 2004), 627. MacCulloch contends that among the reasons Protestant clergy grew beards was to emphasize "that their male sexuality was no different from that of layman ... [and to] symbolize their newly recovered maleness." Ibid.

[236] Reynolds, *Beards: An Omnium Gatherum*, 183. Hugh Latimer, in a sermon preached before Edward VI, said the goal of the papists was "to make the yeomanry slavery, and the clergy shavery." Hugh Latimer, *Sermons by Hugh Latimer, Sometime Bishop of Worcester* (London: J.M. Dent, 1906), 85.

[237] MacCulloch, *The Reformation*, 627.

[238] According to one story, "when John Hopper Worchester's first aggressively Protestant Bishop ... arrived in the diocese in 1552, complete with wife and daughter, one of the few things which a disgusted local chronicler was prepared to note about his repulsive innovations was that he had 'a long beard' presumably previously unknown among the senior clergy." Ibid., 673-74.

[239] Oldstone-Moore, *Of Beards and Men*, 114.

[240] Ibid., 137.

[241] Ibid., 131.

[242] Quoted in Lindsey Hughes, "A Beard Is a Necessary Burden: Peter I's Laws on Shaving and Their Roots in Early Russia," in Roger Bartlett and Lindsey Hughes, eds., *Russian Society and Culture and the Long Eighteenth Century* (Münster: Verlag, 2004), 28. The Stoglav Council further goes on to say that "Apostolic rule states that if a man shaves his beard and dies thus, he is not to be commemorated by a burial service, or on the 40th day, but is to be deemed ... a heretic." Ibid.

[243] Quoted in Reynolds, *Beards: An Omnium Gatherum*, 258. Reynolds traces this position to the belief that men "would not be recognized at the gates of Heaven if they did not wear beards." Ibid.

of the Westerners and, "by shaving, made themselves look like apes and monkeys."[244] However, the days of the Russian beard (and, for that matter, the patriarchate) were numbered.

In 1698 Peter the Great, freshly returned from his embassy to the courts of Europe, decided to bring the fashions and mores of France to the Russian court. Among his first targets were the long beards of the Boyars, which he had forcibly shaved while his jester mocked those who would not comply.[245] In 1705 he instituted a beard tax, charging thirty to one hundred rubles (depending on the wearer's rank) for each beard, and issuing a "beard token" (Бородовой знак) to all those who paid.[246] For Orthodox Russians, many of whom "feared that they would not be allowed to enter heaven without their beards," Peter's actions were intolerable.[247] Trying to win over the people with theological arguments, Peter recruited the bishop of Rostov, who admitted that beards were an ancient custom, but that they were unnecessary. Besides, the laws requiring beards "were founded on the Old Testament and not on the New," meaning that these laws had been superseded by the coming of Christ.[248] Many surrendered to the new fashion, but the Old Believers did not, which is why Peter forced them to wear beards, "clearly identifying them as discredited nonconformists" and isolating them from the rest of Russian society.[249]

In the rest of the Orthodox world, although the old polemics against the beardlessness of the Latins had largely ceased, the issue could still occasionally reappear. Maxim the Greek (d. 1556) wrote, "If those who evade God's commandments are termed accursed, as we hear in the sacred hymns, then those who shave their beards aught be under the same oath."[250] In his nineteenth-century commentary on the Ninety-Sixth Canon of the Council in Trullo, Nicodemus the Hagorite (d. 1809) claimed that the excommunication imposed upon "those who adorn and

---

[244] Quoted in Hughes, "A Beard Is a Necessary Burden," 26.

[245] "The ideological justification of the introduction of beard shaving and 'European' clothing in Peter the Great's Russia was based upon the opposition between the traditional Russian appearance associated with the appearance of 'pagan peoples' and the appearance of European subjects viewed as a Christian one." Evgeny Akeliev, "On the History of Beard Shaving and the Introduction of 'German' Clothing in Peter the Great's Russia," *Quaestio Rossica* 1 (2013): 90.

[246] "Henceforth, in accordance with this, His Majesty's decree, all court attendants ... provincial service men, government officials of all ranks, [and] military men ... must shave their beards and moustaches. But, if it happens that some of them do not wish to shave their beards and moustaches, let a yearly tax be collected from such persons: from court attendants ... provincial service men, military men, and government officials of all ranks—60 rubles per person; from the gosti and members of the wholesale merchants' guild of the first class—100 rubles per person.... As for the peasants, let a toll of two half-copecks per beard be collected at the town gates each time they enter or leave a town; and do not let the peasants pass the town gates, into or out of town, without paying this toll." George Vernadsky, ed., *A Source Book for Russian History from Early Times to 1917*, vol. 2 (New Haven, CT: Yale University Press, 1972), 347. Priests were taxed at the same rate as peasants.

[247] "The Russians regarded this as an enormous sin on the part of the czar and as a thing which tended to the abolition of their religion. These insinuations, which came from the priests, occasioned the publication of many pamphlets in Moscow where for that reason alone the czar was regarded as a tyrant and a pagan; and there were many old Russians who, after having their beards shaved off, saved them preciously, in order to have them placed in their coffins, fearing that they would not be allowed to enter heaven without them." Jean Rousset de Missy quoted in James Harvey Robinson, ed., *Readings in European History*, vol. 2 (Boston: Athenaeum Press, 1906), 310–11.

[248] Oldstone-Moore, *Of Beards and Men*, 142.

[249] Ibid., 144.

[250] Maxim the Greek, *Epistle 137*. Eng. trans.: http://en.rpsc.ru/publications/beard/.

arrange their hair" still applied to the Latins, "who shaved off their mustache and their beard and who look like very young men and handsome bridegrooms and have the face of women."[251]

In the United States the beard became the subject of an interesting intra-Orthodox debate on inculturation when Bishop Tikhon (later patriarch of Moscow), distinguishing between what was "essential" and "accidental" to the Orthodox faith, urged his priests to adopt more "American" styles in clothing and hair.[252] Many priests complied, and for much of the twentieth century it was not uncommon for both Greek and Russian priests in the United States to be beardless.[253] Sometimes there was resistance from the pews. Rev. Joseph Stephanko of Passaic, New Jersey, was accused by the *Little Russian National Union of America*, a local Russian paper, of "making void the Orthodox faith because he shaved himself."[254] As late as 1979 Fr. Seraphim Rose bemoaned the fact that "just a few decades ago almost no Orthodox clergy in America had beards or wore *rassas* on the street," although he noted things were changing.[255] He was right, for by the beginning of the twenty-first century many bishops in the United States were mandating that their clergy be bearded. The clean-shaven Orthodox priest was once again an endangered species.

Among Catholics, beards remained a rarity among the clergy for most of the twentieth century. They were so rare, in fact, that G. K. Chesterton felt the need to explain to non-Catholics that Rome was not tolerating "heresy" by allowing Eastern-rite priests to keep them.[256] The widespread practice of shaving among Latin Catholic clergy is largely attributable to the 1917 Code of Canon Law (136.1), which required

---

[251] Nicodemus the Hagorite, *The Rudder or Pedalion*, 403–5.

[252] In a widely reported story, Fr. Basil Kerbawy, dean of St. Nicholas Syrian Orthodox Cathedral in Brooklyn, in 1911 wrote to the mayor of New York, William Gaynor, about being harassed on account of appearance, asking whether "it is a crime to wear a beard." He complained that his "profession calls for the wearing of a beard," but when he goes out into the street, "The boys and young men mistake me for a Jewish rabbi and insult and assault me." The mayor, himself a bearded man, offered Fr. Basil a detective for his safety. For the incident see Matthew Namee, "To Shave or Not to Shave?," December 11, 2009, http://orthodoxhistory.org/2009/12/11/to-shave-or-not-to-shave/.

[253] Athanasia Papademetriou related a story about her father-in-law, a Greek priest invited to come to America in 1939. "When he arrived his first visit was to the Archdiocese office in New York to receive the blessing of Archbishop Athenagoras (later Ecumenical Patriarch of Constantinople). My father-in-law entered the office of Archbishop Athenagoras dressed in his traditional black cassock, long beard, and tall black hat. Archbishop Athenagoras welcomed him and asked him to sit down. Then the Archbishop gave his instructions regarding the dress code for Greek Orthodox clergy in the United States. He explained that Greek Orthodox priests in America should be clean shaven and wear the black suit and white collar. Archbishop Athenagoras then gave my father-in-law $100 to get a haircut and to buy a new suit." Athanasia Papademetriou, *Presbytera: The Life, Mission, and Service of the Priest's Wife* (Boston: Somerset Hall Press, 2004), 123.

[254] "Pastor Sues for Libel: Jersey Paper Criticized Russian Priest for Shaving," *New York Times*, August 20, 1914. Rev. Stephanko subsequently filed a $25,000 suit against the paper and was awarded $1,000.

[255] Seraphim Rose, "Orthodoxy in America: Its Historical Past and Present," St. Xenia Orthodox Church, http://www.stxenia.org/files/history/ortham.html.

[256] An author unfamiliar with/hostile to Catholicism had written that "Rome tolerates, in her relation with the Russian Uniats, ... strange heresies and even bearded and wedded clergy," as if the two were equal. Chesterton replied: "What is the good of his laboriously beginning to explain that a married clergy is a matter of discipline and not doctrine, that it can therefore be allowed locally without heresy, when all the time the man thinks a beard as important as a wife and more important than a false religion? What is the sense of explaining to him the peculiar historical circumstances that have led to preserving some local habits in Kiev or Warsaw, when the man at any moment may receive a mortal shock by seeing a bearded

priests to "cultivate simplicity in the wearing of hair" (*et capillorum simplicem cultum adhibeant*).[257] Although the canon did not specifically mention facial hair, many bishops chose to interpret it that way and thus enforced the prohibition against beards.[258] Matters changed following the Second Vatican Council and the promulgation of the 1983 code, which said nothing about either hair or beards.[259] Today in the Roman Catholic Church it is a matter of some indifference whether a priest has facial hair, although certain religious orders are still distinguished by their beards.

After centuries of dispute about the merits of shaving, it is interesting to note that East and West are perhaps closer than ever on the issue, insomuch as both are, relatively speaking, pro-beard. In the East, growing secularization in the former Soviet bloc led for calls to return to traditional values, which included (for men at least) the growing of the beard. A 2009 book by Roman Atorin, spokesman for the Old Believers in Russia, denounced shaving as a sin, arguing that "the appearance of a human being needs to match the makeup of his soul," which cannot be done if the man commits the sin of beard-shaving.[260] Less than a decade later, Metropolitan Kornily, primate of the Old Believers, was even more explicit. He said that men with beards were less likely to be "corrupted" by same-sex relationships, and for this reason Russian men should stop shaving to "protect themselves from homosexuality."[261] In the West, especially among Evangelical Christians, the desire for "Bearded Gospel Men"—that is, men who embrace both their faith and their masculinity—has spawned a movement of sorts.[262] Whether this movement has a religious basis or, as Oldstone-Moore argues, a social one, remains open for debate.[263] Yet, by and large, it would appear that today

---

Franciscan walking through Wimbledon or Walham Green? What we want to get at is the mind of the man who can think so absurdly about us as to suppose we could have a horror of heresy, and then a weakness for heresy, and then a greater horror of hair." G. K. Chesterton, "What Do They Think?," in *Collected Works*, vol. 3 (San Francisco: Ignatius Press, 1990), 191, 193.

[257] *Codex Iuris Canonici* (1917) 136 §1. Eng. trans.: Edward Peters, ed. and trans., *The 1917 or Pio-Benedictine Code of Canon Law in English Translation* (San Francisco: Ignatius Press, 2001), 69.

[258] For this interpretation see Charles Seghers, "The Practice of Shaving in the Latin Church," 278–309.

[259] *Codex Iuris Canonici* (1983) Canon 284, which replaced Canon 136 §1 in the old code, simply says that "clerics are to wear suitable ecclesiastical garb according to the norms issued by the conference of bishops and according to legitimate local customs."

[260] R. Atorin, *Problema bradobritiia v pravoslavnoi traditsii* (Moscow: Arkheodoksiia, 2009). Eng. trans.: Oldstone-Moore, *Of Beards and Men*, 141–42. "Beard shaving," Atorin wrote, is contrary to the will of God, for it "tries to remake [man's] appearance according to his own subjective discretion, which does not agree with God's order." Ibid.

[261] According to the article in the *Moscow Times*, Kornily said that "God set down certain rules. The Lord created everyone with a beard. No man can resist his creator." He then lamented that this concept had "completely disappeared from the Catholic West, and yet it's [true] beyond any doubt. After all, in our icons it is impossible for us to imagine Christ or any other saint without a beard. Mankind should not resist his own Creator. This is where sodomy comes from: the always changing men's fashions and hairstyles." "Russian Priest Tells Men Not to Shave to 'Protect from Homosexuality,'" *Moscow Times*, June 19, 2017.

[262] See Jared Brock and Aaron Alford, *Bearded Gospel Men: The Epic Quest for Manliness and Godliness* (Nashville, TN: W Publishing Group, 2017). In their manifesto, the authors good-naturedly poke fun at Christians whose institutions have "created policies that expressly forbid the cultivation of facial manliness ... despite a clear biblical and historical bias toward beardlessness." These include "Bob Jones University, Moody Bible Institute, Pensacola Christian College, and even the Salvation Army—despite General Booth's titanic topical topiary. In fact, Liberty University's 2009 dress code insisted that 'facial hair should be neatly trimmed.' So much for liberty." Ibid., xv.

[263] "The newly sprouted beards of American evangelicals are a social rather than a religious statement. Neither (Rick) Warren nor the Robertsons (of Duck Dynasty fame) have promoted facial hair for

beards are no longer a mark of ecclesial identity, with the arguments once separating East and West on this issue largely relegated to the ash heap of history. Unfortunately, resolving the other issues that have kept them in schism for over a millennium has not been as easy.

---

specifically biblical or theological reasons. They could hardly do so when, for the vast majority of conservative Christians, short hair and a shaven face remain the conventional signs of moral and religious rectitude.... Beards, especially large ones, retain their daring and nonconformist quality, and this is an important part of their appeal to conservative as well as liberal men. A generation ago, conservative evangelicals began appropriating rock music into their worship. Now, finally, it is time for hair." Christopher Oldstone-Moore, "The Right-Wing Beard Revolution: Look Out, Hipsters, Here Come the Counterculture Christians," *Salon*, December 25, 2015, https://www.salon.com/2015/12/25/the_right_wing_beard_revolution_look_out_hipsters_here_come_the_counterculture_christians/.

PART II
AZYMES

3
Bread and Leaven in the Biblical and Patristic Tradition

The debate concerning the type of bread to be used at the Eucharist, that is, whether it should be leavened or unleavened, finds its basis in three distinct historical/theological questions concerning the sacrament as found in Scripture and tradition. The first involves the meaning of "leaven" (ζύμη) and whether it should be understood as a good or bad thing. As Augustine himself noted, Scripture itself sends mixed messages on the subject, for "The Lord talked of yeast in a negative sense when he said, 'Beware of the yeast of the Pharisees' (Mt 16:6), and in a positive sense when he said, 'The kingdom of heaven is like a woman who hid some yeast in three measures of flour, until it was all leavened' (Lk 13:21)."[1] This is why, he warned, "We should not think it is *de rigueur* for us to assume that a thing always has to signify what it happens to signify in one passage by its resemblance to something else."[2] Unfortunately, both East and West forgot Augustine's admonition and chose one interpretation to the exclusion of the other, supporting their respective positions on leaven's meaning with carefully selected biblical and patristic texts.

The second, and perhaps most contentious issue, was the debate surrounding the date of the Last Supper, and whether the meal Jesus shared with the apostles before his death was a Passover meal, as the Synoptics seem to suggest. Much was made of this issue in later polemics—the West arguing that since Jesus would have celebrated Passover with unleavened bread, the Latin church was merely imitating the actions of its Savior, while the Greek tradition (holding to the Johannine dating) held that since it was not a Passover meal, the "new covenant" was made with ἄρτος (bread), not ἄζυμος (unleavened bread).[3] This is proved, the Byzantines claimed, by the fact that ἄρτος, that is, regular bread, was the word used throughout all the descriptions of the Last Supper. Even today there remains lively debate on the issue among biblical scholars, although modern exegesis has largely moved past the old dialectic and opened up new possibilities for understanding the chronological difficulties posed by the gospel accounts.

The third issue, related to the second, was the practice of the undivided church and what type of bread Christians used when "they came together and devoted themselves to the apostles' teaching and fellowship, to the breaking of bread and the prayers" (Acts 2:42). This was a central part of the Byzantines' argument, for if it was the practice of

---

[1] Augustine of Hippo, *Teaching Christianity* 25; Augustine, *Teaching Christianity*, trans. Edmund Hill (Hyde Park, NY: New City Press, 1992), 184.
[2] Ibid.
[3] According to John Erickson, the historical argument was never the East's chief weapon, since ultimately "the Byzantines were less interested in the fact that Christ *instituted* the Eucharist than in the fact that Christ *was* the Eucharist." Erickson, "Leavened and Unleavened," 149.

the universal church to celebrate the Eucharist with leavened bread, then the Latins had departed from the tradition and introduced something new by celebrating with azymes. Historically speaking, on this score the Greeks were probably correct, for the use of azymes seems to have been a relative novelty, most likely introduced in the West at some point in the ninth or tenth century. Yet contrary to the Byzantine belief, the change in Latin practice did not occur in support of any heresy, and still less did it indicate that the Western church had embraced some Judaizing tendency. There was a change, but it was for reasons completely unrelated to any criticisms the Byzantines had to offer.

Leaven in Scriptures

Outside of its descriptions of the Last Supper the New Testament speaks a great deal about bread—for example, "our daily bread" in Matthew 6:11 and Luke 11:13 (τὸν ἄρτον ἡμῶν τὸν ἐπιούσιον), "bread from heaven" in John 6:32 (ἄρτον ἐκ τοῦ οὐρανοῦ), "the bread of life" in John 3:35 (ὁ ἄρτος τῆς ζωῆς), and "living bread" in John 6:51 (ὁ ἄρτος ὁ ζῶν). In Greek "bread" (in Hebrew, *lechem*) is usually described as ἄρτος, which means "cake" or "loaf [of bread]," as distinguished from ἄζυμος, or ἄρτος ἄζυμος ("unleavened bread"), which is the standard Septuagint translation for the Hebrew *maṣṣôt*, *matstsah*, or *matzoh*.[4] It was this latter type of bread, made without *chametz*, or leaven, that was prescribed in Exodus and Deuteronomy for both the Feast of Passover (*Pesah* or *Pesach*)[5] and the seven-day Festival of Unleavened Bread (*Hag Hamatzot*),[6] two celebrations that, for various reasons, were later merged. Deuteronomy 16:3 famously called unleavened bread "the bread of affliction" (*lechem oni*),[7] while the Passover Haggadah says that matzo is eaten during the meal "because the dough of our fathers had not the time to leaven when the King of all kings revealed himself to them and redeemed them."[8] Others have described unleavened bread not only as the "bread of haste"[9] but also as the "bread of redemption" used "to

---

[4] Gerhard Kittel and Gerhard Friedrich, eds., *Theological Dictionary of the New Testament*, trans. and abridged by Geoffrey W. Bromiley (Grand Rapids, MI: Eerdmans, 1985), 73 and 265–66. See also James Strong, *The New Strong's Expanded Exhaustive Concordance of the Bible* (Hendrickson, 1996). The Strong's Reference numbers are H3899/G740 for "bread" and H4682/G106 for "unleavened."

[5] "They shall eat the lamb that same night; they shall eat it roasted over the fire with unleavened bread and bitter herbs" (Ex 12:8).

[6] "You shall observe the festival of unleavened bread, for on this very day I brought your companies out of the land of Egypt: you shall observe this day throughout your generations as a perpetual ordinance. In the first month, from the evening of the fourteenth day until the evening of the twenty-first day, you shall eat unleavened bread" (Ex 12:17–18).

[7] Josephus claimed that this idea went back to the immediate post-Exodus period when the Israelites ate unleavened bread "for thirty days" after leaving Egypt. During this period "they dispensed it to each person, to use so much only as would serve for necessity, but not for satiety. Whence it is that, in memory of the want we were then in, we keep a feast for eight days, which is called the feast of unleavened bread." Flavius Josephus, *The Antiquities of the Jews*, 2.316–17; Eng. trans.: Josephus, *The New Complete Works of Josephus*, trans. William Whiston (Grand Rapids, MI: Kregel Publications, 1999), 107.

[8] Quoted in Joachim Jeremias, *The Eucharistic Words of Jesus*, trans. Norman Perrin (London: SCM Press, 1966), 56.

[9] See Philo of Alexandria, *On the Special Laws* 2.158; Philo, *Works Volume VII*, 628–29. This is only one of several interpretations Philo gave, the others being "that the unleavened bread is 'unfinished' and thus reflects nature before harvest-time ... second, unleavened bread is a gift of nature while leavened bread is

celebrate redemption from Egypt, the victory of the true God over the false gods of the Egyptians, and the nation forming event of the Exodus."[10]

Yet for Joachim Jeremias the most important interpretation of unleavened bread was the eschatological, which linked unleavened loaves to the coming of the messianic age. Already by the first century Rabbi Eliezer ben Hyrcanus spoke of the bread eaten by the Israelites in the desert as a foretaste of what was to come, for when "God miraculously fed Israel during their journey through the desert" he demonstrated the "type of the abundance of bread in the Messianic time."[11] This connection of unleavened bread to the messianic age makes it easy to understand why for early Christians "Leaven and its removal at Passover were symbols of the corruption of the last days.... its purging symbolic of the longed-for eschatological redemption ... [and] final deliverance from this corruption through Jesus, the Passover lamb."[12]

This view of unleavened bread's eschatological significance perhaps helps to clarify 1 Corinthians 5:7–8, where Paul advised his readers to "clean out the old yeast so that you may be a new batch, as you really are unleavened. For our paschal lamb, Christ, has been sacrificed. Therefore, let us celebrate the festival, not with the old yeast, the yeast of malice and evil, but with the unleavened bread of sincerity and truth."[13] Referencing what is thought to be an early Christian Passover Haggadah,[14] Paul explained to the Corinthians that just as one cleans the house of leaven prior to the Feast of Passover (Ex 12:15, 13:7), they must remove the evil and wickedness of the old world and become "new [unleavened] dough"—the very symbol of "the purity and truth that characterizes the new world."[15] He told them that they were "already cleansed of the old leaven of their former selves ... [because] they have entered into a new Exodus through the death of a new Paschal lamb."[16]

Understanding the meaning of "leaven" (ζύμη) or the act of "leavening" (ζυμόω) in the New Testament is made more difficult for modern-day English speakers by the fact that many translations (including the NRSV) render ζύμη as "yeast."[17] Unlike modern store-bought yeast, the leaven used by people of Jesus's time was "a little of the raw dough containing yeast cultures" that was kept aside, during which time "it would begin to ferment," so that when it was added to the new mix "it would infect the new dough and cause it to rise."[18] When it worked, "Only a small amount of leaven was

---

an artificial product ... intended to exhort men to the life of primitive times without artificial demands or needs ... third, that unleavened loaves are the bread of affliction [that] should remind man that a great task can only be accomplished by labour and self-denial ... fourth, the unleavened loaves are a warning to turn away from arrogance." Jeremias, *The Eucharistic Words of Jesus*, 57–58.

[10] Paul Gardner, *1 Corinthians*, 234.
[11] Quoted in Jeremias, *The Eucharistic Words of Jesus*, 59.
[12] Joel Markus, *Mark 1–8, Anchor Bible 27* (New York: Doubleday, 2000), 507.
[13] See Esther Cen, "The Metaphor of Leaven in 1 Corinthians 5," *Dialogismos* 3 (2019): 1–26.
[14] Jeremias, *Eucharistic Words of Jesus*, 59–60.
[15] Ibid., 60. In this passage "ζύμη denotes the moral impurity of the old life, as ἄζυμος liberation from this and therefore truth and purity of the new life." Kittel and Friedrich, *Theological Dictionary of the New Testament*, 266.
[16] Joseph Fitzmyer, *First Corinthians*, 241.
[17] C. Leslie Mitton, "New Wine in Old Wine Skins: IV: Leaven," *Expository Times* 84 (1973): 339–43; Athanase Negoiţă and Constantin Daniel, "L'énigme du levain: Ad Mc. VIII 15; Mt. XVI 6; et Lc. XII 1," *Novum Testamentum* 9 (1967): 306–14.
[18] Gardner, *1 Corinthians*, 232.

needed to impregnate the whole batch of new dough,"[19] thus explaining Jesus's rather positive use of leaven in Matthew 13:33 and Luke 13:21 ("The kingdom of heaven is like ζύμη that a woman took and mixed in with three measures of flour until all of it was leavened [ἐζυμώθη]").[20] Here leaven is a "positive life-giving force" showing "the contrast between the small beginnings of the kingdom and its huge result."[21] According to Joseph Fitzmyer, "The kingdom once present in human history—even in a hidden way, cannot help but leaven the whole because of its characteristic active ingredients. Flour is important for bread, but without leaven there is no real bread!"[22]

The problem, also noted by Fitzmyer, is that the old dough put aside to use as leaven "could easily be contaminated and could dangerously infect the whole batch of new dough into which it was introduced; hence the yearly Jewish practice of destroying old leaven before the celebration of Passover."[23] Old leaven, or leaven that had become contaminated by other organisms, raised "the real danger of sickness,"[24] so that even a small portion hidden in a much larger loaf threatened all who consumed it. In this context leaven, especially old leaven, was a negative, "the symbol of that which is unclean and indeed actively polluting," especially as only a small amount has the power to destroy something far greater.[25] This is why Paul used the image of leaven in 1 Corinthians 5:6 ("Do you not know that a little yeast [ζύμη] leavens [ζυμοῖ] the whole batch of dough?") to convey his concern about certain impure people remaining in the community, and by their actions corrupting the church. For just as "A small quantity of yeast is sufficient to impregnate a whole lump of dough ... one corrupt member is sufficient to corrupt a whole church. The church must therefore exercise discipline

---

[19] Fitzmyer, *First Corinthians*, 241. According to Joachim Jeremias, "In the parable of the leaven [the biblical authors] drastically picture the overflowing mass of dough by borrowing from Gen 18:6 the number of 3 *se'a* (39.4 litres)—3 *se'a* are something like 50 pounds of flour, and the bread baked from this amount would provide a meal for more than 100 persons." Joachim Jeremias, *The Parables of Jesus*, trans. S. H. Hooke (New York: Scribner's, 1963), 147. See also Bernard Brandon Scott, *Hear Then the Parable: A Commentary on the Parables of Jesus* (Minneapolis, MN: Fortress Press, 1989), 321–29. Disagreeing with Jeremias is Klyne Snodgrass, who argues that "the likelihood of an allusion to Gen 18:6 is minimal at best." Klyne Snodgrass, *Stories with Intent: A Comprehensive Guide to the Parables of Jesus* (Grand Rapids, MI: Eerdmans, 2018), 188.

[20] This parable appears in almost identical form in Luke 13:21 ("It is like yeast that a woman took and mixed in with three measures of flour until all of it was leavened") and the *Gospel of Thomas* 96: "Jesus [said]: The kingdom of the Father is like [a] woman; she took a little leaven, [hid] it in dough, (and) made it into large loaves. He who has ears, let him hear." For more see Robert Funk, "Beyond Criticism in Quest of Literacy: The Parable of the Leaven," *Interpretation* 25 (1971): 149–70.

[21] Daniel Harrington, *The Gospel of Matthew*, Sacra Pagina 1 (Collegeville, MN: Liturgical Press, 1991), 205. The purpose of the parable is to "compare the Kingdom of God with the final stage of the finished product ... [that is] the mass of dough wholly permeated by the leaven ... [which in Romans 11:16] is a metaphor for the people of God." Jeremias, *The Parables of Jesus*, 147. C. H. Dodd argued that the parable was about the "power of God's kingdom ... mightily permeating the dead lump of religious Judaism in [Jesus'] time." C. H. Dodd, *The Parables of the Kingdom* (New York: Scribners, 1961), 193.

[22] Joseph Fitzmyer, *Luke X–XXIV*, Anchor Bible 28A (New Haven, CT: Yale University Press, 1985), 1019.

[23] Fitzmyer, *First Corinthians*, 241. According to Joel Markus, "This explanation of the festival's origin is doubtful ... since most harmful organisms would be killed in baking." Joel Markus, *Mark 1–8*, Anchor Bible 27 (New York: Doubleday, 2000), 507.

[24] Gardner, *1 Corinthians*, 232.

[25] Conzelmann, *1 Corinthians*, 98. According to Plutarch: "Yeast is itself also the product of corruption, and produces corruption in the dough with which it is mixed; for the dough becomes flabby and inert, and altogether the process of leavening seems to be one of putrefaction; at any rate if it goes too far, it completely sours and spoils the flour." Plutarch, *Quaestiones Romanae* 109; Eng. trans.: Plutarch, *Moralia, vol. IV*, trans. Frank Cole Babbitt (Cambridge, MA. Harvard University Press, 1936), 163.

in order to maintain its purity; in terms of the metaphor [it must] purge out the old leaven."[26]

Paul employed this proverb again in Galatians 5:9 ("A little yeast leavens the whole batch of dough"), giving strength to the argument that this saying about the corrupting potential of leaven was already well known and came "from popular wisdom, perhaps even from the poets, or both."[27] Here the identity of the "impure leaven" is not as clear as in Corinthians, although from the context Paul may be "identifying the leaven with the doctrine of [his] opponents who, if allowed to introduce the one demand of circumcision, may ruin the entire truth and the whole faith of the Galatians."[28]

It is this idea that leaven was largely a corrupting agent that led early Latin translators of the Bible to render both Galatians 5:9 and 1 Corinthians 5:6 as *Nescitis quia modicum fermentum totam massam corrumpit?* ("Do you not know that a little leaven *corrupts* the whole batch of dough?"). Jerome himself did not agree with translating ζυμοῖ as *corrumpit*, writing:

> Our manuscripts are wrong in reading "A little leaven ruins the whole lump" (*modicum fermentum totam massam corrumpit*), and the translator has rendered his own sense rather than the words of the apostle. For Paul himself uses the same expression to the Corinthians... where he says: "Your boasting is not good; do you not know that a little leaven ruins the whole lump?" or (as we have already corrected it) "leavens the whole dough? (*nescitis quia modicum fermentum totam massam corrumpit? siue [ut iam emendauimus] totam conspersionem fermentat?*)."[29]

Yet despite Jerome's objections the Vulgate maintained the earlier translation, strengthening the link between leaven and corruption in Western theology and reinforcing the idea, seen in 1 Corinthians 5:7–8, that unleavened bread signified purity.

Christ himself acknowledged the corrupting potential of leaven when he warned his disciples to "beware of the yeast of the Pharisees" (Mt 16:6, Mk 8:15, and Lk 12:1), recognizing "the spreading or permeating effect of leaven" but here viewing it as a

---

[26] C. K. Barrett, *The First Epistle to the Corinthians*, 127. Barrett points out that Paul comes back to this point in 1 Corinthians 15:33 when he writes: "Bad company ruins good morals."

[27] Hans Dieter Betz, *Galatians: A Commentary on Paul's Letter to the Churches in Galatia* (Philadelphia: Fortress Press, 1979), 266. According to Archibald Kennedy, "In the view of all antiquity, Semitic and non-Semitic, panary fermentation represented a process of corruption and putrefaction." Archibald Kennedy, *"Leaven" Encyclopedia Biblica* (London: Adam and Charles Black, 1902), 2754. For this reason, Windisch believed, "Paul's metaphor would be readily understandable to Gentile Christians not so well versed in the OT." H. Windisch, "ζύμη," in Kittel and Friedrich, *Theological Dictionary of the New Testament*, 266.

[28] Betz, *Galatians*, 266. Betz continued: "This interpretation stands in a long tradition, beginning perhaps with Ignatius of Antioch ('Put away the deteriorated leaven, leaven stale and sour, and turn to the new leaven, that is, Jesus Christ. Be salted in him to keep any among you from being spoiled, for by your odor you will be tested. It is absurd to have Jesus Christ on the lips, and at the same time live like a Jew.' [*Epistle to the Magnesians* 10.1]) and includes Chrysostom, Theophylactus, Luther, [and] Calvin." Ibid. James Louis Martyn agrees that this verse witnesses to Paul's fear that "all members of the Galatian churches may succumb to the teacher's false gospel." James Louis Martyn, *Galatians, The Anchor Bible 33a* (New York: Doubleday, 1998), 475.

[29] H. A. G. Houghton, "The Biblical Text of Jerome's Commentary on Galatians," *Journal of Theological Studies* 65 (2014): 1–24. According to Houghton this adds weight to the argument that Jerome was not responsible for the Vulgate translation of Paul's letters, which continued to translate ζυμοῖ as *corrumpit*.

danger "and therefore something to be wary of."[30] Mark's gospel reads, "Watch out—beware of the yeast of the Pharisees and the yeast of Herod" (Ὁρᾶτε, βλέπετε ἀπὸ τῆς ζύμης τῶν Φαρισαίων καὶ τῆς ζύμης Ἡρῴδου), a warning that comes shortly after the Pharisees' demand for a sign in Mark 8:11.[31] The apostles themselves fail to understand the saying, believing that all this talk of leaven and bread was due to the fact that they had not brought food. And while Jesus rebukes them for their hardness of heart (Mk 8:17), he does not tell them exactly what the "leaven of the Pharisees" is. Joel Markus suggests it might have been the "Evil Inclination, the destructive and anarchic impulse within the hearts of human beings that causes them to sin.... Jesus, then, is warning his disciples against being infected by the same evil impulse that has hardened the hearts of his enemies."[32] Instead of eating the leavened bread of the Pharisees, they should eat the bread supplied by Christ, the unleavened bread of purity.

Matthew's version replaces Herod with the Sadducees ("Beware of the leaven of the Pharisees and Sadducees"), who for Matthew, together with the Pharisees, are representative of the Jewish leadership. Unlike Mark, where the dangerous "leaven" of the Pharisees and Sadducees is not identified, here the apostles come to understand that it is a reference to their teaching ("Then they understood that he had not told them to beware of the yeast of bread [ἀπὸ τῆς ζύμης τῶν ἄρτων], but of the teaching of the Pharisees and Sadducees" [ἀλλὰ ἀπὸ τῆς διδαχῆς τῶν Φαρισαίων καὶ Σαδδουκαίων] Mt 16:12). What is so intriguing about this statement is the fact that the two groups were well-known adversaries, and that their teaching on so many subjects (e.g., the resurrection of the dead) was dissimilar.[33] However, the one thing they did share is their common misunderstanding of, and opposition to, Jesus rooted in their "preconception of the nature of the messiah and messianic fulfillment."[34] Thus the "leaven" for Matthew is not necessarily a specific teaching of either group, but rather references the "general contest" between their mistaken beliefs and those of the true teacher, Jesus.[35] Matthew is only interested in "the big picture"—that is, their common opposition

---

[30] Donald Hagner, *Matthew 14–28*, Word Biblical Commentary 33b (Dallas, TX: Word Books, 1995), 459.

[31] The inclusion of Herod here is curious. Joel Markus, utilizing the work of Heikki Räisänen, *The "Messianic Secret" in Mark's Gospel*, trans. Christopher Tuckett (Edinburgh: T. & T. Clark, 1990), 200, speculates that Herod was actually the original target of Jesus's saying, wondering "whether Mark has introduced the reference to the Pharisees, Jesus' stereotypical enemies in the gospel, into the [original] dictum." Markus, *Mark 1–8*, 509. Others have argued that "the 'corrupting influence' of Herod may either be an echo of 3:6 where Pharisees and Herodians plot to kill Jesus, or a reference to Herod's misunderstanding of Jesus in 6:14–16." John Donahue and Daniel J. Harrington, *The Gospel of Mark*, Sacra Pagina 2 (Collegeville, MN: Liturgical Press, 2002), 252. Still others speculate that this passage has parallels to "the late Targum 2 to Esther 3:8: 'Just as we remove the leaven, so may the evil rule be removed from us and may we be freed from this foolish king.'" Markus, *Mark 1–8*, 507. See also H. Jacobson, *The Exagoge of Ezekiel* (Cambridge: Cambridge University Press, 1983), 129.

[32] Markus, *Mark 1–8*, 510.

[33] "Here we have not only the strangeness of the linking of two such antithetical groups but the further and more difficult problem of the reference to their teaching.... In terms of their essential religious perspectives, it makes no sense to speak of 'the teaching of the Pharisees and Sadducees.'" Hagner, *Matthew 14–28*, 460.

[34] For Matthew, the two groups' understanding of messianic fulfillment, "a view widely held by the masses and even the disciples ... of necessity would include a national-political dimension." As such it would have "disqualified Jesus from any claim to being the agent of messianic fulfillment" and thus had to be rejected. Ibid.

[35] Rudolf Schnackenburg, *The Gospel of Matthew*, trans. Robert Barr (Grand Rapids, MI: Eerdmans, 2002), 155.

to Jesus—warning against the teaching of the Pharisees and Sadducees as "destructive leaven [simply] because it does not agree with the teaching of the 'one teacher,' Jesus.... That is the issue here."[36]

Luke 12:1 ("Beware of the yeast of the Pharisees, that is, their hypocrisy" [πρῶτον Προσέχετε ἑαυτοῖς ἀπὸ τῆς ζύμης, ἥτις ἐστὶν ὑπόκρισις, τῶν Φαρισαίων]) makes two significant changes from Mark—removing reference to the Herodians and identifying the yeast of the Pharisees as their "hypocrisy."[37] This is strange, since "The Lucan Jesus elsewhere never calls the Pharisees 'hypocrites' as does the Matthean."[38] Luke has also "entirely removed this saying from its narrative context in Mark 8:15" and placed it at the end of a larger attack upon the Pharisees and lawyers, men who "clean the outside of the cup and of the dish, but inside ... are full of greed and wickedness" (Lk 13:39).[39] It is exactly this "dissembling attitude" in their piety that Jesus objects to, warning his disciples "not to let themselves to be so contaminated [for] they should rather cultivate sincerity and openness."[40] As opposed to the Pharisees, who act as a corrupting influence, Jesus teaches his disciples to be "genuine disciples and good leaders, so that they become a positive influence or leaven as co-workers for the kingdom."[41]

The Fathers and Leaven

As might be expected, the patristic corpus sends the same mixed messages on the subject of leaven as do the Scriptures. For example, in commentaries on Matthew 13:33 and Luke 13:21, where leaven was seen as a positive thing, John Chrysostom interpreted the leaven as the church, believing, as he did, that "just as a little leaven leavens the whole lump," so too a small band of committed Christians, by their lives of faith, can change the world. He wrote:

> The righteous have the power of leaven in order that they may transfer the wicked to their own manner of conduct. But the righteous are few, for the leaven is small. But the smallness in no way injures the lump, but that little quantity converts the whole of the meal to itself by means of the power inherent in it.... There were twelve Apostles. Dost thou see how little is the leaven? The whole world was in unbelief. Dost thou see how great is the lump? But those twelve turned the whole world to themselves.[42]

---

[36] Ulrich Luz, *Matthew 8–20: A Commentary* (Minneapolis, MN: Augsburg, 2001), 351.
[37] See D. Bertrand, "Hypocrites selon Luc 12,1–59," *Christus* 21 (1974): 323–33.
[38] Joseph Fitzmyer, *Luke X–XXIV*, 953.
[39] "Leaven works within dough as a hidden yet powerful force; so, we are to understand, is the hidden vice of the opposition beneath their virtuous veneer." Luke Timothy Johnson, *The Gospel of Luke*, Sacra Pagina 3 (Collegeville, MN: Michael Glazier, 1991), 194.
[40] Joseph Fitzmyer, *Luke X–XXIV*, 954.
[41] Pablo Gadenz, *The Gospel of Luke, Catholic Commentary on Sacred Scripture* (Grand Rapids, MI: Baker Academic, 2018), 236.
[42] John Chrysostom, *Homily 3 On the Power of Demons*; NPNF 1.9.192. Elsewhere he wrote, "For as leaven converts the large quantity of meal into its own quality, even so shall you convert the whole world.... [For just as] the leaven leavens the lump when it comes close to the meal ... so you also when you come close to your enemies and are made one with them, then shall you get the better of them [since] the leaven, though it is buried, is not destroyed. Little by little it transmutes the whole lump into its own condition. This happens with the gospel. Do not fear, then, that there will be many dangerous circumstances. Even then you will shine forth and be victorious." John Chrysostom, *Homily on Matthew* 46; NPNF 1.10.289.

In a similar vein he wrote elsewhere:

> This is the reason why He called you leaven: for … little though it is, it affects the whole lump however big it may be. So also do ye: although ye are few in number, yet be ye many and powerful in faith, and in zeal towards God. As then the leaven is not weak on account of its littleness, but prevails owing to its inherent heat, and the force of its natural quality so ye also will be able to bring back a far larger number than yourselves, if you will, to the same degree of zeal as your own."[43]

Irenaeus of Lyon wrote how many of the gnostics interpreted Christ himself as the leaven, who leavened "the lump" (i.e., the church) by blending it with himself.[44] Orthodox writers also understood the leaven to be Christ himself, Ignatius of Antioch writing that we should "put away the deteriorated leaven, leaven stale and sour, and turn to the new leaven, that is, Jesus Christ."[45] According to Hilary of Poitiers, "The Lord compared himself to the yeast that the woman took," so that when he is added into the "three equal measures of flour: namely, of the Law, the prophets, and the Gospels; all is made into one."[46] Ambrose too maintained that "Christ is the leaven that enlivens the virtue which we have received.… The holy church is prefigured in the woman in the gospel. We are her flour, and she hides the Lord Jesus in the inner parts of our mind until the radiance of heavenly wisdom envelops the secret places of our spirit."[47]

However, Ambrose believed that "the doctrine of Christ is [also] fittingly called leaven," writing that "the woman, who prefigures the church," gives to us "the virtue of spiritual doctrine, until the whole hidden inner person of the heart is leavened and the heavenly bread arises to grace."[48] In this he was followed by Rufinus, who similarly saw leaven as holy teaching, arguing that Christ likened the kingdom to leaven not because "the kingdom of heaven is like leaven in all respects, its substance being capable of being handled and perishable," but instead "to demonstrate how, as a result of such an insignificant thing as the preaching of God's word, men's minds can be

---

[43] John Chrysostom, *To Those Who Had Not Attended the Assembly*; NPNF 1.9.224.

[44] "The parable of the leaven, too, which the woman is said to have hidden in three measures of meal, they say, manifests the three classes. According to their teaching, the woman is wisdom; the three measures of meal, the three classes of people, the spiritual, the ensouled, and the earthly. The leaven is Savior himself.… Now they teach that the first fruits are the spiritual class whereas the lump is we, that is, the ensouled church, which lump he assumed and raised up with himself since he was the leaven." Irenaeus of Lyons, *Against the Heresies* 1.8.3; Eng. trans.: Irenaeus of Lyons, *Against the Heresies Book 1*, trans. Dominic Unger, ACW 55 (New York: Newman Press, 1992), 42–43.

[45] Ignatius of Antioch, *Epistle to the Magnesians* 10.1; Eng. trans.: Ignatius of Antioch and Clement of Rome, *The Epistles of St. Clement of Rome and St. Ignatius of Antioch*, trans. James Kleist, ACW 1 (Westminster, MD: Newman Bookshop, 1946), 72.

[46] Hilary of Poitiers, *Commentary on Matthew* 13.5; Eng. trans.: Hilary of Poitiers, *Commentary on Matthew*, trans. D. H. Williams, FC 125 (Washington, DC: Catholic University of America Press, 2012), 155.

[47] Ambrose of Milan, *Exposition of the Gospel of Luke* 7.187; Eng. trans.: Ambrose of Milan, *Exposition of the Holy Gospel According to Saint Luke*, trans. Theodosia Tomkinson (Etna, CA: Center for Traditionalist Orthodox Studies, 1998), 307.

[48] Ambrose of Milan, *Exposition of the Gospel of Luke* 7.191–92; Eng. trans.: Ambrose of Milan, *Exposition of the Holy Gospel According to Saint Luke*, 310. Chrysostom, in his Commentary on 1 Corinthians 5:6–8, where leaven is likened to sin, nevertheless recognized that "Christ also called His doctrine leaven." John Chrysostom, *Homily 15 on First Corinthians*; NPNF 1.12.85.

bound together in unity by the leaven of faith."[49] Jerome also interpreted leaven here as "the leaven of the gospel ... gradually rais[ing] more and more the whole lump of the church,"[50] although elsewhere he wrote that it was the woman who refers "either to the apostolic preaching or to the church, which has been gathered from various nations. She takes the leaven, that is, the knowledge and understanding of the Scriptures, and she buries it in three measures of flower so that the spirit, soul, and body, having been gathered into one, might not discord among themselves, but would agree with two and three and would obtain from the Father whatever they ask for."[51]

Augustine of Hippo, who in his *Questions on the Gospels*, had written that "love [is] the yeast, because it warms and raises up,"[52] elsewhere held that leaven was indeed the Word of God, asking, "Who is that woman, except the flesh of the Lord? What is that leaven, except the gospel?"[53] Cyril of Alexandria also taught that the leaven was the gospel, for just as "leaven is small in quantity ... it seizes upon the whole mass, and quickly communicates to it its own properties. The word of God operates in us in a similar manner; for when admitted within us, it makes us holy and without blame, and pervading our mind and heart, it renders us spiritual."[54] Because of this we receive "the rational and divine leaven in our mind and understanding, that by this precious and holy and pure leaven we may be found spiritually unleavened as having in us none of the wickedness of the world, but being rather pure and holy and partakers of Christ."[55]

While the fathers viewed leaven as a positive thing in some contexts, in others (e.g., when commenting on 1 Cor 5:6-8, Gal 5:9, and "the leaven of the Pharisees") they recognized and condemned leaven's corrupting potential. In particular, they took note of the fact that a small bit of leaven had the ability to corrupt a much larger loaf, leading them to emphasize the destructive power of seemingly insignificant transgressions. According to Marius Victorinus's *Commentary on Galatians*, "All yeast involves a spoiling of bread.... Now, when a little bit of yeast is inserted into a mass, the mass is spoiled.... So your supposed little bit that you have added—namely, that

---

[49] Rufinus, *Commentary on the Apostles' Creed* 7; Eng. trans.: Rufinus, *A Commentary on the Apostles' Creed*, trans. J. N. D. Kelly, ACW 20 (Westminster, MD: Newman Press, 1955), 40.

[50] Jerome, *Letter 66 to Pammachius*; NPNF 2.6.136.

[51] Jerome, *Commentary on Matthew*, 2.13.33; Eng. trans.: Jerome, *Commentary on Matthew*, trans. Thomas Scheck, FC 117 (Washington, DC: Catholic University of America Press, 2008), 159.

[52] Augustine of Hippo, *Questions on the Gospels* 1.12; Eng. trans.: Augustine of Hippo, *The New Testament I and II*, trans. Boniface Ramsey, Kim Paffenroth, and Roland Teske (Hyde Park, NY: New City Press, 2014), 366.

[53] Augustine of Hippo, *Tractates on the Gospel of John* 9.17; Eng. trans.: Augustine of Hippo, *Tractates on the Gospel of John 1–10*, trans. John Rettig, FC 78 (Washington, DC: Catholic University of America Press, 1988), 209.

[54] Cyril of Alexandria, *Homily 96 on the Gospel of Saint Luke*; Eng. trans.: Cyril of Alexandria, *Commentary on the Gospel of Saint Luke*, trans. R. Payne Smith (n.p.: Studion Publishers, 1983), 395. Theophylact of Ohrid, albeit much later, also pursued this line, arguing that "some understand the leaven to be the preaching; the three measures are the three faculties of the soul—the abilities to reason, to be stirred into action, and to desire—and the woman is the soul which hides the preaching within all three of its faculties, so that it is all mixed together, leavened, and sanctified. So every part of us must be leavened and transformed into that which is more Godlike." Theophylact of Ohrid, *Commentary on the Gospel of Matthew*. trans. Christopher Stade (House Springs, MO: Chrysostom Press, 1992),116.

[55] Cyril of Alexandria, *Homily 96 on the Gospel of Saint Luke*; Eng. trans.: Cyril of Alexandria, *Commentary on the Gospel of Saint Luke*, 395.

you would observe circumcision and other things—that little bit of yours, since it is spoiled, spoils the mass of our gospel."[56] Chrysostom imagined Paul's congregation asking, 'Why do you magnify and aggravate the matter ... [for] one commandment only of the Law have we kept, and yet you make this great outcry?' Hear how he terrifies them ... [saying that] this slight error, if not corrected, will have the power (as the leaven has with the lump) to lead you into complete Judaism."[57]

In his commentary on 1 Corinthians 5:6–8 Chrysostom gave an extended meditation on the meaning of leaven, likening its corrupting potential to sinners in the community who go unpunished. For just as "a little leaven leavens the whole lump," one sin has the power "if neglected ... to waste the rest of the body of the Church also."[58] Leaven, "though it be but little, transforms unto its own nature the whole lump; so also this man, if he be let go unpunished and this sin turn out unavenged, will corrupt likewise all the rest."[59] For this reason Paul urged the Galatians, particularly the priests, to "purge out the old leaven, ... [which] is not fornication only, but also sin of every kind. And he said not, purge, but purge out; cleanse with accuracy so that there be not so much as a remnant nor a shadow of that sort."[60] This was foreshadowed in the Passover, when the Jews removed leaven from their houses.

> What then is the hidden meaning [of this]? The believer must be freed from all iniquity. For as among them he perishes with whomsoever is found old leaven, so also with us wheresoever is found iniquity.... For if they so carefully clear their houses of leaven, and pry into mouse-holes; much more ought we to search through the soul so as to cast out every unclean thought.... Wherefore he urges upon them strongly to purge out the leaven, that you may be, says he, a new lump, even as you are unleavened.[61]

Theodoret of Cyrus maintained that "by the old yeast he refers to our [sinful] condition before baptism, from which he bids them be separated and be unleavened, carrying no trace of that condition."[62] Ambrosiaster also understood this passage to refer chiefly to the individual, believing that "just as a little leaven leavens the whole

---

[56] Marius Victorinus, *Commentary on Galatians*, 2.5.9; Eng. trans.: Marius Victorinus, *Commentary on Galatians*, trans. Stephen Adam Cooper (Oxford: Oxford University Press, 2005), 332.

[57] John Chrysostom, *Homily on Galatians* 5.9; NPNF 1.13.37–38.

[58] John Chrysostom, *Homily 15 on First Corinthians*; NPNF 1.12.85.

[59] Ibid.

[60] Ibid. "But I have a strong conviction that the saying about the leaven refers also to the priests who suffer a vast deal of the old leaven to be within, not purging out from their borders, that is, out of the Church, the covetous, the extortioners, and whatsoever would exclude from the kingdom of Heaven." Ibid., NPNF 1.12.87.

[61] John Chrysostom, *Homily 15 on First Corinthians*; NPNF 1.12.86. This echoes Origen, who had earlier written that "just as is done among the Jews, who clean out all the old leaven when the day of unleavened bread dawns, and inspect every place in the house in case any leaven should be there, so should you consider the things stored up in you to prevent there being any leaven there ... eating unleavened bread by refraining from any evil or wickedness." Origen, *Commentary on 1 Corinthians*, in Judith Kovacs, ed., *1 Corinthians: Interpreted by Early Christian Commentators*, The Church's Bible (Grand Rapids, MI: Eerdmans, 2005), 87.

[62] Theodoret of Cyrus, *Commentary on the First Letter to the Corinthians* 5; Eng. trans.: Theodoret of Cyrus, *Commentary on the Letters of Saint Paul*, vol. 1, trans. Robert Charles Hill (Brookline, MA: Holy Cross Orthodox Press, 2001), 177.

lump, so an evil life corrupts the whole man. Therefore, Paul wants us to avoid not only evil acts but all interest in sin."[63] Yet Ambrosiaster also held that "the old leaven has a double meaning. On the one hand, it refers to false teaching, just as Jesus warns his disciples to beware of the leaven of the Pharisees. On the other hand, it also refers to the sin of fornication being dealt with here."[64] Embracing the Passover imagery, Paul spoke of ridding oneself of the old leaven ("bad teaching") and embracing the "new lump, [which] is the teaching of Christ," comparing the post-Exodus Israelites, who "had thrown away the errors of the Egyptians [and] were led into the new law," with the Corinthians, who became unleavened "in the same way ... [and] after being delivered from the errors of the pagans, were led into the gospel of Christ."[65]

Jerome, discussing "the leaven of the Pharisees and the Sadducees," held that it signified "perverse traditions and heretical dogmas ... for leaven has this power, that if it is mixed with flour, that which seemed small grows greater and draws all the dough to its flavor. In the same way, then, heretical teaching, if it casts a little spark into your breast, in a little while rises up as a huge flame and draws to itself the possession of the entire man."[66] Hilary of Poitiers, who believed that "there is complete and total obscurity when it comes to the yeast of the Pharisees and the Sadducees," nevertheless held the passage to be a warning "not to mingle with the teaching of the Jews, because the works of the Law had been established for the prompting of one's faith and as a foreshadowing of events to follow."[67] Having found the truth in Christ, with "no hope of a similar truth lying beyond [what they have received]," the apostles were to avoid the Pharisees and Sadducees and "prevent the[ir] teaching ... ignorant of Christ, from corrupting the realization of the Gospel's truth."[68]

Origen described the leaven of the Pharisees and Sadducees as their teaching, for "you will understand that whenever leaven is named it is put figuratively for teaching."[69] He explained that theirs

> was a certain lump of teaching and of truly ancient leaven,—that according to the bare letter, and on this account not freed from those things which arise from wickedness ... which Jesus does not wish His own disciples any longer to eat, having made for them a new and spiritual lump, offering Himself to those who gave up the leaven of the Pharisees and Sadducees and had come to Him.[70]

The fact that the Jews, adhering to the letter of the Law, continued to commemorate the Passover with unleavened bread was frequently commented upon by the fathers, who often compared (unfavorably, of course) the ceremonies of the Jews with that of the

---

[63] Ambrosiaster, *Commentary on Romans and 1–2 Corinthians*, 142.
[64] Ibid.
[65] Ibid.
[66] Jerome, *Commentary on Matthew* 2.16.6; Eng. trans. Jerome, *Commentary on Matthew*, 187–88.
[67] Hilary of Poitiers, *Commentary on Matthew* 16.3; Eng. trans.: Hilary of Poitiers, *Commentary on Matthew*, 178–79.
[68] Ibid.
[69] Origen, *Commentary on Matthew*, 12.5; ANF 9:452–53. Origen particularly targeted those "many among the heterodox who, because of their unbelief in regard to the resurrection of the dead, are imbued with the leaven of the Sadducees." Ibid.
[70] Ibid.

Christians, who celebrated a new, truly spiritual, Passover. According to Justin Martyr writing to the Jew Trypho, the real "meaning of unleavened bread, [is] that you do not commit the old deeds of the bad leaven. You, however, understand everything in a carnal way, and you deem yourselves pious if you perform such deeds, even when your souls are filled with deceit and every other kind of sin."[71] The Jews, wrote Augustine, "are like Cain with his mark. The sacrifices they used to offer were done away with ... [for] like Cain's mark it has achieved its purpose but they do not know it. They kill a Lamb and eat unleavened bread, but Christ has been immolated as our Passover."[72] Paulinus of Nola similarly wrote that to remember Moses the Jews "even today eat unleavened bread in memory of their flight ... observ[ing] this ancestral ritual under the same form ... but on a sabbath which is superfluous. It is in vain that they observe the empty shell of the old law; Christ alone has fulfilled the true pasch for us.... Because he is with us as living body, the shadow of that symbolism now vanishes."[73]

The Date of the Last Supper

"Easily the most disputed chronological issue in New Testament studies," and (not coincidentally) the biggest point of contention in the later debate over azymes, was the question whether or not the Last Supper, celebrated shortly before Christ's arrest and crucifixion, was a Jewish Passover meal.[74] Although the dating of the Last Supper affects a number of important theological questions, especially the relation of the new

---

[71] Justin Martyr, *Dialogue with Trypho*, 14; Eng. trans.: Justin Martyr, *Writings of Saint Justin Martyr*, trans. Thomas Falls, FC 6 (Washington, DC: Catholic University of America Press, 1948), 169. Origen similarly wrote that "the one who puts off the old man with his practices and who has in himself nothing of the old leaven, having made the new lump in accordance with Christ Jesus—this one has performed the festival of the unleavened bread." Origen, *Commentary on 1 Corinthians* in Kovacs, *1 Corinthians*, 87.

[72] Augustine of Hippo, *Commentary on Psalm* 39.8; Eng. trans.: St. Augustine, *Exposition on the Psalms*, vol. 2, trans. Maria Boulding (Hyde Park, NY: New City Press, 2000), 208–9. He continued, "Should we have found fault with you in earlier days for offering them? No, but we do find fault with you now, and if you attempted to offer them now it would be unseasonable, inopportune, and unfitting. You are still making promises, but I have received what was promised." Ibid.

[73] Paulinus of Nola, *Poem 26*; Eng. trans.: Paulinus of Nola, *The Poems of Paulinus of Nola*, trans. P. G. Walsh, ACW 40 (New York: Newman Press, 1975), 255.

[74] Brant Pitre, *Jesus and the Last Supper* (Grand Rapids, MI: Eerdmans, 2015), 251. Just a sample of the literature includes John C. Lambert, "The Passover and the Lord's Supper," *Journal of Theological Studies* 4.14 (1903): 184–93; F. C. Burkitt, "The Last Supper and the Paschal Meal," *Journal of Theological Studies* 17.4 (1916): 291–97; W. M. Christie, "Did Christ Eat the Passover with His Disciples?," *Expository Times* 43 (1931–32): 515–19; Solomon Zeitlin, "The Last Supper as an Ordinary Meal in the Fourth Gospel," *Jewish Quarterly Review* 42 (1952): 251–60; Hans Lessing, *Die Abendmahlsprobleme im Lichte der neutestamentlichen Forschung seit 1900* (Bonn: Bouvier, 1953); Massey H. Shepherd, "Are Both the Synoptics and John Correct about the Date of Jesus' Death?," *Journal of Biblical Literature* 80 (1961): 123–32; A. R. C. Leaney, "What Was the Lord's Supper?," *Theology* 70 (1967): 51–62; Gordon J. Bahr, "The Seder of Passover and the Eucharistic Words," *Novum Testamentum* 12 (1970): 181–202; Harold Hoehner, *Chronological Aspects of the Life of Christ* (Grand Rapids, MI: Zondervan, 1977); I. Howard Marshall, *Last Supper and Lord's Supper* (Grand Rapids, MI: Eerdmans, 1980); Baruch Bokser, "Was the Last Supper a Passover Seder?," *Bible Review* 3 (1987): 24–33; Matti Myllykoski, *Die Letzten Tage Jesu: Markus und Johannes, ihre Traditionen und die historische Frage*, 2 vols. (Helsinki: Suomalainen Tiedeakatemia, 1991–94); John Hamilton, "The Chronology of the Crucifixion and the Passover," *Churchman* 106 (1992): 323–38; David Instone-Brewer, "Jesus' Last Passover: The Synoptics and John," *Expository Times* 112 (2001): 122–23; Robin Routledge, "Passover and Last Supper," *Tyndale Bulletin* 53 (2002): 203–21; Étienne Nodet, "On Jesus' Last Supper," *Biblica* 91 (2010): 348–69; Andreas J. Köstenberger, "Was the Last Supper a Passover

Passover to the old, for those involved in the azyme debate the issue was whether Jesus would have celebrated this particular meal with unleavened bread (ἄζυμος), which would be the case if it was Passover, or with ordinary bread (ἄρτος), the kind used in a normal meal. At the center of the dispute is the seeming contradiction between the Synoptic Gospels (Matthew, Mark, Luke) who are clear that the Last Supper was a Passover celebration held "on the first day of Unleavened Bread, when the Passover lamb is sacrificed" (Mk 14:12) and the Gospel of John, which places the meal "just before the Passover Festival" (Jn 13:1) with the *crucifixion* taking place on "the day of Preparation for the Passover" (Jn 19:14).[75]

Over the centuries various solutions to this problem have been proposed, which can be grouped into four general categories. They are

1. *The Essene hypothesis*: Both John and the Synoptics are right; the alleged discrepancy a result of the fact that different Jewish liturgical calendars were in use in the first century.
2. *The Johannine hypothesis*: John is right and the Synoptics are wrong. The Last Supper was not a (ordinary) Jewish Passover meal even if John's account of the meal does contain several Passover elements. This was the predominant position of later Eastern writers.
3. *The Synoptic hypothesis*: The Synoptics are right and John is wrong; the Last Supper was a Jewish Passover meal. This was the argument of most later Western authors.
4. *The Passover hypothesis*: Both John and the Synoptics are right; the apparent contradiction being a result of misunderstanding the Passover terminology of John's gospel.[76]

The Essene Hypothesis

The Essene hypothesis, which holds that Jesus and the Essenes used a different calendar than the Temple authorities in Jerusalem and thus celebrated Passover on a different date, has gained many adherents since it was first proposed in Annie Jaubert's 1957 book *La date de la cène (The Date of the Last Supper)*.[77] Among this theory's chief attractions is its ability to reconcile the Synoptic and Johannine chronologies of the

---

Meal?," in Thomas R. Schreiner and Matthew R. Crawford, eds., *The Lord's Supper: Remembering and Proclaiming Christ until He Comes*, NAC Studies in Bible and Theology 10 (Nashville: B&H Publishing Group, 2010), 6–30; Colin Humphreys, *The Mystery of the Last Supper: Reconstructing the Final Days of Jesus* (Cambridge: Cambridge University Press, 2011); Paul Bradshaw, "Did Jesus Institute the Eucharist at the Last Supper?," in Maxwell Johnson, ed., *Issues in Eucharistic Praying in East and West: Essays in Liturgical and Theological Analysis* (Collegeville, MN: Liturgical Press, 2011), 1–19; Joel Marcus, "Passover and Last Supper Revisited," *New Testament Studies* 59 (2013): 303–24; Mariusz Rosik, "The Dispute over the Date of the Last Supper: Its Chronology Revisited," *Verbum Vitae* 38 (2020): 179–98.

[75] "Virtually every introduction to, or discussion of, the infamous 'date of the Last Supper' debate construes the question as a simple choice between the Synoptics (which view it as a Passover meal) and the Gospel of John (which views it as some other kind of meal)." Pitre, *Jesus and the Last Supper*, 253.

[76] See Pitre, *Jesus and the Last Supper*, 258–59.

[77] Annie Jaubert, *The Date of the Last Supper*, trans. Isaac Rafferty (Staten Island, NY: Alba House, 1965). See also her earlier "La date de la dernière Cène," *Revue de l'Histoire des Religions* 146 (1954): 140–73; Annie

passion, assuming as it does that the Synoptics recorded Jesus's celebration of Passover according to the Essene reckoning, while John used the Temple dating, where the feast began later. Jaubert's theory is premised on three interrelated facts:

1) During the first century there was a debate within Judaism over the use of a solar (364-day), rather than lunar (354), calendar to calculate the dates of certain feasts, and thus Jews at that time would have celebrated the Passover on different days depending on which side of this argument they took.[78]
2) Jesus himself adhered to the Essene (i.e., solar) calendar and was thus at odds with the Temple authorities on the dating of Passover.
3) Since the Essence calendar always placed the Passover three days after the Sabbath (i.e., on a Wednesday), the Last Supper actually occurred on a Tuesday evening rather than on Thursday, with the events of the passion (arrest, Jewish trial, Roman trial, crucifixion) spread out over three days.

According to Jaubert, and now widely accepted, a 364 day solar calendar was indeed in use by the Essenes during Jesus's lifetime and is referenced in both the Pseudepigrapha (e.g., *Jubilees* 6:32-38),[79] and the Dead Sea Scrolls.[80] Thus Jaubert's

---

Jaubert, "Le calendrier des Jubilés et les jour liturgiques de la semaine," *Vetus Testamentum* 7 (1957): 35–61. Other advocates of the Essene hypothesis included Eugen Ruckstuhl, *Chronology of the Last Days of Jesus: A Critical Study*, trans. Victor Drapela (New York: Desclée 1965); Patrick Skehan, "The Date of the Last Supper," *Catholic Biblical Quarterly* 20 (1958): 192–99. Although Pope Benedict XVI once referred to it as a "highly plausible hypothesis" (*Homily for the Mass of the Lord's Supper*, April 5, 2007), by 2011 he seems to have changed his mind and claimed that "the traces of tradition to which she refers are too weak to be convincing" and that while it is "so fascinating on first sight" it has been "rejected by the majority of exegetes" and "cannot simply be accepted at face value in view of the various problems that remain unresolved." Joseph Ratzinger, *Jesus of Nazareth: Holy Week: From the Entrance into Jerusalem to the Resurrection* (San Francisco: Ignatius Press, 2011), 111–12.

[78] Paul Billerbeck maintained that there was a calendar dispute, but it was between the Pharisees and Sadducees and revolved around the question of when the month of Nisan began that particular year and thus when the fifteenth of that month would have occurred. See Hermann Strack and Paul Billerbeck, *Kommentar zum Neuen Testament aus Talmud und Midrasch*, vol. 2 (Munich: C.H. Becksche Verlagsbuchhandlung, 1924), 847–53. According to John Meier, Billerbeck believed that "since neither party could prevail against the other, they compromised by having Passover lambs slaughtered on both Thursday and Friday. The Pharisees (and Jesus with them) counted Thursday as the fourteenth of Nisan and so celebrated the Passover meal Thursday evening. The Sadducees instead counted Friday as the fourteenth of Nisan, and so celebrated the Passover meal as the Sabbath was beginning." John Meier, *A Marginal Jew: Rethinking the Historical Jesus*, vol. 3 (New York: Doubleday, 1991), 390–91. Stanislas Dockx held that the dispute was instead between Galileans and Judeans, and that both groups, present in Jerusalem during this week, would have celebrated on different days. Stanislas Dockx, *Chronologies néotestamentaires et vie de l'Eglise primitive: Recherches exégétiques* (Paris-Gembloux: Duculot, 1976). According to John Meier, neither theory is "anchored in the concrete history of Judaism at the time of Jesus" thus both can be dismissed with the dictum that "what is gratuitously asserted may be gratuitously denied." Meier, *A Marginal Jew*, 391. In fact, elsewhere in the book (422–23 n. 74) Meier mentions at least six other versions of the calendar dispute theory, all of which have little evidence to support them. For criticism of these and other theories see also Joachim Jeremias, *The Eucharistic Words of Jesus*, 21–24.

[79] "And you, command the children of Israel so that they shall guard the years in this number, three hundred and sixty-four days, and it will be a complete year. And no one shall corrupt its (appointed) time from its days or from its feasts because all (of the appointed times) will arrive in them according to their testimony and they will not pass over a day, and they will not corrupt a feast." *Book of Jubilees* 6:32 in James Charlesworth, ed., *The Old Testament Pseudepigrapha*, vol. 2 (Garden City, NY: Doubleday, 1985), 68.

[80] According to James VanderKam, "The oldest explicit source for it is 1 Enoch 72–82, where the number 364 is given several times as the length of a solar year (72:32; 74:10, 12, 13; 75:2; 82:6).... It is also attested

first premise—that there was a dispute regarding the calendar and the dates of certain feasts during the Second Temple period—is relatively uncontroversial. However, in maintaining that Jesus himself followed the Essene calendar Jaubert has been widely criticized, both because of lack of evidence—there is no mention in the gospels of this fact—and because John's gospel appears to point in the opposite direction.[81] Even more problematic is the fact that Jaubert's thesis would necessitate a Tuesday Last Supper, as opposed to the Thursday meal attested to in all four gospels, thus calling into question the entire chronology of Jesus's last week. It is true that Jaubert's thesis eliminates the oft-noted problem of how "so many events [could be] compressed into so few hours,"[82] but at the same time it "explicitly contradicts the testimony of both the Synoptics and John that Jesus was crucified the morning after his betrayal and arrest."[83] "In sum, in her effort to explain the divergences of the Synoptics and John on the dating of the Last Supper and the crucifixion, Jaubert ends up with an extremely strange position on the historical reliability of the Gospels."[84]

Jaubert's hypothesis did find support among some archaeologists, who brought forward evidence contending that the site of the Last Supper was near Jerusalem's "Essene gate" identified by Josephus (*Jewish War* 5.145) and thus was in the alleged "Essene quarter" of the city.[85] According to their logic the "proximity to the Essene settlement to the Last Supper room strengthens the assumption that Jesus actually celebrated his last Passover meal according to the calendar of the Essenes."[86] Of course,

---

and assumed in the literature found in the Qumran caves (the two explicit references are 4Q252 ii:3 and 11Q5xxvii:5–6)." Kames VanderKam, *Jubilees 1: A Commentary on the Book of Jubilees Chapters 1–21* (Minneapolis, MN: Fortress Press, 2018), 324. Elsewhere he points out that in *4QCalendrical Document A* frag.4, col. 3:1–9 specific mention is made of the date of Passover, which should be celebrated "on the third day from Sabbath of the course of the sons of Maaziah." James VanderKam and Peter Flint, *The Meaning of the Dead Sea Scrolls: Their Significance for Understanding the Bible, Judaism, Jesus, and Christianity* (San Francisco, CA: Harper San Francisco, 2002), 259. See also James Vanderkam, *Calendars in the Dead Sea Scrolls: Measuring Time* (London: Routledge, 1998); Sacha Stern, *Calendar and Community: A History of the Jewish Calendar 2nd Century BCE–10th Century CE* (Oxford: Oxford University Press, 2001); Jonathan Ben-Dov and Stéphane Saulnier, "Qumran Calendars: A Survey of Scholarship 1980–2007," *Currents in Biblical Research* 7 (2008): 124–68; Stéphane Saulnier, *Calendrical Variations in Second Temple Judaism: New Perspectives on the "Date of the Last Supper" Debate* (Leiden: Brill, 2012).

[81] According to John Meier, it is clear from the Synoptics "and becomes superabundantly clear in the Fourth Gospel" that Jesus celebrates the Jewish feasts (e.g., the Feast of Tabernacles in John 7:1–10) "according to the lunar calendar used in the Temple ... [and thus] at the same time other Jews observe them." Meier, *A Marginal Jew*, 393.

[82] "[Jaubert] points out that the traditional chronologies (Synoptic and Johannine) have to compress a whole series of events into a few hours: the hearing before the Sanhedrin, Jesus being sent over to Pilate, Pilate's wife's dream, Jesus being handed over to Herod, his return to Pilate, the scourging, the condemnation to death, the way of the Cross, and the crucifixion. To accomplish all this in the space of a few hours seems scarcely possible." Ratzinger, *Jesus of Nazareth: Holy Week*, 110.

[83] Pitre, *Jesus and the Last Supper*, 266, 272. It also contradicts the Synoptic Gospels, which clearly identify the Last Supper with "the day when they sacrificed the Passover lamb" (Mk 14:12, Lk 22:7).

[84] Meier, *A Marginal Jew*, 394.

[85] "But if we go the other way westward, it began at the same place, and extended through a place called 'Bethso,' to the gate of the Essenes; and after that it went southward, having its bending above the fountain Siloam, where it also bends again towards the east at Solomon's pool, and reaches as far as a certain place which they called 'Ophlas,' where it was joined to the eastern cloister of the temple." Flavius Josephus, *The Jewish War* 5.145; Eng. trans.: Josephus, *The New Complete Works of Josephus*, 830.

[86] Bargil Pixner, *Paths of the Messiah: Messianic Sites in Galilee and Jerusalem* (San Francisco, CA: Ignatius Press, 2010), 251. See also Rainer Riesner, "Josephus 'Gate of the Essenes' in Modern Discussion," *Zeitschrift des Deutschen Palästina-Vereins* 105 (1989): 105–9; Rainer Riesner, "Jesus, the Primitive Community, and

critics are quick to point out that we do not have any proof that there was an "Essene quarter" in Jerusalem, and while its existence cannot be ruled out, to conclude that "Jesus celebrated the Last Supper in an Essene quarter for which we have no explicit evidence," and that he did so according to a calendar we have no proof he followed, appears largely unsubstantiated by the available data.[87]

The Johannine Hypothesis

Today, among the most widely accepted of the four theories is the belief that John's chronology is substantially correct in claiming that the Last Supper was *not* a Passover meal and that it was only described as such by the Synoptics for theological reasons—that is, in order to dramatize "the pre-Gospel proclamation of Jesus as the paschal lamb."[88] Despite the oft-recognized fact that it contains many "Passover characteristics,"[89] proponents of this theory argue that the Last Supper was either some sort of *ḳiddušš* (Sabbath sanctification)[90] or *ḥaburah* (fellowship) meal,[91] with it being far more likely that "Jesus died on ... the 14th of Nisan, the day on which the paschal lambs were sacrificed, and the eve of the 15th of Nisan, on which the paschal lamb would be eaten."[92]

Among the chief arguments for the accuracy of John's chronology are the apparent lack of a Passover lamb in all four gospel accounts, the improbability that so much activity (e.g., buying/selling of goods, a full Sanhedrin trial) would have taken place "on what should be a solemn feast day,"[93] and the references in the Babylonian Talmud to

---

the Essene Quarter of Jerusalem," in James Charlesworth, ed., *Jesus and the Dead Sea Scrolls* (New Haven, CT: Yale University Press 1992), 198–234; Rainer Riesner, *Essener und Urgemeinde in Jerusalem: Neue Funde und Quellen* (Gießen: Brunnen-Verlag, 1998).

[87] Pitre, *Jesus and the Last Supper*, 278.

[88] Raymond Brown, *The Death of the Messiah*, vol. 2 (New York: Doubleday, 1993).1360. Aside from Brown, notable advocates of this theory include John Meier ("In the end, a number of considerations lead me to favor the basic outline of the Johannine chronology as the most likely." *Marginal Jew*, 386–401), James D. G. Dunn ("As the evidence stands, in this case it is as likely as not that John has been able to draw his theological point from the actual historical sequence." *Jesus Remembered: Christianity in the Making*, vol. 1 [Grand Rapids, MI: Eerdmans, 2003], 772), NT Wright ("There is no reason to suppose that Jesus might not have celebrated what we might call a quasi-Passover meal a day ahead of the real thing." *Jesus and the Victory of God* [Minneapolis, MN: Fortress Press, 1996], 556–59), Markus Bockmuehl ("The 'passover' which Jesus held with his disciples on the night of his arrest was most likely an unofficial meal." *This Jesus: Martyr, Lord, Messiah* [London: T&T Clark, 1994], 93), and Pope Benedict XVI ("Thus with certain reservations, one can agree with Meier's conclusion: "The entire Johannine tradition, from early to late, agrees perfectly with the primitive Synoptic tradition on the non-Passover character of the meal." *Jesus of Nazareth: Holy Week*, 113).

[89] Raymond Brown, *The Gospel According to John XIII–XXI*, Anchor Bible 29a (New York: Doubleday, 1970), 556.

[90] "I venture to suggest, then, that the real Jewish antecedent of the Lord's Supper was the weekly Kiddush." G. H. Box, "The Jewish Antecedents of the Eucharist," *Journal of Theological Studies* 3 (1901–2): 358–60. See also Pierre Batiffol, *L'Eucharistie: La Présence Réelle et la transsubstantiation, études d'histoire et de théologie positive*, vol. 2 (Paris: V. Lecoffre, 1913).

[91] See, for example, Hans Lietzmann, *Mass and Lord's Supper* (Leiden: Brill, 1979), 165–71.

[92] Brown, *Death of the Messiah*, 2:1373.

[93] "Probably the most persuasive argument for those who accept John's dating of the crucifixion is that the many activities described on Thn/Fd do not occur on a feast day." Brown, *Death of the Messiah*, 2: 1360.

Jesus being crucified "on the eve of Passover."[94] Recent reassessments of John's overall historicity, which challenged earlier generations' belief that his gospel contained more "theology" than "history," have also strengthened the case for John's chronology.[95] In fact, according to some scholars, as it pertains to the description of Jesus's last week John's account may be more accurate than the Synoptics, "represent[ing] an independent strain of tradition" that in many ways is "better informed than the tradition behind the Synoptics, whose confused account it clarifies."[96] This is why Raymond Brown, voicing the majority view, concluded that John, rather than the Synoptics, was correct in maintaining that "the Last Supper on Thursday evening was not a legal Passover meal" even though "Christ deliberately imitated many of [its] details."[97] It was only later that "this meal with Passover features became a Passover meal" in the Synoptic tradition, John's dating remaining truer to the actual facts of history.[98]

More recently, however, Brant Pitre and others have tried to challenge the Johannine hypothesis by pointing out that many of the arguments used to support it are substantially incorrect or based on faulty assumptions. For example, while Brown and others maintained that "no Gospel ever mentions that a lamb [ἀρνίον] was part of the meal,"[99] scholars such as C. K. Barrett and Joachim Jeremias pointed out long ago that πάσχα in Greek referred to both the Passover feast and to the lamb itself, and thus when the Synoptics speak of Jesus "eating the *pascha*" (Mk 14:12, Lk 22:15), they were noting the presence of a lamb.[100] Many of the activities allegedly prohibited during Passover were, in fact, permitted, since there was "a distinction [in the Law] between no work whatsoever (Sabbath) and no laborious work (feast day)."[101] Pitre points to the oft-noted improbability that the Sanhedrin would have conducted a trial and

---

[94] "On the eve of the Passover Yeshu was hanged. For forty days before the execution took place, a herald went forth and cried, 'He is going forth to be stoned because he has practiced sorcery and enticed Israel to apostasy. Any one who can say anything in his favour, let him come forward and plead on his behalf.' But since nothing was brought forward in his favour he was hanged on the eve of the Passover." *Sanhedrin* 43a. According to Mark Matson, "If this tradition has any claim to deriving from an early period in the Jewish memory of Jesus—and I think its claim is strong—it clearly suggests that Jesus was crucified (or hung) on the day before the Passover or Nisan 14 in agreement with John's gospel." Mark Matson, "The Historical Plausibility of John's Passion Chronology: A Reconsideration," in Paul N. Anderson, Felix Just, and Tom Thatcher, eds., *John, Jesus, and History*, vol. 2 (Atlanta, GA: SBL Press, 2007–16), 300.

[95] See, for example, Raymond Brown, "The Problem of Historicity in John," in *New Testament Essays* (New York: Doubleday, 2010), 191–221; James Charlesworth and Jolyon Pruszinski, eds., *Jesus Research: The Gospel of John in Historical Inquiry* (London: T&T Clark, 2019).

[96] C. H. Dodd, *Historical Tradition in the Fourth Gospel* (New York: Cambridge University Press, 1963), 120. See also Matson, "The Historical Plausibility of John's Passion Chronology."

[97] Brown, "The Problem of Historicity in John," 220. John Meier, who agreed with Brown's conclusions, maintained that Jesus arranged a "solemn farewell meal with his inner circle of disciples ... taking into account that he might not be able to celebrate the coming Passover meal.... The supper, though not a Passover meal and not celebrated as a substitute Passover meal, was nevertheless anything but an ordinary meal.... The tone would naturally be both solemn and religious, accompanied by all the formalities (reclining at table, drinking wine, singing hymns) that Jeremias uses to prove the Passover nature of the supper." Meier, *Marginal Jew*, 399.

[98] Brown, "The Problem of Historicity in John," 221.

[99] Brown, *Death of the Messiah*, 2:1364.

[100] C. K. Barrett, "Luke XXII.15: To Eat the Passover," *Journal of Theological Studies* 9 (1958): 305–7; Jeremias, *The Eucharistic Words of Jesus*, 17–19.

[101] Pitre, *Jesus and the Last Supper*, 296. Brown conceded that "one can find indications in Jewish tradition allowing every one of these actions on a feast," although he found "the conglomeration of so much activity on a feast day highly implausible." Brown, *Death of the Messiah*, 2:1358.

handed Jesus over to death on the day of Passover—something both Brown and Meier believed "highly implausible"[102]—and argues that Jewish law actually commanded false prophets to be tried on great feast days,[103] with trials on the night before feasts explicitly prohibited.[104] As for the reference in the Babylonian Talmud to Jesus dying on the eve of Passover, this assumes that the "Yeshu" mentioned in the text was Jesus of Nazareth, an unlikely assumption given that most of the details about him (e.g., his mode of death [hanging] and connections with the government) do not match the facts of Jesus's life.[105]

One argument long used to support the Johannine hypothesis deserves special attention, especially as it became a favorite of later Byzantine polemicists—that is, the fact that the gospels all speak of the bread at the Last Supper as ἄρτος (bread) rather than ἄζυμος (unleavened bread), which allegedly proves that Passover was not being celebrated. According to the proponents of this theory, which included Julius Wellhausen[106] and Jack Finegan,[107] "Unleavened bread cannot be designated 'bread' (ἄρτος) ... [and] only 'unleavened bread' (ἄζυμος) could properly be used in describing a Passover meal."[108]

Joachim Jeremias attacked this position on two fronts, first by pointing out that the biblical accounts of the Last Supper may have been colored by the Eucharistic practice of the early church, leading them to describe the loaf used that night as ἄρτος, or "bread," because that is what the first Christians used when remembering it. His second argument was the fact that "the words *lechem* and ἄρτος could be used of both leavened and unleavened bread," and that this "was quite the common practice."[109] Jeremias wrote that this claim can be "decisively proved" by "the extraordinary abundance" of places "in the Old Testament and the Mishnah, in the Targum, in the

---

[102] Meier wrote that it was highly unlikely that "at the time of Jesus, the supreme Jewish authorities in Jerusalem would arrest a person suspected of a capital crime, immediately convene a meeting of the Sanhedrin to hear the case (a case involving the death penalty), hold a formal trial with witnesses, reach a decision that the criminal deserved to die, and hand over the criminal to the Gentile authorities with a request for execution on the same day—all within the night and early day hours of Passover Day, the fifteenth of Nisan! Yet this is what the Synoptic passion chronology and presentation of the Jewish 'process' basically demand. In contrast, John's dating of Jesus' arrest at the beginning of the fourteenth of Nisan and his presentation of a more informal "hearing" before some Jewish officials during the night hours—while not without its own problems—does not labor under the same immense weight of historical improbability." Meier, *Marginal Jew*, 396.

[103] "A rebellious and incorrigible son, a defiant elder, one who leads people astray to worship idols, one who leads a town to apostasy, a false prophet, and perjured witnesses—they do not kill them immediately. But they bring them up to the court in Jerusalem and keep them until the festival, and then they put them to death on the festival" (*Tosefta*, Sanhedrin 11:7).

[104] "In non-capital cases the verdict, whether of acquittal or of conviction, may be reached the same day; in capital cases of verdict of acquittal may be reached on the same day, but a verdict of conviction not until the following day. Therefore trials may not be held on the eve of a Sabbath or on the eve of a festival day" (*Mishnah*, Sanhedrin 4:1).

[105] Johann Maier, *Jesus von Nazareth in der talmudischen überlieferung*, Erträge der Forschung; Bd. 82 (Darmstadt: Wissenschaftliche Buchgesellschaft, 1978), 263–75. For a different view see Peter Schäfer, *Jesus in the Talmud* (Princeton: Princeton University Press, 2007), 63–74.

[106] Julius Wellhausen, "Ἄρτον ἔκλασεν, Mc 14,22," Zeitschrift für die Neutestamentliche Wissenschaft 7 (1906): 182.

[107] Jack Finegan, *Die Überlieferung der Leidens- und Auferstehungsgeschichte Jesu* (Giessen: A. Töpelmann, 1934), 62.

[108] Jeremias, *The Eucharistic Words of Jesus*, 62–63.

[109] Ibid., 63.

Talmud and in the Septuagint" where the shewbread of the Temple, which was unleavened, "is *always* called simply 'bread.'"[110] Jeremias even showed where "the unleavened bread eaten during the feast of Passover could be described as *lechem* or ἄρτος" (e.g., Dt 16:3) in order to demonstrate that the gospels' use of ἄρτος "by no means excludes the possibility that the accounts of the Last Supper are accounts of a Passover meal."[111] Jeremias's position, now accepted by the majority of scholars, means that the old Byzantine argument in favor of John's chronology is no longer given much currency, despite the continued popularity of the Johannine hypothesis among modern exegetes.

The Synoptic Hypothesis

The Synoptic hypothesis—that Mark, Matthew, and Luke were substantively correct in their dating of the Last Supper—found its twentieth-century champion in Joachim Jeremias, whose *Eucharistic Words of Jesus* went to great lengths to defend the Passover nature of the meal.[112] His argument was that the Synoptic chronology was the more accurate, and that it was John who "changed the date of Jesus' execution"[113] in order to associate his death with the slaying of the Passover lambs[114] and show that "Jesus was the true Paschal lamb of God."[115] The strongest argument in favor of the

---

[110] Ibid., 63–64. For example, New Testament (Mk 2:26, Mt 12:4, Lk 6:4) references to the shewbread speak of τοὺς ἄρτους τῆς προθέσεως, using the term "bread" to describe the unleavened cakes. In Exodus 29:31–34 and Leviticus 8:31 Aaron and the priests are commanded to eat a sacrificial meal following the consecration of the priests. "The unleavened bread eaten by the priests on this occasion is called simply 'bread.'" Ibid., 64.

[111] "As a matter of fact, the contention that unleavened bread cannot be called 'bread' is incorrect." Ibid., 63. This view is supported by Joseph Fitzmyer (*Luke X–XXIV*, 1399), John Donahue and Daniel Harrington (*The Gospel of Mark*, 395), and Craig Evans (*Mark 8:27–16:20, Word Biblical Commentary 34b* [Nashville: Thomas Nelson, 2001], 389), among others.

[112] See also his earlier "The Last Supper," *Journal of Theological Studies* 50 (1949): 1–10. Jeremias was hardly alone. Among other supporters of the Synoptic hypothesis were Gerhard Lohfink (*Jesus of Nazareth: What He Wanted, Who He Was*, trans. Lina Maloney [Collegeville, MN: Liturgical Press, 2012]), E. P. Sanders (*The Historical Figure of Jesus* [London: Penguin, 1993], 285–86), C. K. Barrett (*The Gospel According to St. John* [Philadelphia: Westminster Press, 1978], 48–51), Craig Keener (*The Historical Jesus of the Gospels* [Grand Rapids, MI: Eerdmans, 2009], 372–74), Martin Hengel and Anna Marie Schwemer (*Jesus und das Judentum* [Tübingen: Mohr Siebeck, 2007], 582–86), Marcus Borg and John Dominic Crossan (*The Last Week: What the Gospels Really Teach about Jesus's Final Days in Jerusalem* [New York: Harper Collins, 2006], 110), Joachim Gnilka (*Jesus of Nazareth*, trans. Siegfried Schatzmann [Peabody, MA: Hendrickson, 1997], 279–87), and Rudolf Pesch (*Das Abendmahl und Jesu Todesverständnis* [Freiberg: Herder, 1978]).

[113] E.P. Sanders, *The Historical Figure of Jesus*, 285–86.

[114] Raymond Brown made the case that John even times Pilate's sentence of death at noon, "the very hour at which priests began to slaughter the paschal lambs in the temple area." Brown, *The Gospel According to John XIII–XXI*, 556. Pitre rejects this idea, arguing that the Passover lambs were slaughtered between 3:00 and 5:00 p.m. and not at midday and that Brown has no evidence "in support of his claim that the Passover lambs were sacrificed at noon." Pitre, *Jesus and the Last Supper*, 326.

[115] C. K. Barrett, *The Gospel According to St John*, 48–51. Rudolf Schnackenburg disputed this, concluding that "it would be wrong to assume that he deliberately changed the tradition to suit a theological intention. It is usually said that he wanted to present Jesus as the true passover lamb who died on the cross at the same time that the passover lambs were slaughtered in the Temple. Even this idea, however, lacks a firm foundation in the gospel. The evangelist does not in fact say this—it is simply a conclusion drawn from his chronology and his interest in the event of the Passover." Rudolf Schnackenburg, *The Gospel According to St. John*, vol. 3, trans. David Smith and G. A. Kon (New York: Crossroad, 1982), 36.

Synoptic hypothesis is how clearly and repeatedly the evangelists explicitly refer to the meal as a Passover celebration—they do so twelve times[116]—with Jeremias listing fourteen parallels between their accounts of the supper and first-century descriptions of Passover customs.[117] Furthermore, Jesus's interpretation of the bread and wine as his body and blood, which "is extremely difficult to explain in the context of an ordinary meal, however solemn," only makes sense "when his actions are situated in the context of a Jewish Passover meal" where "the act of interpreting the elements of the meal was already in place."[118]

Opposing the Synoptic hypothesis are those who maintain that despite the alleged similarities between Jesus's actions at the Last Supper and first-century Passover rituals, there are too many important elements missing for it to have been a Passover celebration.[119] As for the similarities noted by Jeremias, Jonathan Klawans wrote that "under greater scrutiny they are too general to be decisive.... While such behavior may have been characteristic of the Passover meal, it is equally characteristic of practically any Jewish meal."[120] Enrico Mazza is one of many who held that the Synoptic authors, not John, were the ones who changed the chronology for theological purposes as part of the larger process of "Passoverization" that came to "interpret the very person of Jesus in Passover terms."[121] Because they viewed the Last Supper "as the typological fulfillment of the Jewish Passover ... they gave it a detailed Passover character, even to the point of using a chronology that had the Last Supper being celebrated at the very moment of the Jewish Passover."[122] Yet despite all these critiques, a strong case remains for the Passover or Passover-like nature of the Last Supper, celebrated on, or perhaps in anticipation of, the first night of the feast, some scholars describing it as "something like holding a Christmas party on December 24."[123]

---

[116] Matthew 26:17, 18, 19; Mark 14:12 [2x], 14, 16; Luke 22:7, 8, 11, 13, 15. List taken from Pitre, *Jesus and the Last Supper*, 256.

[117] They include the fact that the meal was eaten (as was customary for Passover) in Jerusalem itself, it was eaten at night, Jesus and the apostles reclined at table, he broke the bread *during* the meal, they drank wine (as opposed to water), and they sang hymns. Jeremias, *The Eucharistic Words of Jesus*, 41–62. Brown, however, claimed these "Passover parallels are weak support. Many of them are drawn from mishnaic descriptions of Passover that are dubiously applicable to Jesus' time." Brown, *Death of the Messiah*, 2:1365.

[118] Pitre, *Jesus and the Last Supper*, 320.

[119] According to Ulrich Luz, "Nothing is said of the Passover lamb, of the bitter herbs and the matzos, nothing of the Passover Haggadah, nothing of the first Hallel.... It is especially strange for Jewish Christian readers that the narrator mentions only one of the four cups that ... absolutely belong to the Passover meal." Ulrich Luz, *Matthew 21–28: A Commentary* (Minneapolis, MN: Fortress Press, 2005), 372.

[120] "That Jesus ate a meal in Jerusalem, at night, with his disciples is not so surprising. It is also no great coincidence that during this meal the disciples reclined, ate both bread and wine, and sang a hymn." Jonathan Klawans, "Was Jesus' Last Supper a Seder?," *Bible Review* 17 (October 2001): 24–33.

[121] Enrico Mazza, *The Celebration of the Eucharist*, trans. Matthew J. O'Connell (Collegeville, MN: Pueblo Books, 1999), 25–26. Eugene La Verdiere noted that Paul does not link the Eucharist to the Passover, but that this first occurs in Mark. There "the theme of Passover ... was clearly related to that of the exodus and the manna as Christians began referencing the eucharist as 'our *epiousios* [daily/supersubstantial] bread.'" Eugene La Verdiere, *The Eucharist in the New Testament and the Early Church* (Collegeville, MN: Liturgical Press, 1996), 192–93.

[122] Enrico Mazza, *The Celebration of the Eucharist*, 25–26.

[123] Harrington, *The Gospel of Matthew*, 371. Jerome Kodell used a similar image, arguing that "It was not a Passover meal as such but had Passover motifs because of the proximity of the feast; as today, a family Christmas meal may take place during the season rather than on the day itself." Jerome Kodell, *The Eucharist in the New Testament* (Collegeville, MN: Liturgical Press, 1991), 42.

The Passover Hypothesis

Brant Pitre, who finds the arguments in favor of a Passover meal "convincing" but is unwilling to admit that John's chronology has been deliberately altered, suggests that the apparent contradictions between the Synoptics and John stem not from rival chronologies, but from a basic misunderstanding of the terminology of Passover, especially as it relates to the Feast of Unleavened Bread, which began immediately following.[124] According to Pitre, during the first century the term "Passover" was used to describe

- The Passover lamb (sacrificed 14 Nisan)
- The Passover meal (celebrated on the eve of 14/15 Nisan)
- The Passover peace offering "sacrificed and eaten during the seven-day feast of Unleavened Bread" (15–21 Nisan)
- The Passover week (15–21 Nisan).[125]

This situation arose because at some point the Feast of Passover and the seven-day Festival of Unleavened Bread were combined—scholars disagree exactly how and when this happened—so that Passover (with the eating of the lamb) became the first day of the Festival of Unleavened Bread.[126] In fact, by the time of Jesus, the two were so closely interconnected that "the term 'Passover' was generally used for both."[127] According to Baruch Bokser the New Testament consistently "treats Passover as part of the Festival of Unleavened Bread ... even using the latter term to refer to the former festival."[128]

This being the case, the alleged contradiction between John and the Synoptics on the dating disappears, because "John's multivalent use of the word 'Passover'" (e.g., in Jn 13:1, 18:28, 19:14) means that depending on the context he could be referring to the Passover meal, the Passover peace offering, or the weeklong celebration that takes place later.[129] For example, in John 13:1 ("Now before the festival of the Passover,

---

[124] Pitre is hardly the first to try to reconcile the two accounts. Aside from Jaubert and those who used calendar disputes to deal with the discrepancies, Brown mentions various other attempts to rearrange the sequence of events or see the Synoptics' description of a "pre-Passover" meal in perfect alignment with John's chronology. According to him, these "various attempts to reconcile the chronological discrepancies between the synoptics and John are implausible, unnecessary, and misleading. The two gospel traditions have given us irreconcilable chronological notices. Logically, then, neither or only one set of notices can be historical." Brown, *Death of the Messiah*, 2:1369.

[125] Pitre, *Jesus and the Last Supper*, 331.

[126] See J. Gordon McConville, "Deuteronomy's Unification of Passover and Maṣṣôt: A Response to Bernard M. Levinson," *Journal of Biblical Literature* 119 (2000): 47–58; Benjamin Kilchör, "Passah und Mazzot—Ein Überblick über Die Forschung Seit Dem 19. Jahrhundert," *Biblica* 94 (2013): 340–67.

[127] "Whereas the Old Testament distinguishes between the Passover, which was celebrated on the night of 14th–15th Nisan, and the feast of Unleavened Bread, held from the 15th to the 21st Nisan, in later Judaism the two were popularly combined and Passover was genuinely used for both. This is the predominant usage in the New Testament (Lk. 22:1; Mt. 26:2; Jn. 11:55, etc.; Acts 12:4)." Joachim Jeremias, "Pascha," Kittel and Friedrich, *Theological Dictionary of the New Testament*, 716 (5:898).

[128] Baruch Bokser, "Unleavened Bread and Passover, Feasts of," *Anchor Bible Dictionary* 6 (New Haven, CT: Yale University Press, 1992), 755–65. Luke, for example, directly makes this connection in 22:1 when he wrote that "the festival of Unleavened Bread, which is called the Passover, was near" even though Mark 14:1 appears to maintain at least a formal distinction between them ("It was two days before the Passover and the festival of Unleavened Bread").

[129] Pitre, *Jesus and the Last Supper*, 340.

Jesus knew that his hour had come to depart from this world and go to the Father") the evangelist is *not* referring to the thirteenth of Nisan (i.e., the day before the Passover lambs were sacrificed) but to the afternoon of the fourteenth—that is, a few hours before the Passover *meal*, which took place later that same night (i.e., on the eve of 15 Nisan) "when the Feast actually begins."[130] Thus for John, like the Synoptics, the supper eaten on the evening of the fourteenth/fifteenth would have been a Passover meal with "the crucifixion of Jesus on 15 Nisan, the first day of the weeklong feast of Passover ... and the day before the sabbath."[131] As for the later reference in John 18:28 that the Passover had not yet been celebrated ("They entered into the judgment hall, lest they should be defiled, but that they might eat the Passover"), Pitre argues that the evangelist here is not referring to the Passover lamb (as traditionally thought) but to the Passover peace offering, which still had to be eaten in a state of ritual purity. Combating the belief of Brown and others that John times Pilate's sentencing of Jesus with the slaughter of the Passover lambs on the fourteenth, Pitre argues that in John 19:14 the phrase "παρασκευὴ τοῦ πάσχα should not be understood as "the day of Preparation for the Passover" (i.e., 14 Nisan) but rather as the "Friday of Passover week," since παρασκευὴ was commonly used to refer to Friday, "the day of the week on which one would prepare for the Sabbath."[132]

If Pitre is correct, then John's gospel contains so many "Passover characteristics"—a fact noted even by proponents of the Johannine hypothesis[133]—because it was indeed a Passover meal. This is why, for example, John describes Jesus reclining at table (Jn 13:23-25), dipping morsels (13:26), and giving to the poor/purchasing last-minute items for the feast (13:29).[134] Thus there is good reason to conclude that despite the seeming discrepancies in their chronologies, both the Synoptics and John paint the

---

[130] Ibid., 343. Among the criticisms made of Pitre's theory is that while he assumes John 13:1 refers to the day of 14 Nisan, just hours before the Passover feast, "John 13:2 ('during supper') refers to the eve of 14/15 Nisan, that is, the Passover feast itself. This requires the sun to set between verse one and verse two, but there are no temporal indicators to suggest this." Daniel Frayer-Griggs, "Jesus and the Last Supper," *Reviews in Religion & Theology* 23 (April 2016): 161.

[131] Pitre, *Jesus and the Last Supper*, 367. Pitre cites previous scholars who proposed variations of his conclusion, such as Roger Beckwith, "The Date of the Crucifixion: The Misuse of Calendars and Astronomy to Determine the Chronology of the Passion," *Calendar and Chronology: Jewish and Christian. Biblical, Intertestamental, and Patristic Studies* (Leiden: Brill, 2001), 276–96; Barry Smith, "The Chronology of the Last Supper," *Westminster Theological Journal* 53 (1991): 29–45; Cullen I. K. Story, "The Bearing of Old Testament Terminology on the Johannine Chronology of the Final Passover of Jesus," *Novum Testamentum* 31 (1989): 316–24; C. C. Torrey, "The Date of the Crucifixion according to the Fourth Gospel," *Journal of Biblical Literature* 50 (1931): 227–441; C. C. Torrey, "In the Fourth Gospel the Last Supper Was the Passover Meal," *Jewish Quarterly Review* 42 (1951–52): 237–50. According to Brown, "Torrey's theory that Passover should be understood as the festival period of seven days and that John is speaking of Friday within Passover week has been refuted by Solomon Zeitlin, 'The Date of the Crucifixion According to the Fourth Gospel,' *Journal of Biblical Literature* 51 (1932): 263–271." Brown, *The Gospel According to John XIII–XXI*, 882.

[132] Pitre, *Jesus and the Last Supper*, 358. Rudolf Schnackenburg also endorsed this translation, arguing that in this verse "the day of preparation for the sabbath (that is Friday) is intended—the normal Jewish usage." Rudolf Schnackenburg, *The Gospel According to St. John* 3, 288.

[133] "That there are Passover characteristics in the meal, even in John, is undeniable." Brown, *Gospel of John* 2: 556.

[134] "The supposed command to give to the poor would be particularly appropriate to Passover night ... so far as the remark is historical it suggests that the event took place on Passover night." C. K. Barrett, *The Gospel According to St. John*, 448–49. According to Jeremias, "Some of the remarks made by John presuppose that this was a Passover meal." Jeremias, *Eucharistic Words of Jesus*, 81.

Last Supper as a Passover meal, which would have been celebrated on the eve of the fifteenth of Nisan with unleavened rather than leavened bread. Whether Pitre's argument achieves widespread acceptance remains to be seen, but given the available evidence, his conclusions on the Passover nature of the meal seem worthy of serious consideration.[135]

The Fathers and the Last Supper

As with most subjects, there is no clear and unambiguous consensus in the patristic corpus when it comes to the Passover nature of the Last Supper, or even the dating of that supper in relation to Christ's crucifixion.[136] For example, the third-century *Didascalia Apostolorum* claimed that Jesus did not celebrate the Passover the night before his death, as is suggested by the Synoptics, but rather on the third day of the week (Tuesday), several days earlier.[137] Allegedly containing the testimony of the apostles, it claimed that

> Judas [came] with the scribes and the priests of the people and delivered up the Lord Jesus. Now this was on the fourth day of the week; for when we were eating the Pascha on the third day of the week in the evening, when we went out to the Mount of Olives, they seized our Lord Jesus at night. And the next day was the fourth day, and he

---

[135] For an opposing view, see Helen Bond, "Dating the Death of Jesus: Memory and the Religious Imagination," *New Testament Studies* 59 (2013): 461–75. Bond claims that "Jesus' death actually took place some time (perhaps up to a week) prior to the day of Passover. I see no good reason to doubt that Jesus was executed on a Friday; the only thing that I want to challenge is the precise link between these events and the Passover.... It is no longer a question of looking for 14th or 15th Nisan, because Jesus' death could have happened at any date round about then perhaps the 11th or the 10th or the 9th Nisan. We simply have no way of knowing."

[136] Debate on these subjects first arose during the Quartodeciman Controversy—i.e., whether Pascha should be celebrated on the fourteenth of Nissan (the Jewish Passover) or on the following Sunday, which was the Roman custom. For the controversy see James Drummond, "The Fourth Gospel and the Quartodecimans," *American Journal of Theology* 1.3 (1897): 601–57; Frank Brightman, "The Quartodeciman Question," *Journal of Theological Studies* 25 (1923–24): 254–70; Nikolay Zernov, "Eusebius and the Paschal Controversy at the End of the Second Century," *Church Quarterly Review* 116 (1933): 24–41; Cyril Richardson, "The Quartodecimans and the Synoptic Chronology," *Harvard Theological Review* 33 (1940): 177–90; Bernhard Lohse, *Das Passafest der Quartadecimaner*, Beiträge zur Förderung christlicher Theologie 54 (Gütersloh: Bertelsmann, 1953); Clifford Dugmore, "A Note on the Quartodecimans," *Studia Patristica* 4 (1961): 411–21; W. H. Cadman, "The Christian Pascha and the Day of Crucifixion: Nisan 14 or 15," *Studia Patristica* 5 (1962): 8–16; Wolfgang Huber, *Passah und Ostern: Untersuchungen zur Osterfeier der alten Kirche*, Beihefte zur Zeitschrift für die neutestamentliche Wissenschaft 35 (Berlin: Töpelmann, 1969); Vittorino Grossi, "La Pasqua quartodecimana e il significato della croce nel II secolo," *Augustinianum* 16 (1976): 557–71; Raniero Cantalamessa, *Easter in the Early Church* (Collegeville, MN: Liturgical Press, 1993); Gerard Rouwhorst, "The Quartodeciman Passover and the Jewish Pesach," *Les Questions Liturgiques: Revue Trimestrielle* 77 (1996): 152–73; Jens Schröter, *Das Abendmahl: Frühchristliche Deutungen und Impulse für die Gegenwart*, Stuttgarter Bibelstudien 210 (Stuttgart: Katholisches Bibelwerk, 2006).

[137] For the *Didascalia Apostolorum* see Alistair Stewart-Sykes, trans. and ed., *The Didascalia apostolorum: An English Version with Introduction and Annotation* (Turnhout: Brepols, 2009). This work largely replaces the earlier R. Hugh Connolly, *Didascalia Apostolorum: The Syriac Version Translated and Accompanied by the Verona Latin Fragments with an Introduction and Notes* (Oxford: Clarendon Press, 1929). See also Paul Galtier, "La Date de la Didascalie des Apôtres," *Revue d'histoire ecclésiastique* 42 (1947): 315–51.

remained under guard at the house of Caiaphas the High Priest. And the same day the chiefs of the people gathered to take counsel against him.[138]

Later, in detailing the rules for fasting, it reaffirmed this chronology:

> You should fast on their behalf on the fourth day of the week, because on the fourth day of the week they began to destroy their souls and apprehended me.... For on the third day of the week I ate my Passover with you in the evening, and at night they seized me. And also you should fast on their behalf on the Friday, since then they crucified me, in the midst of their festival of unleavened bread.[139]

Although often cited as support for the Essene hypothesis, which also posits a Tuesday Passover, the *Didascalia* claims that the reason Jesus celebrated the feast on a Tuesday was not because of a calendar dispute, but rather because

> the priests and the elders determined and ordered and established that they should keep the festival without delay so that they could seize him without disturbance, for the people of Jerusalem were busy with the offering and eating of the Passover and all the people from outside had not yet come since they deceived them with regard to the days. They anticipated the Passover by three days, keeping it on the eleventh day of the month and the third of the week.[140]

Epiphanius, who is aware that many Christians of his time celebrated the Last Supper on a Thursday—he is, in fact, the earliest witness to this phenomenon—rejected this tradition in favor of a Tuesday commemoration.[141] Similar to the *Didascalia Apostolorum*, with which he was probably familiar, he maintained "the Jews came ahead of time and ate the Passover ... two days before its < proper > eating; that is, they ate it in the evening on the third day of the week, a thing that ought to be done at evening on the fifth day.... Jesus was arrested late on that same third day, which was the nighttime of the eleventh of the month, the sixteenth before the Kalends of April."[142] For Epiphanius the fact that Jesus was arrested after the Tuesday night Passover celebration (i.e., on Wednesday eve) helps explain why "we fast till the ninth hour on the fourth day and the eve of the Sabbath, because the Lord was arrested at the beginning of the fourth day and crucified on the eve of the Sabbath. And

---

[138] *Didascalia Apostolorum* 21; Eng. trans.: Stewart-Sykes, *Didascalia apostolorum*, 213–14.
[139] Ibid., 216.
[140] Ibid., 219.
[141] "Assuredly it was not on Thursday that our Lord ate the Passover ... but on Tuesday. That is why the Church commemorates the Lord's captivity on Wednesday.... So do not think it was Thursday evening that he was taken prisoner." Epiphanius, *Letter to Eusebius, Marcellus, Bibianus, and Carpus*, in Karl Holl, "Ein Bruchstück aus Einem Bisher Unbekannten Brief Des Epiphanius," in *Festgabe für Adolf Jülicher* (Tübingen: J.C.B. Mohr, 1927), 159–89; Eng. trans.: Joseph Kavanagh, "The Date of the Last Supper," *Philippine Studies* 6 (1958): 105.
[142] Epiphanius of Salamis, *Panarion*, 51; Eng. trans.: Epiphanius of Salamis, *Panarion of Epiphanius of Salamis, Book II and III (Sects 47–80, De Fide)*, 58. "In other words, Jesus was arrested on our Tuesday night. However, the 'nighttime of the eleventh of the month' should mean Wednesday night; Epiphanius, or the text, is confused here. Epiphanius might have read the phrase, 'late on the third day,' in his version of the *Didascalia*, and taken it as synonymous with 'nighttime of the eleventh.'" Ibid.

the apostles taught us to keep fasts on these days in fulfillment of the saying, 'When the bridegroom is taken from them, that shall they fast on those days.'"[143]

This idea, that the tradition of Wednesday fasting is connected to the day of Jesus's arrest,[144] is also seen in Victorinus of Petau, whose *De Fabrica Mundi* claimed that "the man Christ Jesus ... was taken prisoner [on the fourth day] by wicked hands, by a quaternion of soldiers. Therefore on account of His captivity by a quaternion ... we make the fourth day a station or a supernumerary fast."[145] Because "Victorinus does not appear to depend on the *Didascalia* for his account," the tradition that placed the arrest "on the fourth day of the week, Wednesday," must have "existed in the course of the second century ... [and] antedate both works."[146] Also important to note here is the fact that, like Epiphanius, both works share one key detail—explicitly or implicitly they testify that Jesus celebrated the Passover before his arrest.

Some early authors, many of whom tried to align Jesus's death with certain Old Testament prophecies, were unclear about the timing of Jesus's trial and execution, especially vis-à-vis the Passover. Justin Martyr, writing to the Jew Trypho, told him that "on the day of the Passover (ἐν ἡμέρᾳ τοῦ Πάσχα) you seized Him, and that during the Passover you crucified Him,"[147] which could mean either that Jesus was still at liberty on the first night of the feast (and thus able to celebrate a Passover meal) or that he was arrested before the celebration began.[148] It is also difficult to pin down Tertullian on the issue, as he wrote that Moses prophesied the death of Jesus by foretelling that "the sons of Israel were going to sacrifice a lamb in the evening (*quo agnum occiderunt ad vesperam*)" and eat it with bitterness on "the Passover of unleavened bread."[149] This, he said, foreshadowed "the Passover of the Lord—that is, the suffering of the Christ—because it was fulfilled in such a way that, on the first day of unleavened bread (*prima die azymorum*) you killed the Christ."[150]

---

[143] Epiphanius, *De Fide*, 22; Eng. trans.: Epiphanius of Salamis, *Panarion of Epiphanius of Salamis, Book II and III (Sects 47–80, De Fide)*, 679.

[144] Debate remains whether the *Didascalia*'s chronology influenced the creation of the Wednesday fast, or whether a preexisting fasting tradition found theological justification in a Wednesday arrest. Jeremias was convinced that the "fanciful" chronology "first found in the *Didascalia* is a secondary development out of the fasting practice of the church." Jeremias, *Eucharistic Words of Jesus*, 25. To prove Wednesday fasting came first, he cited the earlier *Didache* (8:1–3), which taught that the Wednesday and Friday fasts were instituted chiefly because they would not coincide with those of Pharisees ("Your fast must not take place at the same time as those of the hypocrites. They fast on Monday and Thursday; you are to fast on Wednesday and Friday"). In opposition, Jaubert's *The Date of the Last Supper* cited Tertullian's *On Fasting* (Wednesday and Friday fasting to commemorate "the taking away of the spouse") and *The Book of Adam and Eve* ("Adam, you have determined in advance the days that suffering will come upon me when I shall become flesh; those days are Wednesday and Friday").

[145] Marius Victorinus, *De Fabrica Mundi* 3 (ANF 7:341).

[146] Saulnier, *Calendrical Variations in Second Temple Judaism*, 35.

[147] Justin Martyr, *Dialogue with Trypho*, 111; Eng. trans.: Justin Martyr, *Writings of Saint Justin Martyr*, 320.

[148] According to George Ogg, Justin accepted the Johannine Chronology and thus the latter option was the more likely. He wrote: "We conclude that according to Justin Jesus was arrested on Thursday after 6:00 p.m. and therefore in the first, i.e., the night portion, and was crucified in the second, i.e., the day portion, of the 14th Nisan." George Ogg, *The Chronology of the Public Ministry of Jesus* (Cambridge: Cambridge University Press, 1940), 241. See also George Ogg, "The Chronology of the Last Supper," in Dennis Nineham, ed., *Historicity and Chronology in the New Testament* (London: SPCK, 1965), 75–96.

[149] Tertullian, *Against the Jews* 10.18; Eng. trans.: Tertullian, *Tertullian*, trans. Geoffrey Dunn, Early Church Fathers (London: Routledge, 2004), 65.

[150] Ibid. Cyril Richardson maintained that Tertullian "thinks that the slaying of the Passover lambs did *not* coincide with the Passion in point of time. If his phrase *prima die azymorum* is accurately used, the

Other fathers were clearer that Jesus did celebrate the Passover, Irenaeus of Lyons affirming that "six days before the day of Passover he came to Bethany. From Bethany he went up to Jerusalem and ate the pasch and suffered on the following day."[151] Origen, writing against those who were keeping Jewish customs, wrote that it was foolish to infer that because Jesus himself celebrated the Passover "according to the customs of the Jews (*more Judaico*), we, as imitators of Christ should do the same."[152] Cyril of Alexandria wrote in his *Commentary on Luke* that "Christ ate [the pascha] with them," interpreting the "lamb of the flock to be slain" as "the type of the true Lamb" who is Christ himself "sacrificed for us."[153] Other witnesses to Jesus's celebration of Passover include Ephrem the Syrian, who, despite a general reliance on the Johannine chronology,[154] explicitly mentions it in his *Sermons on Holy Week*,[155] and Aphraates, who wrote that "our Savior ate the Passover sacrifice with his disciples during the night watch of the fourteenth ... offer[ing] to his disciples the sign of the true Passover sacrifice."[156]

Perhaps the most oft-cited patristic witness to Jesus's celebration of Passover is John Chrysostom, who on several occasions affirmed that Jesus ate the Passover with his disciples "to indicate by all things unto the last day, that He was not opposed to the law."[157] For Chrysostom the Last Supper was a Passover meal where the "old Pasch [became] a type of the Pasch to come, and the reality ... supplant the type. So Christ first showed the foreshadowing and then brought the reality to the banquet table."[158] In his *Third Homily against Judaizing Christians*, Chrysostom held that Christ, a pious Jew, "did keep the Pasch ... so that he might bring the reality to what foreshadowed the reality. He also submitted to circumcision, kept the Sabbath, observed the festival

---

Passion must have followed the Passover meal." Cyril Richardson, "The Quartodecimans and the Synoptic Chronology," 189 n. 17. Conversely, Ogg argued that "the death of Jesus is put *prima die azymorum*; but since this is the day *quo agnum occiderunt ad vesperam* it is 14 and not 15 Nisan." Ogg, *The Chronology of the Public Ministry of Jesus*, 241.

[151] Irenaeus of Lyons, *Against the Heresies* 2.22.3; Eng. trans.: Irenaeus of Lyons, *Against the Heresies Book 2*, trans. Dominic J. Unger, ACW 65 (New York: Newman Press, 2012), 73. Interestingly, while Irenaeus "clearly follows the narrative of John, he follows the Synoptics in putting the crucifixion on the 15th Nissn." Ogg, *The Chronology of the Public Ministry of Jesus*, 241.

[152] Origen, *Commentary on Matthew*, 79; Eng. trans.: Origen, *The Commentary of Origen on the Gospel of St Matthew*, trans. Ronald Heine (Oxford: Oxford University Press, 2018).

[153] Cyril of Alexandria, *Homily 141 on the Gospel of Saint Luke*; Eng. trans.: Cyril of Alexandria, *Commentary on the Gospel of Saint Luke*, 566.

[154] In his *Commentary on the Diatesseron*, Ephrem asked the Jews: "Was it, therefore, necessary that, on the day when the lamb of your salvation was sacrificed, that too should have been [the day on which] the Lamb of our salvation was [likewise] sacrificed?" Ephrem the Syrian, *Saint Ephrem's Commentary on Tatian's Diatesseron: An English Translation of Chester Beatty Syriac MS 709*, trans. Carmel McCarthy (Oxford: Oxford University Press, 1993), 300.

[155] Edmund Beck, ed., *Ephraem Syrus. Sermones in Hebdomadam Sanctam*, 2 vols., CSCO 412-13 (Louvain: Secretariat du Corpus Scriptorum Christianorum Orientalium, 1979), 1.382.

[156] Aphraates, *The Demonstrations of Aphrahat, the Persian Sage*, trans. Adam Lehto (Piscataway, NJ: Gorgias Press, 2010), 282.

[157] John Chrysostom, *Homily 81 on Matthew*; NPNF 1.10.485.

[158] John Chrysostom, *Third Homily against Judaizing Christians* 4.1; Eng. trans.: John Chrysostom, *Discourses against Judaizing Christians*, trans. Paul Harkins, FC 68 (Washington, DC: Catholic University of America Press, 1979), 59.

days, and ate the unleavened bread."[159] Chrysostom even compared Jesus's fidelity to the law with the false piety of the Pharisees, whose hatred for Christ led them to postpone their own celebration of the feast so that they could bring about his death, thus explaining why they had not yet eaten the Passover in John 18:28. He wrote that while "Christ would not have transgressed as to the time of the Passover ... they, who were daring all things [were] trampling underfoot a thousand laws.... Boiling with rage ... [and] having then taken him unexpectedly, they chose even to pass by the Passover for the sake of satiating their murderous lust."[160]

This idea that the Jews postponed their eating of the Passover is also seen in Eusebius, although he gives a different reason. Eusebius believed that Christ wanted to institute "the mystery of his new covenant ... a new custom, and one foreign to the customary Jewish ways."[161] Because he wanted to distinguish new from old, "the Savior did not eat the Pascha along with the Jews," but rather "reclined at table with his disciples and conducted the festival that was desirable to himself" while "they were [still] sacrificing the lamb."[162] Eusebius maintained that this occurred, not because Christ celebrated the Passover early, but rather because the Jews celebrated it late. The Scriptures, he wrote, "present this fact clearly, for they testify that the Lord ate the Pascha on the first day of Unleavened Bread; but they did not eat the Pascha ... [until] the following day, which was the second day of Unleavened Bread and the fifteenth day of the lunar month. They did not eat it on the first day of Unleavened Bread, on which it had to be sacrificed, in accordance with the Law."[163]

However, while some authors believed that the Jews ate the Passover late (on 15 Nisan), others held that it was Jesus who celebrated the feast a day early (i.e., on the eve of the fourteenth). This allowed them to integrate the Synoptics' affirmation that Jesus celebrated the Passover within the Johannine chronology of Holy Week, which was, "down to the beginning of the third century, not only in Asia but throughout the Church generally ... more commonly received than the Synoptic."[164] Clement of Alexandria explained that Jesus, knowing he was to die, ate the Passover early because he desired to teach "the disciples the mystery of the type" and thus a "mystical

---

[159] John Chrysostom, *Third Homily against Judaizing Christians* 3.8; Eng. trans.: John Chrysostom, *Discourses against Judaizing Christians*, 58.

[160] Augustine also commented on the hypocrisy of the Pharisees, noting that because of the feast "it was a defilement for them to enter the dwelling of a foreigner. O ungodly blindness! They would be defiled, of course, by a foreign dwelling-place and would not be defiled by their own crime! They were afraid to be defiled by the praetorium of a foreign judge and were not afraid [to be defiled] by the blood of an innocent brother." Augustine of Hippo, *Tractates on John* 114; Eng. trans.: Augustine of Hippo, *Tractates on the Gospel of John 112–24*, trans. John Rettig, FC 92 (Washington, DC: Catholic University of America Press, 1995), 17.

[161] "The one set of practices, being now ancient and indeed antiquated—the [Pascha] which he used to eat along with the Jews—was not desirable; but the new mystery of his new covenant, which he imparted to his disciples, was desirable to him, quite rightly so." Eusebius of Caesarea, *On the Celebration of the Pascha*, translation by Andrew Eastbourne from *De sollemnitate Paschali* in Angelo Mai, *Novae Patrum Bibliotheca* 4 (1847), 209–16. http://www.tertullian.org/fathers/eusebius_on_easter.htm.

[162] They [i.e., the Jews] were doing this on the Preparation day on which the Savior suffered; for this reason, they did not enter the praetorium, but instead Pilate came out to them. But he [i.e., Jesus] a full day earlier, on the fifth day of the week, was reclining at table with his disciples." Ibid.

[163] Ibid.

[164] Ogg, *The Chronology of the Public Ministry of Jesus*, 239.

anticipation of the true Passover-Passion of the next day."[165] Interestingly, this approach found support in Chrysostom, who argued in his *Commentary on Matthew* that the phrase Τῇ δὲ πρώτῃ τῶν ἀζύμων in Matthew 26:17 should be understood not as "on the first day of unleavened bread" but rather "on the day before the unleavened bread."[166] Noted by modern scholars, and long recognized by later Byzantine polemicists, is the fact that if Jesus did celebrate the Passover on the eve of the fourteenth rather than the fifteenth, then "he could not have done so with unleavened bread, because on this day the leaven had not yet been removed from Israel."[167]

There is another tradition among the fathers, also found in Chrysostom, that while Jesus ate the Passover, his celebration of the feast preceded the institution of the Eucharist, which itself was a separate event that took place only once the meal was ended. In this reading Ἐσθιόντων δὲ αὐτῶν (Mt 26:26) was understood to be not "while they were eating" but rather "when the meal was finished."[168] Thus for Chrysostom, Jesus waited until after the Passover celebration, "after the things of the law should end," and then "abolishes their main festival by seating [the disciples] at another table full of holy awe [saying], 'Take, eat, This is my body, Which is broken for many.'"[169] Similarly Jerome wrote that "after the figurative Passover had been fulfilled and he had eaten the flesh of the lamb with the apostles, he took bread ... and passed over to the true mystery of the Passover."[170] John of Damascus also testifies to this tradition, writing that when Jesus "had eaten the old Pasch with his disciples in the upper chamber ... and fulfilled the old testament, he washed the feet of his disciples.... Then, after he had broken bread, He gave it to them saying ..."[171]

Yet despite all these witnesses to Jesus's celebration of Passover, there was another school of thought that maintained that he did not eat a Passover meal, a view that became increasingly popular as the fathers consciously tried to distinguish the Jewish feast, now abrogated, from the true Pascha celebrated by Christians.[172] Their argument was that since "our paschal lamb, Christ, has been sacrificed" (1 Cor 5:7) and the true

---

[165] "Accordingly, in the years gone by, Jesus went to eat the passover sacrificed by the Jews, keeping the feast. But when He had preached, He, who was the Passover, the Lamb of God, led as a sheep to the slaughter, presently taught His disciples the mystery of the type on the thirteenth day.... It was on this day, then, that both the consecration of the unleavened bread and the preparation for the feast took place.... And on the following day our Saviour suffered, He who was the Passover, propitiously sacrificed by the Jews." Clement of Alexandria, *Fragments from the Chronicon Pascale*; ANF 2:581.

[166] "By the first day of the feast of unleavened bread, he means the day before that feast; for they are accustomed always to reckon the day from the evening, and he makes mention of this in which in the evening the passover must be killed," John Chrysostom, *Homily 81 on Matthew*; NPNF 1.10.485.

[167] "That is an indication that the 'lawful' Passover that Jesus celebrated on the evening prior to the Passover day was not yet the true Passover. It is only a type of the true Passover lamb that he himself became when he was killed on the day of the Passover." Luz, *Matthew 21-28*, 355-56.

[168] According to Luz, "In the church's traditional interpretation there is almost unanimous agreement that the institution of the Eucharist was the institution of a separate ritual that took place after the Passover celebration was completed. It was understood that ἐσθιόντων ... αὐτῶν meant not 'while they were eating' but 'immediately, when the meal was finished, before they got up, before the table was cleared.' Thus the Lord's Supper instituted by Jesus is not a Passover; it replaces the Jewish Passover." Ibid., 372-73.

[169] John Chrysostom, *Homily 82 on Matthew*; Eng. trans.: Luz, *Matthew 21-28*, 372-73.

[170] Jerome, *Commentary on Matthew*, 26.26-27; Eng. trans.: Jerome, *Commentary on Matthew*, 297.

[171] John of Damascus, *On the Orthodox Faith* 4.13; Eng. trans.: John of Damascus, *Writings*, trans. Frederic Chase, FC37 (Washington, DC: Catholic University of America Press, 1958), 356.

[172] In discussing the Ebonites Epiphanius quoted their version of the gospel, in which Jesus did *not* celebrate the Passover, because (as a vegetarian) he would not want to eat the meat of the lamb. "A Passover, as

Passover had arrived, there was no longer need for the type, which was why Jesus himself had dispensed with it. Hippolytus of Rome, for example, argued that "Jesus did not eat the Passover of the law. For he was the Passover that had been of old proclaimed."[173] Apollinaris of Hierapolis claimed that Jesus's last meal was a "supper ... and not yet the Passover food" (δεῖπνον ... καὶ οὔπω τοῦ πάσχα βρῶμα) since he himself was "the true Pascha, the great sacrifice, that was offered in place of the lamb and was buried on the day of Passover."[174] The witness of Scripture (i.e., John's gospel) was clear on the matter, despite the claims of the Quartodecimans, "who assert[ed] that the Lord ate the lamb on the fourteenth day and that he suffered on the great day of unleavened bread; and they interpret Matthew as saying what they imagine to be the case."[175] This understanding is also evident in the *Fragments* of Peter of Alexandria:

> After His public ministry [Jesus] did not eat of the lamb, but Himself suffered as the true Lamb in the Paschal feast.... On that day, therefore, on which the Jews were about to eat the Passover in the evening, our Lord and Saviour Jesus Christ was crucified.... It is not the case, as some who, carried away by ignorance, confidently affirm that after he had eaten the Passover, he was betrayed.... He did not eat of the legal Passover; but, as I have said, He Himself, as the true Lamb, was sacrificed for us in the feast of the typical Passover, on the day of the preparation, the fourteenth of the first lunar month.[176]

While some authors tried to reconcile the alleged differences in the gospels' chronologies, others passed over them in silence. Augustine, for example, recognized potential discrepancies about when Passover occurred, especially in relation to the anointing at Bethany,[177] but gave scant attention to the question of how Jesus could celebrate the Passover when he died on the Day of Preparation.[178]

I said, was meat roasted with fire and the rest. But to destroy deliberately the true passage these people have altered its text—which is evident to everyone from the expressions that accompany it—and represented the disciples as saying, 'Where wilt thou that we prepare for thee to eat the Passover?' and he supposedly saying, 'Did I really desire to eat meat as this Passover with you?'" Epiphanius of Salamis, *Panarion* 30; Eng. trans.: Epiphanius of Salamis, *Panarion of Epiphanius of Salamis, Book I (Sects 1–46)*, 2nd ed., trans. Frank Williams (Leiden: Brill, 2009), 150.

[173] Hippolytus of Rome, *Fragment cited in the Chronicon Pascale*; ANF 5:240. According to Cyril Richardson, this was based on his belief that the legal period for eating the Passover had not yet come and thus it was only an ordinary supper. Richardson, "The Quartodecimans and the Synoptic Chronology," 185 n. 14.

[174] Apollinaris of Hierapolis, *Fragment 131 on Mt 26:20 and 130 on Mt 26:17–18*, in Joseph Reuss, *Matthäus-Kommentare aus der griechischen Kirche* (Berlin: Akademie-Verlag, 1957), 44–45; Eng. trans.: Luz, *Matthew 21–28*, 355.

[175] Apollinaris of Hierapolis, *Fragment Concerning the Pascha* in *Chronicon Pascale*; Eng. trans.: J. van Goudoever, *Biblical Calendars* (Leiden: Brill, 1961), 150. The Quartodecimans were early Christians who calculated the date of Pascha using the fourteenth of Nisan, which meant that their celebration of Easter was not necessarily on a Sunday, as was the custom in Rome.

[176] Peter of Alexandria, *Fragments*; ANF 6:282.

[177] According to Matthew and Mark the anointing took place two days before Passover, but John said it was six. Augustine of Hippo, *Agreement among the Evangelists* 2.78.153; Augustine of Hippo, *The New Testament I and II*, 251–52.

[178] Augustine did address the hour of the crucifixion (since Mark 15:25 described it as the third hour [9:00 a.m.] and John has Jesus condemned at the sixth [noon]), but little about the date. Augustine of Hippo,

Tatian's *Diatessaron* (or at least an early version of it) took a different approach to the problem of harmonizing the chronologies by separating "the Johannine foot-washing meal from the Synoptic Passover meal," creating, "in effect, two Last Suppers."[179] According to Nicholas Zola, Tatian even placed John's meal (the "second-to-last supper") first "for the express purpose of making the actual Last Supper an explicit Passover meal."[180]

In light of the evidence presented, it is clear that despite the claims of later Latin and Byzantine polemicists there is no clear patristic consensus on the Passover nature of the Last Supper, the date on which it was celebrated, or the type of bread that would have been used. Debates on the dating of Easter, the continuing relevance of Jewish tradition, and the relation between the new and old covenants all affected how they thought about the Last Supper and its relation to the Passover. That the fathers, examining the biblical witness, should come to different conclusions on this issue is not surprising. Neither is it surprising that both East and West would later try to truncate the patristic witness and claim only one position as that of the fathers, discounting the richness of the tradition and the questions that helped shape it. Sad, yes, but hardly surprising.

The Bread of the Eucharist in the Early Church

There is one aspect of the later Byzantine argument against azymes—that is, the relative novelty of the Latin practice—that most scholars today do not dispute, as it seems that the use of leavened bread throughout the West was normative until the ninth to tenth centuries.[181] This was recognized by Catholic scholars as far back as the seventeenth century (e.g., in the *Disquisitio de azymo* of Jacques Sirmond [d. 1651]), and today it is almost universally accepted even if it remains unproved. The famed twentieth-century liturgical historian Joseph Jungmann wrote that it was only in the

---

Agreement among the Evangelists 3.13.40–44; Augustine of Hippo, *The New Testament I and II*, 282–84. See also Augustine of Hippo, *Tractate 117 on the Gospel of John*; Augustine of Hippo, *Tractates on the Gospel of John*, 33–35.

[179] Nicholas Zola, "Tatian's Diatessaron and the Passion Chronology" (PhD diss., Abilene Christian University, 2009), 134. Zola comes to this conclusion after studying the manuscript tradition in an effort to reconstruct Tatian's original version, although he acknowledges some of the problems it raises (e.g., two of the earliest witnesses to the *Diatessaron*, Ephrem the Syrian and Aphrahat, do not mention a "'Second-to-Last Supper' solution in their relevant writings"). See also Matthew Crawford and Nicholas Zola, eds., *The Gospel of Tatian: Exploring the Nature and Text of the Diatessaron* (London: T&T Clark, 2019); William Peterson, *Tatian's Diatessaron: Its Creation, Dissemination, Significance, and History in Scholarship* (Leiden: Brill, 1994).

[180] Nicholas Zola, *Tatian's Diatessaron and the Passion Chronology*, 141.

[181] "The same baking method and ovens were used by the Christians for both their daily bread and that which was to be used in worship. It must be made clear that (contrary to practices today in the West) in the Early Christian centuries and in all eastern rites through the ages, except in the Armenian church, the bread used for the Church did not differ from ordinary bread in substance. From the beginning leavened bread was used. Even the Armenians before the seventh century and the Maronites before their union with Rome in the twelfth century used leavened bread. The practice of using unleavened bread for the Eucharist was introduced to the West much later." George Galavaris, *Bread and the Liturgy: The Symbolism of Early Christian and Byzantine Bread Stamps* (Madison: University of Wisconsin Press, 1970), 54.

ninth century that "various ordinances appeared ... all demanding the exclusive use of unleavened bread for the Eucharist" and that this "new custom did not come into exclusive vogue [in Rome] until the middle of the eleventh century" and then only under certain northern influences.[182] Even more polemically minded Catholic texts from the nineteenth and early twentieth centuries were forced to acknowledge that the use of unleavened bread "does not seem to come from the first age. Rather it appears that at Rome too leavened bread was used originally.... Unless there was a principle of using azyme certainly ordinary bread would have been taken. There seems no doubt that this was so."[183]

Supporting this claim is the early church's consistent use of "loaf" (ἄρτος) or "common bread" (κοινὸς ἄρτος) for the Eucharistic offering, especially after the second and third centuries, when Christians became more scrupulous about differentiating ἄρτος (bread) from unleavened bread in order to distinguish their rites from those of the Jews.[184] For many early Christians the use of ἄζυμος was a relic of the old Law that had been done away with, for now that Christ (the reality) had come, there was no further need of the type.[185] For this reason they described azymes as "unclean" (ἀκάθαρτα) and poured scorn on the Jews' continued use of unleavened bread for the Passover.[186] The Jews, who understood Scripture in a "carnal sense," did not know that "like Cain's mark [the old Passover] has achieved its purpose" and should be abolished.[187] In fact, some have even speculated that it was "the great abhorrence of Judaism felt by early Christians" combined with azymes' close association with the Jewish rites that led the church to use leavened bread for its own ceremonies.[188] However, it is far more likely that leavened bread was adopted because the Eucharist

---

[182] Jungmann, *The Mass of the Roman Rite*, vol. 2, 34. "During the first millennium of Church history, however, it was the general custom in both East and West to use normal 'daily bread,' that is, leavened bread, for the Eucharist." Emminghaus, *The Eucharist*, 161.

[183] Adrian Fortescue, *The Mass: A Study of the Roman Liturgy* (New York: Longmans, Green, 1922), 301. John Philoponus (d. 580), in his work *On Pascha*, argued that "if our Lord had used unleavened bread, the church would have kept up the same practice to the present time," which seems to testify that "he knew nothing of the custom" of unleavened bread. W. A. Bulbeck, "The Eucharistic Bread," *Downside Review* 13 (1894): 30–36.

[184] For example, Justin Martyr references the "bread, and a cup of water, and a cup of wine mixed with water" brought up to the "Ruler of the Brethren." Justin Martyr, *First Apology* 1.65; Eng. trans.: Justin Martyr, *The First and Second Apologies*, trans. Leslie William Barnard, ACW 56 (New York: Paulist Press, 1997), 70.

[185] "That both the Passover and Feast of Unleavened Bread were likewise images, Paul the apostle makes plain by saying, 'As our Passover, Christ has been sacrificed,' and, 'that ye may be unleavened, not partaking of leaven'—by 'leaven' here he means evil—'but that ye may be a new lump.'" Ptolemy, *Letter to Flora* 3.9; Eng. trans.: Epiphanius of Salamis, *Panarion of Epiphanius of Salamis, Book I (Sects 1–46)*, 219.

[186] "Surely [Chrysostom] could not have said [this] if he knew of unleavened bread being used in the Eucharist." Reginald Maxwell Woolley, *The Bread of the Eucharist* (London: Mowbray, 1913), 11.

[187] Augustine of Hippo, *Commentary on Psalm* 39.8; Eng. trans.: St. Augustine, *Exposition on the Psalms* vol. 2, 209. See also John Chrysostom, *Discourse* 3.4 (p. 59): "The old pasch was a type of the pasch to come, and the reality had to supplant the type.... Once the reality has come, the type which foreshadowed it henceforth lost in its own shadow and no longer fills the need.... I am showing you that Christ not only did not command us to keep the festival days but even freed us from the obligation to do so." John Chrysostom, *Third Homily against Judaizing Christians* 4.1; Eng. trans.: John Chrysostom, *Discourses against Judaizing Christians*, 59.

[188] "And when we consider the great abhorrence of Judaism felt by early Christians, it is highly probable that in token of this abhorrence, azymes were discontinued." John Mason Neale, *History of the Holy Eastern Church*, 1059.

had its roots in the shared meal, and it was natural for the "common bread" used at table to become the bread broken and blessed by the presider.[189]

The idea that the bread was, throughout most of the patristic period, κοινὸς ἄρτος (common bread, meant for eating), from which the believer received a κλάσμα (broken piece), was interpreted in two different ways.[190] The first was to draw a distinction between the Eucharist before and after the consecration—that is, without necessarily engaging in the metaphysical speculation that would characterize later Western debates on the subject, there was already a recognition that this "common bread" somehow became the bread of life. As early as the mid-second century Justin Martyr maintained that "not as common bread and common drink (κοινὸν ἄρτον οὐδὲ κοινὸν πόμα) do we receive these; but in like manner as Jesus Christ our Saviour, having been made flesh by the Word of God, had both flesh and blood for our salvation."[191] Irenaeus of Lyons, similarly wrote: "For as the bread, which is produced from the earth, when it receives the invocation of God, is no longer common bread, but the Eucharist, consisting of two realities, earthly and heavenly; so also our bodies, when they receive the Eucharist, are no longer corruptible, having the hope of the resurrection to eternity."[192] Ambrose wrote, "You may perhaps say: 'My bread is usual (*Meus panis est usitatus*).' But that bread is bread before the words of the Sacraments; where the consecration has entered in, the bread becomes the flesh of Christ.... Before it be consecrated it is bread; but where the words of Christ come in, it is the body of Christ."[193] Paul the Deacon related a story of Pope Gregory the Great, who was celebrating mass when a woman expressed doubts that this common *panis*, which she had made "by her own hands," could become the body of Christ. Gregory implored God to enlighten her, and just when he finished praying, the bread prepared by the woman changed into flesh.[194]

The second way "common bread" was interpreted was with reference to the church's unity, since by partaking in the Eucharist Christians came to share in and/or become

---

[189] See, for example, David Power, *The Eucharistic Mystery: Revitalizing the Tradition* (New York: Crossroad, 1993); Dennis Smith, *From Symposium to Eucharist: The Banquet in the Early Christian World* (Minneapolis, MN: Fortress Press, 2003).

[190] Concerning the κλάσμα there was frequent reference to the gathering of bread fragments in John 6:12-13, so that even "as this broken bread lay scattered upon the mountains and became one when it had been gathered, So may your church be gathered into your kingdom from the ends of the earth." *Didache* 9:4; Kurt Niederwimmer and Harold W. Attridge, *The Didache: A Commentary* (Minneapolis, MN: Fortress Press, 1998), 144.

[191] Justin Martyr, *First Apology* 1.66; Eng. trans.: Justin Martyr, *The First and Second Apologies*, 70.

[192] Irenaeus of Lyons, *Against the Heresies* 4.18.5; ANF 1:486.

[193] Ambrose of Milan, *The Sacraments* 4.4.14, 4.5.23; Eng. trans.: Ambrose of Milan, *Theological and Dogmatic Works*, trans. Roy J. Deferrari, FC 44 (Washington, DC: Catholic University of America Press, 1963), 302, 305.

[194] As retold in the *Golden Legend*, "A certain woman used to bring altar breads to Gregory every Sunday morning, and one Sunday, when the time came for receiving communion and he held out the Body of the Lord to her, saying: 'May the body of our Lord Jesus Christ benefit you unto life everlasting,' she laughed as if at a joke. He immediately drew back his hand from her mouth and laid the consecrated Host on the altar, and then, before the whole assembly, asked her why she had dared to laugh. Her answer: 'Because you called this bread, which I made with my own hands, the Body of the Lord.' Then Gregory, faced with the woman's lack of belief, prostrated himself in prayer, and when he rose, he found the particle of bread changed into flesh in the shape of a finger. Seeing this, the woman recovered her faith." Jacobus de Voragine, *The Golden Legend: Readings on the Saints*, trans. William Granger Ryan (Princeton: Princeton University Press, 1993), 179-80.

one loaf (εἷς ἄρτος), mentioned in 1 Corinthians 10:17 ("Because there is one bread, we who are many are one body, for we all partake of the one bread"). Cyprian of Carthage wrote that

> the Lord's body can neither be flour alone nor water alone but requires both to be united and fused together so as to form the structure of one loaf of bread (*panis unius*). And under this same sacred image our people are represented as having been made one, for just as numerous grains are gathered, ground, and mixed all together to make one loaf of bread, so in Christ, who is the bread of heaven, we know that there is but one body, and that every one of us has been fused together and made one with it.[195]

Augustine used the same logic, likening the water that joined individual grains to the sacrament of baptism, and the fire that baked the bread to the Holy Spirit. He wrote:

> In this loaf of bread (*in isto pane*) you are given clearly to understand how much you should love unity. I mean, was that loaf made from one grain? (*Numquid enim panis ille de uno grano factus est?*) Weren't there many grains of wheat? But before they came into the loaf they were all separate; they were joined together by means of water after a certain amount of pounding and crushing.... Then came baptism, and you were, in a manner of speaking, moistened with water in order to be shaped into bread. But it's not yet bread without fire to bake it. So what does fire represent? That's the chrism, the anointing. Oil, the fire-feeder, you see, is the sacrament of the Holy Spirit.[196]

Chrysostom commented on the same passage: "For as the bread consisting of many grains is made one, so that the grains nowhere appear ... so are we conjoined both with each other and with Christ: there not being one body for you, and another for your neighbor to be nourished by, but the very same for all ... Now if we are all nourished of the same and all become the same, why do we not also show forth the same love, and become also in this respect one?"[197]

Although it appears likely that the church of the first several centuries used leavened bread for the Eucharist, there seem to have been some exceptions to this general rule. For example, the *Panarion* of Epiphanius mentions the use of unleavened bread by the Ebionites, a Jewish-Christian group whose heresies are chronicled by the author. Epiphanius wrote that "they celebrate supposed mysteries from year to year

---

[195] Cyprian of Carthage, *Letter 63.13*; Cyprian of Carthage, *The Letters of Cyprian of Carthage*, vol. 3, trans. G. W. Clarke, ACW 46 (New York: Newman Press, 1986), 105.

[196] Augustine of Hippo, *Sermon 227*; Eng. trans.: Augustine of Hippo, *Sermons*, vol. III/6, trans. Edmund Hill, O.P. (Hyde Park: New City Press, 1993), 254. He also took up this same theme in a Pentecost sermon: "One bread; what is this one bread? The one body which we, being many, are. Remember that bread is not made from one grain, but from many. When you were being exorcised, it's as though you were being ground. When you were baptized it's as though you were mixed into dough. When you received in the fire of the Holy Spirit, it's as though you were baked. Be what you can see, and receive what you are." Augustine of Hippo, *Sermon 272*; Eng. trans.: Augustine of Hippo, *Essential Sermons*, trans. Edmund Hill (Hyde Park, NY: New City Press, 2007), 318.

[197] John Chrysostom, Homily 24 on First Corinthians; NPNF 1.12.140.

in imitation of the sacred mysteries of the church, using unleavened bread—and the other part of the mystery with water only."[198] The other group were the Armenians, who, we know from the early seventh-century Catholicos Moses II (574–604), refused to "cross the River Azat [and] eat the baked bread or drink the warm water of the Greeks" in Constantinople.[199] When and how the Armenians started using unleavened bread is still an open question—Galavaris argued that they used leavened bread "before the seventh century,"[200] while others claimed that the use of azymes goes all the way back to Gregory the Illuminator (d. 331).[201] During the Council of Manzikert (726), at which the Armenians negotiated union with the Syrian Jacobite Church, canons were issued "exclud[ing] leaven and water from the life-giving mystery" since it was "a pretext for asserting the corruptibility of the flesh of Christ."[202] Important to note about the Ebonites and the Armenians is that because the Greeks connected their use of azymes to the heresies they espoused, later generations of Byzantines were already preconditioned to see unleavened bread in the Eucharist as the manifestation of some greater error. The conclusion they reached was therefore simple—if the Latins used azymes, then they too, like the Ebonites and Armenians, must be heretics.

Yet the Latins of the seventh and eighth centuries were likely still using leavened bread, as witnessed by the Venerable Bede, who wrote of the *panis nitidus* ("pure" or "white" bread) being used in the Eucharist of the English church.[203] Later that century the Sixteenth Council of Toledo (693) demanded that clergy should only use bread specially prepared for the purpose, and that it should be *integer et nitidus* ("whole and pure").[204] Among the first signs that things might have changed occur

---

[198] Epiphanius of Salamis, *Panarion* 30; Eng. trans.: Epiphanius of Salamis, *Panarion of Epiphanius of Salamis, Book I*, 143.

[199] Gérard Garitte, ed., *La Narratio de rebus Armeniae*, Corpus scriptorum Christianorum Orientalium, 132 Subsidia 4 (Louvain: L. Durbecq, 1952), § 102, 40; Eng. trans.: Krzysztof Stopka, *Armenia Christiana: Armenian Religious Identity and the Churches of Constantinople and Rome (4th–15th century)*, trans. Teresa Baluk-Ulewiczowa (Crakow: Jagiellonian University Press, 2016), 79.

[200] See n. 181.

[201] This was the Armenians' position as stated by John IV of Odzun (d. 729) at the Synod of Dvin (719): "It is right to offer unleavened bread and pure wine on the holy altar, according to the tradition handed down to us by St Gregory. And we must not stoop to the traditions of other races of Christians." Cited in Woolley, *The Bread of the Eucharist*, 53–54.

[202] Woolley, *The Bread of the Eucharist*, 55.

[203] After the death of Sabert, king of the East-Saxons, his sons returned to idolatry and began to harass the church. Bede reported: "There is a story that when they saw the bishop, who was celebrating solemn mass in church, give the Eucharist to the people, they said to him, puffed up as they were with barbarian pride, 'Why do you not offer us the white bread which you used to give to our father Saba' (for so they used to call him) 'and yet you still give it to the people in church?' The bishop answered them, 'If you are willing to be cleansed in the same font of salvation as your father was, you may also partake of the holy bread as he did. But if you despise its life-giving waters, you certainly shall not receive the bread of life.' They answered, 'We will not enter the font because we know that we have no need of it, but all the same we wish to be refreshed by the bread.'" Bede, *The Ecclesiastical History of the English People*, 2.5; Eng. trans.: Bede, *The Ecclesiastical History of the English People*, 79. Du Cange considered *panis nitidus* a rendering of καθαρὸς ἄρτος (e.g., as in Ignatius of Antioch's *Letter to the Romans*, where he asked to "be found to be the pure bread [καθαρὸς ἄρτος] of Christ"). Charles Du Cange et al., eds., *Glossarium mediae et infimae latinitatis, Tomos sextus* (Niort: Favre, 1886), 135.

[204] "*Ut non aliter Panis in altari Domini sacerdotali benedictione sanctificandus proponatur, nisi integer et nitidus.*" A similar canon was issued by the Eighth Council of Chelsea (787), demanding that the offerings of the faithful should not be mere crusts of bread (*oblationes quoque fidelium tales fiant ut panis sit non crusta*). This was done, said Woolley, because "frequently, instead of using bread which has specially and reverently been prepared for this holy use, the clergy have just taken bread from their own larders, any piece of a loaf

in the ninth century with Rhabanus Maurus (d. 856), who spoke of the use of *panem infermentatum* in his work *de Institutione Clericorum*.[205] Alcuin of York had earlier mentioned in *Epistle 90* that "the body of Christ is consecrated without addition of any other agent (*absque ferment ullius alterius infectionis*),[206] but this reference seems "to oppose the use of salt" rather than leaven.[207] Yet the custom seems to have been changing, with increased mention of unleavened bread found in the decades that followed.[208] The ubiquity of the practice and how quickly it occurred remains subject to debate. The fact that Photios (d. 893) never mentions the Latins' use of azymes makes it likely that the custom was still unknown to him, which would support the idea that unleavened bread did not achieve widespread acceptance in the West until the late ninth or early tenth century.[209] Within a few decades the old practice seems to have been completely forgotten, and by the eleventh century the use of unleavened bread was accepted in the West as an ancient, indeed apostolic, custom.

As to why this development occurred, there are several hypotheses. The most likely has to do with the reservation of the sacrament, since "leavened bread is much more difficult to keep in anything like a fresh condition than unleavened."[210] The practice of the *sancta* (whereby pieces of the previous day's Eucharist were saved and then placed in the chalice in order to demonstrate continuity in time) and the *fermentum* (where a piece of the consecrated bread from the bishop's mass was taken and distributed to other celebrations in the city) both became part of the Latin liturgical tradition rather early.[211] As a result, "Specific practices developed at the Sunday eucharist regarding

---

being sufficient, and, cutting it into a round cake, have used it in the celebration. It is evident that this is not unleavened bread." Woolley, *The Bread of the Eucharist*, 17.

[205] Rhabanus Maurus, *De institutione clericorum* 1.31 (PL 107:318) "*Ergo panem infermentatum et vinum aqua mistum in sacramentum Corporis et Sanguinis Christi sanctificari oportet, quia ipsasres de se Dominum testificari Dominicum evangelium narrat*." See also Joseph Ernst, *Die Lehre des hl. Paschasius Radbertus von der Eucharistie: Mit besonderer berücksichtigung der Stellung des hl. Rhabanus Maurus und des Ratramnus zu derselben* (Freiburg: Herder, 1896).

[206] Alcuin of York, *Epistle 90* (PL 100:289).

[207] Robert Cabié, *The Church at Prayer*, vol. 2: *The Eucharist*, trans. Matthew O'Connell (Collegeville, MN: Liturgical Press, 1986), 132.

[208] "The use of unleavened bread, already practiced by the Armenians, became general in the West in the eleventh century; this presupposes that it had been introduced here and there a little earlier." Ibid., 132 n. 13. "In the ancient church the use of unleavened loaves, still in practice in the Orthodox churches of the East, was the norm. The same was true in the Western church in some places until the eleventh century. Such loaves can be seen in illustrations in such ancient manuscripts as the Corpus Christi Gospels and Ashburnham Pentateuch, and in the ninth-century Augsburg Gospels, Drogo Sacramentary, and Raganaldus Sacramentary. But a new practice had begun at least by the ninth century in the West, and this later led to the Eucharistic controversies and schism between the Eastern and Western churches in the eleventh century." Roger Reynolds, "Christ's Money: Eucharistic Azyme Hosts in the Ninth Century According to Bishop Eldefonsus of Spain: Observations on the Origin, Meaning, and Context of a Mysterious Revelation," *Peregrinations: Journal of Medieval Art and Architecture* 4.2 (2013): 1–69.

[209] There is the possibility, albeit a very slim one given Photios's other complaints against the Latins, that Photios knew of the practice but did not object to it since the anti-Armenian polemic had not become part of the Byzantine tradition.

[210] Woolley, *The Bread of the Eucharist*, 21. According to Cabié, "Practical reasons, having to do especially with the reservation of the species, must have played a part" in the adoption of unleavened bread. Cabié, *The Eucharist*, 132.

[211] Early references to the practice in Rome come from *Liber Pontificalis*—Pope Miltiades (311–14) "brought about that consecrated offerings from what the bishop consecrated should be sent around to the

the treatment of the consecrated host," with increased sensitivity about the condition/ type of bread being used.[212] Alongside this, the advent of the Eucharistic debates in the West, which took place "precisely at the same moment... the controversy over azymes developed," meant that there was also greater concern to distinguish the Eucharist from "common bread."[213] Whereas earlier fathers had used the idea of κοινός ἄρτος to stress the miraculous change in the elements—from common bread to body of Christ—now "uncommon [i.e., unleavened] bread" was adopted to help Christians believe that what was offered at mass was indeed something extraordinary.[214]

A Quick Note on Spurious Texts

Before leaving, a word should perhaps be said about those spurious or misattributed texts later used in the azyme debate. On the Greek side the most significant were *De Azymis* (Περὶ τῶν Ἀζύμων), which in the eighteenth century was attributed to both Athanasius and Epiphanius,[215] the *Sixth Heresy of the Armenians* (attributed at different times to John of Damascus, Methodius, and Photios, although its author "claims to be quoting a certain Meletius"),[216] and another anti-azymite tract allegedly by John Damascene. On the other side, several eleventh-century Latin authors claimed that in

---

churches," while Pope Siricius (384–99) decreed that "no priest should celebrate mass every week without receiving the guaranteed consecrated element from the designated bishop of the place—this is called the *fermentum*." *Liber Pontificalis: The Book of Pontiffs*, trans. Raymond Davis (Liverpool: Liverpool University, 1989), 13, 29. See John F. Baldovin, "The Fermentum at Rome in the Fifth Century: A Reconsideration," *Worship* 79 (2005): 38–53; Nicholas Paxton, "The Eucharistic Bread: Breaking and Commingling in Early Christian Rome," *Downside Review* 122.427 (April 2004): 79–93. These practices are to be differentiated from the *Malka*, or "the holy leaven" (which ironically contains no leaven) used by the Church of the East. In this rite a "special dough powder" is added to the Eucharistic bread before baking. Containing *khmira* (fermented dough from previous batches), it is said to contain a remainder of the bread used at the Last Supper. See Mar Awa Royel, "The Sacrament of the Holy Leaven (Malkā) in the Assyrian Church of the East," in Cesare Giraudo, ed., *The Anaphoral Genesis of the Institution Narrative in Light of the Anaphora of Addai and Mari: Acts of the International Liturgy Congress Rome 25–26 October 2011* (Rome: Edizioni Orientalia Christiana, 2013), 363–86; Bryan Spinks, "The Mystery of the Holy Leaven (Malka) in the East Syrian Tradition," in Johnson, ed., *Issues in Eucharistic Praying in East and West*, 63–70.

[212] David Grumett, *Material Eucharist* (Oxford: Oxford University Press, 2016), 241. See also Nathan Mitchell, *Cult and Controversy: The Worship of Eucharist outside Mass* (Collegeville, MN: Liturgical Press, 1990).

[213] Brett Whalen, "Rethinking the Schism of 1054: Authority, Heresy, and the Latin Rite," *Traditio* 62 (2007): 9. The logic was that "it was less likely that people should regard the consecrated sacrament as 'mere bread' if the bread [itself] was not common [i.e., leavened]." Woolley, *Bread of the Eucharist*, 21.

[214] This idea that the host was not regular bread is the basis for the oft-told joke that "being a Catholic requires two leaps of faith—believing that that the bread becomes the true body of Christ, and believing that it was really bread to begin with."

[215] Athanasius, *De Azymis* (PG 26:1327–32). According to Mahlon Smith, "It was published first in 1769 under the name of Athanasius, although the editor himself questioned this attribution. Hergenröther noted that the related portions in Niketas's Armenian speech are ascribed by him to Epiphanius. And Schweinburg mentions another related manuscript which in fact claims the great heresiologist as author." Smith, *And Taking Bread*, 63.

[216] Smith maintained that this text "was first edited in 1712 by M. LeQuien as the longer of two anti-azyme tracts he found ascribed to John Damascene in Parisian manuscripts. But since the bulk of the text appears elsewhere ascribed to Methodius and Photios, it is of uncertain authorship and quite possibly pseudonymous." Ibid., 62–63.

119 Pope Alexander I ordered that unleavened bread should be used in the Eucharist, but this testimony is of dubious authenticity. There was also a legend, used frequently throughout the thirteenth century and found in various forms, of Pope Leo (briefly) allowing leavened bread only to fight the Eboniates' Judaizing tendencies, but then returning to the (more ancient) use of leavened bread.[217] Another text with an interesting history is a passage allegedly from Gregory the Great, later included in both the *Tractatus contra Graecos* (1252) and the *Summa Theologica* (P 3, Q 74, Art 4) of Thomas Aquinas. The passage, which Antoine Dondaine argued first appeared in the late twelfth century, was frequently used and cited as part of the *Vita*, although it is now known to be spurious.[218]

---

[217] In its most elaborate form, as given by Thomas of Strassburg (d. 1357), it says that "as a great many doctors relate, from the beginning of the establishment of this sacrament down to Pope Leo, the entire Church of God prepared it with unleavened bread. But in the time of Pope Leo, in order to extirpate the heresy of the Ebionites who were stating that it was necessary for salvation that every human had to observe the ceremonial precepts of the law along with the observation of the gospel, and consequently to consecrate with unleavened bread, the church then ordered it that it be prepared with leavened bread. Next, after the passing of some years, when the aforesaid heresy had been completely extirpated, the priests in Latin regions resumed the first way, namely consecrating with unleavened bread, because it is clearly deduced from the gospel that Christ celebrated with unleavened bread, as was clear above. But the priests of Greece did not resume the first way, but have continued of consecration in leavened bread until the present time. Whence it is clear that these foolish Greeks, asserting that we do not consecrate since we use unleavened bread in consecrating, impute this madness to their fathers and their most holy doctors and all their priests who preceded Pope Leo." Thomas of Strasbourg, *In quartum librum Sententiarum*, d.11, q. 2, a.1 quoted in Schabel, "The Quarrel over Unleavened Bread in Western Theology, 1234–1439," 121.

[218] Dondaine, "Contra Graecos," 357–62. "It is certainly customary to put the question about how in the church some offer leavened and others unleavened bread. We know that the Church is distributed in four orders, namely, that of the Romans, the Alexandrians, the Jerusalemites and the Antiochenes, which are commonly called 'churches.' And while they hold one Catholic faith, they use different mysteries of [divine offices]. Whence it happens that the Roman Church offers unleavened bread because the Lord took up the flesh without any [sexual] union.... Therefore the body of Christ is brought about with unleavened bread. The other churches mentioned above offer leavened bread, because the Word of the Father was clothed in flesh and is true God and true man, so that the leaven is mixed with the flour and the true body of our Lord Jesus Christ is brought about. But when we, both the Roman Church and the other abovesaid churches take both leavened and unleavened bread for the ineffable faith, the one true body of our Savior is brought about." Riedl, ed., *Tractatus contra Graecos* (1252), 82; Eng. trans.: Schabel, "The Quarrel over Unleavened Bread in Western Theology, 1234–1439," 110.

4
The Azyme Debate
The Eleventh and Twelfth Centuries

It is a historical fact that the debate over Eucharistic bread, and not the Filioque or the power of the pope, was the immediate cause of the schism that eventually split the Christian world. Although not part of the ninth century debates between Photios and the Carolingians—probably because at that point there was no difference in practice—by the eleventh century the Latins' use of unleavened bread in the Eucharist was considered by many to be sufficient reason for breaking communion with them. According to Mahlon Smith, this was because the Byzantines believed that

> the azyme question [had] considerable theological significance, [since] the bread is not a peripheral phenomenon in the Eucharist, but rather the focal point in the liturgical *Gestalt*. In the eyes of the faithful it becomes the visible presence of the Lord, the body of Christ, a divine host offered men for their salvation. So any difference in its use or interpretation can alter one's whole understanding of the Christian act of worship and the theology that it implies.[1]

Unfortunately for the cause of Christian unity, the Greeks' first attacks on the Latins' use of azymes occurred precisely at the moment the papacy was emerging from the *saeculum obscurum* and coming to understand its mission in universalist terms. Thus the criticisms of Leo of Ohrid and Michael Keroularios were perceived not only as an assault against the Latins' orthodoxy, but also against the authority of the Roman See, which now saw itself as the "head and mother of the churches" (*caput et mater ecclesiarum*).[2] For this reason Rome took up the challenge and answered accordingly, although (and this is significant) it did not ask the Byzantines to change their practice, but only to recognize the legitimacy of its own.[3]

---

[1] Smith, *And Taking Bread*, 29–30.

[2] "The fact that less compromising voices in the Roman Church ... seized upon the Eucharistic controversy to draw a line in the sand between 'Catholic' Latin and 'heretical' Greeks should hardly provoke surprise. For the supporters of the reformed papacy the dispute over the unleavened Eucharist was linked to the definitions of orthodoxy and authority within their own religious community as well as their universalist vision of Rome's primacy over the universal Church.... Like Berengar of Tours, the Greek patriarch and his followers had challenged Rome's interpretation of the Eucharistic sacrifice and its reading of salvation history. Both were rejected as heretics whose attack on Catholic Christendom was repulsed by the bishops of Rome. In these terms the azyme controversy was more than just a minor liturgical squabble." Whalen, "Rethinking the Schism of 1054," 23.

[3] "The first and most important thing one discovers in the sources is that there is a distinct lack of parallel between the Greek and Latin positions as presented in the Western texts. The Greeks maintain that the Latins cannot perform the sacrament with unleavened bread, that is, the Body of Christ simply cannot be made with unleavened bread. The Latins, on the other hand, universally accept the validity of the Greek sacrament using leavened bread.... For Western theologians, then, the primary reason for the existence of the

The fervor generated by the azyme debate might be hard for moderns to understand, but recent scholarship has gone a long way in explaining the Byzantines' hostility to the change in Latin practice in light of conflicts with groups recently brought back into the empire by conquests—for example, monophysite Syrians and Armenians—who (not coincidentally) also used unleavened bread.[4] The logic was almost algebraic—"If Armenians used unleavened bread, were Judaizers, and denied the formula of Chalcedon regarding the two natures of Jesus Christ, and if Latins also used unleavened bread, then the Latins were also Judaizers and Monophysites."[5] Unlike their shaving and fasting practices, which were often listed with the Latins' other errors without the need for detailed refutation, the use of azymes was countered by the Byzantines with painstakingly thorough argumentation. Even the most irenic of Byzantine churchmen regarded it as an error, although many of them remained unwilling to break communion with Rome, believing the less-enlightened Latins were still capable of instruction by their wiser Eastern kin.

According to Yury P. Avvakumov, the theological case against the Latins' Eucharistic practice, first made in the eleventh century, changed little over the centuries and centered on four major critiques: (1) it was Judaizing, (2) it was "dead" since it lacked the yeast needed to "animate" or "ensoul" the dough, (3) it was contrary to the example of Christ since the Scriptures (i.e., John) were clear that the Last Supper was not a Passover meal, and (4) it was celebrated without ἄρτος (the term applied to the bread Jesus himself used).[6] This last bit was significant, because according to the etymological argument of the Byzantines, "Jesus took ἄρτος. But ἄρτος is derived from αἴρω as well ἐπαίρω, and φέρω ἐπὶ τὰ ἄνω, [meaning] to elevate and raise up and carry to the heights," so therefore it must have contained leaven.[7] However, the most damning criticism might have been that the Latins' introduction of unleavened bread was a novelty, and that in changing the long-standing practice of the church they had signaled the embrace of some new error, or worse, all the errors of the ancient church combined.

The West, in response, claimed that it was only following the example of the Savior, for the Synoptic Gospels were clear that he had celebrated the Last Supper, a Passover meal, with unleavened bread. The Byzantines' argument regarding the symbolic

---

question is the Greeks' denial of the validity of the Latin rite." Schabel, "The Quarrel over Unleavened Bread in Western Theology, 1234–1439," 92.

[4] "These victories brought people into the empire would have been beyond its borders for a century or more. Their reintegration posed a demographic problem, which the 11th century transcribed and prolonged into a religious problem—that is to say, into a crisis of identity.... The groups who re-entered the empire considered themselves orthodox, catholic, apostolic Christians, but theologians in the great capital on the Bosporus tended to label some of them as heretics." Kolbaba, "Byzantine Perceptions of Latin Religious 'Errors,' " 122. The same principle can be applied to the Jews, who in 1051 had revolted against Byzantine rule in Bari and were thus considered a dangerous religious "other." If the Latins used unleavened bread they too, like the Jews at Passover, "revealed that they were too attached to the Old Testament world of shadows and types, and not convinced of the grace of the new dispensation." Ibid., 125.

[5] Kolbaba, "Byzantines, Armenians, and Latins: Unleavened Bread and Heresy in the Tenth Century," 56.

[6] Yury P. Avvakumov, *Die Entstehung des Unionsgedankens. Die lateinische Theologie des Mittelalters in der Auseinandersetzung mit dem Ritus der Ostkirche*, Veröffentlichungen des Grabmann-Institutes zur Erforschung der mittelalterlichen Theologie und Philosophie, 47 (Berlin: Akademie-Verlag, 2002), 103–11.

[7] Erickson, "Leavened and Unleavened," 135–36.

affinity between "yeast" and "soul" was, to their mind, both "bizarre" and "crazy," and the Scriptures themselves spoke of leaven almost exclusively in negative terms.[8] Besides, they claimed, the Eucharist can still be celebrated with leavened bread without harm, so there was no need to dispute the matter provided everyone agreed on what was truly important—the real presence of Christ *after* the consecration.

The Byzantines did not feel similarly, and azymes remained (alongside the Filioque) the chief point of dispute throughout the crusading period. As John Erickson once wrote: "For most Byzantine churchmen of the eleventh and twelfth century, the principal point of disagreement with the Latins was not papal primacy or even the *filioque*, but rather the use of leavened bread in the Eucharist."[9] Latins became "azymites," a derogatory term that would be used for the next several centuries to describe the Christians of the West. Anti-azymite tracts proliferated throughout the twelfth century, and for Greeks living under Latin rule opposition to the azymite Eucharist of the West became the shibboleth of orthodoxy. By the beginning of the thirteenth century, the lines separating prozymite and azymite were clear, with little hope that the gap between them could ever be bridged.

The Eleventh Century

The "heresy of the *fermentacei*, which poured scorn on the holy Roman See, or rather the whole Latin and western church, for offering a living sacrifice to God in unleavened bread,"[10] began in southern Italy, where Greeks and Latins had coexisted in relative peace for many years, albeit with occasional tensions.[11] However, this fragile balance was upset—by whom it is still debated[12]—and a new debate arose at a time when their shared disdain of the Normans should have made Rome and Constantinople natural allies. Some blame Argyros, the Byzantine commander (δούξ) of southern Italy and bête noire of Keroularios, who, it was said, communed with azymes.[13] Others blame the Normans and their desire to suppress Greek customs by replacing "the ordinary

---

[8] Yury Avvakumov, "Sacramental Ritual in Middle and Later Byzantine Theology: Ninth–Fifteenth Centuries," in Hans Boersma and Matthew Levering, eds., *The Oxford Handbook of Sacramental Theology* (Oxford: Oxford University Press, 2015), 259–60.

[9] Erickson, "Leavened and Unleavened," 134. See also Michele Giuseppe D'Agostino, *Il primato della sede di Roma in Leone IX (1049–1054), Studio dei testi latini nella controversia greco-romana nel periodo pregregoriano* (San Paolo: Cinisello Balsamo, 2008).

[10] *The Life of Pope Leo IX*, in Robinson, *The Papal Reform of the Eleventh Century*, 146.

[11] See chapter 2 n. 84 and 85.

[12] For different opinions see Judith Ryder, "Changing Perspectives on 1054," *Byzantine and Modern Greek Studies* 35 (2011): 20–37; Tia Kolbaba, "1054 Revisited: Response to Ryder," *Byzantine and Modern Greek Studies* 35 (2011): 38–44. See also Donald Nicol, "Byzantium and the Papacy in the Eleventh Century," *Journal of Ecclesiastical History* 13 (1962): 1–20.

[13] "Argyros [was] a practitioner of Latin rites and ... esteemed in papal circles, judging by the *Vita* of Leo IX.... Virtually the embodiment of the blurring of culturo-religious identities, [he] became a bête noire in some quarters in Constantinople ... [and] was the object of particular loathing by Michael Keroularios, who on his own avowal often debated with him in Constantinople, 'most of all about azymes.' Complaining that Argyros 'never forgot his own form of worship ... and was ever ill-disposed towards Romania,' he refused him Communion repeatedly," (141). Jonathan Shepard, "Storm Clouds and a Thunderclap: East-West Tensions towards the Mid-eleventh Century," in Marc Lauxtermann and Mark Whittow, eds., *Byzantium in the Eleventh Century: Being in Between* (London: Routledge, 2017).

leavened bread in the eucharist [with] the unleavened bread favoured by the Latins."[14] This practice, which "sharply marked off Greek from Latin ... affected ordinary people, for it concerned what they did when they worshipped," bringing the differences between East and West from the "realm of theory" into the real world.[15]

The initial Greek response to this new situation came from Leo of Ohrid (d. 1056),[16] who in 1053 wrote a letter to John of Trani listing several Frankish practices he found objectionable.[17] Among them were several items that Photios had mentioned centuries earlier, but now a new charge had been added—"the matter of matzos (ἀζύμων) and Sabbaths."[18] This was not the first time the Greeks had objected to unleavened bread in the Eucharist, for the Byzantines had likely attacked its use in their debates with "azymite" non-Chalcedonians a decade earlier.[19] Now the arguments from these earlier encounters were turned against the Latins, whose use of unleavened bread became the focus of Leo's wrath.

---

[14] Andrew Louth, *Greek East and Latin West: The Church AD 681–1071*, The Church in History 3 (Crestwood, NY: St. Vladimir's Seminary Press, 2007), 306–7. Kolbaba disagrees, arguing that there was religious tolerance and that "the popes and Latin bishops of southern Italy did not express contempt for Greek ritual.... Even when the pope recognized Norman sovereignty in southern Italy and asserted his own patriarchal rights in the region, the Latins left the Greek monasteries and many of the Greek churches unmolested.... Greeks and Latins in southern Italy still thought that Christian unity transcended differences of rite. This can be seen in the ways that the Greek monasteries and Greek bishops of southern Italy reacted to Norman rule and a revived papal presence in their region." Kolbaba, "The Virtues and Faults of the Latin Christians," 119.

[15] According to Louth these differences had always been known, but now the differences were "on the doorstep; ordinary people became aware of different customs and had to live with them, or not." *Greek East and Latin West*, 307.

[16] In addition to Büttner see Eleonora Naxidou, "The Archbishop of Ohrid Leo and the Ecclesiastical Dispute between Constantinople and Rome in the mid 11th Century," *Cyrillomethodianum* 21 (2016): 7–19.

[17] Leo hoped his letter would receive wider circulation, claiming that he was writing "to your holiness and through you, to all of the archbishops of the Franks and, through you, to his reverence, the Pope." Leo of Ohrid, *Epistula ad Ioannem Episcopum Tranensem* in Büttner, *Erzbischof Leon von Ohrid*, 180; all the English translations of this letter are by Joseph Ahmad, *First Epistle of the Bishop of Bulgaria Sent to a Certain Bishop under Rome regarding Matzos (Azymes) and Sabbaths*. https://www.academia.edu/39045414/Leo_of_Ochrid_1st_Epistle_to_John_of_Trani_on_azymes_1054_DRAFT.

[18] "Curiously enough, Leo focused on the ritual differences thus, silencing the [older] doctrinal dispute about the procession of the Holy Spirit." Naxidou, "The Archbishop of Ohrid Leo and the Ecclesiastical Dispute between Constantinople and Rome in the mid-11th century," 12.

[19] Kolbaba, "Byzantines, Armenians, and Latins: Unleavened Bread and Heresy in the Tenth Century," 45–57; the exact relation between the anti-Armenian and anti-Latin polemics is the subject of some debate. Kolbaba believes that "in the decade before the more famous events of 1054, a group of anti-Chalcedonian, 'azymite' Christians debated with Chalcedonian, leavened-bread Christians. From these debates came some of the first treatises against azymes. This battle with the Armenians had a negative impact on discussions with Latins." Kolbaba, "Byzantine Perceptions of Latin Religious 'Errors,'" 123. Judith Ryder disagrees, claiming that the "thesis that the Armenian side of the dispute was established well before the controversy with the Latins, and that the Greek polemicists of 1054 were drawing on already-assembled material ... is not strongly supported as presented." Ryder, "Changing Perspectives on 1054," 30 n. 43. This argument echoes the earlier debate between Anton Michel and Joseph Hergenröther, as "Michel claimed the anti-azyme arguments were formulated by Keroularios and his immediate circle for the political struggle with Rome and then disseminated from Constantinople to Antioch, southern Italy etc. Only at a later date was this material adapted for the controversies with the Armenians. Hergenröther seems to affirm the opposite, i.e., that the azyme controversy was already well-developed in ecclesiastical struggles internal to Byzantium before the city of Constantinople came into conflict with Rome." Smith, *And Taking Bread*, 62. See also Anton Michel, "Die vier Schriften des Niketas Stethatos über die Azymen," *Byzantinische Zeitschrift* 35 (1935): 308–36; K. Schweinburg, "Die Textgeschichte des Gesprächs mit den Franken von Niketas Stethatos," *Byzantinische Zetischrift* 34 (1934): 313–47; Hergenröther, *Monumenta graeca ad Photium*, 8–9.

Chief among the charges Leo made was that the Latin practice was Judaizing, for by "celebrating them [i.e., the mysteries] in a Mosaic and unfitting (ἀσυντηρήτως) manner, you have fellowship with the Jews ... [who] were commanded to keep matzos and the Sabbaths by Moses; but Christ is our Pascha, who, lest he be thought impious (ἀντίθεος), both was circumcised and, at first, observed the Pascha of the Law; but then, having put that one to rest, made ours anew (ἐκαινούργησε)."[20] Unlike the Passover of the "unhappy (ἄθλιος) Jews" commemorated with matzo and bitter herbs as "symbols of misery and grief ... our Pascha is joy and mirth entire and it elevates us from the earth through joy (χαρᾶς) to heaven, as even the leaven does to the bread through its own heat, which, in partaking of salt and leaven, is full of sweetness."[21] Leo, citing Matthew's account of the Last Supper, argued that the institution of the new covenant abrogated the old, including the use of azymes, for "having spoken of the new [covenant], he showed that the old has passed away and was put to rest."[22]

Leo then went on to talk about the difference between ἄρτος (bread) and ἄζυμος (unleavened bread), arguing that "the word ἄρτος comes from 'I lift up' (αἴρω) as well as 'I raise' (ἐπαίρω) and 'I bear upward' (φέρω ἐπὶ τὰ ἄνω), having heat and having arisen (ἔπαρσιν) due to the yeast and the salt. Unleavened bread, on the other hand, differs not from a lifeless stone or a brick of clay or a piece of ceramic, compacted with earth and made with dry clay."[23] Leaven in Scripture was a positive thing, "For if the salt and the leaven were evil, why has Christ, having 'salted' the disciples with these names and having 'fermented' them with the grace of the Holy Spirit, named them the light and life (or leaven) of the world?"[24] Paul, when speaking of the remembrance of Christ in the Eucharist, had used ἄρτος, proving that in the use of "unleavened bread neither has *anamnesis* of the Lord, nor does it proclaim His death."[25] Therefore Leo urged the Latins to end the use of matzo and leave "the whole of the Mosaic Law ... to the Jews, some of whom are as the blind feeling for the wall, casting off the light[,] ever resist[ing] it in the darkness as the mindless and stupid."[26]

In a second letter Leo repeated many of the same points, emphasizing that "it was not Moses but Christ who died for us" and that Christ "teaches us to overlook the Mosaic Law as evil and false."[27] He asked the Franks, "why, after the law has been ceased by Christ, do you observe the use of unleavened bread like the Jews and the

---

[20] Leo of Ohrid, *Epistula ad Ioannem Episcopum Tranensem*, in Büttner, *Erzbischof Leon von Ohrid*, 180. For background on the charge of Judaizing see Avvakumov, *Die Entstehung des Unionsgedankens*, 37–46.
[21] Leo of Ohrid, *Epistula ad Ioannem Episcopum Tranensem*, in Büttner, *Erzbischof Leon von Ohrid*, 182, 184.
[22] Ibid., 182. He later reinforced this point, arguing that "the divine Apostle says that 'if perfection were through the Levitical priesthood, Christ would not have been called according to the order of Melchisidech' (Hb. 7:11) and that 'with the change in priesthood, by necessity, there occurs a change in the law' (Hb. 7:12). Thus, according to the same apostle, when the Law had ceased, of necessity even the use of unleavened bread is ceased." Ibid., 186.
[23] Ibid., 182.
[24] Ibid., 184.
[25] Ibid., 186.
[26] Ibid., 192.
[27] Büttner, *Erzbischof Leon von Ohrid*, 212, 218; all the English translations of this letter are by Joseph Ahmad, *Second Epistle of Leo of Ochrid concerning Azymes*, https://www.academia.edu/40414778/Second_epistle_of_Leo_of_Ochrid_concerning_Azymes.

erroneous Armenians?"²⁸ It is true that Christ ate the "legal Pascha," which was the type (τύπος) of the true Pascha, just as "the azymes of the Jews were a type of our Pascha" but Leo stressed that "the type does not save the prototype. Why? Because unleavened bread has neither salt nor leaven nor upward rising, but it is only a clay-like dough made from flour. Moreover, our Pascha is a type of the Heavenly Pascha hereafter: that Pascha is superior to the one we observe now."²⁹ The Scriptures were clear that "bread and wine (ἄρτον καὶ οἶνον) are to be offered in the divine mysteries with prayers, not indeed the azymes (ἄζυμα) or whatever the old Law said" and that if the Latins continued in their ways, they would be "concelebrat[ing] with the Jews, the Armenians, the Jacobites, and the rest" and not with the church of Christ.³⁰

Leo's attack elicited an immediate response from the pope and his allies, who perceived it as a direct assault on Rome's orthodoxy and authority. In reply Cardinal Humbert of Silva Candida (d. 1061) one of the leading lights of the Reform movement, penned a response to Leo and Patriarch Michael Keroularios in the name of Pope Leo IX, although the letter was probably never sent.³¹ He accused Leo and Michael of a "strange presumption, ... incautious reprehension ... [and] evil boasting" for publicly condemning the Latin church because "it dared to celebrate the commemoration of the passion of the Lord from the azymes."³² It was inconceivable that these bishops should presume to teach the Roman church how to celebrate the Lord's Supper as if the See of St. Peter were unaware of such matters.³³ He told them to

> come to your senses from such madness and cease mockingly calling the truly catholic Latins, closer disciples of the most eminent Peter and more devout followers of his teaching, azymites. Stop denying them their churches and stop inflicting the torments, as thus you have begun to do, if you wish now and forever to have your peace and portion.³⁴

---

²⁸ Ibid., 208. "Now, [God] ordered the [Jews] to eat these things [i.e., unleavened bread] with bitter herbs (or with bitterness/repentance) only for seven days, although the Franks and the Lombards do not disdain eating such through the whole of their lives." Ibid.

²⁹ Ibid., 212.

³⁰ Ibid.

³¹ Leo IX, *Epistola ad Michaelem Constantinopolitanum Archiepiscoporum*, in Will, *Acta et Scripta*, 65–85. For debates about the precise authorship of this letter see J. Joseph Ryan, "Cardinal Humbert De s. Romana ecclesia: Relics of Roman-Byzantine Relations 1053/54," *Medieval Studies* 20 (1958): 206–38; Margit Dischner, *Humbert von Silva Candida: Werk und Wirkung des lothringischen Reformmönches* (Neuried: Ars Una, 1996), 51–67. According to Brett Whalen, the "tendency to attribute texts of uncertain authorship to Humbert," which he blames on Anton Michel, "is not necessarily sound. Margit Dischner has persuasively argued that these compositions in defense of the Latin church might best be thought of as 'communal' efforts, overseen perhaps by Humbert, but reflecting input by Pope Leo, as well as by Peter of Amalfi and Frederick of Lorraine, who were Humbert's fellow legates to Constantinople." Whalen, "Rethinking the Schism of 1054," 10.

³² Leo IX, *Epistola*, in Will, *Acta et Scripta*, 68. Eng. trans.: Roy Deferrari, *The Sources of Catholic Dogma* (St. Louis: B. Herder Book Co., 1957), 142.

³³ "You do not weigh carefully how very impudent it is to say that the Father, who is in heaven, hid the worship or rite of the visible sacrifice through the dispensation of his only-begotten Son from Peter, the prince of Apostles, to whom he deigned to reveal himself fully, the ineffable mystery of the invisible divinity of his Son." Leo IX, *Epistola*, in Will, *Acta et Scripta*, 68; Eng. trans.: Whalen, "Rethinking the Schism of 1054," 12.

³⁴ Leo IX, *Epistola*, in Will, *Acta et Scripta*, 76; Eng. trans.: Whalen, "Rethinking the Schism of 1054," 12.

The pope then wrote a more conciliatory letter to the emperor, Constantine IX, with whom he hoped to make common cause against the Normans ("a foreign nation without discipline").[35] Leo waxed lyrically about church unity, but warned the emperor that it was being endangered by Keroularios, whose "presumptions long ago came to our ears," and that, "burning hot against the Latin Church in open persecution, he did not fear to excommunicate all who touched sacraments made from unleavened bread."[36] Leo prayed that the patriarch "shall be found innocent of these things, or if corrected, he shall quickly repent when admonished" and toward that end was sending representatives to Constantinople to resolve the matter.[37]

It is perhaps unfortunate that among those representatives was Cardinal Humbert, a man not temperamentally suited for such a delicate diplomatic mission, having been described by his Latin contemporaries as a "foolish Burgundian" with an "intolerant and overbearing" character.[38] At some point before or during the trip to Constantinople Humbert prepared a response to Leo's charges framed as *A Dialogue between a Constantinopolitan and a Roman*, addressing the Greeks' "blind and hithertofore-unheard-of bravado," which "surpass[ed] the rashness of all the heretics we could catch up till now."[39] By accusing the Latins of Judaizing, Leo and Michael had not only shown themselves ignorant of salvation history, but also proven themselves to be "near-forerunners of the Antichrist" intent on destroying the unity of the church.[40]

In response to the Constantinopolitan's accusation that the Latins communed with the Jews by eating azymes and observing the Sabbath,[41] the Roman cited several Old Testament passages that not only mandated the use of unleavened bread during Passover (e.g., Ex 12:18–20, 13:6–7, Lv 23:58, Nm 28:16–22, and Dt 16:1–4), but also forbade the keeping of any leaven in the home during the celebration. Humbert pointed out that among the Latins "leavened [stuff] is still found, set out, and eaten

---

[35] Leo IX, *Epistola ad Constantinum Monomachum*, in Will, *Acta et Scripta*, 85–89. All English translations of the letter are by William L. North at https://acad.carleton.edu/curricular/mars/leoconst.pdf.
[36] Ibid., 88.
[37] Ibid., 88–89.
[38] Hussey, *The Orthodox Church in the Byzantine Empire*, 133. According to Whalen, most "modern historians of the schism have described the cardinal as 'combative,' 'stiff-necked,' 'hot-tempered,' and 'excitable,' presenting him as a zealot who disliked the Greeks and who was personally responsible for the worsening of the schism." Whalen, "Rethinking the Schism of 1054," 10. According to Gerd Tellenbach, "It is difficult to explain what calculations or feelings led [Leo] ... to make enemies of the Catholic Normans and to seek an alliance against them with the Byzantine Emperor Constantine XI Monomachos (1043–58) only to contradict this by allowing an embassy to Byzantium under Cardinal Humbert of Silva Candida in 1054 to make a major issue out of a secondary question of ritual and thus not to only to wreck his alliance but create the epic-making breach between the Roman and Greek Church." Gerd Teilenbach, *The Church in Western Europe from the Tenth to the Early Twelfth Century*, trans. Timothy Reuter (Cambridge: Cambridge University Press, 1993), 191–92.
[39] Humbert, *Dialogi*, in Will, *Acta et Scripta*, 94; Eng. trans.: Smith, *And Taking Bread*, 148.
[40] Ibid.
[41] "Therefore, in such observance of the Sabbath, where and in what way do we [Latins] have anything in common with the Jews? For they are idle and keep a holiday on the Sabbath, neither plowing nor reaping, and by reason of custom do not work, but they hold a festivity and a dinner, and their menservants, maidservants, cattle, and beasts of burden rest. But we [Latins] observe none of these things, but we do every (sort of) work, as (we do) on the preceding five days, and we fast as we (are wont to) fast on the sixth day [Friday] next to it," Humbert, *Dialogi*, in Will, *Acta et Scripta*, 96–97; Eng. trans.: R. L. Odom, "The Sabbath in the Great Schism of A.D. 1054," *Andrews University Seminary Studies* 1 (1963): 77–78.

each day within our whole territory and borders. Neither do we keep those seven days [i.e., Passover] apart from the rest of the year through matzos.... In what way, therefore, do we communicate with the Jews?" (*In quo ergo communicamus Judaeis?*).[42]

Humbert then addressed the old law, which Christ himself had kept by circumcision and celebrating the old Passover but then abrogated by the institution of the new. According to John Erickson, here one encounters a problem of translation, because in rendering Leo's earlier letter into Latin Humbert translated καταργηθέντα ("abolished") as "cursed" (*maledicta*), which led him to believe that for the Greeks the whole law, both its moral and ceremonial precepts, was accursed.[43] Humbert wrote that the Greeks were thus like the Marcionites who "barked that the very Son of God cursed the law and the azymes which it had established. But O holy, good, and venerable law, with all your commands and observances! Whoever has cursed, curses, or will curse you and what pertain[s] to you even if only a single iota may he be accursed!"[44]

According to both Erickson and Whalen, the underlying issue in the debate was Judaism's place in the economy of salvation, especially as it related to the Law of Moses.[45] According to Whalen, Humbert understood salvation history to be "a series of transitions from the age before the law (*ante legem*) through the age of the Mosaic law (*sub lege*) to the age of Christian grace (*sub gratia*)."[46] There was a "series of progressive relationships: from Jew to Christian, synagogue to church, and flesh to spirit" that characterized salvation history, with each stage building upon the earlier periods that had prefigured it.[47] Since the Jewish Passover prefigured the Christians' Eucharist, just as the other "carnal rituals of the Jews (*carnalia*) ... such as circumcision, prefigured Christian spiritual sacraments (*sacramenta*), such as baptism ... if one maligned those foundations [by disparaging azymes], as the Greeks were doing, one also maligned ... the structure that was erected upon them."[48]

---

[42] Humbert, *Dialogi*, in Will, *Acta et Scripta*, 96; Eng. trans.: Smith, *And Taking Bread*, 148.

[43] Erickson, "Leavened and Unleavened," 143.

[44] Humbert, *Dialogi*, in Will, *Acta et Scripta*, 110–11; Eng. trans.: Erickson, "Leavened and Unleavened," 143. Elsewhere he went further: "Therefore since according to you new things have been made so that the old may be completely abandoned and cursed by Christ, let all those things which we mentioned above ... be thrown far away from the church ... Let there be hatred of God and neighbor! Let mother and father be dishonored! Let man be killed! Let all commit adultery! Steal! Lie! Rape! Let there be no marriages! Let every man approach his nearest kin and have relations with her!" Humbert, *Dialogi*, in Will, *Acta et Scripta*, 116; Eng. trans.: Smith, *And Taking Bread*, 150.

[45] See also Marie-Dominique Chenu, "The Old Testament in Twelfth-Century Theology," in *Nature, Man and Society in the Twelfth Century*, trans. Jerome Taylor and Lester Little (Chicago: University of Chicago Press, 1968), 146–61; Karl-Hermann Kandler, "Evangelium nihil aliud quam expositio Legis. Zum Verhältnis von Gesetz und Evangelium und Altem und Neuem Testament bei Humbert," *Neue Zeitschrift für Systematische Theologie und Religionsphilosophie* 4 (1962): 1–10.

[46] Whalen, "Rethinking the Schism of 1054," 14.

[47] For Humbert the progressive relationship between the Old and New Covenants was made clear during the wedding feast at Cana, when the Lord, the "bearer of both Testaments," did not create wine ex nihilo but rather used water and then changed it. "In this farsighted deed of our Redeemer, we say that the water did not change its substance, but its qualities (that is, taste, color and things of that kind), so we might discern that the Lord himself did not void but renewed the Old Testament, by which he had filled up six ages of the world through the ministry of the earlier fathers, nor did he diminish it after that by his disapproval, but displayed that which lay hidden within it by his approval. For certain things the Law and Gospel proclaim in concord, making allowance only for the change and variation of the times." Humbert, *Dialogi*, in Will, *Acta et Scripta*, 112; Eng. trans.: Whalen, "Rethinking the Schism of 1054," 15.

[48] Whalen, "Rethinking the Schism of 1054," 14–15. "Therefore, the Old Testament is like the basis or foundation whose building or upper part is the New, which must weaken or collapse when the basis on

For Humbert, this "continuity of the two covenants" made Christ the "consummation, rather than destruction of the Law," for Scripture itself testified that Jesus "came not to abolish the Law, but to fulfill it" (Mt 5:17).[49] It is this continuity that helps explains Humbert's defense of the azymes, because he claimed that instead of abandoning (*derelicta*) the old law (like the Greeks) or following its letter (like the Jews), the Latins alone interpreted it properly and saw its fulfillment (rather than its abrogation) in the person of Christ. Thus while the Latins did follow the Old Testament law regarding the use of azymes (for "numerous passages from the Old Testament ... mandated the use of unleavened bread for Passover"), by interpreting these precepts spiritually (*spiritualiter*) rather than carnally (*carnaliter*) they alone properly perceived what they truly represented—that is, "the prefiguration of the Christian celebration of Christ's own sacrifice."[50]

The use of ἄρτος in the New Testament's description of the Last Supper is then touched upon, with Humbert arguing that "in all the Scripture we find 'bread' used indiscriminately, whether [the thing] were matzo or leavened" (e.g., Ps 78:24–25, Ex 16:16).[51] Humbert also argued for the use of azymes on the basis of the incarnation, for Christ was born "free from the corruption of original sin, i.e., from the leaven of malice and wickedness."[52] In support of this association of leaven with wickedness he cited several passages from Scripture that spoke of leaven negatively, especially Matthew 16:6 and 1 Corinthians 5:6–8.[53]

Humbert also employed the historical argument—that is, that Christ himself had used azymes at the Last Supper and thus the Latins were merely following his example—even though he knew that John 18:28 and the entire Johannine chronology seemingly precluded a Passover meal. C. Philipp Nothaft wrote that

> according to the Latin rebuttal offered in the *Dialogues*, the expressions *pascha* and *azyma* or *dies azymorum*, as used by the evangelists, were essentially interchangeable synonyms. ... [Thus] the Jews' mention of the *pascha* in John 18:28 [was] a reference to the *matsot* or *panes azymi*, which were consumed throughout the week of unleavened bread. As a result, the scene at the praetorium and the ensuing crucifixion of Jesus could be understood to have taken place on 15 Nisan, the first day of unleavened bread.... In this scenario, Jesus and his disciples had indeed celebrated the Passover in line with the Mosaic Law on the evening of 14/15 Nisan, which

---

which it was sitting weakens or collapses. And yet when the basis or foundation remains, often the things above it may be completely changed, but when it is lost or ruined they are unable not to be lost or ruined as well." Humbert, *Dialogi*, in Will, *Acta et Scripta*, 112; Eng. trans.: Smith, *And Taking Bread*, 149.

[49] Humbert, *Dialogi*, in Will, *Acta et Scripta*, 114; Eng. trans.: Whalen, "Rethinking the Schism of 1054," 16.

[50] Whalen, "Rethinking the Schism of 1054," 15.

[51] Humbert, *Dialogi*, in Will, *Acta et Scripta*, 99; Eng. trans.: Smith, *And Taking Bread*, 28.

[52] Humbert, *Dialogi*, in Will, *Acta et Scripta*, 107–8; Eng. trans.: Erickson, "Leavened and Unleavened," 136.

[53] "And if you would have examined all the Scriptures you would not ever find leavened used in any place with a good meeting except (that) one place in the gospel where the Lord says that the kingdom of heaven—clearly meeting the teaching of the apostles—is like leaven. But if you mull over all the Scriptures you will not ever find *matsos* used in any place with an adverse meaning but to mean either 'sincerity' or 'truth' (1 Corinthians 5:8)." Humbert, *Dialogi*, in Will, *Acta et Scripta*, 107; Eng. trans.: Smith, *And Taking Bread*, 149.

entailed that they had only used unfermented bread, as was assumed by the Roman rite during the Eucharist.[54]

Humbert "then goes on to give what was probably one of the chief reasons why unleavened bread became general in the West"—the problem of crumbs (*mica*) falling indiscriminately during the breaking of the bread.[55] He asked "what discipline and caution might be had among you over so great a sacrament" when the bread may be prepared "by just any man or woman. You hold to matter little—so little, in fact, that sometimes in the Lord's Supper you might make use of bread that has been bought from the people's shops of trade ... [and] handled by someone's unwashed and filthy hands."[56] Humbert questioned Greek Eucharistic practice, asking why they circumcised the sacrifice with a knife when Scripture says that "the Lord took bread, blessed, and broke it, but not that he cut it either before or after."[57] He asked why they dipped the bread and distributed it with a spoon, when at the Last Supper "dipped bread was extended by the Lord to no disciple except the traitor Judas."[58] However, despite all of these criticisms and his clear preference for the Roman way, Humbert did not dispute the legitimacy of the Greek practice provided the orthodoxy of the Latins was recognized.

Humbert's tolerance on this score was not uncommon. Peter Damian (d. 1073) "dismissed the difference between leavened and unleavened bread for the sacrifice as insignificant,"[59] and Dominic of Grado had argued that "both sacrifices ... were equally meritorious."[60] Because he believed this was the case, Dominic wrote to Peter III of Antioch in early 1054 to see if he could urge the Constantinopolitans to cease their attacks upon the West, arguing that even though the use of azymes was "not only from the apostolic tradition but also from the Lord himself, ... the sacred dough of leavened bread is believed to have been received from the most holy and orthodox fathers of the Eastern churches."[61] Therefore, he asked the East to "faithfully put both customs together and honorably confirm them with a spiritual interpretation. For the mixture of leaven and meal which the Eastern churches use exhibits the substance of the

---

[54] C. Philipp E. Nothaft, *Dating the Passion: The Life of Jesus and the Emergence of Scientific Chronology (200–1600)* (Leiden: Brill, 2012), 143–44. In the book Nothaft goes on to discuss the paschal dating of Reinher of Paderborn (c. 1190), who adapted Humbert's arguments but concluded that the crucifixion took place on 16 Nisan, with the Last Supper occurring on the fifteenth/sixteenth. Ibid., 144–46.

[55] Woolley, *The Bread of the Eucharist*, 25–26.

[56] Humbert, *Dialogi*, in Will, *Acta et Scripta*, 107; Eng. trans.: Smith, *And Taking Bread*, 150.

[57] Humbert, *Dialogi*, in Will, *Acta et Scripta*, 109; Eng. trans.: Smith, *And Taking Bread*, 150.

[58] Ibid.

[59] Whalen, "Rethinking the Schism of 1054," 21. "Just as it makes little difference whether at Mass we offer wine or unfermented grape juice so it seems to me it is all the same whether we offer leavened or unleavened bread. For that 'living bread that came down from heaven' just as he wished to manifest himself under the appearance of a wheat, he did so also under the form of the vine.... Nor am I too careful to inquire whether the bread was preserved in an immature dough until it could ferment or also whether the grape juice was kept in a vat until it could turn into what one calls wine. But since it is not my purpose here to discuss these matters I leave them to be handled by others." Peter Damien, *Letter 41*; Eng. trans.: Peter Damian, *The Letters of Peter Damian 31–60*, trans. Owen Blum, FC Medieval Continuation 2 (Washington, DC: Catholic University of America Press, 1990), 215.

[60] Whalen, "Rethinking the Schism of 1054," 21.

[61] Dominic of Grado, *Epistula ad Petrum Antiochensem*, in Will, *Acta et Scripta*, 207; Eng. trans.: Smith, *And Taking Bread*, 55.

incarnate Word. And the plain unleavened dough which the Church of the Romans maintains presents—without contradiction—the purity of the human flesh which the deity was pleased to join to itself."[62]

Although generally an irenic figure, on the matter of the azymes Peter was unbending, holding that in this matter Rome was clearly in error, for the use of leavened bread was an ancient practice observed by "the four [other] holy patriarchs."[63] Rome, as the "odd man out," should therefore conform itself to the rest of the church, "For everyone knows that you are [otherwise] orthodox ... being lame in this one thing alone."[64] He argued that unleavened bread (ἄζυμα) was "prescribed for the Hebrews in remembrance of the history of flight from Egypt ... but the perfectly leavened loaf which through the ritual is made over into the undefiled body of our Lord and Savior Jesus Christ is given in remembrance of his dispensation in the flesh."[65] The matter was simple—the old covenant was celebrated with azymes, the new with bread. Therefore, "If we still partake of matzos, it is evident that we are still under the shadow of the Law of Moses and we eat a Jewish meal rather than the Logos-filled (λογικὴν) and living flesh of God."[66] Elsewhere, paraphrasing Paul ("If you are circumcised Christ will be of no value to you"—Gal 5:2), he put it even more starkly: "If you eat matzos, Christ will be of no value to you. For these were commanded in memory of the flight from Egypt, and not (in memory) of His saving Passion."[67]

Peter asked Dominic to reread 1 Corinthians 11.26 ("For whenever you eat this loaf and drink this cup," he says, "you proclaim the death of the Lord until He comes") and

> notice, most holy brother-in-spirit, that in all these places a loaf (ἄρτος) and not matzo is proclaimed to be the Body of the Lord, because it is complete and full (ἄρτιον). But matzo is dead and lifeless and in all ways incomplete. But when the leaven is introduced to the wheaten dough it becomes, as it were, life and substance in it. Now tell me, how is it not out of place for those who believe in our Lord and Savior Jesus Christ to receive something incomplete and dead and lifeless as his living and life-giving flesh?[68]

---

[62] Ibid.
[63] Peter III of Antioch, *Epistola ad Dominicum Gradensem*, in Will, *Acta et Scripta*, 214. "Now for God's sake stop resisting manifest truth like this ... [and] follow the four [other] holy patriarchs by employing the practice we received as pupils of the church, so that the vote of the majority might prevail. Now one [alone] is nothing, but two are better than one (Ecl 4:9). And where four, thinking alike, fall in line like this who doubts that God to is among them?" Peter III of Antioch, *Epistola ad Dominicum Gradensem*, in Will, *Acta et Scripta*, 224; Eng. trans.: Smith, *And Taking Bread*, 58. Elsewhere Peter had questioned Dominic's use of the title "patriarch of Grado" since he knew of only five patriarchs.
[64] Peter III of Antioch, *Epistola ad Dominicum Gradensem*, in Will, *Acta et Scripta*, 214; Eng. trans.: Smith, *And Taking Bread*, 55. He later speculated that perhaps the Roman tradition had been introduced as a concession, "because most of these Christians who were in Rome were Hebrew, as the book of The Acts of the Apostles makes clear. But afterwards, when [that] moment was ended, these things were too." Peter III of Antioch, *Epistola ad Dominicum Gradensem*, in Will, *Acta et Scripta*, 227; Eng. trans.: Smith, *And Taking Bread*, 58–59.
[65] Peter III of Antioch, *Epistola ad Dominicum Gradensem*, in Will, *Acta et Scripta*, 215–16; Eng. trans.: Smith, *And Taking Bread*, 56.
[66] Ibid.
[67] Peter III of Antioch, *Epistola ad Dominicum Gradensem*, in Will, *Acta et Scripta*, 217; Eng. trans.: Smith, *And Taking Bread*, 56–57.
[68] Peter III of Antioch, *Epistola ad Dominicum Gradensem*, in Will, *Acta et Scripta*, 215; Eng. trans.: Smith, *And Taking Bread*, 56.

Because the azymes were "death-dealing" and "life-less," containing neither leaven (representing soul) nor salt (representing mind), they "could not properly serve as man's daily 'food of life,' which was what the Logos offered men in the flesh."[69] This was because "our Lord Jesus Christ, who is himself perfect God and perfect man ... assumed a besouled and also beminded body from the ever-virgin, handed over as an image of this mystery of the new covenant through a perfect loaf."[70] This gave the use of unleavened bread Christological implications, for by partaking of azymes one "unwittingly runs the risk of falling into the heresy of Apollinaris ... [who] dared to say that the Son and Word of God received only a soul-less and mindless Body from the Holy Virgin, saying that the Godhead took the place of the mind and soul."[71]

Knowing that the Latins grounded their practice in the Lord's example, Peter reminded Dominic that Christ was also circumcised and kept the Sabbath, but Paul had ended these practices because of the coming of the gospel of grace.[72] He then began an extended defense of the Johannine chronology of the passion, "since it was necessary that Christ suffer on the very day of the Torah's Pasch during the hour when the lamb was slain by the Jews."[73] It was on the evening before that he celebrated his own Pasch with his disciples, which he did, according to Luke, with "a loaf, and not matzo. For there was none as yet, it being Thursday [the thirteenth] and there were no matzos yet since the removal of the loaf had not yet occurred for according to the Torah matzos began on the fifteenth day and on the fourteenth the lamb was slain."[74]

When Cardinal Humbert reached Constantinople in summer of 1054, his main opponent, aside from the patriarch, was a Studite monk named Niketas Stethatos (d. 1090), whose works, *Adversus Latinos et Armenios de azymis* (Κατὰ Ἀρμενίων καὶ Λατίνων καὶ περὶ ἀζύμων),[75] the *Libellus contra Latinos*,[76] and the *Dialexis et antidialogus de azymis*,[77] catalogued the "horrible infirmities" of the Western church, emphasizing especially the use of azymes.[78] Humbert made Niketas the particular focus of his ire, calling him (among other things) a "pestiferous pimp," a "drunk," and

---

[69] Peter III of Antioch, *Epistola ad Dominicum Gradensem*, in Will, *Acta et Scripta*, 225; Eng. trans.: Smith, *And Taking Bread*, 58.

[70] Ibid.

[71] Ibid.

[72] "But those who want to eat matzos, why do they not also circumcise insomuch as Christ too was circumcised? And why do they not keep the Sabbath according to the ancient tradition?" Peter III of Antioch, *Epistola ad Dominicum Gradensem*, in Will, *Acta et Scripta*, 217; Eng. trans.: Smith, *And Taking Bread*, 56.

[73] Peter III of Antioch, *Epistola ad Dominicum Gradensem*, in Will, *Acta et Scripta*, 220; Eng. trans.: Smith, *And Taking Bread*, 57. He refers to this as the "godkillers' (θεοκτόνων] day of preparation."

[74] Peter III of Antioch, *Epistola ad Dominicum Gradensem*, in Will, *Acta et Scripta*, 221; Eng. trans.: Smith, *And Taking Bread*, 57. To the possible criticism that the Synoptic Gospels appeared to be at variance with John, Peter claimed there was no contradiction, since when they spoke of "the First of Matzoth" they did not mean the fourteenth, but "the 10th day of the first month, which along with the eleventh and the next three days, i.e., the 11th 12th and 13th—was the Preparation for Pasch as it had been recorded in the book of Exodus." Peter III of Antioch, *Epistola ad Dominicum Gradensem*, in Will, *Acta et Scripta*, 223; Eng. trans.: Smith, *And Taking Bread*, 58.

[75] Hergenröther, *Monumenta graeca ad Photium*, 139–54.

[76] Will, *Acta et Scripta*, 127–36.

[77] Michel, *Humbert und Kerullarios* 2, 320–42.

[78] For more on Niketas's writings see Jean Darrouzès, "Trois documents de la controverse gréco-arménienne," *Revue des Etudes Byzantines* 48 (1990): 89–92; Jean Darrouzès, "Un faux περὶ τῶν ἀζύμων de Michel Cérulaire," *Revue des Etudes Byzantines* 25 (1967): 288–91; Jean Darrouzès, *Nicétas Stéthatos. Opuscules et lettres*, SC 81 (Paris: Les éditions du Cerf, 1961).

"more dense than an ass."[79] In fact, Humbert was so eager to humiliate his opponent that he asked that Niketas be forced to watch while his anti-Latin writings were publicly burned, a request the emperor granted.[80]

Reconstructing the sources of Niketas's arguments remains difficult, but they were likely derived from earlier disputes with the Armenians,[81] Peter of Antioch's *Epistola ad Dominicum Gradensem*, and materials provided him by the archbishop of Bari.[82] Like Peter he defended the Johannine chronology that would have precluded the institution of the Eucharist with unleavened bread, for if Christ was sacrificed on Friday the fourteenth, and the Sabbath was the Feast of Unleavened Bread, when did he eat matzos?[83] The gospels and Paul were clear that Christ did not break and distribute ἄζυμος, but rather ἄρτος, explaining why the church has always used bread rather than matzo for the sacrifice.[84] Niketas then turned to the canons, claiming that the Council in Trullo (692) had prohibited both laymen and those in priestly orders from eating the unleavened bread of the Jews (Μηδεὶς τῶν ἐν ἱερατικῷ καταλεγομένων τάγματι ἢ λαϊκὸς τὰ παρὰ τῶν Ἰουδαίων ἄζυμα ἐσθιέτω),[85] and since Pope Agatho

---

[79] "But woe to you Sarabaite! You who are inspired by no monastic rule, led by our own will and lust, your barking against the holy Roman and apostolic Church and the councils of all the holy fathers makes one's hair stand on end (*horribiliter latrasti*)! More dense than an ass, you try to shatter the lion's brow and the wall of steel! In this attempt, at any rate, you have not overcome error but have been overcome by error. (You are) not an elder but a hold-over from evil days and a boy cursed with a hundred years! You should be called 'drunk' (*Epicurus*) rather than 'monk' (*monachus*)! One would not think that you live in the Studite monastery but in a ring or brothel, where—as one of your fathers has said—whoever wishes, enters and lets the ass loose! You are also rightly named 'Pectoratus.' ... For, with the serpent of old, you move on your belly!" Humbert, *Responsio sive condradicto adversus Nicetae Pectorati Libellum*; Eng. trans.: Smith, *And Taking Bread*, 98.

[80] "At the insistence of these Roman legates, at the monastery of Studios within the city of Constantinople in the presence of the emperor and his princes, the monk Niketas anathematized a certain text against the apostolic see and the entire Latin Church which had been circulated under his name.... Furthermore, he anathematized all those who denied that the Roman Church was the first of all churches and who presumed to rebuke its ever-orthodox faith in any respect. After this, at the suggestion of these same Roman legates and in the sight of all, the orthodox emperor ordered that the aforementioned text be burned and so was it destroyed.... On the following day, the aforementioned Niketas left the city and approached these legates ... [and] after receiving from them a complete answer to his questions, he willingly anathematized all words, attempts, and deeds against the first and apostolic see. And so, after they had received him into communion, Niketas became their intimate friend." Humbert, *Brevis et succincta commemoratio eorum quae gesserunt apocrisarii sanctae Romanae et apostolicae sedis in regia urbe*, in Will, *Acta et Scripta*, 15; Eng. trans.: William L. North. See also Richard Mayne, "East and West in 1054," *Cambridge Historical Journal* 11 (1954): 133–48.

[81] For different views of Niketas's dependence on the anti-Armenian polemic see n. 19.

[82] "The revolt of Bari's Jews in 1051 would have made local Greek authorities suspicious of all supposed forms of 'Jewishness,'" which gave the "Archbishops of Trani and Bari reason to seek out authoritative Orthodox pronouncements on the subject [of unleavened bread] and to share their findings with Constantinople." Smith, *And Taking Bread*, 117. According to Hergenröther (*Monumenta graeca ad Photium*, 8–9), these might have included the texts De Azymis (Περὶ τῶν Ἀζύμων) and "The Sixth Heresy of the Armenians," although both Michel ("Die vier Schriften des Niketas Stethatos über die Azymen," 332) and Schweinberg ("Die Textgeschichte des Gesprächs mit den Franken von Niketas Stethatos," 344) "view all these tracts as later echoes of a writing composed by Niketas for the controversy with the Latins." Hergenröther, *Monumenta graeca ad Photium*, 63.

[83] "*Si autem Christus immolatus est et crucifixus in decima quarta die lunae, feriae sextae, in sabbato autem erat festum azymorum, quando azyma comedit?*" Niketas Stethatos, *Libellus contra Latinos*, in Will, *Acta et Scripta*, 130.

[84] Niketas Stethatos, *Adversus Latinos et Armenios de azymis*, in Hergenröther, *Monumenta graeca ad Photium*, 139.

[85] Heinz Ohme, ed., *Concilivm Constantinopolitanvm A. 691/2 In Trvllo Habitvm (Concilivm Qvinisextvm)* (Berlin: Walter de Gruyter, 2013), 29.

had accepted Trullo's decisions, Rome was wrong to assert that the use of azymes was apostolic.[86]

Niketas followed Peter of Antioch in associating the Latins' use of unleavened bread with the Armenians, whose use of azymes reflected their Apollinarian Christology, for using bread without leaven implied that Christ assumed flesh from the Virgin Mary without soul and mind.[87] For Niketas the bread, in order to represent Christ, must be "animated and dynamic, in full possession of the living energies of humanity" (i.e., leavened) rather than the "soulless" or "dead" matzos used by heretics.[88] According to Yury P. Avvakumov, this argument was premised on

> the concept of ἀντίτυπον ("that which bears an image of something corresponds symbolically to something").... [That meant that] between the material substance of bread and the body of Christ there must be some correspondence and symbolic affinity; bread should be ἀντίτυπον of the body of Christ. Unleavened bread, however, lacks a "soul" because it lacks yeast; yeast "animates" the dough, gives "life" to it; unleavened bread is therefore "dead" and cannot function as ἀντίτυπον of Christ's body because the divine *Logos* took on a human body with a soul.[89]

For this reason Niketas came to the conclusion that the Latins' dead sacrifice could not become Christ's body and thus remained bread and wine even after the consecration.[90] He asked the Latins how they could possibly hope to "enter into communion with Christ, the living God, while eating the dead unleavened dough of the shadow of the law and not the yeast of the new covenant?"[91] Referencing the "supersubstantial" (ἐπιούσιος) bread Christ spoke of in the Lord's Prayer,[92] Niketas told them that

---

[86] "But you resist the truth in vain brothers, for if the eating of matzos were handed on to you by the apostles, St. Agatho—*your pope*—would have naturally introduced it when he was president of the holy sixth (ecumenical) council before the emperor Constantine (IV) ... when the godly fathers of this holy council put forth a law against matzos." Niketas Stethatos, *Antidialogus*, in Michel, *Humbert und Kerullarios* 2, 333; Eng. trans.: Smith, *And Taking Bread*, 97.

[87] Niketas Stethatos, *Adversus Latinos et Armenios de azymis*, in Hergenröther, *Monumenta graeca ad Photium*, 151. "In accordance with this the four evangelists say that in the holy mysteries the Lord handed over a perfect loaf—and not matzo—so that they might believe him to have a perfect body from the holy virgin. Now [by perfect] I mean [one that was] with soul and mind and not—as the heretic Apollinaris said—that he took only a body." *De Azymis* (PG 26:1328); Eng. trans.: Smith, *And Taking Bread*, 137.

[88] John Meyendorff, *Byzantine Theology: Historical Trends and Doctrinal Themes* (New York: Fordham University Press, 1974), 95. "For the body without breath is dead. And matzo only—which does not have leaven—is dead, and not a living loaf. For the leaven gives life and oneness to the dough, just as the spirit does to the body and salt to the mind." *De Azymis* (PG 26:1328); Eng. trans.: Smith, *And Taking Bread*, 137.

[89] Avvakumov, *The Oxford Handbook of Sacramental Theology*, 259–60. Avvakumov goes on to assert that "among all [the] Greek anti-azymite objections this one made Latins especially annoyed and angry owing to its unscientific, 'bizarre,' and 'crazy' character." For most of the Latin theologians it was completely irrelevant "whether the bread is leavened before the consecration," since "after the consecration it is no longer bread but the body of Christ." Ibid. See also Avvakumov, *Die Entstehung des Unionsgedankens*, 109–11.

[90] "Therefore he who partakes of matzos does not eat ... of Christ our Savior, for what is without leaven is clearly also without soul, as the nature of the matter very clearly shows. For leaven is added to the wheaten dough and kneaded into it. And when leaven has spread to the whole it warms it with its life-giving power and produces, as it were, living motion; whereas in the unleavened leaven of the Pharisees, which the Word also commands us to avoid, this will never happen." Niketas Stethatos, *Adversus Latinos et Armenios de azymis*, in Hergenröther, *Monumenta graeca ad Photium*, 141; Eng. trans.: Smith, *And Taking Bread*, 68.

[91] Ibid.

[92] There remains great scholarly debate about the proper translation of ἐπιούσιος, which Davies and Allison called "one of the great unresolved puzzles of NT lexicography." William Davies and Dale Allison,

those who still partake of the azymes ... eat of the table of the Jews, not of the reasonable and living table of God nor of the bread which is both supersubstantial [ἐπιούσιος] and consubstantial to us men who have believed. For we have been taught to ask for supersubstantial bread from on high. For what is supersubstantial if not that which is consubstantial to us? But the bread which is consubstantial to us is nothing other than the body of Christ, who was born consubstantial to us according to his humanity. But if our lump's nature (which the word assumed) is living [i.e., possesses a soul] you, by partaking of the azymes do not eat bread which is supersubstantial and consubstantial to us.[93]

Humbert did not take these charges lightly, and during the "pamphlet war" that erupted in Constantinople in the summer of 1054 he issued a *Responsio* to Niketas, claiming (among other things), that he should be excommunicated for interfering in ecclesiastical affairs in violation of the canons.[94] He maintained that while there was no need to repeat his earlier arguments against Leo, he did want to address some of the issues Niketas had raised, including Trullo's prohibition against "eating the unleavened bread of the Jews."[95] Trullo's authority had long been questioned in the Latin world, but Humbert claimed that even if one granted the canon's validity, the Latins' practice had nothing to do with the festivals of the Jews, so the legislation did not apply.[96] Humbert then addressed the relation between consubstantial and supersubstantial, as he felt "compelled to deny Stethatos' claim that the consecrated elements of the Eucharist remain consubstantial to ordinary human breads."[97] For Humbert this would have denied the idea of substantial change (and thus the doctrine of real presence) and come "dangerously close to Berenger's contention that the bread of the eucharist is merely a figure of the body of Christ."[98] He wrote:

A Critical and Exegetical Commentary on the Gospel according to Saint Matthew 1 (Edinburgh: T&T Clark, 1991), 607. It is used in both Matthew's and Luke's version of the Our Father, although Jerome translated it as "supersubstantial" (*supersubstantialem*) in Matthew 6:11, and "daily" (*quotidianum*) in Luke 11:3, with the latter translation becoming the more common. For more on the debate and possible resolutions see Pitre, *Jesus and the Last Supper*, 171–78.

[93] Niketas Stethatos, *Dialexis*, in Michel, *Humbert und Kerullarios* 2, 322; Eng. trans.: Erickson, "Leavened and Unleavened," 137–38.

[94] The canon in question was Canon 4 of Chalcedon: "Those who truly and sincerely enter on the solitary life are to be accorded to honor. But since some people use a cloak of monasticism to disrupt both the churches and public affairs ... [they] are to embrace silence and devote themselves to fasting and prayer alone, persevering in the places where they renounce the world; they are not to cause annoyance in either ecclesiastical or secular affairs, or take part in them, leaving their own monasteries, unless indeed for some compelling need they be permitted to do so by the bishop of the city." Canon 4 of the Council of Chalcedon; Eng. trans.: Richard Price and Michael Gaddis, eds., *The Acts of the Council of Chalcedon*, vol. 3 (Liverpool: Liverpool University Press, 2005), 95.

[95] Humbert also addressed the controversies surrounding the celebration of the Sabbath and the marriage of priests, since Niketas (citing Trullo's Canon 13) had attacked the Latins, asking: "Who is it, who taught you to prohibit and dissolve the marriage of priests? Which of the Church's doctors handed such depravity on to you?" Niketas Stethatos, *Libellus contra Latinos*, in Will, *Acta et Scripta*, 133.

[96] Humbert, *Responsio sive contradictio adversus Nicetae Pectorati Libellum*, in Will, *Acta et Scripta*, 140.

[97] Erickson, "Leavened and Unleavened," 139.

[98] Ibid.

As for what you also said—that the consubstantial and the supersubstantial are the same—it is altogether worthless. For although the Lord Jesus is consubstantial to us in humanity, in Divinity, in which he is consubstantial to the Father, he is supersubstantial to us. Thus, although the breads of a human table are consubstantial to themselves, the bread of the Divine table is supersubstantial to them.[99]

On July 16, 1054, frustrated because "Michael was avoiding their presence and conversation and persevering in his stupidity," Humbert decided to act.[100] Along with his fellow delegates he "entered the church of Holy Wisdom on July 16 ... as the clergy was preparing for the Mass in their customary way at the third hour of the morning ... [and] placed the charter of excommunication upon the principal altar under the gaze of the people and clergy who were present."[101] Shaking the dust from their feet and saying, "Let God see and judge" (*Videat Deus et judicet!*), they left, leaving the excommunication to be translated into Greek for the patriarch.[102] Among its list of charges was that like "the Severians, [Keroularios] maintain[ed] that the law of Moses is accursed ... [and] that anything fermented is alive ... forbidding [us the use of] churches to celebrate Mass, just as earlier he had closed the Latin churches [in Constantinople] and, calling the Latins 'azymites' he hounded them everywhere in word and deed."[103] In another excommunication, spoken in the presence of the emperor, Humbert declared that anyone who "has stubbornly opposed the faith of the Roman Church and its sacrifice, let them be anathema ... let them not be considered a catholic Christian, but a prozymite heretic. Let it be done, let it be done!"[104]

It was now Keroularios's turn, for upon reading the excommunication issued by these "wicked, abominable and (for right believers) downright unspeakable men who have come up out of the darkness," he gathered the bishops with the emperor's permission and issued a synodal edict against Humbert.[105] Interesting to note is that despite the centrality of azymes in the debates up to this point, aside from a quick reference

---

[99] Humbert, *Responsio sive contradictio adversus Nicetae Pectorati Libellum*, in Will, *Acta et Scripta*, 137–38; Eng. trans.: Erickson, "Leavened and Unleavened," 139.

[100] Humbert, *Brevis et succincta commemoratio*, in Will, *Act et Scripta*, 151; Eng. trans.: North. Humbert had also likely heard of Pope Leo's death in April, giving him impetus to act before word of this began to spread.

[101] Ibid., 152.

[102] Ibid.

[103] Humbert, *Excommunicatio*, in Will, *Acta et Scripta*, 153–54; Eng. trans.: Geanakoplos, *Byzantium*, 209. The claim that Keroularios threatened to close the Latin churches in Constantinople unless they adopted the Greek rite is now highly suspect. See Tia Kolbaba, "On the Closing of the Churches and the Rebaptism of Latins: Greek Perfidy or Latin Slander?," *Byzantine and Modern Greek Studies* 29 (2005): 39–51.

[104] Humbert, *Item alia Excommunicatio*, in Will, *Acta et Scripta*, 154; Eng. trans.: North. According to the *Brief and Succinct Account*, after they left Hagia Sophia they prepared to depart for Italy, "But because of the excessive pressure of the entreaties of Michael, who promised that he would finally debate with them, the emperor was compelled to summon them back. [But] when the heresiarch Michael learned that they had returned, he tried to lead them on the following day into the church of Holy Wisdom as if to a council so that, when their charter was displayed, which he had utterly corrupted in translating it, they might be destroyed there by the people. Taking precautions against this, the prudent emperor did not want any council to be held unless he himself was present. And since Michael opposed this in every way, the Emperor ordered that these legates quickly depart." Humbert, *Brevis et succincta commemoratio*, in Will, *Act et Scripta*, 152; Eng. trans.: North.

[105] Keroularios, *Edictum Pseudosynodi Constantinopolitanae*, in Will, *Acta et Scripta*, 157; Eng. trans.: Geffert and Stavrou, *Eastern Orthodox Christianity*, 247.

to the Greeks erroneously being labeled prozymites, unleavened bread is barely mentioned in the document. Instead, Humbert's charge that "like Pneumatomachians or Theoumachians, the [Greeks] have *deleted* from the creed the procession of the Holy Spirit from the Son," completely changed the focus of the Byzantine attack.[106] Overnight the Filioque, and not the use of azymes, became the Latins' chief error, although the issue of the Eucharistic bread would not be forgotten.

Soon after Humbert's departure from Constantinople, Kerularious wrote to the other Eastern patriarchs to enlist their help in resisting the heresies of the Latins. Among the recipients was Peter III of Antioch, whose earlier letter to Dominic of Grado on the use of azymes seemed to make him a natural ally. Keroularios wondered why Peter had limited his earlier criticism of the Latins only to azymes, "omitting the other Roman errors, which are much more serious … [For] you know very well that the Romans are not spitted on only one pike—the one regarding unleavened bread, which is clearly known to all—but on many and various ones."[107] Keroularios then listed his other charges, including the Latins' "Judaizing" tendencies like the shaving of the beard and "the aforementioned accusation regarding azymes."[108] He even asked Peter to investigate the patriarchs of Alexandria and Jerusalem, for "[We have also heard] that the two aforementioned bishops not only accept people who partake of the unleavened bread, but also themselves celebrate the divine mystery with unleavened bread."[109]

Peter, whose earlier letter had been quite critical of the Latins, now shifted gears. After dismissing the obviously erroneous charges, he differentiated between those errors that "seem abominable and should be fled; others [that] are curable; [and] still others [that] can be overlooked."[110] Most he placed in the latter two categories, except for that "evil, even the evilest of evils … their addition to the creed."[111] As for the azymes, it was a question that "has already been sufficiently scrutinized by us, and has been overturned and discarded on the grounds that it does not conform to ecclesiastical tradition."[112] For Peter the question was whether "we [can] turn that proud and haughty race away from their own customs" when "they say that the custom of azymes is ancient among them."[113] Even if the Latins continued using azymes, he told

---

[106] Humbert, *Excommunicatio*, in Will, *Acta et Scripta*, 153; Eng. trans.: Geanakoplos, *Byzantium*, 208–9.

[107] Michael Keroularios, *Epistula I ad Petrum Patriarcham Antiochenum*, in Will, *Act et Scripta*, 179; all translations of this letter are found in Tia Kolbaba, Medieval Sourcebook, https://sourcebooks.fordham.edu/source/1054michael-kerularious-to-peter-of-antioch1.asp.

[108] Ibid., 180–81.

[109] Ibid., 179.

[110] Peter of Antioch, *Epistola ad Michaelem Cerularium*, in Will, *Acta et Scripta*, 193; all translations of this letter are from Tia Kolbaba, Medieval Sourcebook, https://sourcebooks.fordham.edu/source/1054peter-of-antioch-to-michael-kerularious1.asp.

[111] Ibid., 196. Peter speculated that this error probably stemmed from the fact that the Latins had for too long been under the control of the barbarian Vandals and consequently had lost their copies of the Acts of Nicaea. Besides, "They are our brothers, even if it happens that, through rusticity and lack of education, they have frequently fallen from what is seemly, following their own will. We do not demand the same accuracy in barbarous peoples as we demand among those who have been brought up in doctrine." Ibid., 197–98.

[112] Ibid., 199. Peter told Kerularios that in this earlier letter he had "clearly demonstrated … that the meal in which our Lord and Savior Jesus Christ offered the mystery of the holy teaching to his disciples took place before Passover, at which time it was not required to eat unleavened bread." Ibid., 203.

[113] Ibid., 200, 199.

Keroularios, he would maintain communion with them, for it was enough "if the divine is preached correctly among them, and if he is praised and glorified in accordance with the word of truth and in common with us."[114] This is why Peter asked only that they correct "the addition to the holy creed ... leaving as a matter of indifference, along with all the other matters, even their fault regarding the unleavened bread. And this also I exhort Your Divine Blessedness to accept, so that you may not, by demanding everything, lose everything."[115]

Although the Filioque took center stage in the years that followed, the debate over azymes remained very much alive. From the West, we have the 1070 letter written by Laycus of Amalfi "about how to defend the sacrifice with azymes against Greek accusations."[116] After providing several passages allegedly proving that Christ had celebrated the Passover with unleavened bread at the Last Supper, he went on to discuss the relation between the old and new covenants. The old Law, he maintained, "was a sign ... [that] prefigured our times," so that those things "which [were] hidden in shadow" would be allowed to shine "brightly in the light of the New Testament.... For just as the passion of our Redeemer was prefigured in the sacrifice of the lamb, baptism in the Red Sea, the Holy Spirit in the pillar of cloud, the gift of heavenly grace in manna ... so certainly the sacrifice of our times is prefigured in the azyme bread."[117] Besides, as Humbert had argued years earlier, Rome knew better than anyone how the Eucharist should be celebrated, since this had been taught by Christ himself to Peter, and then passed on to his successors.

One of those successors, Pope Gregory VII (1073-85), in a 1080 letter to the Armenian Catholicos Gregory II Vkayaser, wrote that he "learned that your church sacrifices with unleavened bread and on this account is censured by the Greeks, ignorant as they are."[118] The pope urged Gregory not to "depart from your custom," noting that the Greeks not only

> throw this up ... as a slander against you, but also... against the holy Roman church, which through blessed Peter, as if by a special privilege, is asserted by the holy fathers to be the mother of all the churches.... As for them, when commending their leavened bread, they do not desist from contemptuously launching against us the most idle words of criticism. Yet we, while defending our unleavened bread according

---

[114] Ibid., 200.
[115] Ibid., 203.
[116] Whalen, "Rethinking the Schism of 1054," 18. See Laycus of Amalfi, *Epistola Layci clerici missa Sergio abbati ad defendendum se de azimis contra Graecos*, in Anton Michel, *Amalfi und Jerusalem im Griechischen Kirchenstreit (1054-1090): Kardinal Humbert, Laycus von Amalfi, Niketas Stethatos, Symeon II, von Jerusalem und Bruno von Segni uber die Azymen* (Rome: Pontificium Institutum Orientalium Studiorum, 1939), 35-47. According to Whalen, the letter "was redacted with minor changes by Bruno of Segni (*De sacrificio azymo*, PL 65:1087-90)," who addressed it to a monk named Leo of the Benedictine monastery of St Maria de Latina in Constantinople. Whalen, "Rethinking the Schism of 1054," 19.
[117] Laycus of Amalfi, *Epistola*, in Michel, *Amalfi und Jerusalem*, 38; Eng. trans.: Whalen, "Rethinking the Schism of 1054," 18.
[118] Gregory VII, *Letter to Catholicos Gregory II Vkayaser*, in H. E. J. Cowdrey, *The Register of Pope Gregory VII, 1073-1085: An English Translation* (Oxford: Oxford University Press, 2002), 363. See also Charles Frazee, "The Christian Church in Cilician Armenia: Its Relations with Rome and Constantinople to 1198," *Church History* 45 (1976): 166-84.

to God's incontrovertible argument, neither abuse nor reject their leavened bread, following the apostle when he says that to the pure all things are pure.[119]

From the East, where the issue generated far more "heat," we have the treatise of Leo, metropolitan of Pereyaslavl, "To the Romans or Latins on the Azymes" (Πρὸς 'Ρωμαίους ἤτοι Λατίνους περὶ τῶν ἀζύμων), written in the 1060s, with twelve of the nineteen questions dedicated to the proper matter of the Eucharist.[120] The text shows a clear dependence on the works of Leo of Ohrid, Niketas, and Peter of Antioch, and is generally moderate in its tone.[121] However, to their earlier charge that azymes manifested monophysitism, the author wrote that "to employ bread without leaven is to deny that Christ was God as well as man," thus making the Latins Nestorians as well.[122] A few decades later, John II of Kyiv (1080–89) added that the use of azymes also manifested "the heresies of Manes, Valentinus, Apollinaris, Paul of Samosata, Eutyches, Dioscorus, Severus, Sergius, and Pyrrhus."[123] For the East the heresies of the Latins were multiplying at an alarming rate, which perhaps explains why clerics in Russia believed it completely unacceptable "for Orthodox Christian princes to marry their daughters to husbands who live in countries where they use azymes and do not reject unclean foods."[124]

One bishop not convinced by these arguments was Theophylact of Ohrid (d. 1107), who railed against overzealous defenders of orthodoxy accusing the West of heresy even though most of their charges stemmed solely from differences in custom.[125] On

---

[119] Gregory VII, *Letter to Catholicos Gregory II Vkayaser*, in Cowdrey, *The Register of Pope Gregory VII*, 363.

[120] André Poppe, "Le traité des azymes Λέοντος μητροπολίτου τῆς ἐν Ῥωσίᾳ Πρεσθλάβας: Quand, où et par qui a-t-il été écrit?," *Byzantion* 35 (1965): 508. According to Poppe, the text comes from Λέοντος μητροπολίτου τῆς ἐν Ῥωσίᾳ Πρεσθλάβας, who was earlier thought to be Leontius, the (legendary) first metropolitan of Kiev, Leontius, or Leo of Preslav. For the text see Pavlov, *Kriticheskie opyty*, 115–32.

[121] Poppe, for example, notes how the author "follows Nicétas Stéthatos and Peter of Antioch, placing the [Last] Supper on the third day of the moon, one day before Passover proper. In this 'the first day of the azymes' in the Synoptics is understood as the tenth of the month, which would open the pre-feast of Passover. "Le traité des azymes, 509.

[122] Pavlov, *Kriticheskie opyty*, 127; Eng. trans.: Erickson, "Leavened and Unleavened," 137.

[123] John II of Kiev, *Letter to Clement of Rome* in Pavlov, *Kriticheskie opyty*, 181; Eng. trans.: Erickson, "Leavened and Unleavened," 137. For a discussion of this text see Bernard Leib, *Rome, Kiev, et Byzance à la fin du XIe siècle: Rapports religieux des Latins et des Gréco-Russes sous le pontificat d'Urbain II (1088–1099)* (Paris: Auguste Picard, 1924), 32–37; Jannis Spiteris, *La Critica Bizantina del Primato Romano nel secolo XII, Orientalia Christiana Analecta 208* (Rome: Pontificium Institutum Orientalium Studiorum, 1979), 38–44.

[124] "Kanonicheskie otvety mitropolita Ioanna II," in Andrei Pavlov, ed., *Pamiatniki drevnerusskogo kanonicheskogo prava, Russkaia istoricheskaia biblioteka*, 6 (Saint Petersburg: Arkheograficheskaia komissiia, 1880), col. 7; Eng. trans.: Catherine Philippa Sykes, Latin Christians in the Literary Landscape of Early Rus, c. 988–1330 (PhD dissertation, Newnham College, University of Cambridge, 2017), 39. According to the Philippa-Sykes, "The prominence of azymes in Early Russian writing seems likely to be, at least in part, a reflection of the privileging of this issue in the higher echelons of ecclesiastical culture in Byzantium and Rus. However, this is perhaps not the whole story. In Russian writing, two words are used for 'azymes': *opresnoki* and *oplatki* (from Latin *oblatum*).... It is the term derived from Latin and most likely adopted into Slavonic via Poland that seems to him to be the more natural designation, not the term used in most anti-Latin polemic. This suggests that Russian awareness of azymes might have derived not from anti-Latin polemical texts alone, but from the cultural proximity of Rus to the Latin world. After all, the issue of azyme use was both easily comprehensible (at least on a basic level) and immediately visible to any Rus who might be present at services at Latin churches." Ibid., 48.

[125] See chapter 2 nn. 99 and 100.

the azymes, he lamented the fact that on this issue many of his coreligionists burned with "a very hot zeal, hotter than fire itself and would sooner part with their lives than give up their opinion on this point."[126] Despite his own belief that the use of leavened bread was genuinely apostolic, Theophylact urged the East to tolerance and argued that it was futile to dispute with the "obstinate" Latins over azymes, not unlike "clapping one tile against another, without putting glue in between, and trying to get them to stick."[127] Interestingly, unlike most of his contemporaries Theophylact accepted that Jesus *did* eat the pascha the night before he died[128] and that after the meal, he "passed on the mystery of his own *pascha* ... with the bread he had on hand, which happened to be unleavened."[129]

The First Crusade

Despite the hopes that a joint campaign against the Turk might help heal the growing division between East and West, increased contact between Latins and Greeks during the Crusades only brought about a heightened awareness of their "otherness," especially when it came to their celebration of the liturgy.[130] Not surprisingly, this was particularly true of those Byzantine churchmen like the Patriarch of Antioch, John IV ("the Oxite"), who were at odds with the Latins over ecclesiastical jurisdiction in the newly established crusader kingdoms. John was initially in communion with the Latins for two years following their capture of Antioch—he even consecrated its first Latin bishop, Peter of Narbonne—but apparently underwent a change of heart after being exiled from his See by Prince Bohemond I in 1100.[131] By 1101 he was writing

---

[126] Theophylact of Ohrid, Προσλαλιά τινι τῶν αὐτοῦ ὁμιλητῶν περὶ ὧν ἐγκαλοῦνται Λατῖνοι, in Gautier, *Théophylacte d'Achrida: Discours, traités, poésies*, 261; Eng. trans.: Palmer, *Dissertations on Subjects Relating to the "Orthodox" or "Eastern Catholic" Communion*, 26.

[127] Ibid., 277–79.

[128] Theophylact held that Jesus "allowed His disciples to eat the paschal meal a day early, reserving Friday as the day on which He Himself—the true Paschal Lamb—would be slaughtered, and the types of the old Pascha fulfilled." Theophylact of Ohrid, *The Explanation of Blessed Theophylact Archbishop of Ochrid and Bulgaria of the Holy Gospel according to Saint John*, trans. Christopher Stade (House Springs, MO: Chrysostom Press, 2007), 275.

[129] Theophylact of Ohrid, Προσλαλιά τινι τῶν αὐτοῦ ὁμιλητῶν περὶ ὧν ἐγκαλοῦνται Λατῖνοι, in Gautier, *Théophylacte d'Achrida: Discours, traités, poésies*, 263. This position is also found in his scriptural commentaries: "From this some believe that the Lord did not eat the Pascha that year. For they say that only while standing was the Paschal lamb to be eaten. Yet Christ sat down; hence it could not have been the Pascha which He ate. But we might say that first He ate the Pascha standing, and then He sat down and gave them His own Mystery and Sacrament. For having first kept the Pascha in type, He then kept it in truth." Theophylact of Ohrid, *The Explanation by Blessed Theophylact Archbishop of Ochrid and Bulgaria of the Holy Gospel according to Saint Matthew*, trans. Christopher Stade (House Springs, MO: Chrysostom Press, 2006), 227.

[130] See Johannes Pahlitzsch, "Die Bedeutung der Azymenfrage fur die Beziehungen zwischen griechisch-orthodoxer und lateinischer Kirche in den Kreuzfahrerstaaten," in Walter Beltz, ed., *Die Folgen der Kreuzzuge fur die orientalischen Religionsgemeinschaften, Hallesche Beiträge zur Orientwissenschaft 22* (Halle: Martin-Luther-Universität, Institut für Orientalistik, 1996), 75–93.

[131] John was exiled during a war between Bohemond and the Emperor Alexios I, with whom John was said to be conspiring. Although he clearly saw himself as exiled, later Latin historians like William of Tyre (who called John "a true confessor of Christ") interpreted John's exit as an abdication because "as a Greek he could not conveniently rule over Latins." William of Tyre, *History of Deeds Done beyond the Sea* 1; see Ralph-Johannes Lilie, *Byzantium and the Crusader States, 1096–1204*, trans. J. C. Morris and Jean Ridings (Oxford: Clarendon Press, 1993). For the dating of John's *Treatise on the Azymes*, which may have

"derisive reports—if not lampoons—of the Italians' eucharist, rites which he claims to have seen with his own eyes (αὐτόπτης)."[132] The work, Λόγος περὶ τῶν ἀζύμων πρὸς τὸν Ἀδριανουπολίτην, famously described their use of azymes as "the chief and primary cause of the division between them and us.... The matter of azymes involves in summary form the whole question of true piety; if it is not cured, the disease of the church cannot be cured."[133]

According to Bernard Leib, John's "originality does not consist in the discovery of new lines of argument, but in the manner he develops the themes" of earlier authors and utilizes their arguments—for example, unleavened hosts do not have the nourishing, living, or life-giving qualities of bread, it was Judaizing, and historically Christ instituted the Eucharist with ἄρτος.[134] He also took pains to refute the Italians' arguments about the corrupting nature of azymes, their misreading of the passion chronology, and their claim that azymes were apostolic.[135] He complained that the Italians, when confronted by these "irrefutable arguments ... resort to vomiting forth subtleties, analogies, [and] symbols.... [But] when I approach the holy and fearsome table, I no longer see symbols or figures, for I receive in my hands the very flesh of my Lord, free from all veils."[136] For John the Italians' mass was more a pantomime than a sacrifice and could not even be described as a true "communion," since Latin priests, after consuming the azymes, merely embraced the congregation in lieu of giving them the consecrated host.[137]

John was certainly not alone in objecting to the Eucharistic practices of the Latins, a fact demonstrated by the large number of anti-azyme tracts written in the first decade of the twelfth century. There is the treatise *On Azymes* (Περὶ τῶν ἀζύμων), attributed to

---

been composed as late as 1112, see Bernard Leib, "Deux inédits byzantins sur les azymes au début du xii e siècle: Contribution à l'histoire des discussions théologiques entre Grecs et Latins," *Orientalia Christiana* 9 (1924): 191; Paul Gautier, "Jean V l'Oxite, patriarche d'Antioche: Notice biographique," *Revue des études byzantines* 22 (1964): 132–35.

[132] Jonathan Shepard, "Hard on Heretics, Light on Latins: The Balancing-Act of Alexios I Komnenos," in *Mélanges Cécile Morrisson, Travaux et Mémoires 16* (Paris: Association des Amis du Centre d'Histoire et Civilisation de Byzance, 2010), 768. Leib points out the significance of the continued reference to the "Italians" (as opposed to "Latins") since Antioch's ruler, Bohemond, was a Norman. Leib, "Deux inédits byzantins," 192–93.

[133] John the Oxite, Λόγος περὶ τῶν ἀζύμων πρὸς τὸν Ἀνδρινουπολίτην, in Leib, "Deux inédits byzantins," 245; Eng. trans.: Kolbaba, "Byzantine Perceptions of Latin Religious 'Errors,'" 126.

[134] Leib, "Deux inédits byzantins," 192.

[135] For example, he granted that the Lord may have celebrated the Passover, but argued that Christ anticipated the feast in order to die on the day the Jews ate the Passover. Since it was before the legal Passover, John asked how azymes could have been present. John the Oxite, Λόγος περὶ τῶν ἀζύμων πρὸς τὸν Ἀνδρινουπολίτην, in Leib, "Deux inédits byzantins," 252–54. Also, like Peter of Antioch, he granted that azymes may have been allowed early on in Rome because of the presence of so many Jewish Christians, but that this practice had ceased soon after. Ibid., 259–60.

[136] Ibid., 256–57.

[137] Ibid., 262. For a discussion of this charge and the *Pax* as a sort of "spiritual communion" see ibid., 199–200. Leib quotes from Thomas à Kempis: "Receive the *Pax* with reverence and devotion, for it is a contact with the Body of the Lord through the mouth of the priest.... In the Primitive Church all the faithful were wont to communicate, and in place of such communion the *Pax* is given as being in some measure a receiving of Christ's Body. The reason (as I hold) that His Body is not now given so generally is that in the Primitive Church when His Blood was but lately shed, men were better, and religious fervour was in full vigour and at its height: but this is now grown old." Thomas à Kempis, "Life of Gerhard the Great," in *The Founders of the New Devotion*, trans. J. P. Arthur (London: Kegan Paul, Trench, Trübner, 1905), 66.

Symeon II, patriarch of Jerusalem and dated from 1095 to 1105, that while "mild and courteous" was also unambiguous in its condemnation of the azymes.[138] Charitably, he maintained that the Latins simply required instruction in order to recognize the truth, which is why he decided to teach them how azymes were introduced in the West by the heretic Lucius (Λεύκιός), also known as Felix (Φῆλιξ), an Apollinarian who fled from the East, spread his heresy in Agrigento, and then went to Rome, where he tricked the Romans into electing him pope.[139] Symeon also schooled them on the proper interpretation of Scripture, for nowhere in the gospels does it say that Christ ate the legal Passover, or that he used anything except ἄρτος.[140] Symeon's work, which like John's is not terribly original ("aside from a willingness to admit that Latins and the Greeks jointly celebrated the liturgical office in the first centuries"),[141] relied heavily on the first part of Bishop Nicholas of Andida's Νικολάου ἐπισκόπου Ἀνδίδων λόγος κατὰ τῶν ἄζυμα προσφερόντων ἐν τῇ θείᾳ ἱερουργίᾳ, although in general Nicholas is far less charitable.[142] Nicholas had written his work sometime between 1095 and 1100 as a response to the conduct of the "crowd of Latins together with like-minded Venetians" who had come Rhodes and "founded churches there with the consent and command of the emperor."[143] These Latins not only used azymes in their churches but also "seduced ... the simpler among the orthodox" to do the same, using "specious arguments and misrepresentation of the holy scriptures" to claim that "their form of offering was more pleasing to God."[144]

Symeon's story about the introduction of azymes in the West was only one of many circulating in the East, for there was also *A Tale, Briefly Told, about How and What for the Latins Split and Were Excluded from Their Primacy and from the Commemorative Books in Which the Orthodox Patriarchs Are Listed*, which was originally written in

---

[138] Symeon of Jerusalem, Περὶ τῶν ἀζύμων, in Leib, "Deux inédits byzantins," 217–39. According to Yury P. Avvakumov, "Most recently, Peter Plank convincingly demonstrated that the patriarch could have died at the earliest in 1105 because he mentioned the antipope Silvester IV in the treatise against the azymes." Avvakumov, *Die Entstehung des Unionsgedankens*, 102. See Peter Plank, "Patriarch Symeon II. von Jerusalem und der erste Kreuzzug," *Ostkirchliche Studien* 43 (1994): 277–327. Anton Michel contended that the work was Symeon's answer to the writings of Laycus of Amalfi, not Bruno of Segni, as Leib contended. Anton Michel, *Amalfi und Jerusalem*, 28–33.

[139] Symeon of Jerusalem, Περὶ τῶν ἀζύμων, in Leib, "Deux inédits byzantins," 220–21. This tale appears in various forms throughout the East. See, for example, the third of the three *Opuscula de origine schismatis* found in Hergenröther, *Monumenta graeca ad Photium*, 171–81, with a revised edition and translation in Luigi Silvano, "'How, Why and When the Italians Were Separated from the Orthodox Christians': A Mid-Byzantine Account of the Origins of the Schism and Its Reception in the 13th–16th Centuries," in Marie-Hélène Blanchet and Frédéric Gabriel, eds., *Réduire le schisme? Ecclésiologies et politiques de l'Union entre Orient et Occident (XIIIe–XVIIIe siècle* (Paris: Centre de recherche d'histoire et civilisation de Byzance, 2013), 117–50. According to Silvano, "In adding the name Felix to that of Lucius, Symeon might have had in mind Felix II, antipope from 355 to 365" since Niketas of Nicaea (PG 120:716 A–B) blamed a "Pope Felix responsible for a schism with Constantinople." Ibid., 121.

[140] Symeon of Jerusalem, Περὶ τῶν ἀζύμων, in Leib, "Deux inédits byzantins," 226.

[141] Leib, "Deux inédits byzantins," 185.

[142] Jean Darrouzès, "Nicolas d'Andida et les azymes," *Revue des études byzantines* 32 (1974): 199–210. Avvakumov noted that the first part of Nicholas's work corresponds to chapters 15–31 of Symeon's tract. Avvakumov, *Die Entstehung des Unionsgedankens*, 102.

[143] Darrouzès, "Nicolas d'Andida et les azymes," 208; Eng. trans.: Sheppard, "Hard on Heretics, Light on Latins," 770–71.

[144] Ibid.

Greek and then translated into Slavonic.[145] The story blamed the introduction of azymes and the Filioque on Charlemagne, whose monks and priests came to Rome in order to spread their heresies. Opposing these efforts, "Pope Benedict III (855–858) sent a letter to the four eastern patriarchs in which he asked them not to recognize any of the popes to succeed him ... [until] they had received written testimony confirming his adherence to the orthodox faith."[146] The last pope to do so was allegedly Stephan VI (885–91), so that by refusing to commune with the azymite Latins the East was merely "complying with the will of the former pope" and maintaining the purity of the ancient faith.[147]

The *Opusculum contra Francos* exerted great influence on subsequent polemical literature, not only becoming the basis for similar anti-Latin lists, but also serving as chief source for later Latin responses thanks to the Latin translation of Hugo Ethenarius.[148] The *Opusculum* claimed that "The Roman Pope" as well as the "Italians, Langobards, Franks, also called Germans, Amalphitans, Venetians and others" have left "the Catholic church and [become] strangers to the evangelical, apostolic, and patristic traditions, because they hold onto unlawful and barbaric rites,"[149] chief among them being that "they offer azymes and slander the apostle Peter and the holy fathers by saying that they received such a tradition from them."[150] Konstantinos Stilbes (d. 1204), who would later go on to produce one of the longest lists of Latin errors ("The Faults of the Latin Church") based in part on the *Opusculum*, added to this charge that they also "do not take a large loaf and break it and distribute it as the Lord offered at the mystical supper, but [rather] take a coin-shaped bit of unleavened bread and this bit unbroken the celebrant alone consumes."[151]

From the same period there are also the largely derivative "Errors of the Franks" by the monk Nikon of the Black Mountain, written shortly after the crusaders' arrival in Antioch,[152] and three treatises against azymes attributed to Patriarch John VIII of Jerusalem, authored at some point before he went into exile in 1106–7.[153] The

---

[145] For a discussion of this text, found in BAR Ms. Slav. No 330, f. 132v–133v, I rely largely on the analysis of Nikolov, "Mediaeval Slavonic Anti-Catholic Texts." See also Angel Nikolov, "'A Useful Tale about the Latins': An Old Bulgarian Translation of a Lost Byzantine Anti-Latin Text of the End of 11th–Early 12th Century," *Scripta & E-Scripta* 1 (2003): 99–119; Lara Sels, "Lawless, Forbidden and Abominable Customs: О Латинѣхъ сирѣчь Фроугохъ, a Slavonic List of Latin Errors," in Michel De Dobbeleer and Stijn Vervaet, eds., *(Mis)understanding the Balkans: Essays in Honour of Raymond Detrez* (Ghent, Belgium: Academia Press, 2013), 271–88.

[146] Nikolov, "Mediaeval Slavonic Anti-Catholic Texts," 266.

[147] Ibid.

[148] *Opusculum contra Francos*, in Hergenröther, *Monumenta graeca ad Photium*, 62–71.

[149] Ibid., 62–63; Eng. trans.: Milka Levy Rubin, "'The Errors of the Franks' by Nikon of the Black Mountain: Between Religious and Ethno-cultural Conflict," *Byzantion* 71 (2001): 433–34. Levy-Rubin points out that certain groups in the West (e.g., the Calabrians and the Alemannians) were exempted from this censure since "they are Orthodox Christians from the first and were reared by our Apostolic church." Ibid.

[150] *Opusculum contra Francos*, in Hergenröther, *Monumenta graeca ad Photium*, 64; Eng. trans.: Kolbaba, *The Byzantine Lists*, 37.

[151] Darrouzès, "Le mémoire de Constantin Stilbès contre les Latins," 63; Eng. trans.: Kolbaba, *The Byzantine Lists*, 37.

[152] See Levy-Rubin, "'The Errors of the Franks' by Nikon of the Black Mountain," 422–37.

[153] For John's life and work see Johannes Pahlitzsch, *Graeci und Suriani im Palästina der Kreuzfahrerzeit: Beiträge und Quellen zur Geschichte des griechisch-orthodoxen Patriarchats von Jerusalem*, Berliner historische Studien 33 (Berlin: Duncker and Humblot, 2001), 101–33. According to Bernard Hamilton, John had been bishop of Tyre before coming to Jerusalem and being elected its bishop by the

third of these treatises is framed in terms of a dialogue with a "Latin philosopher" in Jerusalem, which may (or may not) have actually occurred,[154] while the first (Περὶ ἀζύμων λόγος πρῶτος) is probably the work of Eustratios of Nicaea,[155] the author of *Oratio ad Latinos de azymes* (Λόγος πρὸς τοὺς Λατίνους περὶ τῶν προσφερομένων ἀζύμων, ἅτε παρὰ τοὺς θείους κανόνας ταῦτα ποιοῦντας),[156] who famously debated Peter Grossolanus on the Filioque and azymes in 1112.[157] The debate, which involved Eustratios, John Phournos, and Niketas Seides (among others), had been organized by Alexios I to ease growing East-West tensions, but to the emperor's horror it instead "let loose a torrent of polemical arguments from the Greek ecclesiastics,"[158] with a large number of them specifically aimed at the Latins' use of unleavened bread.[159] In the aftermath, almost all of the Greek participants authored anti-azymite texts, including Seides (*Adversus Latinos*),[160] Theodore of Smyrna (Λόγος περὶ τῶν

Orthodox community. From here there may have been a misunderstanding, since "the Latin patriarch might well have welcomed an Orthodox coadjutor who could, under his authority, undertake the supervision of the Orthodox communities in his charge; whereas John may have considered that he was lawful Orthodox patriarch." Hamilton, *The Latin Church in the Crusader States*, 180.

[154] According to Andrew Jotitcxhsjy, "There is no record of a dialogue with the Latin but the opportunity in John's case makes it not implausible." Andrew Jotitschky, "Greek Orthodox and Latin Monasticism around Mar Saba during Crusader Rule," in Joseph Patrich, ed., *The Sabaite Heritage in the Orthodox Church from the Fifth Century to the Present* (Leuven: Peeters, 2001), 91. See also Pahlitzsch, *Graeci und Suriani im Palästina*, 120-31.

[155] This treatise was first attributed to John in the Τόμος ἀγάπης of Patriarch Dositheos in 1698. See Jotitschky, "Greek Orthodox and Latin Monasticism," 109-19.

[156] Text in Andronicus Demetracopoulos, Ἐκκλησιαστικὴ Βιβλιοθήκη, vol. 1 (Leipzig, 1866), 100-127. Despite his attacks on the Latins, Eustratios was later charged with heresy and in 1117 suspended from his office, a fact that may have more to do with his "friend and champion" Emperor Alexios I than with his theological views. Hussey, *The Orthodox Church*, 151.

[157] See V. Grumel, "Autour de voyage de Pierre Grossolanus, archevêque de Milan, à Constantinople en 1112," *Echos d'Orient* 32 (1933): 22-33; Jean Darrouzès, "Les documents byzantins du XIIe siècle sur la primaute romaine," *Revue des études byzantines* 23 (1965): 51-59.

[158] Of this period Steven Runciman wrote, "Amongst the unhappy delusions of mankind is the belief that a dispute can be settled by a debate." Steven Runcimann, *The Eastern Schism: A Study of the Papacy and the Eastern Churches during the XIth and XIIth Centuries* (London: Oxford University Press, 1955), 108. However, according to some accounts (see Demetracopoulos, Ἐκκλησιαστικὴ Βιβλιοθήκη 1:46.27-47.6), "The debate ended amicably, with Phrounos rhetorically inviting Grossolanus to move permanently to Byzantium." A. P. Kazhdan and Ann Wharton Epstein, *Change in Byzantine Culture in the Eleventh and Twelfth Centuries* (Berkeley: University of California Press, 1985), 188. For different evaluations of dialogue during this period see Averil Cameron, *Arguing It Out: Discussion in Twelfth-Century Byzantium* (Budapest: Central European University Press, 2016); Averil Cameron and Niels Gaul, eds., *Dialogues and Debates from Late Antiquity to Late Byzantium* (London: Routledge, 2017); Denis Searby, ed., *Never the Twain Shall Meet? Latins and Greeks Learning from Each Other in Byzantium* (Berlin: Walter de Gruyter, 2018).

[159] Kazhdan and Epstein, *Change in Byzantine Culture*, 188. Jonathan Shepard contextualized this discussion in light of earlier dialogues that had taken place between traveling Latin ecclesiastics and various Byzantine churchmen. For example, he wrote that "only from a passing allusion in a discourse by Niketas Seides does one learn of a discussion in Constantinople on the subject of azymes sometime between 1100 and 1102 [where] Niketas had heard 'one of those who are called cardinals' hold forth." Shepard, "Hard on Heretics, Light on Latins," 769.

[160] Niketas Seides, *Adversus Latinos* / Νικήτα τοῦ Σείδου, ὃς ἦν ἐν τοῖς χρόνοις Ἀλεξίου βασιλέως τοῦ Κομνηνοῦ ἐφ' οὗ καὶ οἱ Λατῖνοι κατὰ τὴν Κωνσταντινούπολιν ἦλθον ἐπισκόπους μεθ' ἑαυτῶν ἔχοντες, ὧν εἷς ἦν καὶ ὁ Μεδιολάνων ἀδόμενος ἐπὶ λόγων ἰσχύι, λόγος σχεδιασθεὶς πρὸς Ῥωμαίους καὶ δύο ταῦτα ἀποδεικνύων, ὅτι αἰδεσιμώτερα τὰ νέα τῶν παλαιῶν καὶ ὅτι ἐκ τοῦ πατρὸς μόνου, οὐχὶ δὲ καὶ ἐκ τοῦ υἱοῦ, ὡς αὐτοὶ λέγουσιν ἐκπορεύεται τὸ πνεῦμα τὸ ἅγιον. ἐγράφη δὲ ὁ λόγος οὗτος ἐν Κωνσταντινουπόλει ὅτε ἐνεδήμει ταύτῃ ὁ ῥηθεὶς ἐπίσκοπος Λατῖνος ἐν ἔτει ϛχκ. See Gahbauer, *Gegen den Primat des Papstes*.

ἀζύμων),[161] and John of Claudiopolis (περὶ τῶν ἀζύμων).[162] It seemed that wherever the Latins went, an anti-azymite treatise was sure to follow.

Some anti-azymite works of the period were composed, not against the Latins, but rather against the Armenians, whose continued use of unleavened bread in the Eucharist remained a sore point. There was the *Panoplia Dogmatike* of Euthymius Zigabenus, whose section 23 dealt with their use of unleavened bread,[163] and the work of Dionysius Barsalībi (d. 1171), whose writings repeated many of the old arguments ("How would Christ make his body from dead azyme when this same body is living and has a soul?") while adding others.[164] He argued that despite the Armenian claim that in Scripture "leavened" meant sinful, "leaven is a word of neutral morality, like wealth, poverty, sun, north, mountain, and health. Sometimes it denotes sin and wickedness, and sometimes goodness."[165] In the Eucharist it represented "true faith, because [just] as it draws the dough to its savour, so also Christ draws all to Himself through faith in Him."[166] He allowed that Jesus ate azymes on the night before he died "for the fulfillment of the old Law," but Barsalībi claimed that he also told his apostles

---

Seides listed twelve significant differences between the two churches, only three of which (azymes, the Filioque, and the Latins' alleged unwillingness to call Mary *Theotokos*) he regarded as genuinely problematic. See Hans-Georg Beck, *Kirche und theologische Literatur im Byzantinischen Reich* (Munich: C.H. Beck, 1959), 617–18.

[161] This was probably part of a larger treatise dealing with both azymes and the Filioque originally entitled Λόγος περὶ τῶν ἀζύμων καὶ περὶ τῆς λεγομένης παρὰ Ῥωμαίοις τοῦ Πνεύματος ἐκ τοῦ Υἱοῦ ἐκπορεύσεως. See Beck, *Kirche und theologische Literatur*, 616–17.

[162] Text in Pavlov, *Kriticheskie opyty*, 189–91. This work may have influenced (or it may have been influenced by) the *Opusculum contra Francos*, but that depends on the dating. Darrouzès argued that the text was composed by "the John ... known at the end of the eleventh century ... [who] was together with John Phournos, Eustratios of Nicaea, Theodoros Smyrnaios, and John of Antioch, a protagonist in the discussions of 1112." Darrouzès, "Le mémoire de Constantin Stilbès contre les Latins," 53, quoted in Kolbaba, *The Byzantine Lists*, 177. Hans-Georg Beck assigns this to "the John who signed a synodal act in 1166" and thus dates the work much later. Beck, *Kirche und theologische Literatur*, 627. Kolbaba accepts Darrouzès; Avvakumov (*Die Entstehung des Unionsgedankens*, 95) accepts Beck.

[163] Euthymius Zigabenus, *Panoplia Dogmatike* (PG 130:1174–89); Erich Trapp, "Die Quellen von Zigabenos' Panoplia, Tit. 23 (Gegen die Armenier)," *Jahrbuch der Österreichischen Byzantinistik* 29 (1980): 159–64. For a critical edition of chapters 23–28 see Metin Berke, "An Annotated Edition of Euthymios Zigabenos, Panoplia Dogmatikē, Chapters 23–28" (PhD diss., Queen's University Belfast, 2011). See also Nadia Miladinova, *The Panoplia Dogmatike by Euthymios Zygadenos: A Study on the First Edition Published in Greek in 1710, Texts and Studies in Eastern Christianity* (Leiden: Brill, 2014). Among his arguments was the idea that whenever Scripture referred to a man (ἄνθρωπος), it meant a "living man" unless it was qualified by another adjective (e.g., "a dead man"), and in the same way whenever Scripture spoke of bread (ἄρτος), it meant "leavened bread" unless qualified by the adjective "unleavened" (PG 130:1180).

[164] Alphonse Mingana, ed. and trans., *The Work of Dionysius Barsalībi against the Armenians* (Piscataway, NJ: Gorgias Press, 2009), 23.

[165] Ibid., 24. "Some ignorant Armenians advance and unsavory and nauseating opinion: 'When Shem, son of Noah, was little he mixed his digested food with dough which was immediately leavened and leaven dates from this act. This is the reason why we do not mix leaven with the Eucharistic bread.'" Ibid., 28.

[166] Ibid., 27. Barsalībi supported his position with quotations from several patristic authors, including Ephraim the Syrian ("And in the place of this heavy azyme, which weighs on the stomach, I will give you living bread, which is leavened with the Holy Spirit") and John Chrysostom ("He did not give his body without purpose; because the first nature of the body that was fashioned from earth was overtaken by sin to death, and was straying from life, he introduced, so to speak, another dough and leaven, his body, which by nature was identical with its prototype but which was free from sin and full of life and he gave it for all to take"). Ibid., 24.

to prepare "leavened bread and wine for the inauguration of the new."[167] This is why, Barsalībi reminded his readers, Christ called himself the bread of life, not the azyme of life.[168]

The Greeks' opposition to azymes took many forms, and included not only the writing of anti-Latin treatises, but also hagiography.[169] For example, the *Life of St Luke, Bishop of Isola Capo Rizzuto* (c. 1100) recalled the bishop's disputation with some Latins, where he accused them of "interpreting the Scripture like the Pharisees [and] celebrat[ing] with unleavened bread in the Jewish manner."[170] In response, the Latins "put him in a hut and set fire to it on all sides," although the author assures us that (miraculously) Luke survived to fight another day.[171]

In the West these attacks met with a relatively measured, but no less firm, response. According to Geofreddo Malaterra, in 1088 Pope Urban II had already "paternally admonished" Alexios I because the emperor "had forbidden the Latin Christians who lived in his territory from sacrificing with unleavened bread, ordering them to use leavened bread—which our rite never uses—in their sacrifices just as the Greeks did."[172] Malaterra wrote that the emperor "received this reprimand with humility," and invited the pope "to come to Constantinople with Latin churchman," where a council would assemble and "remedy once and for all that schism—whereby the Greeks sacrifice with leavened bread while the Latins use unleavened—so that, with one common prescription aimed at the entire church of God, the one church would henceforth observe one custom."[173] Malaterra even claimed that Alexios agreed to "observe ... whatever might be decided, in accordance with true doctrine, as agreed upon by the Greeks and Latins present, whether that meant sacrificing with leavened or unleavened bread."[174]

Guibert of Nogent's account of the First Crusade, *Gesta Dei per Francos*, had noted that there were differences between East and West "in the preparation of the Eucharist," but maintained that it was not too problematic an issue since "making the sacrament out of leavened bread is defended with the appropriate or apparently

---

[167] Ibid., 22. In this he followed those earlier writers who had speculated that there was a second table to which Christ led the apostles after dinner, instituting the Eucharist with leavened bread there and commanding them to eat "because it was not their habit to eat leavened bread on that evening." Ibid., 23.

[168] Ibid.

[169] See Martin Hinterberger, "A Neglected Tool of Orthodox Propaganda? The Image of the Latins in Byzantine Hagiography," in Hinterberger and Schabel, *Greeks, Latins, and Intellectual History, 1204–1500*, 129–50.

[170] Giuseppe Schirò, *Vita di S. Luca vescovo di Isola Capo Rizzuto* (Palermo, 1954), 106–9; Eng. trans.: Schabel, "The Quarrel over Unleavened Bread," 92–93.

[171] Ibid.

[172] Goffredo Malaterra, *Historia Sicula* 4.13; Eng. trans.: Malaterra, *The Deeds of Count Roger of Calabria*, 188–89.

[173] Ibid. Malaterra told how the emperor "also set the time when the pope was to come to Constantinople, that is, a year and a half later. The count (Roger of Sicily) advised the pope to go, so that such a schism might be removed from the Church of God. But, impeded by enemies of the holy church of God, who persisted in making Rome dangerous for him, the pope was prevented from undertaking the journey." Ibid. For the correspondence between them see Walther Holtzman, "Die Unionsverhandlungen zwischen Kaiser Alexios I und Papst Urban II im Jahre 1089," *Byzantinische Zeitschrift* 28 (1928): 38–67.

[174] Goffredo Malaterra, *Historia Sicula* 4.13; Eng. trans.: Malaterra, *The Deeds of Count Roger of Calabria*, 188–89.

reasonable argument that using yeast is not harmful when it is done in good faith."[175] Guibert wrote that although the Greeks accepted the paschal nature of the Last Supper and Christ's own use of unleavened bread to institute the sacrament, they did not feel bound to follow his example since they believed the use of azymes was not "a central part of the mystery."[176]

Shortly after the Latins established themselves in the East,[177] Anselm of Canterbury wrote a letter to Walram, bishop of Naumburg, titled *The Sacrifice of Unleavened and Leavened Bread* (*Epistola de Sacrificio Azimi et Fermentati*), on the debate concerning Eucharistic bread.[178] He acknowledged that "to many judicious Catholics, it seems that what the Greeks do is not contrary to the Christian faith" since "unleavened bread and leavened bread do not differ in substance" and thus in the Eucharist Christ's body gives "eternal life, irrespective of whether [it] is leavened or unleavened."[179] Nevertheless, wrote Anselm, "It is perfectly clear that it is better to consecrate unleavened bread than to consecrate leavened bread—not only because to do so is much more suitable, pure, and exact, but also because the Lord did this. Hence, it is not to be passed over in silence that when the Greeks anathematize the 'azimites'—for this is what they call us—they are anathematizing Christ."[180]

Anselm then dealt with the charge that the use of azymes was Judaizing, for since Christ certainly used unleavened bread at the Last Supper, "If they say that we Judaize, let them likewise say that Christ Judaized.... For we consecrate unleavened bread not in order to observe the Old Law but in order to perform the rite more exactly and to imitate the Lord who performed it without Judaizing."[181] Not everyone who eats azymes does so in observance of the Law, just as a man "required to circumcise his foreskin" for health reasons is not necessarily Judaizing.[182] "Therefore, when we

---

[175] Guibert of Nogent, *Gesta Dei per Francos* 1.2; Eng. trans.: Robert Levine, *The Deeds of God through the Franks: A Translation of Guibert de Nogent's "Gesta Dei per Francos"* (Woodbridge, Suffolk: Boydell Press, 1997), 31. William of Tyre, perhaps a bit less charitably, wrote that the Greeks were "insolently separated from the Church of Rome [and] regard everyone who does not follow their worthless traditions as a heretic." William of Tyre, *History of Deeds Done beyond the Sea*, 2:1021. To this the Old French translator of the *Historia* added, "Although they said they were Christians they nevertheless did not agree with the Latins on the manner of preparing the sacrifice and did not want to obey the Roman Church in any way. They called all those who did not follow their customs in the church service false Christians and heretics (*faus crestiens et popelicans*)." Guillaume de Tyr, *L'Estoire de Eracles, empereur, et la conqueste de la Terre d'Outre-Mer, c'est la continuation de "l'Estoire" de Guillaume, arcevesque de Sur.—Continuation de Guillaume de Tyr, de 1229 à 1261*, vol. 2 (Paris: Académie des inscriptions et belles-lettres., 1859), 424. Eng. trans.: Savvas Neocleous, *Heretics, Schismatics, or Catholics: Latin Attitudes to the Greeks in the Long Twelfth Century* (Toronto: Pontifical Institute of Medieval Studies, 2019), 225–26.

[176] According to Guibert, "The Lord had put an end to the old ways by eating lamb with unleavened bread, and celebrating the sacrament of his own body with the same bread, because there was no other bread, and he could not fulfill the law at that time in any other way, to them the use of unleavened bread, necessary at the time, did not seem a central part of the mystery, just as the dipping of the mouthful was an indication not of the carrying out of the sacrament but of Judas's betrayal." Guibert of Nogent, *Gesta Dei per Francos* 1.2: Eng. trans.: Levine, *The Deeds of God through the Franks*, 31.

[177] No later than December 1105.

[178] Anselm of Canterbury, *Epistola de sacrificio azimi et fermentati*; Eng. trans.: Jasper Hopkins and Herbert Richardson, eds. and trans., *Complete Philosophical and Theological Treatises of Anselm of Canterbury* (Minneapolis, MN: Arthur J. Banning Press, 2000), 515–22. Anselm had probably become familiar with the Greek objections during his 1098 encounter in Bari.

[179] Ibid., 515–16.
[180] Ibid., 516.
[181] Ibid., 516–17.
[182] Ibid., 517.

consecrate unleavened bread ... we in no way thereby observe the oldness of the Law but we render honor to the truth of the Gospel." For Anselm the Latins simply deemed azymes "more suitable for producing the reality of the Lord's Body" since this was the bread used in the old Law to prefigure the sacrifice.[183]

As for the Greeks' emphasis on symbolism, they should realize that "the word 'leaven' both [in] the Old Testament and the New signif[ies] sin."[184] This is why the Latins used unleavened bread, for it symbolizes that the Messiah has come into the world, but without the "leaven" of sin.[185] The West maintained that unleavened bread is not only a better symbol for Christ, whose "body ... was unleavened (i.e., free from the stain of sin)," but also a better reminder that "we who partake of His Body ought to be unleavened, in accordance with the words of the apostle.... Therefore, whether our consecration of unleavened bread has a symbolic significance or whether it has no symbolic significance, the Greeks cannot at all show us to be blameworthy. Instead, either we alone act rightly and they act wrongly, or else if they act rightly we act more rightly and more correctly."[186]

Anselm then offered an extended meditation on the relation between "the Spirit and the letter" of the Law, since the Greeks "say that Christians ought not to use symbols because the old things (wherein symbols were necessary) have passed away.... Thus they try to show that the letter which the old Passover commands to be celebrated with unleavened bread kills us when we observe the letter by consecrating unleavened bread."[187] Unlike the Jews, who could not properly understand the Old Testament because in adhering to the letter "a veil is placed over their hearts" (2 Cor 3:15), Latins grasped the spirit of the Law since in Christ the veil is taken away.[188] Anselm then went on to note the irony that the Greeks often quoted the Old Testament—"Offer a sacrifice of praise with leaven" (Am 4:5)—to support their teaching, demonstrating that it was the Greeks who were observing the old Law, "For in observance of the letter they sacrifice with leavened bread.[189]

A few years later, in 1110, Rupert of Deutz (d. 1129) wrote *The Book on the Divine Offices* (*Liber de divinis officiis*), which addressed the use of unleavened bread in the Western liturgy and the Greek objections to this practice.[190] Employing a bit of word-play, Rupert wrote that "Greece was spoilt [*fermentata est*] by so many heresies" that it was not surprising "that it sacrifices with leavened bread (*de fermento*)" and accuses the Romans of all sorts of errors.[191] Constantinople, which had "produced not only heretics, but even many heresiarchs," presumptuously called the Latins azymites and

---

[183] Ibid., 517–18.
[184] Ibid., 518. Anselm cited 1 Corinthians 5:8 to prove this.
[185] Ibid. For Anselm the Greeks seemed to "to favor the pagans, who think that Jesus was leavened by sin, as are other men." Ibid.
[186] Ibid., 519.
[187] Ibid., 520.
[188] Ibid., 521.
[189] Ibid.
[190] Rupert of Deutz, *Liber de divinis officiis*, ed. Rhaban Haacke, CCM 7 (Turnhout: Brepols, 1967), 52–56. On Rupert's career and his composition of this liturgical commentary, see John Van Engen, *Rupert of Deutz* (Berkeley: University of California Press, 1983), 362.
[191] Rupert of Deutz, *Liber de divinis officiis*, 52–53; Eng. trans.: Neocleous, *Heretics, Schismatics, or Catholics*, 47.

disdained "the customs of the Roman church ... founded higher upon the rock of apostolic faith."[192] Yet despite his sharp invective in defense of the Roman rite, Rupert never denied the validity of the Greek Eucharist and "stopped short of declaring that one could not perform the sacrament with leavened bread."[193]

A similar position was held by Alger of Liège (d. 1131), who used the theology of transubstantiation to argue that because the bread ceased to be bread after the consecration, its accidental properties (i.e., leavened or unleavened) ultimately mattered little.[194] For this reason Alger held that despite the debates and name-calling ("Azymites" vs. "Fermentarians") Christ's body became present, "whether the bread is unleavened or leavened," which is why it was "not against the Christian faith" to use either in the sacrifice of the altar.[195]

The Mid-Twelfth Century

The continued Latin presence in the Levant ensured that exchanges on the use of azymes remained a regular feature of twelfth-century theology and polemics, among which the 1136 debate between Anselm of Havelberg and Niketas of Nicomedia holds a special place.[196] Arranged by Emperor John II ("the Beautiful"; 1118–43), it covered three of the most controversial religious issues of the day: the procession of the Holy Spirit, the primacy of Rome, and the use of unleavened bread.[197] Niketas contended that Rome had once used leavened bread, that this practice had been confirmed "by the popes Melchiades and Siricius," and that only later had the use of azymes been "established and promulgated" by later popes.[198] He then asked Anselm, tongue in cheek, if the East—allegedly bound to obey the authority of the popes in all things—should follow the teachings of the earlier popes or the later. Niketas seems to have believed that both in the apostolic church and in Rome itself, "everyone used unleavened or

---

[192] Ibid. Rome, which had a "direct chain of transmission from Christ to Peter, and from Peter to the bishops of the Roman church," was an "impregnable wall against all heresies" and had "always confounded the heretics of both Greece and the entire world." Ibid.

[193] Schabel, "The Quarrel over Unleavened Bread," 96.

[194] Alger of Liège, *De sacramentis de corporis et sanguinis Dominici: Libri Tres* (London: David Nutt, 1873), 298–307.

[195] Ibid., 299; Eng. trans.: Schabel, "The Quarrel over Unleavened Bread," 96. Schabel also mentions the work of Pierre de Celle (*Liber de Panibus* PL 202:943-51), who similarly defended the Latin rite without denying the validity of the Greek rite. Ibid.

[196] Anselm of Havelberg, *Anticimenon: On the Unity of the Faith and the Controversies with the Greeks*, trans. Ambrose Criste and Carol Neel, Cistercian Studies 232 (Collegeville, MN: Liturgical Press, 2010), 162–63. Whether the *Anticimneon* is a literary production or a verbatim account is the subject of some debate. For recent scholarship see Norman Russell, "Anselm of Havelberg and the Union of the Churches," *Sobornost* 1 (1979): 19–41; Jay Lees, *Deeds into Words in the Twelfth Century* (Leiden: Brill, 1997); Sebastian Sigler, *Anselm von Havelberg: Beiträge zum Lebensbild eines Politikers, Theologen und königlichen Gesandten im 12. Jahrhundert* (Aachen: Shaker, 2005); Alex Novikoff, "Anselm of Havelberg's Controversies with the Greeks: A Moment in the Scholastic Culture of Disputation," in Cameron and Gaul, *Dialogues and Debate from Antiquity to Late Byzantium*, 105–22; Yury P. Avvakumov, "Anselm of Havelberg as 'Ecumenist': Fiction and History," in Irene Bueno and Camille Rouxpetel, eds., *Les récits historiques entre Orient et Occident (XIe–XVe siècle)* (Rome: École française de Rome, 2019), 207–36.

[197] For brief descriptions of the other two sections see Siecienski, *The Filioque*, 121–23, and *The Papacy and the Orthodox*, 268–71.

[198] Anselm of Havelberg, *Anticimenon*, 185.

leavened bread indifferently according to the judgement of those who presided or offered it, without any scandal among those so communicating, whether they were Greek or Latin."[199] He argued that the dispute was actually the Latins' fault since it was they who first began to "blaspheme our leavened bread, judging it unworthy for the sacrifice of the altar, calling us heretics ... [and] refusing to communicate with us."[200]

Anselm began his presentation appealing to the custom of the Roman church, an argument he thought necessary since so many Easterners, including the Ruthenians ("virtual idiots ignorant of all divine Scriptures"), "imitate your rite by custom alone."[201] He would not believe that Rome "once used leavened bread and later, setting this practice aside, took up unleavened bread," choosing to ground the Roman practice in the example of Christ himself, since he "himself used unleavened bread in that first consecration of his most sacred body ... establishing this as the model they should follow in commemorating him."[202] Scripture was clear that it was Passover, and "according to the commandant of the law leavened bread was to be found in no house of Israel in those seven days but only unleavened bread, and because Christ came not to abolish the law but to fulfill it, clearly he used unleavened bread consecrating it in the Paschal Supper, so fulfilling the ancient Passover and inaugurating the new."[203] He asked Niketas: "Does this reasoning not seem sufficient to you? [Surely] Christ, as author of the sacrament, he whom we must follow in all things, should suffice for you as a model and example."[204]

Niketas acknowledged that Anselm had "adduced the reasoning that you promised, supporting it with great authorities," but then raised the question of language, since "we read thus in the Gospel: ἄρτον εὐλόγησεν, that is 'He blessed bread.' When the text says ἄρτος it seems to indicate mere bread, common bread, that is, leavened bread such as men use everywhere and which they named by the usual term ἄρτος, that is, 'bread.'"[205] Anselm replied that in the Old Testament that "nowhere in the law is leavened bread offered to the Lord in sacrifice, instead always unleavened bread or the purest fine flour, without any leaven. So we must believe too that the Son of God himself, because he knows best how God the Father must be appeased, used unleavened bread in the consecration of his most sacred body."[206] Leaven in Scripture, he contended, was "nowhere understood to signify goodness," which is why we are told to "beware the leaven of the Pharisees."[207]

It was at this point that Niketas astonishingly (and somewhat unbelievably) surrendered, conceding that Anselm was essentially correct that all "the authorities and

---

[199] Ibid., 186–87. "We can be the surer of this because we read that when the great number of Greeks and Latins lived together in the city of Rome, not only Latins but many Greeks were heads of the holy Roman Church. Pope Anacletus was a Greek, as were his successors.... Do you imagine that these Greek prelates and their Latin subjects had daily conflict about sacrificing unleavened or leavened bread so that the Greek pontiffs offered only leavened bread and the Roman Church never communicated with them through it?" Ibid., 186.
[200] Ibid., 188.
[201] Ibid., 189–90.
[202] Ibid., 193–94.
[203] Ibid., 194–95.
[204] Ibid., 195.
[205] Ibid., 196.
[206] Ibid., 197.
[207] Ibid., 198.

the logical arguments" taught "we ought to offer an unleavened host."[208] While the East's use of leavened bread was indeed ancient and "could not be changed without great scandal to many," he admitted to Anselm, "I think it should be changed ... [and] no Greek sages disagree with me in this conclusion."[209] Niketas himself said that he would be happy to participate in an azymite Eucharist, and that "if it happened that I were in a place where no leavened bread whatsoever were available but unleavened bread was ready at hand, and I wished to sing Mass, offering the Lord the sacrifice of the altar, I would certainly not shrink from unleavened bread, rather would confidently consecrate it for offering as an immaculate sacrifice to God."[210]

Niketas, knowing that the "faint-hearted" and uneducated would never give up their ancient practice without resistance, held that the only way to resolve the issue was

> to celebrate a general council at a suitable place and time convening as the one body and for all to adopt, in uniformity, universally, either the rite of unleavened bread or of leavened bread universally. Or if neither one nor the other might be accepted universally without some scandal ... they might at least agree in this—that neither this side nor that rashly condemn the other for the usage of leavened or unleavened bread to which it is respectively accustomed, rather offer each other mutual peace.[211]

Believing that there would still be resistance, Niketas concluded that "it would be well to allow what has been done among us for a long time, especially since leavened and unleavened bread are alike bread, although differing in form, still in substance no different in being leavened or unleavened."[212] Christ, that "living bread who came down from heaven may aptly be figured in either," which is why the host "may be rightly made from either for the salvation of those believing in it, and those faithfully offering it, if not for the salvation of those wickedly disputing about it."[213]

Other dialogues—whether fictional or real—were rarely as amiable, as Peter the Deacon's *Altercatio pro Romana Ecclesia contra Graecum quendam* (1137) attests.[214] After discussion on the papacy and the procession the parties moved on to azymes, Peter cited the earlier accusation that "like the Manicheans the [Greeks] think that what is fermented is alive" (*Sicut Manichaei, inter alia, quodlibet fermentatum fatentur animatum esse*).[215] The Greeks then upbraided Peter for his youth, which

---

[208] Ibid., 200.
[209] Ibid., 199–200.
[210] Ibid., 199.
[211] Ibid., 199–200.
[212] Ibid., 200.
[213] Ibid. Unfortunately for Anselm, his later debate with Basil of Ohrid in Thessalonica (1154) did not end as happily. However, in 1156 Basil responded to a letter of Pope Hadrian IV that the issues separating the churches (including the use of azymes) were not so great that a general council could not settle them, as long as "bishops under your [i.e., the pope's] direction and those of us in the East" acted in a spirit of genuine goodwill. See Josef Schmidt, ed., *Des Basilius aus Achrida, Erzbischofs von Thessalonich, bisher unedierte Dialog* (Munich: J. J. Lentner, 1901), 16–23.
[214] Jean-Marie Martin, "*Petri Diaconi Altercatio pro Romana Ecclesia contra Graecum quendam (1137) Édition, traduction et commentaire*," in Olivier Delouis, Sophie Métivier, and Paule Pagès, eds., *Le saint, le moine et le paysan: Mélanges d'histoire byzantine offerts à Michel Kaplan* (Paris: Éditions de la Sorbonne, 2016), 407–56.
[215] Ibid., 428.

made him "talk foolishly, attacking the unchanging faith of the Greeks and praising the Roman Church ... which Judaizes with the azymes."[216] They told him only Jews "keep the unleavened because of the prescription of Moses" and "it was necessary to adhere to the use of unleavened bread until the Last Supper of the Lord, when the shadow of the Old Testament passed away and the New [dispensation] started."[217] "Why you sacrifice with unleavened bread we do not know, for azymes do not differ from stone," while "leavened bread is, so to speak, an animated object," which is why, according to the evangelist "the Lord Jesus Christ gave his disciples leavened, and not unleavened, bread."[218]

To counter these arguments Peter referred his interlocutor to the earlier works of Cardinal Humbert, reminding him that "at the Last Supper the Lord, with his disciples, ate unleavened bread, not fermented bread. For he did not come to abolish the law, but to fulfill it; and he did it as he commanded us to do, saying, Do this in memory of me."[219] As for the Greeks' notion of "animated bread," this confirmed that the Greeks were Manichaeans rejecting the notion that

> the man Jesus Christ ... celebrated the Mosaic Passover ... [and] ate unleavened bread with his disciples.... This is why our holy and truly apostolic lord, Pope Innocent II, father, master, doctor and universal prince of all Christians, who possesses through the apostle Peter, after God, full power on earth and in heaven, accepts the sacrificial rite transmitted by the Savior to his disciples, and scorns the ungodly innovations of the Greeks as dung and considers them null.[220]

Occasionally voices were raised urging moderation, including that of the philosopher Theorianos, who had been sent by the emperor Manuel I Komnenos (d. 1180) to negotiate union with the Armenians.[221] For Theorianos the question of azymes was not church-dividing, for if the elements were changed into the body and blood of Christ, it was "superfluous to dispute whether they were from azymes or enzymes, or from red or white wine (ἡ εξ αζύμων ἡ ενζύμων ἠν, ἡ λευκού, η ερυθρού τυχόν οίνου) or to pursue such curious and futile enquiries with respect to the tremendous mysteries."[222] Similarly, John IX, Orthodox patriarch of Jerusalem in exile (1156–66), compared the controversy over azymes to the early church's debate over

---

[216] Ibid., 429.
[217] Ibid.
[218] Ibid.
[219] Ibid.
[220] Ibid., 430.
[221] See Theorianos, *Disputatio cum Armeniorum Catholico* (PG 133:120–212); Theorianos, *Disputatio secunda cum Nersete Patriarcha Generali Armeniorum* (PG 133:212–97); Theorianos, *Epistola ad sacerdotes in monte degentes*, in Raymond-Joseph Loenertz, "L'epitre de Theorien le Philosophe aux pretres d'Oreine," in Institut français d'études byzantines, *Memorial Louis Petit: Melanges d'histoire et d'archeologie byzantines* (Bucharest, 1948), 317–35. The *Tractatus contra Graecos* attributed quotations from Theorianos to John Chrysostom, explaining why he appeared so often (albeit misattributed) in later Latin polemical works.
[222] Quotation in Angelo Mai, ed., *Novae Patrum Bibliothecae, Tomos Quintus: Sancti Nicephori Patriarchae Constantinopolitani Opera Adversus Iconomachos. Sancti Theodori Studitae scripta varia quae in Sirmondi editione desunt* (Rome, 1849), 125; Eng. trans.: John Mason Neale, *History of the Eastern Church: Introduction pt 2* (London: Joseph Masters, 1850), 1074.

circumcision, for just as neither "circumcision profited anything nor uncircumcision... so neither in Christ does leaven profit anything, or azymes, but faith."²²³

Emperor Manuel's generally pro-Latin policies were designed with the hope that continued dialogue could help "diffuse the schism with Rome, which those who sought to justify attacks on the empire had used to such good effect."²²⁴ The emperor even expressed a willingness to "root out practices that had so shocked Odo of Deuil at the time of the Second Crusade," among which was the Greeks' "treatment of the eucharist," and the washing of any altar on which a Latin celebrated an [azymite] eucharist as if to purify it from defilement.²²⁵ Unfortunately, Manuel's efforts had the opposite effect, as theological encounters (like one in 1166 over the phrase "the Father is greater than I") generally brought about more conflict than goodwill, especially if "the emperor supported what was seen to be a Latin interpretation.²²⁶ Out of such encounters came Gerhoh of Reichersberg's (d. 1169) *Tractatus contra Graecorum errorem*,²²⁷ Leo Tuscus's 1177 work *De haeresibus et praevaricationibus Graecorum*,²²⁸ and Hugh Eteriano's, *De sancto et immortali Deo*, all of which took aim at the Greeks,²²⁹ Niketas of Thessolinike's (aka Niketas of Moroneia) *Six Dialogues against the Filioque*,²³⁰ and Nicholas of Methone's anti-Latin works,²³¹ which attacked the West. Nothing really new was

---

[223] John IX in Patriarch Dositheos, ed., Τόμος ἀγάπης (Jassy, 1698), 505; Eng. trans.: Neale, *History of the Eastern Church*, 1074. See Foteini Spingou, "John IX Patriarch of Jerusalem in Exile," *Byzantinische Zeitschrift* 109 (2016): 179–206.

[224] Harris, *Byzantium and the Crusades*, 119.

[225] Ibid. "For instance, if our priests celebrated mass on Greeks altars, the Greeks afterwards purified them with propitiatory offerings and ablutions, as if they had been defiled.... But, oh dreadful thing! We heard of an ill usage of theirs which should be expiated by death; namely, that every time they celebrate the marriage of one of our men, if he has been baptized in the Roman way, they rebaptize him before they make the pact. We know other heresies of theirs, both concerning their treatment of the Eucharist and concerning the procession of the Holy Ghost... and because of this they were judged not to be Christians, and the Franks considered killing them a matter of no importance." Odo of Deuil, *De Profectione Ludovici VII in Orientem*, 55–57.

[226] Michael Angold, *Church and State in Byzantium under the Comneni, 1081-1261* (Cambridge: Cambridge University Press, 1995), 513. "Treatises concerning the Latin church were all, without exception, occasioned by imperial attempts at rapprochement with the papacy." Magdalino, *The Empire of Manuel I Komnenos*, 369. See also Peter Classen, "Das Konzil von Konstantinopel 1166 und die Lateiner," *Byzantinische Zeitschrift* 48 (1955): 339–68.

[227] Friederic Scheibelberger, *Gerhohi Reichersbergensis praepositi: opera hactenus inedita. Tomus I. Libri III De investigatione Antichristi, unacum tractatu adversus Graecos* (Lincii: M. Quirein, 1875), 341–57.

[228] See chapter 2 n. 183.

[229] Pietro Podolak and Anna Zago, eds., *Hvgonis Eteriani Epistolae, De sancto et immortali Deo, Compendiosa expositio, fragmenta Graeca, qvae extant*, Corpus Christianorum Continuatio Mediaevalis, CCCM 298 (Turnhout: Brepols Publishers, 2020).

[230] Alessandra Bucossi and L. D'Amelia, eds., *Nicetas Thessalonicensis, Dialogi sex de processione Spiritus Sancti*, Corpus Christianorum Series Graeca, CCSG 92 (Turnhout: Brepols Publishers, 2021). See also Alessandra Bucossi, "The Six Dialogues by Niketas 'Of Maroneia': A Contextualising Introduction," in *Cameron and Gaul, Dialogues and Debate from Antiquity to Late Byzantium*, 137–52.

[231] Arsenij Ivanenko and Athanasios Angelou, "Nicholas of Methone: The Life and Works of a Twelfth-Century Bishop," in Margaret Mullett and Roger Scott, eds., *Byzantium and the Classical Tradition: University of Birmingham Thirteenth Spring Symposium of Byzantine Studies 1979* (Birmingham: Centre for Byzantine Studies, University of Birmingham, 1981), 143–48; Arsenij Ivanenko and Athanasios Angelou, *Nicholas of Methone, Refutation of Proclus' Elements of Theology: A Critical Edition with an Introduction on Nicholas' Life and Works* (Leiden: Brill, 1984).

offered by either side, as the anti-Filioque and anti-azymite arguments first brought forward in earlier centuries were simply restated.[232] For all his efforts Manuel's attempts to improve relations probably had the opposite effect, feeding the general anti-Latinism that boiled over into the Constantinopolitan riots of 1182 that killed thousands of the city's Latin residents.[233]

Before leaving, there are two works that touch on the use of azymes that are worth mentioning, if only because of their authors. Baldwin of Forde (d. 1190), the archbishop of Canterbury who crusaded with Richard I, wrote a treatise on the Eucharist (*De sacramento altaris*), arguing that it was important to remember that not only had Christ instituted the sacrament with unleavened bread, but also that the Old Testament signs (e.g., Passover azymes) maintained their significance even if superseded by the reality (Christ).[234] Although Baldwin did not necessarily condemn the Greek practice, others did, including the future Pope Innocent III (d. 1216), whose own work on the Eucharist, *De sacro altaris mysterio libri sex*,[235] took aim at the Greeks for celebrating the sacrament with leavened bread despite the fact that "Christ, without doubt, consecrated unleavened bread."[236] The proper celebration of the sacrament was then passed on "to the blessed apostles Peter and Paul" and maintained inviolable in the Roman Church, where "no storm of heretical perversity was able to shake ... the rock of apostolic faith."[237] It was the Greeks who changed the practice, just one of the many "heresies [that] fermented the Church of Constantinople," where they dared "to call Latins, among other things, azymites, when, more truly, they should be known as fermentarians."[238] For Innocent the matter was simple: "Christ consecrated unleavened bread when he established the sacrament," the apostles and fathers followed his example, and unlike those who "still sacrifice with leavened bread ... the Roman Church is in communion with these true Catholics."[239]

Innocent, despite his genuine desire for unity, albeit on his terms, would eventually launch the crusade that consummated the schism brewing since the first Greek attacks on the azymes centuries earlier. Although the Latins' use of unleavened bread

---

[232] For a list of Latin works in this period that, at least tangentially, touched on the azyme debate, see Avvakumov, *Die Entstehung des Unionsgedankens*, 118–24. For Greek anti-Latin works see ibid., 91–103.

[233] "The emperor's support for the Latin position caught many of the Greeks off-guard and put them on the defensive. Probably more people now found Latin ideas threatening and were prepared to resist them at all cost." Tia Kolbaba, "The Orthodoxy of the Latins in the Twelfth Century," in Andrew Louth and Augustine Casiday, eds., *Byzantine Orthodoxies: Papers from the Thirty-Sixth Spring Symposium of Byzantine Studies, University of Durham, 23–25 March 2002* (Aldershot: Ashgate, 2006), 214.

[234] Baldwin of Forde, *Tractatus De Sacramento Altaris* (Turnhout: Brepols Publishers, 2010). See also Jean Leclercq, John Morson, and E. de Solms, eds., *Le Sacrement de l'autel, Tomes I and II*, SC 93 and 94 (Paris: Les éditions du Cerf, 1963); Jeremiah Grosse, "Abbot Baldwin of Ford on the Sacrament of the Altar," *Downside Review* 127 (2009): 269–78. However, like all before and after him, Baldwin never explicitly condemned the Greek practice.

[235] Innocent III, *De sacro altaris mysterio libri sex* (PL 217:773–916). For the discussion on azymes see PL 217:854–58.

[236] Innocent spoke about the five potential meanings of *pascha* in Scripture (the day, the festival, the lamb, the time, the azymes) to prove the Greek understanding of the paschal chronology was in error. Schabel, "The Quarrel over Unleavened Bread in Western Theology, 1234–1439," 99.

[237] Ibid., 100.
[238] Ibid.
[239] Ibid.

would remain an important issue in the years to come, the pope's continued demands for obedience eventually meant that the primacy, and not unleavened bread, came to stand alongside the Filioque as the chief theological causes of the division. Azymes were still an issue, of that there is no doubt, but as the thirteenth century progressed, it was clear that it was now running a distant third behind the other two.

5

The Azyme Debate

The Fourth Crusade to the Modern Era

The long-simmering hostility between East and West, which occasionally boiled over into violence as it did in 1182 and 1185, entered a new phase in 1204 following the crusaders' sack of Constantinople and the establishment of the Latin empire. Anti-Latin polemical works proliferated, although it was during this period that the papacy and the Filioque, rather than azymes, became the Greeks' chief complaints.[1] That does not mean that the azymes were forgotten—on the contrary, anti-azymite tracts were plentiful, and the Latins' use of unleavened bread in the Eucharist remained among the most common charges in the lists of Latin errors.[2] According to Yury P. Avvakumov, by the end of the thirteenth century the Orthodox had produced no fewer than forty-three works addressing the use of azymes, most of them polemically charged attacks on the Latin practice.[3]

The Latins naturally countered with tracts of their own—Avvakumov mentions no less than forty-nine, although that number would be much larger should we count the hundreds of unedited works in which azymes were treated, if only briefly.[4] Latin authors argued not only for the legitimacy of unleavened bread, but also for its superiority over the Greek practice, maintaining that the latter was merely tolerated for the sake of religious peace. Yet despite all their efforts to get the Greeks to admit the validity of an azymite Eucharist, for most it remained, along with commemoration of the pope and the recitation of the Filioque, the clearest manifestation of the Latins' heretical nature. As a consequence, the Greeks scrubbed any altar on which a Latin priest had celebrated an azymite Eucharist, "and would not offer sacrifice on them until they had washed them, as if the altars had been defiled thereby."[5]

---

[1] This was largely the result of Pope Innocent's ongoing demands for obedience, leading the Greeks to question the whole idea of Rome's primacy and the theological arguments that supported it. As Joseph Gill wrote, it was during this period that the debate about the papacy began to generate "heat"—i.e., no longer was it a academic matter "carried on without a sense of urgency"; it became an intense intra-Byzantine debate about the acceptability of Roman primacy and all that went along with it. Joseph Gill, *Byzantium and the Papacy, 1198–1400* (New Brunswick, NJ: Rutgers University Press, 1979), 12. See also Donald Nicol, "The Papal Scandal," in Derek Baker, ed., *The Orthodox Churches and the West, Studies in Church History 13* (Oxford: Oxford University Press, 1976), 141–68; A. Edward Siecienski, "Byzantium and Papacy from the Fifth to Fifteenth Centuries: The Three Stage Response," in Alessandra Bucossi and Anna Calia, eds., *Contra Latinos et Adversus Graecos: The Separation between Rome and Constantinople from the Ninth to the Fifteenth Century* (Leuven: Peeters, 2020), 1–30.

[2] Kolbaba, *The Byzantine Lists*, 190.

[3] Avvakumov, *Die Entstehung des Unionsgedankens*, 91–103.

[4] Ibid., 118–24.

[5] Constitutions of the Fourth Lateran Council; Eng. trans.: Tanner, ed., *Decrees of the Ecumenical Councils* 1, 236. This charge echoes Odo of Deuil's *De profectione Ludovici VII in Orientem*. See chapter 4 n. 225.

By the time negotiations began for the Council of Ferrara-Florence, it was clear that the West's use of azymes would be on the agenda, even if its significance had diminished relative to other issues. At the council itself very little time was spent discussing the matter, as the old debate was replaced with a relatively new one—the moment of consecration (aka the *epiclesis* debate)—which occurred in large part because the scholastics' rediscovery of Aristotle brought with it an increased interest not only in the proper "matter" (*materia*) of the Eucharist, but also its "form" (*forma consecrationis*).[6] Christ became present in the Eucharist—on this East and West were united—but questions remained on exactly when and how this happened. Of course the West's use of unleavened bread was not forgotten, and Mark of Ephesus still hoped to persuade the Latins to return to the ancient ways, but by Florence the issue that had caused the schism had become little more than a distraction.

This trend continued in the centuries after Florence as the papacy and Filioque took center stage, although anti-azyme works occasionally appeared (e.g., the writings of Metrophanes Kritopoulos and Eustratios Argenti stand as prime examples). As late as 1895 the Orthodox replied to Pope Leo XIII that they could not imagine the restoration of communion while "one [church] uses leavened bread in the sacrament of the Holy Eucharist, and another unleavened."[7] It was only later, with the rapprochement that occurred in the mid-twentieth century, that azymes all but completely disappeared as an ecumenical issue and more serious concerns became the focus of the dialogue.

The Fourth Crusade

If one were to make a movie about the 1204 Latin conquest of Constantinople, one might be tempted to call it *Attack of the Azymites*, for indeed, that is how many Byzantines saw it. Describing the 1189 encounter between Frederick Barbarossa and the Armenians, Niketas Choniates called it a meeting of friends, because the Germans and Armenians "agree with one another in most of their heresies," including the shared "use [of] azymes in their Divine liturgies," along with "other perverse doctrines which are rejected by Orthodox Christians."[8] To his great shame, in exchange for the crusaders' help Alexios IV had agreed to accept these perverse doctrines, "abjur[ing] his faith" and "agree[ing] to ... the altering of the sacred customs of the Romans" by introducing unleavened bread.[9] In April 1204, when he was unable to meet his obligations, the Franks and Venetians moved into the city to take what they were owed, cutting a swathe of destruction wherever they went. Especially galling for Niketas was how the crusaders treated the Greek Eucharist, bemoaning "how horrible it was to see the Divine body and blood of Christ poured out and thrown to the ground" and the

---

[6] See especially the recent work of Christiaan Kappes, *The Epiclesis Debate at the Council of Florence* (Notre Dame, IN: University of Notre Dame Press, 2019).

[7] Anthimos VII, "A Reply to the Papal Encyclical of Pope Leo XIII on Reunion," in Eustathius Metallinos, ed., *Orthodox and Catholic Union: The Reply of the Holy Orthodox Church to Roman Catholic Overtures on Reunion and Ecumenism* (Seattle: St. Nectarios Press, 1985), 3.

[8] Niketas Choniates, *O City of Byzantium*, 222.

[9] Ibid., 296.

"precious chalices and patens ... seized as plunder" while "the remaining vessels [were set] on their tables to serve as bread dishes and wine goblets."[10]

Because of the strong anti-Latin line followed by Niketas in the *Annals*, it often surprises readers that in his *Dogmatic Panoply*, based largely on the *Panoplia Dogmatike* of Euthymius Zigabenus, he seems to moderate his position, especially on azymes.[11] The Filioque, he was clear, was a nonnegotiable barrier to reunion that had created an "abyss of disagreement" which now opened before them "like a chasm."[12] However, in his treatment of the azymes (22nd *Tomos*), while Niketas maintained "that the Greek usage of leavened bread is certainly "more suitable for the mystic sacrifices," he nevertheless admitted that the West's use of azymes is an "old tradition and is so thus undoubtedly also valid."[13] Azymes, which Niketas had described in the *Annals* as a "heresy" and "perverse doctrine," were now written off as an insignificant difference, citing the earlier views of Peter of Antioch and Theophylact of Ohrid, who in their efforts to overcome the schism "did not persist in splitting hairs on the other heresies we blame on the Latins."[14]

There is some evidence that Niketas was not alone in his irenicism, and that even after the Fourth Crusade many Greek clerics still recognized a degree of kinship with their Latin cousins.[15] For example, Thietmar, a Westphalian cleric who led a pilgrimage to the Holy Land in 1217–18, recounted the many kindnesses of Greek Christians and the conversations he had with the pious bishops and monks he met.[16]

---

[10] Ibid., 314–25.

[11] According to Luciano Bossina, this stems from the different genres of the two works (history vs. theology), and from the times when they were written. The *Dogmatic Panoply*, he argues, was written "at the very moment in which a Latin patriarch was raised to the Constantinopolitan throne," and "the idea of a reappraisal of the relationship between the two Churches was a pressing item on the agenda.... It is as if Niketas was saying: this is the history of heresies, these are the dogmatic grounds on which the ecclesiastical tradition has been founded and these are the bases on which we can undertake a theological debate with the Latins. These are the negotiable principles and these are the non-negotiable ones." Luciano Bossina, "Niketas Choniates as a Theologian," in Alicia Simpson and Stephanos Efthymiades, eds., *Niketas Choniates: A Historian and a Writer* (Geneva: Pomme d'or, 2009), 174.

[12] Niketas Choniates, *Dogmatike Panoplia*, in Bossina, "Niketas Choniates as a Theologian," 180.

[13] Ibid.

[14] Ibid., 181.

[15] Many bishops, for example, those of Rhaedestos (Rodosto) and Euboea (Negroponte), submitted to papal authority in 1205, and over the next few years "a number of monasteries submitted to the pope and received, in return, papal protection for their rights and properties." Kolbaba, "Byzantine Perceptions of Latin Religious 'Errors,'" 129. Some undoubtedly did so under great pressure, but as Kolbaba reminds us, "one cannot (as much scholarship has done) write off such men as 'merely weak or evil, willing to sell their souls for safety or political preference. Maybe some were craven traitors, but we need not take their opponents' word for it. It is equally likely that some men honestly believed that an oath of obedience to the pope was no stain on their orthodoxy. That belief, however, made their definition of orthodoxy quite different from that of the anti-Latin, anti-papal rigorists." Ibid., 130. At the same time, Nicholas Coureas noted that "not all Greek prelates submitted to the incoming Latin clergy. In Athens, Corinth, Patras and Crete, the Greek metropolitan archbishops fled to Nicaea," where they remained protected by the empire-in-exile. Nicholas Coureas, "The Latin and Greek Churches in Former Byzantine Lands under Latin Rule," in Nickiphoros Tsougarakis and Peter Lock, eds. *A Companion to Latin Greece* (Leiden: Brill, 2015), 151. See also Christopher Schabel, "*Ab hac hora in antea*: Oaths to the Roman Church in Frankish Cyprus (and Greece)," in M. Sinibaldi, K. J. Lewis, B. Major, and J. A. Thompson, eds., *Crusader Landscapes in the Medieval Levant: The Archaeology and History of the Latin East* (Cardiff: University of Wales Press, 2016), 361–72.

[16] Thietmar, *Peregrenatio*, in Denys Pringle, ed., *Pilgrimage to Jerusalem and the Holy Land, 1187–1291* (London: Routledge, 2012), 95–133.

It was during one of these encounters that "a Greek bishop explained [the procession of the Holy Spirit] to me and said that it was not like that, but that the Greeks believed in the same way as the Latins except that they consecrated leavened bread."[17] As for the rumor that the Greeks "wash the altars after the celebration of the Latins ... the same bishop openly denied this."[18]

Demetrios Chomatenos, archbishop of Ohrid, also addressed the question of unleavened bread when he was asked whether "the azymes of the Latins, the vessels used in their church service, and their priestly vestments be considered common or sacred."[19] Chomatenos responded that while the canons had indeed prohibited eating the azymes of the Jews, "the Latin azymes are mentioned nowhere by any canon."[20] Thus while "many of our people, of an excessive zeal, have in private writings among themselves exploded this as a monstrosity," the use of azymes in the Eucharist was "never synodically debated nor were the Latins publicly condemned as heretics. But they eat with us and pray with us."[21] Citing Theophylacht's *Liber de iis quorum Latini incusantur* at length, he urged his coreligionists to charity, claiming that minor deviations in ritual should not be turned into church-dividing issues.[22] The azymes of the Latins and the vessels they used should be considered holy, for how could it be otherwise when "they are sealed by the invocation of the Lord's name, and hallowed, as we hear, by the holy prayers of James, the Lord's brother."[23] Chomatenos concluded that since the Latins "consider what we consecrate as holy, so we also consider what they consecrate as holy" and for this reason if they come "seeking to communicate at our hands of the holy oblation which is made with leavened bread, show[ing] plainly that they cannot think much of their azymes," they should be able to partake.[24]

---

[17] Ibid., 131.

[18] Ibid.

[19] Demetrios Chomatenos, *Responses to Constantine Kavasilas* in Joannes Baptista Pitra, *Analecta Sacra et Classica Spicilegio Solesmensi. Juris Ecclesiastici Graecorum VI* (RomE, 1891), 625-30. Sections of this work have been translated into English in William Palmer, *Dissertations on Subjects Relating to the "Orthodox" or "Eastern-Catholic" Communion* (London: Joseph Masters, 1853), 25-31. See also Eleonora Naxidou, "The Latin West in the Eyes of the Orthodox East: The Paradigm of the Archbishop of Ohrid Demetrios Chomatenos," *Church Studies* 15 (2018): 329-41. For the relation of this work to that of Ioannes of Kitros see Jean Darrouzès, "Les réponses canoniques de Jean de Kitros," *Revue des Etudes Byzantines* 31 (1973): 319-34.

[20] Demetrios Chomatenos, *Responses to Constantine Kavasilas*; Eng. trans.: Palmer, *Dissertations*, 25.

[21] Demetrios Chomatenos, *Responses to Constantine Kavasilas*; Eng. trans.: Savvas Neocleous, *Heretics, Schismatics, or Catholics? Latin Attitudes to the Greeks in the Long Twelfth Century* (Toronto: Pontifical Institute of Medieval Studies, 2019), 234.

[22] Naxidou points out that there were inconsistencies in Chomatenos's view of the Latins, which appeared to change years later during a dispute between Greek and Iberian monks on Mount Athos. The issues were ritual and papal authority, and Chomatenos wrote to the Greeks that they should cut off communion with the Iberians since the papal church was in schism with the Eastern patriarchates "because of its many different religious beliefs and practices, of which the most objectionable were the filioque and the use of the azymes." For this reason, he assumed that whoever embraced the western dogma and customs did not belong to the Orthodox community, but should be considered alien." Naxidou, "The Latin West in the Eyes of the Orthodox East," 335.

[23] Demetrios Chomatenos, *Responses to Constantine Kavasilas*; Eng. trans.: Palmer, *Dissertations*, 28.

[24] Ibid., 30. Theodore Balsamon had addressed the question of intercommunion in 1185, arguing that a Latin prisoner should not be permitted to partake of the Holy Mysteries "unless he first promises to refrain from Latin dogmas and customs, is instructed in the canons, and is made equal to the Orthodox." Patrick Demetrios Viscuso, ed., *Guide for a Church under Islam: The Sixty-Six Canonical Questions Attributed to Theodoros Balsamon* (Brookline, MA: Holy Cross Orthodox Press, 2014), 85.

However, if some in the East expressed a certain openness to the West, the vast majority did not, with Constantinopolitans slandering their Latin overlords, clerical and secular, as both "azymites and pneumatomachoi."[25] The bishop of Acre, Jacques de Vitry (d. 1240), wrote in his *Historia orientalis* that the Greeks' contempt for the Latin sacraments was such that they even refused to rise when a Latin priest entered a room with the Eucharist to distribute it to the sick.[26] Fueling hostility to the Latin church and its sacraments was the new patriarch's "foreignness" (Thomas Morisini was beardless and could not speak Greek), disputes over ecclesiastical jurisdiction, and the obvious differences in rite, which most Byzantines still viewed as heretical. To ease these tensions, and to aid in Pope Innocent's plan for the *reductio Graecorum*, the Latins once again resorted to dialogue and disputation, believing they could win the Greeks over to their way of thinking through force of logic.[27]

Among those who participated in these debates was Nicholas of Otranto (aka Nektarios of Casole), who served as translator in many of these meetings, and whose work against beards (Περὶ Γενείων) we encountered earlier.[28] Nicholas was also author of an anti-azyme tract (Τρία Συντάγματα), which stressed that leavened bread was once used by all, and that by changing the universal custom Rome was to blame for destroying the unity of the church.[29] As proof he brought forth passages from the *Dialogues* of Pope Gregory to prove that even the great Roman pope had once used leavened bread.[30] One of these texts related the story of how a repenting soul, now returned to earth, claimed that because he could no longer eat holy bread it should given to the church for the Eucharist (*Iste panis sanctus est, ego hunc manducare non possum*),[31] which proved to the bilingual Nicolas that Gregory celebrated Eucharist with fermented bread (*panis*) rather than *azymus*.

One memorable debate occurred in November 1214 when Cardinal Pelagius of Albano "assembled his whole council" for the purpose of debating Nicholas Mesarites on the subject of azymes."[32] Mesarites attacked the Latin practice as Judaizing, since

---

[25] Michael Angold, ed., *Nicholas Mesarites: His Life and Works in Translation* (Liverpool: Liverpool University Press, 2018), 180. The *pneumatomachoi* were an early Christian sect, opposed by Basil the Great, who denied the divinity of the Holy Spirit.

[26] Bird, ed., *Jacques de Vitry's History of the East*.

[27] According to Jeff Brubaker, the different ways these encounters were described probably says something about the way each side approached them. The Latins, more often than not, used the term *disputatio* to refer to these meetings. Among the Greeks, Nicholas Mesarites described the discussions in late 1204 as διαλαλία, "discourse," and διάλεξις, "conversation," while the meetings in 1206 and 1214 were ἄθλος, meaning "contests" or "spiritual struggles." Jeff Brubaker, *The Disputatio of the Latins and the Greeks 1234* (Liverpool: Liverpool University Press, 2023). See also Jean Richard, "The Establishment of the Latin Church in the Empire of Constantinople (1204–1227)," in Benjamin Arbel, Bernard Hamilton, and David Jacoby, eds., *Latins and Greeks in the Eastern Mediterranean after 1204* (London: Frank Cass, 1989), 45–62; Coureas, "The Latin and Greek Churches in Former Byzantine Lands," 145–84.

[28] See pages 62–63.

[29] "Nicholas's argument is clear: if the Latins ended this ancient custom, they are responsible for breaking the unity of the Church, which remained unchanged until the time of Pope Gregory the Great, who had been the guarantor of that unity." Schiano, "Omnes civitates nostre obedient veneration," 176.

[30] See page 110,n. 194.

[31] This story, which was later employed as a prooftext for Purgatory, will be covered in more detail in the next chapter.

[32] Angold, *Nicholas Mesarites: His Life and Works*, 270. See also August Heisenberg, *Neue Quellen zur Geschichte des lateinischen Kaisertums und der Kirchenunion 3: Der Bericht des Nikolaos Mesarites über die politischen und kirchlichen Ereignisse des Jahres 1214* (Munich: Verlag der bayer. Akad. der Wissenschaften, 1923).

the use of azymes had its roots in the Old Testament rather than the New. He told the cardinal that "we understand the word bread as something separate from unleavened bread.... If, therefore, you find in Mosaic text the word bread without closer definition then it will be bread pure and simple," while during Passover the Jews were specifically told to eat "unleavened bread with bitter herbs."[33] But the Latins erroneously held that the word *artos*, used during the institution of the Eucharist, meant unleavened [bread], which meant they celebrated the shadow [Passover] rather than reality [the new Pascha].[34] This was manifestly ridiculous, for while the Latins bore "a cross on [their] shoulders and [claimed to] have abolished Jewish customs," they simultaneously observed the old Jewish rites.[35] Even the Latins' own prayers showed them to be "transgressors against ... conscience," for during the anaphora the priest "ceaselessly and uncomplainingly" spoke under his breath of the "holy bread of the life everlasting (*panem sanctum vitae sempiternae*)," an obvious reference to "leavened bread and not the unleavened bread that you, being Roman, offer to the perfect and life-giving Trinity."[36] According to Nicholas's own account of the encounter, the cardinal was stuck dumb by the eloquence of Mesarites's speech, and "not [being] equal to the task" of replying, simply "limited himself to extravagant praise of what he had heard."[37] A clear victory for orthodoxy, or so it seemed.

Although many of the debates between Latins and Greeks during this period focused on the Filioque and the primacy—Pope Innocent's ongoing demands for "obedience" had now brought the latter issue to the fore—azymes continued to remain divisive. Innocent's policy was generally to leave the rites of the Greeks alone, but in May 1205 he wrote a letter to the Latin emperor Baldwin, in which he allegedly contemplated a change in strategy.[38] This action, should he have taken it, would have constituted "a break not only with long established papal policies towards the Greeks, but also with [the pope's] own attitudes" up until that point.[39] Fortunately, Innocent never acted on this impulse, and a year later (August 1206) confirmed his earlier view in a letter to Constantinople's Latin patriarch. Morisini had written asking the pope whether he "should permit the Greeks to practice the sacrifices and other sacraments according to their custom (*more suo*) or rather compel them to practice according

---

[33] Angold, *Nicholas Mesarites: His Life and Works*, 270.
[34] Ibid.
[35] Ibid.
[36] Ibid., 271. It was at this point that Mesarites claimed that the crowd "were at a loss among themselves because 'no Greek had ever spoken to us in so forthright a manner.'" Ibid.
[37] Ibid., 275.
[38] Innocent III, *Register 8.56 (55)*; Eng. trans.: Andrea, *Contemporary Sources for the Fourth Crusade*, 154-57. Innocent wrote that "the Greek Church which by virtue of age ought to have been the teacher appears, on the contrary, to stand in need, so that it must be taught the first principles of the beginning of God's Words because it has sinned against Him.... With the Greek empire transferred from the disobedient and the superstitious to the sons of obedience and the pious, it is necessary that the priestly rites be transferred so that Ephraim, who has returned to Judah, might feast upon the azymes of sincerity and truth, the old leavened bread having been thrown away." Ibid., 155-56.
[39] Neocleous, *Heretics, Schismatics, or Catholics?*, 179. "After his election as Pope in January 1198 and up to 1205 Innocent never tried to latinize the Greek rite in areas rule by Latins such a Sicily, Cyprus, or Hungary.... In his letters of 12 and 13 November 1199 to the Byzantine emperor and patriarch, the pope had asked the patriarch of Constantinople to show obedience to Rome 'regardless of disparity in rites.'" Ibid., 180-81.

to that of the Latins."⁴⁰ Innocent declared that "if he could not win them over," the patriarch should "maintain them in their rite until the apostolic see agreed to a different settlement after mature reflection."⁴¹ In a 1208 revision of his earlier *De sacro altaris mysterio*, he acknowledged that "there are many who sacrifice with leavened bread with whom, as truly catholics, the Roman Church is in communion."⁴² This anticipated the decision of the Fourth Lateran Council (1215), where the church recognized "one faith but different rites and customs" (*varii ritus et mores*) as a way of "cherish[ing] and honor[ing] the Greeks who in our days are returning to the obedience of the apostolic see" while still "preserving their customs and rites."⁴³

Despite Innocent's misplaced optimism, not everyone in the East was eager to return to Roman obedience, usually manifesting their resistance by refusing to commemorate the pope in the liturgy and to recognize the validity of Latin sacraments.⁴⁴ This was especially the case on Cyprus, where the martyrdom of several monks for refusing to accept the azymite Eucharist became a cause célèbre.⁴⁵ The incident began in 1227–28 when the Kantara monks welcomed Master Andrew, a Dominican, to discuss various issues surrounding the sacraments, including the use of azymes. The monks argued for the exclusive use of leavened bread, which Andrew interpreted as a slight against the Latins' Eucharist.⁴⁶ After Andrew reported this to Archbishop Eustorge (ca. 1214–50), the monks were interrogated and jailed for three years, during which time they continued to label the Latin practice as heretical.⁴⁷ Finally, at the urging of Pope Gregory IX (d. 1241), the monks were handed over to be punished as heretics, resulting in their torture and public burning in 1231.⁴⁸ They became, in the memory of the Greeks, martyrs and heroes for the faith.

---

⁴⁰ Innocent III, *Register 9.255*; Eng. trans.: Neocleous, *Heretics, Schismatics, or Catholics?*, 181.

⁴¹ Ibid.

⁴² Innocent III, *De sacro altaris mysterio libri sex* (PL 217:878); Eng. trans.: Neocleous, *Heretics, Schismatics, or Catholics?* 181.

⁴³ Tanner, *Decrees of the Ecumenical Councils* 1, 239, 235. However, Alfred Andrea cautioned that "if we infer ... that Innocent and the council embraced the entire body of Byzantine church customs and rites, we would be wrong, quite wrong." Alfred J. Andrea, "Innocent III and the Byzantine Rite, 1198–1216," in Angeliki Laiou, ed., *Urbs Capta: The Fourth Crusade and Its Consequences (La IVe croisade et ses conséquences)* (Paris: Lethielleux, 2005), 113.

⁴⁴ Chrysovalantis Kyriacou describes such actions, not as a manifestation of an inherent "anti-Latinism," but rather as a part of the necessary "boundary building" that helped the Cypriots (and others) maintain their identity during periods of occupation. See Chrysovalantis Kyriacou, *Orthodox Cyprus under the Latins, 1191–1571: Society, Spirituality, and Identities* (Lanham, MD: Lexington Books, 2018).

⁴⁵ For details see Hinterberger, "A Neglected Tool of Orthodox Propaganda?" 129–50; Christopher Schabel, "Martyrs and Heretics, Intolerance of Intolerance: The Execution of Thirteen Monks in Cyprus in 1231," in Schabel, *Greeks, Latins, and the Church in Early Frankish Cyprus* (London: Routledge, 2010), 1–33; Schabel, "Religion," in Angel Nicolaou-Konnari and Christopher Schabel, *Cyprus: Society and Culture, 1191–1374* (Leiden: Brill, 2005), 157–218 (esp. 196–98). The incident is recorded in both Greek and Latin sources. The main Greek source for the martyrdom is the anonymous "Narrative of the Thirteen Holy Fathers of Kantara," composed between 1275 and 1282.

⁴⁶ At one point the monks suggested an "ordeal by fire" in which a monk of each church, carrying either the leavened or unleavened host, would enter the flames to see which one God would protect. Ordeal by fire, however, had been prohibited in the Latin church since 1215. Elena Kaffa, *The Greek Church of Cyprus, the Morea and Constantinople during the Frankish Era (1196–1303): A New Perspective* (Newcastle, UK: Cambridge Scholars, 2014), 93.

⁴⁷ The monks' Confession of Faith, publicly read out on the day of their martyrdom (May 19, 1231) is published in Kyriacou, *Orthodox Cyprus under the Latins*, 233–37.

⁴⁸ "Further, you added that certain Greek monks, thinking badly of the Catholic faith, publicly protested that the sacrament of the Eucharist does not exist on our altar, and that the Body of Christ should not

In March 1238, in an effort to avoid similar incidents, "Pope Gregory IX wrote to the Latin patriarchs of Antioch and Jerusalem, and to the Latin archbishop of Nicosia, instructing them not to allow any of the Orthodox clergy to celebrate any of their offices, unless they first took an oath of obedience to Rome, renouncing all heresy, 'and especially that where the Latins are regarded as heretics for celebrating mass with unleavened bread.'"[49] Led by Archbishop Neophytos, most of the higher clergy, unwilling to obey, stripped their monasteries and churches of all their valuables and left for Armenia, threatening excommunication against those who remained and submitted.[50] Supported by Patriarch Germanos II in Nicaea, resistance on the island stiffened, forcing Latin authorities to rule that any who called the use of azymes heretical would themselves be condemned as a heretic.[51] Instead, Cypriot clergy were instructed to "admonish and exhort the common people ... to show reverence when the host of the Eucharist is raised at the altar in the churches of the Latins, bowing and uncovering their heads and to do the same when a priest brings the host to the sick."[52]

In 1234, shortly after the execution of the Kantara monks and perhaps as a response to it, Pope Gregory sent a delegation of Dominicans and Franciscans to Nicaea in order to meet with Patriarch Germanos.[53] Gregory's earlier letter to Germanos had indicated that he was perfectly willing to concede the orthodoxy of the Greeks' Eucharistic practice if they would only do likewise.[54] Employing the earlier logic of

---

be made of unleavened bread but rather of leavened bread, publicly pronouncing many other outrageous things that they know to be manifest error.... Against the aforesaid monks you will proceed as if against heretics, invoking for this the help of the secular arm against them." Christopher Schabel, *The Synodicum Nicosiense and Other Documents of the Latin Church of Cyprus, 1196–1373* (Nicosia: Cyprus Research Center, 2001), 296–97.

[49] Nicholas Coureas, *The Latin Church in Cyprus, 1195–1312* (London: Routledge, 1997), 286. For the letter see Aloysius L. Tăutu, ed., *Acta Honorii III (1216–1227) et Gregorii IX (1227–1241)* (Rome: Typis Polyglottis Vaticanis, 1950), 310–11.

[50] According to Nicholas Coureas, the Latins tried to take over the abandoned churches and install their own clergy, but this was "easier said than done, as most of them did not know Greek." Coureas, *The Latin Church in Cyprus*, 286–87.

[51] "For many years many Greek priests and monks on the island of Cyprus were notorious suspects of heretical wickedness, and were often warned to abjure all heresies—and especially the one that damns the sacrament of the Eucharist prepared with unleavened bread.... Therefore, so that we are not found negligent or remiss surrounding this pestilence by the authority of the council we judge that those already mentioned are heretics." Schabel, *The Synodicum Nicosiense*, 142–45. Germanos had been writing how pleased he was with the Cypriots' opposition "against the godless Latins ... for let no one deceive even you, most holy brethren, into thinking that the heresy of the godless Latins is of small moment or that the subjects of their heresy are confined to one or two or three errors.... For the introduction of unleavened bread [in the Eucharist] infiltrates the heresy of those two impious enemies of Christ, Apollinaris and Arius.... The unfermented sacrifice of Jewish-minded Latins, being deprived of [salt and ferment], makes them prone to lapse into the above-mentioned heresies together with their Judaizing." Joseph Gill, "An Unpublished Letter of Germanos, Patriarch of Constantinople," *Byzantion* 44 (1974): 143–45.

[52] Schabel, *The Synodicum Nicosiense*, 100–101.

[53] Both Christopher Schabel and Jeff Brubaker connect the friars' mission to Nicaea with the execution of the Kantara monks. Schabel, "The Quarrel over Unleavened Bread," 86 n. 3; Jeff Brubaker, "You Are the Heretics!' Dialogue and Disputation between the Greek East and the Latin West after 1204," *Medieval Encounters* 24 (2018): 613–30.

[54] "Still, if your rite, different from ours, induces a thought of doubt about the most sacred Sacrament of the Eucharist, then hear that the mystery of our salvation, celebrated alike by Greeks and Latins, is not other or a different mystery, belonging as it does to the one Lord Jesus Christ." Gregory then compared the two churches to the apostles John and Peter running to the tomb of Christ. "The Greek—running ahead to the faith with the younger of the disciples ... established the host be offered in the leaven.... But the Latin,

Alger of Liège, Gregory maintained that the type of bread one used was ultimately insignificant since the "bread, simple before the sacrifice ... by means of transubstantiation ... is made through the words of the Lord ... not bread, and therefore it may be called neither leavened nor unleavened."[55]

First in Nicaea and then in Nymphaeum (or Nymphaion) the friars engaged the patriarch and his representatives (who included Demetrios Karykes and Nikephoros Blemmydes (d. 1272) in debate over the Filioque and the azymes.[56] The friars' approach was simple—they were not there to debate but rather to answer Greek "doubts" about those things the Church of Rome knew to be true.[57] After prolonged back and forth over the Filioque, which the Greeks claimed was the more important issue,[58] the friars put forward the central question: "Are we able to accomplish the body of Christ in azymes, or not?"[59]

---

obeying the monument of the letter with the elder Peter, from which proceeds spiritual thought ... [chose] to celebrate the more marvelous sacrament of the glorified body in the azymes of purity." Pope Gregory IX to Patriarch Germanos II (May 18, 1233) in Tăutu, *Acta Honorii III (1216–1227) et Gregorii IX (1227–1241)*, 266–68; Eng. trans. in Brubaker, *The Disputatio of the Latins and the Greeks 1234*. My thanks to Dr. Brubaker for allowing me to use pre-publication drafts of his translations.

[55] Ibid. This last statement has led Tia Kolbaba and others to argue that the real issue in the debate was the Latin teaching on transubstantiation, for not only did the pope want the Greeks to accept the legitimacy of the Latins' Eucharist, but also the Western teaching on Christ's presence as defined by the Lateran Council. "In this context the papal letter's stress on the Eucharist is illuminating: the pope is not worried about whether the bread is leavened or unleavened, but seeks rather to ensure that the doctrine of transubstantiation is accepted. The Greeks, however, completely miss this point." Tia Kolbaba, "Theological Debates with the West, 1054–1300," in Anthony Kaldellis and Niketas Siniossoglou, eds. *The Cambridge Intellectual History of Byzantium* (Cambridge: Cambridge University Press, 2017), 490–91. According to the Fourth Lateran Council (1215), "His body and blood are truly contained in the sacrament of the altar under the forms of bread and wine, the bread and wine having been changed in substance (*transsubstantiatis*), by God's power, into his body and blood." Tanner, *Decrees of the Ecumenical Councils* 1, 230.

[56] Aside from Brubaker's recent studies and translation see Girolamo Golubovich, "Disputatio Latinorum et Graecorum seu Relatio Apocrisariorum Gregorii IX de gestis Nicaeae in Bithynia et Nymphaeae in Lydia 1234," *Archivum Franciscanum Historicum* 12 (1919): 418–70; Paul Canart, "Nicéphore Blemmyde et la mémoire adressé aux envoyés de Grégoire IX (Nicée, 1234)," *Orientalia Christiana Periodica* 25 (1959): 310–25; Joseph Munitiz, ed. and trans., *Nikephoros Blemmydes: A Partial Account* (Leuven: Spicilegium Sacrum Lovaniense, 1988); Joseph Munitiz, "A Reappraisal of Blemmydes First Discussion with the Latins," *Byzantinoslavica* 51 (1990): 20–26.

[57] "We have not been sent to debate with you about some article of faith, about which we or the Roman Church are in doubt, but rather that with you we may have a friendly debate about your doubts. Therefore it will be yours to reveal and ours, by the grace of God, to illuminate." If the filioque and azymes were the reasons, "Why have you removed yourselves from obedience to the Church of Rome? Let us see if these are or ought to be sufficient causes for such disobedience." Brubaker, *The Disputatio of the Latins and the Greeks 1234*. All of the translations of the *Disputatio* are from the pre-publication drafts of this book. According to Henry Chadwick, the Dominican friars were especially eager to discuss the Eucharist, since they felt the Greeks were "on the run" over the issue, as they had recently gotten the abbot of St. Mamas to end his objections to azymes. Henry Chadwick, *East and West: The Making of a Rift in the Church* (Oxford: Oxford University Press, 2003), 239.

[58] Chadwick speculated that this was because the Greeks believed that they "were on far stronger ground with the *filioque* than with *azyma*." Ibid., 241.

[59] "Now we have determined that you think badly of our Sacrament in azymes. We know this first through your writing, which was full of this heresy. Second, because you do not intend to answer the question put forward on the Sacrament, lest your heresy be laid bare. Third, because your deeds prove it. You wash your altars after the Latins celebrate on them. Fourth, because you compel Latins who come to your Sacrament to forsake and repudiate the Sacraments of the Roman Church." Brubaker, *The Disputatio of the Latins and the Greeks 1234*.

The Greek response was simple: "You ask if the body of Christ can be completed in azymes; and we answer that it is impossible.... It cannot be done at all because we know that the Lord did perform it in leavened bread.... [I]t cannot be done in another bread, that is, in the bread of the other nature (i.e., unleavened)."[60] The Greeks then submitted a document claiming that sacrificing with azymes was impossible for those under "the new grace in accordance with the tradition of the Savior, which is from the beginning." For Christ had "passed [the mysteries] on to his own holy disciples and apostles through leavened bread, ... [and] they likewise passed [it] on ... as they themselves received it," and that even "elder Rome also received [it] thus" before changing. "For this reason we say that one cannot consume the sacrifice through azymes."

For the friars, this was clearly heresy, "But because a defense of heresy makes a heretic, we wish to know why you say such things." There then followed a detailed discussion of whether ἄρτος exclusively meant "bread" or whether it could also refer to unleavened bread. For the Greeks, "When it is put by itself, it stands in place of leavened bread" but "when placed with an adjective [i.e., "unleavened"] there is, so to speak, a contradiction in the adjective as when one says 'a dead man.'" The friars leaped upon this point, because if ἄρτος could be used to describe either leavened or unleavened bread, requiring a modifier to differentiate the two, then when the gospels say that "Jesus took bread" (λαβὼν ὁ Ἰησοῦς ἄρτον) (Mt 26:26) they could be referring to either type. However, since it occurred "on the first day of azymes ... we prove through the gospel, that the Lord made his body in azymes, and not in leavened bread." Then the friars brought forth patristic texts, especially Chrysostom's *Homilies on Matthew*, to prove that Jesus "fulfilled the Passover through everything, showing to the last day that he was not contrary to the law." The Greeks, in response, cited John, but then the hour got late and the debate was ended.

It was at this point that the emperor suggested a quid pro quo—given that there were two issues in dispute, in the name of peace the Latins "ought to give up one of these two. We will worship and hold your sacrament, while you, on the other hand, give up to us your creed, and say with us just as we say." The friars replied that "the Lord Pope and the Roman Church will not abandon a single iota of their faith." What was required was for the Greeks "to faithfully believe ... that the body of Christ can be completed in azymes just as in leavened bread ... [and for] all books which you have written against our creed to be condemned and burnt." When the Greeks refused, the friars proclaimed, "You believe and say that the body of Christ cannot be made in azymes. But this is heretical, therefore, you are heretics. Thus we found you heretics and excommunicates, and as heretics and excommunicates we leave you." The Greeks shouted back, "It is you who are the heretics!" and the debate was at an end.

The mutual hostility created by these debates spilled over into the polemical literature such as the 1252 *Tractatus contra Graecos*, where the azymes was treated after the Filioque and the issue of Purgatory that had emerged only a few years earlier.[61] It

---

[60] According to the friars, "Listening to this heresy, we asked separately from each one, first from the Patriarch of Nicaea, next from [the Patriarch] of Antioch, then from each prelate, if this was their faith, and if they believed that. And they answered separately: 'This is our faith, and we believe this.'"

[61] See chapter 2 n. 182.

began with a short introduction of the debate, giving both its progenitor (identified as Michael Keroularios) and a summary of recent events on Cyprus.

> Therefore, following this Michael [Keroularios] until today, the Greeks do not shrink from publicly calling the Latins "azymites." Whence among them the mystery of the sacrament has become so accursed and scorned that not only do they refuse to take it when in danger of death, but they choose to endure the torture of the flames rather than acknowledge the sacrament. This Cyprus proves, which in our time made twelve Greek monks, laboring under this error, into new martyrs of the devil through the flame of fire. For the aforesaid monks were saying that the Latin sacrament was mud, and not a sacrament, and that those who eat it are sacrificing to demons in the way of the gentiles.[62]

According to the *Tractatus*, the Greeks rejected azymes because Christ passed on the mysteries "not in azymes, but with leavened bread" and this was confirmed not only by the language (i.e., the consistent use of ἄρτος in the Last Supper accounts), but also by the Johannine chronology, where Jesus celebrated the meal with his disciples "before the festival of Passover" (*ante diem festum Paschae*).[63] The Greeks also maintained that in Christ there was a perfect union of divinity, soul, and body, and that this union was reflected in the flour, leaven, and water used in the making of the perfect (i.e., fermented) bread.[64] In response, the author of the *Tractatus* cited both John Chrysostom and Theophylacht of Ohrid to support Jesus's celebration of the Passover, later quoting the spurious text from Gregory the Great discussed earlier to justify the use of both leavened and unleavened bread.[65]

Bonacursius of Bologna's (d. late thirteenth century) *De erroribus Graecorum* treated azymes only after six other errors (including the Filioque and the primacy), citing the Greeks' belief that the sacrament ought to be celebrated exclusively with leavened bread (*quod sacramentum altaris non debet fieri in azymo, sed tantummodo in fermento*).[66] In many ways it was similar to the *Tractatus*, "using reason and authorities from the Greek as well as from the Latin saints" to establish that Christ instituted the sacrament in azymes and passed it down to his disciples in this form, and that the successors of Peter faithfully kept and transmitted this custom.[67]

One relatively new feature of Bonacursius's work was the growing need to explain why the Greeks would change their practice when Scripture and history were so clear that unleavened bread was to used.[68] For this Bonacursius relied on a story, which later

---

[62] Andrea Riedl, *Tractatus contra Graecos*, 70; Eng. trans.: Chris Schabel and Alexander Beihammer, "Two Small Texts on the Wider Context of the Martyrdom of the Thirteen Monks of Kantara in Cyprus, 1231," in Encarnatió Motos Guirao and Morfakidis Filactós, eds., *Polypthychon: Homenaje al Profesor Ioannis Hassiotis* (Granada: Centro de Estudios Bizantinos, 2008), 71.

[63] Andrea Riedl, *Tractatus contra Graecos*, 71.

[64] Ibid., 72.

[65] Ibid., 73, 82. See chapter 3 n. 218.

[66] Stegmüller, "Bonacursius Contra Graecos," 71.

[67] Ibid. See also Wilhelm von Auxerre, *De discordia quae est inter Graecos et Latinos in confectione eucharistiae* (Book 4, tract 7, cap 8), in Jean Ribaillier, ed., *Magistri Guillelmi Altissiodorensis Summa aurea*, vol. 4, Spicilegium Bonaventurianum 19 (Paris: Editions du Centre National de la Recherche Scientifique, 1980-87), 185-93.

[68] See Avvakumov, *Die Entstehung des Unionsgedankens*, 325-34.

developed into the "Pope Leo legend," that told how the popes had once conceded the use of leavened bread to fight certain Judaizing heresies in the East.[69] In Bonacursius's account, an expanded version of the one found in the *Quaestiones antequam* (q 51, disp 2, mem 1) of Alexander of Hales,[70] Peter's successor as bishop of Antioch, a man named Euvodius, was shocked to hear that some of the Jews he brought to the faith were backsliding and giving consecrated hosts to dogs.[71] Euvodius wrote to the pope for advice, and it was he who suggested that the Christians should begin using leavened bread, especially at Easter when the Jews (then celebrating Passover) could only have matzo in their homes. However, once the heresy was stamped out and the Latins returned to using azymes, the Greeks, forgetting the reasons behind the concession, did not. Their continued use of leavened bread was not, in itself, problematic according to Bonacursius, for "the Greeks do this with good intentions in order to express that the Son of God received a soulful body from the Virgin," while "the Latins ... offer unleavened bread to show that the Savior, without the defilement of the male seed, adopted a soulful body from the Virgin."[72] The current debate only arose because the haughty Greeks insisted on calling Latins "azymites" when in reality the West's practice was the more reasonable, ancient, and (given its dominical institution and papal backing) well established.

In the West, the rise of scholasticism occasioned great interest in the Eucharist, with theologians debating both the "matter" (*materia*) and "form" (*forma consecrationis*) necessary for a valid celebration. According to Chris Schabel, scholastic theologians universally recognized the legitimacy of using leavened bread for the Eucharist, although they were unanimous in their condemnation of the Greeks for refusing to admit the validity of the Latin practice.[73] Some, like William of Meliton and Pierre d'Ailly, believed the Greeks were "justly judged to be heretics" for questioning the

---

[69] See Schabel, "The Quarrel over Unleavened Bread," 115–22. In this section Schabel detailed how early writers identified Pope Leo as the source for this story ("Pope Leo says ..."") but by the time of Peter of Tarentaise (the future Pope Innocent V), Leo was wrongfully identified as the pope who ruled in favor of leavened bread on account "of the Ebionite heretics who were saying that the law must be observed with the Gospel." Ibid., 118.

[70] Latin with German translation in Avvakumov, *Die Entstehung des Unionsgedankens*, 327–28. Christopher Schabel notes that Mahlon Smith cited Alexander of Hales's *Summa Theologica* as a witness to this story, but that the section quoted from Book IV of the *Summa* was not written until after Alexander's death in 1245. Schabel, "The Quarrel over Unleavened Bread," 116. Mahlon's English translation of Alexander's *Summa* (IV, q. 32 mem 3) reads: "When the error concerning Torah observance was flourishing, the fathers of old determined that the church should not make the preparation from unleavened, but from leavened bread, until such time as that error should cease. Hence the church first made preparation from unleavened bread, only secondly from leavened. Thirdly, when this cause had ceased, the Roman Church returned to the first rite and made preparation from unleavened bread. But the Greeks, having become high and mighty, as it were, did not want to return to the first rite and on this account they were compelled to defend themselves by saying that they had received this rite from the fathers. But since this was not enough, they added in the second place another reason: lest they should Judaize. Since this was not enough, if the Lord had made preparation with matzos they dare to say that the Lord had made preparations with leavened bread. And since the evangelists say the opposite, they dare to say that the latter were wrong in reporting and that they were corrected by John." Smith, *And Taking Bread*, 48–49 n. 52.

[71] Stegmüller, "Bonacursius Contra Graecos," 74–75. German translation in Avvakumov, *Die Entstehung des Unionsgedankens*, 330–32.

[72] Ibid., 74–75.

[73] Schabel, "The Quarrel over Unleavened Bread," 103.

West's teaching on the matter,[74] while more charitable voices maintained that because the Greeks' error was grounded in their "stupidity" or "haughtiness," they were unaware of "what they are saying, just as on so many other matters."[75]

Dominican Guerric of Saint-Quentin (d. 1245) believed that it was "permitted to prepare [the Eucharist] with leavened and unleavened bread" and insisted that the Greeks should not "be scolded because they prepare it with leavened."[76] Yet, like Meliton and Pierre d'Ailly, Guerric held the Greeks were justly considered heretics because "they exclude that it can be prepared with unleavened. For that is a heresy: to say what is allowed is not allowed."[77] A similar view was expressed by William of Auvergne (d. 1249), who wrote in his *De septum sacramentis libellus* that the Eucharist can be celebrated with both leavened and unleavened bread "according to the custom of various churches" (*consuetudo diversarum Ecclesiarum*), even if the Latins' use of azymes was the more reasonable (*rationabilior*)" practice.[78] While Matthew Paris (d. 1259) considered the Greeks schismatics for their refusal to acknowledge the "motherhood" of Rome,[79] he held that the Greek church was still orthodox in its faith, its faults found more in "its acts [rather] than its sayings" (*magis tamen eius facta quam dicta*]), such as "consecrat[ing] the eucharist from fermented bread."[80]

Matthew of Aquasparta's *Commentary on the Sentences* had little influence on later Eucharist debates, as they were only a small part of an early work that was neither widely known nor widely distributed.[81] In the work he detailed the thirteen arguments used by the Greeks, nine of which focused on the chronology, and four that touched upon issues of language, symbolism, and the "Judaizing" nature of the Latin practice. According to Christopher Schabel, what makes Matthew's text noteworthy is the fact that Matthew, unlike almost all of his contemporaries, accepted the Greeks' passion chronology, and readily admitted that Christ anticipated the Passover and ate it on the thirteenth of the month. However, since it was a true Passover, it was celebrated with

---

[74] William of Meliton, *Quaestiones de sacramentis* IV, pars III, q. 9; Eng. trans.: Schabel, "The Quarrel over Unleavened Bread," 103.

[75] Albert Magnus, *In quartum librum Sententiarum*, d. 12, c, a. 8; Eng. trans.: Schabel, "The Quarrel over Unleavened Bread," 103.

[76] Guerric of Saint-Quentin, *Quaestio de controversia Graecorum et Latinorum*; Eng. trans.: Schabel, "The Quarrel over Unleavened Bread," 102.

[77] Ibid.

[78] William of Auvergne, *De septum sacramentis libellus*; Eng. trans.: Neocleous, *Heretics, Schismatics, or Catholics?* 234. Like Bonacursius, William believed that the Greeks' use of leavened bread stemmed from the desire to avoid some Judaizing heresy, in this case "an aversion to heresy of the Nazarenes, who mixed the Gospel with the law." William of Auvergne, *De septum sacramentis libellus*; Eng. trans.: Schabel, "The Quarrel over Unleavened Bread," 116.

[79] Neocleous, *Heretics, Schismatics, or Catholics?*, 237. He complained the Greeks regarded Rome only as "sister," refusing to acknowledge her as the "mother" of all churches. For the importance of familial language in the relationship between Rome and the East see A. Edward Siecienski, "Father, Mother, Brother, Sister: Primacy and Familial Language," *International Journal of Systematic Theology* 23 (2020): 1–16.

[80] Matthew Paris, *Chronica Majora* 3:446–47; Eng. trans.: Neocleous, *Heretics, Schismatics, or Catholics?*, 236.

[81] Christopher Schabel claimed that "it is quite possible that no one read his discussion on the bread of the Eucharist until I began working on this paper." Schabel, "The Quarrel over Unleavened Bread," 108. For the Latin text see Christopher Schabel, Fritz Pedersen, and Russell Friedman, "Matthew of Aquasparta and the Greeks," in Kent Emery, Russell Friedman, and Andreas Speer, eds., *Philosophy and Theology in the Long Middle Ages: A Tribute to Stephen F. Brown* (Leiden: Brill, 2011), 813–53.

unleavened bread, thus proving that the Lord instituted the sacrament with azymes.[82] Matthew's conclusions were echoed half a century later by Gerald Odonis, who held that Christ ate the Passover early but "prepared it with unleavened bread," because "he anticipated the time of eating the paschal lamb."[83] Even though "they were not supposed to eat [the paschal meal], Christ gave a dispensation" and celebrated with unleavened bread, although Odonis, like Matthew, accepted the legitimacy of using either type.[84]

While Matthew of Aquasparta's work played little role in later debates, the writings of the three greatest scholastic theologians, Bonaventure (d. 1274), Thomas Aquinas (d. 1274), and Albert Magnus (d. 1280), were far more influential. In his *Commentary on the Sentences* Bonaventure began his treatment of the issue by asking whether Christ himself confected with unleavened bread, arguing that he did because it was clear from the gospels (Mt 26:17, Mk 1412, Lk 22:7) that he celebrated a legal Passover on the fourteenth of Nisan.[85] Others (i.e., the Greeks) erroneously held that he anticipated the Passover and celebrated the Last Supper on the thirteenth with leavened bread, based largely on their misreadings of John 18:28 and Luke 23:56.[86] They further maintained that since "the Lord did not wish that we observe a Jewish rite," he would not have observed it himself.[87] Bonaventure answered these objections by correcting the Greek misunderstanding of John 18:28, arguing that "Passover" was used several ways in the Scripture and when used here it was a reference not to the feast, but to the "unleavened bread" eaten for seven days.[88] As for the charge that Christ "made us Judaizers," by giving us unleavened bread "it must be said that the Lord did not take

---

[82] "I say with the Greeks that Christ anticipated the time of Passover, but nevertheless I say with the Latins and assert without any doubt the Christ prepared it with unleavened bread. Seeing this, the response to the argument adduced for both sides is clear: that those that prove that he prepared it with unleavened bread are to be granted and so are those that prove that Christ anticipated the time of Passover." Schabel, "The Quarrel over Unleavened Bread," 107.

[83] Gerald Odonis, *In quartum librum Sententiarum*, d. 12, q. 3; Eng. trans.: Schabel, "The Quarrel over Unleavened Bread," 109.

[84] Ibid.

[85] "It must be said that the Lord celebrated the Passover on the fourteenth of the month. It follows that he did not anticipate it, as the three evangelists expressly agree. Nor should he have anticipated it. If therefore the eating of the figurative lamb is emptied out ... by the eating of the true lamb, the eating of the true lamb had to come after the figurative one, not before it. Hence because he observed the Passover on the fourteenth of the month, when only unleavened bread was eaten, it is clear that he celebrated with unleavened bread." Bonaventure, *Commentaria in quatuor libros Sententiarum Magistri Petri Lombardi*, Lib. IV, dist. 11, pars 2, art. 2, q. 1; Eng. trans.: Wayne Hellmann, Timothy LeCroy, and Luke Townsend, eds. and trans., *Works of Saint Bonaventure: Commentary on the Sentences: Sacraments* (St. Bonaventure, NY: Franciscan Institute Publications, 2016).

[86] "Then they returned, and prepared spices and ointments. On the sabbath they rested according to the commandment." According to Bonaventure, this allegedly demonstrated "that it was not permitted to prepare anything according to the Law [and] therefore the great festival day was the one following the crucifixion." Ibid.

[87] Ibid.

[88] "To the objection that they did not enter the praetorium lest they become impure, it must be said that Passover can be understood in three ways. In one way the Passover is called the Paschal food, such as unleavened bread, which was eaten by the Jews for seven days. Another meaning is the Paschal Lamb in Luke 22:7.... The third meaning of Passover means the true lamb, as in 1 Corinthians 5:7.... In John 18 he references the first meaning." Ibid.

it over from the Law but instituted it anew," for "the Lord came not to abolish the Law but to fulfill it."[89]

Bonaventure then asked: "From whence did the controversy between the Greeks and Latins arise? It would seem that this controversy should not have happened. They both received from the apostles, and the apostles from their one Lord. Therefore, either the apostles were in error or the Greeks made it up."[90] To explain the origin of the dispute Bonaventure referenced the story found earlier in Bonacursius and Alexander of Hales, where "the fathers of old" briefly allowed the use of leavened bread to keep Christians from observing Jewish rites.[91] "But when that situation ended, the Roman Church returned to the earlier rite... [while] the Greeks, proud as they are, were unwilling to return to the earlier rite."[92] When finally forced to defend the practice, the Greeks began "by saying that this was what they had received. Then second, because this did not suffice, they added a reason, to the end that they not become Judaizers. Third, since this did not suffice ... they dare to say that the Lord confected with leavened bread ... [and] because the evangelists say the opposite, they dared to say that they were mistaken."[93] In their stubbornness the Greeks had thus turned a "minor error" into "a great one," and yet Bonaventure still insisted that "they confect just as we do. For [the type of bread used] is not the substance of the sacrament, but part of its fittingness."[94]

Thomas Aquinas (d. 1274) addressed the proper matter for the Eucharist at several points in his career, including his *Commentary on the Sentences*,[95] the *Summa Theologiae*,[96] and his *Contra errores Graecorum*.[97] In the *Summa* (P 3, Q 74, Art 4) Aquinas asked "whether this sacrament ought to be made of unleavened bread," addressing the four chief objections to this practice.

1. According to John 13:1, Christ instituted the sacrament in leavened bread.[98]
2. "Legal observances ought not to be continued in the time of grace."[99]

---

[89] "It is just as apparent in the case of baptism, for they were purified with water, just as we are purified with water." Ibid.

[90] Ibid.

[91] "It must be said, just as Pope Leo says, because the feast of unleavened bread was an institution of the Jews, when the error of continuing observance of the law was common, the fathers of old decreed with the council of the Holy Spirit that it should cease. This was to allow that error of continuing to observe the Law to lessen.... Hence at first every Church celebrated with unleavened bread, and later for this reason with leavened bread." Ibid.

[92] Ibid.

[93] Ibid.

[94] Ibid.

[95] Thomas Aquinas, *Scriptum super libros Sententiarum IV* d. 11, q. 2, a. 2; Eng. trans.: Thomas Aquinas, *Commentary on the Sentences, Book IV, Distinctions 1–13*, trans. Beth Mortensen (Green Bay, WI: Aquinas Institute, 2017), 490–97.

[96] Thomas Aquinas, *Summa Theologiae* III, q 74 art 4; Eng. trans.: Thomas Aquinas, *Summa Theologica*, vol. 5, trans. Fathers of the English Dominican Province (Westminster: Christian Classics, 1981), 2435–36.

[97] Thomas Aquinas, *Contra Errores Graecorum* pars 2 c 39; Eng. trans.: James Likoudis, *Ending the Byzantine Greek Schism* (New Hope: Catholics United for the Faith, 1992), 185–87.

[98] See also John Joy, "Ratzinger and Aquinas on the Dating of the Last Supper: In Defense of the Synoptic Chronology," *New Blackfriars* 94 (2013): 324–39.

[99] Thomas Aquinas, *Summa Theologiae* III, q 74 art 4; Eng. trans.: Thomas Aquinas, *Summa Theologica*, 2435–36.

3. The Eucharist is the sacrament of charity, and the "fervor of charity is signified by fermented bread."[100]
4. Just as the validity of baptism is not affected by the use of warm or cold water, because leavened or unleavened are mere accidents of bread, which do not vary the species," ultimately it does not matter which type of bread is used for the sacrament.[101]

Aquinas then distinguished between "what is necessary, and what is suitable" arguing that "it is necessary that the bread be wheaten ... [but] it is not, however, necessary for the sacrament that the bread be unleavened or leavened, since it can be celebrated in either."[102] "Nevertheless," Aquinas argued,

> the custom of celebrating with unleavened bread is more reasonable. First, on account of Christ's institution ... secondly, because bread is properly the sacrament of Christ's body, which was conceived without corruption, thirdly, because this is more in keeping with the sincerity of the faithful which is required in the use of this sacrament, ... [since we] feast ... with the unleavened bread of sincerity and truth. However, this custom of the Greeks is not unreasonable both on account of its signification ... and in detestation of the heresy of the Nazarenes, who mixed up legal observances with the Gospel.[103]

In the *Contra Errores Graecorum* Aquinas refuted the claims of those "misguided persons" who believed that the "Body of Christ cannot be consecrated from unleavened bread" by using "texts from the Greek doctors" (i.e., John Chrysostom and Theophylact of Ohrid) to prove Christ celebrated the legal Passover.[104] He then attempted to reconcile the Synoptic and Johannine chronologies to show the Last Supper was a Passover meal,[105] invoked the authority of Gregory Nazianzus to

---

[100] Ibid.
[101] Ibid. In replying to this objection Aquinas argued that, in fact, "there is a wider difference between unleavened and leavened bread than between warm and cold baptismal water: because there might be such corruption of fermented bread that it could not be validly used for the sacrament." Ibid.
[102] Ibid. He further held that just as "a priest sins by celebrating with fermented bread in the Latin Church, so a Greek priest celebrating with unfermented bread in a church of the Greeks would also sin, as perverting the rite of his Church." Ibid.
[103] This last sentence references the story found in Bonacursius and Alexander of Hales.
[104] Thomas Aquinas, *Contra Errores Graecorum* pars 2 c 39; Eng. trans.: Likoudis, *Ending the Byzantine Greek Schism*, 185–86.
[105] Thomas believed that the evangelists could not contradict one another, and it was one of the Greeks' heresies to believe that they could. In his *Commentary on the Gospel of John* (Lecture 13:1), Aquinas addressed the chronology dispute: "And indeed, the Greeks ... say that our Lord suffered on the fourteenth, when the Jews were supposed to celebrate the Passover, and that our Lord, knowing that his passion was near, anticipated the celebration of the Passover and celebrated his own Passover on the day before the Passover feast of the Jews. And because it is commanded ... [that] the Hebrews should not have any leavened bread, they further say that the Lord celebrated not with unleavened bread, but with leavened bread, because Hebrews did have leavened bread on the thirteenth day, that is, before the Passover. But the other three Evangelists do not agree with this, for they say the time was the first day of Unleavened Bread, when the lamb was to be sacrificed (Mt 26:17; Mk 14:12; Lk 22:7). It follows from this that our Lord's Supper took place on the very day that the Jews sacrificed the lamb. The Greeks ... [claim] that the other Evangelists did not report this truly; and so John, who wrote the last of the Gospels, corrected them. But it is heresy to say that there is anything false not only in the Gospels but anywhere in the canonical Scriptures. Consequently, we have to say that all the Evangelists state the same thing and do not disagree."

emphasize the purity of unleavened bread,[106] and used a spurious quote by Gregory the Great to prove that one could confect with either type of bread.[107]

Albert the Great, who (like Bonaventure) would later attend the Council of Lyons (1274), also addressed the debate between the "Greek and Latin doctors over whether Christ handed over his body in unleavened or leavened bread."[108] In his book, *On the Body of the Lord*, Albert began with the Greek case, which primarily used John's gospel to show that "Christ gave his body to his disciples on the ... thirteenth of the month ... [when] there was no unleavened bread in the dwellings of the Jews ... therefore, as it seems, he gave it in leavened bread."[109] Albert naturally disagreed, arguing that the term "Passover" was used seven different ways in Scripture, and that these varied meanings were even made into a verse—"week, hour, day, feast, drink, unleavened bread, Christ" (*hebdomas, hora, dies, epulae, potus, azyma, Christus*).[110] Thus there was no discrepancy in the gospel accounts because Christ gave his body "on the fourteenth of the month when the leavened bread had already been removed from the dwellings of the Jews," with John 18:28 referring to the fifteenth—that is, the day "the unleavened bread was eaten for seven days."[111] Albert maintained that this chronology allowed "the truth to correspond to the shadow ... for it was fitting that Christ, the true lamb, began to be immolated on the fourteenth day of the month, when he was taken captive and betrayed, since the feast of Passover began at evening, which was counted as the fifteenth day."[112]

Albert then made the claim that because the Eucharist was the sacrament of strengthening and since "leavened bread ... is less effective than unleavened for strengthening," it was more appropriate to receive "the sacrament in unleavened rather than in leavened" form.[113] Yet in the end, Albert answered the question "whether it is possible to consecrate it in leavened bread" in the affirmative, for although it "should be consecrated in unleavened ... it can be consecrated in leaven, and if it is consecrated in leavened, the true body of Christ is consecrated" even if "he who does it is to blame, since he does not maintain the apostolic rite appropriate to the sacrament."[114]

Thomas Aquinas, *Commentary on the Gospel of John*, vol. 3, trans. Fabian Larcher and James A. Weisheipl (Washington, DC: Catholic University of America Press, 2010), 2.

[106] The passage, taken from *Oration* 1, reads: "Today we have clean escaped from Egypt and from Pharaoh; and there is none to hinder us from keeping a Feast to the Lord our God—the Feast of our Departure; or from celebrating that Feast, not in the old leaven of malice and wickedness, but in the unleavened bread of sincerity and truth, carrying with us nothing of ungodly and Egyptian leaven." Gregory Nazianzus, *Oration* 1; NPNF 2.7.203.

[107] Here Aquinas employed the same spurious text also found in the *Tractatus contra Graecos*. See chapter 3 n. 218.

[108] Albert the Great, *On the Body of the Lord*, trans. Albert Marie Surmanski, FC Medieval Continuation 17 (Washington, DC: Catholic University of America Press, 2017), 409.

[109] Ibid., 411. Albert also mentions the Greeks' use of Luke 23:55–56.

[110] Ibid., 419.

[111] Ibid.

[112] Ibid., 420.

[113] Ibid., 421.

[114] According to Christopher Schabel, Albert's attitude, like that of most scholastics, was "a sort of 'you can but you may not.'" Schabel, "The Quarrel over Unleavened Bread," 104. For Albert the Greek Eucharist was valid, but nevertheless they "sin against the law with respect to what is fitting." Albert the Great, *In quartum librum Sententiarum* d. 12, c, a. 8.

Although theologians were unanimous in accepting the validity of the Eastern practice, the canonists of the period tended to be far less tolerant. While legislation continued to recognize both types of bread as valid mater for the sacrament, individual writers such as Huguccio of Pisa (d. 1210), Geoffrey of Trani (1245), Hostiensis (d. 1270 or 1271), and William of Pagula (d. 1332) all argued that bread with yeast was incapable of being transubstantiated. According to Huguccio, only unleavened wheaten bread was capable of being transubstantiated because the Eucharist's validity depended on the priest using the same matter as Christ when he instituted the sacrament.[115] For Hostiensis, at the Last Supper Christ had offered "not in the old leaven, but in the unleavened bread of sincerity and truth" (*iuxta illud non in fermentato veteri, sed in azymis synceritatis et veritatis*),[116] which meant that adding anything to it (e.g., yeast) "made it no longer what Christ used," thus preventing transubstantiation.[117] According to Thomas Izbicki, the views of these canonists were among "the most negative ... in the West, where the use of leavened bread by the Greeks was accepted grudgingly by [most] others."[118]

Guido de Monte Rochen's (d. 1333) *Handbook for Curates* instructed priests that "the body of Christ can be made from leavened bread," and yet warned them that because "the head and mother and teacher of all the churches" taught that it "ought to be unleavened ... anyone who celebrates with leavened bread sins mortally and is to be severely punished."[119] John of Freiburg and Nicholas of Ausimo nuanced this view a bit, claiming that while a Latin priest would sin by using leavened bread, a Greek priest would sin "if he did not," for he would then be "perverting the rite of his church (*peruertens sue ecclesie ritum*).[120] On Cyprus, where the difference in Eucharistic bread had been a casus belli since the death of the Kantara monks in 1231, Archbishop Ranulph of Nicosia continued to acknowledge the legitimacy of the Greek rite, telling the Cypriots in 1280 that "as long as [the sacrament] is done by the priest according to the procedure of the church, it does not matter whether they perform it with leavened

---

[115] "*Et ideo propter iudeorum credendus est Christus tunc usus fuisse tantum azimis et ideo nos in sacramento altaris azimis uti debemus*." Huguccio, *Summa decretorum* in Thomas Izbicki, *The Eucharist in Medieval Canon Law* (Cambridge: Cambridge University Press, 2015), 68. This view was later echoed in William of Pagula's *Oculus Sacerdotis*. See ibid., 50–51.

[116] Ibid., 74.

[117] Ibid., 67–68. Hostiensis followed Geoffrey of Trani in accepting that even the mixing of leavened with unleavened dough (*si panis fit ex fermentato et azimo simul mixto*) prevented transubstantiation. Hostiensis, *Summa*, in Izbicki, *The Eucharist in Medieval Canon Law*, 74.

[118] Ibid., 50.

[119] "Know too that by this precept and custom of the Roman Church, which by the Lord's determination is the head and mother and teacher of all the churches, and therefore all churches ought to obey her in everything as both mother and teacher, the bread from which the body of Christ is confected ought to be unleavened because although by the power of the sacrament the body of Christ can be made from leavened bread, anyone who celebrates with leavened sins mortally and is to be severely punished." Guido de Monte Rochen, *Handbook for Curates: A Late Medieval Manual for Pastoral Ministry*, trans. Anne Thayer (Washington, DC: Catholic University of America Press, 2011), 50.

[120] John of Freiburg, *Summa Confessorum*, in Izbicki, *The Eucharist in Medieval Canon Law*, 80. John de Burough disagreed, and in his *Pupilla oculi* argued that any priest, Latin or Greek, who offered unleavened bread contravened the custom of the Roman church and thus sinned gravely. Ibid. Peter of Palude wrote, "Some say that a Greek sins if he prepares it with unleavened bread, because when in Rome, do as the Romans do. But because they are schismatics, no one—not even one of them—is obliged to stick with them." Petrus de Palude, *In quartum librum Sententiarum*, d. 11, q. 1, a. 5; Eng. trans.: Schabel, Pedersen, and Friedman, "Matthew of Aquasparta and the Greeks," 818.

or unleavened bread so long as they believe that in both ways it is the true body of Christ."[121]

The Second Council of Lyons (1274) and the Aftermath

The Second Council of Lyons, although still reckoned an ecumenical council by the Roman Catholic Church, is perhaps better understood, not as a true reunion council, but rather as Emperor Michael VIII's personal submission to Rome, with the resulting "union" being little more than his unsuccessful attempt to bring the Eastern church along with him.[122] In Humbert of Romans's *Opusculum tripartitum*, which was written in preparation for the council, Humbert detailed the history of the schism, including the debate over "the matter of the sacrament of the eucharist," which he believed had been exacerbated by both mutual misunderstanding and an appalling lack of Christian charity.[123]

The profession of faith that Michael eventually signed, largely derived from the 1267 document Pope Clement IV (1265–68) had prepared for him, was unambiguous about both the legitimacy of unleavened bread and the real presence of Christ in the Eucharist. It stated that the "Roman Church prepares the sacrament ... from unleavened bread (*ex azymo conficit*), holding and teaching that in the same sacrament the bread is changed into the body, and the wine into the blood of Jesus Christ."[124] Michael, in an effort to make the unpopular union more palatable, requested that the Greeks "be permitted to recite the sacred creed as it had been before the schism and up to our time [i.e., without the Filioque], and that we may remain in observance of the rites we had before the schism—these rites not being contrary to the faith declared above nor to the Divine commandments."[125] The pope accepted these terms, writing that "the Roman Church gladly proposes that the Greeks observe [their rites] to the full extent that God allows and permits them to continue in those rites which in the

---

[121] Schabel, *The Synodicum Nicosiense*, 127.

[122] For more on Michael's reasons for negotiating union see chapter 2, n. 188. For the Second Council of Lyons see Hans Wolter and Henri Holstein, *Lyon I et Lyon II* (Paris: Editions de l'Orante, 1966); Antonio Franchi, ed., *Il Concilio II di Lione (1274) secondo la ordinatio concilii generalis Lugdunensis, Studi e Testi Francescani 33* (Rome: Edizioni Francescane, 1965); Burkhard Roberg, *Die Union zwischen der griechischen und der lateinischen Kirche auf dem II Konzil von Lyon, Bonner historische Forschungen 24* (Bonn: L. Röhrscheid, 1964). For their part the Orthodox have never understood Lyons to be either ecumenical (four of the five ancient patriarchates were unrepresented) or a proper reunion council, since discussion of the theological issues dividing the churches never took place. In fact, the statement on the procession of the Holy Spirit, arguably the chief dogmatic dispute, was formulated weeks before the Byzantine delegation even arrived. See Siecienski, *The Filioque*, 134–38.

[123] Elliott, "The Schism and Its Elimination in Humbert," 72.

[124] Aloysius L. Tăutu, ed., *Acta Urbani IV, Clementis IV, Gregorii X (1261–1276)* (Rome: Typis Polyglottis Vaticanis, 1953), 61–69; Eng. trans.: Deferrari, *The Sources of Catholic Dogma*, 185.

[125] Roberg, *Die Union zwischen der griechischen und der lateinischen Kirche*, 227–28; Eng. trans.: Geanakoplos, *Byzantium*, 218. This allowed Michael to assure the anti-unionists that the union would leave their church "untouched by innovation," aside from the inclusion of the pope's name in the diptychs. He told the pope: "This is not crucial to your holiness but for us it is a matter of vital importance because of the immense multitude of our people." Ibid.

decision of the Apostolic See do not injure the integrity of the Catholic faith or detract from the holy decrees of the Canons."[126] The Greeks need not become azymites.

When the Byzantine delegation left Lyons in July 1274 they knew full well that the union would not be popular, especially among the clergy. A year earlier, Patriarch Joseph and the synod had specifically cited the Filioque and the azymes as reasons for rejecting union with the Latins, giving the usual arguments in favor of leavened bread (e.g., Christ's use at the Last Supper, the old Law vs. the law of grace), using quotations from Chrysostom and Peter III of Antioch in support.[127] They wrote that "on the subject of the sacrifice whose purity for us resides in the offering of leavened bread" the Greek position was "completely correct ... supported and confirmed by irrefutable witnesses—the declarations of the divine and sacred canons, of the holy apostles, and of the seven divine ecumenical councils and even of the local councils," while "ancient Rome, I know not why, takes no account of these witnesses ... [and] follows the opposite way."[128] When Michael later tried to enforce the union, many of these priests and bishops endured prison rather than recognize the legitimacy of an azymite Eucharist.[129]

In making their case to the Constantinopolitan populace, opponents of the union had the advantage that the Latins' liturgy was obviously "different," an important fact since issues of identity were key during these debates.[130] "They" were not like "us," and although the Latins' use of unleavened bread had largely been displaced by the Filioque and the primacy in the theological literature, ritual differences became easy targets for the polemicists, who once again began to ply their trade. Among the most interesting works in this genre was the comically anti-Latin *Dialogue of Panagiotes with an Azymite*, which was aimed "not only against the Latins, but, even more, against the emperor and his followers, including the new unionist patriarch John Bekkos."[131] In this fictional encounter cardinals of the Roman church arrive in Constantinople at the bidding of the pope, who has sent them "so that all Christians may partake of the communion of unleavened bread."[132] Despite the fact that this was clearly a "heresy," the *Dialogue* goes on to list several leading unionists, "men of bad conscience," who then communed with the Latin delegation using azymes.[133] At this point the hero of

---

[126] Later, Pope Nicholas III (Pope Gregory's successor) did demand that the Greeks adopt the Filioque, since "unity of faith does not permit diversity in its confessors or in confession ... especially in the chanting of the creed." Jules Gay, *Les Registres de Nicolas III 1277-1280* (Paris: Bibliothèque des Ecoles Françaises d'Athènes et de Rome, 1904), no. 376, p. 128; Eng. trans.: Geanokoplos, *Emperor Michael Palaeologus and the West*, 313.

[127] Vitalien Laurent and Jean Darrouzès, eds., *Dossier Grec de l'Union de Lyon 1273-1277* (Paris: Institut Français d'Etudes Byzantines, 1976), 308-13.

[128] Ibid., 309-10.

[129] For example, at the trial of Nikephoros in 1277 a Latin (Thomas of Lentini) engaged with Nikephoros over the issue, pointing out that Christ had celebrated Passover for thirty-three years with unleavened bread. Nikephoros responded that Christ was also circumcised and kept the other precepts of the Law, yet we are not required to do the same. Ibid., 492-95.

[130] See chapter 2, n. 201.

[131] Geanokoplos, "A Greek Libellus against Religious Union with Rome," 156-70. See also Donald Nicol, "The Byzantine Reaction to the Second Council of Lyons, 1274," in G. J. Cuming and Derek Baker, eds., *Councils and Assemblies: Papers Read at the Eighth Summer Meeting and the Ninth Winter Meeting of the Ecclesiastical History Society* (Cambridge: Cambridge University Press, 1971), 113-46.

[132] Geanokoplos, "A Greek Libellus against Religious Union with Rome," 159.

[133] Ibid.

the story stepped forward (Panagiotes) to defend the orthodox faith against one of the cardinals, who was derisively addressed throughout the debate as "Azymite," a term which, by 1274, "had become highly significant in the Byzantine mind as connoting one with Latin or 'Latinizing' views."[134] Panagiotes then lectured those present on a wide range of issues, including (but not limited to) the structure of the universe,[135] why Latins ate hedgehogs and made the sign of the cross incorrectly,[136] and the fact that Western priests kept concubines[137] and urinated during mass.[138]

Other anti-Latin works included Pseudo-Athanasios's *Letter to All Christians*, which listed the orthodox beliefs currently under attack, including that the "the accomplishment of the sacrifice with fermented bread ... [was] perfectly and very clearly transmitted to us by the holy apostles and evangelists."[139] *The Heresies of the Franks and Their Neighbors* (c. 1281) also mentioned azymes, as did Meletios Homologetes's *On the Customs of the Italians*, which described the "offering of azymes" as the Italians' "second evil" after the Filioque.[140] This practice was forbidden by the sixty-second canon of the apostles, and those canons condemning the Armenians, for in offering with azymes the Italians, like the "terrible Apollinaris, [who] foolishly babbled that the body of the Lord was without a soul and without a mind ... accomplish with deeds ... what he accomplished with words."[141]

Sections 23–37 of *Refutation of the Errors of the Latins* by Matthew Blastares dealt with azymes at great length, beginning with an extended treatment of the "the creation of the world and man with the symbolism of leaven."[142] According to Blastares, "Humankind needed leaven in order for it to be re-modelled, and the rejection of this leaven ... , for [Christ] calls himself thus, ... introduces the denial of the incarnation of the *Logos*."[143] The soul, he argued, "needs to be fermented and transformed in order

---

[134] Ibid., 160.
[135] According to Panagiotes, "Three hundred angels hold up the sky with twelve columns and twelve arches, and three hundred angels hold up the earth with twelve columns and twelve arches.... It is for this reason that heaven is called twelve hilled and seven hilled." The sun rises because "Christ, the Son of God, gives the crown to the angels and they put it on the sun and it rises, and, at once, two birds called griffins, of which one is called phoenix, with each other dampen the sun, so that the sun may not scorch the earth. And because of the heat of the fire the feathers of the birds are burnt and only their flesh remains. And again they fly toward the ocean and wash themselves and once more grow feathers." Ibid., 165.
[136] For more on this issue see Andreas Andreopoulos, *The Sign of the Cross: The Gesture, the Mystery, the History* (Brewster, MA: Paraclete Press, 2006), 34–37.
[137] "Instead you have concubines, and your priest sends his servant to bring him his concubine and he puts out the candle and then he mounts her for the whole night. Then he goes out of his cell and asks forgiveness before his fellow priests who do the same, offering as an excuse, 'Forgive me, my brothers, but I have had an erotic dream' and he receives pardon. Then he enters into the church to celebrate the liturgy." Ibid., 168.
[138] "Removing his robes he goes to satisfy the needs of the body whereupon he again enters the church." Ibid.
[139] Laurent and Darrouzès, *Dossier Grec de l'Union de Lyon 1273–1277*, 341.
[140] Kolbaba, "Meletios Homologetes: On the Customs of the Italians," 144; Eng. trans.: 151.
[141] Ibid.
[142] Palaiologos, *An Annotated Edition of the Refutation of the Errors of the Latins*, 58. "It is the Logos, Matthaios stresses, Who, as if He were a kind of leaven joined with a dough which carries many riddles (ὡς ἄν τις ζύμῃ, πολυσχεδεῖ ἑνωθεῖσα φυράματι),unites and brings together all in concordance, communion, unanimity and union, lifting up towards the apprehension of Him Who is greater, from Whom men have been granted their existence (τὸ εἶναι) and their preservation (τὸ διαμένειν)." Palaiologos, *An Annotated Edition of the Refutation of the Errors of the Latins*, 353–54 (Eng. trans on page 60).
[143] Ibid., 366–67; Eng. trans.: 65.

to become more divine (ζυμοῦσθαι καὶ μεταποιεῖσθαι πρὸς τὸ θειότερον), through God the Logos."[144] Leaven for the Eucharist is suggested in both the Old and New Testaments, and the Latins are wrong to use Paul as an argument against it, for the apostle never commanded the use of unleavened bread, but instead "used the image of leaven metaphorically (τροπικῶς) in an excellent way, as a method of moral teaching, inviting each one of us to do better actions, at the same time advising us to keep away from the worse actions."[145]

As for Christ himself, Blastares was convinced that he did not use unleavened bread, "for eating azymes had not yet come when the Last Supper was taking place—for it was in that very day when the Jews celebrated their feast that the Lord visited Hades chasing and plundering its elements."[146] When Jesus ate the meal, he called the elements "bread (ἄρτον) but 'not unleavened' (οὐκ ἄζυμον), since bread is life-giving (ζωτικὸν) and stimulating motion (κινητικόν), and it can introduce sufficient natural warmth to those who come close to it."[147] According to Konstantinos Palaiologos, in a "a word-play which is full of symbolism, Blastares remarks that properly speaking Christ would be said to be bread (ἄρτος) as he is complete (ἄρτιος), for he is not lacking anything."[148] This is why Paul too in 1 Corinthians called the divine gift bread and not something else (ἄρτον καὶ οὐκ ἄλλό τι).[149] The church followed his example, explaining why the seventieth Apostolic canon and the eleventh canon of the Sixth Ecumenical Council (680) prohibited Christians from consuming Jewish azymes (τὰ παρὰ τῶν Ἰουδαίων ἄζυμα), a canon the Latins were clearly violating.[150] That they believed it was a sign of Christ's incarnation without human seed showed their folly, for azymes were "a symbol not of the birth of the Lord from the Virgin but of his salvific passion, the life-giving Cross."[151]

The fourteenth-century dialogues and schemes aimed at reuniting the churches manifested what Edward Gibbon famously described "as the thermometer of the [Byzantines'] prosperity or distress," as several emperors dangled church union before the pope in the hopes of receiving military aid in exchange.[152] The primacy and the Filioque remained the chief divisive issues, and the popes were unambiguous that there could be no negotiation on either, for in their eyes the doctrines of the holy Roman Church were "certain ... [and] may not be brought to the sifting of doubt and of prying discussion and that by useless debate we may not replace the old faith by a new."[153] However, concerning the bread of the Eucharist, the Latins remained clear

---

[144] Ibid.
[145] Ibid., 370–73; Eng. trans.: 67.
[146] Ibid., 376–77; Eng. trans.: 69.
[147] Ibid., 380; Eng. trans.: 70.
[148] Ibid., 71.
[149] Ibid., 382; Eng. trans.: 71.
[150] Ibid., 388–89; Eng. trans.: 74.
[151] Ibid., 398; Eng. trans.: 78.
[152] Edward Gibbon, *The Decline and Fall of the Roman Empire*, vol. 3 (New York: Modern Library, 1995), 2272. For Gibbons's views of Byzantine church history see Deno Geanakoplos, "Edward Gibbon and Byzantine Ecclesiastical History," *Church History* 35 (1966): 170–85.
[153] Aloysius Tăutu, ed., *Acta Urbani PP. V (1362–1370)*, 311–13; Eng. trans.: Gill, *Byzantium and the Papacy 1198–1400*, 220.

that they would allow the Greeks to keep their rites unchanged provided only that they accept the legitimacy of the Western practice.

By the late fourteenth and early fifteenth centuries the flow of Greek anti-azymite tracts, once a torrent, had slowed to a trickle, despite the fact that the West's use of unleavened bread remained a sticking point. Symeon of Thessalonike (d. 1429), in his *Dialogus contra Omnes Haereses* (also known as the *Dialogue in Christ*) complained that the Latins offered azymes, "which was the custom of the Jews," while the Orthodox celebrated with the living bread, representing the "perfect God and perfect man" who told us that "the Kingdom of God is like leaven."[154] Elsewhere, drawing on language already present in Nicholas of Andida,[155] Symeon used leaven to emphasize the full humanity of Christ by likening the ensouled (leavened) bread to the "leavening" or impregnating of Mary by the Holy Spirit, so that when "the priest cuts this leavened bread out of the middle, [he] represents in this also that the Savior was incarnated of our nature, not of another essence, and from one woman, the blessed, holy, and ever virgin maiden."[156] Symeon even complained that the shape of the Latins' Eucharist was wrong, for instead of being square and perfect, it was round, which, the Latins claimed, "signifies both the being without beginning and the being without end of the divinity."[157]

From the West came John-Jerome of Prague's *De Erroribus Graecorum* (1532), a work that "provides some indication of the depth of the antipathy between the two sides, as well as the limited knowledge of many in the Latin West about the details of ... Greek theology of the eve of the council of Florence."[158] Highly polemical in tone,[159] John-Jerome's work listed among the Greeks' chief errors the fact that they

---

[154] Symeon of Thessalonica, *Dialogue in Christ against All Heresies* (PG 155:101). "And the bread is leavened, because it is in a sense living on account of the leaven, and it is truly complete, leavened bread for it witnesses that the human nature which the Word of God assumed for us was fully complete." Symeon of Thessalonika, *The Liturgical Commentaries*, trans. Steven Hawkes-Teeples (Toronto: Pontifical Institute of Medieval Studies, 2011), 186–87.

[155] "Therefore, in this way, the blessed ones continued to make remembrance of him [Christ], so that through the divine symbols the body was consecrated (ἀποτελεῖν) sound and whole, with mind and soul (ἔννουν καὶ ἔμψυχον), through the leaven put into the dough, and filled with divinity in essence." Nicholas of Andida, *Protheoria* (PG 140:420); Eng. trans.: Maria Evangelatou, "Krater of Nectar and Altar of the Bread of Life: The Theotokos as Provider of the Eucharist in Byzantine Culture," in Thomas Arentzen and Mary Cunningham, eds., *The Reception of the Virgin in Byzantium: Marian Narratives in Texts and Images* (Cambridge: Cambridge University Press, 2019), 110.

[156] Symeon of Thessalonika, *The Liturgical Commentaries*, 204–5.

[157] Ibid., 188–89. "The bread is four-sided, and not round and unleavened, as that sacrificed by the Latins, because, as we said, it is fully complete since God took on a fully complete human nature, with a soul and the four elements; and because all the world is four-part and the Word itself is the creator of the world; and because the body which Christ took on is made of four elements, and because the incarnate Word sanctified all the ends of the world, both the heavenly and the earthly, and because the shape of this typifies the cross, having been crucified and died on which, He restored us and the whole world." Ibid.

[158] William Hyland, "John-Jerome of Prague (1368–1440) and the *Errores Graecorum*: Anatomy of a Polemic against Greek Christians," *Journal of Religious History* 21 (1997): 249. John-Jerome had first given a sermon against the Greeks in 1409, while a confessor at the Polish court, condemning all those "who do not believe in the articles of faith," including "Greeks, Wallachians, Armenians, Besermanians, Bosnians, Jacobites, Nicolaites, and others from the East who are damned because of their disbelief." Ibid., 253–54.

[159] "I found all of the Greeks to be so obstinate and pertinacious in their heresy, that they publicly professed that they would rather receive the faith of the Turks then that of the Latins." John-Jerome of Prague, *De erroribus graecorum* in J-B Mittarelli and A. Costadoni, eds., *Annales Camuldulenses* (Venice 1755–73), vol. 9, col. 916; Eng. trans.: Hyland, "John-Jerome of Prague (1368–1440) and the *Errores Graecorum*," 259.

"deny that the Catholics can consecrate the body of Christ in unleavened bread,'"[160] and he claimed to have seen "with mine own eyes in Nicosia and Rhodes, that when the Catholic priest made the elevation during the mass, some Greeks who were then present turned their backs and an obscene part of the body against the sacrament of the altar."[161] This heresy, he claimed, was caused by the Greeks' "lack of understanding," for Scripture was clear that Christ "came to fulfill the law rather than abolish it. Thus, during the Passover supper Christ must have used unleavened bread, as the law required."[162] Besides, "if Christ had violated Jewish law in the way the Greeks assumed he did, then he would have been so accused when brought before Pontius Pilate."[163]

Because John-Jerome did not believe that union could be achieved through negotiation, his exclusion from Ferrara-Florence was both understandable and propitious.[164] Although his views were popular in some circles, if the upcoming council was going to succeed, it would require a different approach, such as the one taken by Hermann Zoest in his *De fermento et Azymo* (1436).[165] Discounting the "Leo legend" as nonhistorical ("for going through the decrees of the holy synods or of Roman pontiffs over and over, one does not find this at all"), the author urged both sides to charity in the name of peace.[166] He argued that even if the legend was true, it merely provided "an argument that [the Eucharist] *can* be prepared with leavened bread," and that "those who bark assaults against the Greeks should cease, and the Latin should stop gnawing on the Greeks with iron teeth ... and the Greeks should not despise the Latins. Let us seek what is for the Peace of Jerusalem, so that love is preserved."[167]

Zoest's work dealt chiefly with the chronology of the passion—that is, the question of whether Jesus had celebrated the Passover—a longtime point of contention between Latins and Greeks. After laying out the Latin and Greek cases with supporting texts from the fathers, he argued that in Jesus's day the rabbis often postponed

---

[160] John- Jerome of Prague, *De erroribus Graecorum*, 918; Eng. trans.: Schabel, "The Quarrel over Unleavened Bread," 123.

[161] John-Jerome of Prague, *De erroribus Graecorum*, 917; Eng. trans.: Hyland, "John-Jerome of Prague (1368–1440) and the *Errores Graecorum*," 259.

[162] Ibid., 256.

[163] Ibid.

[164] His solution to ending the schism was more drastic: "Complete union with the Greeks [cannot] be hoped for unless first the Lord Pope or a general council would seize that sacrilegious city of Constantinople, which is a den of heretics, and would hand that city into the possession of the master and brothers of St John of Rhodes, commanding the said master and brothers under the threat of anathema, to eliminate the Greek patriarch, bishops, and priests. And in their place would be placed a Catholic Archbishop and clergy. So the Catholic Church would triumph, and the inveterate heresy of the Greeks, having been constrained, would cease, to the praise of Christ. Amen." Ibid., 262. Hyland noted that his exclusion may have come because of rumors he spoke badly of both Ambrogio Traversai and Pope Eugene IV while at the Council of Basel. Ibid., 252.

[165] I am grateful to C. Philipp Nothaft and Christopher Schabel, who allowed me to see an early draft of their new book, now published as C. Philipp Nothaft and Chris Schabel, *The Cistercian Hermann Zoest's Treatise on Leavened and Unleavened Bread:* De fermento et azimo. *Oecumenism, Exegesis, and Science at the Council of Basel*, Recherches de Théologie et Philosophie médiévales – Bibliotheca, 21 (Leuven: Peeters, 2022).For Hermann Zoest see C. Phillipp Nothaft, "A Tool for Many Purposes: Hermann Zoest and the Medieval Christian Appropriation of the Jewish Calendar," *Journal of Jewish Studies* 65 (2014): 148–68; C. Phillipp Nothaft, *Medieval Latin Christian Texts on the Jewish Calendar: A Study with Five Editions and Translations* (Leiden: Brill, 2014); C. Phillipp Nothaft, *Dating the Passion: The Life of Jesus and the Emergence of Scientific Chronology (200–1600)* (Leiden: Brill, 2012).

[166] *Libellus de fermento et azymo*; Eng. trans.: Schabel, "The Quarrel over Unleavened Bread," 122.

[167] Ibid.

Passover to avoid celebration on Fridays, and that the alleged discrepancy in the gospels' chronology came about because Jesus and the apostles ignored their decision.[168] According to Zoest, Jesus and the disciples

> decided to celebrate their Passover on the evening of the fourteenth day of the lunar month ... without observing the postponement that the Jewish calendar demanded for that particular year. Since Jesus had eaten the Passover Lamb before the official beginning of the feast, it could not be inferred with any certainty whether fermented or unleavened bread had been available on the table during the Last Supper.[169]

Because the type of bread Jesus himself used remained uncertain, Zoest "took a pointedly irenic stance in the azymes controversy, defending the legitimacy of the Greek rite and calling on both sides to tolerate all that could be tolerated."[170] Ceremonial differences were unimportant, and if there were differences in faith these should be discussed between brothers in mutual charity, and not disputed by those who lived only to sow discord.[171]

The Council of Ferrara-Florence and Beyond

When the Council of Ferrara-Florence began, there was little doubt that azymes would be on the agenda, as the five church-dividing issues listed in the 1252 *Tractatus contra Graecos* (Filioque and its addition to the creed, primacy, Purgatory, azymes) all remained unresolved.[172] When the council began, Mark Eugenikos of Ephesus wrote an impassioned letter to Eugene IV praising the pope's genuine desire for unity, but then undiplomatically raised the issue of azymes, asking the Latins to end the "imperfect and dead" sacrifice in unleavened bread in order to avoid giving scandal to their brothers in the East.[173] When Emperor John VIII discovered the contents of the

---

[168] "Back in the 12th century, Rupert of Deutz and Reiner of Paderborn both noticed how the Jewish postponement rules, which prohibited the celebration of Passover on a Friday, implicitly backed the Johannine account of the passion, which set the Last Supper on the evening of 13/14 Nisan. This version of events was later endorsed by Rodger Bacon and Robert of Leicester, who realized that the events described in the gospels were in conflict with the obligation of sabbatical rest on 15 Nissan, thus backing the Greek position." Nothaft, *Medieval Latin Christian Texts on the Jewish Calendar*, 482.

[169] Ibid., 484. Hermann was originally not aware of the work of Paul of Burgos, who had come to a similar conclusion just a few years earlier. When he did, Hermann added texts from Paul and cited him and Reinher of Paderborn "as the only two scholars known to him to have paid any attention to the Jewish postponement rules in their treatment of the Passion chronology." Ibid., 485.

[170] "Que omnia sancta mater Ecclesia toleravit ac tolerat." Ibid., 484.

[171] "Non curemus cerimonialium differentias. Abiciamus multitudinem errorum contra Grecos a diversis collectorum. Si qua differentia est in hiis que sunt fidei, hec in karitate mutua plenius disputentur. O utinam non essent, aut fuissent, discordias inter fratres venenose seminantes." Ibid.

[172] Preparing for the council, Mark of Ephesus and the majority of the Greeks had decided that the interpolation should be the focus of the debates and that its removal would pave the way for restored communion, although they brought with them other works (e.g., those of Nilus Cabasilas) if it became necessary to discuss the dogmatic issues.

[173] Joseph Gill, *Quae supersunt Actorum Graecorum Concilii Florentini: Res Ferrariae gestae*, CF 5.1.1 (Rome: Pontifical Oriental Institute, 1953), 32. See also Vitalien Laurent, ed., *Les "Mémoires" du Grand Ecclésiarque de l'Église de Constantinople Sylvestre Syropoulos sur le Concile de Florence (1438–1439)*, CF 9 (Rome: Pontifical Oriental Institute, 1971), 258.

letter, he was furious, and might have hauled "Mark before the synod for punishment if Bessarion had not intervened to pacify him."[174] The emperor did not want the old dispute to endanger the union, which perhaps explains why, when both sides met to discuss the agenda, it was he who ruled against beginning with azymes.[175] This was in May 1438. The Eucharist would not be discussed again until June 1439, following a yearlong debate on the procession of the Holy Spirit.

What is so interesting about the Eucharistic debates at Florence, which began on June 9, is how quickly the issue of the azymes, a point of contention for almost four hundred years, receded so quickly into the background to be replaced by a new dispute, the *epiclesis* debate—that is, whether consecration of the elements took place after the words of institution (the Latin position) or the after the invocation of the Spirit (the Greek argument).[176] Essentially the Eucharistic debate shifted from matter to form, with very little time given to the former. With both sides eager to wrap up proceedings, and a new problem suddenly emerging, most of the Greeks, who "felt no great objection to the Latin custom," were willing to move on without too much comment.[177]

The man charged with putting forward the Latin case was the Dominican cardinal John of Torquemada, whose presentation echoed the arguments used two centuries earlier by Thomas Aquinas. Like Thomas he described the use of azymes as the more "reasonable" (*rationabilitor*) practice since Christ himself used unleavened bread at the Last Supper,[178] yet accepted that the Greek custom was valid since it had a "reason and significance" (*rationem et significationem*) of its own.[179] John spoke about both the matter and form of the Eucharist, distinguishing between what was necessary and what was becoming (*quid sit necessarium et quid sit conveniens*).[180] For John the *necessary* matter of the sacrament was wheaten bread without addition, and as such was valid whether leavened or unleavened.[181] Like Thomas, he held that priests belonging to both churches, East and West, were bound to confect the body of Christ according to their own custom, so that while the Latins would not ask the Greeks to give up their rite, neither should the Greeks regard the Latin practice as heretical.[182]

---

[174] Joseph Gill, *The Council of Florence* (Cambridge: Cambridge University Press, 1959), 114. Incident found in Laurent, Les "*Mémoires*", 260.

[175] Ibid., 270–72.

[176] Aside from Kappes, *The Epiclesis Debate at the Council of Florence*, see also John McKenna, *The Eucharistic Epiclesis: A Detailed History from the Patristic to the Modern Era* (Chicago: Hildebrand Books, 2009).

[177] Gill, *The Council of Florence*, 275. Gill noted that this did not apply to Mark of Ephesus, "who would have liked to have unfermented bread altogether forbidden." Ibid.

[178] Emmanuel Candal, ed., *Apparatus super decretum Florentinum unionis Graecorum*, CF B.2.1 (Rome: Pontificum institutum orientalium studiorum, 1942), 66–71. John used the standard arguments and prooftexts (including the spurious Leo legend and pseudo–Gregory the Great text) to defend the synoptic chronology and the use of unleavened bread in the ancient church. Ibid.

[179] Ibid., 71.

[180] Ibid., 70.

[181] Ibid. Thomas Izbicki noted that John had taken a similar stance in his commentary on Gratian's *Decretum* (Juan de Torquemada, *Commentaria super decreto* 5.61 A-B). Izbicki, *The Eucharist in Medieval Canon Law*, 85.

[182] "*Sacerdototes in altero ipsum debere corpus Christ conficere, ecclesie tamen sue sive Orientalia sive Occidentalia servata consuetudine.*" Candal, ed., *Apparatus super decretum Florentinum unionis Graecorum*, 68.

The final decree, *Laetentur Caeli*, signed on July 6, 1439, essentially repeated John's position as outlined in his *cedula*,[183] stating that "the body of Christ is truly confected in both unleavened and leavened wheat bread, and priests should confect the body of Christ in either, that is, each priest according to the custom of his western or eastern church."[184] Given the complete victories the West had achieved on all the other disputed issues, the concession that the Greeks should be allowed their own rites seemed almost generous. Yet "in truth the compromise was all on the side of the Greeks," wrote Christopher Schabel, since the decree merely echoed the position Aquinas's *Summa Theologica*, which the Greeks were now asked to swallow whole.[185]

Although agreement on the azyme issue had allegedly been reached, at the concluding liturgy, which was celebrated according to the Latin rite, not a single Greek bishop accepted the unleavened host.[186] This had actually been subject to some discussion the day before, when the pope, having heard that many Greeks wanted to receive the Holy Mysteries, instructed them that they should "keep continence, purify themselves, and prepare for this act."[187] Apparently the unionist bishop of Mytilene, Dorotheos, had initially indicated that he would be willing to partake of the unleavened host, but after a "spectacular about-face" he and the whole Greek delegation decided against it.[188] The emperor then asked that there be a Greek liturgy immediately following the Latin one, in order to demonstrate the equality of the rites, but when this was rejected for lack of time, he suggested it should take place the next day.[189] Eugene, pleading ignorance of the Greek liturgy, asked if some of his representatives might first view it in private and decide on its suitability.[190] The emperor, insulted at the suggestion that the Eastern liturgy might somehow be found lacking or inappropriate, immediately withdrew the proposal.[191]

---

[183] As given by Gill, it read, "We define also that the body of the Lord is truly effectuated in unfermented or in fermented bread, which the words of the Savior pronounced in the effectuating of it, and also that priests should effectuate the very body of the Lord in one of these according to the custom of his church, weather Latin or Oriental." Gill, *The Council of Florence*, 274. Latin original in Georg Hofmann, ed., *Andreas de Santacroce, advocatus consistorialis, Acta Latina Concilii Florentini*, CF 6 (Rome: Pontifical Oriental Institute, 1955), 231.

[184] "*Item, in azimo sive fermentato pane triticeo, corpus Christi veraciter confici, sacerdotesque in altero ipsum Domini corpus conficere debere, unumquemque scilicet iuxta sue ecclesie sive occidentalis sive orientalis consuetudinem.*" Laetentur Caeli; Tanner, ed., *Decrees of the Ecumenical Councils* 1, 527–28.

[185] Schabel, "The Quarrel over Unleavened Bread," 124.

[186] Laurent, *Les "Mémoires"*, 501. See Miguel Arranz, "Circonstances et conséquences liturgiques du Concile de Ferrare-Florence," in Giuseppe Alberigo, ed, *Christian Unity: The Council of Ferrara-Florence 1438/9* (Leuven: Leuven University Press, 1991), 407–27, esp. 414–18.

[187] "To the Pope's recommendations, the Bishop of Nicaea replied: 'Our people live in perpetual continence and spend all the time of their lives in piety. They have just heard the prescriptions of your Holiness and if anyone wants to commune, he will prepare for it with even more attention.'" Laurent, *Les "Mémoires,"* 496.

[188] "We had, in fact, heard that the bishop of Mytilene wanted to receive communion with the unleavened bread of the Latins and we had not believed it. But then we believed it because of the words of the Pope. The Bishop of Mytilene was quite confused and in a spectacular about-face gave up the idea of taking communion." Ibid.

[189] Ibid., 500–502.

[190] Ibid., 502.

[191] Ibid.

According to reports, by the time the Greek delegates returned to Constantinople, almost all had come to regret signing the decree, allegedly crying out upon their arrival, "We have betrayed our faith. We have exchanged piety for impiety. We have renounced the pure sacrifice and become azymites."[192] Mark of Ephesus, who had not subscribed to the union, derided those who did as "Greco-Latins," (Γραικολατῖνοι), "Latin-minded" (Λατινόφρονες), and "split people," who "like the mythical centaurs, confess together with [the Latins] ... that unleavened bread is the Body of Christ, and yet together with us do not dare to commune with it."[193] How could there be union if there was no shared faith, which was obviously the case when two diverse creeds are recited and two different sacrifices offered "one confected with leavened bread, the other with azymes."[194] The orthodox rightly shun the unleavened bread of the Jews, "For we obey the canons of the apostles which have prohibited it," unlike the unionists who affirm that what the Latins sacrifice is truly the Body of Christ.[195] Mark's premise was simple: "Ritual difference undermin[ed] the supposed unity of the churches," and thus "to be united, Greeks and Latins must observe one rite."[196]

Mark's opponents, like the unionist John Plousiadenos, took issue with this premise and emphasized that the unity of the church is evident in the shared faith of all "catholics" (καθολικοί) regardless of culture and rite.[197] According to Plousiadenos, just as we do not say that "[Christ] is Greek, or that [Christ] is Latin," we do not say that "the mystery of the New Testament, of the holy consecration, is twofold, so that the Body of the Lord Itself is divided into two, saying the one is leavened, the other unleavened; but both of these we confess to be the Body of Christ, and we proclaim to be the Body

---

[192] "As soon as the hierarchs disembarked from the triremes, the Constantinopolitans, as was customary, embraced them and inquired, 'How are you? What news do you bring us of the synod? Have we perchance gained the victory?' They replied, 'We have betrayed our faith. We have exchanged piety for impiety. We have renounced the pure sacrifice and have become azymites.' These and other statements, more abominable and foul, were heard. And who were they who made these confessions? Why, the very ones who had subscribed to the horos—Antony, the metropolitan of Heraklea, and all the rest! When questioned, 'Why did you subscribe?' they answered, 'Because we feared the Franks.'" Doukas, *Decline and Fall of Byzantium to the Ottoman Turks: An Annotated Translation of the "Historia Turco-Byzantina"*, trans. Harry Magoulias (Detroit: Wayne State University Press, 1975), 181. See also George Demacopoulos, "The Popular Reception of the Council of Florence in Constantinople (1439–1453)," *St. Vladimir's Theological Quarterly* 43 (1999): 37–53.

[193] *Marci Ephesii epistola encyclica contra Graeco-Latinos ac decretum synodi Florentiae*, in Petit, ed. *Marci Eugenici, metropolitae Ephesi, opera antiunionistica*, 142.

[194] Ibid., 142–43.

[195] Ibid., 150.

[196] Yost, "Neither Greek nor Latin, but Catholic," 54, 56. This Greek intolerance toward foreign liturgical rites is sometimes described as "Byzantinism" and according to scholars like Yury P. Avvakumov results "from a failure to separate the accidental, non-essential aspects of sacramental rituals from the transcendent truths to which those rituals supposedly point." Ibid., 56–57. See also Yury P. Avvakumov, "Die Fragen des Ritus als Streit- und Kontroversgegenstand. Zur Typologie der Kulturkonflikte zwischen dem lateinischen Westen und dem byzantinisch-slavischen Osten im Mittelalter und in der Neuzeit," in Rainer Bendel, ed., *Kirchen- und Kulturgeschichtsschreibung in Nordost- und Ostmitteleuropa: Initiativen, Methoden, Theorien, Band 2* (Berlin: LIT Verlag, 2006), 191–233.

[197] The term "catholic," which was already being used as an insult, was for Plousiadenos "a badge of honor. "We are catholics and we want to be called catholics, even if you give us this name sarcastically and consider it an insult; for believing in one, holy, catholic, and apostolic Church, we are and are called catholics; and we call those [who] are not called 'catholics,' or not following her [i.e. the Church], 'schismatics' and, I think, justly." John Plousiadnenos, *Expositio pro sancta et oecumenica synodo florentina quod legitime congregata est, et defensio quinque capitum quae in decreto ejus continentur* (PG 159:1281). Eng. trans.: Yost, "Neither Greek nor Latin, but Catholic," 55–56.

of Christ, reckoning them to be one and the same thing, even if consecrated differently by either side."[198] For Charles Yost,

> Though he asserts that as a matter of historical fact Christ sacrificed in unleavened bread, Plousiadenos maintains the reality of the Eucharist as the Body of Christ as transcending the material difference between leavened and unleavened bread.... One and the same Body of Christ is constituted by leavened or unleavened bread, Byzantine or Latin liturgical rites. The reality of the Body of Christ is not constrained to one quality of bread or rite, and thus transcends both without excluding either ... [just as] the same Church, the Body of Christ, comprises Latins as well as Greeks, but is not restricted to or exclusively identified with either.[199]

Among the Latin defenders of Florence was Fantinus Vallaresso, who wrote a commentary on the council's decisions claiming that Christ instituted the sacrament with bread without specifying type, and for this reason, "It did not matter whether the bread was white or black square or round in form (*albus vel niger aut in forma quadratra vel rotunda*)" as long as it was made of wheat.[200] Even if Christ himself used unleavened bread (which, according to Fantinus was the more likely scenario), he "did not wish to restrain the sacrament to unleavened or leavened bread alone, but he granted and conceded power that it could be confected from any wheat bread."[201]

The Latins' frustration, as it had been for centuries, was that while they were willing to concede the legitimacy of leavened bread, the Greeks continued to deny the validity of an azymite Eucharist. For this, Andreas de Escobar argued, they were "heretics and schismatics" who believed "the Latin Church had sinned and was therefore not holy."[202] For if "the host consecrated of unleavened is not the true body of Christ, [then] neither the pope, nor cardinals, nor patriarchs, who are priests, nor the other Latin clerics have ever celebrated mass" and all Christians who show it reverence are little more than "idolaters."[203]

Yet Mark remained adamant that the Latins' rite could never be accepted as orthodox and continued to press home the point in his polemical works. In his *Epistola ad Georgium Presbyterum Methonensem contra Ritus Ecclesiae Romanae* Mark employed quotations from Maximos the Confessor's *Mystagogia* and Basil's *Liturgy* to demonstrate that what is offered at liturgy is not an antitype of what is dead, but what is life-giving and Spirit-filled.[204] In 1440, to counter Mark's charges, Andreas

---

[198] Plousiadenos, *Expositio* (PG 159:1189); Eng. trans.: Yost, "Neither Greek nor Latin, but Catholic," 53–54.
[199] Ibid., 54.
[200] Bernard Schultze, ed., *Libellus de ordine generalium conciliorum et unione Florentina*, CF 2 (Rome: Pontifical Oriental Institute, 1944), 61; Eng. trans.: Izbicki, *The Eucharist in Medieval Canon Law*, 84.
[201] Ibid.
[202] Andreas de Escobar, *Tractatus polemico-theologicus de Graecis errantibus*, in Emmanuel Candal, ed., *Documenta et Scriptores*, CF B.4.1 (Rome: Pontifical Oriental Institute, 1952), 47–55. Eng. trans.: Johnna Sturgeon, "Cares at the Curia: Andreas de Escobar and Ecclesiastical Controversies at the Time of the Fifteenth-Century Councils" (PhD diss., Northwestern University, 2017), 195–96.
[203] Sturgeon, *Cares at the Curia*, 195–96.
[204] Mark of Ephesus, *Epistola ad Georgium Presbyterum Methonensem contra Ritus Ecclesiae Romanae*, in Petit, ed., *Marci Eugenici, metropolitae Ephesi, opera antiunionistica*, 163–64.

Chrysoberges, archbishop of Rhodes, composed a fictional *Dialogue against Mark, Pontiff of the Ephesians, Who Damns the Rites and Sacrifices of the Roman Church*.[205] Andreas went through the usual arguments in favor of unleavened bread in order to counter Mark's claim that the Latins' Eucharist was a "dead sacrifice" (*mortuum sacrificium*) performed according to the Law of Moses. Accepting the historicity of the Leo legend, Andreas chided Mark for rejecting the use of azymes when it was actually the more ancient of the two customs and universally held before the Greeks refused to return to the older way.[206] There followed a prolonged discussion of the Filioque and the epiclesis controversy, after which Andreas expressed frustration with Mark's unwillingness to accept the council's teaching on azymes, especially given the Latins' liberality in allowing leavened hosts, and warned him that if he failed to acknowledge his errors and repent, he would join the other heresiarchs in the fires of Hell.[207]

Although the debate over azymes lost most of its "heat" in the years after Florence, the people of Constantinople kept it very much alive, praying not only for relief against the infidel, but also to be kept "far away from the worship of the azymites!"[208] Even after the fall of the city in 1453 and the formal repudiation of Florence in 1484, the Latin use of unleavened bread remained a point of contention. When the Ruthenian bishops began the negotiations that led to the Union of Brest in 1595, they insisted that "the most holy sacraments of the body and blood of Our Lord Jesus Christ should be preserved for us intact, as we have celebrated them until now, under both species— bread and wine; that this be preserved in perpetuity, completely and without violation."[209] This was not a problem, as the Florentine decree had made clear, but the Ruthenians wanted assurances, lest by entering into communion with azymites they should become azymites themselves.[210]

In 1574, following the Protestant Reformation, a group of Tübingen theologians began a correspondence with Patriarch Jeremiah II (1572–79, 1580–84, 1586–95) in the hope of finding common cause against the Roman church.[211] The patriarch was cordial and responded to these "wise German men and spiritual sons" by engaging them in a discussion over those things that divided them, especially the Filioque and

---

[205] Andreas Chrysoberges, *Dyalogus in Marcum, Ephesiorum pontificem, damnantem ritus et sacrificia Romane Ecclsie, habitus a fratre Andrea, archiepiscopo Colossensi, ad cives Methonenses*; Martin Hinterberger and Christopher Schabel, "Andreas Chrysoberges' Dialogue against Mark Eugenikos," in Alison Frazier and Patrick Nold, eds., *Essays in Renaissance Thought and Letters: In Honor of John Monfasani* (Leiden: Brill, 2015), 492–545.

[206] Ibid., 501.

[207] Ibid., 545.

[208] "They beseeched [the Mother of God] to protect and defend the City against Mehmed as she had done in the past against Chosroes and Chagan and the Arabs. "We have need neither of the Latins' help nor of the Union. Keep far away from us the worship of the Azymites!" Doukas, *Decline and Fall of Byzantium to the Ottoman Turks*, 204–5.

[209] Articles of Union, 3; Eng. trans.: Borys Gudziak, *Crisis and Reform: The Kyivan Metropolitanate, the Patriarchate of Constantinople, and the Genesis of the Union of Brest* (Cambridge, MA: Harvard University Press, 1998), 264.

[210] It should be noted that although some Greek-rite parishes in southern Italy began using unleavened bread in the late seventeenth century, for the most part there was no large-scale effort to convert the Eastern Catholics to this practice despite all the other "latinizations" that eventually crept into their liturgies.

[211] For the English translation of the correspondence see George Mastrantonis, ed., *Augsburg and Constantinople: The Correspondence between the Tübingen Theologians and Patriarch Jeremiah II of Constantinople on the Augsburg Confession* (Brookline, MA: Holy Cross Orthodox Press, 1982).

the role of free will. Among the issues he raised was the type of bread used in the Eucharist, which was offered "not as unleavened, but as leavened, which in truth is bread; for the saints of the East, Chrysostom as well as others, interpret and prove that it is necessary to offer not the unleavened, but leavened bread."[212] The patriarch did not elaborate further, admitting that "a discourse concerning this subject is a major one and requires a lengthy dissertation," although he promised he would instruct them further if they desired.[213]

In their response, the Tübingen theologians wrote that they did not "wish to quarrel with anyone" about the type of bread used at the Eucharist, and yet they wanted the patriarch to understand their position.[214] The East believed that only "the leavened is truly and correctly called bread ... [while] we say that the flour which has been mixed with water and kneaded truly becomes bread, whether mixed with leaven or not."[215] They argued that "since our Pascha is Christ, the true lamb, who in the holy supper becomes our meat, we with good reason use unleavened bread not only to remind ourselves of the faultlessness and purity of that heavenly bread, but forthwith also so that we may be alerted to cleanse the old leaven of evil and wickedness and then celebrate the Passover with the unleavened bread of sincerity and truth."[216]

By the seventeenth century the papacy had replaced both azymes and the Filioque as the focus of Orthodox polemics, as antipapal treatises, like Elias Miniati's *The Rock of Scandal* (Πὲτρα Σκανδάλου) and Eustratios Argenti's (c. 1687–c. 1758) *Manual Concerning the Latin Pope and Anti-Christ*, proliferated.[217] Yet azymes were not forgotten, and in the *Confessio* (1625) of Metrophanes Kritopoulos, extensive space was given defending the use of leavened bread against its "opponents."[218]

---

[212] Ibid., 189.

[213] Ibid.

[214] Ibid., 263. Although most of the reformers kept using unleavened bread in the Eucharist, in 1523 Ulrich Zwingli and Conrad Grebel separated over Grebel's belief that leavened bread was preferred since *panis* was the word used in Scripture. John Wenger, *Glimpses of Mennonite History and Doctrine* (Eugene, OR: Wipf and Stock, 2000), 20. In the *Institutes of the Christian Religion* (4.17.43) John Calvin wrote that "whether the bread is leavened or unleavened; the wine red or white—it makes no difference. These things are indifferent, and left at the church's discretion.... The histories narrate that common leavened bread was used before the time of the Roman Bishop Alexander, who was the first who delighted in unleavened bread." John Calvin, *Institutes of the Christian Religion*, trans. Ford Lewis Battles (Louisville, KY: Westminster John Knox Press, 1960), 1420.

[215] Mastrantonis, *Augsburg and Constantinople*, 263.

[216] Ibid. Ultimately, the exchange with the Lutherans seems to have convinced Jeremiah that, at least on a theological level, he had more in common with the Catholics than with the Protestants, whose views on many of the contested issues (e.g., good works, free will, prayers for the dead, saints, icons) were at odds with the Orthodox position. He concluded his final letter with "Therefore, we request that from henceforth you do not cause us more grief, nor write to us on the same subject if you should wish to treat these luminaries and theologians of the Church in a different manner. You honor and exalt them in words, but you reject them in deeds. For you try to prove our weapons, which are their holy and divine discourses, as unsuitable. And it is with these documents that we would have to write and contradict you. Thus, as for you, please release us from these cares. Therefore, going about your own ways, write no longer concerning dogmas; but if you do, write only for friendship's sake. Farewell." Ibid., 306.

[217] "If the procession of the Holy Spirit formed the chief topic in polemics between east and west before the fall of Constantinople, the Orthodox in the Turkish period came to place greater emphasis upon the papal claims, considering it the fundamental point at issue." Kallistos Ware, *Eustratios Argenti: A Study of the Greek Church under Turkish Rule* (Oxford: Clarendon Press, 1964), 161.

[218] See Metrophanes Kritopoulos, *Confession of Faith*, in Jaroslav Pelikan and Valerie Hotchkiss, eds., *Creeds and Confessions of Faith in the Christian Tradition*, vol. 1 (New Haven, CT: Yale University

In many ways there was little new in the *Confessio*, as Kritopoulos merely repeated many of the arguments used since the eleventh century (e.g., that "the Lord appears to have used leavened bread," "you will not find unleavened bread called simply bread in the Holy Scriptures," "the Evangelists all say of the Lord that he took bread not unleavened bread").[219] He cited the story of Emmaus as a potential proof of the Latin case, since "the Lord is said to have taken bread at Emmaus ... and this was done during the Passover festival when everyone was forbidden to eat leavened bread."[220] Kritopoulos speculated that Emmaus "was a Gentile city ... where the use of unleavened bread was not known," and perhaps the disciples Jesus met "were proselytes, who had only recently come to the Lord, and therefore were not yet bound to keep the Jewish custom" or that they had "learned from the Lord not to make too much of such useless customs as the strict observance of the Sabbath."[221] Interestingly, unlike many before him, Kritopoulos accepted that Jesus did celebrate the lawful Passover on the fourteenth of the new moon, "for if he had celebrated the feast unlawfully, those sycophants, who fabricated so many charges against him, would have made this their strongest point."[222] Echoing Chrysostom, Kritopoulos maintained that it was the Jews who postponed their celebration, either to "vent their rage on the Savior, since it was not possible for them to go to the courts and accuse and plead cases during the feast of Passover ... or else in accordance with some traditions of their fathers. For there is some such tradition, as those who are conversant with the Hebrew books tell us."[223]

Kritopoulos argued that the use of azymes must be rejected because it was instituted by heretics, and was "practiced first among the arch heretic Apollinaris ... [who] taught that the Lord took flesh without soul or a mind."[224] As for Paul's admonition "to throw away the old leaven and celebrate the feast with unleavened bread in singleness of heart," Kritopoulos answered that "there are many things in the inspired scriptures which are both praised and blamed, not in the same place but in different places. For instance, the serpent was first pronounced accursed and condemned to crawl on his

---

Press, 2003), 516–20. See also Colin Davey, *Pioneer for Unity: Metrophanes Kritopoulos, 1589–1639, and Relations between the Orthodox, Roman Catholic and Reformed Churches* (London: British Council of Churches, 1987).

[219] Kritopoulos, *Confession of Faith*, in Pelikan and Hotchkiss, *Creeds and Confessions* 1, 516.

[220] If it was the Passover, then "the bread he broke must have been unleavened," and yet Scripture simply calls it "bread." Ibid.

[221] Ibid., 517. To prove that the disciples were not following the letter of the Law, Kritopoulos calculated how far they walked, which would have been in excess of what was allowed. He wrote: "This is clear from the fact that having journeyed so many stadia during the time of the festival, when it was only possible to go a sabbath days journey, which is 2040 paces. But they, it appears, had gone sixty stadia that day, which was the second day of the Jewish Passover, and each stadium is 625 paces. So they appear to have broken the Jewish custom by their journey and also in their failure to use unleavened bread." Ibid.

[222] Ibid.

[223] Ibid., 518. The Jews "had agreed that when the Passover fell on the sixth day of the week, to postpone it to the next day, which is the Sabbath; and if it fell on Sunday, to bring it forward again to the Sabbath. That this was the case can be seen from two places in the gospel: first where the Evangelist writes that the high priest on the morrow did not come 'into the praetorium, so that they should be undefiled, and able to eat the Passover'—and clearly they had not yet eaten it—and also where he names the Sabbath day as 'great' for he says, 'That Sabbath was a high day.' What can this mean except that day was both the Sabbath, the weekly feast of the Jews, and also the first day of the Passover." Ibid.

[224] Ibid.

belly, but later in the time of Moses he is used as an image of Christ.... so too with leaven. It seems to be blamed by the apostle, but [elsewhere] it was praised by the Lord and likened to the kingdom of heaven."[225]

Other confessions, such as the *Orthodox Confession of the Catholic and Apostolic Eastern Church* written by the metropolitan of Kyiv, Peter Mohyla (d. 1647), spent little time discussing the proper matter for the Eucharist, stating only that "the purest leavened bread, made of grain" was necessary for validity.[226] The same is true of the *Longer Catechism of the Orthodox, Catholic, Eastern Church*, issued by Philaret of Moscow in 1823, which maintained the type of bread to be used should be "such as the name itself of bread, the holiness of the Mystery, and the example of Jesus Christ and the Apostles all require; that is, leavened, pure, wheaten bread."[227] The *Confession* of Patriarch Dositheus and the Synod of Jerusalem (1672) never even mentioned azymes, emphasizing instead the real presence of Christ in the sacrament against the Protestant position.[228]

Although azymes took on less importance with every passing decade, the eighteenth century did manage to produce one of the last great anti-azymite tracts, Eustratios Argenti's *Treatise against Unleavened Bread* (Σύνταγμα κατὰ Ἀζύμων), which Kallistos Ware called "the most thorough and detailed attack on the defects of the modern Roman eucharistic practice that any Orthodox controversialist has ever composed."[229] Argenti focused his attack on the historical questions—that is, the type of bread used at the Last Supper and the type of bread used by the ancient church.[230] He defended the Johannine chronology and reconciled it to the Synoptics by affirming that the Last Supper took place on 13 Nisan, which Matthew 26:17 had described as Τῇ δὲ πρώτῃ τῶν ἀζύμων—that is, "on the day *before* the unleavened bread," not "on the first day of unleavened bread."[231] Because the Passover of the Jews had not yet begun, Christ instituted the "new Passover" with ἄρτος, not ἄζυμος. He later supported this position by arguing that "Christ is a priest after the order, not of Aaron, but of Melchizedek; but azymes belong to the Aaronic priesthood, while Melchizedek is said in Genesis to have offered not *azyma* (azymes) but *artos* (bread)."[232] The fathers, with the possible exception of Chrysostom (whose chronology of the passion was "ambiguous, careless, and contradictory"), all agreed that "Christ was sacrificed on the cross on the actual day and hour when the Passover of the law was sacrificed, so that according to the holy fathers Christ instituted the Lord's Supper before the

---

[225] Ibid., 519.
[226] Peter Mohyla, *Orthodox Confession of the Catholic and Apostolic Eastern Church*, in Pelikan and Hotchkiss, *Creeds and Confessions* 1, 604. For more on Mohyla see Ihor Ševčenko, "The Many Worlds of Peter Mohyla," in *Ukraine between East and West: Essays on Cultural History to the Early Eighteenth Century* (Edmonton: Canadian Institute of Ukrainian Studies Press, 2009), 164–86.
[227] Philaret of Moscow, *Longer Catechism of the Orthodox, Catholic, Eastern Church*, in R. W. Blackmore, ed., *Doctrine of the Russian Church* (London: J. Masters, 1905), 73–74.
[228] Patriarch Dositheus, *Confession*, in Pelikan and Hotchkiss, *Creeds and Confessions*, 615. See also J. N. W. B. Robertson, *The Acts and Decrees of the Synod of Jerusalem* (New York: AMS Press, 1969).
[229] Ware, *Eustratios Argenti*, 108.
[230] "He makes virtually no use of symbolical arguments, and one cannot but feel that he was wise in this." Ibid., 114.
[231] Ibid., 115.
[232] Ibid., 117.

beginning of the period of unleavened bread."[233] Yet even if Christ had used unleavened bread, "it would not follow that the Church must do the same ... [for] he was circumcised and as a rule observed the sabbath, but these ordinances do not apply to his followers."[234]

Argenti then claimed that leavened bread had been used throughout the church until the Latins decided to change their practice at some point after the Photian Schism, probably by Pope Leo IX.[235] He wrote that nowhere

> in the whole of divine scripture, in all the councils, ecumenical and local, orthodox and heretical, and all the holy fathers, and all the historians, ... [is there] any mention of unleavened bread or use of the word in connection with the Lord's Supper. So far as I have been able to examine the matter (and I have examined many things), I have found no trace of unleavened bread in any writer save only in the case of the heretical Ebionites.[236]

The Eastern church continued to observe this custom, just as the Western church had done "in the time of her orthodoxy."[237] By introducing azymes, the Latins had lost the symbolism of sharing the one loaf, "which strengthens men's hearts" and "represents the oneness of Christ's members in his mystical body."[238] He urged the West to return to the ancient custom and partake "not from [the] many, but from [the] one loaf, as the Catholic Church did and still does, and as Christ and the apostles did, that you may become one body with your head—not the pope, but Christ—and with the members of Christ, the Orthodox."[239]

Despite occasional condemnations of the "azymites" during this period, the reality on the ground was often quite different, for "Greeks and Latins continued in practice quietly to ignore the separation and to behave as if no breach in communion had occurred. Instances of *communicatio in sacris* are especially abundant in the seventeenth century, and if we are to speak of a 'final consummation' of the schism, perhaps this should not be placed earlier than the years 1725-50."[240] A definitive date could even be 1755, when the patriarchs of Constantinople, Jerusalem, and Alexandria decided that all converts from Latin Christianity should be rebaptized, a policy that even today remains in force in many parts of the Orthodox world.[241] The Latins' use of azymes

---

[233] Ibid.

[234] Ibid., 118.

[235] "The most holy Photios, writing to Pope Nicholas and enumerating in detail the differences between the liturgies, says nothing about azymes from which we learn that in the time of Photios the great the use of azymes had not yet arisen among the Latins." Ibid., 119. Here, Argenti was "reject[ing] the earlier Byzantine view that the Latins' use of azymes had been introduced by one Leucius, a disciple of Apollinaris. In its place he constructs a fairly plausible argument that azymes were first used in Rome sometime between the ninth and eleventh centuries." Erickson, "Leavened and Unleavened," 149.

[236] Ware, *Eustratios Argenti*, 119.

[237] Ibid.

[238] Ibid., 120.

[239] Ibid.

[240] Kallistos Ware, "Orthodox and Catholics in the Seventeenth Century: Schism or Intercommunion?," in Derek Baker, ed., *Studies in Church History*, vol. 9: *Schism, Heresy and Religious Protest* (Cambridge: Cambridge University Press, 1972), 259-76.

[241] For the relative novelty of this approach see George Dragas, "The Manner of Reception of Roman Catholic Converts into the Orthodox Church with Special Reference to the Decisions of the Synods of

were not necessarily given as the reason for this decision, but it was cited among those practices which were considered "opposed ... to the ordinance of God ... [and] a serious innovation, which has caused scandal and schism."[242]

In January 1848, soon after his election, Pope Pius IX (1846–78) addressed an apostolic letter to the East on the subject of Christian unity (*In Suprema Petri Apostoli Sede*), calling them back to the church their forebears had left.[243] The Orthodox hierarchy responded to Pius's letter by issuing one of its own, *The Encyclical of the Eastern Patriarchs*, which vehemently rejected the pope's overtures and his claims to headship over the church.[244] Among his many errors was that in introducing the Filioque "disgraceful fruits ... [and] other novelties" were brought forth, among which "may be numbered sprinkling instead of baptism, denial of the divine Cup to the Laity, elevation of one and the same bread broken, the use of wafers, [and] unleavened instead of real bread."[245]

In 1894 Pope Leo XIII (1878–1903) issued a similar, but perhaps more irenic, apostolic letter on Christian unity (*Praeclara Gratulationis*) urging Eastern Christians to "return to the fold they have abandoned," assuring them that there was no "reason for you to fear that we or any of our successors will ever diminish your rights ... or the established rite of any of your Churches."[246] In his response, Patriarch Anthimos VII of Constantinople (1895–97) echoed Mark of Ephesus in maintaining that unity of faith could not exist when "in one and the same Church one believes that the Holy Ghost proceeds from the Father, and another that He proceeds from the Father and the Son ... one uses leavened bread in the sacrament of the Holy Eucharist, and another unleavened."[247] Anthimos challenged the pope to find any proof that the once-orthodox Roman church "read the Creed with the addition, or used unleavened bread" before the ninth century, knowing that "for more than a thousand years throughout the East and West" the Eucharist was celebrated "with leavened bread, as the truth-loving papal theologians themselves also bear witness."[248] The change, as

---

1484 (Constantinople), 1755 (Constantinople), and 1667 (Moscow)," *Greek Orthodox Theological Review* 44 (1999): 235–71.

[242] As early as 1484 Latin converts were forced to "turn completely away from the gatherings of the Latins in their churches, or even of those who are Latin-minded, and of those who use azymes in a Jewish fashion, or celebrate these [mysteries] in an Apollinarist way, regarding them as heretics." Ibid.

[243] "Return without further delay," Pius begged them, "for it will never be possible for those who wish to be separated from the solidity of the Rock on which the Church itself was divinely built, to be in communion with the One, Holy, Catholic, and Apostolic Church." Should they return they would be received with "most lovingly and with extraordinary paternal benevolence" with both their faith and rites (apart from those things "that may have crept in during the time of separation that are at odds with the same faith and catholic unity") preserved intact. Pius IX, *In Suprema Petri Apostoli Sede*, trans. Patrick Brannan, in James Likoudis, *Eastern Orthodoxy and the See of Peter: A Journey towards Full Communion* (Waite Park, MN: Park Press, 2006).

[244] *Encyclical of the Eastern Patriarchs: A Reply to the Epistle of Pope Pius IX*, in Pelikan and Hotchkiss, *Creeds and Confessions*, vol. 3, 266–88.

[245] Ibid.

[246] Leo XIII, *Praeclara Gratulationis*, in Josef Neuner and Jacques Dupuis, eds., *The Christian Faith* (New York: Alba Houe, 1982), 258–59.

[247] Anthimos VII, *A Reply to the Papal Encyclical of Pope Leo XIII on Reunion*, in Metallinos, ed., *Orthodox and Catholic Union*, 3.

[248] Ibid., 5–6.

scholars were now admitting, came in the eleventh century, when "the papal church made an innovation ... in the sacrament of the divine Eucharist by introducing unleavened bread."[249]

Epilogue

As with beards, by the twentieth century azymes had completely disappeared as an ecumenical issue after almost a millennium of debate.[250] While quite understandable on one level, given how prominently the Eucharist has figured in the recent theological dialogues between the Catholic and Orthodox Churches, its omission does seem strange.[251] Scouring the subreddits and YouTube channels of Orthodox polemicists, one can find thousands of references to the papacy and the Filioque—this I know—but almost nothing about unleavened bread, once considered the casus belli in the East-West dispute. In fact, one is far more likely to read about the desacralization of the Roman rite following Vatican II than about the use of azymes in that rite. While there have been some excellent historical studies of the issue, many of them cited liberally in this book, Sergei Sveshnikov's *Break the Holy Bread, Master: A Theology of Communion Bread*, remains a rarity, treating the debate over communion bread as an ongoing symbolic, theological, and sacramental issue.[252] Unapologetically Orthodox, but without indulging in the polemics of the past, the author ultimately concludes that not only should communion bread be handmade, salted, and leavened, for "how can we see the risen Lord in a flat azyme," but also that the yeast should be natural as opposed to store-bought.[253]

If the old debates about unleavened bread are really over, maybe we have finally arrived at a point when the "endless controversaries" that reduced the Eucharist into "elements" and "formulas" required for validity can be settled, allowing both East and West to see the Eucharist as it was meant to be—as the "one organic, all-embracing and all-transforming act of the whole church."[254] There are still issues that prevent Catholics and Orthodox from standing together at the Eucharistic table, but perhaps the type of bread used at that table is no longer one of them.

---

[249] Ibid., 6.

[250] Although the Romanian Orthodox Church's rite for the "Reception of the Other Believers in Orthodoxy," revised as recently as 2014, asks Catholic converts to reject their heresies, which include the Filioque, the primacy of the Roman pope, Purgatory, and the use of the azymes.

[251] The first joint statements, both from the US Theological Consultation (1969) and the Joint International Commission (1982), concerned the Eucharist.

[252] Sergei Sveshnikov, *Break the Holy Bread, Master: A Theology of Communion Bread* (San Francisco: Booksurge, 2009).

[253] Ibid., 74. "The process of preparing the starter, as if waiting for the dead Christ to rise and come forth from his tomb before mixing the living in three measures of flour and watching the miracle take place not only offers an old-fashioned link to those who came before us, but also is more orthodox. Indeed, using distilled commercially-produced yeast is akin to performing CPR on Christ instead of waiting for him to rise." Ibid., 74–75.

[254] Alexander Schmemann, *For the Life of the World* (Crestwood, NY: St. Vladimir's Seminary Press, 1995), 33–34.

PART III
PURGATORY

6
Purgatory in the Biblical and Patristic Tradition

According to Jacques Le Goff, the word "Purgatory" did not appear as a noun until sometime between 1170 and 1180, a fact used for centuries by critics, both Orthodox and Protestant, who claimed that the dogma had no biblical and patristic basis.[1] Yet Catholic authors since the Middle Ages have maintained that although the word "Purgatory" itself is not present, the teaching that departed souls can be cleansed of their sins after death is "explicitly taught in Scripture ... found in the writings of the early church fathers ... [and] is part of the deposit of faith 'which was once for all delivered to the saints' (Jude 1:3)."[2] The Orthodox, while acknowledging the importance of prayers for the dead, remained unconvinced by this argument, and interpreted the writings of certain fathers (e.g., Gregory of Nyssa) on "the crucible of purifying fire" differently than their Catholic counterparts.[3] Protestants went even further, rejecting not only the doctrine of Purgatory, but also (to varying degrees) all prayers for the deceased.[4]

The question of Purgatory, and the extent to which it is treated in both the biblical and patristic corpus, is intimately bound up with the larger question about the state of souls after death and how the early church thought about the issue. Christianity

---

[1] Le Goff, *The Birth of Purgatory*, 130–32. Other modern scholars suggest the doctrine's origins lay in the ninth to twelfth centuries (Adriaan Bredero, "Le Moyen Âge et le purgatoire," *Revue d'histoire ecclésiastique* 78 [1983]: 429–52), and Peter Brown goes as far back as the seventh (Peter Brown, "Vers la naissance du purgatoire. Amnistie et pénitence dans le christianisme occidental de l'Antiquité tardive au haut Moyen Âge," *Annales. Histoire, Sciences Sociales* 52 [1997]: 1247–61; an English version of this article appeared as "The Decline of the Empire of God: Amnesty, Penance, and the Afterlife from Late Antiquity to the Middle Ages," in Caroline Walker Bynum and Paul Freedman, eds., *Last Things: Death and the Apocalypse in the Middle Ages* [Philadelphia: University of Pennsylvania Press, 2000], 41–59). See also Graham Robert Edwards, "Purgatory: Birth or Evolution," *Journal of Ecclesiastical History* 36 (1985): 634–46.
[2] John Salza, *The Biblical Basis for Purgatory* (Charlotte, NC: Saint Benedict Press, 2009), 12.
[3] See Gregory of Nyssa, *De mortuis non esse dolendum* (PG 46:524).
[4] *The Westminster Confession* (1647) XXI stated: "Prayer is to be made for things lawful; and for all sorts of men living, or that shall live hereafter: but not for the dead, nor for those of whom it may be known that they have sinned the sin unto death." *The Westminster Confession* in John Leith, ed., *Creeds of the Churches* (Louisville: John Knox Press, 1963), 217. In the earlier *Apology of the Augsburg Confession* (1530), in Article XXIV Philip Melancthon maintained: "Our opponents quote the Fathers on offerings for the dead. We know that the ancients spoke of prayer for the dead. We do not forbid this, but rather we reject the transfer of the Lord's Supper to the dead *ex opere operato*." Philip Melancthon, "Apology of the Augsburg Confession," in Theodore Tappert, ed., *The Book of Concord* (Philadelphia: Fortress Press, 1959), 267. Yet when later Lutherans wrote to Patriarch Jeremiah II in 1577, they maintained that they did "not approve of prayers and alms offered for the dead. If they have truly believed in Christ, we do not doubt that they do live with Christ, enjoying the gladness in heaven.... But if they have departed without true and living faith, they cannot be helped neither by prayers nor by alms.... As long as we are here, we have good hopes. But as soon as we depart to that place, we can no longer repent nor cleanse ourselves from our iniquities." Mastrantonis, *Augsburg and Constantinople*, 135–36.

has always been an eschatological faith, with Christians holding that "the end was near ... because they believed Jesus had risen from the dead, and because they were convinced that the community's new experience of the charisms of the Spirit was the first taste of the Kingdom of God."[5] Yet as time passed and the timeline for the eschaton shifted, questions arose about the fate of those who had died and a more developed eschatological system was needed. One can see the beginnings of this process in Paul (e.g., 1 Thes 4:13–18),[6] but it would take centuries before many of the questions Christians had about the next world received doctrinal formulation. Purgatory arose out of this conversation, with writers searching the Scriptures for hints of what happened after death, how sins committed after baptism were forgiven, and how the church on earth was linked in prayer to those who had gone before.

Certain biblical texts lent themselves to this discussion, and these would become the battleground in the fight over Purgatory for the next thousand years: 2 Maccabees 12:39–45, Matthew 12:32, Revelation 21:27, and 1 Corinthians 3:11–15 would be the chief prooftexts used by the Latins, bolstered by other passages (like Dt 25:2, Ez 33:14–15, Ws 7:25,) that dealt with punishment, forgiveness, and the necessity of purity upon entrance to the kingdom. Still later other New Testament texts—Matthew 5:25–26, Luke 12:47–48, 1 Corinthians 15:28–29, Hebrews 12:22–23—would be employed by defenders of the doctrine who hoped to ground the teaching in the words of Jesus and Paul.

As the church fathers continued to explore these questions, they were guided by several factors, including not only the Scriptures, but also their understanding of the universe and the pastoral needs of those to whom they wrote. Here, at times, speculation reigned, as the church had not yet framed its teaching on the world to come in great detail. For example, the Bible talked about God's universal salvific will and spoke of how God would be "all in all" at the end (1 Cor 15:28), leading certain authors, most notably Origen and Gregory of Nyssa, to advocate a form of universal reconciliation (*apokatastasis*) that was later condemned by the church. God's punishments, they believed, had a purpose—they were pedagogical, not punitive. When the Latins later cited Nyssa as a witness to Purgatory, the Greeks were torn, for although they revered him, his references to a "sleepless" and "purifying" fire seemed to flirt with heresy. This occasioned great debate, for if the writings of the great saints could contain errors, where was the line that separated a father who erred from a notorious heretic?[7]

---

[5] Brian Daley, *The Hope of the Early Church: A Handbook of Patristic Eschatology* (Peabody, MA: Hendrickson Publishers, 1991), 3.

[6] "But we do not want you to be uninformed, brothers and sisters, about those who have died, so that you may not grieve as others do who have no hope. For since we believe that Jesus died and rose again, even so, through Jesus, God will bring with him those who have died. For this we declare to you by the word of the Lord, that we who are alive, who are left until the coming of the Lord, will by no means precede those who have died. For the Lord himself, with a cry of command, with the archangel's call and with the sound of God's trumpet, will descend from heaven, and the dead in Christ will rise first. Then we who are alive, who are left, will be caught up in the clouds together with them to meet the Lord in the air; and so we will be with the Lord forever. Therefore encourage one another with these words."

[7] A. Edward Siecienski, "Avoiding the Sin of Ham: Dealing with Errors in the Works of the Fathers," in *Studia Patristica: Proceedings of the Fifteenth International Conference on Patristic Studies* XLV (Leuven: Peeters, 2010), 175–79.

Of course, the Latins had other weapons at their disposal, especially those Western saints who from the fourth century on began to make a clearer distinction between the temporary punishment meted out to sinners and the eternal fires of Hell. Yet while the West moved toward clarity, the Byzantines appeared "in no great hurry to impose ... systematic definition" on the afterlife, seemingly content to let the middle state of souls (i.e., the state between death and resurrection) remain "more muddle than mystery."[8] Latin theology may have discerned an emerging patristic consensus on the fate of souls after death, but the Greeks remained skeptical, believing that precise descriptions of what happened when one died were "not only elusive, but perhaps undesirable."[9]

The Bible and Purgatory

Although Latin theologians and apologists have for centuries asserted that the doctrine of Purgatory is clearly found in Scripture, modern Roman Catholic scholars have been more circumspect, most acknowledging that "the Scriptures [do] not yield a systematic or exhaustive doctrine of Purgatory in any way comparable to the achievement of later theologies."[10] Some have gone even further, holding that "there is no clear textual basis in Scripture for the later doctrine of Purgatory"[11] and that "in the final analysis the Catholic doctrine of Purgatory is based on tradition, not Sacred Scripture."[12] That said, the Bible does contain many passages that lent themselves to discussions of postmortem purgation or to the fate of souls after death, although oftentimes these texts were not always the same ones used by later defenders of the doctrine.[13]

According to Isabel Moreira, the most frequent scriptural image used in support of Purgatory was "the refiner's fire and scorching oven imagery of Malachi 3:3" ("He will sit as a refiner and purifier of silver, and he will purify the descendants of Levi and refine them like gold and silver, until they present offerings to the Lord in righteousness").[14] Similar images are also found in Zechariah 13:9,[15] Wisdom 3:5–6,[16] and a host of other verses throughout the Old Testament (Is 4:4 and 48:10, Jb 23:10, Prv 17:3, Sir 2:1–9, Ps 66:10, Dn 12:10), where the purification of souls is likened to the

---

[8] Constas, "To Sleep, Perchance to Dream," 94.
[9] Ibid.
[10] Robert Ombres, *Theology of Purgatory* (Butler, WI: Clergy Book Service, 1978), 15.
[11] Zachary Hayes, *Four Views on Hell* (Grand Rapids, MI: Zondervan, 1996), 107. Hayes did add that "neither is there anything [in Scripture] that is clearly contrary to that doctrine." Ibid.
[12] J. F. X. Cevetello, "Purgatory," *New Catholic Encyclopedia*, vol. 11 (New York: McGraw Hill, 1967), 1034.
[13] Robert Bellarmine, for example, adduced ten passages from the Old Testament that allegedly spoke about Purgatory, including several that referenced the fasts of David following the deaths of Saul, Jonathan, and Abner (2 Kgs 1:12, 3:35), arguing that "although these seem to be done as a sign of sorrow and sadness, nevertheless it is believable that it was especially done to help the souls of the dead." Robert Bellarmine, *On Purgatory*, trans. Ryan Grant (Post Falls, ID: Mediatrix Press, 2017), 22–23.
[14] Isabel Moreira, *Heaven's Purge: Purgatory in Late Antiquity* (Oxford: Oxford University Press, 2010), 18.
[15] "And I will put this third into the fire, refine them as one refines silver, and test them as gold is tested."
[16] "Having been disciplined a little, they will receive great good, because God tested them and found them worthy of himself; like gold in the furnace he tried them, and like a sacrificial burnt offering he accepted them."

refining of precious metals, with impurities removed by the fire of God's love.[17] Psalm 66:12 ("We went through fire and through water; yet you have brought us out to a spacious place") was also widely used to support Purgatory, with Catholic commentators emphasizing the purifying effects of both water (baptism) and fire (Purgatory).[18]

Yet despite this plethora of Old Testament references to a cleansing fire, it was a passage from the New Testament, 1 Corinthians 3:10–15, that would later become the critical prooftext for the doctrine of Purgatory.[19] It reads:

> For no one can lay any foundation other than the one that has been laid; that foundation is Jesus Christ. Now if anyone builds on the foundation with gold, silver, precious stones, wood, hay, straw—the work of each builder will become visible, for the Day will disclose it, because it will be revealed with fire, and the fire will test what sort of work each has done. If what has been built on the foundation survives, the builder will receive a reward. If the work is burned up, the builder will suffer loss; the builder will be saved, but only as through fire.

Joachim Gnilka's 1955 book *Ist 1 Kor 3, 10–15 ein Schriftzeugnis für das Fegfeuer?* is perhaps the most detailed study of the text, and begins by examining how "fire" was first used in Jewish literature to describe both God's glory and God's wrath (Jer 21:12, Ps 89:47, Ez 22:31).[20] Gnilka argued that in 1 Corinthians 3:10–15 Paul simply brought together these two uses of fire to describe the Parousia, when God will come in fiery judgment. At that time the All-Holy and Inaccessible One, who does not tolerate anything impure, will be accompanied by the fire and majesty of the divine glory.[21] It was

---

[17] For a full discussion of all these texts, and their influence on New Testament writings, see Daniel Frayer-Griggs, *Saved through Fire: The Fiery Ordeal in New Testament Eschatology* (Eugene, OR: Pickwick Publications, 2016).

[18] Bellermine, *On Purgatory*, 21–22. Modern commentators are almost unanimous that in this passage "'fire and water' is a merism for extreme danger, as in Isa 43:2" and not a reference to Purgatory. See Frank Lothar Hossfeld and Erich Zenger, *Psalms 2: A Commentary on Psalms 51–100*, trans. L. M. Maloney (Minneapolis, MN: Fortress Press, 2005), 146.

[19] Another New Testament text, 1 Peter 1:7 ("So that the genuineness of your faith—being more precious than gold that, though perishable, is tested by fire—may be found to result in praise and glory and honor when Jesus Christ is revealed"), never achieved the same status despite the reference to fire. See John Elliott, *1 Peter*, Anchor Bible 37b (New Haven, CT: Yale University Press, 2000), 341–42.

[20] Joachim Gnilka, *Ist 1 Kor 3, 10–15 ein Schriftzeugnis für das Fegfeuer? Eine exegetisch-historische Untersuchung* (Düsseldorf: Triltsch, 1955). See also Gisbert Greshake, ed., *Ungewisses Jenseits? Himmel, Hölle, Fegfeuer* (Düsseldorf: Patmos, 1986). Particularly important in this regard was the influence of those apocalyptic texts (e.g., the *Testament of Isaac*) that spoke of the river of fire and the fiery judgment to come: "Then he brought me to a river of fire. I saw it throbbing, with its waves rising to about thirty cubits and its sound was like rolling thunder. I looked upon many souls being immersed in it to a depth of about nine cubits. They were weeping and crying out with a loud voice and great groaning, those who were in that river. And that river had wisdom in its fire. It would not harm the righteous but only the sinners by burning them. It would burn every one of them because of the stench and repugnance of the odor surrounding the sinners." James Charlesworth, ed., *The Old Testament Pseudepigrapha*, vol. 1: *Apocalyptic Literature and Testaments* (Garden City, NY: Doubleday, 1983), 909. Similarly, in the *Sibylline Oracles*: "And (He) shall sit on the right hand of Majesty, judging on his throne, the life of the pious and the ways of impious men.... And then shall all pass through the burning river and unquenchable flame; and the righteous shall all be saved but the impious shall perish for whole ages." Ibid., 351. Gnilka noted that the river of fire seen in these and similar texts tests and punishes sinners, but it was not purificatory. Gnilka, *Ist 1 Kor 3, 10–15 ein Schriftzeugnis für das Fegfeuer?*, 15–16.

[21] Gnilka, *Ist 1 Kor 3, 10–15 ein Schriftzeugnis für das Fegfeuer?*, 126.

only in the period after Origen ("rightly regarded as the founder [*Begründer*] of the doctrine of Purgatory") that a shift took place and the "saving fire" described by Paul began to be interpreted as a purifying fire through which the righteous had to pass.[22] Thus Gnilka concluded that 1 Corinthians 3:10–15 was not, as later Catholic apologists maintained, a witness to the purifying fires of Purgatory, describing only "an aspect of God's coming in judgment" rather than "an instrument of that judgment."[23]

Despite some notable exceptions,[24] Gnilka's conclusions were largely accepted by exegetes, with the "prevailing consensus" of biblical scholars "insist[ing] that the fire of 1 Cor 3:13–15 plays no soteriological function in the purification of individuals whatsoever."[25] Joseph Fitzmyer, for example, thought these verses referenced a "testing of constancy and a subsequent deliverance" rather than "a purification or refining by fire,"[26] while Raymond Collins believed Paul was speaking about a "testing by fire" by which each person's work was "evaluated in light of the eschaton."[27] As for Purgatory, Collins was clear that "there is no need to see in [this text]—nor is there any exegetical warrant for seeing in it!—a reference to the Christian idea of Purgatory."[28] It should be noted, lest these conclusions be thought denominationally biased, that all three exegetes—Gnilka, Fitzmyer, and Collins—are Roman Catholics.[29]

---

[22] Ibid., 115.

[23] Frayer-Griggs, *Saved through Fire*, 14. According to Joseph Ratzinger, "Gnilka ... excludes any interpretation of the text in terms of Purgatory. There is no fire, only the Lord himself. There is no temporal duration involved, only eschatological encounter with the judge. There is no purification, only the statement that such a human being 'will be saved only with exertion and difficulty.'" Joseph Ratzinger, *Eschatology: Death and Eternal Life*, trans. Michael Waldstein (Washington, DC: Catholic University of America Press, 1988), 229.

[24] Among those who disagreed with Gnilka were Johannes Michl, "Gerichtsfeuer und Purgatorium, zu I Kor 3,12–15," in *Studiorum Paulinorum Congressus Internationalis Catholicus*, vol. 1 (Rome: Pontificio Istituto Biblico, 1963), 395–401; S. Cipriani, "Insegna 1. Cor. 3, 10–15 la dottrina del Purgatorio?," *Rivista Biblica* 7 (1959): 25–43; John Townsend, "1 Cor 3:15 and the School of Shammai," *Harvard Theological Review* 61 (1968): 500–504; E. B. Allo, *Premiere Epitre aux Corinthiens* (Paris: Gabalda; Lecoffre. 1934), 60–63, 66–67. Joachim Jeremias was among those who speculated that the rabbinic "conception of a purificatory character of the final fire of judgment" was behind the use of fire in both Mark 9:49 ("For everyone will be salted with fire") and 1 Corinthians 3:10–15. See Joachim Jeremias, "Géenna," in Gerhard Kittel, ed., *Theologisches Wörterbuch zum Neuen Testament*, vol. 1 (Stuttgart: W. Kohlhammer Verlag, 1966), 657–58.

[25] Frayer-Griggs, *Saved through Fire*, 201. Paul O'Callaghan was more nuanced, arguing that while the passage offers "a good description of the general dynamic of Christian purification ... [albeit with] an undeniable eschatological cadence ... personal repentance as such is not envisaged ... [even if] purification of the sinner is effected." Paul O'Callaghan, *Christ Our Hope: An Introduction to Eschatology* (Washington, DC: Catholic University of America Press, 2011), 291.

[26] Fitzmyer, *First Corinthians*, 201. "Paul is using a proverbial saying to make the point that only by the skin of one's teeth, and not without great peril, will the one concerned attain to eternal salvation." Ibid.

[27] Raymond Collins, *First Corinthians, Sacra Pagina* 7 (Collegeville, MN: Liturgical Press, 1999), 151. Collins argued that Paul's use of fire imagery "is particularly apropos" in light of his discussion of the church as an edifice, since "some building materials withstand fire; others do not. The activities of each member of the community are subject to divine scrutiny for which fire serves as a symbol. With the fire motif Paul exhorts the community to consider that each of its members stands under eschatological judgment." Ibid., 151–52.

[28] Ibid., 153.

[29] Hans Conzelmann (a Protestant) also believed that it was "misguided" to interpret this verse as a reference to Purgatory, believing that in using the expression οὕτως δὲ ὡς διὰ πυρός "Paul is obviously borrowing from the common phrase, 'barely escaped from the fire.'" This fire, which punishes but "nevertheless does not cancel our eternal salvation ... has to be understood in the wider context of the doctrine of justification.... Unsatisfactory works performed by the Christians as a Christian do not cause his damnation. This is the reverse side of the fact that works do not bring about salvation. But we remain responsible for our works before God for the life of believers is service." Conzelmann, *1 Corinthians*, 77. See also

All that said, the apparent reference to two fires, one "probative" and the other "the fire through which imperfect Christians will be saved," has made this text a rich source for patristic and later medieval reflection on the state of souls after death.[30] In fact, Le Goff claimed that "the development of Purgatory in the Middle Ages... can be followed simply by attending to the successive exegesis of this text from Paul."[31] The problem, often noted, was that "the passage posed more questions than it answered," such as who gets judged (Christians or everyone), when it happens (immediately or during the Last Judgment), and how long the "saving fire" would burn (fleetingly or until the Last Judgment).[32] Patristic and medieval writers, in trying to come up with the answers, laid the foundations upon which the doctrine of Purgatory was built.

Alongside the idea of purification by fire were the biblical ideals of God's justice (in Hebrew *mishpat, tsedeq, tsedeqah*) and mercy (*chesed*). God was the "God of justice" who "judges the people with equity," and this required that his punishments be somehow proportional to the offense (e.g., Dt 25:2).[33] This idea of proportional punishment appears also in the New Testament (e.g., Lk 12:47–48) where the more guilty of two slaves (the one "who knew what his master wanted, but did not prepare himself or do what was wanted") received a "severe beating," while the one who erred out of ignorance received only a "light beating."[34] Although modern exegetes believe this story is chiefly about the believer's "obligation of service"[35] because it occurred in the "explicit framework" of the "eschatological judgment,"[36] Catholic authors have long maintained that Jesus is here differentiating between the two punishments—eternal and temporal—meted out to sinners *in the afterlife*.[37] Jesus, they argue, was teaching about Purgatory.

While Scripture teaches that God is always just, it also tells us that he is merciful, and that his temporary chastisements are followed by forgiveness, especially for those who repent (e.g., Mi 7:9)[38] and make restitution for their crimes (Ez 33:14–15).[39]

Hans Bietenhard, "Kennt das Neue Testament die Vorstellung vom Fegefeuer?," *Theologische Zeitschrift* 3 (1947): 101–22.

[30] Moreira, *Heaven's Purge*, 18.

[31] Le Goff, *The Birth of Purgatory*, 43. This, of course, is exactly what Gnilka had set out to do.

[32] Moreira, *Heaven's Purge*, 19.

[33] "If the one in the wrong deserves to be flogged, the judge shall make that person lie down and be beaten in his presence with the number of lashes proportionate to the offense."

[34] "Punishment is meted out according to the knowledge and culpability involved." Fitzmyer, *Luke X–XXIV*, 992. According to Nolland, "The principle is that answerability is proportionate to awareness. Reference may be made to the OT distinction between witting and unwitting sins (Num 15:30; Deut 17:12; Ps 19:13; cf. 1QS 5:12; 7:3; CD 8:8; 10:3; etc.)." John Nolland, *Luke 9:21–18:34*, Word Biblical Commentary 35b (Dallas, TX: Thomas Nelson, 1993), 704.

[35] Fitzmyer, *Luke X–XXIV*, 991.

[36] Johnson, *The Gospel of Luke*, 205.

[37] The Catholic apologist John Salza claimed that "Jesus makes a clear distinction between temporal and eternal punishments in the life to come. Those who sin mortally will receive the eternal punishment of damnation. Those who sin only venially will receive temporal punishments to make satisfaction for their sins, but will still be saved.... In short, Jesus presents a continuum of punishments in the afterlife—either eternal or temporal—depending upon the person's deeds." Salza, *The Biblical Basis for Purgatory*, 111.

[38] "I must bear the indignation of the Lord, because I have sinned against him, until he takes my side and executes judgment for me. He will bring me out to the light; I shall see his vindication."

[39] "Again, though I say to the wicked, 'You shall surely die,' yet if they turn from their sin and do what is lawful and right—if the wicked restore the pledge, give back what they have taken by robbery, and walk in the statutes of life, committing no iniquity—they shall surely live, they shall not die."

Often this recompense is spoken about as payment of a "debt" to God, which is why, according to Gary Anderson, "by the close of the Old Testament period and on into the New, the predominant metaphor [for sin] is that of a debt."[40] This linking of sin to debt can clearly be seen in Matthew's version of the Lord's Prayer, where Jesus says, "Forgive us our debts" [τὰ ὀφειλήματα] (6:12), as opposed to Luke's version where he says, "Forgive us our sins" [τὰς ἁμαρτίας]) (11:4), although "both have reference to debts in their second clauses" ("for we ourselves forgive everyone indebted to us").[41] Matthew 18:23–35 (the story of a servant who is forgiven his debts but refuses to forgive another) also speaks to this relationship, but it was Matthew 5:25–26 ("Come to terms quickly with your accuser while you are on the way to court with him, or your accuser may hand you over to the judge, and the judge to the guard, and you will be thrown into prison. Truly I tell you, you will never get out until you have paid the last penny") that eventually became one of the key biblical prooftexts for the doctrine of Purgatory.

In context this verse has nothing to do with the afterlife, but rather appears amid a series of sayings about anger and the need for reconciliation. In verses 25–26 the subject is the "uncontrolled anger that has set them [i.e., the two parties] against each other," and the potentially ruinous consequences if they do not reconcile before going to court.[42] It presumes that one of the parties is in debt to the other ("the background here seems to be non-Jewish since the Jews did not imprison for debt")[43] and suggests as a matter of "simple prudence" that it would be better for the debtor to "come to terms" rather than face imprisonment.[44] Yet despite the seeming irrelevance of this passage to a discussion of eschatology, Rudolf Schnackenburg and others have noted that because it invokes the concept of justice ("giving to each their due") it is natural that "the mind [should] move to the thought of divine judgment."[45] Debts must be paid "to the last penny" for justice to reign, and while this lesson applies to this world, it "does not exclude eschatological applications" since "'paying one's debts in full' is part of eschatological justice, just as everyone receives from the deity his or her due."[46]

---

[40] Gary Anderson, "Is Purgatory Biblical? The Scriptural Structure of Purgatory," *First Things*, November 2011, 41.

[41] Charles Nathan Ridlehoover, *The Lord's Prayer and the Sermon on the Mount in Matthew's Gospel* (New York: T&T Clark, 2019), 157.

[42] "By gaining control over that anger and by changing it into friendliness, they will find they have no reason to go to court and can part as friends rather than foes. In this way, the commandment of Jesus (vs. 22a*), the Torah commandment (vs. 21b*), is fulfilled in a positive and beneficial way, that is, in accordance with the overall purpose of God's Torah." Hans Dieter Betz, *The Sermon on the Mount: A Commentary on the Sermon on the Mount, including the Sermon on the Plain (Matthew 5:3–7:27 and Luke 6:20–49)* (Minneapolis, MN: Fortress Press, 1995), 228.

[43] Donald Hagner, *Matthew 1–13, Word Biblical Commentary 33a* (Dallas, TX: Word Books, 1993), 117.

[44] Betz, *The Sermon on the Mount*, 226. Betz, citing the work of Bernard S. Jackson (*Theft in Early Jewish Law* [Oxford: Clarendon, 1972] 144,) refers to Plato Leg. 9, 857A: "For the thief also, whether he steals a great thing or a small, one law and one legal penalty shall be enacted for all alike: first he must pay twice the value of the stolen article, if he loses his case and possesses enough property over and above his allotment wherewith to pay; but if not, he must be put in prison until either he has paid the sum or has been let off by the prosecutor." Ibid.

[45] Schnackenburg, *The Gospel of Matthew*, 55. Donald Hagner similarly concludes that "it is a mistake to allegorize the details and to identify the adversary or the judge with God. At the same time, however, since God's judgment is in view in verses 21–22, it is impossible to avoid at least the suggestion of the same in the present passage." Hagner, *Matthew 1–13*, 118.

[46] Betz, *The Sermon on the Mount*, 229.

Very often payment of this debt took the form of charity to the poor, as it did in the case of King Nebuchadnezzar, who was told by Daniel to "atone for your sins with righteousness, and your iniquities with mercy to the oppressed" (Dn 4:27).[47]

It should be noted that in none of the preceding passages is there any mention of punishment or repayment occurring after death, temporal chastisement for sin usually taking the form of a personal affliction (2 Sm 12:13–14)[48] or a national tragedy (Jer 31:18).[49] Because punishment was thought to have a pedagogical function, believers were taught to be grateful when God admonished them (Jb 5:17),[50] since it was a sign not only of God's desire for justice, but also of his paternal benevolence (2 Sm 7:14).[51] A loving father taught through discipline, and therefore God's chastisement was a blessing not to be despised (Ps 94:12, Prv 3:11–12).[52]

However, there is evidence that by the beginning of the Christian era, as a more developed "geography" of the afterlife began to appear in Jewish apocalyptic literature, people came to believe that these temporal punishments could also be meted out after death. Jacques Le Goff called this development "decisive for the subsequent history of the idea of Purgatory," with authors drawing distinctions between *Eden*, *Sheol* ("the world of the dead"), and *Gehenna*, which was described as a place of both temporal and eternal punishment.[53] Rabbinical texts dating from AD 70 to 135, spoke of three groups of people on the day of judgment ("one of the truly holy, another of the truly wicked, and a third in between"), and how those who "are neither entirely good nor entirely bad ... will be punished for a time [in *Gehenna*] after their death and then go to *Eden*."[54] It was this "intermediate *Gehenna* of an atoning or purifying nature" that Le Goff argued morphed into the medieval doctrine of Purgatory.[55]

---

[47] For Gary Anderson, "This counsel reflects a major revolution in the way in which the Bible understands sin. Whereas David had to make amends for what he had done by graciously enduring the consequences, Nebuchadnezzar can take active steps in the repair of his own soul. Forgiveness is no longer dependent on awaiting what suffering will come. One can make one's own ordeals of penance, as it were, by inflicting on oneself the pain of giving up a portion of one's wealth for the sake of those in need." Anderson, "Is Purgatory Biblical?," 41.

[48] "David said to Nathan, 'I have sinned against the Lord.' Nathan said to David, 'Now the Lord has put away your sin; you shall not die. Nevertheless, because by this deed you have utterly scorned the Lord, the child that is born to you shall die.'"

[49] "I have surely heard Ephraim grieving, 'You have chastised me, and I was chastised, Like an untrained calf; Bring me back that I may be restored, For You are the LORD my God.'"

[50] "How happy is the one whom God reproves; therefore do not despise the discipline of the Almighty."

[51] "I will be a father to him, and he shall be a son to me. When he commits iniquity, I will punish him with a rod such as mortals use, with blows inflicted by human beings."

[52] "Blessed is the man whom You chasten, O LORD, And whom You teach out of Your law." "My child, do not despise the Lord's discipline or be weary of his reproof, for the Lord reproves the one he loves, as a father the son in whom he delights."

[53] Le Goff, *The Birth of Purgatory*, 39. "In the material presented by the Strack-Billerbeck collection, part of which goes back to the second century of the Christian era, there are clear signs of the idea of an intermediate *Gehenna*, understood as a Purgatory where souls, in their atoning suffering, are prepared for definitive salvation." Ratzinger, *Eschatology*, 221. The reference is to texts contained in Hermann Leberecht Strack and Paul Billerbeck eds., *Kommentar zum Neuen Testament aus Talmud und Midrasch, Book 4/2: Exkurse zu einzelnen Stellen des NT* (Munich: Beck, 1928), 1036–49.

[54] "It is immediately written and sealed that the truly holy shall live until the end of time, and it is likewise written and sealed that the truly wicked shall remain in Gehenna.... As for the third group, they shall go down to Gehenna for a time and then come up again ... for it is written that He who is abundant in mercy inclines toward mercy." BT.Rosh Hashanah 16b–17a, quoted in Le Goff, *The Birth of Purgatory*, 40.

[55] Fitzmyer, *First Corinthians*, 202. Both Le Goff and Fitzmyer cited the school of Shammai as an early example of this belief. According to Fitzmyer, this school "interpreted Zech 13:9 ('I will put this third [i.e.,

The idea that one's status in the afterlife could change did not go unchallenged, as can be seen in 4 Ezra, an apocryphal book written around this same period.[56] Here the belief was that "once judgment has commenced, the wicked will no longer be able to repent ... [since] divine judgment is decisive and final."[57] This view, according to M. E. Stone, differed from other apocalyptic texts, such as the *Testament of Abraham*, where during the "intermediate judgment of souls ... [Abraham's] prayer of intercession redeems one soul whose good and evil deeds are equally balanced."[58] Importantly, this latter view came to predominate medieval rabbinic Judaism, with intercessory prayers (*kaddish*) and alms offered for the dead.[59]

The idea of efficacious prayer and alms offered on behalf of the dead is at the heart of 2 Maccabees 12:39–45, perhaps the most consistently cited biblical text in favor of the Catholic teaching on Purgatory.[60] The passage itself describes the actions of Judas Maccabees and his soldiers following the battle against Gorgias, governor of Idumea:

---

human beings, neither righteous nor godless, but those whose merit and guilt hung in the balance] into the fire and refine them as one refines silver, and test them as gold is tested. They will call on my name, and I will answer them') and 1 Sam 2:6 ('The Lord kills and brings to life; he brings down to Sheol and raises up') and concluded to such an afterlife purification." Ibid.

[56] According to M. E. Stone, 4 Ezra is generally dated "between 70 C.E. and the end of the second century," although he argued that this can be narrowed down even further, and that it was probably composed "in the time of Domitian (81–96 C.E.)." M. E. Stone, *Fourth Ezra: A Commentary on the Book of Fourth Ezra* (Minneapolis, MN: Fortress Press, 1990), 10.

[57] "And if it is one of those who have shown scorn and have not kept the ways of the Most High, and who have despised his law, and who have hated those who fear God—such souls shall not enter into treasuries, but shall immediately wander about in torments, ever grieving and sad in seven ways. The first way, because they have scorned the law of the Most High. The second way, because they cannot now repent and do good that they may live." Ibid., 235.

[58] Ibid., 241. "And Abraham said to the angel, 'My Lord, Commander-in-chief, how is it that the soul which the angel held in his hand was sentenced to be (placed) in the middle?' The Commander-in-chief said, 'Hear, righteous Abraham, (it was) because the judge found its sins and its righteous deeds to be balanced and he gave it over neither to judgment nor to salvation—until the judge and God of all comes.' Abraham said, 'And what yet does the soul need in order to be saved?' The Commander-in-chief said, 'If it could get one righteous deed more than (the number of its) sins, it will come to salvation.' Abraham said to the Commander-in-chief, 'Come, Michael, Commander-in-chief, let us pray for the soul, and let us see if God will hear us.' And the Commander-in-chief said, 'Amen, so be it.' And they made petition and prayer to God for the soul. And God heard their prayer ... and Abraham said to the angel, 'Where is the soul?' The Commander-in-chief said, 'It was saved by your righteous prayer.' And behold! a glorious Angel took it and carried it into Paradise." Dale Allison, ed., *Testament of Abraham* (Berlin: Walter de Gruyter, 2003), 294.

[59] "Rav Sherira Gaon ... writing in the tenth century, said that alms given in the name of a particular deceased man could provide benefit. 'If a Holy Man seeks mercy for the deceased whether with alms for the poor or without [that is, by prayer],' he writes, 'it is possible that the Holy One (Blessed be He!) will lighten his punishment in recognition of that meritorious person's merit. But if no [such person is available], we take the poor [who received alms on his behalf] to [his grave] to petition that he be granted mercy. If one of them has [sufficient] merits ... they may possibly help him; but there is no presumption that it will help: May it be God's will that He accede to their petition.' What comes out clearly in this responsum is that rabbinic Judaism clearly imagines that the state of the person is not always settled at the time of death and that there is a period of time in which further purgation from sin is possible. Judaism, like early Christianity, imagines that specific human actions like prayer and the offering of alms could have an effect." Anderson, *Is Purgatory Biblical*, 43.

[60] I leave aside here the later Reformation debates concerning the canonicity of 2 Maccabees, for these go far beyond the scope of this book. Both Orthodox and Roman Catholics accept it as canonical, although there were debates up to, and at, the Council of Trent on its status. Luther himself believed that 2 Maccabees was "not among the books of Holy Scripture, and, as St. Jerome says, it is not found in a Hebrew version.... In other respects, too, this book deserves little authority, for it contradicts the first Book of Maccabees ... and contains many other fables which destroy its credibility.... [It is] the least important and

Judas and his men went to take up the bodies of the fallen and to bring them back to lie with their kindred in the sepulchers of their ancestors. Then under the tunic of each one of the dead they found sacred tokens of the idols of Jamnia, which the law forbids the Jews to wear ... [So] they turned to supplication, praying that the sin that had been committed might be wholly blotted out.... He also took up a collection, man by man, to the amount of two thousand drachmas of silver, and sent it to Jerusalem to provide for a sin offering. In doing this he acted very well and honorably, taking account of the resurrection. For if he were not expecting that those who had fallen would rise again, it would have been superfluous and foolish to pray for the dead. But if he was looking to the splendid reward that is laid up for those who fall asleep in godliness, it was a holy and pious thought. Therefore he made atonement for the dead, so that they might be delivered from their sin.

Several modern commentators maintain that what is at stake in this passage is not the eternal fate of those found with idols, but rather the purity of the community, which had "unknowingly been tainted with the sin of idolatry through the secret misconduct of the soldiers."[61] This idea, also found in Leviticus 4:13 ("If it is the anointed priest who sins, thus bringing guilt on the people, he shall offer for the sin that he has committed a bull of the herd without blemish as a sin offering to the Lord") meant that because an individual's sin endangered the holiness of the whole community, Judas's real reason for making expiation was "to protect and purify the survivors," not to change "the postmortem fate of the sinners."[62] If the offering had been made only for those soldiers who had possessed the idols, "there would have been an offering for each sinner."[63] Furthermore, several scholars argue that under rabbinic law "the principle holds that sacrifices do not secure expiation for the dead [since] the experience of death itself is their expiation."[64] However, there are others who, while accepting that the sacrifice was not *solely* for the fallen, nevertheless hold that because Judas wanted to make atonement for the *whole* community, this would also have included both the living and those "beyond the grave"—that is, "those dead who [had] acted against the law" and thus required further purification.[65]

---

most despised book." Martin Luther, "Defense and Explanation of All the Articles," in George W. Forell, ed., *Luther's Works*, vol. 32: *Career of the Reformer II* (Philadelphia: Concordia Publishing House, 1958), 95–96. For more see Timothy H. Lim, *The Formation of the Jewish Canon* (New Haven, CT: Yale University Press, 2013); F. F. Bruce, *The Canon of Scripture* (Downer's Grove, IL: Intervarsity Press, 1988).

[61] Jonathan Goldstein, *II Maccabees*, Anchor Bible 41a (New Haven, CT: Yale University Press, 1983), 449.

[62] Jeffery Trumbower, *Rescue for the Dead: The Posthumous Salvation of Non-Christians in Early Christianity* (Oxford: Oxford University Press, 2001), 27.

[63] Goldstein, *II Maccabees*, 449.

[64] Ibid., 450. Opposing this position was Daniel Schwartz, who held that "what was crucial was that atonement be worked for each of the dead ... due to the fear that ... death was not enough to atone for the sins of the fallen and they were in need of more merit supplied by the sacrifice. The assumption is that if their sin is not atoned they suffer even more, and might even be excluded from resurrection. This implies that sinners are punished after their death, an implication that easily begets the notion of a place where that happens—Gehenna/Purgatory." Daniel Schwartz, *2 Maccabees, Commentaries on Early Jewish Literature* (Berlin: Walter De Gruyter, 2008), 443–44.

[65] Rober Doran, *2 Maccabees* (Minneapolis, MN: Fortress Press, 2012), 247. "For the Jews, the rite of Kippur (Lv 4–5) was used to redeem sins not only of the living, but also of the dead." O'Callaghan, *Christ Our Hope*, 289.

Today, most Catholic exegetes, even those who accept that the prayers and sacrifices were made on behalf of the dead, are generally hesitant about using 2 Maccabees as scriptural proof for Purgatory, instead citing it as evidence for "a tradition of piety which ... served as the basis for ... the Christian practice of praying for the dead and performing good works, with the expectation that this might be of some help to the dead."[66] Yet there remain others who see in Judas's actions clear "evidence that those who die piously can be delivered from unexpiated sins that impede their resurrection" and thus the genesis "vaguely formulated ... of what would [later] become ... the teaching on Purgatory."[67]

Prayers and suffrages for those who have died is also at the heart of 1 Corinthians 15:29, where Paul speaks of "those people ... who receive baptism on behalf of the dead" (οἱ βαπτιζόμενοι ὑπὲρ τῶν νεκρῶν).[68] This practice, which appears nowhere else in the New Testament, probably "indicates a general concern for the dead among the Corinthian population ... and likely took place only in first century Corinth, where religious syncretism was a fact of life."[69] Throughout the centuries scholars have developed several theories as to what this practice was and why it occurred,[70] although Fitzmyer contended that "the majority of interpreters today ... accept that it refers to living Christians [who] underwent vicarious or proxy baptism, i.e., water baptism in the Christian rite on behalf of persons (e.g., relatives) who had died without being baptized, so that those persons might be saved or gain access to the Kingdom of

---

[66] Hayes, *Four Views on Hell*, 104–5. The text "seems to be more concerned with helping the fallen soldiers to participate in the resurrection of the dead," and thus cannot be seen as a "direct statement of the later doctrine of Purgatory." Ibid.

[67] Neil McEleney, "1–2 Maccabees," in Raymond Brown, Joseph Fitzmyer, and Roland Murphy, eds., *New Jerome Biblical Commentary* (Englewood Cliffs, NJ: Prentice Hall, 1990), 446. See also Elmer O'Brien, "Scriptural Proof for the Existence of Purgatory from 2 Maccabees—12:43–45," *Sciences Ecclesiastiques* 2 (1949): 80–108.

[68] Hans Conzelmann called this verse "one of the most hotly disputed passages in the epistle." Conzelmann, *1 Corinthians*, 275. For various treatments see Herbert Preisker, "Die Vikariatstaufe 1 Cor 15:29—ein eschatologischer—nicht sakramentaler Brauch," *Zeitschrift für die neutestamentliche Wissenschaft* 23 (1924): 298–304; Bernard M. Foschini, *"Those Who Are Baptized for the Dead," 1 Cor. 15:29: An Exegetical Historical Dissertation* (Worcester, MA: Heffernan, 1951); Maria Raeder, "Vikariatstaufe in 1 Cor 15:29," *Zeitschrift für die neutestamentliche Wissenschaft* 46 (1955): 258–61; G. R. Beasley-Murray, *Baptism in the New Testament* (Grand Rapids, MI: Eerdmans, 1962); Mathias Rissi, *Die Taufe für die Toten: Ein Beitrag zur paulinischen Tauflehre* (Zurich: Zwingli, 1962); Rudolf Schnackenburg, *Baptism in the Thought of St Paul*, trans. G. R. Beasley-Murray (Oxford: Basil Blackwell, 1964), 95–102; J. K. Howard, "Baptism for the Dead: A Study of 1 Corinthians 15:29," *Evangelical Quarterly* 37 (1965): 137–41; Jerome Murphy-O'Connor, "Baptized for the Dead (1 Cor., XV, 29): A Corinthian Slogan?," *Revue Biblique* 4 (1981): 532–43; John D. Reaume, "Another Look at 1 Corinthians 15:29, 'Baptized for the Dead,'" *Bibliotheca Sacra* 152 (1995): 457–75; Joel R. White, "'Baptized on Account of the Dead': The Meaning of 1 Corinthians 15:29 in Its Context," *Journal of Biblical Literature* 116 (1997): 487–99; Adam English, "Mediated, Mediation, Unmediated: 1 Corinthians 15:29: The History of Interpretation, and the Current State of Biblical Studies," *Review & Expositor* 99 (2002): 419–28; Michael F. Hull, *Baptism on Account of the Dead (1 Cor 15:29): An Act of Faith in the Resurrection* (Atlanta: Society of Biblical Literature, 2005); James E. Patrick, "Living Rewards for Dead Apostles: 'Baptized for the Dead' in 1 Corinthians 15.29," *New Testament Studies* 52 (2006): 71–85; William O. Walker, "1 Corinthians 15:29–34 as a Non-Pauline Interpolation," *Catholic Biblical Quarterly* 69 (2007): 84–103; Daniel Sharp, "Vicarious Baptism for the Dead: 1 Corinthians 15:29," *Studies in the Bible and Antiquity* 6 (2014): 36–66.

[69] Collins, *First Corinthians*, 556–57.

[70] Anthony Thiselton, *The First Epistle to the Corinthians: A Commentary on the Greek Text* (Grand Rapids, MI: Eerdmans, 2000), 1242–49, details and critiques thirteen different views.

God."⁷¹ Paul, it seems, neither approves of, nor criticizes, the practice, but only uses it "to score a point" about belief in the resurrection.⁷² And while later generations would associate baptism on behalf of the dead with certain heretical sects, the idea that the actions/prayers of the living could somehow affect the deceased remained an important part of orthodox Christian belief.⁷³

Another important principle in the later development of Purgatory, seen in both the Old and New Testaments, was that God's purity was such that nothing entering the divine presence could be blemished by sin. Scripture had taught that because wisdom was the "breath of the power of God.... nothing defiled gains entrance into her" (Ws 7:24–25) and that God's eyes were "too pure to behold evil ... [He] cannot look on wrongdoing" (Hb 1:13).⁷⁴ Revelation 21:27, later a powerful prooftext for Catholic apologists, echoed Isaiah 52:1 ("O Jerusalem, the holy city; for the uncircumcised and the unclean shall enter you no more"),⁷⁵ and held that "nothing unclean will enter [the heavenly Jerusalem], nor anyone who practices abomination or falsehood, but only those who are written in the Lamb's book of life." According to exegetes, the author has taken "ritual impurity, a central religious category in early Judaism (Lev 10:10; 1 Macc 1:47, 62; 4 Macc 7:6) ... [and] transformed it into an exclusively moral category."⁷⁶ This passage thus becomes a warning to those who "live before the end, when the forces of evil are still active ... that those who adopt the ways of evil defile themselves, making themselves unfit to enter God's presence."⁷⁷ Yet there is no mention of those

---

⁷¹ Fitzmyer, *First Corinthians*, 578. Among those he cites in favor of this consensus are Barrett, Barth, Beasley-Murray, Collins, Conzelmann, Downey, Edwards, Fee, Hays, Horsley, Hurd, Lietzmann, Orr-Walther, Rissi, Schrage, Senft, Taylor, Tuckett, Wedderburn, Weiss, and Wolff. Dissenters from this position (Raeder, Thiselton, G. G. Findlay, Howard, Jeremias, Reaume, Robertson-Plummer, and Schnackenburg), understanding ὑπὲρ to mean "for the sake of" rather than "on behalf of," hold that baptism is undergone "not in order to remedy some deficiency on the part of the dead, but ... refers to the decision of a person or persons to ask for, and to receive, baptism as a result of the desire to be united with their believing relatives who have died." Thiselton, *The First Epistle to the Corinthians*, 1248.

⁷² Fitzmyer, *First Corinthians*, 580. Some commentators assume Paul "cannot have approved" of this practice, despite the lack of evidence for such a statement. See Gardner, *1 Corinthians*, 692.

⁷³ Tertullian (*De resur, mortuorum* 48.11 and *Adv. Marc.* 5.10:1–2) mentioned it, as did Epiphanius and John Chrysostom. Speaking of the followers of Cerinthus (sect. 28), Epiphanius wrote: "I also heard of a tradition which said that when some of their people died too soon, without baptism, others would be baptized for them in their names, so that they would not be punished for rising unbaptized at the resurrection and become the subjects of the authority that made the world." Epiphanius of Salamis, *Panarion* 28; Eng. trans.: Epiphanius of Salamis, *The Panarion of Epiphanius of Salamis Book I (Sects 1–46)*, 120. Chrysostom, in *Homily 40 on First Corinthians*, told how there were certain people who, when a "catechumen departs among them, having concealed the living man under the couch of the dead ... approach the corpse and talk with him, and ask him if he wishes to receive baptism; then when he makes no answer, he that is concealed underneath says in his stead that of course he should wish to be baptized; and so they baptize him instead of the departed, like men jesting upon the stage" (NPNF 1.12:244).

⁷⁴ Among the other passages often adduced to support this point are Ezekiel 44:9, "Thus says the Lord God: No foreigner, uncircumcised in heart and flesh, of all the foreigners who are among the people of Israel, shall enter my sanctuary," and Matthew 5:8, "Blessed are the pure in heart, for they will see God."

⁷⁵ See also Isaiah 35:8 and Ezekiel 44:9.

⁷⁶ David Aune, *Revelation 17–22*, Word Biblical Commentary 52c (Grand Rapids, MI: Zondervan, 1998), 1174.

⁷⁷ Craig Koester, *Revelation*, Anchor Bible 38A (New Haven, CT: Yale University Press, 2014), 833. Wilfrid Harrington also interprets this passage as "a pastoral warning to John's hearers" so that they avoid all those things that are unclean, e.g., those items listed in Mk 7:20–23: "It is what comes out of a person that defiles. For it is from within, from the human heart, that evil intentions come: fornication, theft, murder, adultery, avarice, wickedness, deceit, licentiousness, envy, slander, pride, folly. All these evil things come

entering the New Jerusalem receiving purification, the assumption being that "only those who are written in the Lamb's book of life" are permitted to enter—that is, those who have kept themselves unblemished by sin.[78]

One text often cited in favor of a postmortem purification is Hebrews 12:22–23, where it speaks of all those who dwell in "the city of the living God, the heavenly Jerusalem," including "the spirits of the righteous *made perfect* [τετελειωμένων]."[79] According to scholars, "made perfect" in this context can either "be understood eschatologically, in reference to those who have already passed through judgment (cf. 9:27) and have obtained the verdict that they are righteous, or soteriologically, in reference to those who have been decisively purged and consecrated to God by the sacrificial death of Jesus."[80] It is clearly linked to the work of Christ, since "in Hebrews's understanding human hearts, minds, and spirits have been 'perfected' and granted access to God's own realm [only] by the cleansing sacrifice of Christ,"[81] as seen previously in verse 10:14.[82] F. F. Bruce speculates the righteous mentioned in this passage are "most probably believers of pre-Christian days, like those mentioned in 11:39–40,[83] who could not attain perfection until Christ came in the fulness of time" and by his sacrifice brought them to God.[84] "They have been 'made perfect' in the same way that contemporary believers 'have been made perfect.' Both have been cleansed from sin and thus brought into the presence of God through the work of Christ."[85]

Matthew 12:32 ("Whoever speaks a word against the Son of Man will be forgiven, but whoever speaks against the Holy Spirit will not be forgiven, either in this age or in the age to come") is a problematic passage in many respects,[86] and one that most

---

from within, and they defile a person." Wilfrid Harrington, *Revelation*, Sacra Pagina 16 (Collegeville, MN: Liturgical Press, 1993), 215.

[78] See Robert Mounce, *The Book of Revelation*, New International Commentary on the New Testament (Grand Rapids, MI: Eerdmans, 1998), 397.

[79] "But you have come to Mount Zion and to the city of the living God, the heavenly Jerusalem, and to innumerable angels in festal gathering, and to the assembly of the firstborn who are enrolled in heaven, and to God the judge of all, and to the spirits of the righteous made perfect." According to Harold Attridge, "The connotations of the verb here closely parallel that of its first occurrence (2:10), where it obviously referred to Christ's exaltation." Harold Attridge, *The Epistle to the Hebrews: A Commentary on the Epistle to the Hebrews* (Philadelphia: Fortress Press, 1989), 376.

[80] William Lane, *Hebrews 9–13*, Word Biblical Commentary 47b (Grand Rapids, MI: Zondervan, 1991).

[81] Attridge, *The Epistle to the Hebrews*, 376. "The description of the souls as 'perfected' sounds once again Hebrews's characteristic and complex theme of perfection." Ibid. See also David Peterson, *Hebrews and Perfection: An Examination of the Concept of Perfection in the "Epistle to the Hebrews"* (Cambridge: Cambridge University Press, 1982).

[82] "For by a single offering he has perfected for all time those who are sanctified."

[83] "Yet all these, though they were commended for their faith, did not receive what was promised, since God had provided something better so that they would not, apart from us, be made perfect."

[84] F. F. Bruce, *The Epistle to the Hebrews*, The New International Commentary on the New Testament (Grand Rapids, MI: Eerdmans, 1990), 360. Gareth Lee Cockerill agreed, maintaining that "'Spirits of . . . righteous people' is an apocalyptic term for the people of God who have already died and await resurrection. . . . Thus, this term encompasses people like the heroes of faith . . . who lived before Christ, as well as the faithful who have died since his coming." Gareth Lee Cockerill, *The Epistle to the Hebrews*, The New International Commentary on the New Testament (Grand Rapids, MI: Eerdmans, 2012), 657.

[85] Cockerill, *The Epistle to the Hebrews*, 657.

[86] Donald Hagner held that this passage "does not encourage optimism in the exegete." Donald Hagner, *Matthew 1–13*, Word Biblical Commentary 33a (Dallas, TX: Word Books, 1993), 347. W. D. Davies and Dale C. Allison wrote: "As it stands [it] has no obvious meaning. Perhaps here we have an example of a saying whose Greek form misrepresents the Aramaic original. Because the sayings of Jesus were regarded

exegetes today "see as having little if anything to do with Purgatory."[87] Yet for centuries is was among the most-cited prooftexts in favor of the doctrine, for by denying postmortem forgiveness to those who blasphemed the Spirit it seemingly implied that other sins *could* be forgiven in the world to come. This saying is found, in similar form, in Mark 3:28-29 and Luke 12:10,[88] although it is only Matthew who uses the formula "either in this age or in the age to come" (οὔτε ἐν τούτῳ τῷ αἰῶνι οὔτε ἐν τῷ μέλλοντι).[89] Most scholars believe that this construction is used here solely for emphasis—that is, to indicate "that blasphemy against the Holy Spirit can *never* be forgiven."[90] Yet Rudolf Schnackenburg was among those who posited that Matthew accepted the Jewish belief, discussed earlier, that there was an "interim place of punishment" to which sinners were relegated before the Judgment.[91] Just as Jewish tradition had "definitively excluded ... the generation of the great Flood" from God's future world, those who blasphemed against the Spirit were to be similarly barred, a point Matthew "underscored" by the use of "either in this age or in the age to come."[92]

When all is said and done, examination of the biblical witness yields few (if any) proofs of the doctrine of Purgatory as later Western theology understood it. At the same time, it must also be admitted that many of the concerns that helped shape belief in a "purifying state after death"—for example, testing and cleansing by fire, God's justice, sin and recompense, punishment and mercy, concern for the salvation of the dead, God's perfection—are all present in the Bible, if only in nascent form. For this reason, just as it would be inaccurate to say that Purgatory is explicitly affirmed in the Bible, it would be equally inaccurate to say that there is absolutely no scriptural basis for it.[93] This ambiguity in large part explains why the fathers, in wrestling with the

---

as authoritative, some of the more obscure ones just might have been passed on out of respect for the tradition, even when they were not comprehended.... We remain stumped." W. D. Davies and Dale C. Allison, *Matthew 8-18*, International Critical Commentary (London: T&T Clark, 1991), 348. According to Ulrich Luz, this passage two important questions: "First, the exegetical question is: Of what does the blasphemy against the Spirit consist? The texts do not elaborate on it but presuppose that it is understood.... Second, the theological question is: Is there a limit to grace? Does this sentence not contradict the boundless love of God—thus the center of the proclamation of Jesus—and therefore also the conviction of the boundless power of the Holy Spirit?" Luz, *Matthew 8-20*, 206.

[87] Hayes, *Four Views on Hell*, 105.

[88] Mark 3:28-29: "Truly I tell you, people will be forgiven for their sins and whatever blasphemies they utter; but whoever blasphemes against the Holy Spirit can never have forgiveness, but is guilty of an eternal sin." Luke 12:10: "And everyone who speaks a word against the Son of Man will be forgiven; but whoever blasphemes against the Holy Spirit will not be forgiven."

[89] "This two-age language is common in Judaism and in Matthew; 13:22, 39, 40; 24:3." Hagner, *Matthew 1-13*, 347. According to R. T France, "'This age' and 'the age to come' are Jewish terms which apply primarily to the contrast between this life and the next rather than to successive phases of life on earth.... Here, then, the consequences of the unforgivable sin apply not only to this life but also to the life to come, when judgment will finally have been given." R. T. France, *The Gospel of Matthew*, The New International Commentary on the New Testament (Grand Rapids, MI: Eerdmans, 2007), 484.

[90] Harrington, *The Gospel of Matthew*, 184. See also Luz: "From the context it is clear that by accusing Jesus of casting out demons in the name of the devil the Pharisees blaspheme not only Jesus but Jesus as the bearer of the Spirit who works through the Spirit of God. Jesus' pronouncement thus applies to them: Your sin is not abolished—by God—for all eternity." Luz, *Matthew 8-20*, 209.

[91] Schnackenburg, *The Gospel of Matthew*, 116.

[92] Ibid.

[93] This conclusion is now accepted by the vast majority of Roman Catholic exegetes and theologians, and was endorsed by no less a figure than Joseph Ratzinger (later Pope Benedict XVI) in his own treatment of the subject: "The New Testament left open the question of the 'intermediate state' between death and the

church's teaching on the state of souls after death, did not achieve anything akin to unanimity, and why later generations, East and West, could read the Scriptures and come to such startlingly different conclusions.

The Eastern Fathers on Purgatory

If there is a difference in how the Greek and Latin churches addressed the question of cleansing/punishment after death, it might be that "the Greek fathers basically preserved the irresolution of the Scriptures on this question," while the Latin fathers strove for clarity.[94] It is not that the Greeks were unconcerned with questions concerning the fate of souls after death, as they affirmed the efficacy of prayer for the dead, the possibility of postmortem remission of sins, and even, in some cases, a cleansing fire. And while many in the West later chose to interpret these teachings as supporting the doctrine of Purgatory, Eastern writers have always been more reluctant to read the Greek fathers that way, instead viewing those passages that "mention a punishment by fire in the hereafter" as "ambiguous" at best.[95]

Among the chief factors that gave rise to discussions about the postmortem fate of souls in the early church was the growing "preoccupation," already seen in Paul (1 Thes 4:13–18), with "the collective fate of humanity" and the "the fate of individuals, especially those Christians who died before the Parousia."[96] Believers wondered whether they had to wait until the return of Christ to be judged and rewarded, and whether all went together to Sheol or instead (like the rich man and Lazarus [Lk 16:23–31]) each received an "anticipatory reward or punishment," in places like the "bosom of Abraham" or Hades.[97] Several Eastern fathers speculated that because no person receives reward or punishment until the final judgment, there must be an "interim state" in which souls exist until then.[98] Aphrahat, for example, believed that the souls of the

---

general resurrection on the Last Day ... [which] remained in an unfinished condition since it could only be clarified by the gradual unfolding of Christian anthropology and its relation to christology." Ratzinger, *Eschatology*, 219.

[94] James Jorgenson, "The Debate over Patristic Texts on Purgatory at the Council of Ferrara Florence," *St. Vladimir's Theological Quarterly* 30 (1986): 326.

[95] Jean-Claude Larchet, *Life after Death According to the Orthodox Tradition*, trans. G. John Champoux (Rollingsford, NH: Orthodox Research Institute, 2012), 174–75. For Larchet, all the scriptural and patristic evidence gathered by the Latins in support of the doctrine merely affirmed one undeniable truth, long admitted by the Orthodox: that "Scripture and the fathers deem the Church's prayers advantageous to the deceased." Ibid.

[96] Robert Eno, "The Fathers and the Cleansing Fire," *Irish Theological Quarterly* 53 (1987): 186.

[97] The terms used to denote "places" or "states" in the afterlife varied according to time and author. John Nolland wrote that in Luke, Hades represented "the place of the dead quite generally" even if it came "increasingly to include the idea of a preliminary experience of what is to be the individual's ultimate fate at the final judgment." Nolland, *Luke 9:21–18:34*, 829. Joseph Fitzmyer agreed, and claimed that the use of Hades in the story of the rich man and Lazarus should be taken to mean "death's abode ... a locale distinct from Abraham's bosom ... [although] it may be that two different locales in Sheol are really meant." Fitzmyer, *Luke X–XXIV*, 1132.

[98] "From all these things, my friend, understand and be certain that no person has yet received his reward or punishment. The righteous have not inherited the kingdom, nor have the evil gone to torment. The shepherd has not yet divided his flock.... Those virgins who are waiting for the Bridegroom [continue] to sleep right up to the present; they are waiting for the shout, and [then] they will wake up. And those

departed reside in a kind of "sleep state" in which they dream until they awake on the Last Day—the good anticipating their rewards, the evil fretting over their punishment.[99] Ephrem the Syrian also accepted this idea of a sleep state before the resurrection of the body, since "the soul cannot have perception of Paradise without its mate, the body, its instrument and lyre."[100] Yet Ephrem saw this sleep state as a period of complete inactivity, for "without its companion [the soul] lacks true existence; it fully resembles an embryo still in the womb, whose existence is as yet bereft of word or thought."[101] According to scholars, Ephrem's understanding "left no room for the purification of sinners after death although he hints at it in one passage of *Hymns on Paradise* (10.14) and urges his hearers to pray for their dead."[102]

The central question, raised in large part by Christians' concern for their departed relatives and friends, was whether the living could somehow improve the condition of those in this intermediate state insomuch as they had not yet received definitive judgment.[103] If, as the evidence suggests, Jews had already come to accept intercessory prayers and alms on behalf of the dead as efficacious, it is not surprising that Christians "seemed to have acquired the habit of praying for their dead at a very early date."[104] Although the New Testament does not mention it,[105] John Chrysostom thought the practice went back to the apostles, who had ordered memorials "in the terrible mysteries for those who had departed [for] they knew that great gain would accrue to them, great benefit."[106] When prayer for the dead actually began remains

who have gone before and laboured in the faith will not be perfected until the last ones arrive." Aphrahat, *The Demonstrations of Aphrahat the Persian Sage* (8.22), trans. Adam Lehto (Piscataway, NJ: Gorgias Press, 2010), 234–35.

[99] "While he is sleeping, the servant for whom his master is preparing punishments and fetters does not want to wake up, since he knows that when the morning comes and he wakes up his master will punish and bind him. But the good servant, to whom his master has promised gifts, waits for the coming of the morning so that he might receive presents from his master. Even though he is truly sleeping, he sees in his dream how his master would give to him what he had promised him; he rejoices in his dream, and is exultant and gladdened. The sleep of the wicked person, however, is not pleasant for him." Aphrahat, *The Demonstrations of Aphrahat* (8.19), 232. See also F. Gavin, "The Sleep of the Soul in the Early Syriac Church." *Journal of the American Oriental Society* 40 (1920): 103–20; J. Edward Walters, "Sleep of the Soul and Resurrection of the Body: Aphrahat's Anthropology in Context," *Hugoye: Journal of Syriac Studies* 22 (2019): 433–65.

[100] Ephrem the Syrian, *Hymns on Paradise* (8.2), trans. Sebastian Brock (Crestwood, NY: St. Vladimir's Seminary Press, 1990), 132.

[101] Ibid. (8.5), 133.

[102] Daley, *The Hope of the Early Church*, 74. In the passage Ephrem wrote: "As I reflected I was fearful again because I had presumed to suppose that there might be between the Garden and the fire a place where those who have found mercy can receive chastisement and forgiveness." Ephrem the Syrian, *Hymns on Paradise* (10.14), 153.

[103] Le Goff, *The Birth of Purgatory*, 48.

[104] Ibid., 45. See Joseph Fischer, *Studien zum Todesgedanken in der alten Kirche* (Munich: Hueber 1954); Salomon Reinach, "L'Origine des prières pour les morts," *Revue des études juives* 41 (1900): 161–73.

[105] Outside of 2 Maccabees, one text often cited as scriptural warrant for such prayers is 2 Timothy 1:16–18, where Paul prayed for Onesiphorus ("May the Lord grant mercy to the household of Onesiphorus, because he often refreshed me and was not ashamed of my chain; when he arrived in Rome, he eagerly searched for me and found me—may the Lord grant that he will find mercy from the Lord on that day! And you know very well how much service he rendered in Ephesus"). Martin Dibelius and Hans Conzelmann argued that while this text has been used by Catholics as "a proof-text for the intercession for the dead ... nothing of the sort is implied." Martin Dibelius and Hans Conzelmann, *The Pastoral Epistles: A Commentary on the Pastoral Epistles* (Philadelphia: Fortress Press, 1972), 106.

[106] "They were not considered to be in vain by the apostles—holding a memorial in the terrible mysteries for those who had departed. They knew that great gain would accrue to them, great benefit. I mean, when

unclear, but by the end of the second century there is evidence that the practice was already well established. There is the epitaph of Bishop Abercius of Hieropolis (c. 190), which asked that anyone "who understands and believes this pray for Abercius."[107] The *Acts of Paul and Thecla*, also second century, included a passage about Falconilla, a righteous pagan who had died and appeared to her mother asking her to take in "the abandoned stranger Thecla ... in order that she might pray on my behalf and I might be transferred to the place of the righteous."[108] By the fourth century prayers for the dead had entered the liturgy, commemorating "all the faithful dead who have died in the true faith."[109]

Behind this practice was the belief that one could, through prayer, move "Christ our God, who took their souls and spirits to Himself ... [to] pardon the faults" of the dead and grant them remission of their sins.[110] In fact, almost all references to prayer for the dead in the ancient church explicitly connect it with the forgiveness of sins. Pseudo-Dionysius wrote that prayers for the dead are "to the Divine goodness, asking pardon for the deceased for all the sins caused by human frailty, begging that he be established 'in the light in the land of the living.'"[111] Epiphanius maintained that "even though the prayer we offer for them cannot root out all their faults [αἰτιαμάτων]— [how could it], since we often slip in this world, inadvertently and deliberately—it is still useful as an indication of something more perfect."[112] The *Apostolic Constitutions* enjoined Christians to "pray for our brethren that are at rest in Christ, that God, the lover of mankind, who has received his soul, may forgive him every sin, voluntary and

---

the entire people is present, holding up their hands, the full complement of priests [is present], and the terrible sacrifice is set up in front, how shall we not importune God when we intercede on their behalf?" John Chrysostom, *Homily 4 on Philippians*, in John Chrysostom, *Homilies on Philippians*, trans. Pauline Allen (Atlanta, GA: Society for Biblical Literature, 2013), 73–75.

[107] *Epitaph of Abercius*, in Johannes Quasten, *Patrology*, vol. 1: *The Beginnings of Patristic Literature* (Westminster, MD: Christian Classics, 1986), 172. In his *Testament*, now believed to be inauthentic, Ephrem the Syrian allegedly implored believers "in the name of that God who commands me to leave you, to remember me when you assemble to pray. Do not bury me with perfumes. Give them not to me, but to God. Me, conceived in sorrows, bury with lamentations, and instead of perfumes assist me with your prayers; for the dead are benefited by the prayers of living Saints." For the authenticity of the testament see Edmund Beck, *Des heiligen Ephraem des Syrers Sermones IV*, CSCO 335 (Louvain: Secretariat du CSCO, 1973).

[108] See Trumbower, *Rescue for the Dead*, 61. Trumbower provides a translation of the much-expanded fifth-century *Life and Miracles of St Thecla*, which was "the first Greek work in a long series of texts that highlight the prayer for Falconilla and invoke it to justify prayer for the dead generally, sometimes even including dead pagans." Ibid., 72.

[109] *Syriac Liturgy of St. James* in C. E. Hammond, *The Saint James Liturgy* (Piscataway, NJ: Gorgias Press, 2009), 75. The prayer further asked, entreated, and prayed that "Christ our God, who took their souls and spirits to Himself, that by His many compassions He will make them worthy of the pardon of their faults and the remission of their sins."

[110] Ibid.

[111] Pseudo-Dionysius, *The Ecclesiastical Hierarchy* 7.4, in Pseudo-Dionysius, *The Complete Works*, trans. Com Luibheid (Mahwah, NJ: Paulist Press, 1987), 253.

[112] "And then, as to naming the dead, what could be more helpful? What could be more opportune or wonderful than that the living believe that the departed are alive and have not ceased to be but exist, and live with the Lord—and that the most sacred doctrine should declare that there is hope for those who pray for their brethren as though they were off on a journey? And even though the prayer we offer for them cannot root out all their faults—[how could it], since we often slip in this world, inadvertently and deliberately—it is still useful as an indication of something more perfect. For we commemorate both righteous and sinners. Though we pray for sinners, for God's mercy." Epiphanius of Salamis, *Panarion* 75; Eng. trans.: Epiphanius of Salamis, *The Panarion of Epiphanius of Salamis Books II and III*, 509.

involuntary, and may be merciful and gracious to him."[113] Cyril of Jerusalem gave a more detailed rationale in the *Mystical Catechesis*, using an image he hoped they could understand.

> Then we commemorate also those who have fallen asleep ... believing that this will be of the greatest benefit to the souls of those on whose behalf our supplication is offered in the presence of the holy, the most dread Sacrifice. Let me use an illustration for an argument. For I know that many of you say: "What does it avail a soul departing this world, whether with or without sins, to be remembered at the Sacrifice?" Well, suppose a king banished persons who had offended him, and then their relatives wove a garland and presented it to him on behalf of those undergoing punishment, would he not mitigate their sentence? In the same way, offering our supplications to Him for those who have fallen asleep, even though they be sinners, we, though we weave no garland, offer Christ slain for our sins, propitiating the merciful God on both their and our own behalf.[114]

Like Cyril, John Chrysostom also enjoined prayer for the dead at the Eucharist, telling his congregants that "if the children of Job were purged by the sacrifice of their father," there was no doubt "that when we too offer for the departed, some consolation arises to them since God is wont to grant the petitions of those who ask for others.... Let us not then be weary in giving aid to the departed, both by offering on their behalf and obtaining prayers for them."[115] The reasons for these prayers were simple: "If [the deceased] had departed a sinner, it may do away his sins; but if righteous, that it may become an increase of reward and recompense."[116] Chrysostom thought believers should be particularly solicitous "for those who had the possibility of washing away their sins and didn't want to do it. Let's mourn them, let's help them as much as we can, let's devise some assistance for them—paltry, but let's help anyway. How and in what way? By praying and encouraging others to offer prayers on their behalf and by giving frequently to the poor on their behalf. This act can provide some consolation."[117]

That the faithful departed might be in need of consolation was hinted at in several gnostic texts (e.g., *Apocryphon of John*, *Pistis Sophia*), where the dead were said to receive purifying punishment "until [they were] liberated from [their] forgetfulness and acquired knowledge."[118] In the *Pistis Sophia* the disciples ask Jesus about the

---

[113] *Apostolic Constitutions* 8:4,41; ANF 7:497.

[114] Cyril of Jerusalem, *Mystagogical Lecture 5*; Eng. trans.: Cyril of Jerusalem, *Works*, vol. 2, trans. Leo McCauley and Anthony Stephenson, FC 64 (Washington, DC: Catholic University of America Press, 1970), 197–98.

[115] "It is possible from every source to gather pardon for them, from our prayers, from our gifts in their behalf, from those whose names are named with theirs. Why therefore dost thou grieve? Why mourn when it is in thy power to gather so much pardon for the departed?" John Chrysostom, *Homily 41 on First Corinthians*; NPNF 2.12.254.

[116] John Chrysostom, *Homily 31 on The Gospel of Matthew*; NPNF 2.10. 209.

[117] John Chrysostom, *Homily 4 on Philippians* in John Chrysostom, *Homilies on Philippians*, 73.

[118] "And I said, 'Lord, those, however, who have not known to whom they belong, where will their souls be?' And he said to me, 'In those [people] the despicable spirit has gained strength when they went astray. And he burdens the soul and draws it to the works of evil, and he casts it down into forgetfulness. And after it comes out of (the body), it is handed over to the authorities, who came into being through the *archon*, and they bind it with chains and cast it into prison and consort with it until it is liberated from the forgetfulness

punishments for specific crimes (e.g., blasphemy, robbery, pederasty), after which he gives a detailed account of their sufferings, specifying the length of each punishment down to the hour.[119] In almost all of these descriptions, the instrument of punishment is fire.[120]

The image of testing and cleansing by fire also appears in the *Didache*, which states that humanity "will pass into the testing fire and many will be scandalized and perish, but those who persevere in their belief will be saved by the curse itself."[121] According to most commentators, "What is being presented here ... is probably the threat of persecution" in which some will become apostates and perish while others "remain faithful, ... withstand the test," and are saved by Christ, who (according to Gal 3:13) "became a curse for us."[122] Yet there are those who have interpreted "the curse that saves" as the purifying fire itself, arguing that the *Didache* "offers an overlooked testimony to the dual function of eschatological [and purifying] fire more than a century prior to Tertullian and Clement of Alexandria."[123] In support they cite the *Shepherd of Hermas* (4.1.10), which also has references to a fire that purifies and refines believers like gold in the furnace.[124] Perhaps this is why *Hermas*, in its discussion of

---

and acquires knowledge. And if thus it becomes perfect, it is saved.'" *Apocryphon of John*; Eng. trans.: James Robinson, ed., *The Nag Hammadi Library in English* (New York: HarperCollins, 1990), 120.

[119] "Peter said, 'My Lord, a robber and thief whose sin has continued to be this, when he comes forth from the body, what is his punishment?' Jesus answered, 'When the time of such a one is completed ... they take it down to Amente to the presence of Ariel, and he takes revenge on it in his punishments for three months and eight days and two hours. After these things they take it to the Chaos to the presence of Jaldaboath with his 49 demons and each one of his demons takes revenge on it for another three months and eight days and two hours. After these things they take it upon the way to the Midst, and each of the archons of the way of the Midst takes revenge on it by means of his dark smoke and his wicked fire for another three months and eight days and two hours.'" *Pistis Sophia*, Book 4, 146; Eng. trans.: Carl Schmidt, ed., *Pistis Sophia*, trans. Violet MacDermot, Nag Hammadi Studies 9 (Leiden: Brill, 1978), 377–78.

[120] "After these things [the soul] is taken through rivers of fire and seas of fire and the soul is punished in them for another six months and eight days. After these things it is taken upon the way of the Midst, so that each one of the *archons* of the way of the Midst punishes it with his punishment for another six months and eight days.... Mariam continued again and said: 'My Lord, the man who continuously slanders, when he comes forth from the body, where will he go, or what is his punishment?' Jesus said: 'A man who slanders continuously ... [is taken down] to the Chaos to the presence of Jaldaboath with his 49 demons and each one of his demons attacks it for another eleven months and twenty-one days as they flagellate with fiery scourges.' ... Bartholomew asked, 'A pederast, what is the vengeance on him?' Jesus said, 'The measure of the pederast and of the man with whom he sleeps is the same as that of the blasphemer ... they take them forth to rivers of fire and seas of boiling bitumen, which are full of pig-faced demons which devour them and immerse them in the rivers of fire for another eleven years.'" Ibid., 374–75.

[121] *Didache* 16:5; Eng. trans.: Kurt Niederwimmer and Harold Attridge, *The Didache: A Commentary* (Minneapolis, MN: Fortress Press, 1998), 221.

[122] Ibid.

[123] Aaron Milavec, "The Saving Efficacy of the Burning Process in Didache 16.5," in Claton Jefford, ed., *The Didache in Context: Essays on Its Text, History, and Transmission* (Leiden: Brill, 1995), 131. See also Aaron Milavec, "The Birth of Purgatory: Evidence of the Didache," in Terrance Callan, ed., *Proceedings of the Eastern Great Lakes Biblical Society* 12 (Cincinnati: Eastern Great Lakes and Midwest Bible Societies, 1992), 91–104. For a different view see Nancy Pardee, "The Curse That Saves" in Jefford, *The Didache in Context*, 156–76.

[124] "The gold portion is you who have fled from this world. Just as gold is tried by fire and becomes useful, so also you who live among them are being tested. Those who endure and are consumed by flames will be purified by them. As gold drops off its dross, so you will let fall all sadness and anguish, and you will be purified and become useful for the building of the tower." Carolyn Osiek, *The Shepherd of Hermas: A Commentary* (Minneapolis, MN: Fortress Press, 1999), 90.

postbaptismal repentance, is sometimes cited as an early witness to Purgatory,[125] although debate remains over whether the torments described in the text occur in this world or the next.[126]

By the late second and early third centuries, Christian writers increasingly came to link the postmortem punishments incurred for sin with the purifying fire, which, while painful, nevertheless gave meaning to the suffering involved. This was especially the case with the two great Alexandrians, Clement and Origen, who are, rightly or wrongly, regarded by many as the "founders of Purgatory."[127] According to Joseph Ratzinger, Clement viewed "Christian existence at large in terms of the ... idea of *paideia* (i.e., education)" and unlike his Valentinian opponents saw the fires of judgment as "purifying" and "educative" rather than as "punishing" or "destructive."[128] For Clement, "God does not take vengeance (for vengeance is a retaliation of evil), but he chastens with a view to the good ... of those who are chastened."[129] God's chastisements, both in this world and the next, had a purpose.[130]

This was particularly the case for the fires of judgment, which were only part of the larger "process of man's pneumatic purification, that catharsis which will fit him for God, begins with baptism and reaches into eternity."[131] Both Ratzinger and Eno noted that for Clement the "expiatory aspect of [the] cleansing after death is very minor" and

---

[125] The passage that is often cited: "I asked her if all those stones that had been thrown away and did not fit into the tower really had the opportunity for conversion and a place in this tower. 'They will have the chance for conversion,' she said, 'but they cannot fit into this tower. They will fit into another much inferior place, and this after they have been tormented and have filled up the time of their sins. But then they will be changed to a different place because they had a part in the righteous word. Then it will happen that they will be taken out of the torments in which they were placed because of their evil deeds.'" Ibid., 67. See also Karl Rahner, "The Penitential Teaching of the Shepherd of Hermas," in *Theological Investigations* 15 (New York: Crossroad, 1982), 57–113.

[126] While Osiek believed that "the torment that must afflict these late arrivals to conversion" is "likely some kind of eschatological punishment" (Osiek, *The Shepherd of Hermas*, 75), she noted that other authors (e.g., E. C. Dewick) disagreed. See E. C. Dewick, *Primitive Christian Eschatology* (Cambridge: Cambridge University Press, 1912), 349.

[127] Robert Eno noted that it was the Protestant scholar Gustav Anrich who in 1902 first called Clement and Origen the "founders of the idea of Purgatory." Eno, "The Fathers and the Cleansing Fire," 182. See Gustav Anrich, "Clemens und Origenes als begründer der lehre vom Fegfeuer," *Theologische Abhandlungen. Eine Festgabe zum 17. Mai 1902 für H.J. Holtzmann* (Tübingen: Mohr Siebeck, 1902), 97–120.

[128] Ratzinger, *Eschatology*, 225. Ratzinger wrote that Clement's views were worked out in controversy with the Valentinians, who believed that the gnostic could not be touched by the fire of judgment "since s/he carries the two extinguishing agents—the water of baptism and the 'Wind,' (i.e., the Spirit).... The ordinary man, however, ... is caught in the fire's blaze, with results at once curative and destructive." Ibid.

[129] "For there are also partial forms of discipline, which are called chastisements, into which most of us, who have trespassed from among the Lord's people, slip and fall. But as children are chastened by their teacher or their father, so are we by Providence. For God does not take vengeance (for vengeance is a retaliation of evil), but he chastens with a view to the good, both public and private, of those who are chastened." Clement of Alexandria, Stromata 7:16; Eng. trans.: Henry Chadwick and J. E. L Oulton, *Alexandrian Christianity* (Louisville, KY: John Knox Press, 2006), 159–60.

[130] This idea, according to Le Goff, comes from the ancient Greek idea that "the chastisement inflicted by the gods is not punishment but rather a means of education and salvation, part of a process of purification. In Plato's view it is a boon offered by the gods." Le Goff, *The Birth of Purgatory*, 52.

[131] Ratzinger, *Eschatology*, 225. For Clement this "fire sanctifies, not flesh or sacrifice, but sinful souls, understanding by fire not the all-devouring flame of common life, but the discerning flame which pierces through the soul that walks through fire." Clement of Alexandria, *Stromata* 7:6; Eng. trans.: Chadwick and Oulton, *Alexandrian Christianity*, 114. See W. C. van Unnik, "The 'Wise Fire' in a Gnostic Eschatological Vision," in Patrick Granfield and Josef Jungmann, eds., *Kyriakon. Festschrift Jahannes Quasten*, vol. 1 (Munster Westfalen: Verlag Aschendorf, 1970), 277–88.

must be seen in light of the lifelong "drama" or "ascent" that began "with the planting of the seed at the baptism ... and continued developing through the purification after death."[132] At the end of this process,

> The believer, through great discipline, divesting himself of the passions, passes to the mansion which is better than the former one, viz., to the greatest torment, taking with him the characteristic of repentance from the sins he has committed after baptism. He is tortured then still more—not yet or not quite attaining what he sees others to have acquired.... And though the punishments cease in the course of the completion of the expiation and purification of each one, yet those have very great and permanent grief who are found worthy of the other fold, on account of not being along with those that have been glorified through righteousness.[133]

Two interesting issues raised by Clement's writings are the degree to which he acknowledged the punitive nature of the fires of judgment, and whether some sinners were so incorrigible that they would be punished without end. Most scholars are agreed that "the essential role of punishment in purifying the soul after death is not found in Clement's nonretributive, intelligent fire"[134] and that for Clement "all punishment, including punishment after death, [is seen as] purification rather than retribution."[135] Yet despite the fact that Clement "generally viewed punishment after death as a medicinal and therefore temporary measure," there are texts where he spoke of "the punishment of eternal fire,"[136] which would seem to allow for the existence of two fires—a "'devouring and consuming' one for the incorrigible, and for the rest a fire that 'sanctifies' and 'does not consume, like the fire of the forge.'"[137]

Origen's thinking on the afterlife was built upon his exegesis of 1 Corinthians 3:11–15 and centered on a pastoral question—"What if we finish our life with sins [i.e., wood, hay, stubble] but also with what is commendable [i.e., gold, silver, precious stones].... Will we be saved through what is commendable and acquitted concerning those sins which were knowingly committed? Or will we be punished for the sins but receive no recompense for what is commendable?"[138] Origen began his answer to

---

[132] Eno, "The Fathers and the Cleansing Fire," 187. It is a process "whereby the soul is transformed into a *sōma*, (body) of ever greater pneumatic perfection" until the time when the person achieved "the highest level of pneumatic bodiliness ... [and] entered *sunteleia*, (perfection)" on the eschatological "Day of God." Ratzinger, *Eschatology*, 226.

[133] Clement of Alexandria, *Stromata* 6:14; ANF 2:504.

[134] Moreira, *Heaven's Purge*, 28.

[135] Daley, *Hope of the Early Church*, 47. According to Daley, "In this consistent interpretation of all punishment ... as purification rather than retribution, Clement can be considered the first Christian exponent of the doctrine of purgatorial eschatological suffering." Ibid.

[136] Ibid. "It is possible for you to neglect those that are loved by God; the penalty for which is the punishment of eternal fire" (κόλασις ἐμπυρος αἰώνιος). Clement of Alexandria, *Quis Dives Salvetur*, 33.

[137] Le Goff, *The Birth of Purgatory*, 54. Moreira disagreed with this assessment, arguing Clement's theology of the afterlife did *not* allow for "a place of eternal punishment without correction and without respite." Moreira, *Heaven's Purge*, 28.

[138] "For suppose that you have built, after the foundation which Christ Jesus has taught, not only gold, silver, and precious stones... but also wood and hay and stubble, what does he wish you to become after your final departure? To enter afterwards then into the holy lands with your wood and with your hay and stubble so that you may defile the Kingdom of God? But again, do you want to be left behind in the fire on account of the hay, the wood, the stubble, and to receive nothing due you for the gold and the silver and precious stone? This is not reasonable. What then?" Origen of Alexandria, *Homily 16 on Jeremiah*, 5; Eng. trans.: Origen,

this question with a reflection on the revealing fire described by Paul, which he interpreted, not as "a fire which has already been kindled by another or existed before," but rather as a spiritual fire that "every sinner kindles for himself" and consists "of the tortures of conscience in the sinful soul that knows itself to have fallen away from God."[139] For Origen, "The food and material of this fire are our sins, which are called, by the apostle Paul, wood and hay and straw."[140] Just as a man who eats and drinks too much suffers illness in proportion to his intemperateness,

> So also, when the soul has gathered together a multitude of evil works and an excess of sins in itself, at a suitable time all that assembly of evils boils up to punishment and is set aflame to chastisements; at which time the intellect itself, or the conscience, bringing to memory by divine power all those things ... will see exposed before its eyes a history, as it were, of its evil deeds, of every single act it had done, whether foul or shameful, and had even impiously committed; then the conscience itself is agitated and pierced by its own stings and becomes its own accuser and witness.... From which it is understood that, in what concerns the substance of the soul, certain torments are produced from the hurtful affections of the sins themselves.[141]

"The degree and duration of [this] suffering for those confined in [this fire] varied depending on their guilt" (i.e., the amount of "wood, hay, and stubble" they had accumulated),[142] with the fire of conscience "tortur[ing] body and soul ... [with] great suffering,"[143] until it eventually consumed all sin, leaving only those materials fit to

---

Homilies on Jeremiah and Homily on 1 Kings 28, trans. John Clark Smith, FC 97 (Washington, DC: Catholic University of America Press, 1998), 173–74. For Origen and Purgatory see Albert Michel, "Origène et le dogme du purgatoire," in *Questions ecclésiastiques* (Lille, 1913): 407–32; Henri Crouzel, "L'Hadès et la Géhenne selon Origène," *Gregorianum* 59 (1978): 291–331; Henri Crouzel, "L'éxégèse origénienne de 1 Cor. 3, 11–15 et la Purification Eschatologique," in Jacques Fontaine and Charles Kannengiesser, eds., *Epektasis: Melanges patristiques offerts au Cardinal Jean Danielou* (Paris: Beauchesne, 1972), 272–83.

[139] "Now we find in the prophet Isaiah that the fire by which each one is punished is described as his own; for he says, 'Walk in the light of your fire and in the flame which you have kindled for yourself.' It seems to be indicated, by these words, that every sinner kindles for himself the flame of his own fire, and is not plunged into some fire which has already been kindled by another or existed before himself." Origen of Alexandria, *On First Principles* 2.10.4; Eng. trans.: Origen, *On First Principles*, vol. 2, trans. John Behr (Oxford: Oxford University Press, 2017), 261. See also Hans Urs Von Balthasar, *Dare We Hope That All Men Be Saved*, trans. David Kipp and Lothar Krauth (San Francisco: Ignatius Press, 1988), 47–72; Hans-Jürgen Horn, "Ignis aeternus. Une interprétation morale du feu éternel chez Origène," *Revue des Études Grecques* 82 (1969): 76–88.

[140] Origen of Alexandria, *On First Principles* 2.10.4; Eng. trans.: Origen, *On First Principles*, 261.

[141] Ibid.

[142] Origen also used the image of impure metals, which must be separated from the gold and silver by the purifying fire: "For when from our evils we cause vices and passions to come upon God's creation, which is good from the beginning, then we are mixing brass, tin, and lead with silver and gold. Fire then becomes necessary to purify it. And that is the reason one must take great care that, when we come to that fire, we may pass through it unscathed. Like gold, silver, and precious stone that are without a trace of adulteration, may we not so much burn in the conflagration as be tested [cf. 1 Cor 3:12]." Origen of Alexandria, *Homily 1 on Ezekiel*, 13; Eng. trans.: Origen, *Homilies 1–14 on Ezekiel*, trans. Thomas Scheck, ACW 62 (New York: Newman Press, 2010), 43.

[143] Daley, *The Hope of the Early Church*, 57. "Blessed, then, is the one who is baptized in the Holy Spirit and does not need the baptism by fire, but three times unhappy is that man who has need to be baptized in fire, though Jesus takes care of both of them.... God is a consuming fire and God is light, a consuming fire to sinners, a light to the just and holy ones." Origen of Alexandria, *Homily 2 on Ezekiel*, 3; Eng. trans.: Origen,

enter the kingdom.¹⁴⁴ Yet for Origen this pain was therapeutic, explaining why he ultimately viewed the purgatorial fires "as a house of healing, not a torture chamber; as a hospital, not a prison."¹⁴⁵ They were simply a "part of a larger *schola animarum*—a process of divine education wherein the angels themselves would act as teachers—in preparation for the final reunification with God on the last day."¹⁴⁶

The question raised by Origen's system is whether this fire had the potential to cleanse even the most hardened sinners, thus eliminating the need for a permanent state of punishment called "Hell."¹⁴⁷ In most of his writings Origen appears to assume that "the soul steadily improves after death, and no matter how sinful it may have been at the outset, [it] eventually makes sufficient progress to be allowed to the eternal contemplation of God."¹⁴⁸ Like Clement, Origen also taught that "all punishment is medicinal and educational," and thus it made no sense for God to impose an eternal punishment from which the sinner could not profit.¹⁴⁹ For these reasons the majority of scholars are comfortable asserting that for Origen Hell is not necessarily a permanent state but rather "a temporary abode" that exists "as a kind of Purgatory," where even the worst sinners can "be completely purified and allowed to enter Heaven."¹⁵⁰

Homilies 1–14 on Ezekiel, 26. "But you will find many who are thought to believe who have unstrained words, actions, and thoughts. For this reason, 'fire will devour their carnal actions as straw' tormenting even the soul together with the body because of the inveterate physical transgressions in it. For just as it is not possible to cut away innate growths on bodies without great pain and suffering by those who are afflicted, so it is with the carnal sins committed by those who (if I may speak this way) have made their souls flesh." Origen, *Series Commentariorum on Matthew*, 20; Eng. trans.: Origen, *The Commentary of Origen on the Gospel of St Matthew*, vol. 2, trans. Ronald Heine (Oxford: Oxford University Press, 2018), 571.

¹⁴⁴ "It follows that you receive the fire first due to the wood, which consumes the wood and the hay and the stubble. For to those able to perceive, our God is said to be in reality a consuming fire.... For he does not consume what is according to the image and likeness, he does not consume his own creation but the accumulated hay, the accumulated wood, the accumulated stubble.... [He] renders what is due for the evil things, in order that through the disappearance of evil things, he may bring an end to the punishment of those who suffer, so that after this, he may render what is due for the good things." Origen of Alexandria, *Homily 16 on Jeremiah*, 6; Eng. trans.: Origen, *Homilies on Jeremiah*, 74.

¹⁴⁵ Kallistos Ware, "Dare We Hope for the Salvation of All," in *The Inner Kingdom*, vol. 1 of *The Collected Works of Kallistos Ware* (Crestwood, NY: St. Vladimir's Seminary Press, 2001), 205.

¹⁴⁶ Moreira, *Heaven's Purge*, 29. "Those gradually making progress and ascending in order and measure shall arrive first at that other Earth and the training that is in it ... [so that] they may be prepared for those better ordinances.... The Lord Jesus Christ, who is king of all, will himself assume the kingdom; that is, after their training in the holy virtues, he himself will instruct those who are capable of receiving him in respect to his being Wisdom, reigning in them until he subjects them to the Father, who has subjected all things to himself." Origen of Alexandria, *On First Principles* 3.6.9; Eng. trans.: Origen, *On First Principles*, 453–55.

¹⁴⁷ See M. F. Egan, "The Two Theories or Purgatory," *Irish Theological Quarterly* 17 (1951): 24–34; John R. Sachs, "Apocatastasis in Patristic Theology," *Theological Studies* 54 (1993): 617–40.

¹⁴⁸ Le Goff, *The Birth of Purgatory*, 55.

¹⁴⁹ Daley, *The Hope of the Early Church*, 58. "God's wrath is not so much wrath as necessary governance. Hear what the action of God's wrath is for: to rebuke, to chasten, to improve ... the reason it is administered is to cure the sick, to improve those who have despised listening to his words.... Everything that comes from God is good and we deserve to be chastened.... Everything that comes from God that seems to be bitter is advanced for instruction and healing. God is a physician, God is a Father, he is a Master, and he is not a harsh but a mild Master." Origen of Alexandria, *Homily 1 on Ezekiel*, 2; Eng. trans.: Origen, *Homilies 1–14 on Ezekiel*, 27–28. "How much more is it to be understood that God, our physician, desiring to wash away the ills of our souls, which they had contracted through a variety of sins and crimes, should employ penalties of this sort and even apply the punishment of fire to those who have lost their soul's health." Origen of Alexandria, *On First Principles* 2.10.6; Eng. trans.: Origen, *On First Principles*, vol. 2, 263.

¹⁵⁰ Le Goff, *The Birth of Purgatory*, 55.

However, if it was true that "the purifying fire could restore all beings to God," it meant that "Hell, in a traditional sense, [did] not exist,"[151] a teaching that was later condemned by the Fifth Ecumenical Council (553) along with Origen, its alleged progenitor.[152] Accurate or not, this perhaps explains why, when the Greeks were confronted with the Latin doctrine of Purgatory centuries later, they immediately connected it to the "madness of Origen" and condemned it.

Whether Origen was truly one of the founders of Purgatory remains an open question, although his writings do preview many of the central concepts around which Purgatory was later constructed. According to Le Goff:

> It was Origen who clearly stated for the first time the idea that the soul can be purified in the other world after death. For the first time a distinction was drawn between mortal and lesser sins. We even see three categories beginning to take shape: the righteous, who pass through the fire of judgment and go directly to heaven; those guilty of the lesser sins only, whose sojourn in the "fire of combustion" is brief; and "mortal sinners," who remain in the flames for an extended period.[153]

John Chrysostom, in his own commentary on 1 Corinthians 3:11–15, took aim at Origen's understanding of a temporary "Hell" by reaffirming that Christ himself taught that hellfire was eternal.[154] This fiery punishment, which Chrysostom often

---

[151] Moreira, *Heaven's Purge*, 30. However, Brian Daley noted that there are places in Origen's writings, "particularly in his homiletic works," where he "refers to the need for divine punishment of sinners (Hom in Jer 12.5) and paints the prospect of 'eternal fire' in thoroughly traditional terms.... Origen even speaks approvingly in Homilies on Ezekiel 4.8 of the 'common understanding' that this punishment is final, in contrast with the 'foolishness of some' who believe that anyone can be saved from Gehenna by the prayers of holy intercessors." Daley, *The Hope of the Early Church*, 56. That said, "Origen raises serious questions about the eternity of the punishment of sinners ... and is careful to point out, in several places, that Scripture designates 'eternal fire' expressly 'for the devil and his angels,' as if implying that it is not meant for human souls (so Hom in Jos 14.2)." Ibid., 57. Daley also pointed out that Origen explicitly denied that he taught the redemption of the devil although he also recognized that certain ambiguities in Origen's allow one to speculate "that Origen himself remained undecided on the subject." Ibid., 59.

[152] David Bentley Hart denied Origen had actually been condemned: "It is true that something remembered by tradition as 'Origenism' was condemned by someone in the sixth century, and that Origen was maligned as a heretic in the process; and it is also true that for well more than a millennium both those decisions were associated with the Council of 553 by what was simply accepted as the official record. But, embarrassingly, we now know, and have known for quite some time, that the record was falsified.... Even if the anathemas had actually been approved by the council, they no more constitute a serious condemnation of Origen than they do a recipe for brioche." David Bentley Hart, "Saint Origen," *First Things*, October 2015, 72. See also A. Edward Siecienski, "(Re)defining the Boundaries of Orthodoxy: The Rule of Faith and the 20th Century Rehabilitation of Origen," in Ronnie Rombs and Alex Hwang, eds., *Tradition and the Rule of Faith in the Early Church: Festschrift for Joseph Lienhard* (Washington, DC: Catholic University of America Press, 2010), 286–307.

[153] Hart, "Saint Origen," 72; Le Goff, *The Birth of Purgatory*, 57. Although Le Goff clarified that "in this vision of the other world a number of ingredients of the true Purgatory are lacking" (e.g., a clear distinction between Hell and Purgatory, no clear mention of Purgatory as a "place"). Ibid.

[154] "For that it has no end Christ indeed declared when he said, 'Their fire shall not be quenched, and their worm shall not die' [Mk 8:44, 46, 48.] ... Paul also says, in pointing out the eternity of the punishment, that the sinners shall pay the penalty of destruction, and that forever [2 Thes 1:9]. And again, 1 Corinthians 6:9: 'Be not deceived; neither fornicators, nor adulterers, nor effeminate, shall inherit the kingdom of God.' And also unto the Hebrews he says [Heb 12:14], 'Follow peace with all men, and the sanctification without which no man shall see the Lord.' And Christ also, to those who said, 'In your Name we have done many wonderful works,' says, 'Depart from Me, I know you not, you workers of iniquity [Mt 7:22].' And the virgins too who were shut out, entered in no more. And also about those who gave Him no food, He says [Mt25:46],

described in vivid detail as a way of discouraging immoral behavior, Paul called "salvation," only because it was "his custom in things which have an ill sound to use fair expressions."[155] Others, like Cyril of Jerusalem, continued to speak of the fire not as punishing but as probative, describing the moment on the Day of Judgment when "the Son of Man will come to the Father, in the clouds of heaven, trailing a stream of fire, which shall try men. A man whose works are golden shall be made more splendid; if a man's actions have been unsubstantial like stubble, he shall be burned by fire."[156] Theodoret of Cyrus (d. 453) interpreted the passage as a reference to teachers, who will receive salvation if they have "taught what is proper."[157] At the same time, their works (i.e., their students) will either be made resplendent like precious metals or be burned up like stubble depending on the choices they have made, the teacher himself being blameless for any evils students have committed "by their [own] free will."[158]

Although "the Cappadocians do not have a great deal to say on this subject [of purgative fire]," their writings often appeared in the later debates over Purgatory given the universal respect they were accorded.[159] Basil of Caesarea, for example, was an oft-cited witness to some sort of "way station" on the believer's heavenly journey where "noble athletes of God, who have wrestled considerably with the invisible enemies during the whole of their lives ... are examined by the prince of the world in order that, if they are found to have wounds from the wrestling or any stains or effects of sin, they may be detained; but, if they are found unwounded and stainless, they may be brought by Christ into their rest as being unconquered and free."[160] Also frequently cited was his Pentecost prayer, which asked God to "give rest to the souls of Your Servants who have departed this life, in a place of light, a place of renewed life, a joyous place, shunned alike by pain and sorrow and sighing. And place their spirits where the righteous dwell, counting them worthy of peace and repose ... [for] it is we the living who ... offer You propitiatory prayers and sacrifices for their souls."[161]

'They shall go away into everlasting punishment.'" John Chrysostom, *Homily 9 on First Corinthians*; NPNF 1.12.49.

[155] John Chrysostom, *Homily 9 on First Corinthians*; NPNF 1.12.52. Explaining Chrysostom's relative silence on the world to come, Vasileios Marinis speculated that despite writing "four discourses on the parable of the rich man and Lazaros," John was generally unconcerned with "the geography of the afterlife," because "his main concern was charity" and encouraging good behavior in his congregants. Vasileios Marinis, *Death and the Afterlife in Byzantium: The Fate of the Soul in Theology, Liturgy, and Art* (Cambridge: Cambridge University Press, 2017), 4.

[156] Cyril of Jerusalem, *Catechesis* 15.21; Eng. trans.: Cyril of Jerusalem, *Works*, vol. 2, 67.

[157] Theodoret of Cyrus, *The First Letter to the Corinthians*, 3; Eng. trans.: Theodoret of Cyrus, *Commentary on the Letters of St Paul*, vol. 1, trans. Robert Charles Hill (Brookline, MA: Holy Cross Orthodox Press, 2001), 170–71.

[158] Ibid. When this text was brought forward at the Council of Florence, it included the sentence "For this, we believe this fire is Purgatory (τοῦτο πῦρ πιστεύομεν καθαρτήριον) in which the souls are purified like gold in the smelting furnace." If this addition were genuine (and few believe it is), it would have been an "unusual use of Purgatory as a substantive noun (hence a place or state) in Greek patristic literature." Jorgenson, "The Debate over Patristic Texts on Purgatory," 316.

[159] Eno, "The Fathers and the Cleansing Fire," 193.

[160] Basil the Great, *Homily 11 on Psalm 7*; Eng. trans.: Saint Basil, *Exegetic Homilies*, trans. Sister Agnes Clare Way, FC 46 (Washington, DC: Catholic University of America Press, 1963), 167–68.

[161] Third Kneeling Prayer at Vespers. Latins and Greeks, including Mark of Ephesus in his post-Florentine writings, used this text to support for the universally agreed-upon belief that suffrages on behalf of the dead were efficacious.

Despite being deeply influenced by Origen, Basil was clear that these prayers could not grant release from Hell, for from the eternal fire there was "no pardon whatsoever, no matter the command in question, for those who fail to repent of their disobedience, unless it is possible to venture a different conclusion in the face of such bald, plain, and unconditional statements" as contained in Scripture.[162]

Like Origen, Gregory of Nazianzus accepted that the chief suffering of sinners in the afterlife "is spiritual in nature and consist[ed] in alienation from God, and the 'boundless shame of conscience' which understands ... its own responsibility in bringing it about.'"[163] He also spoke of the cleansing fire, which Gregory identified with Christ himself, writing, "For I know also a purifying fire, which Christ came to cast upon the earth. And he himself is called a fire in an anagogical sense [which] consumes matter and evil habits."[164] Elsewhere, however, Gregory appears to break with Origen by denying the possibility of postmortem purgation, warning that it was "better to be punished and cleansed now than to be transmitted to the torment to come, when it is the time of chastisement, not of cleansing ... for God has confined life and action to this world, and to the future the scrutiny of what has been done."[165] Yet Gregory allowed that "some [may] prefer even here to understand this fire as showing more love to humankind, in a way worthy of the punisher,"[166] leaving the door open to an Origenist interpretation—that is, if postmortem punishment was pedagogical rather than punitive, "It hardly seems possible that it could be eternal."[167]

---

[162] Basil of Caesarea, *On the Judgment of God*; Eng. trans.: Basil the Great, *On Christian Ethics*, trans. Jacob Van Sickle (Crestwood, NY: St. Vladimir's Seminary Press, 2014), 63.

[163] John Sachs, "Apocatastasis in Patristic Thought," *Theological Studies* 54 (1993): 629. The author quotes from *Oration 16*, where Gregory wrote of the judgment to come: "Some will be welcomed by the unspeakable light and the vision of the holy and royal Trinity, which now shines upon them with greater brilliancy and purity and unites itself wholly to the whole soul, in which solely and beyond all else I take it that the kingdom of heaven consists. The others among other torments, but above and before them all must endure the being outcast from God, and the shame of conscience which has no limit." Gregory of Nazianzus, *Oration* 16.9; NPNF 2.7.250.

[164] "For I know also a purifying fire, which Christ came to cast upon the earth. And he himself is called a fire in an anagogical sense. This consumes matter and evil habits, and Christ wants to kindle it swiftly, for he desires that we do good quickly, since he even gives us burning coals as a help. I know also a fire that does not purify but indeed punishes: either the fire of Sodom, which the Lord reigns down on all sinners mixed with brimstone and tempest, or that prepared for the devil and his angels; or that which goes forth before the face of the Lord and burns up his enemies all around; and, what is even more fearful than these, that which does not rest and is deployed with the worm, which is not extinguished but remains forever for the wicked." Gregory of Nazianzus, Oration 40.36; Eng. trans.: Gregory of Nazianzus, *Festal Orations*, trans. Nonna Verna Harrison (Crestwood, NY: St. Vladimir's Seminary Press, 2008), 132.

[165] Gregory of Nazianzus, *Oration* 16.9; NPNF 2.7.249–50.

[166] Gregory of Nazianzus, *Oration* 40.36; Eng. trans.: Gregory of Nazianzus, *Festal Orations*, 132. According to the translator, "Gregory is saying that he considers universal salvation, which would follow as much purification as is needed after death, as a possibility. However, like his friend Gregory of Nyssa, whom he probably has in mind here, he stops short of affirming it as a necessary outcome of God's infinite goodness and patience with creaturely freedom." Ibid.

[167] "What makes Gregory hedge here, even in face of the biblical language concerning (eternal) punishment, is his conviction that punitive punishment is simply unworthy of God. And if punishment is remedial in nature, it hardly seems possible that it could be eternal." Sachs, "Apocatastasis in Patristic Thought," 630. For this reason Sachs (quoting Brian Daley) concluded that Gregory "offers a cautious, undogmatic support of the Origenist position." Ibid., 632. See also Daley, *Hope of the Early Church*, 84. For an opposing view see Donald Winslow, *Dynamics of Salvation: A Study in Gregory of Nazianzus* (Cambridge, MA: Philadelphia Patristic Foundation, 1979), 165–67.

Perhaps the most important, and simultaneously the most complicated, Greek patristic witness in the whole Purgatory debate is Gregory of Nyssa, who, like Origen, advanced a form of *apocatastasis* (universal salvation) based on his belief that the "renewal of all things" brought about by the return of Christ would restore "all things to their original condition before the appearance of sin, and, consequently [bring about] the total destruction of evil."[168] According to Gregory, because the human soul "will always long for God as its ultimate good" and "it [is] axiomatic that this capacity cannot be permanently frustrated," it followed that no one could forever lose the possibility of knowing and loving God.[169] Hell, understood as eternal exile from God, made no sense, nor did punishment that had no benefit.

Yet Gregory also believed that the reality of sin made it impossible to know and love God without purification, a painful process that began at baptism, took place throughout our lives by "the practice of voluntary penance and asceticism," and continued after death.[170] Even though Gregory exhorted believers in this life "to clear away every passionate and irrational burden of nature and ... be purified ... through prayer and philosophy," he recognized that some would remain "inclined to the irrational pressure of the passions" and require further cleansing after death.[171] Gregory used "a number of vivid similes" to speak about this postmortem purification; however, it was the image of "purgative fire" that has remained the most enduring.[172] This fire, which was sometimes described as "sleepless," "purifying," or "purifying sleepless," "purged [people] of the filthy contagion in [their] soul"[173] and refined them like gold, so that "the pure is melted with the adulterated and the one remains while the

---

[168] Sachs, "Apocatastasis in Patristic Thought," 633. For Gregory's writings on apocatastasis, see Jean Daniélou, "L'apocatastase Chez Saint Grégoire de Nysse," *Recherches de Science Religieuse* 30 (1940): 328–47; A. Mouhanna, "La Conception du Salut Universel selon Saint Grégoire de Nysse," in Adel-Theodor Khoury and Margot Wiegels, eds., *Weg in Die Zukunft: Festschrift für Prof. Dr. Anton Antweiler zu Seinem 75. Geburtstag* (Leiden: Brill, 1975), 135–54; Morwenna Ludlow, *Universal Salvation: Eschatology in the Thought of Gregory of Nyssa and Karl Rahner* (Oxford: Oxford University Press, 2000); Ilaria L. E. Ramelli, "Christian Soteriology and Christian Platonism: Origen, Gregory of Nyssa, and the Biblical and Philosophical Basis of the Doctrine of Apokatastasis," *Vigiliae Christianae* 61 (2007): 313–56.

[169] Daley, *Hope of the Early Church*, 87.

[170] Ibid. "And since it was necessary for its stains, implanted by sins, to be removed by some sort of healing, on account of this, in the present life the medicine of virtue is applied for the therapy of such wounds; but if it should remain without therapy, the therapy is dispensed in the afterlife." Gregory of Nyssa, *Great Catechetical Oration* 8; Eng trans. Gregory of Nyssa, *Catechetical Discourse: A Handbook for Catechesis*, trans. Ignatius Green (Crestwood, NY: St. Vladimir's Seminary Press, 2019), 86.

[171] Gregory of Nyssa, *De mortuis*; PG 46:524; Eng. trans.: Daley, *Hope of the Early Church*, 89. "Some of us are purged of evil in this life, some are cured of it through fire in the afterlife ... the extent of healing will depend on the amount of evil present in each person. The healing of the soul will be purification from evil and this cannot be accomplished without suffering.... After a long period of time, they will assume again the form which they received from God in the beginning." Gregory of Nyssa, *On the Soul and the Resurrection*; Eng. trans.: Gregory of Nyssa, *Ascetical Works*, trans. Virginia Woods Callahan, FC 58 (Washington, DC: Catholic University of America, 1967), 267–68.

[172] In his work *On Virginity*, Gregory used the image of water, likening sinners to "those who slip and fall into the mud and, having smeared themselves with mire, become unrecognizable even to their companions, so the one who falls into the mire of sin no longer is the image of the incorruptible God, and he is covered through sin with a corruptible and slimy form which reason advises him to reject. However, if, purged by the water, so to speak, of his way of life, the earthly covering can be stripped off, the beauty of the soul may reappear again." Gregory of Nyssa, *On Virginity* 12; Eng. trans.: Gregory of Nyssa, *Ascetical Works*, 44.

[173] Gregory of Nyssa, *De mortuis*; PG 46:525; Eng. trans.: Jorgenson, "The Debate over Patristic Texts on Purgatory," 316.

other is consumed ... [and just as] wickedness is consumed by a sleepless/purifying fire, so also it is entirely necessary that the soul which is united to wickedness be in fire until the intermingled counterfeit and material and adulterated is consumed with the eternal fire."[174]

Before leaving the Greek fathers, final note should be taken of "Concerning Those Who Have Fallen Asleep in the Faith" (*De his qui in fide dormierunt*), a text long attributed to John of Damascus but probably written in the late ninth or early tenth century.[175] This influential work was meant to encourage commemoration for the dead, a practice which "the interpreters and eye-witnesses of the word, the disciples of the Savior and the apostles of God" had instituted and which "the universal, apostolic, and catholic Church of Christ has retained ... firmly and without any controversy from then until now and even to the end of the world."[176] To show the power of such prayer, even its ability to save pagans, the author included the story, well known in both East and West, about Gregory the Great interceding for the soul of the emperor Trajan and by these prayers releasing his soul from Hell.[177] Western versions of the story explained that Gregory's prayer was efficacious because the emperor, though a pagan, was an otherwise virtuous man.[178] This text omits reference to the

---

[174] Gregory of Nyssa, *De consolatione et statu animarum post mortem*; PG 46:100. Eng. trans.: Jorgenson, "The Debate over Patristic Texts on Purgatory," 316. "And the furnace is appropriate for gold that has been alloyed with dross, so that ... the vice mingled in them being melted, after long ages its nature might be restored pure to God. Since, then, there is some purgative power in fire and in water, those who have washed away the filth of vice by the mystic water do not need other forms of cleansing, but those who are not initiates in this purification are necessarily purified by fire." Gregory of Nyssa, *Great Catechetical Oration* 35; Eng. trans.: Gregory of Nyssa, *Catechetical Discourse*, 143–44.

[175] For the argument in favor of authenticity see F. Diekamp, "Johannes von Damaskus 'Über die im Glauben Entschlafenen,'" *Römische Quartalschrift* 17 (1903): 371–82.

[176] Pseudo-Damascene, *De his qui in fide dormiunt*, 3 (PG 95:249); Eng. trans.: Jorgenson, "The Debate over Patristic Texts on Purgatory," 317.

[177] "Gregory the Dialogist, the senior bishop of Rome, as everybody knows, was a man well known for his righteousness and knowledge. They even say that the divine angel assisted him when he was conducting the liturgy. One day this Gregory, while taking a walk among the stones, stood carefully still and uttered a mighty prayer directed toward the soul-loving Lord for the forgiveness of the sins of Trajan the king. Immediately after saying these things he heard a voice borne to him from God: 'I have heard your prayer, and I grant forgiveness to Trajan. But you should not again put forward prayers addressed to me on behalf of pagans.' And that this story is true and blameless, the whole of East and West is witness. Look, this even surpasses what happened to Falconilla. For she was a party to no other evil (beyond idolatry), but Trajan brought about the deaths of many martyrs." Pseudo-Damascene, *De his qui in fide dormiunt*, 16; Jeffrey Trumbower, *Rescue for the Dead*, 145. See also Gordon Whatley, "The Uses of Hagiography: The Legend of Pope Gregory and the Emperor Trajan in the Middle Ages," *Viator* 15 (1984): 25–64; Marcia L. Colish, "The Virtuous Pagan: Dante and the Christian Tradition," in William Caferro and Duncan G. Fisher, eds., *The Unbounded Community: Papers in Christian Ecumenism in Honor of Jaroslav Pelikan* (New York: Garland, 1996), 43–92. There are several versions of this story, preserved in the earliest life of Gregory by the anonymous monk of Whitby and the *Vita Sancti Gregorii Magni* by John the Deacon.

[178] "Some of our people also tell a story related by the Romans of how the soul of the Emperor Trajan was refreshed and even baptized by St. Gregory's tears, a story marvelous to tell and marvelous to hear.... One day as he was crossing the Forum, a magnificent piece of work for which Trajan is said to have been responsible, he found on examining it carefully that Trajan, though a pagan, had done a deed so charitable that it seemed more likely to have been the deed of a Christian than of a pagan.... When Gregory discovered the story ... [and] did not know what to do to comfort the soul of this man who brought the words of Christ to mind, he went to St. Peter's church and wept floods of tears, as was his custom, until he gained at last by divine revelation the assurance that his prayers were answered, seeing that he had never presumed to ask this of any other pagan." Anonymous Monk of Whitby, *The Earliest Life of Gregory the Great*, trans. Bertram Colgrave (Cambridge: Cambridge University Press, 1985), 127–29.

emperor's virtue,[179] and yet the author was clear that while anyone who has died "unrepentant and with an evil life cannot be helped by anyone in any way," those who have "departed even with the slightest virtue, but who had no time to increase this virtue because of indolence, indifference, procrastination, or timidity," will not be forgotten.[180]

Without a doubt, many Eastern fathers appear to support certain important aspects of what would become the doctrine of Purgatory. After all, they taught about "an intermediate state of souls" in which "the prayers, the liturgies and the suffrages ... of the Church contribute to their salvation."[181] The Greek fathers also spoke about the need for postmortem purification, and the pains of the testing/cleansing fire that accomplished it.[182] Yet what was largely missing from their discussions of the "middle state" was the notion of satisfaction for sin, a subject that would later come to dominate Western literature on the subject, especially in the Middle Ages. Perhaps this fact explains why later Byzantine theology found so many elements of the Latin teaching on the afterlife familiar, and other parts so completely and utterly foreign.

The Western Fathers on Purgatory

It should not surprise us that the Western fathers, wrestling with the same pastoral questions as the East concerning the state of souls after death, came to many of the same conclusions, albeit with some differences in emphasis. For example, while the efficacy of prayer for the deceased was taught by all, in the West there is early evidence that the chief purpose of these prayers was to relieve the suffering of the dead, for whom the middle state was a place of punishment. One can see early hints of this in the *Passion of Perpetua and Felicity*, an influential early third-century text which circulated in both Latin and Greek.[183] In the story, shortly before her death Perpetua was inspired to pray for her long-dead brother Dinocrates:

> I began to pray intensely for him and groan before the Lord. Immediately, on that very night this vision was shown to me. I saw Dinocrates coming out of a dark place where there were many others; he was very hot, thirsting, and his face was covered with dirt and his skin was pale. And he had that wound on his face which was there when he died.... And I awakened, and I knew that my brother was suffering. But

---

[179] In an email exchange with the author, Demetrios Bathrellos wrote that this was an important detail, "not only because to be virtuous is significant and decisive for the salvation of non-Christians, but also because this reference to the emperor's virtue seems to be an attempt to justify something not easily justifiable."

[180] Pseudo-Damascene, *De his qui in fide dormiunt*, 21; Eng. trans.: Jonathan Munn, *Anglican Catholicism: Unchanging Faith in a Changing World* (Anglican-Catholic Church, 2019), 228.

[181] Bathrellos, "Love, Purification, and Forgiveness versus Justice, Punishment, and Satisfaction," 114.

[182] Demetrios Bathrellos cautioned that the Greek fathers interpreted the suffering this process caused "not as [a] divine punishment, but rather as the self-inflicted consequence of sin"—e.g., what Origen called "the tortures of conscience," which was quite different than the Latin conception of suffering endured as satisfaction of a debt. Ibid., 115.

[183] See Jan Bremmer and Marco Formisano, eds., *Perpetua's Passions: Multidisciplinary Approaches to the Passio Perpetuae et Felicitatis* (Oxford: Oxford University Press, 2012); Thomas J. Heffernan, ed. and trans., *The Passion of Perpetua and Felicity* (Oxford: Oxford University Press, 2012).

I trusted that I could help him in his suffering.... And I prayed day and night for my brother with groans and tears so that this gift might be given to me. On the day on which we were kept in the stocks, this vision was shown to me. I saw that place which I had seen before, but now there was Dinocrates, his body clean, well dressed and refreshed, and where the wound was, I saw a scar.... He began to play in the water, rejoicing in the manner of children. And I woke up. I knew then that he was freed from his suffering.[184]

Curiosity about this middle state and the general geography of the afterlife sometimes led to other, more speculative, visions of the world to come, like the third-century *Apocalypse of Paul* (*Visio Sancti Pauli*).[185] This work "had the greatest influence on medieval literature concerned with the afterlife and with Purgatory in particular,"[186] despite its rejection by both Augustine and the Gelasian Decree.[187] Purporting to give an account of Paul's tour of the afterlife, several versions of the *Visio* survive, and include vivid descriptions of Heaven, Hell, and the various tortures inflicted upon sinners.[188] The author told how the suffering begged the archangel Michael to intercede for them before God, after which Christ granted them "a night and day of respite" not only for Michael's sake, but also "for the sake of your brethren who are in the world and offer oblations."[189] According to Le Goff, these notions—"the infernal tortures ... the distinction between a lower and upper Hell ... and a felt need to mitigate

---

[184] *The Martyrdom of Perpetua and Felicity* 7–8; Eng. trans.: Heffernan, *The Passion of Perpetua and Felicity*, 128–29.

[185] Although originally written in Greek, it appeared early in Latin translation, and greatly influenced later Western theology. For more see Theodore Silverstein, *Visio Sancti Pauli: The History of the Apocalypse in Latin Together with Nine Texts* (London: Christophers, 1935); Jan Bremmer and István Czachesz, eds., *The Visio Pauli and the Gnostic Apocalypse of Paul* (Leuven: Peeters, 2007); Lenka Jiroušková, *Die Visio Pauli: Wege und Wandlungen einer orientalischen Apokryphe im lateinischen Mittelalter unter Einschluß der alttschechischen und deutschsprachigen Textzeugen* (Leiden: Brill, 2006).

[186] Le Goff, *The Birth of Purgatory*, 35.

[187] "With a most foolish presumption, certain vain persons have devised an *Apocalypse of Paul*, which the sound Church does not accept, full of some fables or other, asserting that this it is about which he had said that he had been caught up to the third heaven and there had heard 'unspeakable words, which it is not granted to man to utter.'" Augustine of Hippo, *Tractates on the Gospel of John* 98.8; Eng. trans.: Augustine of Hippo, *Tractates on the Gospel of John*, 55–111, trans. John Rettig, FC 90 (Washington, DC: Catholic University of America Press, 1994), 217.

[188] "And I saw there a river boiling with fire, and in it a multitude of men and women immersed up to the knees, and other men up to the navel, others even up to the lips, others up to the hair. And I asked the angel and said, 'Sir, who are those in the fiery river?' And the angel answered and said to me, 'They are neither hot nor cold, because they were found neither in the number of the just nor in the number of the godless. For those spent the time of their life on earth passing some days in prayer, but others in sins and fornications, until their death.'" *Apocalypse of Paul* 31; Eng. trans.: J. K. Elliott, ed., *The Apocryphal New Testament: A Collection of Apocryphal Christian Literature in an English Translation* (Oxford: Oxford University Press, 1993), 633.

[189] "'Now, however, for the sake of Michael the archangel of my covenant and the angels who are with him, and because of Paul the well-beloved, whom I would not grieve, for the sake of your brethren who are in the world and offer oblations, and for the sake of your sons, because my commandments are in them, and more for the sake of my own kindness, on the day on which I rose from the dead, I give to you all who are in punishment a night and a day of refreshment forever.' And they all cried out and said, 'We bless you, Son of God, that you have given us a night and a day of respite.'" *Apocalypse of Paul* 44; Eng. trans.: Elliott, *The Apocryphal New Testament*, 639.

the tortures inflicted in the other world" by intercessory prayer all helped shape the description of Purgatory as it later emerged in the Middle Ages.¹⁹⁰

Tertullian, like many of the Eastern fathers, speculated that between death and the Last Judgment the souls of the just exist in a type of waiting area, which Luke had described as the bosom of Abraham (Luke 16:22).¹⁹¹ According to Tertullian, this temporary refreshment or refuge (*refrigerium interim* or *temporale receptaculum*) "although not in heaven ... is yet higher than hell and is appointed to afford an interval of rest to the souls of the righteous until the consummation of all things."¹⁹² He believed that martyrs alone entered Heaven upon their deaths,¹⁹³ while all other souls "are consigned to Hell ... [where] they suffer either punishment or reward [i.e., the *refrigerium interim*], according to the story of Lazarus and Dives."¹⁹⁴ Unlike Clement and Origen, Tertullian held that this postmortem suffering was neither "purgatorial" nor "pedagogical"—it was simply a preview of the punishment sinners would suffer for all eternity in the flesh.¹⁹⁵ He made clear that the chief purpose of this suffering was recompence for sin, for "if we understand the 'prison,' of which the Gospel (Matt 5:25–26) speaks, as Hell, and 'the last farthing' as the smallest defect that has to be atoned for there before the resurrection, there will be no doubt that the soul suffers in Hell some retributory penalty, without denying the complete resurrection, when the body also will pay or be paid in full."¹⁹⁶ From this prison "there is no release until every sin has been expiated in the period before the resurrection."¹⁹⁷

Interestingly, while holding that a person's position in the afterlife could not be improved, Tertullian still accepted that Christians should "make offerings for the dead on their anniversary to celebrate their birthday [into eternal life]."¹⁹⁸ He advocated

---

¹⁹⁰ Le Goff, *The Birth of Purgatory*, 37.

¹⁹¹ "Hades therefore has a place ('hell') for the souls of the wicked where they undergo punishment. Correspondingly, Hades also has a place for the souls of the faithful, called 'Abraham's bosom,' 'in which there exists already in outline an image of that which is to be' (*in quo iam delinietur futuri imago*) (Tertullian, *Against Marcion*, 4.34). Eliezer Gonzalez, *The Fate of the Dead in Early Third Century North African Christianity: The Passion of Perpetua and Felicitas and Tertullian* (Tübingen: Mohr Siebeck, 2014), 187.

¹⁹² Tertullian, *Against Marcion*, 4.34; ANF 3:406. "As long as the earth remains, Heaven is not open; in fact, the gates are barred. When the world shall have passed away, the portals of Paradise will be opened." Tertullian, *On the Soul* 55; Eng. trans.: Tertullian, *Apologetical Works and Minucius Felix Octavius*, trans. Rudolph Arbesmann, Sister Emily Joseph Daly, and Edwin A. Quain, FC 10 (Washington, DC: Catholic University of America Press, 1950), 299.

¹⁹³ "Those who die this new death for God, and violently as Christ did, are welcomed into a special abode." Ibid.

¹⁹⁴ Tertullian, *On the Soul* 58; Eng. trans.: Tertullian, *Apologetical Works*, 307. "Why don't you want to believe that souls are punished or rewarded in the meantime while awaiting the judgment to glory or damnation? There they remain in hopeful confidence while anticipating their fate. You feel that God's judgment ought to be definitive, and that no inkling of His sentence should be betrayed beforehand, and that punishment or reward must await the restoration of the flesh which should share the retribution of the deeds performed when they were together." Ibid.

¹⁹⁵ "It is most fitting that the soul, without waiting for the restoration of the flesh, should be punished for the sins it committed without help from the body. Likewise, it will be rewarded before the flesh is restored for the pious and kindly thought elicited independently of the body." Tertullian, *On the Soul* 58; Eng. trans.: Tertullian, *Apologetical Works*, 308.

¹⁹⁶ Tertullian, *On the Soul* 58; Eng. trans.: Tertullian, *Apologetical Works*, 309.

¹⁹⁷ Tertullian, *On the Soul* 35; Eng. trans.: Tertullian, *Apologetical Works*, 263.

¹⁹⁸ Tertullian, *On the Crown*, 3.3; Eng trans. Tertullian, *Disciplinary, Moral, and Ascetical Works*, trans. Rudolph Arbesmann, Sister Emily Joseph Daly, and Edwin A. Quain, FC 40 (Washington, DC: Catholic University of America Press, 1959), 237.

prayer for the deceased, telling widows that they should offer annual sacrifices and pray for the souls of their husbands, asking that "during the interval, [they] may find rest and ... share in the first resurrection."[199] Ultimately, however, Tertullian recognized that "if you demand a precise scriptural precept for these and other practices of church discipline, you will find none. Tradition, you will be told, has created it, custom has strengthened it, and faith has encouraged its observance."[200]

Cyprian of Carthage's *Letter to Antonianus* has traditionally been viewed as a witness to Purgatory, especially where he distinguished between those Christians "awaiting the granting of pardon" and those "achieving the heights of glory."[201] "It is one thing," he wrote,

> for [a person] to be thrown into prison and not emerge until he pays the very last farthing, and quite another thing for him to receive all at once the rewards for faith and valour; it is one thing for a man to be wracked by long grieving over his sins and to be purged and purified over a lengthy period of time by fire, and it is quite another thing for him to have purged away all his sins by a martyr's death. In a word, to hang in doubt on the day of judgment awaiting the verdict of the Lord is far different from being crowned by the Lord without a moment's delay.[202]

Modern scholarship, however, has been more hesitant, believing that Cyprian here is not referencing a postmortem place of purgation, but rather using "metaphorical language" to talk about the "cleansing works of penance" practiced by the *lapsi*.[203] The *lapsi*'s need for penance and forgiveness is compared with the instant glory awaiting the martyrs, and thus in this passage "It is not a question of 'Purgatory' in the hereafter, but of penitence here below."[204] One notable dissent from the new consensus was

---

[199] Tertullian, *On Monogamy* 10; Eng. trans.: Tertullian, *Treatises on Marriage and Remarriage: To His Wife, An Exhortation to Chastity, Monogamy*, trans. William Le Saint, ACW 13 (New York: Newman Press, 1951), 91–92.

[200] Tertullian, *On the Crown*, 4.1; Eng trans. Tertullian, *Disciplinary, Moral, and Ascetical Works*, 238.

[201] Cyprian of Carthage, *Letter 55.20*; Eng. trans.: Cyprian of Carthage, *The Letters of Cyprian of Carthage*, vol. 3, trans. G. W. Clarke, ACW 46 (New York: Newman Press, 1986), 45. "This purificatory suffering, this fire beyond the grave, can only be Purgatory. Though Cyprian has not yet achieved the clarity of expression that we find in later periods, he has already advanced beyond Tertullian." Albert Michel, "Purgatoire," *in* Alfred Vacant, Eugène Mangenot, and Émile Amann, eds., *Dictionnaire de théologie catholique, fasc CXVI-CXXI* (Paris: Letouzey, 1936), 1214.

[202] Cyprian of Carthage, *Letter 55.20*; Eng. trans.: Cyprian of Carthage, *The Letters of Cyprian of Carthage*, vol. 3, 45.

[203] The *lapsi* were those Christians who gave in during the persecutions. Cyprian of Carthage, *The Letters of Cyprian of Carthage*, vol. 3, 196. G. W. Clarke posits that Cyprian chose fire because it was "suitably painful yet purifying." Ibid. See esp. CHANGE CHECK IBIDPierre Jay, "Saint Cyprien et la doctrine du purgatoire," *Recherches de théologie* 27 (1960): 133–36.

[204] Le Goff, *The Birth of Purgatory*, 58. Brian Daley agreed, noting that Cyprian elsewhere explicitly denied the possibility of postmortem repentance, writing: "When there has been a withdrawal hence, then there is no opportunity for repentance, no accomplishment of satisfaction. Here life is either lost or kept; here by the worship of God, and by the fruit of faith provision is made for eternal salvation. Let no one either by sins or by years be retarded from coming to the acquiring of salvation. To him who still remains in this world no repentance is too late." Cyprian of Carthage, *Ad Demetrianum*, 25; Eng. trans.: Cyprian of Carthage, *Treatises*, trans. Roy Deferrari et al., FC 36 (Washington, DC: Catholic University of America Press, 1958), 190.

Joseph Ratzinger, who continued to see in this passage reference to a "penitential way of purification... [both] in this world [and] in the world to come."[205]

As Joachim Gnilka previously noted, central to the development of Purgatory in the West were the commentaries and glosses on 1 Corinthians 3:11–15, with its descriptions of a trial and refining by fire, an idea that became both "widespread and popular among ordinary Christians" during the patristic period.[206] Lactantius, for example, wrote how the just,

> when God will judge them, will be tried by Him with fire. Then, those whose sins shall warrant it, either by their weight or number, will be scorched with fire and burned. And when the fullness of their justice and maturity of virtue has been boiled free of dross, they will not feel the fire, for they have something of God in them which may, then, repel and ward off the power of the flame. So great is the power of innocence that that fire shrinks from it without doing harm, because it has received this power from God to burn the impious, and to refresh the just.[207]

Hilary of Poitiers maintained that each person was judged at death, and then "consigned either to Abraham's bosom or to punishment" until the final judgment.[208] On the Last Day, according to Hilary, the righteous will go directly to Heaven, unrepentant sinners and unbelievers will go Hell, and the rest will face 'the purification that burns us by the fire of judgment,'[209] which seems to indicate that "it is only the sinful believer, the person who is neither a committed disciple nor a hardened reprobate, who will actually need to be judged [by fire] at Christ's Second Coming."[210] Paulinus of Nola also spoke about this "judgmental" (*arbiter*), or "intelligent" (*sapiens*) fire, at which

> the great crowd of sinners not hostile to God will rise again, not to glory, but to be submitted to scrutiny.... Fire will be the judge and rush through every deed. Every act that the flame does not consume but approves will be allotted eternal reward. He who has done deeds which must be burned will suffer injury but will safely escape the flames; yet wretched because of the marks of his charred body.[211]

---

[205] Ratzinger, *Eschatology*, 224. "Certainly they [i.e., the *lapsi*] cannot, in their present condition, enter into definitive communion with Christ. Their denial, their half-heartedness, stands in the way. But they are capable of purification.... With this interpretation, that there is purification in the future life, the root concept of the Western doctrine of Purgatory is already formulated clearly enough." Ibid.

[206] Eno, "The Fathers and the Cleansing Fire," 191.

[207] Lactantius, *Divine Institutes* 7:21:6; Lactantius, *The Divine Institutes, Books I–VII*, trans. Sister Mary Francis McDonald, FC 49 (Washington, DC: Catholic University of America Press, 1964), 525. Unlike other Latin authors Lactantius denied that "souls are judged immediately after death. All are detained in one common custody, until the time will come when the Great Judge is to hold examination of merits." Ibid., 526.

[208] Trumbower, *Rescue of the Dead*, 103. During this period the mercy of God remains active, even if it is too late for confession and repentance: "There is hope of mercy in time and eternity; but there is confession in time only, and not in eternity." Hilary of Poitiers, *Commentary on Psalm 51.23*; Eng. trans.: Trumbower, *Rescue of the Dead*, 103.

[209] Le Goff, *The Birth of Purgatory*, 59.

[210] Daley, *Hope of the Early Church*, 98.

[211] Paulinus of Nola, *Carmina 7*; Eng. trans.: Paulinus of Nola, *The Poems of St Paulinus of Nola*, trans. P. G. Walsh, ACW 40 (New York: Newman Press, 1975), 51–52. Paulinus indicated later in the passage that as long as the sinner was "conquered by the flesh but not perverted in mind... in spite of his denying to the law

At times Ambrose of Milan appeared to agree with Hilary that the righteous went directly from the bosom of Abraham to Heaven without the need for further judgment,[212] although in several other texts he insisted that "*everyone* has to be tested by fire if they want to return to paradise ... even John the Evangelist."[213] The flaming sword of judgment, he wrote, passed through us all like a "consuming fire ... burning out of us the lead of iniquity and the iron of sin, making us pure gold."[214] While the saints were tested like silver (i.e., quickly and painlessly) most were tested like lead, "burning until the lead melts away."[215] Yet after experiencing it, "Each one of us, consumed but not destroyed by that fiery sword, will enter into the pleasures of paradise ... [for] he who has gone through fire will enter into rest."[216] Ambrose taught that this medicinal fire was different from the eternal fire, where those who had no silver or gold within them "shall, like straw, be totally burnt,"[217] rotting "in the place of fire and brimstone, where the fire is not quenched."[218]

While Ambrose believed the process of purification should ideally occur here on earth, he followed Gregory of Nyssa in teaching that cleansing would continue after death, since "those who are purified here must also be purified hereafter."[219] He even held that the prayers of the church could assist those completing this process—for example, the "tears and prayers" he offered for the emperor Theodosios so that he might "lead the man whither his merits summon, unto the holy mountain of God,

---

the allegiance which was its due by his frequent involvement in many sins, he will never be exiled from the shores of salvation, for he preserves the eternal glory of the faith." Ibid.

[212] "And so while we await the fullness of time, the souls await their due reward. Some await punishment and others glory. And yet in the meantime the one group is not without harm nor the other without gain.... [For the first group] have overcome the flesh and have not bent to its enticements. Then, that as the reward of their perseverance and their innocence they possess a composure ... [and are not] tormented with the recollection of their vices or tossed about, as it were, on tides of anxiety.... They are supported by God's testimony that they have kept the law so that they have no fear of any uncertain outcome of their deeds at the last judgment." Ambrose of Milan, *De bono mortis*; Eng. trans.: Ambrose of Milan, *Seven Exegetical Works*, trans. Michael McHugh, FC 65 (Washington, DC: Catholic University of America Press, 1972), 103–4.

[213] Ambrose of Milan, *In Psalmum CXVII, Sermo 20.12*; Eng. trans.: Ambrose of Milan, *Homilies of Saint Ambrose on Psalm 118 (119)*, trans. Íde M. Ní Riain (Dublin: Halcyon Press, 1998), 290. Concerning John, Ambrose knew that "some were doubtful that he would die, but that he had to pass through fire we cannot doubt, because he is in paradise and is not separated from Christ.... but the fiery sword will soon be turned aside for John, for no evil can be found in him whom justice loved. Had there been an element of human vice in him, divine love would have melted it away." Ibid.

[214] Ambrose of Milan, *In Psalmum CXVII, Sermo 3.16*; Eng. trans.: Ambrose of Milan, *Homilies of Saint Ambrose on Psalm 118 (119)*, 32.

[215] Ambrose of Milan, *In Psalmum CXVII, Sermo 20.13*; Eng. trans.: Ambrose of Milan, *Homilies of Saint Ambrose on Psalm 118 (119)*, 290.

[216] Ambrose of Milan, *In Psalmum CXVII, Sermo 3.16*; Eng. trans.: Ambrose of Milan, *Homilies of Saint Ambrose on Psalm 118 (119)*, 32.

[217] Ambrose of Milan, *In Psalmum CXVII, Sermo 20.13*; Eng. trans.: Ambrose of Milan, *Homilies of Saint Ambrose on Psalm 118 (119)*, 290.

[218] Ambrose of Milan, *De Fide* 2.13.119; NPNF 2.10.239. Ambrose made the distinction between the two types of fire in several places throughout his work: "This is a fire prepared by the Lord Jesus himself for his little servants to cleanse them by this delay from faults they have incurred among the Dead. There is another fire prepared for the devil and his angels." Ambrose of Milan, *In Psalmum CXVII, Sermo 3.17*; Eng. trans.: Ambrose of Milan, *Homilies of Saint Ambrose on Psalm 118 (119)*, 32.

[219] Ambrose of Milan, *In Psalmum CXVII, Sermo 3.16*; Eng. trans.: Ambrose of Milan, *Homilies of Saint Ambrose on Psalm 118 (119)*, 32.

where there is eternal life, where there is no corruption, no sickness, no mourning, no sorrow."[220]

Ambrosiaster's exegesis of 1 Corinthians 3:11–15, which was later quoted as the work of Ambrose himself, "had considerable influence on the medieval commentators ... [and] played a key role in the inception of Purgatory."[221] He equated the gold and silver Paul described with good teaching, and the baser materials with bad teaching, the latter "which will perish" in the flame even though "the man [i.e., the teacher] himself will be saved, because his substance will not perish in the same way his bad teaching will."[222] Yet if he is saved it is because "he will suffer punishments of fire and be saved only by being purged. Unlike complete unbelievers, he will not be tortured in eternal fire" because he was, despite his various shortcomings, a man of faith.[223] Important to note here is that for Ambrosiaster, as with Ambrose himself, salvation for all but unbelievers and the most hardened sinners was possible after cleansing, an eschatological optimism explained, in large part, by the influence of Origen.[224]

The individual who is often regarded as "the true father of Purgatory" is Augustine of Hippo, a saint also credited (or blamed) as the chief patristic witness to the Filioque, another divisive East-West issue.[225] Yet in many of his early works Augustine's views on the subject are actually "quite traditional," especially his understanding of the cleansing fire of 1 Corinthians 3:11–15.[226] In these texts Augustine's work echoed the optimism of Ambrose, maintaining that as long as Christ remained believers' foundation, they should not despair their eventual salvation, for "those who have built on this foundation in wood, hay, and stubble will be corrected, that is purged, [and] though they will suffer loss, they will be saved as if they had passed through fire."[227]

---

[220] Ambrose of Milan, *De Obit Theodosii*; Eng. trans.: Saint Gregory Nazianzen and Saint Ambrose, *Funeral Orations*, 323.

[221] Le Goff, *The Birth of Purgatory*, 61. In fact, at Ferrara-Florence it was one of the key Latin prooftexts for the doctrine.

[222] Ambrosiaster, *Commentary on Romans and 1-2 Corinthians*, 134.

[223] Ibid.

[224] According to Daley, "In general, Ambrose seems to sympathize with the Origenist doctrine of universal salvation, although he never makes it entirely clear how strictly universal he expects it to be. In the treatise on the resurrection that forms the second book *On the Death of his Brother* (*De Excessu Fratris*), he asserts that 'all who are considered to be joined to the holy church by being called by the divine name, shall obtain the privilege of the resurrection and the grace of eternal bliss.' (116) Other passages extend the certainty of salvation to all human beings. Ambrose never suggests, however, that the devils will also be included in that ultimate reconciliation." Daley, *Hope of the Early Church*, 99.

[225] Le Goff, *The Birth of Purgatory*, 61. See Pierre Jay, "Saint Augustin et la doctrine du purgatoire," *Recherches De Théologie Ancienne Et Médiévale* 36 (1969): 17–30; Joseph Ntedika, *L'évolution de la doctrine du purgatoire chez Saint Augustin* (Paris: Études augustiniennes, 1966).

[226] Eno, "The Fathers and the Cleansing Fire," 194.

[227] Augustine of Hippo, *Commentary on Psalm* 6.3; Eng. trans.: St. Augustine, *Exposition on the Psalms* vol. 1, trans. Maria Boulding (Hyde Park, NY: New City Press, 2000), 106. "By wood, clay, and straw we can recently understand desires for worldly things ... so strong that they cannot be lost without mental agony. And since such agony burns us, if Christ's foundation is in our heart, that is, in such a way that nothing is put before him, and the person on fire with this agony would rather be deprived of the things he so loves than be deprived of Christ, he is saved by fire.... The fire of which the apostle speaks in that place must be understood to be of such a kind that both pass through it—those who build on this foundation with gold, silver, and precious stones, and those who build with wood, clay, and straw ... so fire will test the work not only of one of the groups but of both.... [For the former] the pain of losing things he loves burns him, but without ruining or consuming him, since he has the protection of a foundation that is firm and without

Elsewhere he distinguished those who built with "gold, silver, and precious stones" by living upright lives, and those who "have been building in wood, hay, and straw by their self-indulgence and worldly concerns; nonetheless, because they had Christ as the foundation on which they built, he set fire to the hay and they remained firm on the foundation."[228] Significantly, he allowed "that something of the same kind could happen also after this life ... that some of the faithful are saved by a purifying fire (*ignem quemdam purgatorium*) more or less quickly depending on whether they have loved perishable good things more or less."[229]

Augustine also accepted without question the long-standing practice observed by "the whole church ... [and] received from the fathers, that prayer should be offered for those who have died in the communion of the body and blood of Christ."[230] For "Whenever their names are mentioned at the sacrifice ... [or] works of mercy are performed for their sakes, who can doubt that this benefits those for whom [the] prayers" are said."[231] Famously, in relating the story of his mother's death in Book 9 of the *Confessions*, Augustine wrote how Monica's last request to her sons was that they should "remember [her] at the altar of the Lord, wherever you may be,"[232] an obligation Augustine readily accepted,[233] asking his readers to do the same.[234]

As for the benefits of these prayers, they fell chiefly on those who were "neither so good that these things are not necessary after death, nor so bad that they are of no use."[235] For just as it was pointless to pray for the martyrs ("to whose prayers we ought rather to commend ourselves"),[236] it was useless to pray for "those whose lives [were]

---

decay." Augustine of Hippo, *Enchiridion on Faith, Hope, and Charity* 18.68–69; Eng. trans.: St. Augustine, *On Christian Belief*, trans. Edmund Hill (Hyde Park, NY: New City Press, 2005), 314–15.

[228] Augustine of Hippo, *Exposition 2 on Psalm 29.9*; Eng. trans.: St. Augustine, *Exposition on the Psalms* vol. 1, 308.

[229] Augustine of Hippo, *Enchiridion on Faith, Hope, and Charity* 18.68–69; Eng. trans.: St. Augustine, *On Christian Belief*, 315.

[230] Augustine of Hippo, *Sermon 172*; Eng. trans.: Augustine of Hippo, *Essential Sermons*, trans. Edmund Hill (Hyde Park, NY: New City Press, 2007), 234.

[231] Ibid. The genesis of this practice, according to Augustine, can be traced back to "the books of the Maccabees [where] we read of sacrifice offered for the dead. Howbeit even if it were nowhere at all read in the Old Scriptures, not small is the authority, which in this usage is clear, of the whole Church, namely, that in the prayers of the priest which are offered to the Lord God at His altar, the commendation of the dead has also its place." Augustine of Hippo, *De cura pro mortuis*; NPNF 1.3.540. See also Paula Rose, *A Commentary on Augustine's De cura pro mortuis gerenda: Rhetoric in Practice* (Leiden: Brill, 2013), 107–13.

[232] Augustine of Hippo, *Confessions* 9.11.27; Eng. trans.: Augustine of Hippo, *Confessions*, trans. Vernon Bourke, FC 21 (Washington, DC: Catholic University of America Press, 1953), 254.

[233] "I now pray to Thee for the sins of my mother. Hear me through the remedy of [y]our wounds, who hung upon the Cross, and who, sitting at Thy right hand, intercedes with Thee for us. I know that she acted mercifully and from her heart, 'forgave her debtors their debts': do Thou also forgive her her debts, if she contracted any during the many years following the water of salvation.'" Augustine of Hippo, *Confessions* 9.13.35; Eng. trans.: Augustine of Hippo, *Confessions*, 260.

[234] "And inspire, O my Lord, my God, inspire Thy servants, my brethren, Thy children, my masters, those whom I serve with heart and voice and pen, so that, as many as read these words may remember at Thy altar Thy servant Monica, and Patricius her onetime spouse, those through whose flesh Thou didst introduce me to this life." Augustine of Hippo, *Confessions* 9.13.37; Eng. trans.: Augustine of Hippo, *Confessions*, 261–62.

[235] Augustine of Hippo, *Enchiridion on Faith, Hope, and Charity* 29.110; Eng. trans.: St. Augustine, *On Christian Belief*, 336.

[236] "That's why, as the faithful know, Church custom has it that at the place where the names of the martyrs are recited at God's altar, we don't pray for them, while we do pray for the other departed brothers and sisters who are remembered there. It is insulting, I mean, to pray for martyrs, to whose prayers we

so evil that ... such things cannot help them."²³⁷ However, the bulk of humanity, awaiting the resurrection and final judgment "in hidden places of rest or punishment," did benefit in some way from "the piety of their loved ones who are alive when the sacrifice of the mediator is offered for them or alms are given them in the church."²³⁸

According to Joseph Ntedika, Augustine's views on the afterlife underwent a change following his post-413 battles with the *misericordes* ("the merciful-hearted who refuse to believe that the punishments of hell will be eternal"), when he began to speak more forcefully about the eternal punishments meted out to sinners in the world to come.²³⁹ It was during this period that Augustine, combating those who "insist[ed] that *all* punishments are meant to serve remedial purposes,"²⁴⁰ "adopted a tripartition [of the afterlife] into hell, Purgatory, and paradise," more clearly distinguishing the *poenae sempiternae* (eternal punishments) of Hell from the *poenae temporariae* (temporary punishments) and *tormenta purgatoria* (purgatorial torments) undergone in the *ignis purgatorius* (purgatorial fire).²⁴¹ For his part Augustine was clear that the eternal fire, where Christ himself thrice affirmed that the "worm dies not, and the fire is not

---

ought rather to commend ourselves. They have tackled sin, after all, to the point of shedding their blood." Augustine of Hippo, *Sermon 159*; Eng. trans.: St. Augustine, *Sermons*, vol. III/5, trans. Edmund Hill (Hyde Park: New City Press, 1992), 121.

²³⁷ Augustine believed that it was only on earth "that we accrue all the merit or demerit that can either support a person or weigh him down.... Nobody should hope to gain in the sight of the Lord after death what he has neglected here." Augustine of Hippo, *Enchiridion on Faith, Hope, and Charity* 29.110; Eng. trans.: St. Augustine, *On Christian Belief*, 336. This meant that "there can be no doubt at all that [prayers and oblations] are of value to the departed; but [only] to such of them as lived in such a way before they died, as would enable them to profit from these things after death. For those, you see, who have departed from their bodies without the faith that works through love and its sacraments, acts of piety of this sort are performed in vain. While they were still here they lacked the guarantee of this faith either because they did not receive God's grace at all, or received it in vain.... So no new merits are won for the dead when their good Christian friends do any work on their behalf.... [For] [i]t was only while they lived here that they could ensure that such things would be of help to them after they ceased to live here." Augustine of Hippo, *Sermon 172*; Eng. trans.: Augustine of Hippo, *Essential Sermons*, 234. For similar statements see Augustine of Hippo, *City of God* 21.24; Eng. trans.: Saint Augustine, *The City of God Books 11–22*, trans. William Babcock (Hyde Park, NY: New City Press, 2013), 479.

²³⁸ Augustine of Hippo, *Enchiridion on Faith, Hope, and Charity* 29.110; Eng. trans.: St. Augustine, *On Christian Belief*, 336–37. Augustine was clear that these prayers "are not [equally] beneficial ... because of the differences between the life that each person lived in the body. So when sacrifices, whether that of the altar or sacrifices of alms, are offered for all the baptized who are dead, for the truly good they are acts of thanksgiving, for those who are not truly good they are propitiatory, and, as far as the truly evil are concerned, although they are of no help to the dead, they offer some kind of consolation to the living." Ibid. Le Goff pointed out that "not a single sentence in any of Augustine's writings suggests a connection between these suffrages and purgatorial fire." Le Goff, *The Birth of Purgatory*, 66.

²³⁹ Ntedika, *L'évolution de la doctrine du purgatoire chez Saint Augustin*, 19. Le Goff believed that prior to this controversy Augustine showed a general "lack of interest in the fate of the soul between death and the Last Judgment," his later interest perhaps brought about by the realization that "the Bible was imprecise, not to say contradictory" on the subject of the hereafter." Le Goff, *The Birth of Purgatory*, 62–63.

²⁴⁰ "The Platonists, of course, although they want to maintain that no sins go unpunished, still insist that all punishments are meant to serve remedial purposes whether they are imposed by human or Divine laws, and whether they are imposed in this life or after death." Augustine of Hippo, *City of God* 21.13; Eng. trans.: Saint Augustine, *The City of God Books 11–22*, 467–68.

²⁴¹ These distinctions, according to Le Goff, later became the chief "ingredients" in the doctrine of Purgatory. Le Goff, *The Birth of Purgatory*, 63. See also Ilaria Ramelli, "Origen in Augustine: A Paradoxical Reception," *Numen* 60 (2013): 280–307.

quenched" (Mk 9:43–48) was both real and material, and should not be interpreted merely as the anguish of a soul that "repented too late and thus uselessly."[242]

In *De fide et operibus*, written in 413, Augustine "strongly and clearly rejected an interpretation of the cleansing fire and of 1 Cor 3:15" that would have "maintained that all orthodox Christians would be saved—eventually—however evil their lives may have been."[243] Mere belief was not enough since "Scripture testified in the clearest terms that faith achieves nothing, unless it is faith as the apostle defines it, namely, the faith that works through love."[244] For Augustine, only when the foundation was "Christ's faith, the faith of Christian grace, the faith that works through love" could the believer avoid perishing in the eternal flame, meaning that those who committed acts of "murder, adultery, fornication, idolatry, and anything like that ... [would] not be saved by fire ... [but would] suffer torment in the eternal fire."[245] The purifying fire was not meant for serious sinners, but rather for good, but imperfect, Christians who only required that the last of their worldly attachments be burned away.[246] It was also for those who died with penalties for sin yet unpaid, as Augustine was among the first to explicitly make "the connection between penitence and Purgatory, which would assume such great importance in the twelfth and thirteenth centuries."[247]

Because postmortem purification was painful as well as salvific, Augustine warned that Christians should by no means trivialize the "correcting fire" (*emendatorio igne*), for although "it will be for some the means of salvation, [it] will nevertheless be harder to bear than anything we can endure in this life.... How much better advised would [believers] be to do what God orders them to escape far more severe penalties!"[248]

---

[242] "But some people want both of these—that is, both the fire and the worm—to refer to the punishment not of the body but of the soul. They claim that those who will be separated from the kingdom of God, because they repented too late and thus uselessly, will burn with anguish of soul; and so they contend that fire could not unsuitably be used for this burning anguish.... I still find it easier to hold that both worm and fire refer to the body than that neither does. And in my view, the reason why the Divine Scripture does not specifically mention the soul's pain using these terms is that it is understood to follow (even if it is not explicitly stated) that, when the body is in so much pain the soul will also be tormented by fruitless repentance." Augustine of Hippo, *City of God* 21.9; Eng. trans.: Saint Augustine, *The City of God Books 11–22*, 463–64.

[243] Eno, "The Fathers and the Cleansing Fire," 196. See Augustine of Hippo, *On Faith and Works*, 15.24–16.30; Eng. trans.: Saint Augustine, *On Christian Belief*, 243–48.

[244] Ibid., 245.

[245] Ibid., 246–47.

[246] Augustine of Hippo, *Enchiridion on Faith, Hope, and Charity* 18.69; Eng. trans.: St. Augustine, *On Christian Belief*, 315. According to Le Goff, although he did not detail the kinds of sins that needed to be cleansed in the purgatorial fire, in differentiating serious (i.e., damnable) "crimes" (*crimina*) from "slight" "minor" "petty" and "quotidian" sins (*levia, minuta, minutissima, minora, minima, modica, parva, brevia, quotidiana*) that do not necessarily destroy the possibility of salvation, Augustine recognized the distinction between what would later be called "mortal" and "venial" sins." Le Goff, *The Birth of Purgatory*, 70.

[247] Le Goff, *The Birth of Purgatory*, 73. This move, from the "amnesty of God" to the need for penitential satisfaction, is traced by Peter Brown in "Vers la naissance du purgatoire. Amnistie et pénitence dans le christianisme occidental de l'Antiquité tardive au haut Moyen Âge," 1247–61. According to Isabel Moreira, Augustine "insisted that all humans owed a debt of pain, and so all, with the possible exception of martyrs, must suffer some punishment after death." Moreira, *Heaven's Purge*, 32. See also Robert Atwell, "From Augustine to Gregory the Great: An Evaluation of the Emergence of the Doctrine of Purgatory," *Journal of Ecclesiastical History* 38 (1987): 173–86.

[248] Augustine of Hippo, *Commentary on Psalm* 37.3; Eng. trans.: St. Augustine, *Exposition on the Psalms*, vol. 2, trans. Maria Boulding (Hyde Park, NY: New City Press, 2000), 147–48. Both Eno and Le Goff noted that Augustine's description of the fire as a sort of "temporary Hell" paved the way for the medieval infernalization of Purgatory. See Eno, "The Fathers and the Cleansing Fire," 196; and Le Goff, *The Birth of Purgatory*, 84.

He told his listeners to avoid sin and build "on gold, or silver, or precious stones," in order to be "safe from both kinds of fire: not only the eternal fire which will torture the impious forever, but even that which will chasten those who are to be saved through it."[249] Instead of enduring punishments after death, believers should "cultivate" their souls here and now, so that like the farmer who has tilled the field and earned his "bread even though with much toil" he ensured that his pains were "only sensed, only experienced, in this life alone" and thus could "rest rather than suffer at the end of [his] journey."[250] For Augustine, those who "fail[ed] to cultivate the field, and allow[ed] it to be overrun with thorns and thistles ... after this life will have to face either the fires of Purgatory or eternal punishment [*habebit vel ignem purgationis vel poenam aeternam*]."[251]

Yet despite his running battle with the *misericordes* Augustine continued to advocate prayer for the deceased as a way of bringing about either "full remission of [their] punishment" or making "condemnation itself more tolerable."[252] This implied that in the intermediate state before the Last Judgment there were "two classes of people suffering.... the damned and those who are in reality saved but need to be punished for their lesser sins and purified by fire."[253] In the *City of God* he wrote:

> As for temporal punishments some suffer them only in this life, others after death, and still others both in this life and after death, but always prior to the final and most severe judgment [*ante iudicium illud severissimum novissimumque*]. Nor does everyone who undergoes temporal punishments after death come under the eternal punishments which will follow that judgment. For, as we have already said, there are some for whom what is not forgiven in this world will be forgiven in the world to come and these will not be punished in the eternal punishment of the world to come.[254]

---

[249] Augustine of Hippo, *Commentary on Psalm 37*.3; Eng. trans.: St. Augustine, *Exposition on the Psalms* vol. 2, 148.

[250] Augustine of Hippo, *On Genesis: A Refutation of the Manichees* 2.20.30; Eng. trans.: Saint Augustine, *On Genesis*, trans. Matthew O'Connell (Hyde Park, NY: New City Press, 2002), 91–92.

[251] Ibid.

[252] Augustine of Hippo, *Enchiridion on Faith, Hope, and Charity* 29.110; Eng. trans.: St. Augustine, *On Christian Belief*, 337.

[253] Eno, "The Fathers and the Cleansing Fire," 197. Those suffering these temporary punishments endured what Ntedika called "a provisionary condemnation" (*condemnation provisoire*) which did not anticipate, as it did for others, their ultimate condemnation to the eternal fire. Ntedika, *L'évolution de la doctrine du purgatoire chez Saint Augustin*, 12.

[254] Augustine of Hippo, *City of God* 21.13; Eng. trans.: Saint Augustine, *The City of God Books 11–22*, 468. Later in the same work he wrote that "even after the resurrection of the dead has taken place, there will be some to whom mercy will be granted after they have suffered the punishments inflicted on the spirits of the dead, and they will not be thrown into eternal fire. For it could not be true to say that some will not be forgiven, either in this world or the world to come, unless it were also true to say that some will be forgiven in the world to come, even though they were not forgiven in this world." Augustine of Hippo, *City of God* 21.24; Eng. trans.: Saint Augustine, *The City of God Books 11–22*, 479. Interesting to note in this text is the fact that for Augustine release from these temporary punishments appears to take place only at the resurrection, although in other places he wrote that the time spent in the purgatorial fire was slow or quick "depending on whether they [i.e., the dead] have loved perishable good things more or less."

Among the things Augustine did not address was where these temporary punishments took place—that is, the location of the purgatorial fire, especially in relation to Hell. Le Goff speculated that this was because "in order to do so he would have had to echo more or less 'popular' beliefs ... embedded in the apocalyptic and apocryphal tradition that he rejected."[255] Yet in detailing the nature of the purgatorial fire and the pains associated with it, Augustine laid the foundation for the later Western teaching, creating a "pre-Purgatory" of fire upon which the Latin doctrine was built.[256]

Caesarius of Arles, in two influential sermons later attributed to Augustine, spoke of those who "have committed deeds worthy of temporal punishments" and before entering Heaven must first "pass through the stream of fire ... through the river of flame and a terrible lake of boiling masses ... [where] the reasonable discipline of flames will punish a man as much as his guilt demands, and wise punishment will range as long as foolish iniquity committed sin."[257] In *Sermon 179* he railed against those who used 1 Corinthians 3:11–15 in order to deny the reality of eternal punishment, "deceiving themselves with a false assurance" because they believed "that if they build serious sins (*capitalia crimina*) upon the foundation of Christ, those very offenses can be purified by transitory flames (*per ignem transitorium*), and they themselves can later reach eternal life."[258] According to Caesarius, Paul deliberately excluded serious sins (e.g., "sacrilege, murder, adultery. false testimony, theft, robbery. pride, envy, avarice ... anger, [and] drunkenness") from those that could be purged in the fire, intending only certain "petty" (*parva*) or "daily" (*quotidiana*) sins such as "rising too late for church" or "knowing [one's] wife without the desire for children."[259] Yet even these slight offenses (*minuta peccata*) required redemption "by constant prayer, frequent fasting, [and] more abundant almsgiving" so that "whatever remains of these sins" after our efforts can be "purged in that fire of which the Apostle" spoke and "consumed like wood, hay, and straw."[260] Like Augustine, Caesarius warned Christians not to delay their efforts because of an overreliance on the fire's cleansing power, for "the fire of Purgatory will be more difficult than any punishment in this world can be seen or imagined or felt.... For this reason, let each one labor with all his strength to avoid serious sins, and to redeem his slight offenses by good works in such a way that either very little or nothing of them may be seen to remain for that fire to consume."[261]

Perhaps the most quoted patristic passage in support of Purgatory is found in the *Dialogues* of Pope Gregory the Great, the "eschatological pastor"[262] who in Book Four wrote about the visions and miracles that proved the soul's survival after death and the

---

[255] Le Goff, *The Birth of Purgatory*, 84.
[256] Ibid.
[257] Caesarius of Arles, *Sermon 167*; Eng. trans.: Saint Caesarius of Arles, *Sermons, Volume II (81–186)*, trans. Sister Mary Magdeleine Mueller, FC 47 (Washington, DC: Catholic University of America Press, 1963), 407.
[258] Caesarius of Arles, *Sermon 179*; Eng. trans.: Saint Caesarius of Arles, *Sermons, Volume II (81–186)*, 450.
[259] Ibid., 450–51.
[260] Ibid., 452.
[261] Ibid., 453.
[262] Le Goff, *The Birth of Purgatory*, 88. "In all his words and acts Gregory considered that the final day and coming judgment were immanent; the closer he felt the end of the world was coming with its numerous disasters the more carefully he pondered human affairs." Paul the Deacon, *Vita Sancti Gregorii Magni* 4.65; Eng. trans.: Daley, *Hope of the Early Church*, 211.

reality of the *purgatorius ignis* for certain minor sins.[263] Asked by Peter the Deacon "if we have to believe in a cleansing fire after death,"[264] Gregory answered:

> It is clear that each one is presented in judgment just as he is when he departs from here. Nevertheless, we should believe that there is a purgatorial fire (*purgatorius ignis*) for certain minor faults, for the truth says that if anyone should have blasphemed against the Holy Spirit, it will be forgiven him neither in this age nor in the future (Matthew 12:32). In such a statement one is given to believe that some faults are forgiven (*laxari*) in this age and some in the future. For if it is denied for one then it logically follows that it is granted for others. As I have said, this must be believed to be a possibility for small and slight sins (*peccata minima atque levissima*) such as persistent idle talking, immoderate laughter, sinful care of property, which can hardly be administered without fault even by those who know the fault to be avoided, or the error of ignorance in non-important matters. For all these are burdensome after death if they are not forgiven while still in this life.... Although [the fire mentioned in 1 Cor 3:11–15] may be understood as the fire of suffering (*igne tribulationis*) applied to us in this life, yet if one may also take this as the fire of future purgation (*igne futurae purgationis*) it should be pondered carefully that Paul said that one can be saved through fire—not he who builds on this foundation in iron, bronze, or lead, that is, major sins (*peccata maiora*) which are more burdensome and therefore indestructible—but he who builds in wood, hay, or straw, which are the little and small sins, which fire easily consumes. Therefore, we should know that no one will obtain purgation of even the smallest sins there unless through good works while here in this life he should merit to obtain it there.[265]

Gregory then went on to illustrate the teaching using the story of Paschasius, "a deacon of the Apostolic See ... [and] a man of outstanding sanctity" who, "through ignorance and not through malice," took the wrong side in a disputed papal election.[266] After Paschasius's death the bishop of Capua went to the baths and saw him working as a lowly attendant, sentenced to do so for the sin of having endorsed the wrong candidate. "Pray for me to the Lord," he begged the bishop. "When you come back and no longer find me here you will know that your prayers have been heard."[267] After days of fervent prayer the bishop returned and did not see Paschasius, who (according to Gregory) "through his previous almsdeeds ... obtained the grace of receiving forgiveness at a time when he was no longer able to do meritorious works."[268] Later Gregory told of another spirit, disguised as a man, who because of his sins was sent back to earth to work at a bathhouse. When a grateful priest gave him some bread as a gift, he refused it, saying, "If you wish to do something for me, then offer this bread to

---

[263] See Marilyn Dunn, "Gregory the Great, the Vision of Fursey, and the Origins of Purgatory," *Peritia* 14 (2000): 238–54.
[264] Gregory the Great, *Dialogues*, 4.4; Eng. trans.: Gregory the Great, *Dialogues*, trans. Odo John Zimmerman, FC 39 (Washington, DC: Catholic University of America Press, 1959), 247.
[265] Ibid., 248–49.
[266] Ibid., 249–50.
[267] Ibid., 250.
[268] Ibid., 249–50.

Almighty God, and so make intercession for me, a sinner.... The priest spent the entire week in prayer and tearful supplications, offering mass for him daily. When he returned to the bath, the man was no longer to be found."[269] For Gregory these stories proved "the great benefits souls derive from the sacrifice of the mass ... and even show us by signs that it was through the mass that they were pardoned."[270]

Interesting to note in both of these stories is how the spirits of the dead were sent back to suffer in *this* world, for it seemed fitting to Gregory that "men should be punished where they sinned," and the sight of their crimes become a "penal place" (*in hoc loco poenali*).[271] In later centuries, when "the spectacles of Purgatory ... were transferred to a special theater, not of this world but of the next," these ideas about an earthly purgation were among "the first to be sacrificed" even though these stories still had a great effect on subsequent piety.[272] While Gregory had no doubt that the eternal fire was real, his desire "to save as many people as possible" before the end simply led him to share stories of how the fate of the departed could be ameliorated by the prayers and actions of the faithful, which were just as real and just as important.[273]

Another of Gregory's contributions concerned the geography of the afterlife, for by distinguishing between an "upper hell ('what may have been what was later identified as the Limbo of the Fathers') where the righteous reside, and lower hell, where the wicked reside" one gets the first hints of Purgatory's location.[274] By the end of the seventh century "the concept of a special place of atonement in the otherworld from which a soul could be freed even before Judgment Day by the prayers and masses offered by the living was already clearly formulated in the Anglo-Saxon *Vision of Dryhthelm*."[275]

---

[269] Ibid., 267.

[270] Ibid. Gregory told a similar story of a monk in his own monastery named Justus who had died and was found to have kept a secret stash of gold. After thirty days of masses the monk appeared to one of the brothers and told how "up to this moment I was in misery ... but now I am well, because this morning I was admitted to communion [in Heaven]." Ibid., 268.

[271] Le Goff, *The Birth of Purgatory*, 94.

[272] Ibid. According to Moreira, these stories were reminders that because "the dead are still visible to the living and can be recalled to mind, the living are still a recourse for them and can improve their fate." Moreira, *Heaven's Purge*, 91.

[273] Jerry Walls, *Purgatory: The Logic of Total Transformation* (Oxford: Oxford University Press, 2012), 16. "In the years that followed his death ... the power of the Holy Sacrifice was to assume near-magical proportions, and the assistance of the saints was to be seen not simply as advantageous but vital." Atwell, "From Augustine to Gregory the Great," 186.

[274] Walls, *Purgatory*, 16.

[275] Marina Smyth, "The Origins of Purgatory through the Lens of Seventh-Century Irish Eschatology," *Traditio* 58 (2003): 126. "The valley that you saw, with its awful flaming fire and freezing cold, is the place in which those souls have to be tried and chastened who delayed to confess and make restitution for the sins they had committed until they were on the point of death; and so they died. But because they did repent and confess, even though on their deathbed, they will all come to the kingdom of heaven on judgment day; and the prayers of those who are still alive, their alms and fastings and specially the celebration of masses, help many of them to get free even before the day of judgment." Bede, *The Ecclesiastical History of the English People*, 5.12; Eng. trans.: Bede, *The Ecclesiastical History of the English People*, 256. A similar vision was recounted by Boniface in the "Vision of the Monk of Wenlock," in which souls came to the New Jerusalem by crossing a bridge placed over a river of boiling pitch (*Tartareum flumen*). When some fell in they emerged more beautiful than ever, since their "light sins" were removed "by the kindly chastisements of a merciful God." Moreira, *Heaven's Purge*, 150. See also Andrew Rabin, "Bede, Dryhthelm, and the Witness to the Other World: Testimony and Conversion in the *Historia Ecclesiastica*," *Modern Philology* 106 (2009): 375–98.

Although Le Goff claimed that little happened in the development of Purgatory from Gregory until the twelfth century, more recent research has examined the pivotal role played by the Venerable Bede (c. 672–735). For scholars such as Isabel Moreira, Bede provides "evidence that the rise of Purgatory ... [was] a direct response to, and repudiation of, universal salvation and the Origenist views of purgation that had supported it."[276] It was "an orthodox variation on universalism" that affirmed the reality of the eternal fire while still offering "the hope of salvation to a wider range of persons, including those guilty of serious sins, so long as they partook of the sacraments, confessed their sins, and were willing to do penance."[277] She noted that Bede's view, although still solidly Augustinian, effectively meant "that many more persons were eligible for final salvation than he [i.e., Augustine] had allowed," with particular emphasis on the power of intercession by one's "faithful friends" (*amici fideles*) to speed one's journey through the pain of purgation.[278] Presenting Purgatory as doctrine rather than speculation, Bede wrote in his *Homilies for Advent* that

> there are some who are preordained to the lot of the elect on account of their good works, but on account of some evils by which they were polluted went out from the body after death to be severely chastised and were seized by the flames of the fire of Purgatory (*flammis ignis purgatorii*). They are either made clean from the stains of their vices and their long ordeal (*examinatione*) up until Judgment Day, or, on the other hand, if they are absolved from their penalties by the petitions, almsgiving, fasting, weeping, and oblation of the saving sacrificial offering by their faithful friends, they may come earlier for the rest of the blessed.[279]

In summary, the writings of the Latin fathers make it clear that they, like the Greeks, accepted many of the teachings upon which the medieval doctrine of Purgatory would be built—for example, the intermediate state of souls before the Last Judgment, the benefits of prayers, liturgies, and suffrages for the dead, and the judgment by fire during which sins, especially minor sins, could be cleansed. However, the Latin tradition stressed, far more than the Greek, the penitential nature of this process, as the purgative fire came to be described in more punishing and painful terms than Basil's

---

[276] Moreira, *Heaven's Purge*, 164–65.
[277] Ibid., 165. Marina Smyth cited the *Vision of Fursey* and Adomnan's *Life of Columba* as witnesses to "an awareness and even endorsement of [the] point of view ... that a finite period of painful purification immediately follows the death of most Christians." Smyth, "The Origins of Purgatory through the Lens of Seventh-Century Irish Eschatology," 91. See also Sarah Foot, "Anglo-Saxon 'Purgatory,'" *Studies in Church History* 45 (2009): 87–96.
[278] Moreira, *Heaven's Purge*, 165–66.
[279] Bede, *Homily for Advent*; Eng. trans.: Bede the Venerable, *Homilies on the Gospels: Book One—Advent to Lent*, trans. Lawrence Martin and David Hurst, CS 110 (Athens, OH: Cistercian Publicans, 1991), 17. Moreira, citing the work of Henry G. J. Beck ("A Ninth-Century Canonist on Purgatory," *American Ecclesiastical Review* 111.4 [1944]: 250–56) and M. Thomas Aquinas Carroll ("An Eighth-Century Exegete on Purgatory," *American Ecclesiastical Review* 112.1 [1945]: 261–63) noted that Bede's use of *flammis ignis purgatorii* could be the earliest use of Purgatory as a noun.

"way station" on the way to Heaven.[280] By the medieval period, Latin theologians concluded that since the punishments endured by the wicked in Hell were eternal, whatever temporary pains were endured by those undergoing penance and purification must take place somewhere else. Purgatory, understood as a separate place of cleansing and restitution in the "fire that saves," was the result.

---

[280] See n. 245.

7
Purgatory in the Thirteenth and Fourteenth Centuries

By the beginning of the thirteenth century there were already a host of issues dividing Christian East and West. The Filioque, azymes, and the primacy were by this time already major points of contention, not to mention the dozens of liturgical and canonical differences that filled the lists of Latin errors produced after 1204. There was enough fuel to keep the fires of hatred burning on both sides, which is why the addition of a new fire, the *ignis purgatorius*, seemed remarkably unnecessary. Yet very soon after its introduction as an ecumenical stumbling block in the 1230s Purgatory became a regular feature of the polemical literature on both sides, soon eclipsing clerical marriage, fasting regulations, and other ritual differences as a chief point of division.

As it had been with the Filioque, the problem for the Greeks was that the Latins came to the debate better prepared, in that Western theology had spent the previous century—what Le Goff called "the century of the great advance"—developing both a far more detailed penitential system and geography of the afterlife than their Greek counterparts.[1] By the time the debate began, Purgatory already played a key role in Latin theology, intimately connected to prayers and masses for the dead, the granting of indulgences, and medieval notions of retributive justice. The Greeks, who had remained content with the fathers' ambiguity on the fate of souls after death, were puzzled by the language and concepts being employed by their Latin counterparts and responded with more questions than answers. One particular question the Greeks had concerned Purgatory's alleged relationship to Origenism (i.e., the doctrine of *apocatastasis*, or universal salvation), since the belief that sinners' punishments in the fire would eventually end sounded very much like the teaching of the condemned Alexandrian. The Latins tried to explain and defended their position, differentiating the cleansing fire of Purgatory from the eternal fires of Hell, but the Greeks remained leery, especially since the infernalization of Purgatory made it sound more like a temporary Hell than Heaven's waiting room.

By the mid-thirteenth century the *Tractatus contra graecos* listed Purgatory as one of the chief dogmatic issues preventing the union of East and West. For the Latins, Purgatory had become a central tenet of the Catholic faith and a nonnegotiable for union, and thus the relative flexibility they exhibited during the beard and azyme debates was not in evidence here. In fact, it was Pope Innocent IV's desire to impose the teaching on the Greeks that led to the 1254 definition of Purgatory that eventually became the doctrine's "birth certificate."[2] Yet despite the pope's efforts, and those of the Greek unionists writing after Lyons, Purgatory never found widespread acceptance

---

[1] Le Goff, *The Birth of Purgatory*, 130.
[2] Ibid., 283.

in the East, and debate on the issue continued throughout the fourteenth century and into the fifteenth.

The Latin Background

Aside from the writings of the Venerable Bede mentioned in the last chapter, several other developments took place in the early medieval period that helped prepare the groundwork for Purgatory as it would later be formulated. Among these was the celebration of the "Day of the Dead" or "All Souls Day" (November 2) that began at Cluny at some point between 1024 and 1033.[3] Inspired by the necrologies ("lists of the dead kept in the margins of a calendar and read out at the office of prime") that encouraged monastic prayers for the deceased by name, the feast seems to have been inaugurated to widen the practice and "extend the benefits of the liturgy to all the dead," regardless of rank.[4] Once it spread, the day was "set aside to perform suffrages for the dead in the form of prayers, masses, and alms for the poor, in order to hasten their respite from the purging fires ... creat[ing] a solemn bond between living and dead."[5] "The dead, especially those in need of suffrages, now had a day of their own in the calendar of the Church, ... mark[ing] an essential milestone" in the creation of Purgatory.[6]

Two other key developments were the growth of the penitential system, whereby specific sins were assigned particular penances based on their severity, and the birth of indulgences, allowing the church to reduce or remit these penalties in exchange for the performance of some holy act (e.g., fasting or pilgrimage).[7] In 1095 that act became a heavily armed pilgrimage to Jerusalem "to liberate the church of God," in exchange for which the pilgrim received an indulgence for the complete remission of "all penances." Modern scholars debate the meaning of this phrase—whether it was intended to apply only to ecclesiastically imposed penances or extended also to temporal punishments one might suffer in the hereafter[8]—but whatever the original intention it was not long before the "*remissio peccatorum* promised to the crusaders" came to include both.[9] The fathers had been clear that the debt for sin must be paid,

---

[3] Walls, *Purgatory*, 18.

[4] Le Goff, *The Birth of Purgatory*, 125.

[5] Walls, *Purgatory*, 18. See Brian Patrick McGuire, "Purgatory, the Communion of Saints, and Medieval Change," *Viator* 20 (1989): 61–84.

[6] Le Goff, *The Birth of Purgatory*, 127.

[7] See Atria Larson, *Master of Penance: Gratian and the Development of Penitential Thought and Law in the Twelfth Century* (Washington, DC: Catholic University of America Press, 2014); Rob Meens, *Penance in Medieval Europe, 600–1200* (Cambridge: Cambridge University Press, 2014); Abigail Firey, *A New History of Penance* (Leiden: Brill, 2008).

[8] Ane Bysted wrote that until recently "most crusade historians who have occupied themselves with the crusade indulgences have followed 'The Gottlob thesis' (Adolf Gottlob, *Kreuzablass und Almosenablass. Eine studie über die frühzeit des ablasswesens* [Stuttgart: F. Enke, 1906]) or at least certain aspects of it ... that states that the crusade indulgences were not intended to have transcendental effects before the pontificate of Eugenius III and his crusading bull *Quantum praedecessores*." Ane Bysted, *The Crusade Indulgence: Spiritual Rewards and the Theology of the Crusades, c. 1095–1216* (Leiden: Brill, 2015), 31.

[9] Ibid., 276. "Because of this, those crusaders who prepare themselves for the service of God, truly confessed and contrite, are considered true martyrs while they are in the service of Christ, freed from venial and also mortal sins, from all the penitence enjoined upon them, absolved from the punishments for their sins in this world and the punishment of Purgatory in the next, safe from the tortures of Hell, in the glory and honour of being crowned in eternal beatitude." Jacques De Vitry, *Sermon 2.18*; Eng.

either in this world or in the purgatorial fire to come,[10] but through the indulgence one could satisfy the debt with less pain and suffering than would be required later.[11] This deal was so good that by the mid-twelfth century the crusader indulgence was being advertised as a "real bargain" (*bonum forum*) whereby one could obtain "an immense reward for modest labour."[12]

Among the other theological developments leading "to the acceptance of Purgatory as a distinct place" was the gradual collapsing of Augustine's "fourfold classification of persons—martyrs/saints (*valde boni*), those not altogether good (*non valde boni*), those not altogether evil (*non valde mali*), the godless/wicked (*valde mali*)—into three, permitting each type of person to be placed quite neatly into a suitable location in the afterlife—Heaven, Hell, or Purgatory.[13] This occurred

---

trans.: Christopher Maier, ed., *Crusade Propaganda and Ideology: Model Sermons for the Preaching of the Cross* (Cambridge: Cambridge University Press, 2000), 113.

[10] *Liber de vera et falsa poenitentia*, long quoted as the work of Augustine but now believed to have been authored "by an anonymous author ... in the second half of the eleventh century," was clear that "punishments that are not expiated in this life will be transferred to Purgatory, where they will be harder than those of this life." Bysted, *The Crusade Indulgence*, 88, 92.

[11] "Be so reconciled with God here by chastening your misdeeds with a worthy atonement, that thereafter he doesn't find anything to punish anymore. Forestall graver penalties by gentler ones. For as blessed Augustine says: 'The future life's penalties, even though they are purgatorial, are graver than all the present life's ones.' Thus great care should be taken with them, and great deeds done, so that in accordance with the stipulations of the holy fathers such atonement might be undergone here that there remains nothing to be expurgated there." Peter Abelard, *Ethics*, 200; Eng. trans.: Peter Abelard, *Ethical Writings: "Ethics" and "Dialogue Between a Philosopher, a Jew and a Christian"*, trans. Paul Vincent Spade (Indianapolis: Hackett, 1995), 48.

[12] Telling the story of a man reluctant to join the crusade, Jacques de Vitry described his change of heart when he heard what a good deal it was: "When I preached in some town, one man did not want to come to the sermon with the others since his wife objected. But he began to watch through a window in the loft out of curiosity and listen secretly to what I would say. When he heard that through the properties of the Cross and without any other penitence people received such a great indulgence as people mostly do not obtain who fast and wear a hair shirt for sixty years and that nothing less than the whole may be remitted ... [and] when he also heard that for the labour of a short time dependent in this world and the punishment of Purgatory were remitted, the punishment of Hell avoided and the Kingdom of Heaven gained, he was full of remorse and inspired by God ... [he] jumped out into the crowd and was the first to come to the cross." Jacques De Vitry, *Sermon 2.37*; Eng. trans.: Christopher Maier, ed., *Crusade Propaganda and Ideology*, 121.

[13] Walls, *Purgatory*, 18. One can see this movement as early as Alcuin of York (d. 804), where he divided the dead into saints, righteous, and wicked. Concerning the purgatorial fire he wrote that "this affects the wicked differently, the saints differently, and the righteous differently. Now indeed, from the wracking of this fire, the wicked are drawn down to the flames of the perpetual fire. The saints, who are without any stain of sin, will be resurrected together with their bodies, because they built gold, silver, and precious stones on the foundation, which is Christ, and they will triumph over that fire with as much ease as they had integrity of faith and love of Christ.... The righteous, who die still tainted by minor sins, will endure some pain: There are still certain people, the righteous, obligated [merely] for certain minute sins because they built on the foundation that is Christ, wood, hay, and straw, which are purged by the ardor of that fire, by which, once they are cleansed, they are made worthy by the glory of eternal felicity." Alcuin of York, *De fide sanctae et individuae Trinitatis*, Libri tres 3.21 (PL 101:53); Eng. trans.: Alan Berstein, *Hell and Its Rivals: Death and Retribution among Christians, Jews, and Muslims in the Early Middle Ages* (Ithaca, NY: Cornell University Press, 2017), 189. To these distinctions "Peter Lombard [in *Sentences*, Book 4, Distinction 45] added a distinction of his own in order to shed further light upon the benefits that the 'not very wicked ones,' *non valde mali*, might derive from our prayers and sacrifices. Unlike the saints, who do not need our prayers, and the damned, whose conduct during this life renders our actions on their behalf pointless for them after they have died, a large group of people directly benefits from our prayers and sacrifices. The 'moderately wicked' (*mediocriter mali*) might be granted mitigation of their punishment, while we may hope that our supplications will move God to grant the 'moderately good' (*mediocriter boni*) complete absolution of their sins." Philipp Rosemann, *Peter Lombard* (Oxford: Oxford University Press, 2004), 183. Hugh of St. Victor added

alongside the distinction increasingly made in the twelfth century between venial and mortal sins, which allowed purgation for those who died with minor sins, provided they were burned away in the fire to come.[14] According to Peter Lombard, these were precisely the sins Paul had spoken about in 1 Corinthians 3:10–15, where he "insinuates overtly that those who build of wood, hay, and straw carry with them flammable structures, that is to say, venial sins, which must ultimately be consumed in purgatorial fire."[15]

Another factor in Purgatory's development was the popularity of stories, like the earlier *Apocalypse of Paul* and *Visio sancti Fursei*, where the living were granted visions of the world to come. Among the most influential of this genre was the best-selling *Tractatus de Purgatorio Sancti Patricii* (c. 1190), called by Le Goff Purgatory's "literary birth certificate,"[16] in which Christ allegedly showed St. Patrick a hole (*fossa*) and told him that "whoever, being truly repentant and armed with true faith, would enter and remain for the duration of one day and one night, would be purged of all the sins of his life. Moreover, while going through it, he would see not only the torments of the wicked, but also ... the joys of the blessed."[17] Patrick built a church nearby, which became a pilgrimage site visited by many, including, in 1153, an Irish knight named Owein whose journey though the afterlife is recounted in great detail. After meeting demons and undergoing a series of trials, he encountered a group in the "earthly paradise" who told Owein that they were there in order

> to obtain remission of our sins through penance. But the penance we received either before our death or at the point of death and that we did not carry out during our lives, we repaid after the dissolution of the flesh by undergoing tortures in the places of punishment which you have seen, some of us for a long period, others for a shorter time.... None of those who are in torment knows for how long he will be tortured. Yet, through masses, psalms, prayers, and alms, whenever they are made for them, their torments are alleviated or else they are converted into lesser and more tolerable ones until they are completely freed by such favors.[18]

---

the category of imperfectly wicked (*imperfecti sive minus mali*) who seemed to be biding their time before eventually entering Hell. Le Goff, *The Birth of Purgatory*, 144.

[14] This distinction found its biblical basis in 1 John 5:16–17, "If you see your brother or sister committing what is not a mortal sin, you will ask, and God will give life to such a one—to those whose sin is not mortal. There is sin that is mortal; I do not say that you should pray about that. All wrongdoing is sin, but there is sin that is not mortal."

[15] Peter Lombard, *Sentences*, Book 4, Distinction 21; Eng. trans.: Peter Lombard, *The Sentences, Book 4: On the Doctrine of Signs*, trans. Guilio Silano (Toronto: Pontifical Institute of Medieval Studies, 2010).

[16] Le Goff, *The Birth of Purgatory*, 181.

[17] Jean-Michel Picard, ed. and trans., *Saint Patrick's Purgatory: A Twelfth Century Tale of a Journey to the Other World* (Dublin: Four Courts Press, 1985), 47–48.

[18] Ibid., 69. He then added, "And as the length of their stay in the places of punishment is given according to the number of their sins, likewise we who are here will stay in this place of rest more or less according to our good merits. And although we are completely free from torments we are not yet worthy of rising to the higher joy of the saints. Yet none of us knows the day and the starting point of our advancement to a better state." Ibid.

Another important, yet oft-neglected text, in this genre is Hildegard of Bingen's *Liber vitae meritorum*, written between 1158 and 1163.[19] Hildegard, described by Barbara Newman as one of Purgatory's "midwives," told how punishments in the hereafter

> cleanse these souls who, living in this changing world, have earned in a non-changing way the cleansing of their sins through punishment. But these torments have not cleansed them from the death which comes to the body; these torments do not prevent them from being weighed in the world by the divine scourges of the merciful God. But these torments will cleanse them unless they are snatched away from these punishments by the labors of men or by the virtues of the holy ones which God works in those men when they call upon the piety of divine grace.[20]

Although a number of eleventh- and twelfth-century authors spoke with regularity about the "purgatorial fire" and "purgatorial punishments"—Le Goff mentions Honorius Augustodunenis, Geuric of Igny, Hugh of St. Victor, Bernard of Clairvaux, Gratian, and Peter Lombard, among others—there remained some ambiguity about exactly where and when these punishments occurred.[21] The one belief they all shared, and which "helped to prepare the way for the inception of Purgatory, was this: that the souls of the dead could be helped by prayer, and more particularly by suffrages. In these the faithful found what they needed both to satisfy their desire to support their relatives and friends beyond the grave, and to sustain their own hopes of benefiting in turn from similar assistance."[22]

The duration and severity of one's time in the purgatorial fire often depended on how much suffering one had undergone in *this* world, for purgation actually began as "a bodily torture which the wicked inflict upon [us] in this life. For others it is the afflicting of their own bodies with fasting, vigils and other labors. Some lose their loved

---

[19] English translation of the work in Hildegard of Bingen, *The Book of the Rewards of Life: Liber Vitae Meritorum*, trans. Bruce Hozeski (Oxford: Oxford University Press, 1997). See also Barbara Newman, "Hildegard of Bingen and the 'Birth of Purgatory,'" *Mystics Quarterly* 19.3 (1993): 90–97. Newman was critical of Le Goff's general disregard for the work of women in chronicling Purgatory's birth, including such figures as Elisabeth of Schönau, who "was both praying for sisters in Purgatory and worrying about her own potential sojourn there" as early as 1155. Ibid., 91.

[20] Hildegard of Bingen, *The Book of the Rewards of Life*, 47. Interestingly, Newman pointed out that for Hildegard, aside from Purgatory and Hell "there is also a kind of limbo for infidels who die without baptism, but unencumbered by grave sins. Souls freed from Purgatory enter the earthly paradise, since Heaven is reserved for the saints until Judgment Day. The vision thus includes five possible destinations for the dead." Newman, "Hildegard of Bingen and the 'Birth of Purgatory,'" 92.

[21] "All in all, there was much hesitation about the nature of this intermediary place. Although almost everyone agreed that some sort of fire, distinct from the eternal fire of Gehenna, played a role, few tried to locate that fire, or if they did, were quite vague about it. From the fathers to the final representatives of the Carolingian church, the problem of the hereafter was essentially that of distinguishing between those who would be saved and go to heaven and those who would be damned and sent to hell." Le Goff, *The Birth of Purgatory*, 134.

[22] Ibid. Aside from repeating Augustine's teaching in the *Enchiridion on Faith, Hope, and Charity* (discussed last chapter) Gratian in his *Decretum* also clarified how people were aided: "The souls of the dead are delivered in four ways: by the sacrifices of the priests, the prayers of the saints, by the alms of dear friends, and by the fasting of relatives" (*Animae defunctorum quatuor modis soluuntur, aut oblationibus sacerdotum, aut precibus sanctorum, aut karorum elemosinis, aut ieiunio cognatorum*). Gratian, *Decretum*, Pars Secunda, Causa 13, Chapter 22; Eng. trans.: Le Goff, *The Birth of Purgatory*, 147.

ones or fortunes. Some suffer sadness or sickness" or some other misfortune.²³ For those who did not experience these things on earth, after death there was

> either too much fiery heat or a terrible freezing cold or some other type of punishment, of which the least is greater than the greatest imaginable in this life. While they are there, angels or some of the saints in whose honor they did something in this life occasionally appear to them and comfort them with a breeze or sweet smell or some other solace. When they are freed, their benefactors will lead them into that court which accepts no blemish.²⁴

Yet while there was widespread belief that suffering the fires of Purgatory was a state endured by many after death, "Purgatory" as a proper noun, describing the place where these pains were suffered, did not yet exist. That development, according to Le Goff, occurred at some point between 1170 and 1180 at the school at Notre-Dame, and probably in the works of Peter Comester ("Manducatur," or "Peter the Eater," d. 1178).²⁵ In a sermon on Psalm 122:3 ("Jerusalem—built as a city that is bound firmly together"), long attributed to Hildebert of Lavardin, Peter spoke of the dead being cleansed "in Purgatory" (*in purgatorio*), where they "obtain either complete absolution or else a mitigation of the penalty."²⁶ Although in other works he used the more traditional formula "in the fires of Purgatory" (*in igne purgatorio*),²⁷ if Le Goff is correct, this sermon marks Peter as the "inventor ... or at least one of the earliest

---

²³ Honorius Augustodunensis, *Elucidarium* Book 3, Q. 8; critical edition in Yves Lefèvre, *L'Elucidarium et les Lucidaires*, Bibliothèque des écoles Françaises d'Athènes et de Rome, 180 (Paris: Boccard, 1954). Eng. trans.: Clifford Teunis Gerritt Sorensen, *The Elucidarium of Honorius Augustodunensis: Translation and Selected Annotations* (MA thesis, Brigham Young University, 1979), 145.

²⁴ Ibid. This view is also found in Werner von Ellerbach's *Deflorationes sanctorum Patrum*, where he wrote that "after death, too, we are told, there is a purgatorial fire (*ignis quidam purgatorius*) which purges and cleanses those who have begun to purify themselves in this life but who have not finished their work.... These tortures are hard to endure even if they are but of minor degree. Thus, it is better to finish here the work that one is supposed to do. But if one has not finished it, provided he has begun, he should not despair, because 'he shall be saved yet so as by fire.' Your crimes will burn in you until they are consumed. But you will be saved because the love of God has remained in you as your foundation" (PL 157:1035–36). English translation in Le Goff, *The Birth of Purgatory*, 140. See also Paul Glorieux, "Les Deflorationes de Werner de Saint-Blaise," in *Mélanges Joseph de Ghellinek*, vol. 2 (Gembloux: J. Duculot, 1951), 699–721.

²⁵ Le Goff set forth his case in Appendix 2 of *The Birth of Purgatory* (362–66). As mentioned earlier (chapter 6 n. 1), these conclusions have not gone unchallenged. According to Barbara Newman, "Few medievalists, for example, share his conviction that the emergence of the noun *purgatorium*, circa 1170, marks a definitive change in beliefs about the afterlife, or that the increasing emphasis on Purgatory and prayers for the dead signals a shift from a binary to a ternary model of the cosmos. Nor have many critics accepted his claim that a circle of Parisian scholastics—Odo of Ourscamp, Peter Comestor, and Peter Cantor—were decisive innovators in purgatorial doctrine." Newman, "Hildegard of Bingen and the 'Birth of Purgatory,' " 90.

²⁶ Peter Comestor, *Sermon 85*; Eng. trans.: Le Goff, *The Birth of Purgatory*, 155. This sermon is found in PL 171:739–44, attributed to Hildebert. For the attribution of this sermon to Peter see Peter Harris Tibber, "The Origins of the Scholastic Sermon, c. 1130–c. 1210" (DPhil thesis, Oxford University, 1984); André Wilmart, "Les sermons d'Hildebert," *Revue Bénédictine* 47 (1935): 12–51; M.-M. Lebreton, "Recherches sur les manuscrits contenant des sermons de Pierre le Mangeur," *Bulletin d'information de l'Institut de Recherche et d'Histoire des Textes* 2 (1953): 25–44.

²⁷ In his work *Sententiae de sacramentis* Peter described the dead *in igne purgatorio* being cleansed for different periods of time depending on their sins, penances, and contrition. Peter Manducator, *De Sacramentis, De penitentia*, in Heinrich Weisweiler, ed., *Maitre Simon et son groupe*, Spicilegium sacrum Lovaniense, 17 (Louvain: Spicilegium sacrum lovaniense bureaux, 1937), 81–82.

users" of the word "Purgatory" (*purgatorium*) as a noun.²⁸ This development was "revolutionary,"²⁹ for while "Christians had spoken about purgation from the earliest generations of Christian history, the idea that Purgatory was a specific place" was something genuinely new.³⁰ This was literally a universe-defining moment, for in moving "from a vaguely defined sense of purgation to the specific place where that process occurs ... the geography of the otherworld was expanded from the two-level vision of heaven and hell to a three-level vision, which [now] included an intermediate place."³¹

Given its relative novelty, it is remarkable how quickly Purgatory was embraced, becoming, within three decades, a regular feature of both theological and devotional literature.³² Odo of Ourscamp (d. 1171), "the second (or, chronologically speaking, possibly the first) theologian to speak of Purgatory,"³³ wrote about the soul "enter[ing] immediately into Purgatory" (*intrat purgatorium statim*), where "it is purged, and thus benefits."³⁴ In the works of Peter Cantor ("the Chanter" d. 1197), "the man who first integrated Purgatory into theological teaching,"³⁵ the tripartite division of the afterlife is simply assumed, with each class of person assigned their appropriate spot:

> The good either go at once to Paradise (*patria*) if they have nothing with them to burn, or they go first to Purgatory (*purgatorium*) and then to Paradise, as in the case of those who bring venial sins along with them. No special receptacle is set aside for the wicked, who, it is said, go immediately to Hell.³⁶

Despite its rapid acceptance, there were still some who resisted Purgatory's rise, including certain heretical groups who rejected all prayers for the departed, believing that the dead "are either damned or saved from the moment they die."³⁷ As a

---

²⁸ Le Goff, *The Birth of Purgatory*, 157.
²⁹ Ibid.
³⁰ Hayes, *Four Views on Hell*, 110.
³¹ Ibid.
³² Jerry Walls cites a number of reasons this may have happened—societal, intellectual, legal (especially new thinking regarding guilt and punishment), eschatological, and psychological (i.e., the growing belief that suffering had "productive potential" to "forge identity and meaning"). Walls, *Purgatory*, 20–21. Andrew Skotnicki associated the development of Purgatory with the idea of prisons. See "God's Prisoners: Penal Confinement and the Creation of Purgatory," *Modern Theology* 22 (2006): 85–110.
³³ Le Goff, *The Birth of Purgatory*, 158.
³⁴ Odo of Ourscamp, *De anima in Purgatorio*, in J. Pitra, ed., *Questiones Magistri Odonis Suessionis*, Analecta novissima Spicilegii Solesmensis. Continuatio altera 2 (Paris and Frascati, 1888), 137–38. Le Goff believed that Odo himself did not use the word, suggesting that the *Quaestiones* were actually compiled from his students' notes, and that it was they who included the term—i.e., "Where Odo still spoke of purgatorial fire, his students were already speaking of Purgatory." Le Goff, *The Birth of Purgatory*, 159.
³⁵ Le Goff, *The Birth of Purgatory*, 165.
³⁶ Peter Canter, *Summa De Sacramentis et Animae Consiliis*, in Jean-Albert Dugauquier, ed., *Summa De Sacramentis et Animae Consiliis* (Louvain: Louvain University Press, 1957), 103–4; Eng. trans.: Le Goff, *The Birth of Purgatory*, 165. Peter wanted to emphasize that despite the opinions of some, only the elect go to Purgatory since the damned have no need of it.
³⁷ This was the opinion of Pierre de Bruys and his disciple Henri of Lausanne in the first part of the twelfth century. An anonymous treatise attacked these views, insisting that "there are some sins which will be erased in the future by the alms of friends and the prayers of the faithful or by purgatorial fire." Text in Raoul Manselli, "Il monaco Enrico e la sua eresia," *Bolletino dell' Istituto Storico Italiano per il medio evo e Archivo Muratoriano* 65 (1953): 44–62; Eng. trans.: Le Goff, *The Birth of Purgatory*, 169. For Pierre and Henri see James Fearns, "Peter von Bruis und die religiöse Bewegung des 12. Jahrhunderts," *Archiv*

response, orthodox writers like Bernard of Fontcaude emphasized that most souls did not go "immediately after their separation from the flesh, to either Heaven or Hell," and that most went instead to "the purgatorial fire" intended for "those who are neither entirely good or entirely wicked ... a place that is moderately bad ... [where] it is less harsh than Hell but worse than the world."[38] Alan of Lille (d. 1203) went a step further, writing of both the purgatorial fire and of Purgatory itself, emphasizing that if we do not take care to undergo the purgatorial fire (*ignis purgatories*) in this life (through penance), we will suffer punishment in Purgatory itself after death.[39] As for those who have started this process but left it uncompleted, Alan assured his readers that "beyond any doubt [they] will complete this satisfaction in Purgatory, but how long [they] will be there, only he who weighs the punishments in the balance can tell."[40]

By the beginning of the thirteenth century, the scholastic movement had given Purgatory its full-throated endorsement, as had the Cistercians.[41] William of Auvergne (d. 1249) closely associated the pains of Purgatory with penance and the demands of divine justice, for by completing penances in this world ("by torturing itself not only in spiritual ways, ... but even with corporeal afflictions such as fasts, works, lashings, and other things of this sort, which are called sacred exercises") the soul comes to know that "all these do not suffice to satisfy the justice of the Creator fully."[42] Purgatory thus became the place where "perfect purgation was attained" and the demands of divine justice were satisfied by penitential punishments (*poena purgatoriae et poenitentiales*) that differed little from those suffered by the damned except that in Purgatory, these torments "would last only long enough to complete the atonement interrupted by death. In hell, they would endure forever."[43] This postmortem cleansing would probably be "necessary for many souls" (*necessariae sunt multis animabus*) since "unforeseen death, imperfect repentance prior to death, and death in a state of lesser sin" was all too common.[44]

---

für Kulturgeschichte 48 (1966): 311–35; Raoul Manselli, *Studi sulle eresie del secolo XII*, Studi Storici 5 (Rome: Istituto storico italiano per il medio evo, 1953).

[38] Bernard of Fontcaude, *Liber adversus Waldensium sectam*; Eng. trans.: Mary Cesilia Hilferty, "The *liber adversus Waldensium sectam* of Bernard, Abbot of Fontcaude: A Translation with Critical Introduction" (MA thesis, Catholic University of America, 1963).

[39] Jean Longere, ed., *Alan of Lille: Liber poenitentialis*, vol. 2 (Louvain: Editions Nauwelaerts, 1965), 174–77; Eng. trans.: Le Goff, *The Birth of Purgatory*, 172–73.

[40] Ibid.

[41] Bernard of Clairvaux, whom Le Goff called "Purgatory's putative father," is often credited as one of the first to employ the term, but Le Goff disagreed. The works in which he did so are, in Le Goff's opinion, misattributed. While he spoke of "purgatorial places" (*in locis purgatoriis*) and "places of purgation" (*in purgabilibus locis*), the noun "Purgatory" is not found in his authentic works. Le Goff, *The Birth of Purgatory*, 145–46. See also Carlos de la Casa and Elena de la Casa, "La idea del Purgatorio y Bernardo de Claraval," *Revista Cistercium* 223 (April–June 2001): 343–56.

[42] William of Auvergne, *De universo*, in F. Hotot, ed., *Opera omnia*, vol. 1 (Frankfurt am Main: Minerva, 1963), 679; Eng. trans.: Alan Bernstein, "Esoteric Theology: William of Auvergne on the Fires of Hell and Purgatory," *Speculum* 57 (1982): 511.

[43] Ibid., 512.

[44] Le Goff, *The Birth of Purgatory*, 243. "In other words, Purgatory is quite likely to be heavily populated. Though the point is not spelled out, it is obvious that, on this view, the population of Purgatory has been swelled at the expense of Hell." Ibid.

As for the nature of these penitential punishments, Alan Bernstein has argued that for William of Auvergne, Purgatory's fires were largely metaphorical or immaterial, since the "pains of Purgatory" were so closely associated with "the torments of penance."[45] He argued that William used the image of fire to convey "the anguish of the contrite soul, which tortures itself with feelings of guilt and inadequacy," the chief difference between the fires of Hell and Purgatory being "that the pains of hell are inflicted against the will of the damned"—that is, people suffered the agony of Purgatory willingly because they knew it was ultimately beneficial.[46] Yet Bernstein also noted that William sometimes did use more materialist terms when writing for more popular audiences, probably because "he wanted the uneducated to take the fire literally; otherwise its deterrent force would be diminished."[47]

William's contemporary Alexander of Hales (d. 1245) spoke about Purgatory as the place where venial sins could be remitted (*purgans a venialibus*), just as they were "purged in this life by love" and the sacraments, and the penalties due for mortal sins satisfied (*et a poenis debitis mortalibus nondum sufficienter satisfactis*).[48] These penalties were more severe than anything on earth, yet because Purgatory was the "antechamber of paradise" where people awaited the beatific vision, it was ultimately a place of hope.[49] Alexander believed that Purgatory was "the temporary holding place ... [for] the majority of men ... in the other world" since there are few "whose merits are sufficient that they need not pass through it."[50] While there, they benefit from the suffrages "of the universal church" which prays and laments for them, and by these actions aid the dead in making satisfaction.[51] Great acts of holiness (e.g., going on crusade, pilgrimages) were powerful enough not only to atone for one's own sins, but also help satisfy the debt owed by those now suffering in Purgatory.[52] The theology that would later undergird the selling of indulgences in the sixteenth century was beginning to take shape.

The Byzantine Background

Although they never achieved the precision of the scholastics on the how and where of postmortem purgation, Greek theologians continued to speak about the state of souls

---

[45] Bernstein, "Esoteric Theology," 530.
[46] Ibid.
[47] Ibid. Bernstein admitted that William did speak of the fire that "corporeally and really tortures the bodies of souls (*corporaliter et vere torqueat corpora animarum*), which is why Le Goff rejected Bernstein's thesis and maintained that William "believed and taught that the fire of Purgatory is real [and] material." Le Goff, *The Birth of Purgatory*, 245.
[48] Alexander of Hales, *Glossa in quatuor libros sententiarum Petri Lombardi*, Liber 4 (Quaracchi: Collegium S. Bonaventurae, 1957), 349–65; Eng. trans.: Le Goff, *The Birth of Purgatory*, 247.
[49] Ibid., 247–48.
[50] Ibid., 248.
[51] "Just as specific pain entails satisfaction for sin, so the common pain of the universal Church, crying for the sins of dead believers, praying and lamenting for them, is an aid to satisfaction; it does not create satisfaction in itself, but with the pain of the penitent aids in satisfaction, which is the very definition of suffrage. Suffrage is in fact the merit of the church, capable of diminishing the pain of one of its members." Alexander of Hales, *Glossa in quatuor libros sententiarum*, 354; Eng. trans.: Le Goff, *The Birth of Purgatory*, 249.
[52] "But those who, in love, go to the aid of the Holy Land may be in such devotion and generosity of alms that, themselves liberated from all their sins, they are able to liberate their relatives from Purgatory, by obtaining satisfaction for them." Ibid.

after death and how they are aided by the prayers of the living. There was the work of Michael Psellos (1018–81), who authored *On the Separation of the Body and Soul*,[53] and the writings of Michael Glykas, whose *Theological Chapters on the Problem of the Holy Scripture* (Εἰς τὰς ἀπορίας τῆς Θείας Γραφῆς κεφάλαια) addressed a number of inquiries about the afterlife.[54] Among the most important of these concerned the question of "where the souls of the departed go once they are separated from the body after death."[55] Glykas answered that immediately upon death

> souls are forcefully carried down to Hades by demons ... [who] stand nearby and fight it out to take the soul with them, and especially those who do not deny committing wicked deeds.... [This is] in accordance with what the great Maximos says, that, after the departure from this life, wicked powers stand against our souls as they proceed on the upward journey. And they prevail over those who have performed bad deeds, but they are defeated by the righteous through the angelic alliance.[56]

This idea—that angels and demons attended a person at the hour of death, after which they would fight for possession of the soul—"had worked its way deep into the imagination and the structure of eschatological expectations of the Byzantines."[57] In fact, the threat of the awaiting demons was often used to inculcate good behavior,[58] as a host of writers warned readers, usually in gruesome detail, of the tortures that awaited them if they continued in their life of sin."[59]

---

[53] Michael Psellos, *De omnifaria doctrina: A Critical Text and Introduction*, ed. Leendert Gerrit (Nijmegen: Centrale Drukkerij, 1948).

[54] Michael Glykas, *Εἰς τὰς ἀπορίας τῆς Θείας Γραφῆς κεφάλαια*, ed. S. Eustratiadis, 2 vols. (Athens, 1906 and 1912). See also Eirini-Sophia Kiapidou, "Chapters, Epistolary Essays and Epistles: The Case of Michael Glykas' Collection of Ninety-Five Texts in the 12th Century," *Parekbolai* 3 (2013): 45–64; Yannis Papadogiannakis, "Michael Glykas and the Afterlife in Twelfth-Century Byzantium," *Studies in Church History* 45 (2009): 130–42.

[55] Papadogiannakis, "Michael Glykas and the Afterlife," 133.

[56] Marinis, *Death and the Afterlife in Byzantium*, 39.

[57] Papadogiannakis, "Michael Glykas and the Afterlife," 134. This idea of a battle waged for Christian souls can be seen as early as a fifth-century homily incorrectly attributed to Cyril of Alexandria ("On the Departure of the Soul, and on the Second Coming" [PG 77:1072–90]). See Brian Daley, "At the Hour of Our Death': Mary's Dormition and Christian Dying in Late Patristic and Early Byzantine Literature," *Dumbarton Oaks Papers* 55 (2001): 76. The author of the homily wrote of "the army of heavenly powers on one side, and the powers of darkness on the other," both standing ready at the moment of death to take possession of the soul. "What fear and trembling do you think the soul will experience on that day, when it gazes on the dreadful, fierce, cruel, merciless, untamable demons circled around it, as dark as Ethiopians? The very thought of them is more oppressive than any punishment! Just by looking at them, the soul will be cast into turmoil, terrified, racked with pain, and made to shrink with horror and distress, and will flee for refuge to the angels of God. The soul will be protected by the holy angels, as it makes its way forward and upward through the air." PG 77:1073; Eng. trans.: Daley, "At the Hour of Our Death," 77.

[58] According to Nicholas Constas, "The salutary utility of these terrible little tales was not lost on their authors. The Life of Antony, for instance, notes that: 'Having seen this [i.e., the vision of the ascending soul] ... [Antony] struggled the more to daily advance,' adding that the saint shared the vision with others 'for whom the account would be beneficial, that they might learn that discipline bore good fruit.'" Constas, "To Sleep, Perchance to Dream," 109.

[59] "When the soul of a man departs from the body, a certain great mystery is there enacted. If a person is under the guilt of sin, bands of demons and fallen angels approach along with the powers of darkness which capture that soul and drag it as a captive to their place. No one should be surprised by this fact. For if, while a man lived in this life, he was subject to them and was their obedient slave, how much more, when he leaves this world, is he captured and controlled by them?" Macarius of Egypt, Homily 22; Eng.

Glykas then touched on a concept long present in Byzantine thinking on the afterlife "even though ... [it was] never officially endorsed by the Orthodox church"—that is, "the possibility of changing or at least alleviating the verdict on one's soul after death while it was passing through the τελώνια,—the heavenly toll houses."[60] The idea, present as early as the fifth century,[61] was that following a person's death an "infernal revenue service staffed by a swarm of archons, cosmocrats, teloniarchs, logothetes, and praktopsephistai (fiscal officials of low rank)" examined the soul at a series of τελώνια—"aerial toll houses," "weigh-stations," or "heavenly custom-houses"—at which "each of the bodily senses was closely scrutinized ('from the time of one's youth until the hour of death') beginning with sins of the mouth, followed by those of the eyes, the ears, the sense of smell, and touch."[62]

Jean-Claude Larchet, who chronicled the rise of the tollhouse tradition, saw its genesis in the *Apophthegmata Patrum*,[63] where Theophilus spoke of demons accusing "souls, as in a lawsuit, bringing before [the soul] all the sins it has committed, whether deliberately or through ignorance ... [while] the divine powers stand on the other side and they present the good deeds of the soul."[64] In some later texts "These encounters often take the form of prosecution by demons in the charged setting of a courtroom, with angels acting as counsels for the defense. At other times, the scene shifts to an aerial 'tollgate' where souls ascending to heaven are detained by passport control and have their moral baggage inspected by demonic customs officials."[65] At these "heavenly custom houses ... correspond[ing] to a particular passion ... or a kind of sin of which a certain type of demon is the inspirer... the demons appointed ... stop the soul and examine it ... demanding that it account for what they find."[66]

---

trans.: George Maloney, ed. and trans., *Pseudo-Macarius: The Fifty Spiritual Homilies and the Great Letter* (New York: Paulist Press, 1992), 109.

[60] Angold, *Church and State in Byzantium under the Comneni, 1081–1261*, 445–46. See also George Every, "Toll Gates on the Air Way," *Eastern Churches Review* 8 (1976): 139–50; Eirini Afentoulidou, "Gesellschaftliche Vorstellungen in den byzantinischen Berichten von posthumen Zollstationen," *Zeitschrift für Religions- und Geistesgeschichte* 67 (2015): 17–42.

[61] In a fifth-century homily attributed to Cyril of Alexandria (see n. 57 above) we read: "The [angels] take the soul then and carry it away into the air. But it finds there a cordon of duty collectors that bar the route, that sees and stop souls from passing. Now to each station is assigned a particular kind of sin. Here are the sins of the tongue and mouth: lies, swearing and perjury, useless words and vain pleasantries, immoderate libations of wine, excessive and misplaced laughter, immodest kisses and lewd songs. But the holy angels that are leading the soul extol it in their turn all the good speech that our mouth and tongue have pronounced: prayers, thanksgiving, psalms, hymns and spiritual canticles, lessons in Scripture, in short anything we have offered to God by mouth and tongue." Pseudo-Cyril of Alexandria, *Homily 14* (PG 77:1073–76); Eng. trans.: Larchet, *Life after Death According to the Orthodox Tradition*, 92.

[62] Constas, "To Sleep, Perchance to Dream," 107–8.

[63] Larchet, *Life after Death According to the Orthodox Tradition*, 80–81.

[64] *Apophthegmata Patrum*, Theophilus 4; Eng. trans.: Benedicta Ward, ed. and trans., *The Sayings of the Desert Fathers*, CS 59 (Kalamazoo, MI: Cistercian Publications, 1975), 81.

[65] Constas, "To Sleep, Perchance to Dream," 105. Constas described the eleventh-century *Life of Lazaros Galesiotes*, which "narrates the tale of a sinful layman who in a vision beheld his soul being tried in a courtroom after death, after which he resolved to become a monk." Ibid., 107.

[66] Larchet, *Life after Death According to the Orthodox Tradition*, 86–87. Larchet noted that "Like some corrupt tax collectors ... the demons sometimes demand reckoning from the soul for misdeeds it did not commit," which Michael Angold claimed made "the journey of the soul after death [like] the difficulties the ordinary citizen faced in his dealings with 'the customs officers, logothetes, and tax-collectors." Angold, *Church and State in Byzantium under the Comneni, 1081–1261*, 446.

The best-known story within the tollhouse tradition is the tenth-century "Vision of Theodora," part of the *Life of Basil the Younger* written by Gregory of Thrace.[67] The vision tells how Theodora's soul, as soon as it left her body, was met by demons ("in the guise of Ethiopians") who carried documents and confronted her with her sins.[68] Although angels stood nearby and "examined the works I had performed, to see if somehow they could find a good deed among them ... to bring forth as compensation," her fate remained unsettled until Basil arrived with a "scarlet bag full of gold" (representing his "excess spiritual wealth") in order to tip the scales in her favor.[69] At this point in the vision Theodora was taken "upward on the road to the east," to a series of twenty-one tollgates, each one representing a specific sin and each manned by demons, where she was confronted by her sins while angels argued her case.[70] Basil's prayers, the angels tell her, are of great help, "For you would have suffered, had not the great servant of Christ, Basil, succeeded in rescuing you."[71] Finally after the last station, Theodora and her angelic companions "departed from the [demons], rejoicing and filled with the greatest joy, because we were not penalized by them in any way, and we entered joyfully within the gate of heaven."[72]

While there currently exists an interesting intra-Orthodox debate about the dogmatic status of the tollhouse tradition (more on this in the next chapter), for our purposes the relevant question is the degree to which it affected the Byzantines' response to the eschatology of the West, especially since later authors contended that "the trial of the tollgates was, in fact, the Byzantine equivalent of Purgatory, minus the fireworks."[73] Hans-Georg Beck, who posited "a nearly complete separation of popular views on death from those held by the clergy and the educated elite," minimized the importance of these stories since they were "impregnated with a monastic outlook, which, he asserts, did not command the allegiance of the people as a whole."[74] In contrast, Michael Angold believed "monastic explanations of death ... [were] deeply

---

[67] Denis F. Sullivan, Alice-Mary Talbot, and Stamatina McGrath, eds. and trans., *The Life of Saint Basil the Younger: Critical Edition and Annotated Translation of the Moscow Version* (Washington, DC: Dumbarton Oaks Research Library and Collection, 2014).

[68] "I looked and behold, like a swarm of bees, those gloomy and savage Ethiopians surrounded the divine youths holding me and said amid shouting, 'We have on record great and very terrible transgressions of hers, and so she must defend herself extensively to us concerning them.'" Ibid., 205.

[69] "'My lords, this soul has been allotted to me, for she served me for a long time, giving me comfort in my old age; therefore I petitioned the Lord on her behalf, and His goodness granted her to me.' And taking from the fold of his garment a scarlet bag full of pure gold, he gave it to the two young men and said to them, 'Take this and use it to redeem this woman as you proceed through the tollhouses of the air; for by the grace of Christ I have great spiritual wealth.'" Ibid., 207.

[70] The twenty-one stations were Slander, Verbal abuse, Envy, Falsehood, Wrath and anger, Pride, Idle chatter, Usury and deceit, Ennui and vainglory, Avarice, Excessive wine drinking and inebriation, Malice, Magic and divination, Gluttony, Idolatry and heresy, Homosexuality and pederasty, Adultery, Murder, Theft, Fornication, Heartlessness and cruelty.

[71] Sullivan, Talbot, and McGrath, *Life of Saint Basil*, 245.

[72] Ibid., 249.

[73] Constas, "To Sleep, Perchance to Dream," 109. Constas was quoting the work of Gennadios Scholarios, who exposed the "cover-up" of the tollhouse teaching during the debates at Florence. Constas wrote that despite the fact that "Mark Eugenikos (d. 1445), was undoubtedly familiar with the tradition of the demonic tollgates, [he] failed to mention it in his polemics against Purgatory." Ibid., 108.

[74] Angold, *Church and State in Byzantium under the Comneni 1081–1261*, 446. See Hans-Georg Beck, *Die Byzantiner und ihr Jenseits. Zur Entstehungsgeschichte einer Mentalitat* (Munich: Verlag der Bayerischen Akademie der Wissenschaften, 1979).

engrained in the popular consciousness" and that "Beck was wrong to be so dismissive."[75] Nicholas Constas accepted the importance of the tollhouse tradition, but more for its "power to catalyze religious conversion" than its subsequent influence on the Byzantine reaction to Purgatory.[76]

Three other questions touched upon by Glykas did impact the later debate about Purgatory, the first being whether souls enjoy their full reward or punishment after their trial in the air. Citing a text from Pseudo-Athanasius's *Quaestiones ad Antiochum ducem*, likely composed in the seventh or early eighth century,[77] Glykas answered that "the souls of the righteous ... after Christ's arrival [on earth] are in paradise, as we learn from the thief on the cross. Because Christ our God did not open paradise just for the soul of the holy thief but for all the rest of the souls of saints."[78] The wicked, he argued, "are in Hades below the whole earth and the sea ... where they contemplate the evils that they have committed during their lives."[79] In affirming this, however, Glykas followed Pseudo-Athanasius in clarifying that the just did not receive the *full* reward that would come at the Last Judgment, but instead entered "Adam's Paradise, which was opened by the repentance of the thief; it is incorruptible and located above the earth. This, however, is different from the Kingdom, which is much more excellent."[80] It was, in the words of Pseudo-Athanasius, only a

> partial enjoyment, like the sorrow that the sinners have [is] a partial punishment. It is like when the emperor summons his friends to eat together and, in like manner, [he summons] the condemned to punish them. Those invited to lunch await in front of the emperor's house in delight until the time comes. Thus we should think about the souls of the deceased, of both the righteous and the sinners.[81]

Opposing Glykas was Niketas Stethatos, a central figure in the azyme debate who also authored a treatise *On the Soul* (c. 1075).[82] He "assert[ed] that Adam's Paradise

---

[75] Angold, *Church and State in Byzantium under the Comneni. 1081–1261*, 453.

[76] Constas, "To Sleep, Perchance to Dream," 109. "The mere thought of rapacious tax collectors and grasping lawyers created great anxiety among the Byzantine populace and, as symbolic devices, were judged effective in fostering a sense of final reckoning and ultimate accountability." Ibid.

[77] This incredibly influential text relied on the work of Anastasius of Sinai. See Marcel Richard and Joseph A. Munitiz, eds., *Anastasii Sinaitae: Quaestiones et responsiones* (Turnhout: Brepols, 2006), lii–lv.

[78] Pseudo-Athanasius, *Quaestiones ad Antiochum ducem* (PG 28:609); Eng. trans.: Marinis, *Death and the Afterlife in Byzantium*, 26. Theophylact of Ohrid also maintained this distinction in his exegesis of Luke 23:39–43, claiming that "the repentant thief did obtain paradise, but he had not yet obtained the Kingdom. But he will obtain the Kingdom, along with all those whom Paul enumerated. In the meantime, he has paradise, which is a place of spiritual rest (χωρίον πνευματικῆς ἀναπαύσεως)." Theophylact allowed that "even if the Kingdom of Heaven and paradise are one and the same" and "the good thief is in paradise, that is, in the Kingdom ... he does not yet enjoy the full inheritance of good things." Theophylact of Ohrid, *The Explanation of Blessed Theophylact Archbishop of Ochrid and Bulgaria of the Holy Gospel according to Saint Luke*, trans. Christopher Stade (House Springs, MO: Chrysostom Press, 2004), 311.

[79] Pseudo-Athanasius, *Quaestiones ad Antiochum ducem* (PG 28:609); Eng. trans.: Marinis, *Death and the Afterlife in Byzantium*, 26.

[80] Marinis, *Death and the Afterlife in Byzantium*, 41.

[81] Pseudo-Athanasius, *Quaestiones ad Antiochum ducem* (PG 28:609); Eng. trans.: Marinis, *Death and the Afterlife in Byzantium*, 26.

[82] Nicetas Stethatos, *On the Soul*, in Darrouzès, *Nicétas Stéthatos Opuscules et lettres*, 56–152. Niketas was chiefly concerned with the faculties of the soul (e.g., imagination, memory, bodily, and intellectual sensation) after death. See Dirk Krausmüller, "What Is Mortal in the Soul? Nicetas Stethatos, John Italos and the Controversy about the Care of the Dead," *Mukaddime* 6 (2015): 1–17.

has been closed for it served no purpose because, with Christ's Resurrection, the door of the Kingdom was open to all."[83] Gone are all the demons and angels associated with the provisional judgment, "because he deems one's conduct and deeds to be sufficient in themselves," with the just taken immediately "to the Trinity," where they "join the angelic powers in offering praise."[84] As it concerns sinners, they too receive the fullness of their punishment, "led away against their will by punishing and dark angels, in the midst of a horrible fear, with frightened trembling, toward the depths of Hell as into a gloomy and pitiless prison."[85]

A second inquiry concerned "whether one should give credence to those who say that the departed souls of the saints rest in some place and do not pray on our behalf before Christ."[86] The question stemmed from the story of Dives and Lazarus (Luke 16:19–31), which in the Byzantine tradition "provided the main scriptural guide to the fate of the soul after death—the righteous gathered into the bosom of Abraham and the rich man amid the torments of Hell."[87] However, the inability of Abraham to provide the rich man with any comfort, or for the rich man to help his family, seemingly denied the power of the saints to intercede on our behalf.[88] To answer the question Glykas relied on the work of Eustratios of Constantinople, who had written a

---

[83] Marinis, *Death and the Afterlife in Byzantium*, 41. See also M. Chalendard, "Nicétas Stéthatos: Le Paradis spirituel et autres textes annexes" (doctoral dissertation, Université de Paris, 1944).

[84] Marinis, *Death and the Afterlife in Byzantium*, 41. "If the soul has completed the present life in piety and purity, in the exercise of every good and the practice of the commandments of God, it pitches its tent in the places of the glory of God.... It is full of gladness and experiences a perfect joy in the hope of enjoying the eternal blessings of God, even before the future resurrection and the final return of things divine.... Among the souls that emigrate, some are pure and perfumed, alike to God, filled with divine glory and absolutely immaculate light: these are the saints; upon departing the body they shine like the sun because of the works of Justice, wisdom, and purity. These, by the intermediacy of the angel friends who lead them away toward the primal, super essential and immaterial light, a light incomprehensible even to angels, God himself glorified and adored in Father, Son, and Holy Spirit by the infinite Powers." Nicetas Stethatos, *On the Soul*, 13–14; Eng. trans.: Larchet, *Life after Death According to the Orthodox Tradition*, 145–47.

[85] "They are handed over to the unclean and evil spirits that guard this prison, there where the Prince of Darkness is held fast by eternal bonds to be prey to the fire with his fellows, the angels of darkness. They are delivered up to them to remain with them eternally in the future." Nicetas Stethatos, *On the Soul*, 14; Eng. trans.: Larchet, *Life after Death According to the Orthodox Tradition*, 146–47. Marinis did acknowledged that Stethatos's "opinions on the intermediate state are not always clear. In his letters to a certain Gregory the Sophist, Stethatos vehemently opposes any notion of the earthly paradise as an intermediate state and claims, again, that the souls of the righteous are already with Christ. Elsewhere, however, he concedes that the souls await full restoration in the future (τῆς μελλούσης τῶν θείων ἐκείνων πραγμάτων ἀποκαταστάσεως), but he does not explain how this is different from the previous state." Marinis, *Death and the Afterlife in Byzantium*, 41.

[86] Michael Glykas, *Theological Chapters*, Q. 21; Eng. trans.: Papadogiannakis, "Michael Glykas and the Afterlife," 138.

[87] Angold, *Church and State in Byzantium under the Comneni, 1081–1261*, 448. According to Angold, the story "gave hope to the poor and threatened the complacency of the rich and powerful. The lessons of the parable provided the church with some of its best ammunition against the indifference of lay society. The parable also constituted the strongest evidence for supposing that soon after death a decision was made about the soul's fate. The bosom of Abraham was the immediate reward in the next world for good works done in this." Ibid.

[88] Pseudo-Athanasius, upon whom Glykas relied, had claimed that the parable of the rich man and Lazarus "should not be taken literally, because it would not be possible for sinners in Gehenna to see the righteous with Abraham; indeed, it would be impossible to see anyone because they live in darkness. The souls of the saints remember those who are still alive, but those of the sinners do not, as they are concerned about their expected punishment." Marinis, *Death and the Afterlife in Byzantium*, 26.

defense of the cult of the saints centuries earlier.[89] Glykas believed that despite having received only a "deposit (ἀρραβῶνα) of the[ir] future enjoyment without being perfected, [the dead] can stand with confidence (μετὰ παρρησίας) before Christ on behalf of those still living."[90] This allowed the saints "to pray for us and bring down to us all kinds of spiritual gifts" since "they are alive and active after death ... interceding for us on our behalf."[91]

A third question raised by Glykas was whether the pains of the afterlife could be ameliorated by the suffrages of the living and "whether good works done on behalf of the dead could wipe away their sins entirely."[92] Glykas, citing Theophylact of Ohrid's *Commentary on Mark*, maintained that the sufferings of the afterlife were chiefly the pains of conscience caused by one's actions in this world.[93] Because he believed that hellfire was not corporeal, Glykas questioned the view of Gregory the Great on the subject, rejecting his position as unscriptural and even suggesting that it might have been placed in Gregory's text by scribal error.[94] Instead he maintained belief in a metaphorical fire that gave light to the good deeds of the just, and consumed the iniquities of sinners, although ultimately "only God knows ... what kind of fire this will be and how it will burn the wicked in the Day of the Last Judgment."[95]

Despite the fact that prayers, commemorations, and alms for the dead "had been the practice of the Christian church, in both East and West, from early on," the Byzantine tradition remained unclear on their benefits, especially as concerned the remission of

---

[89] Nicholas Constas, "An Apology for the Cult of Saints in Late Antiquity: Eustratius Presbyter of Constantinople, On the State of Souls after Death (CPG 7522)," *Journal of Early Christian Studies* 10 (2002): 267–85. Eustratius claimed his opponents were philosophers who taught that "human souls, after their departure from their bodies, are inactive." In response, Eustratius insisted that the souls of the saints were "even more active in death than they were in life, having transcended the spatial and temporal restrictions of the body." Ibid., 272, 274.

[90] Michael Glykas, *Theological Chapters*, Q. 21; Eng. trans.: Marinis, *Death and the Afterlife in Byzantium*, 42.

[91] Michael Glykas, *Theological Chapters*, Q. 21; Eng. trans.: Papadogiannakis, "Michael Glykas and the Afterlife," 139. Glykas interpreted the story of Dives and Lazarus as proof that the dead *did* act on behalf of the living, which is why "the rich man ... begged Abraham to send Lazarus to the house of his father, so that his five brothers might be saved." Michael Glykas, Theological Chapters, Q. 21; Eng. trans.: Angold, *Church and State in Byzantium under the Comneni, 1081–1261*, 450.

[92] Michael Glykas, *Theological Chapters*, Q. 50; Eng. trans.: Angold, *Church and State in Byzantium under the Comneni, 1081–1261*, 450.

[93] "The worm and the fire which punish the sinners are each person's conscience and the memory of the shameful things done in this life, for they consume like the worm and burn like fire. Everyone shall be salted with fire, that is, shall be tested. Paul also says that all things shall be tried by fire." Theophylact of Ohrid, *The Explanation of Blessed Theophylact Archbishop of Ochrid and Bulgaria of the Holy Gospel according to Saint Mark*, trans. Christopher Stade (House Springs, MO: Chrysostom Press, 2008), 80–81. According to Constas: "A passage from Dorotheos of Gaza ... (Theological Chapters, Q. 20) states that the thoughts of sinful souls eternally return to the scenes of their crimes, and they can remember only those whom they sinned against so that murderers, for example, can remember only the faces of their victims." Constas, "To Sleep, Perchance to Dream," 102.

[94] Michael Glykas, *Theological Chapters*, Q. 85; Eng. trans.: Angold, *Church and State in Byzantium under the Comneni, 1081–1261*, 451.

[95] Michael Glykas, *Theological Chapters*, Q. 69; Eng. trans.: Papadogiannakis, "Michael Glykas and the Afterlife," 140. According to Papadogiannakis, "Glykas turns to the language of refining gold, asserting that if the light shines upon gold (i.e. the righteous), the gold will become more resplendent. By contrast, if it shines upon wood or hay (i.e. the sins of the wicked), it will set it on fire." Ibid.

sin.⁹⁶ Eustratios's earlier defense of the cult of the saints had cited 2 Maccabees 12:39–45 as biblical proof that sins could be forgiven after death, and selections by John Chrysostom and Pseudo-John of Damascus (discussed in the previous chapter) provided patristic witnesses to the efficacy of prayers and alms for the deceased.⁹⁷ Glykas did not disagree, but gave a "not unqualified" endorsement of the position, using the authority of Pseudo-Dionysius to argue that while prayers and alms could bring about the forgiveness of sins, this applied only to minor sins committed by the otherwise righteous, not to serious sins.⁹⁸

As for the alleviation of suffering, there were plenty of witnesses to the idea that prayers somehow lessened the pains suffered by the dead, even if they were not Christians. Aside from the story of Gregory the Great's prayers for Trajan, popularized in the East in the *Oratio de his qui in fide dormierunt* of Pseudo-Damascene,⁹⁹ there was the story of Makarios the Great, whose prayers brought consolation (παραμυθία) to the soul of a pagan high priest as he stood "in the midst of the fire, from the feet up to the head."¹⁰⁰ One story, "repeated only in Glykas ... comes from the life of John Eleemon ... [and] concerns a person imprisoned by the Persians whose family ... considers him dead and offers liturgical commemorations for him three times a year."¹⁰¹ When the prisoner escaped and returned to his family, he told them "that three times a year, the days on which the liturgy was offered on his behalf, an angel freed him from prison, although the next day he had to return."¹⁰² The moral of the story was simple—if liturgical commemorations had the power to free the living from their prisons, imagine how much more they aided those suffering in the hereafter.

---

⁹⁶ Marinis, *Death and the Afterlife in Byzantium*, 97. "Glykas endorses what had been standard practice in Byzantium (and in Eastern Christianity to date), *mnemosyna*, a series of memorial services—accompanied by memorial meals at the house of the deceased—which were conducted on the third, ninth and fortieth days after death and again on the first anniversary." Papadogiannakis, "Michael Glykas and the Afterlife," 139.

⁹⁷ Cited by both Eustratios and Glykas was the selection from Chrysostom's *Homilies on Matthew*: "If [the deceased] had departed a sinner, it may do away his sins; but if righteous, that it may become an increase of reward and recompense." John Chrysostom, *Homily 31 on The Gospel of Matthew*; NPNF 2.10. 209.

⁹⁸ Papadogiannakis, "Michael Glykas and the Afterlife," 139. "The truthful traditions of the Scriptures teach us that even prayers of the just are efficacious in the course of this life—to say nothing of after death—only for those worthy of holy prayer." Pseudo-Dionysius, *Ecclesiastical Hierarchy* 7.6. Glykas paraphrased this passage to read: "If [the deceased] have still minor [sins], they benefit from the good works; if [the sins] are grievous, God has shut them off because of them." Michael Glykas, *Theological Chapters*, Q. 50; Eng. trans.: Marinis, *Death and the Afterlife in Byzantium*, 98, 162.

⁹⁹ See last chapter.

¹⁰⁰ "Walking in the desert one day, I found the skull of a dead man, lying on the ground. As I was moving it with my stick, the skull spoke to me. I said to it, 'Who are you?' The skull replied, 'I was high priest of the idols and of the pagans who dwelt in this place; but you are Macarius, the Spirit-bearer. Whenever you take pity on those who are in torments, and pray for them, they feel a little respite.' The old man said to him, 'What is this alleviation, and what is this torment?' He said to him, 'As far as the sky is removed from the earth, so great is the fire beneath us; we are ourselves standing in the midst of the fire, from the feet up to the head. It is not possible to see anyone face to face, but the face of one is fixed to the back of another. Yet when you pray for us, each of us can see the other's face a little. Such is our respite.'" *Apophthegmata Patrum*, Macarius the Great 38; Eng. trans.: Ward, *The Sayings of the Desert Fathers*, 136–37.

¹⁰¹ Michael Glykas, *Theological Chapters*, Q. 50; Eng. trans.: Marinis, *Death and the Afterlife in Byzantium*, 99.

¹⁰² Ibid.

The Beginnings of the Dispute

One could easily make the argument that given their shared beliefs and practices concerning the afterlife—both East and West offered prayers and alms for the deceased, both believed that these suffrages were beneficial, both associated them with the forgiveness of sins and the alleviation of postmortem suffering—that there was no reason why the fate of souls after death should ever have become a point of contention. Yet Latin theology's embrace of a "third place" between Heaven and Hell where souls suffered until their penitential debts were paid introduced concepts—for example, satisfaction and expiation—that were largely missing from Eastern thinking on the subject.[103] Perhaps in a less contentious atmosphere a calm discussion of the issues involved would have resolved any alleged discrepancies, but in the years following the Fourth Crusade this was simply not possible. Purgatory, when it was finally introduced, immediately stirred debate.

The first encounter, according to the report later given by metropolitan of Corfu George Bardanes, took place in 1231 (or 1235–36) at a Greek monastery near Otranto in Italy.[104] It was there that Bardanes learned that the Franciscans "teach and lay down falsely as doctrine that there is a purifying fire, where those who died having confessed but do not have time to mourn deeply for their sins are taken and are purified before the Last Judgment by obtaining deliverance from the punishment before the Last Judgment. They present Saint Gregory Dialogos as an ally of such an idea."[105]

The conversation began when a Franciscan friar named Bartholomew wanted to know the Greek view of "where souls go when they die without doing penance and have not had time to complete the *epitimies* their confessors have ordered."[106] Bardanes, speaking for the Greeks, repeated the ancient Greek tradition that sinners do not receive their full punishment until the Last Judgment, because "he who is to judge the whole universe has not yet come with his glory to distinguish the just from the sinners."[107] Until that time, "They go to dark places (εἰς τόπους σκυθρωποτέρους) which give a foretaste of the tortures that sinners must undergo. For, since several

---

[103] See especially Yves Congar, "Le purgatoire," in *Le mystère de la mort et sa célébration, Lex orandi*, 12 (Paris: Les éditions du Cerf, 1951), 279–336. Elsewhere Congar had noted that "the word 'satisfaction' practically does not exist in Greek." Yves Congar, *After Nine Hundred Years: The Background of the Schism between the Eastern and Western Churches* (New York: Fordham University Press, 1959), 31.

[104] For discussions of the dating of the encounter see Martiniano Pellegrino Roncaglia, *Les discussions sur le purgatoire entre Georges Bardanès, Métropolite de Corfou, et frère Bartélemy, franciscain (15 oct.–17 nov. 1231): étude critique avec texte inédit*, Studi e testi francescani 4 (Rome: Scuola tipografica italo-orientale, 1953); Gilbert Dagron, "Byzance et l'union," in *Centre national de la recherche scientifique, 1274: Année charnière: mutations et continuités* (Paris: Editions du C.N.R.S., 1977), 191–202; Gilbert Dagron, "La perception d'une différence: Les débuts de la querelle du purgatoire," in *Actes du XVe Congrès International d'Études Byzantines, Athènes, Septembre 1976* (Athens: Association international d'études byzantines, 1979), 84–92; Johannes Hoeck and Raymond-Joseph Loenertz, *Nikolaos Necktarios von Otranto, Abt von Casole. Beiträge zur Geschichte der ost-westlichen Beziehungen unter Innozenz III. und Friedrich II* (Ettal: Buch-Kunstverlag, 1965), 117–25, 147–235.

[105] Roncaglia, *Les discussions sur le Purgatoire*, 56; Eng. trans.: Marinis, *Death and the Afterlife in Byzantium*, 74.

[106] Roncaglia, *Les discussions sur le Purgatoire*, 56–58; Eng. trans.: Le Goff, *The Birth of Purgatory*, 282.

[107] Roncaglia, *Les discussions sur le Purgatoire*, 58.

places and several rests have been prepared for the just in the house of the father ... so to do various punishments exist for the sinners."[108]

It was at this point in the discussions, which Andrea Riedl described as "confrontational, but polite,"[109] that Bartholomew introduced the Latin teaching on Purgatory, or at least the "purgatorial fire,"[110] "that is to say, a fire that purifies, and that through this fire those who passed from this world without repenting, such as thieves, adulterers, murderers, and all who commit venial sins, suffer in this (purificatory) fire for a certain time and purify themselves of the taint of their sins, and are then delivered from punishment."[111]

That, said Bardanes, was the madness of Origen and his followers, for it embraced the teaching "of the end of hell" where "even demons are supposed to obtain their pardon after several years and be delivered from eternal punishment."[112] This was clearly contrary to the gospel, where Christ spoke of summoning "the just to resurrection of Life, whereas sinners are summoned to the resurrection of judgment," where they [will] depart "into everlasting fire, prepared for the devil and his angels."[113] Bardanes told his "excellent friend" that Christ held out "many threats ... over those who leave this life with wicked actions and crimes unpurified by penance," and thus it was impious to believe that there is "a purificatory fire and a so-called end to punishment prior to the decision of the Judge."[114] Referencing the story of the rich man and Lazarus, he asked Bartholomew, if sinners could be released, "what would have prevented the very faithful Abraham, most beloved of God, from releasing from the fire the rich man without mercy, when he begged, with words capable of moving the depths of one's heart, for a mere drop of water from the tip of one finger to cool his tongue?"[115]

What then was the point of prayers and suffrages for the deceased? Bardanes explained that "the alms and liturgies performed by the relatives of the deceased serve him who has repented not only to avoid the punishment of the purifying fire, as some believe, but [also] to receive the perfect restoration of the first bliss, that is the bliss of paradise and the enjoyment of the goods."[116] Bardanes then produced the writings of Scriptures and the holy fathers "so that, seized by respect before the authority of the greatest masters, he might give up his objections," but the friar remained unpersuaded and "stopped up his ears."[117] The debate was at an end.

---

[108] Ibid., 58.

[109] Andrea Riedl, "Das Purgatorium im 13. Jahrhundert: Schlaglichter auf ein Novum der ost-westlichen Kontroverstheologie am Vorabend des II. Konzils von Lyon (1274)," *Annuarium Historiae Conciliorum* 46.1 (2014): 355-70.

[110] Roncaglia, *Les discussions sur le Purgatoire*, 58-60; Eng. trans.: Le Goff, *The Birth of Purgatory*, 282. According to Mîrşanu, "Here appears for the first time in Greek the 'neologism' πῦρ πουργατόριον, no doubt reflecting Bartholomew's use of *ignis purgatorius*." Mîrşanu, "Dawning Awareness of the Theology of Purgatory in the East," 182.

[111] Roncaglia, *Les discussions sur le Purgatoire*, 58-60; Eng. trans.: Le Goff, *The Birth of Purgatory*, 282.

[112] Roncaglia, *Les discussions sur le Purgatoire*, 60.

[113] Ibid., 60.

[114] Ibid., 60-62.

[115] Ibid., 62; Eng. trans.: Le Goff, *The Birth of Purgatory*, 283.

[116] Roncaglia, *Les discussions sur le Purgatoire*, 68; Eng. trans.: Marinis, *Death and the Afterlife in Byzantium*, 75.

[117] Roncaglia, *Les discussions sur le Purgatoire*, 62; Eng. trans.: Le Goff, *The Birth of Purgatory*, 283.

Bardanes's report of the debate was sent to Patriarch Germanos II (1223–40), who was then residing in Nicaea negotiating with, and battling against, the Latin occupying powers. Recent debates between Latins and Greeks, like those in 1234, had dealt chiefly with the Filioque and azymes,[118] and now suddenly there was a new issue that required attention. Germanos penned a response, now lost, which some Latins interpreted as proof that the Greeks rejected both the cleansing fire and any judgment prior to the Last.[119] However, Germanos may have also been the source of a sermon, later cited by the author of the *Tractatus contra Graecos*,[120] which spoke about the sick being "assayed ... like gold in a furnace and purified [in] their souls," arguing that it was better for them to "purify their souls here below through this the best of furnaces."[121] Although, in context, this was not a reference to the afterlife but to physical trials in this world, the text led the Latins to believe that the Byzantines were not too far removed from their own views on the subject. The fact that the Greeks continued to reject the doctrine thus became a constant source of frustration, especially for the Dominicans living in Constantinople, who saw it as another example of Byzantine bloody-mindedness.[122]

This frustration is evident in the *Tractatus contra Graecos* (1252), which now added Purgatory to the chief doctrinal issues that divided East and West.[123] The author began his discussion with the alleged Greek denial that there was any judgment for the deceased before the Day of Judgment.[124] This was contrary to Scripture, he argued, for Jesus had promised the thief that he would be with Christ in paradise (Luke 23:43) proving that "Christ's paradise was opened not only for this one, but also for all saints, while the gates of Hell were also opened for the damned ... where no human memory reached them, and intercession was no longer effective."[125] The author claimed that the Greeks too believed this, and pointed to the many icons and mosaics in Constantinople that showed "angels of light escorting the souls of saints to heaven and the angels of Satan separating with a fair degree of force the souls of the sinners

---

[118] See chapter 5.

[119] See Daniel Stiernon, "Le Problème de l'union gréco-latine vu de Byzance: De Germain II à Joseph Ier (1232–1273)," in *1274—Année charnière. Mutations et continuités*, 139–66.

[120] The sermon was used as proof that even the Greek doctors (*quidam doctorum suorum*) were favorable to the idea of an *ignis mundificatorius*. Riedl, *Tractatus contra Graecos (1252)*, 62.

[121] Sp. Nik Lagopatēs, *Germanos ho 2., Patriarchēs Kōnstantinoupoleōs-Nikaias, 1222-1240: vios, syngrammata kai epistolai to prōton ekdidomenai*, ed. Sp. Nik Lagopatēs (Tripolei: Ek tōn Typographeiōn tēs Ephēmeridos "Moreas", 1913), 285:9–10; Eng. trans.: Angold, *Church and State in Byzantium under the Comneni 1081–1261*, 452.

[122] According to Michael Angold, "It is easy to sympathize with the Dominican[s]. The Greeks were so evasive. There were elements in the orthodox tradition which pointed in the direction of the doctrine of Purgatory. However, the challenge of the Latin church left orthodox theologians increasingly reluctant to commit themselves on the matter." Ibid.

[123] For more on the *Tractatus* see chapter 2 n. 182. According to Andrea Reidl, while the material about the afterlife "only makes up about a fifth of the total content of the tract in comparison to the other three topics (the *filioque*, azymes, primacy), it is nevertheless surprising that a comparatively recent point of conflict is already so prominently featured." Riedl, "Das Purgatorium," 364.

[124] The fact that the particular judgment was the first issue raised is evidence for Riedl that Purgatory was "only part of the larger eschatological conflict between Eastern and Western Churches." "Das Purgatorium," 364.

[125] Riedl, *Tractatus contra Graecos*, 57–58. See also Riedl, "Das Purgatorium," 366.

from their bodies and bearing them away with them to hell."[126] Surely, he argued, despite their objections, they must accept the particular judgment.

He then went on to affirm the fact that there were "four receptacles of the dead" (Heaven, Hell, Limbo,[127] and Purgatory), the last of these attested to by the testimony of many holy fathers.[128] Using primarily Eastern authors, the author of the *Tractatus* tried to demonstrate "that the contemporary Greeks were not only ignorant of the Latin tradition, but also their own."[129] He began with Macrina the Younger, who had said that "the soul which is made in the likeness of God ... does not return unless cleansed; it is purged either by afflictions in this life or by fire after death (*purgatio uero erit per afflictionem in uita ista, uel per ignem post mortem*)."[130] He then cited Gregory of Nyssa's homily for the first Sunday after Pentecost ("*uel post hanc vitam positus per purgatorii ignis conflationem purgetur*"), Basil's Office for the Dead ("*purga propter uiscera misericorie tue*"), and Pseudo-Damascene's *Oratio de his qui in fide dormierunt*, which spoke about "Purgatory as a river of fire (*fluuio igneo*)" and showed that "the living can use prayer to have a positive influence on the purification of the deceased."[131] Then, to counter the Greek allegation that the Latin teaching was Origenist, he introduced the authority of Athanasius, to clarify the types of sins—only "*subtilia et leuia*"—that can be erased by the purifying fire.[132]

The author then dealt with some of the language of the debate, arguing that the word σωθήσεται in 1 Corinthians 3.15 did not mean *conservatio* (as if souls were simply stored or preserved until judgment) but rather *salvatio*, understood here as an act of cleansing or healing.[133] He maintained that the use of the preposition *per* was also important, since the fire's liberating effect came not from itself, but rather acted "instrumentally, as a tool," at God's command (*Deo iubente*).[134] "So we say that man is saved by fire (*per ignem*). This means that through that temporal and purifying fire (*igne temporali et purgatorio*) he is freed from the stains of forgivable sins

---

[126] Riedl, *Tractatus contra Graecos*, 59; Eng. trans.: Angold, *Church and State in Byzantium under the Comneni 1081–1261*, 452. Marinis speculated that the author of the Tractatus simply "misunderstood depictions of the Last Judgment." Marinis, *Death and the Afterlife in Byzantium*, 75.

[127] Limbo, as described by the author, is the *receptaclum* "that contains the souls of unbaptized children and of the children of unbelieving parents (*non baptizati autem et etiam gentilium pueri*). He relates it to Abraham's bosom ... which was used to house the righteous of the Old Covenant, especially the patriarchs and prophets, until for the resurrection of Christ. Although the *limbus partum* was now empty and closed because Christ redeemed its former residents, in reconceiving it as the *Limbus puerorum*, the "womb of Abraham" was given new residents." Riedl, "Das Purgatorium," 366. For the doctrine of limbo and its history see Christopher Belting, "The Development of the Idea of Limbo in the Middle Ages" (PhD thesis, Oxford University, 1997).

[128] Riedl, *Tractatus contra Graecos*, 61. According to Riedl, "In this first section, the author focuses exclusively on the fate of the righteous on the one hand and the damned on the other, thereby addressing Heaven and Hell without yet considering Purgatory as a third place... The subsequent presentation of the four receptacles implies a categorization of the deceased according to their earnings and behavior during their lifetimes, which is decisive for their allocation to the proper *receptaculum*." Riedl, "Das Purgatorium," 365.

[129] Riedl, "Das Purgatorium," 365.

[130] Riedl, *Tractatus contra Graecos*, 63. "The author anticipated that the Greeks may not attribute the same authority to a woman's testimony as to a man's, and consequently substantiated Macrina's statements with those of her brothers Basil and Gregory of Nyssa." Riedl, "Das Purgatorium," 367.

[131] Riedl, *Tractatus contra Graecos*, 63–64.

[132] Ibid., 65.

[133] Ibid., 67.

[134] Ibid., 68.

(*peccatorum uenialium*), so that the soul cleaned from stain can be presented worthily to the Judge."[135]

The debate over Purgatory initially found the Latins far better prepared than their Greek counterparts, as they set out assembling patristic florilegia to support their position. Among them was the *Libellus de fide ss. Trinitatis* of Nicholas of Cotrone, a Greek-speaking bishop of the Latin church, which was later used by Thomas Aquinas in his own *Contra errores Graecorum*.[136] Here only two texts were cited in favor of Purgatory, from Gregory of Nyssa[137] and Theodoret of Cyrus,[138] both of which are now known to be spurious.

The battle over Purgatory soon shifted to Cyprus, where the Latins' use of azymes and the enforcement of papal primacy had long been the source of tension. And while Rome "had wrought radical changes in the structure [and] episcopal hierarchy of the Orthodox church ... [it had actually] interfered little in its internal life and workings."[139] That changed in 1254 when Pope Innocent IV, more "enlightened"[140] and yet "markedly more interventionist than ... his predecessors," wrote to the papal legate, Cardinal Odo (Eudes) of Châteauraoux, "telling him which rites of the Orthodox church were tolerable and which were not."[141] Most of the letter dealt with sacramental practice (e.g., that the Cypriots should postpone chrismation until it could be performed by the bishop), but in the eighteenth article he addressed the issue of Purgatory, providing what Le Goff called "the birth certificate of Purgatory as a doctrinally defined place."[142]

---

[135] Ibid.

[136] The work was probably composed at the request of the emperor Theodore Laskaris (1254–1258), who had asked Nicholas for the Latin positions on the theological points in dispute. See Antoine Dondaine, "Nicolas de Cotrone et les sources du Contra errores Graecorum de Saint Thomas" *Divus Thomas* 28 (1950): 313–40; Mark Jordan, "Theological Exegesis and Aquinas's Treatise 'Against the Greeks,'" *Church History* 56 (1987): 445–56. According to Jordan: "The collection gives by far the greatest weight to trinitarian citations, numbering 93 of the 112 passages in the Leonine edition. Eleven more concern primacy, six leavening, and two Purgatory." "Theological Exegesis," 447.

[137] "If anyone here in his frail life has been less than able to cleanse himself of sin, after departing hence, (*post transitum hinc*),through the blazing fire of Purgatory (*per Purgatorii ignis conflationem*) the penalty is the more quickly paid, the more and more of the ever-faithful bride offers to her spouse in memory of his passion gifts and holocaust on behalf of the children she has brought forth for that spouse by word and sacrament just as we preach in fidelity to this dogmatic truth so we believe." Nicholas of Cotrone, *Libellus de fide ss. Trinitatis* 111; Eng. trans.: Likoudis, *Ending the Byzantine Greek Schism*, 188.

[138] "The apostle states that one is saved thus as through a blazing fire cleansing whatever accumulated through carelessness in life's activities or at least from the dust of the feet of earthly living. In this fire one remains so long as any earthly and bodily affections are being purged (*in quo igne tandiu manet, quandiu quidquid corpulentiae et terreni affectus inhaesit, purgetur*). For such a person holy mother Church prays and devoutly offers peace offerings, and so through this such a one emerging clean and pure assists immaculate before the most pure eyes of the Lord of hosts." Nicholas of Cotrone, *Libellus de fide ss. Trinitatis* 112; Eng. trans.: Likoudis, *Ending the Byzantine Greek Schism*, 188.

[139] Coureas, *The Latin Church in Cyprus, 1195–1312*, 293.

[140] Michael Angold, "Greeks and Latins after 1204: The Perspective of Exile," in Arbel, Hamilton, and Jacoby, *Latins and Greeks in the Eastern Mediterranean after 1204*, 74.

[141] Coureas, *The Latin Church in Cyprus, 1195–1312*, 293. Innocent was already engaged in negotiations with Emperor John III Vatatzes and Patriarch Manuel II, reaching an agreement that Joseph Gill called "the most promising opportunity of restoring unity to the church during all the long years of schism" (Gill, *Byzantium and the Papacy, 1198–1400*, 95). Unfortunately, the death of all three parties in quick succession prevented the deal from going forward. For more see Siecienski, *The Papacy and the Orthodox*, 294–96.

[142] Le Goff, *The Birth of Purgatory*, 284.

Since the Greeks themselves, it is said, believe and profess truly and without hesitation that the souls of those who die after receiving penance but without having had time to complete it, or who die without mortal sin but guilty of venial [sins] or minor faults are purged after death and may be helped by the suffrages of the Church (*qui, suscepta paenitentia, ea non peracta, vel qui sine mortali peccato, cum venialibus tamen et minutis decedunt, purgari post mortem, et posse suffragiis Ecclesiae adiuvari*); we, considering that the Greeks assert that they cannot find in the works of their doctors any certain and proper name to designate the place of this purgation (*quia locum purgationis*), and that, moreover, according to the traditions and authority of the Holy Fathers, this name is Purgatory (*purgatorium nominantes*); we wish that in the future this expression be also accepted by them (*quod de caetero apud illos isto nomine appelletur*). For, in this temporary fire, sins, not of course crimes and capital errors, which could not previously have been forgiven through penance, but slight and minor sins, are purged (*sed parva et minuta purgantur*); if they have not been forgiven during existence, they weigh down the soul after death.[143]

It is clear that the pope genuinely believed that the Greeks already accepted the reality of postmortem purgation, and that the only difference between East and West was that the Latins had achieved a greater degree of clarity in describing where it took place.[144] Innocent, hoping to appeal to this "broad consensus ... on the matter of postmortem purging of sins," thus penned a statement "notable for its modesty and its minimalism."[145] Unfortunately, "The spirit of reconciliation did not survive Innocent IV's death," and his successors became more insistent that the Greeks accept the doctrine in terms defined by the Latin scholastics.[146]

Central to the scholastic development of Purgatory were Albert Magnus and Bonaventure, both of whom built upon the foundations already established by William of Auvergne and Alexander of Hales. Albert was key, for he had the ability "to synthesize the popular, empirical account of Purgatory, which accounted so much for its broad appeal, with the rational academic arguments of the theologians.... [This] gave it a staying power it could not have enjoyed had it been only the bailiwick of storytellers and visionaries with colorful imaginations or merely the product of arid arguments of intellectuals."[147] In his *De Resurrectione* Albert spoke about the various abodes of the dead, distinguishing between the limbo of children and the limbo of the fathers, locating Purgatory "next to Hell and in the upper part of Hell," although

---

[143] Innocent IV, *"Sub Catholicae,"* 23; Eng. trans.: Le Goff, *The Birth of Purgatory*, 283–84.

[144] "In his opinion, Greeks' views about the fate of a sinner's soul after death were not so very different from Latin teaching. All that the Orthodox had failed to do was to elaborate an appropriate terminology. He therefore insisted that for want of a proper Greek word they should use the term Purgatory." Angold, "Greeks and Latins after 1204: The Perspective of Exile," 74.

[145] Walls, *Purgatory*, 23.

[146] Angold, "Greeks and Latins after 1204: The Perspective of Exile," 74.

[147] Walls, *Purgatory*, 22. According to Le Goff, Albert's work "shows the rationalization of a belief which ... rose as much from imagery as from reasoning, as much from fantastic tales as from authorities, and which did not develop in any straightforward way, but rather through countless meanderings, hesitations, and contradictions, culminating finally in a tightly knit fabric of beliefs." Le Goff, *The Birth of Purgatory*, 259.

in many ways it was "closer to Heaven, to God, than to Hell."[148] For Albert the chief difference between Hell and Purgatory was "not of intensity but of duration," so that Purgatory's residents suffered only until such time as their venial sins were remitted.[149]

In his later *Commentary on the Sentences*, Albert speculated that most would experience the pains of Purgatory, since death itself was rarely enough to atone for all one's venial sins, martyrs being the exception to the rule.[150] As long as one has built on the foundations of faith, hope, and love, then these venial sins ("customarily called wood, hay, and stubble") could be burned up, which raised the issue of the purgatorial fire (*purgatorius ignis*), and the place where that fire necessarily existed, Purgatory (*purgatorium*).[151] It had to be fire, Albert argued, for cold was a punishment of the damned, while only fire had the power to be both "purgative and consumptive."[152] Souls willingly submitted to this process because they wanted to be saved, and while demons gleefully looked on during these purgatorial sufferings, they were not responsible for inflicting them.[153] Purgatory itself was not a terminal place, but was rather a place of passage, itself divided between those suffering "from a lack of proper merit or from a failure to have paid the price."[154]

It was in article 10 that Albert discussed "the error of certain Greeks who say that no one enters heaven or hell before Judgment Day and that everyone must wait in intermediate places (*in locis mediis*) to be transferred to one or the other."[155] Albert was convinced that the denial of Purgatory was a "wicked heresy" (*haeresis pessima*), for it

---

[148] Le Goff, *The Birth of Purgatory*, 259. Le Goff cites Albert as a witness that not "all thirteenth century thinking in regard to Purgatory tended in the direction of infernalization." Ibid. See Wilhelm Kübel, ed., *Alberti Magni Opera Omnia Tomus XXVI: De Sacramentis. De Incarnatione. De Resurrectione* (Münster: Aschendorff, 1958), 315–18, 320–21; Eng. trans.: Albert the Great, *On Resurrection*, trans. Irven M. Resnick and Franklin T. Harkins, FC Medieval Continuation 20 (Washington, DC: Catholic University of America Press, 2020), 225. "*De Resurrectione* ... is actually an independent work, although it has been added to the other works *De Sacramentis, De Incarnatione,* [*De Resurrectione*], *De IV Coaequavis, De Homine,* and *De Bono.* Together, these works form the larger *Summa Parisiensis*, which was comprised of Albertus' public disputations while he was a master at the University of Paris." Christopher Beiting, "The Nature and Structure of Limbo in the Works of Albertus Magnus." *New Blackfriars* 85 (2004): 493.

[149] Le Goff, *The Birth of Purgatory*, 257–58. Albert distinguished between temporary and permanent receptacles for the deceased, and whether they involved punishment (damnation and/or punishment) or glory. Purgatory was the temporary place of damnation and punishment, while the limbo of children was a permanent place of damnation but not punishment. Hell was the permanent place of damnation and punishment, while Heaven was the permanent place of glory.

[150] Albert the Great, *Commentary on Book IV of the Sentences*, Dist 21, Art 1 in Auguste Borgnet, ed., *Alberti Magni Opera Omnia Tomos XXIX* (Paris, 1894), 862–63.

[151] Albert the Great, *Commentary on Book IV of the Sentences*, Dist 21, Art 4 in Borgnet, ed., *Alberti Magni Opera Omnia Tomos XXIX*, 865–67. Albert made the argument that although the word "Purgatory" was missing from the works of the fathers, "It is necessary, according to all reason and faith, that there be a purgatorial fire," from which "it follows in a concordant way that there is a Purgatory." Ibid., 866; Eng. trans.: Le Goff, *The Birth of Purgatory*, 261.

[152] "To the question concerning icy cold, we say that they do not suffer an icy cold. In fact, this is a quality (*passio*) of those whose love has cooled, but this does not occur in souls being purged." Albert the Great, *On Resurrection*, 231.

[153] "To the question concerning demons, whether they are their tormentors, one must say that they are not in any way other than by leading them to punishment." Ibid.

[154] Albert the Great, *Commentary on Book IV of the Sentences*, Dist 44, Art 45, in Auguste Borgnet, ed., *Alberti Magni Opera Omnia Tomos XXX* (Paris, 1894), 603–4; Eng. trans.: Le Goff, *The Birth of Purgatory*, 263.

[155] Albert the Great, *Commentary on Book IV of the Sentences*, Dist 21, Art 10 in Auguste Borgnet, ed., *Alberti Magni Opera Omnia Tomos XXIX* (Paris, 1894), 875; Eng. trans.: Le Goff, *The Birth of Purgatory*, 262.

prohibited Christians from receiving the wages promised by Christ as reward for their faith.[156] For Albert, once people had been cleansed of sin, a process expedited by the prayers and suffrages of the church militant, they could leave Purgatory and immediately enter paradise. This position, clearly supported by both Scripture (Lk 25:43, 16:22, Rv 6:2, Heb 2:40) and the fathers, was contrary to the Greek belief that "the dead form a community and that, as in urban communities where decisions are made in common, the decision regarding both the saved and the damned must be taken and executed in a single moment," that is, at the Last Judgment.[157]

Bonaventure, a student of Alexander of Hales, dealt with Purgatory both in his *Commentary on the Sentences*[158] and also in the *Breviloquium*, where he summarized his position:

> The fire of Purgatory is a physical fire which torments the spirits of the just who in this life did not fulfill the penance and due satisfaction [for their sins]. These are punished to a greater or lesser degree according as they took with them from this life more or less of what must be burned away.[159] They are afflicted less severely than in Hell, but more so than in this present world.[160] ... By means of this suffering, inflicted by a physical fire, their spirits are purified of the guilt and dregs of sin, as well as its after-effects. When they are wholly cleansed, they take flight immediately and are brought into the glory of paradise.[161]

Like Albert, Bonaventure denied that the punishments of Purgatory were inflicted by demons[162] and believed Purgatory was, in many ways, closer to Heaven than to Hell,[163] because "there is more certainty of glory in Purgatory" than there is during our earthly pilgrimage (i.e., "on the way [*via*]").[164] The punishments of Purgatory were severe, but they were "far different and far milder than damnation" since "these souls know without the possibility of doubt that their state is not the same as ... those who

---

[156] Albert the Great, *Commentary on Book IV*, 877. Walls noted that "Albert took perhaps the strongest stand among his contemporaries declaring it a heresy to deny the doctrine of Purgatory." Walls, *Purgatory*, 22.

[157] Albert the Great, *Commentary on Book IV*, 876; Eng. trans.: Le Goff, *The Birth of Purgatory*, 262.

[158] Bonaventure, *Commentaria in Quatuor Libros Sententiarum* IV Dist 20, pars 1 in *Bonaventurae Opera Omnia Tomos IV* (Rome: Collegium S. Bonaventurae, 1889), 517–29.

[159] Bonaventure, *Brevlloqulum*, Part 7, chap 2; Eng. trans.: Bonaventure, *Texts on Translation Series Vol IX: Breviloquium*, trans. Dominic Monti (Bonaventure, NY: Franciscan Institute Publications, 2005), 269. "Now some just persons die before having wholly satisfied their penance in this life. But the beauty of eternal order cannot be disturbed, and so the merit of eternal life cannot go to them undeservedly and the stain of sin cannot remain unpunished. Therefore, even though they will be rewarded ultimately, it is still necessary that they be temporarily punished according to their deserts and the guilt of their sin." Ibid., 270.

[160] Ibid., 269. "This penalty is not so severe as to deprive them of hope and of the knowledge that they are not in Hell, although because of the greatness of their punishments they might not always avert to this." Ibid., 269–70.

[161] Ibid., 270.

[162] Bonaventure, *Commentaria in Quatuor Libros Sententiarum* IV Dist 20, pars 1, q 5, in *Bonaventurae Opera Omnia Tomos IV*, 524–25.

[163] Nevertheless, in terms of its location Bonaventure follows the traditional Latin view that Purgatory is "below, but it is in the middle" between the two. Bonaventure, *Commentaria in Quatuor Libros Sententiarum* IV Dist 20, pars 1, q 6, in *Bonaventurae Opera Omnia Tomos IV*, 525–27.

[164] Bonaventure, *Commentaria in Quatuor Libros Sententiarum* IV Dist 20, pars 1, q 4, in *Bonaventurae Opera Omnia Tomos IV*, 523.

are tortured in Hell with no remedy."[165] Yet Albert and Bonaventure had some important differences as well. For example, while Albert had taught that souls undergo Purgatory willingly, Bonaventure believed that they merely "tolerate it ... desiring the opposite" (*Poena purgatorii minimam habet rationem voluntarii, quia est a voluntate tolerante quidem sed oppositum desiderante*).[166]

Bonaventure taught that the punishments of Purgatory, inflicted by a physical fire,[167] "must be justly punitive, duly atoning, and sufficiently cleansing," although it could be argued that he emphasized the first two aspects far more than the third.[168] He believed that "just as supreme goodness suffers no good to remain unrewarded, so it cannot suffer any evil to go unpunished," which is why those who "die before having wholly satisfied their penance in this life" cannot inherit eternal life before being "temporarily punished according to their deserts and the guilt of their sin."[169] This temporal punishment was meted out only to those who died "in the state of grace" (i.e., burdened by venial as opposed to mortal sin), with its severity and duration determined "as the measure of their guilt demands."[170] Purification, however, is not forgotten, for "the fire of Purgatory [also] possesses ... the very power of indwelling grace, assisted by the external punishment," which "effectively cleanses the soul, which is thereby punished for its offenses and relieved of the burden of its guilt."[171] Once "there remains nothing unfit for glory," souls are immediately lifted up by "a fire of love" to "the gates of heaven," for it would not befit "the divine mercy or justice further to delay glory once God finds the vessel to be suitable."[172]

As for the suffrages of the church, Bonaventure followed the traditional view that "such suffrages benefit the dead ... [but] not all the dead indiscriminately," just " 'the moderately good,' [*mediocriter boni*] that is, the souls in Purgatory. They are of no use for 'the entirely evil,' the souls in hell, nor for 'the entirely good,' those that are in heaven."[173] The prayers and sacrifices of the church benefited souls depending on a number of factors, including "the charity of the living, who may be more solicitous of

---

[165] Bonaventure, *Brevlloqulum*, Part 7, chap 2; Eng. trans.: Bonaventure, *Breviloquium*, 272.

[166] Bonaventure, *Commentaria in Quatuor Libros Sententiarum* IV Dist 20, pars 1, q 6, in *Bonaventurae Opera Omnia Tomos IV*, 522. Because "the punishment of Purgatory must be atoning ... the element of satisfaction that is lacking—namely, freely choosing to undergo it—must be compensated by the bitterness of the punishment itself." Bonaventure, *Brevlloqulum*, Part 7, chap 2; Eng. trans.: Bonaventure, *Breviloquium*, 271.

[167] Ibid., 270. "Therefore the order of divine justice demands that a material fire punish the spiritual soul. For, as the soul is united to the body in the order of nature for the sake of vivifying it, so it should be united to material fire in the order of justice for the sake of receiving punishment—for one who is to be punished must be united to a punishing agent." Ibid., 271.

[168] Ibid., 270.

[169] Ibid.

[170] Ibid., 271. "To quote the great doctor Augustine, 'It is necessary that the sinner suffer pain in proportion to his or her inordinate love.' The more deeply a person has loved the things of this world in the inner depths of his or her heart, the harder it will be for that person to be cleansed." Ibid.

[171] Ibid., 272.

[172] Ibid. In the *Commentary on the Sentences* he cited Luke 23:43 ("Today you shall be with me in Paradise") as proof of this assertion against the Greeks.

[173] Bonaventure, *Brevlloqulum*, Part 7, chap 3; Eng. trans.: Bonaventure, *Breviloquium*, 273. "By the word 'suffrages' I mean all those things the Church does on behalf of the dead, such as sacrifices, fasts, alms, and other prayers and voluntary penances performed for the purpose of facilitating and hastening the expiation of their sins." Ibid.

some souls than others. This benefit either alleviates their suffering or hastens their release, as divine providence sees fit for each soul's good."[174]

Thomas Aquinas, undoubtedly the most influential of all the scholastics, addressed the subject of Purgatory in both his theological writings (*Commentary on the Sentences*,[175] *Summa Contra Gentiles*,[176] *Summa Theologiae*,[177] *De Malo*[178]), and in his polemical works aimed specifically at the Greeks—the *Contra Errores Graecorum* and *De Rationibus Fidei Contra Saracenos, Graecos, et Armenos ad Cantorem Antiochenum*.[179] What is evident in Thomas's thinking, which "grew partly out of the debate with Eastern Christians," is how rapid the "doctrinal development and ecclesial assimilation" of Purgatory had been, so much so that Thomas "could say with ease that to deny Purgatory is to speak against divine justice and to resist the authority of the church."[180] For Thomas it was self-evident that sin "involves [both] guilt (*culpa*) and punishment (*poena*), the making of satisfaction[181] ... [and] because sin violates an order, a state of relations between God and men, that violation has to be overcome either in this life or after death."[182] Simply put, one had to pay now or pay later.

---

[174] Ibid. "Therefore, while the severity of divine justice demands that the just in whom there remains some guilt of sin must be cleansed after this life by the pains of Purgatory, the sweetness of divine mercy dictates that they should also be lifted up and given assistance and comfort." Ibid., 274.
[175] Thomas Aquinas, *Scriptum super libros Sententiarum IV* d.45; Eng. trans.: Thomas Aquinas, *Commentary on the Sentences, Book IV, Distinctions, 43–50*, trans. Beth Mortensen (Green Bay, WI: Aquinas Institute, 2018).
[176] Thomas Aquinas, *Summa Contra Gentiles*, Book 4, chap 91; Eng. trans.: Thomas Aquinas, *Summa Contra Gentiles Book 4: Salvation*, trans. Charles O'Neil (Garden City, NY: Image Books, 1957), 334–38.
[177] The subject of Purgatory in the *Summa* is covered in the Supplement, which itself was gleaned from Thomas's earlier treatment of the subject in the *Scriptum super libros Sententiarum*.
[178] Thomas Aquinas, *De Malo*, q 7, art 11; Eng. trans.: Thomas Aquinas, *On Evil*, trans. Richard Regan (Oxford: Oxford University Press, 2003), 308–14.
[179] Thomas Aquinas, *On Reasons for Our Faith against the Muslims, and a Reply to the Denial of Purgatory by Certain Greeks and Armenians to the Cantor of Antioch*, trans. Peter Damien Fehlner (New Bedford, MA: Franciscans of the Immaculate, 2002).
[180] Robert Ombres, "The Doctrine of Purgatory According to St. Thomas Aquinas," *Downside Review* 99 (1981): 279. "Wherefore those who deny Purgatory speak against the justice of God: for which reason such a statement is erroneous and contrary to faith. Hence Gregory of Nyssa ... adds: 'This we preach, holding to the teaching of truth, and this is our belief; this the universal Church holds, by praying for the dead that they may be loosed from sins.' This cannot be understood except as referring to Purgatory: and whosoever resists the authority of the Church, incurs the note of heresy." Thomas Aquinas, *Summa Theologiae*, app 2, q 1, art 1; Eng. trans.: Thomas Aquinas, *Summa Theologica*, 3010. Yet despite the firm place Purgatory seems to have achieved in Thomas's understanding of church doctrine, Le Goff made the argument that it did not occupy a very *important* place. "My impression is that Thomas dealt with Purgatory because the question was obligatory, because, to lapse for a moment into academic jargon, it was 'in the syllabus' and not because he thought the issue was a crucial one. To Thomas, Purgatory seemed, to use a word that was not part of his vocabulary, 'vulgar.'" Le Goff, *The Birth of Purgatory*, 268.
[181] "The act of sin makes a man deserving of punishment insofar as he transgresses the order of divine justice, to which he does not return except through some recompense of punishment, which restores the equality of justice, namely so that he who indulged his will more than he ought to, acting against the command of God, should, according to the order of divine justice, suffer, willingly or unwillingly, something contrary to that which he would want." Thomas Aquinas, *Summa Theologiæ* I-II, q. 87, a. 6; Eng. trans.: Thomas Aquinas, *Summa Theologica*, 977.
[182] Ombres, *Theology of Purgatory*, 41. "For, if after guilt is effaced through contrition, the debt of punishment is not entirely taken away, nor are venial sins always taken away when mortal ones are forgiven, and God's justice requires that sin be ordered by the due punishment, a person who dies after contrition and absolution for sin but before making the due satisfaction must be punished after this life." Thomas Aquinas, *Summa Theologiae*, app 2, q 1, art 1; Eng. trans.: Thomas Aquinas, *Summa Theologica*, 3010.

Sin, because it creates this debt, constituted an obstacle on our return to God ("*redditus*"), which is the end toward which all intellectual beings tend.[183] Thomas taught that the frustration or accomplishment of our proper end results from choices we make in life, many of which, because of concupiscence, are contrary to our true *telos*—that is, they are sinful to a greater (mortal) or lesser (venial) degree.[184] Mortal sin, which is a loss of charity, resulted in a total falling away from God, and those who died in this state were rightly consigned to the "destructive punishments" of Hell.[185] However, "to die with forgiven mortal sin, but before all the punishment due has been met, or to die in venial sin," is different, for these souls "still have the virtue of charity and so can conclude their turning to God."[186] Yet before one could approach God, all "impediments" needed to be removed/purified, and although this was normally done here on earth "by penance and the other sacraments ... [sometimes] such purification is not entirely perfected in this life [and] one remains a debtor for the punishment, whether by reason of some negligence, or business, or even because a man is overtaken by death."[187] Such people needed to be "held back from the achievement of their reward while they undergo cleansing punishments ... purged after this life ... by punishments ... which satisfy the debt."[188] This was the raison d'être of Purgatory.

This explained the "why" of Purgatory, but Thomas also had to address the when, where, and how. The answer to the "when" question was partly worked out in opposition to "the error of some of the Greeks, who deny Purgatory and say that before the resurrection souls neither ascend into heaven nor descend into hell."[189] Echoing Albert, Thomas argued that "there can be no reason for deferring reward or punishment beyond the time at which the soul is first capable of receiving either the one

---

[183] "Now, the ultimate end of man, and of every intellectual substance, is called felicity or happiness, because this is what every intellectual substance desires as an ultimate end, and for its own sake alone. Therefore, the ultimate happiness and felicity of every intellectual substance is to know God." Thomas Aquinas, *Summa Contra Gentiles*, Book 3, chap 25; Thomas Aquinas, *Summa Contra Gentiles Book 3, Part 1: Providence*, trans. Charles O'Neil (Garden City, NY: Image Books, 1957), 102.

[184] "Both mortal and venial sin prevent perfect happiness, mortal sin in one way, venial sin in another way. For human beings by mortal sin suffer diminution of goodness by being deprived of the chief thing that leads to their end, namely, charity. And human beings by venial sin suffer diminution of goodness and an impediment by reason of something unbecoming in the sinful act.... There is also a difference regarding the liability to punishment, since one by mortal sin merits destructive punishment as an enemy, and one by venial sin merits corrective punishment." Thomas Aquinas, *De Malo*, q 7 art 11; Eng. trans.: Thomas Aquinas, *On Evil*, 311.

[185] Thomas refuted any hint that Purgatory is Origenist by affirming on several occasions that "in the future life, mortal sin can never be remitted regarding moral fault, since no new infusion of grace and charity transforms the soul essentially after this life ends. And because the moral fault has not been remitted, neither is the punishment." Ibid.

[186] Ombres, *Theology of Purgatory*, 41. Such a person "is not entirely cut off from his reward, because such things can happen without mortal sin, which alone takes away the charity to which the reward of eternal life is due." Thomas Aquinas, *Summa Contra Gentiles*, Book 4, chap 91; Eng. trans.: Thomas Aquinas, *Summa Contra Gentiles Book 4: Salvation*, 336.

[187] Ibid. "Nonetheless, one must weigh the fact that in the case of the good there can be an obstacle to keep the souls from receiving their ultimate reward, which consists in the vision of God, right after their release from the body. To that vision no rational creature can be elevated unless it be thoroughly and entirely purified, since that vision exceeds the whole of the creature's natural powers." Ibid.

[188] Ibid.

[189] Ibid.

or the other, that is, as soon as it leaves the body."[190] He denied that there was a difference between the "paradise" promised to the thief on the cross and "the ultimate reward, which will be in heaven," for if one "considered rightly the words of sacred Scripture ... he will find that the final recompense promised to the saints in heaven is given immediately after this life."[191] The only delay one might experience was the time spent in Purgatory, where the deferment of eternal joy corresponded "to the firmness with which sin has taken root in its subject."[192]

Concerning Purgatory's location, Thomas admitted that "nothing is clearly stated in Scripture about [it] ... nor is it possible to offer convincing arguments on this question."[193] Nevertheless he thought it "probable" that Purgatory was situated "below and in proximity to Hell, so that it is the same fire which torments the damned in Hell and cleanses the just in Purgatory; although the damned being lower in merit, are to be consigned to a lower place."[194] This fire, eternal in substance but temporary in effect, burned off the guilt of venial sin like "wood, hay, stubble," releasing a person "from his indebtedness" to God by paying the debt of punishment incurred by sin.[195] This punishment, he emphasized, was not administered by demons, for it would be unjust if "he who has triumphed over someone should be subjected to him after victory ... [and] those who are in Purgatory have triumphed over the demons, since they died without mortal sin."[196]

The pains of Purgatory for Thomas were twofold—"one of loss, namely, inasmuch as souls are held back from the divine vision; the other, of sense, according as they are physically punished by fire. And in both, the least punishment of Purgatory exceeds the greatest punishment of this life."[197] Although they endured great suffering, the residents of Purgatory were consoled by the fact that their punishments, unlike those experienced by the damned, were temporary and ultimately beneficial.[198] That said,

---

[190] Thomas compared the Christian's reception of his/her eternal reward/punishment to "warfare and the days of the hireling.... But, after the state of warfare and the labor of the hireling, the reward or punishment is straightway due those who have fought well or badly.... Immediately after death, therefore, the souls receive either reward or punishment." Ibid., 335.

[191] Ibid., 337.

[192] Thomas Aquinas, *Summa Theologiae*, app 1, q 2, art 6; Eng. trans.: Thomas Aquinas, *Summa Theologica*, 3009. "Some venial sins cling more persistently than others, according as the affections are more inclined to them, and more firmly fixed in them. And since that which clings more persistently is more slowly cleansed, it follows that some are tormented in Purgatory longer than others, for as much as their affections were steeped in venial sins." Ibid.

[193] Thomas Aquinas, *Summa Theologiae*, app 2, q 1, art 2; Eng. trans.: Thomas Aquinas, *Summa Theologica*, 3011.

[194] Ibid. He allowed that "some are punished in various places, either that the living may learn, or that the dead may be succored," explaining the stories told by Gregory the Great and others about visions and apparitions. Yet Thomas dismissed the idea that "the place of Purgatory is where man sins. This does not seem probable, since a man may be punished at the same time for sins committed in various places." Ibid.

[195] Thomas Aquinas, *Summa Theologiae*, app 1, q 2, art 5; Eng. trans.: Thomas Aquinas, *Summa Theologica*, 3009. "Whosoever is another's debtor, is freed from his indebtedness by paying the debt. And, since the obligation incurred by guilt is nothing else than the debt of punishment, a person is freed from that obligation by undergoing the punishment which he owed. Accordingly, the punishment of Purgatory cleanses from the debt of punishment." Ibid.

[196] Thomas Aquinas, *Summa Theologiae*, app 1, q 2, art 3; Eng. trans.: Thomas Aquinas, *Summa Theologica*, 3007.

[197] Thomas Aquinas, *Summa Theologiae*, app 1, q 2, art 1; Eng. trans.: Thomas Aquinas, *Summa Theologica*, 3006.

[198] "Consequently there is no hope either in the blessed or in the damned. On the other hand, hope can be in wayfarers, whether of this life or in Purgatory, because in either case they apprehend happiness as a

Thomas did not believe people suffered them willingly, for "no one begs to be freed from suffering that he willingly endures. But those who are in Purgatory beg to be freed," which is why the suffrages of the church were there to aid them.[199]

According to Robert Ombres, Thomas's position on suffrages shows the "humanness" of his writings on Purgatory, for behind everything he wrote "is the conviction that the souls in Purgatory are fixed in charity," and that the "bonds of charity which unites believers ... survive death ... [It was] a form of friendship ... [wherein] a dead man can be helped by a living one because what one does through a friend one does oneself."[200] We cannot "change their state from unhappiness to happiness or vice versa," but we can attain for them the "diminution of punishment, or something of the kind"[201] "through masses, through almsgiving, and through prayers."[202] Thomas was clear that those who are without charity (i.e., the damned) cannot profit from the actions of the living, which is why it was useless to pray for them, yet for those in Purgatory, who remain fixed in charity, these suffrages were of great benefit.[203]

Thomas's writings aimed specifically against the criticisms of the Greeks, the *Contra Errores Graecorum* and *De Rationibus Fidei*, both addressed the subject of Purgatory, albeit briefly. The *Contra Errores Graecorum* merely repeated the quotations from the *Libellus de fide ss. Trinitatis* of Nicholas of Cotrone, adding that the denial of Purgatory denigrated the power of the Eucharist, which offered "the souls in Purgatory [the] special healing ... conferred by this sacrament."[204] The treatment of

---

future possible thing." Thomas Aquinas, *Summa Theologiae*, II-II, q 18, art 3; Eng. trans.: Thomas Aquinas, *Summa Theologica*, 1243.

[199] Thomas Aquinas, *Summa Theologiae*, app 1, q 2, art 2; Eng. trans.: Thomas Aquinas, *Summa Theologica*, 3006. "Now some people say that it is not voluntary in any way, for the souls are so absorbed by their sufferings that they do not know they are being purified by them, but they believe themselves to be damned. But this is false: for unless they knew they would be freed, they would not beg for prayers, which they often do." Ibid., 3006–7.

[200] Ombres, *Theology of Purgatory*, 42. "Charity, which is the bond uniting the members of the Church, extends not only to the living, but also to the dead who die in charity. For charity, which is the life of the soul even as the soul is the life of the body, has no end: charity never falls away (1 Cor 12:8). Moreover, the dead live in the memory of the living: wherefore the intention of the living can be directed to them. Hence the suffrages of the living profit the dead in two ways even as they profit the living, both on account of the bond of charity and on account of the intention being directed to them." Thomas Aquinas, *Summa Theologiae*, Supp, q 71, art 2; Eng. trans.: Thomas Aquinas, *Summa Theologica*, 2833.

[201] Ibid.

[202] Thomas Aquinas, *On the Apostles' Creed*; Eng. trans.: Thomas Aquinas, *The Sermon-Conferences of St Thomas Aquinas on the Apostles' Creed*, trans. Nicholas Ayo (Notre Dame, IN: University of Notre Dame Press, 1988), 85. "We should not wonder, because even in the world one friend can make satisfaction for another. We should understand the same thing about those in Purgatory." Ibid. Thomas also recognized that "fasting can profit the departed by reason of charity, and on account of the intention being directed to the departed. Nevertheless, fasting does not by its nature contain anything pertaining to charity or to the directing of the intention, and these things are extrinsic thereto as it were, and for this reason Augustine did not reckon, while Gregory did reckon, fasting among the suffrages for the dead." Thomas Aquinas, *Summa Theologiae*, Supp, q 71, art 9; Eng. trans.: Thomas Aquinas, *Summa Theologica*, 2841.

[203] "The punishment of Purgatory is intended to supplement the satisfaction which was not fully completed in the body. Consequently, since ... the works of one person can avail for another's satisfaction, whether the latter be living or dead, the suffrages of the living without any doubt profit those who are in Purgatory." Thomas Aquinas, *Summa Theologiae*, Supp, q 71, art 6; Eng. trans.: Thomas Aquinas, *Summa Theologica*, 2838.

[204] Thomas Aquinas, *Contra Errores Graecorum* pars 2 c 40; Eng. trans.: Likoudis, *Ending the Byzantine Greek Schism*, 187.

Purgatory in *De Rationibus Fidei* is longer and addressed the Greek position, which "while wishing to avoid Origen's error of holding all punishment after death to be purgative (and none vindictive), fall into the opposite error of saying no punishment after death is purgative."[205]

To address the Greek critique that souls do not enjoy their eternal reward or punishment at death, Thomas cited several biblical texts (e.g., the story of Dives and Lazarus, Jb 21:13 and 22:17, Gn 37:35, and Ps 16:10) allegedly demonstrating that "those who die in mortal sin are immediately subjected to the torments of Hell," while "those who die without stain immediately receive the wages of eternal compensation."[206] Thomas insisted that God would not frustrate the desire for our heavenly dwelling, explaining why "the vision of God is not postponed until the Day of Judgment when [the saints] resume their bodies."[207]

To show the need for a purifying state, Thomas cited Wisdom 7:25, Isaiah 35:8, and Revelation 21:7, which he interpreted as proof that those guilty of venial sins must "endure a postponement of glory" and be cleansed before they could enter the presence of God.[208] Since it would be "too great a punishment ... for minor sins" if the dead had to wait until Judgment Day to receive their reward, the length of this postponement was determined by the time necessary to complete the appropriate penances, and this differed depending upon the person and the sins.[209] Until released, these souls were supported by the "ritual of the Church introduced by the Apostles" and the prayers of the whole church, for it was precisely for those suffering the "temporal and cleansing penalties after this life" that the church prayed.[210] Paul himself attested to this, for when he spoke of those saved through fire, "This cannot be understood of the fire of Hell, because those who suffer that fire are not saved. Hence, it must be understood as referring to some purifying fire."[211]

The Second Council of Lyons and Its Aftermath

While Thomas wrote, both Pope Urban and his successor, Clement IV (1265–68), engaged in negotiations with Emperor Michael VIII, who had recaptured

---

[205] Thomas Aquinas, *On Reasons for Our Faith*, 57. In contrast, "Between these opposite errors the holy, Catholic and apostolic Church has carefully traced a middle position ... [and] confesses that in the state of souls after death some punishments are purgative, for those, namely, who leave this world without mortal sin in the state of charity and grace. Moreover, the Church does not with Origen confess all punishments after death to be purgative, but asserts those who die with mortal sin are afflicted by eternal torment together with the devil and his angels." Ibid., 57–58.

[206] Ibid., 58–59.

[207] Ibid., 62.

[208] "It happens, however, that some in the hour of death are defiled by some stains of sin, on account of which, nevertheless, they do not merit eternal damnation in Hell, for instance, venial sins such as idle words or other things of this kind. Therefore, those who died defiled by such faults cannot immediately on death enter heavenly glory. They could, however ... do so, were such things not in them. At the least then, they endure a postponement of glory on account of venial sins." Ibid., 63.

[209] Ibid., 64.

[210] Ibid., 65.

[211] Ibid.

Constantinople in 1261, but needed papal assistance to keep it.[212] Clement, perhaps aware of his strong bargaining position, was far less willing than his predecessors to equivocate when it came to the doctrinal issues that divided them, believing it was neither "proper nor permissible to call into question the purity of the faith" once it had been defined.[213] Thus it was that he decided, in March 1267, to send Michael a confession of faith that detailed, in no uncertain terms, what the emperor must accept if the union were to proceed. However, while the statements on the Filioque and the primacy were quite strong,[214] the section on Purgatory was "less advanced than that of Innocent IV's letter" and "the word '*purgatorium*' (Purgatory) does not appear ... [nor is there] mention of either a place or a fire (*ignis purgatorius*)."[215] The confession read:

> Because if they [i.e., the baptized] die truly repentant in charity before they have made satisfaction by worthy fruits of penance for [sins] committed and omitted, their souls are cleansed after death by purgatorial or purifying punishments (*poenis purgatoriis, sive catherteriis*) as Brother John[216] has explained to us. And to relieve punishments of this kind, the offerings of the living faithful are of advantage to these, namely, the sacrifices of Masses, prayers, alms, and other duties of piety, which have customarily been performed by the faithful for the other faithful according to the regulations of the Church.[217]

---

[212] See Donald Nicol, "Greeks and the Union of the Churches: The Preliminaries to the Second Council of Lyons, 1261–1274," in John Watt, John Morrall, and Francis X. Martin, eds., *Medieval Studies Presented to Aubrey Gwynn* (Dublin: Lochlainn, 1961), 454–80. Nicol pointed out that Urban had "Charles of Anjou at hand, ready and willing to lead any crusade for the reorganization of the Latin Empire." Ibid., 458.

[213] Tăutu, ed., *Acta Urbani IV, Clementis IV, Gregorii X (1261–1276)*, 61–69. Bonaventure had argued against a holding a council, maintaining "that it was not opportune to call them, because the Church could [define matters] without them; it was laborious, on account of the distance; it was unfruitful, because there was no longer the great wisdom among the Greeks (as there once was) since it had passed over to the Latins; it was dangerous, because it was dangerous to put into doubt what was already held certain." Bonaventure, *Commentaria in Quatuor Libros Sententiarum* I Dist. 11, a. 1, q. 1, in *Bonaventurae Opera Omnia* 1 (Rome: Collegium S. Bonaventurae, 1882), 212.

[214] According to Donald Nicol, as it concerned the primacy this profession was groundbreaking, for "seldom had the [papacy's] terms and conditions for union been so forcibly expressed." Nicol, "Greeks and the Union of the Churches," 459.

[215] Le Goff, *The Birth of Purgatory*, 286. Le Goff conjectured that this "backpedaling" might be attributed "solely to the hostility of the Greeks," but that it also could have occurred because of "the doubts of some Western theologians. The latter is not out of the question, particularly in light of the fact that some documents suggest that the Byzantine imperial chancery, at any rate, was prepared to accept the word 'Purgatory.'" Ibid.

[216] This was the Greek-born and very popular Franciscan John Parastron, who had been sent to instruct Michael in the Latin faith. An irenic figure, he prayed publicly with the Byzantine clergy and (according to Pachymeres) even received the antidoron ("blessed bread") following the divine liturgy. His popularity was such that upon his death the Greek emperor and clergy allegedly petitioned the pope to proclaim him a saint. See Girolamo Golubovich, "Cenni storici su Fra Giovanni Parastron," *Bessarione* 10 (1906): 295–304.

[217] Tăutu, ed., *Acta Urbani IV, Clementis IV, Gregorii X (1261–1276)*, 61–69; Eng. trans.: Deferrari, *The Sources of Catholic Dogma*, 184. The statement went on to clarify that "the souls of those who after having received holy baptism have incurred no stain of sin whatever, also those souls who, after contracting the stain of sin, either while remaining in their bodies or being divested of them, have been cleansed, as we have said above, are received immediately into heaven. The souls of those who die in mortal sin or with original sin only, however, immediately descend to hell, yet to be punished with different punishments. The same most holy Roman Church firmly believes and firmly declares that nevertheless on the day of judgment 'all' men will be brought together with their bodies 'before the tribunal of Christ' 'to render an account' of their own deeds." Ibid.

Even if the "restrained tone" of this formula was, as some scholars speculate, an "attempt at irenicism," it still remained too much for Greek sensibilities.[218] The election of Gregory X (1271–76) brought the hope of a better deal, but to Michael's great disappointment the new pope offered essentially the same terms as his predecessor, although Gregory seems to have been more sensitive to the emperor's delicate position.[219] Out of options, in 1273 Emperor Michael finally committed himself and his church to union with Rome, knowing full well that the cause had little support from either the Greek clergy or the people.[220] On Christmas Day of 1273 he issued a chrysobull defining the terms under which the upcoming union would proceed—conspicuously avoiding the doctrinal points—and soon the Greek delegates were on their way to Lyons to swear, in the emperor's name, to uphold the catholic faith as defined by the council.

The council itself began on May 7, although the Greek delegation did not arrive until June 24, delayed due to a storm that had destroyed one of their ships.[221] When the fourth session began on July 6, the emperor's profession of faith—the one drafted in 1267 by Clement IV—was read aloud, as was a letter from those bishops who had acquiesced to the chrysobull. George Akropolites[222] then stepped forward on behalf of the emperor, promising to "profess and preserve [the faith] inviolate as the sacrosanct Roman Church teaches and holds it."[223] Despite the presence of both Albert the Great and Bonaventure, both of whom had written extensively on Purgatory, no formal debate on the subject ever took place at Lyons.[224]

---

[218] Aidan Nichols, *Rome and the Eastern Churches*, 2nd ed. (San Francisco: Ignatius Press, 2010), 293.

[219] According to Joseph Gill, "Union with the Greeks, good though it was in itself, was for him (i.e., Gregory) more a means than an end," that end being a joint crusade against the Turks. Gill, *Byzantium and the Papacy 1198–1400*, 123. See also Vitalien Laurent, "La croisade et la question d'Orient sous le pontificat de Grégoire X," *Revue historique du Sud-Est européen* 22 (1945): 105–37.

[220] Patriarch Joseph, it should be noted, was against the union but eschewed some of the nastier anti-Latin polemics of his contemporaries. He wrote: "After all, they [i.e., the Latins] were formerly our brothers, reborn brothers of the same font of holy baptism; if they are sick, if they are eccentric, they nevertheless merit more pity than hate." Laurent and Darrouzès, *Dossier Grec de l'Union de Lyon 1273–1277*, 299; Eng. trans.: Aristeides Papadakis, *Crisis in Byzantium: The Filioque Controversy in the Patriarchate of Gregory II of Cyprus, 1283–1289* (Crestwood, NY: St. Vladimir's Press, 1996), 21.

[221] Aboard this ship was not only the official translator George Berroiotes, but also the gift that had been especially chosen for the pope—an altar cloth taken by the emperor from Hagia Sophia.

[222] Ironically, Acropolites, charged with securing union with Rome on the emperor's behalf, had once written tracts against the Latins. See George Acropolites, "Τοῦ μεγάλου λογοθέτου Γεωργίου τοῦ Ἀκροπολίτου λόγος κατὰ Λατίνων, γραφεὶς αὐτῷ ὅτε ἐν τῇ δύσει κατάσχετος ἦν" and "Λόγος δεύτερος περὶ τῆς ἐκ πατρὸς τοῦ ἁγίου πνεύματος ἐκπορεύσεως," in August Heisenberg, ed., *Georgii Acropolitae Opera*, vol. 2 (Lipsiae: Teubner, 1903), 30–66.

[223] "I George Acropolites, Grand Logothete, envoy of our lord the Greek emperor, Michael Dukas Angelos Comnenos, possessing the latter's full mandate for what follows, do entirely abjure schism. The statement of faith to which we have subscribed, as it has been fully read out and faithfully set forth, in my said lord's name I do recognize to be the true, holy, catholic, and orthodox faith. I accept it. In my heart I with my lips I profess it, and I do promise that I shall preserve it inviolate, as the sacrosanct Roman Church truly holds, faithfully teaches and preaches it, and I promise that I shall never at any time abandon it or deviate from it or disagree with it in any way whatsoever." Franchi, *Il Concilio II di Lione*, 88–90; Eng. trans.: Kenneth Setton, *The Papacy and the Levant 1204–1571*, vol. 1 (Philadelphia: American Philosophical Society, 1976), 117.

[224] Despite this, Franciscan chroniclers attributed Bonaventure's sudden death during the council "to his intensive negotiations with the Greeks." Deno Geanakoplos, "Bonaventura, the Two Mendicant Orders, and the Greeks at the Council of Lyons (1274)," in *Constantinople and the West* (Madison: University of Wisconsin Press, 1989), 216.

The purgatorial process, if not Purgatory itself, was now simply assumed to be part of the Greeks' faith.[225]

After Gregory X died in 1276, his successors—four in less than two years[226]—continued to press the emperor for proof of his sincerity, suspicious that Michael was being less than genuine in his desire for union. To assure them Michael sent confessions to both Pope John XXI (1276–77) and Nicholas III (1277–80) affirming his own belief in "the penalties of Purgatory" (*poenis purgatorii* or ποιναῖς πουργατορίου), which went further than his earlier confession in that it acknowledged Purgatory as a place.[227] Michael's new patriarch, John IX Bekkos (1275–82), also affirmed the orthodoxy of the doctrine in his 1277 profession of faith, writing to the pope that "since the said holy Roman Church reverences and preaches all these tenants, we believe and say that the same holy Roman Church teaches and preaches them with sound faith, orthodoxy, and truth."[228]

If Michael and his patriarch were willing to accept the Latins' orthodoxy, the vast majority of the Greek clergy were not, leading to the depositions, trials, and imprisonments of anyone who would not subscribe to the union.[229] One of these was Nikephoros the Hesychast, who was arrested following a 1276 "sweep of [Mount] Athos ... one of the leading centers of resistance."[230] Michael, to demonstrate his allegiance to the union, handed Nikephoros and his companion Clement over to the papal legate, Thomas Agni of Lentini, who in 1277 questioned them about the issues under dispute.[231] The discussion of Purgatory, as recorded by Nikephoros,[232] began with Thomas ("The Latin") asking: "And Purgatory? What do you say about that?"[233]

---

[225] According to Mîrșanu, when one compares this text to "the earlier letter of Pope Innocent IV, which had explicitly asked ... for the recognition by the Greeks of the term 'Purgatory' proper, ... we can wonder about the reason behind the cautious expression in the conciliar text.... It may be that the westerners in Lyons ... decided to express the doctrine as neutrally as possible (i.e. with respect to the noun and its implied physicality), to give the union a better chance for being accepted in Graecia." Mîrșanu, "Dawning Awareness of the Theology of Purgatory in the East," 187.

[226] Innocent V, Haridan V, John XXI, and Nicholas III.

[227] Le Goff, *The Birth of Purgatory*, 286. The confession of Michael's son and co-emperor, Andronikos II, employed the same language.

[228] Jean Gouillard, "Michel VIII et Jean Beccos devant l'Union," in *1274: Année charnière. Mutations et continuities* (Paris: CNRS, 1977), 183. For more on Bekkos see Peter Gilbert, "Not an Anthologist: John Bekkos as a Reader of the Fathers," *Communio* 36 (2009): 259–304; Joseph Gill, "John Beccus, Patriarch of Constantinople," *Byzantina* 7 (1975): 251–66; Romulad Souarn, "Tentatives d'union avec Rome: un patriarche grec catholique au XIIIe siècle," *Echos d'Orient* 3 (1899/1900): 229–37, 351–70; V. Grumel, "Un ouvrage recent sur Jean Beccos, patriarche de Constantinople," *Echos d'Orient* 24 (1925): 229–37; Alexandra Riebe, *Rom in Gemeinschaft mit Konstantinopel: Patriarch Johannes XI. Bekkos als Verteidiger der Kirchenunion von Lyon (1274)* (Wiesbaden: Harrassowitz Verlag, 2005).

[229] Michael's cruelty toward the anti-unionists became the stuff of legend. One story told how Michael traveled to Mt. Athos in October 1274 and burned twenty-six monks of the Zographou Monastery for their refusal to accept the union. Another story claimed that the pope himself came to Athos and beheaded the abbot of Vatopedi for his opposition. See Richard McGillivray Dawkins, *Monks of Athos: Life and Legends of the Holy Mountain* (London: G. Allen & Unwin, 1936).

[230] Le Goff, *The Birth of Purgatory*, 286–87.

[231] The encounter is found in Laurent and Darrouzès, *Le dossier grec de l'Union de Lyon (1273–1277)*, 486–507. Thomas of Lentini was not only papal legate, but also patriarch of Jerusalem and bishop of Acre.

[232] For the argument that Nikephoros's text is not a verbatim account of the trial see Jonathan Rubin, *Learning in a Crusader City Intellectual Activity and Intercultural Exchanges in Acre, 1191–1291* (Cambridge: Cambridge University Press, 2018), 157–58.

[233] Laurent and Darrouzès, *Le dossier grec de l'Union de Lyon (1273–1277)*, 497; Eng. trans.: Le Goff, *The Birth of Purgatory*, 287.

Nikephoros ("The Christian") responded by asking a question of his own—"What is Purgatory and from which Scripture did you learn it?"[234] Thomas replied that the teaching came from Paul (1 Cor 3:15), who taught that

> if someone after having sinned, goes to confess, receives a penance for the guilt, and dies before completing this penance, the angels cast his soul into the purificatory fire, that is, into that river of fire, until it has completed the time that remains of what has been set by his spiritual [father] the time it was unable to complete owing to the unpredictable suddenness of death. It is after completing the time that remains, it goes purified into this eternal life. Do you believe this too: Is this the way it is, or not?[235]

Nikephoros responded that "not only do we not accept this, we anathematize it, as do the fathers in council."[236] He then used Ezekiel,[237] Psalms,[238] and the gospels[239] to show that the Latins' teaching was contrary to Scripture, for "If we say that the punishment ends, then the enjoyment of the righteous should also end.... [Rather] God shut and sealed both, those who ended their lives well for the resurrection to life, those who acted badly for a resurrection to judgment."[240] It is true, he acknowledged, that there are stories of how the intercession of the saints and the suffrages of the living benefited the dead (e.g., Gregory the Great and Trajan, Thecla, and Falconilla), but

> these dreams and reveries ... offer no certainty. This is why Basil the Great, with a number of fathers, said "Present your living offering; do not lay a corpse at the altar." That means [you should] do good during your lifetime, for everything is inert after death, and because of that prayer for those who have not done good during their own life is not granted.[241]

Thomas then asked the crucial question about where "the souls of the righteous currently repose, and in what place are the sinners."[242] Nikephoros responded that "the righteous such as Lazarus are in the bosom of Abraham, and the sinners such as the Rich Man without pity are in the fires of Gehenna."[243] Thomas answered, "Many simple believers in our church have difficulty accepting this. The restoration

---

[234] Ibid.
[235] Ibid.
[236] Ibid.
[237] "Where I will find you there also I will judge you: if it is in the way of righteousness, for life, if it is in the way of sin, for eternal punishment." This is probably a paraphrase of Ezekiel 18:30.
[238] "In Sheol who can give you praise?" (Ps 6:5).
[239] "Night is coming when no one can work" (Jn 9:4).
[240] Laurent and Darrouzès, *Le dossier grec de l'Union de Lyon (1273–1277)*, 499; Eng. trans.: Marinis, *Death and the Afterlife in Byzantium*, 76. Nikephoros did make an exception for those Christ took from Scheol following his descent among the dead.
[241] Laurent and Darrouzès, *Le dossier grec de l'Union de Lyon (1273–1277)*, 499; Eng. trans.: Le Goff, *The Birth of Purgatory*, 287.
[242] Ibid.
[243] Laurent and Darrouzès, *Le dossier grec de l'Union de Lyon (1273–1277)*, 499; Eng. trans.: Le Goff, *The Birth of Purgatory*, 288.

[ἀποκατάστασις], they say, has not yet come and for this reason souls experience neither punishment nor rest there."²⁴⁴

The manuscript breaks off at this point, and we are left to wonder what was said next, but it was already clear at this point that Greek hostility to the doctrine of Purgatory was far more entrenched than the Latins and their unionist allies were willing to admit. This became evident in the lists of Latin errors that appeared after 1274, many of which now included Purgatory among the heresies taught by Rome. Meletios Homologetes's *On the Customs of the Italians* (c. 1276–80) claimed that "they [i.e., the Latins] say that all sinners must get purification in the cleansing fire of Purgatory, and they learned this from the frightful Origen."²⁴⁵ *The Heresies of Franks and Their Neighbors* (c. 1281) also linked Purgatory with the doctrine of *apocatastasis*, maintaining that the Latins "say also that sinners who are to be chastened with the devil in the age to come will have an end [to their punishment] after sufficient time. The devil and his angels will come back to their former nobility, and sinners will come with the just into [eternal] life."²⁴⁶

Among the more interesting anti-Latin works was *Dialogue of Panagiotes with an Azymite*, in which "the tendency towards 'trivialization' and denigration of the religious dispute... by outright lies and fabrications, so characteristic of the Byzantine polemical literature, reaches one of its peaks."²⁴⁷ The *Dialogue* covered a wide range of issues, including Purgatory, for when the Latin cardinal asked Panagiotes where the souls of the just resided, he responded, "In Paradise, those of sinners in Hell," thereby denying the possibility of a third option.²⁴⁸ This led to a discussion of their respective cosmologies, "in which Panagiotes amaze[d] his opponent with his deep knowledge of the secrets of life and the structure of the world."²⁴⁹ The universe was, in Panagiotes's view, a multilayered reality with several levels above the heavens, and several below the earth (ending with Tartarus, "which the sinners deserve"), but nowhere was there anything akin to Purgatory.

With the Greek resistance to Purgatory stiffening, the Latins, led by the Dominicans, increased their efforts to prove the Western doctrine correct. For example, Bonacursius of Bologna's *De erroribus Graecorum* criticized the Greeks on several fronts, including their insistence that (number 8) "up to the Day of Judgment, no one descends to Hell," (number 9) "up to the Day of Judgment no one goes to Paradise, not even the blessed Virgin and the good thief," and (number 10) "no one goes to Purgatory."²⁵⁰ Bonacursius then went on to refute them using "authorities from both

---

²⁴⁴ Laurent and Darrouzès, *Le dossier grec de l'Union de Lyon (1273–1277)*, 499–501; Eng. trans.: Le Goff, *The Birth of Purgatory*, 288. Le Goff speculated that Thomas raised the specter of Origenism at this point simply to emphasize the fact that "many simple believers were no longer content with the contrast between Gehenna and the bosom of Abraham, the stark division between Hell and Paradise from the moment of individual death. The need for Purgatory, for a final episode between death and resurrection, for a continuation of the process of penitence and salvation beyond the bogus boundary of death was a requirement rooted in the masses, a need voiced—in the West, at any rate—by the *vox populi*." Ibid.
²⁴⁵ Tia Kolbaba, "Meletios Homologetes On the Customs of the Italians," 167.
²⁴⁶ Juliette Davreux, "Le Codex Bruxellensis (Graecus) II 4836 (De Haeresibus)," *Byzantion* 10 (1935): 105; Eng. trans.: Kolbaba, *The Byzantine Lists*, 199.
²⁴⁷ Nikolov, "Mediaeval Slavonic Anti-Catholic Texts," 275.
²⁴⁸ Geanakoplos, "A Greek Libellus against Religious Union with Rome," 161.
²⁴⁹ Nikolov, "Mediaeval Slavonic Anti-Catholic Texts," 275.
²⁵⁰ Stegmüller, "*Bonacursius contra Graecos: Ein Beitrag zur Kontroverstheologie*," 76–78.

the New and Old Testaments, as well as the authority of the saints, Greek as well as Latin."[251]

For the immediacy of punishment Bonacursius produced Numbers 16:33 ("So they with all that belonged to them went down alive into Sheol"), Psalm 106:17 ("The earth opened and swallowed up Dathan, and covered the faction of Abiram"), Job 21:13 ("They spend their days in prosperity, and in peace they go down to Sheol"), and the Lucan story of the rich man and Lazarus. He then cited Athanasius and Gregory of Nyssa as Greek patristic witnesses, although the former citation is from the Pseudo-Athanasian *Quaestiones ad Antiochum ducem*,[252] and the latter (where the "saints are fully conformed to the divine glory" while sinners go in fear and trembling to the "place of darkness") appears to be spurious.[253]

For the reward of the just Bonacursius quoted Psalm 127:2–3 ("For he gives sleep to his beloved"), 2 Corinthians 5:1 ("For we know that if the earthly tent we live in is destroyed, we have a building from God, a house not made with hands, eternal in the heavens"), Luke 16:9 ("And I tell you, make friends for yourselves by means of dishonest wealth so that when it is gone, they may welcome you into the eternal homes"), John 16:26 and 17:24 ("Where I am, there will my servant be also"), Philemon 1:23 ("My desire is to depart and be with Christ"), and, of course, the story of Dives and Lazarus. For patristic sources he quoted Epiphanius and John Chrysostom,[254] but once again the first quotation was not genuine but instead from Pseudo-Epiphanius's *Second Homily on Holy Saturday* ("The enemy led you out of the earthly paradise. I will not restore you in that paradise, but in the heavenly kingdom").[255]

While his choice of texts to prove the immediacy of judgment was unconventional, to support the existence of Purgatory Bonacursius relied on scriptural passages that had already become regular features of the Latin polemic (e.g., Mt 12:32, 1 Cor 3:13, and 2 Mc 12:43).[256] As with most literature of the genre, the purpose of the work was not to encourage discussion, but rather to overwhelm opponents with biblical and patristic texts in order to force their assent. By the dawn of the fourteenth century the West was clearly in a better position to do this, for while the Greeks "rejected Purgatory because, in their opinion, it had no scriptural or patristic basis ... they did not [yet]

---

[251] Ibid., 76.

[252] "*Quoniam quidem peccatorum animae in inferno sunt deorsum, subtus omnem terram et mare.*" The quotation is from the Pseudo-Athanasiuan, *Quaestiones ad Antiochum ducem* (PG 28:609), the work earlier used by Gkykas.

[253] Stegmüller, "*Bonacursius contra Graecos: Ein Beitrag zur Kontroverstheologie*," 77.

[254] "For on what account, tell me, do you thus weep for one departed? Because he was a bad man? You ought on that very account to be thankful, since the occasions of wickedness are now cut off. Because he was good and kind? If so, you ought to rejoice; since he has been soon removed, before wickedness had corrupted him; and he has gone away to a world where he stands ever secure, and there is no room even to mistrust a change. Because he was a youth? For that, too, praise Him that has taken him, because he has speedily called him to a better lot. Because he was an aged man? On this account, also, give thanks and glorify Him that has taken him.... Consider to whom the departed has gone, and take comfort. He has gone where Paul is, and Peter, and the whole company of the angels." John Chrysostom, *Homily 5 on Lazarus* (PG 48:1020–21); Eng. trans.: Henry Jones Ripley, "The Blessings of Death," in William Jennings Bryan, ed., *The World's Greatest Orations*, vol. 7 (New York: Funk and Wagnalls, 1906), 4, 6.

[255] Stegmüller, "*Bonacursius Contra Graecos: Ein Beitrag zur Kontroverstheologie*," 77.

[256] For patristic support he followed the author of the *Tractatus* by quoting Macrina and Gregory of Nyssa's *De mortuis*, adding to it the spurious quote from Gregory seen earlier in the *Libellus* of Nicholas of Cotrone.

have a sufficient theology regarding prayers for the dead to offer in its stead."[257] The Latins were convinced that the Greeks shared their faith, even if—and this was a constant source of frustration—they stubbornly refused to admit it. Yet while theologians on both sides busied themselves debating Purgatory's existence, it was an Italian poet who would usher in the next stage of the doctrine's development. The "fireworks" were about to begin.

The Road to Ferrara-Florence

At some point before 1319 Dante Alighieri completed the first two parts of his *Divina Commedia*, the *Inferno* and the *Purgatorio*, which detailed the author's imagined tour of Hell and Purgatory guided by the Roman poet Virgil.[258] In his travels through Purgatory ("that second realm where man's soul goes to purify itself and become worthy to ascend to Heaven")[259] Dante climbed a mountain through seven kingdoms, witnessing "the souls of those who purge themselves of guilt" by different means.[260]

> First, by material punishment that modifies the wicked passions and instills virtue. Second, by meditation on the sin to be purged and its correlative virtue.... Third and last, purgation is accomplished through prayer, which purifies the soul, strengthens it by the grace of God, and expresses its hope.[261]

As souls made their painful ascent up the mountain, their "punishment was alleviated ... as if the climb became easier, the mountain less steep, as the soul shed its burden of sins."[262] Interestingly, unlike the theologians, Dante allowed for the purgation of both venial *and* mortal sins during this process, since it was the seven capital sins (Envy, Wrath, Greed, Sloth, Pride, Gluttony, and Lust) that were cleansed in Purgatory, not simply the "slight" sins mentioned by the scholastics. While the damned suffered eternal torment for their sins, the residents of Purgatory experienced only a "Hell of limited duration," either "because they had partly effaced their sin by repentance and penance, or because they were less inveterate sinners, or because their sins were mere blemishes on lives otherwise animated by the love of God."[263]

---

[257] Marinis, *Death and the Afterlife in Byzantium*, 76.
[258] Le Goff noted how Dante placed the righteous pagans (Virgil, Plato, Aristotle), as well as unbaptized infants, in the first circle of Hell in a "noble castle," safeguarding the Christian doctrine that baptism was required for salvation but granting them an existence of "fruitless yearning" where one hears "not shrieks of pain, but hopeless sighs." Le Goff, *The Birth of Purgatory*, 336.
[259] Dante Alighieri, *The Divine Comedy*, vol. 2: *Purgatory*, trans. Mark Musa (New York: Penguin Books, 1985).
[260] Ibid., 3.
[261] Le Goff, *The Birth of Purgatory*, 339.
[262] Ibid. "As we were climbing up the sacred steps, I seemed to feel myself much lighter now than I had been before on level ground. 'Master,' I said, 'tell me, what heavy thing has been removed from me? I feel as if to keep on climbing would be effortless.' He answered: 'When the P's [meaning *peccato* or sin] that still remain (though they have almost faded) on your brow shall be erased completely like the first, then will your feet be light with good desire; they will no longer feel the heavy road but will rejoice as they are urged to climb.'" Dante, *Purgatory*, 131.
[263] Le Goff, *The Birth of Purgatory*, 341.

How long one spent in Purgatory, or how long one had to wait at the foot of the mountain in order to begin the purgatorial climb, was dependent on a number of factors, including the lateness of one's earthly repentance.[264] During their ascent, souls sought the aid of the saints and the suffrages of the living, reciprocating (as much as they were able) by their own prayers for friends and family left behind.[265] Angels, not demons, were in charge of Purgatory, guiding souls through their progress until such time as all memories of sin were washed away, "evil forgotten, and all that remained in memory was that which is immortal in man, the good."[266] It is true that Dante's Purgatory had many Hell-ish features (e.g., fire, suffering, pain), and that his descriptions of its punishments could be both "colorful and creatively frightful,"[267] yet Le Goff claims that it was ultimately Dante who

> rescued Purgatory from the infernalization to which the church subjected it in the thirteenth century. Dante was in a sense more orthodox than the church, more faithful to Purgatory's underlying logic. He depicts Purgatory as a place between two extremes, but closer to one of them, straining in the direction of paradise. For him it is a place of hope, of initiation into joy, of gradual emergence into the light.[268]

Yet while Dante imbued Purgatory with both "hope and anticipation," other artists tended to do the opposite, portraying it, with all of its fires and punishments, "as a frightful place hardly distinguishable from Hell."[269] Thus what one tended to see in Western art was "an infernalized version that played more on fear than on hope ... reproducing the imagery of Hell, but adding an image of rescue."[270] Unsurprisingly, "this frightful picture of Purgatory ... readily lent itself to the sale of indulgences for persons willing to pay any (at least financial) price to avoid or shorten such horrific suffering."[271] Simply put, the more hellish Purgatory became, the more eager people were to avoid it.

Their chance came in the year 1300, when Pope Boniface VIII initiated the Jubilee Year, granting "all pilgrims who came to Rome a plenary indulgence (*plenissima venia peccatorum*), complete pardon of all sins, a favor that heretofore had been extended only to crusaders."[272] Boniface then extended this indulgence "to all those who had died while on their pilgrimage to Rome as well as to those who sincerely intended to take the pilgrimage but were unable to do so," marking the first time that "a pope employed the presumed power to liberate souls from Purgatory, a power that had been

---

[264] "Before I start, the heavens must revolve as many times as while I was alive, for I put off repenting till the end." Dante, *Purgatory*, 44.
[265] "Prayers could, of course, make my rime shorter here: prayers from a heart that lives in grace-the rest are worthless, for they go unheard in Heaven!" Ibid.
[266] Le Goff, *The Birth of Purgatory*, 355.
[267] Walls, *Purgatory*, 25–26.
[268] Le Goff, *The Birth of Purgatory*, 355. "How different are these passageways from those of Hell! One enters here to music—there, below, to sounds of violent laments." Dante, *Purgatory*, 131.
[269] Walls, *Purgatory*, 24.
[270] Ibid., 25. Walls cited the work of Stephen Greenblatt for this conclusion. See Stephen Greenblatt, *Hamlet in Purgatory* (Princeton, NJ: Princeton University Press, 2013), 53–54.
[271] Walls, *Purgatory*, 25.
[272] Le Goff, *The Birth of Purgatory*, 330.

articulated before but until this time had never actually been exercised."[273] This was a critical development, for now the doctrine of Purgatory was forever linked to the pope's authority over it, meaning that denial of the teaching became a de facto challenge to the primacy of the bishop of Rome. And while there were still doubters in the West who questioned "the great presumption and dangerous error" that through "their works, their words, and their offerings" they can "pluck souls from Purgatory after a certain period of time," the chief opponents to the doctrine remained the Greeks.[274]

The Byzantines continued to reject "the suggestion that there was a third choice in the afterlife other than heaven or hell [because it] seemed to blunt the stark choice offered in the Gospels."[275] However, if one broke down this rejection "into its constituent parts the[ir] position becomes less clear" and far less antithetical to the Latin position.[276] For example, the Greeks generally—but not universally—accepted the idea of a particular judgment, and while they rejected "the existence of a *place* intermediate between heaven and hell ... the idea of an intermediate *state*, neither heaven nor hell, seems generally to be assumed, especially in popular Orthodox beliefs about the afterlife."[277] They largely rejected the Latin contention that souls in this "intermediate state ... undergo expiratory suffering and, in particular, [that] this suffering takes place through the agency of [a material purgatorial] fire," and yet they did hold that "the soul undergoes purification before the last judgment, ... that this purification involves suffering ... [and that] prayers for the departed" can benefit the dead during this process.[278]

Perhaps the biggest hurdle for the Byzantines was the notion that the suffering one endured in this intermediate state was expiratory, and that "by such suffering, the soul renders satisfaction of sins forgiven."[279] According to John Meyendorff, this was *the* fundamental difference in the way East and West approached the issue of Purgatory, for while "legalism, which applied to individual human destiny the Anselmian doctrine of 'satisfaction,' is the *ratio theologica* of the Latin doctrine on Purgatory," the same could not be said of the Orthodox.[280] In the debates over Purgatory, "The Latins took for granted their legalistic approach to Divine Justice—which, according to them, required a retribution for every sinful act," while "the Greeks interpreted sin

---

[273] Walls, *Purgatory*, 25.

[274] Jacopo Passavanti, *Lo Specchio di vera penttenza*, ed. Maria Lenardon (Florence: Libreria Editrice Florentina, 1925), 387–91; Eng. trans.: Le Goff, *The Birth of Purgatory*, 333. Le Goff noted that opposition in the West came both from heretical groups (e.g., the Waldensians and Cathari) and more conservative churchmen afraid that the teaching had pagan roots.

[275] Andrew Louth, "Eastern Orthodox Eschatology," in Jerry Walls, ed., *Oxford Handbook of Eschatology* (Oxford: Oxford University Press, 2007), 243. For the Byzantines "the souls of the righteous dwell in the Spirit as in a kind of light-space" as if "standing in God's holy fire" and between this light and the absence of it (i.e., Hell) "there can be no middle ground. In death, as in life, the soul can stand only on either side of a 'great chasm which none may cross' (Luke 16:26). There can thus be no purgatorial 'third place' because there can be no middling, intermediate relationship with God (cf. Matt. 12:30; Rev. 3:15–16)." Constas, "To Sleep, Perchance to Dream," 117.

[276] Louth, "Eastern Orthodox Eschatology," 243.

[277] Ibid.

[278] Ibid.

[279] Ibid.

[280] Meyendorff, *Byzantine Theology*, 220.

less in terms of the acts committed than in terms of a moral and spiritual disease which was to be healed by Divine forbearance and love."[281] Although one could argue that the lines are too sharply drawn, today scholars on both sides acknowledge that in the medieval debates over Purgatory "the Latin emphasis ... on God's justice and punishment" often stood in sharp contrast with the "Greek emphasis ... on God's love and forgiveness."[282]

Another fundamental difference harkened back to the earlier debates between Glykas and Niketas Stethatos and concerned the speed with which a soul received its full reward or punishment. In general, "The Greeks ... without denying a particular judgment after death ... maintained that neither the just nor the wicked ... attain[ed] their final state of either bliss or condemnation before the last day."[283] Byzantine authors tended to use words like "partial" "incomplete," and "temporary" to describe both "the happiness of the just" and the "suffering of sinners."[284] And yet while words like "sleep" and "repose" still found their way in Orthodox descriptions of the afterlife,[285] far more influential was the idea of *epectasis*, or "perpetual progress," present in Gregory of Nyssa and others, which taught that "the souls of the righteous, despite their state of bliss, are nevertheless incomplete ... [for] their souls are merely on their way to the palace—they have not yet arrived at the banquet. Their 'share in the joy of the kingdom,' therefore, remained only 'partial and incomplete.' "[286]

Interestingly, Latin Christianity became engaged in an internal debate on this very subject after Pope John XXII (d. 1334) began preaching, not unlike the Orthodox, that because of the saints' "perpetual progress" toward God, the righteous did not attain the beatific vision until the Last Judgment.[287] Although Pope John later retracted his views, Benedict XII (d. 1342), felt the need to condemn his predecessor's positions in the encyclical *Benedictus Deus*, teaching that

---

[281] Ibid.

[282] Bathrellos, "Love, Purification, and Forgiveness versus Justice, Punishment, and Satisfaction," 118. "Whereas the Greeks highlighted God's love and forgiveness as well as the purification of the soul, the Latins emphasized divine justice and the punishment of the sinner for the sake of offering satisfaction. In spite of some common ground, the two approaches were hardly compatible." Ibid.

[283] Meyendorff, *Byzantine Theology*, 220. As Mark of Ephesus would later put it, "The kingdom is prepared, [but] it has not yet been given; the fires, too, have been prepared, but they are not yet occupied." Mark Eugenikos, *Oratio altera de igne purgatorio*, in Georg Hodmann and Ludovico Petit, eds., *De Purgatorio disputationes in Concilio Florentino habitae*, CF 8.2 (Rome: Pontifical Oriental Institute, 1969), 64; Eng. trans.: Constas, "To Sleep, Perchance to Dream," 117–18.

[284] Larchet, *Life after Death According to the Orthodox Tradition*, 151.

[285] Larchet rejected the "sleep state" as the work of "some marginal theologians, chiefly of Syriac origin and of Nestorian persuasion," for while "the fathers certainly speak at times of sleep in connection with death ... the soul is in a state of repose but is not, as it would be if entirely dead, completely inactive. It is only inactive with respect to this world, but in fact displays another form of activity in the hereafter." Ibid., 164–65.

[286] Constas, "To Sleep, Perchance to Dream," 115.

[287] Pope John's thoughts on the subject are contained in his book *On the Glory of the Souls* (*De gloria animarum*) and a series of sermons. See John Weakland, "Pope John XXII and the Beatific Vision Controversy," *Annuale Mediaevale* 9 (1968): 76–84; Marc Dykmans, *Les Sermons de Jean XXII sur la vision béatifique, Miscellanea Historiae Pontificiae* 34 (Rome: Presses de l'Université Grégorienne, 1973); F. A. van Liere, "Johannes XXII en het conflict over de visio beatifica," *Nederlands Theologisch Tijdschrif* 44 (1990): 208–22; Christian Trottmann, *La Vision béatifique des disputes scolastiques à sa définition par Benoît XII, Bibliothèque des écoles françaises d'Athènes et de Rome 289* (Rome: École française de Rome, 1995); Hans Boersma, *Seeing God: The Beatific Vision in Christian Tradition* (Grand Rapids, MI: Eerdmans, 2018).

the souls of all the saints who departed from this world ... provided they were not in need of any purgation when they died ... [will be with Christ in heaven] immediately (*mox*) after their death ... even before the resurrection of their bodies and the general judgment ... [Moreover] the souls of those who depart in actual mortal sin immediately (*mox*) after their death descend to Hell where they are tortured by infernal punishments.[288]

Although this dispute did not originally involve the Greeks, it helped to put the positions of the two churches into sharp relief—that is, the Western belief in "the state of the blessed" as something "static" versus the Eastern view of "a never-ending ascent" into which it was difficult to place people into neat categories. This perhaps explains why John-Jerome of Prague mocked the Greeks for their belief that "the souls of the dead ... fly in the air awaiting the coming of Christ at the judgment" when they will be joined with their bodies."[289] The immediacy of judgment, he told them, was clearly taught in Scripture, as both the story of Lazarus and the words of Christ to the good thief attested.

For the Greeks, the idea that the saints enjoyed "eternal life and rest" implied that they were no longer in need of our prayers, a belief incompatible with the church's liturgical tradition, in which the "bloodless sacrifice" was offered for "patriarchs, prophets, apostles, and every righteous spirit made perfect in faith."[290] The Byzantines instead held that the saints were ever "advancing forward to God ... like the friends of a king who have received invitations to a royal banquet. They move toward God with joy, beholding the palace looming on the horizon and contemplating with delight the hour of celebration."[291]

Symeon of Thessalonica (d. 1429) addressed many of these questions in his writings, including the *Dialogus contra Haereses, De Ordine Sepulturae,* and *Responsa ad Gabrielem Pentapoletanum*,[292] Symeon believed that the souls of the deceased were in a temporary state, and distinguished between paradise (παραδείσου, where, for example, the good thief went) and heaven (οὐρανοῦ, where the saints who fully imitated Christ will be).[293] He accepted that unrepentant sinners go to Hades, where they are tortured by demons, but held that they "have not yet been delivered to the full punishment" that awaits them after the Last Judgment, when they will be joined to the bodies that committed the sin.[294] While rejecting Purgatory as a Latin innovation,

---

[288] Benedict XII, *Benedictus Deus*; Eng. trans.: Deferrari, *The Sources of Catholic Dogma*, 197–98.

[289] Hyland, "John-Jerome of Prague (1368–1440) and the *Errores Graecorum*," 256. The Greeks "assert[ed] that sins committed in the flesh need to be punished corporeally, and before the day of judgment human souls are lacking bodies, and thus cannot be punished in such a place as Purgatory.... [The Greeks] conclude from this therefore that they are not punished and will not be punished before the day of judgment ... [and that] after judgment day evil souls with their bodies will go to Hell and good souls, united with their bodies, will go to the kingdom of heaven." Ibid.

[290] Liturgy of St John Chrysostom.

[291] Mark of Ephesus, *Oratio altera de igne purgatorio*, in Petit, *Documents relatifs au concile de Florence*, 111; Eng. trans.: Constas, "To Sleep, Perchance to Dream," 114.

[292] Symeon of Thessalonica, *Dialogus contra Haereses*, 23 (PG 155:116–17), *De Ordine Sepulturae*, 370 and 373 (PG 155:688 and 692–93], and *Responsa ad Gabrielem Pentapoletanum*, 4 (PG 155:841–48).

[293] Demetrios Bathrellos, Σχεδίασμα Δογματικῆς Θεολογίας μὲ βάση τό συγγραφικό ἔργο τοῦ Ἁγίου Συμεὼν Θεσσαλονίκης (†1429) (Athens: En Plo, 2008), 300.

[294] Ibid., 302.

Symeon nevertheless accepted the possibility of postmortem purification, teaching that through prayers, the holy mysteries, and good works one could obtain remission and a relaxation of punishments for the departed.[295] This was especially true of those who "have sinned moderately and left this life in repentance, [for] through the most holy sacrifice and good works and the rest, it might be possible for them to find freedom before the judge comes. Because the church accepts this, she performs prayers and sacrifices for the deceased."[296] In this way Symeon provided a rationale for the various prayers and offerings for the dead that had become traditional in the East, including those offered during the prothesis,[297] and the *kolyva*, "a kind of boiled wheat cake" offered on certain anniversaries.[298]

Symeon's position, although thoroughly traditional, thus shows, in the words of Demetrios Bathrellos, a "fundamental convergence" with many aspects of the Latin teaching, especially as it regarded the possibility of nonserious sinners eventually approaching God.[299] The key difference remained the idea of expiatory suffering, for while Symeon accepted that sinners "are tormented by sorrow, fear, and expectation of their final punishment," he believed that "it was not this pain that helps the deceased to draw closer to God, but rather the benefits they derive from the divine liturgy, the prayers, the blessings and the other good deeds" offered by the living.[300] Categories like satisfaction and expiation, which had become so important in the Latin system, had no place in his thought. Yet Symeon's work evidences that East and West did share common ground, despite the important differences that remained. It also showed that the East was slowly moving toward consensus in its thinking about the afterlife, even if it would take the whetstone of Ferrara-Florence to sharpen its views and provide the clarity they sought.

---

[295] "But there is no earlier hell [i.e., Purgatory] into which the souls of sinners are thrown and pay a penalty commensurate with their wickedness, and are then freed from punishment, as some babble." Symeon of Thessalonica, *De Ordine Sepulturae*, 373 (PG 155:693); Eng. trans.: Marinis, *Death and the Afterlife in Byzantium*, 105.

[296] Ibid.

[297] According to Marinis, "Symeon immediately differentiates ... between the particles of the saints that are for the saints' 'glory and honor and the augmentation of their worthiness and greater acceptance of their Divine illumination' and those of the dead and the living. The former are offered for the remission of sins and eventual union with the divine grace, the latter for deliverance from difficulties, forgiveness of sins, and for the hope of eternal life." Marinis, *Death and the Afterlife in Byzantium*, 100.

[298] Symeon of Thessalonica, *De Ordine Sepulturae* (PG 155:688–92). See Larchet, *Life and Death According to the Orthodox Tradition*, 206.

[299] Bathrellos, Σχεδίασμα Δογματικῆς Θεολογίας, 301.

[300] Ibid., 303. To prove his point Symeon cited the story of Gregory the Great assisting the emperor Trajan, although Symeon does not mention the emperor by name.

8
Purgatory from Ferrara-Florence to Modern Times

The initial stages of the Purgatory debate had found the Latins better prepared, with the doctrine firmly ensconced in Western theology and culture as part of the afterlife's three-tiered system, toured and described by so beautifully by Dante in the *Divine Comedy*, "the noblest representation of Purgatory ever conceived by the mind of man."[1] The Greeks had only begun to formulate a positive response to Latin queries about the afterlife—Symeon of Thessalonica evidences that the process was already underway before Ferrara-Florence—but knew, almost instinctually, that the Western theology of Purgatory was not an acceptable option. This dynamic changed in 1438–39, during the conciliar debates on Purgatory, when the East took a huge step beyond a simple rejection of the Latin teaching. Thanks in large part to Mark of Ephesus, the East finally had something positive to offer in response and a framework within which subsequent Orthodox authors could work.

The reformers' rejection of Purgatory in the sixteenth century, which was based on different theological arguments than those used by the Greeks, made Rome more determined than ever to have the doctrine accepted as part of the church's faith. Even if the arguments of Robert Bellermine and others were aimed chiefly at the Protestants, they were often employed against the Orthodox, whose eighteenth- and nineteenth-century confessions sometimes took positions that were theologically inconsistent in order to avoid any hint of the Roman teaching. Yet they all agreed that "the fires of Purgatory" could have no place within Orthodoxy,[2] and as late as 1895 the pope's "innovations concerning purgatorial fire" were listed among the teachings separating Rome from the faith of "the one holy, catholic and apostolic Church of the seven Ecumenical Councils."[3]

As with so many of the issues that divided East from West, the twentieth century provided new opportunities to move the dialogue on Purgatory beyond the polemics of the past. Among Roman Catholic theologians, including the future Pope Benedict XVI, discussion of Purgatory once again began to emphasize its purificatory rather than punishing aspects, with far less emphasis placed on the fires and pains involved.

---

[1] Le Goff, *The Birth of Purgatory*, 334.
[2] According to Kallistos Ware, "Most Orthodox writers seem to attach an altogether inordinate importance to this question of purgatorial fire, turning it into a major issue in their controversy with Rome ... overlook[ing] the fact that the Church of Rome, while making belief in Purgatory *de fide*, has never put out any dogmatic statement concerning purgatorial fire.... It is surely a mistake on the Orthodox part to make a major issue out of something which Rome has never formally defined." Ware, *Eustratios Argenti*, 152–53.
[3] Anthimos VII, *A Reply to the Papal Encyclical of Pope Leo XIII on Reunion* in Metallinos, ed., *Orthodox and Catholic Union*.

Orthodox theologians, mostly free of the anti-Romanism that colored earlier generations, began to recognize how close the modern Catholic teaching was to their own, despite remaining differences in vocabulary. Yet, interestingly, it was not the dialogue with Rome that reignited discussion about the afterlife in Orthodox circles, but rather intra-Orthodox debates over the tollhouse tradition and the rehabilitation of Origen. Because both of these debates rely on arguments once used in the contest with the Latins over Purgatory (at least to some degree), Orthodox theology continues to wrestle with the teaching, keeping the fate of souls after death very much alive as an ecumenical issue.

The Council of Ferrara-Florence (1438–39)

The agenda for the Council of Ferrara-Florence—that is, the list of theological issues requiring resolution before union could proceed—had been laid down almost two centuries earlier in the 1252 *Tractatus contra Graecos* and was set forward once again by Cardinal Julian Cesarini early on in the proceedings: "The first concerns the procession of the Holy Spirit (i.e., the *filioque*), the second is the sacrifice with unleavened or leavened bread, the third is the fire of Purgatory, and the fourth is the primacy of the pope."[4] Armed with dozens of pro- and anti-azymite tracts, patristic florilegia on the Filioque, and centuries of polemical works for/against the primacy, both parties now had to decide which to tackle first. It is perhaps odd that they chose to start with the newest of the four, Purgatory, with Mark of Ephesus asking Cesarini to provide an explanation of both the doctrine and its sources.[5] Thus began the conciliar debate on Purgatory, for which we have "such abundant sources ... as to be able to reconstruct their history fairly completely."[6]

---

[4] "When several people disagree on certain points, if they live far from each other and do not examine the reasons for their divergences, each of them comes to believe that the difference between them is great. But, let them meet and examine the reasons for their separation, and what was thought to be great often happens to be small and not very considerable. It seems to me that this is what has happened in our case. Indeed, because the separation has grown both because of great distance and the passage of many years, and because we have not met to discuss them for a long time, it seems that the gap between us is great. But now that you are here, with God's help, if we move on to a discussion of what caused the scandal and the disunity between us, the dispute between us ... could easily be remedied. ... There are, I believe, four things that separate us ... [and while] there are also some other differences, these are nevertheless the main and the most serious." Laurent, *Les "Mémoires"*, 270.

[5] Cardinal Cesarini had used "all his powers of persuasion" to urge the Greeks to begin the doctrinal discussions, at least informally (Gill, *The Council of Florence*, 115), but the Byzantines, supported by the emperor, continued to refuse. When they did finally agree to choose one of the four issues, Syropoulos recorded that the Greeks went to the emperor, who ruled out both the Filioque and the azymes until the plenary sessions had begun. They then offered to discuss either Purgatory or the primacy, with Cesarini and the Latins choosing the former. Laurent, *Les "Mémoires"*, 270–72.

[6] "Both the *Acta Graeca* and Syropoulos provide information about what went on behind the scenes among the Greeks, the Greek *Acta* furnishing also a few precious dates; both, too, synopsize part of the arguments exposed, though this is of less value since the five main speeches are preserved, because happily at the end of the first of the conferences it was agreed that each side should furnish the other in writing with the arguments propounded on each occasion." Gill, *The Council of Florence*, 117–18.

On June 4 Cardinal Cesarini set forth the Latin teaching in words that echoed (almost verbatim) the earlier *Confessio* of Michael VIII.[7] He stated:

> The souls of the faithful who are truly penitent (*vere poenitentes*), when they have died in charity (*in caritate*) before having made satisfaction by worthy fruits of penance for their faults of commission and omissions, are purified after death by the pains of Purgatory (*poenis purgatoriis*). They can be alleviated by the suffrages of the faithful who are living: sacrifices of the Mass, prayers, alms, and other works of piety. The souls of those who after baptism have not committed any fault, or who having committed faults have expiated them fully, whether during this life or after death in Purgatory, are immediately received into heaven (*in coelum mox recipiuntur*). The souls of those who die in mortal sin, or with only original sin, immediately descend into Hell (*mox in infernum descendunt*), there to be subjected to chastisements more or less rigorous. This is without prejudice to the final judgment where all men appear with their bodies at the tribunal of Christ to render account for their works.[8]

Cesarini supported the Latin position with seven arguments from Scripture (e.g., 2 Mc 12:46, Mt 12:32, 1 Cor 3:13–15) and the tradition of the universal church, "whether Latin or Greek, which prays and has always prayed for the dead. Unless there is a purification after death, this prayer would be in vain; for this prayer is neither for those who are already in glory nor for those in Hell."[9] He then cited authorities, arguing that Purgatory had always been taught by the Roman church "trained and formed by the holy apostles Peter and Paul" and the holy fathers, both Latin (Ambrose, Augustine, and Gregory the Great) and Greek (Basil the Great, Gregory of Nyssa, Dionysius the Areopagite, Epiphanius of Cyprus, Theodoret of Cyrus, and John of Damascus).[10] Finally, in an argument based on theological reasoning (*ratio theologica*), Cesarini argued that "divine justice ... does not permit any faults to go unpunished, but it proportions the expiation to the offense."[11] Full satisfaction (*satisfaciat*) must be made, in this life or the next. For all these reasons, "One must ... admit that, between Heaven and Hell, there is another place for purification to be accomplished where the soul can clear away its offenses and become worthy to enter the presence of God."[12]

---

[7] The Latin and Greek versions of Cesarini's speech are found in Georg Hofmann and Ludovico Petit, eds., *De Purgatorio disputationes in Concilio Florentino habitae*, CF 8.2 (Rome: Pontifical Oriental Institute, 1969), 1–12. According to Hoffman, the two versions are almost identical except for two missing references to Thomas Aquinas (*beatus Thomas*). See also Adhémar D'Alès, "La question du Purgatoire au concile de Florence en 1438," *Gregorianum* 3 (1922): 9–50; André de Halleux, "Problèmes de méthode dans les discussions sur l'eschatologie au Concile de Ferrare et de Florence," in Giuseppe Alberigo, ed., *Christian Unity: The Council of Ferrara-Florence 1438/9* (Leuven: Leuven University Press, 1991), 251–301.

[8] Hofmann and Petit, *De Purgatorio disputationes*, 1–2; Eng. trans.: Jorgenson, "The Debate over Patristic Texts on Purgatory," 310.

[9] Hofmann and Petit, *De Purgatorio disputationes*, 4; Eng. trans.: Jorgenson, "The Debate over Patristic Texts on Purgatory," 311.

[10] Ibid.

[11] Hofmann and Petit, *De Purgatorio disputationes*, 12; Eng. trans.: Jorgenson, "The Debate over Patristic Texts on Purgatory," 311–12. Among the texts cited is Deuteronomy 25:2: "If the guilty man deserves to be beaten, the judge shall cause him to lie down and be beaten in his presence with a number of stripes in proportion to his offense." Also cited were Ezekiel 33:14–15 and Wisdom 7:25.

[12] Ibid.

Cesarini's argument "largely depend[ed] on and reflect[ed] the established penitential practice of the Roman Church at that time ... [which] included three stages: contrition, confession, and satisfaction."[13] Its basic premise, seen already in Albert, Bonaventure, and Aquinas, was that sin, even if confessed and forgiven, "leaves behind it punishments to be undergone in compensation, which can be compared to a debt."[14] If one has not made adequate satisfaction in this world for one's sins (i.e., paid the debt), then one must do so in the next. This idea, which Demetrios Bathrellos called "irredeemably forensic," depended largely on Western medieval concepts of divine justice, perhaps explaining why it continued to confound the Greeks, who wondered why and how one could be punished for sins already forgiven.[15]

When Cesarini was finished, "Mark of Ephesus said a few courteous words, affirming that there was apparently little to divide the churches on this doctrine," and the session closed.[16] When they received a written copy of Cesarini's remarks (for it had been "agreed that each side should furnish the other in writing with the arguments propounded"), both Mark and Bessarion of Nicaea wrote responses, with the emperor deciding to combine "the urbanity of Nicaea's exordium ... with the force of Mark's arguments" in the official reply, which Bessarion delivered on June 14.[17]

Mark's *Memorandum* began by acknowledging that "those who have entered their rest while confessing the faith are, without any doubt, assisted by liturgies, prayers, and alms done for their intention" and that this has been believed "from the earliest times," supported by "a host of testimonies ... from both Latin and Greek doctors."[18] However, he rejected the notion that "souls are delivered thanks to a certain purgative suffering and by a temporary fire possessed by Purgatory," an idea found "neither in the Holy Scriptures, the prayers of the church, and the hymns for the dead, or in the words of the doctors."[19] He allowed that souls "who have quit this life with faith and love, yet bearing away with them certain sins, either minor sins for which they have not repented at all, or major sins for which, although they had repented of them, they had not have ever undertaken to show the fruits of repentance," can be "cleansed or whitened of these kinds of sin, but not by means of some purgatorial fire."[20] Instead they were "made clean at the very time of their departure from the body, thanks to the

---

[13] Bathrellos, "Love, Purification, and Forgiveness versus Justice, Punishment, and Satisfaction," 84.

[14] Roncaglia, *Les discussions sur le Purgatoire*, 43.

[15] Bathrellos, "Love, Purification, and Forgiveness versus Justice, Punishment, and Satisfaction," 87. See also de Halleux, "Problèmes de méthode," 265.

[16] Gill, *The Council of Florence*, 118.

[17] Ibid. See Laurent, *Les "Mémoires"*, 284.

[18] Mark of Ephesus, *Oratio prima de igne purgatorio* in Louis Petit, ed., *Documents relatifs au concile de Florence: La question du purgatoire à Ferrare, Documents I–VI* (Paris: Firmin-Didot, 1921), 39–40; Eng. trans.: Larchet, *Life after Death According to the Orthodox Tradition*, 181. Citing the story of Macarius and the skull (see chap 7 n. 100), Mark insisted these prayers were not for those allegedly in Purgatory, but rather for those "held in Hades and already subject to eternal torment, either in fact and experience, or in a hopeless expectation of torment" since they can receive "a certain minor relief, even though this cannot deliver them completely from torment, or give them hope for a final deliverance." Ibid.

[19] Ibid.

[20] Petit, *Documents relatifs au concile de Florence*, 41; Eng. trans.: Larchet, *Life after Death According to the Orthodox Tradition*, 182–83. Mark insisted that the allusions to fire in the prayers of the church referred not to "a temporary fire that holds sway in Purgatory, but rather to that eternal fire of everlasting punishment." Petit, *Documents relatifs au concile de Florence*, 42; Eng. trans.: Larchet, *Life after Death According to the Orthodox Tradition*, 184.

fright of death" or after "abiding in the same earthly place... or, if their sins are more serious... kept in Hades, but not in such a way as to remain forever in fire in torment, but as if imprisoned there, confined and under guard."[21]

For Mark, the punishments of the afterlife did not come from a purifying fire, but rather from fear and conscience, which "gnaws... with more torment than any fire whatsoever might bring; still others are made clean by the great terror experienced before the Divine glory and the uncertainty about what the future will be. Experience shows that this torments and punishes much more than anything else."[22] Postmortem purgation was possible, for even the funeral hymns of the church asked God to cleanse the deceased of their sins, but cleansing came about thanks to God's goodness and compassion, not through a fire.[23] And if these sins are forgiven by divine love, why is there need for further chastisement, for "Once one is forgiven, one is also immediately released from punishment."[24]

In reading Mark's *Memorandum* modern scholars can discern at last three key differences between his position and that of Cesarini. "First, [Mark] believes that punishment is meaningless unless it leads to purification"—that is, the concept at satisfaction as developed by the scholastics was simply foreign to him.[25] Second, Mark emphasized God's willingness to forgive sins far more than the demands of divine justice, "For if this were not so... no one would ever escape the pains of the afterlife."[26] Third, "Mark had a different concept of punishment" whereby the torments of sinners are "self-inflicted side-effects of the committed sins rather than as punishments imposed by divine justice for the sake of satisfaction."[27]

Bessarion's presentation of the formal Greek reply, which utilized many of Mark's arguments, was far more reserved, laying forth why the Greeks rejected the Latin

---

[21] Petit, *Documents relatifs au concile de Florence*, 41; Eng. trans.: Larchet, *Life after Death According to the Orthodox Tradition*, 182–83.

[22] Ibid.

[23] "The hymn speaks clearly of purgation, yet not of purgation through fire, but through divine goodness and compassion alone. For it would be in vain if we asked that this which is still purged by fire be also purged by compassion. But the hymn is asking for the blotting out of the stains [of sin], on account of which [the deceased] is alienated from the vision and enjoyment of God. This blotting out takes place through divine goodness alone, and the hymn calls it purgation." Petit, *Documents relatifs au concile de Florence*, 52–53; Eng. trans.: Bathrellos, "Love, Purification, and Forgiveness versus Justice, Punishment, and Satisfaction," 92.

[24] Petit, *Documents relatifs au concile de Florence*, 55; Eng. trans.: Bathrellos, "Love, Purification, and Forgiveness versus Justice, Punishment, and Satisfaction," 93. Demetrios Bathrellos echoed Joseph Gill in his assessment that "Eugenicus does not admit the debt of temporal punishment due to sins forgiven that the Latins hold to be one of the main reasons for a Purgatory." Bathrellos, "Love, Purification, and Forgiveness," 93.

[25] Bathrellos, "Love, Purification, and Forgiveness," 90. Although, to be clear, he did not reject the idea of eternal punishment.

[26] Ibid. Mark himself wrote that "divine goodness overpowers the logic of justice." Petit, *Documents relatifs au concile de Florence*, 56.

[27] Bathrellos, "Love, Purification, and Forgiveness," 90. "As [Martin] Jugie has argued, these pains are of a moral order and originate from within the soul. They are not inflicted from outside and therefore, according to the terminology of Mark, they are not properly speaking a punishment." See Martin Jugie, "La Question du Purgatoire au Concile de Ferrare-Florence," *Echos d'Orient* 20 (1921): 278.

teaching yet "without revealing much information about Byzantine attitudes."[28] He stated that the whole debate centered around two questions:

> Is there remission of sins in the afterlife? If this is so, how is it accomplished? Simply as an effect of God's love for man (φιλανθρωπία) responding to the prayers of the Church, or by means of punishments. If these sins are forgiven through punishment, what kind of punishment is it? Are the souls kept in jail, in darkness, and in ignorance, or are they punished by material fire as you [the Latins] affirm?[29]

Both sides agreed that the answer to the first question was yes, but for the Greeks postmortem cleansing was accomplished by God's *philanthropia* rather than by punishments inflicted by the fires of Purgatory, especially as the Eastern church "has never encountered among their doctors the belief in a material or temporary fire."[30] Belief in such a fire was dangerous, since it "encouraged moral laxity amongst the living"[31] and favored "the origenist heresy of apocatastasis, which denied the eternity of Hell and of eternal punishments for the wicked."[32]

Bessarion then dealt with the scriptural and patristic texts the Latins had employed, claiming that some were irrelevant (e.g., 2 Mc 12:46 never mentions a cleansing fire, only the benefits of prayer for the dead), others were misinterpreted (the verb σωθήσεται 1 Cor 3:15 refers to being "preserved" rather than "saved" by fire), and still others were obscure (e.g., the spurious text from Theodoret of Cyrus).[33] Among the Greek fathers this left only the witness of Gregory of Nyssa, whose writings could be seen as supporting the Latin position. Rather than questioning the authenticity of the text, Bessarion instead argued that the writings of one father, tinged by the heresy of Origen—which, to be fair, had not been formally condemned when Gregory was writing—could not be used to usurp the "common teaching of the Church and the rule of the Scriptures."[34] He claimed that we should remain silent about this error "out of respect for this father, who is renowned for his holiness and learning," since anyone, including a great saint, could occasionally be mistaken.[35]

---

[28] Marinis, *Death and the Afterlife in Byzantium*, 76. Gill's assessment was similar: "Bessarion's arguments had been mostly negative, rebutting the reasons alleged by the Latins ... witness[ing] to Greek teaching only in so far as they denied certain positions of their adversaries." Gill, *Council of Florence*, 121.

[29] Hofmann and Petit, *De Purgatorio disputationes*, 14–15; Eng. trans.: Bathrellos, "Love, Purification, and Forgiveness versus Justice, Punishment, and Satisfaction," 96. Larchet, *Life after Death According to the Orthodox Tradition*, 186.

[30] Hofmann and Petit, *De Purgatorio disputationes*, 15; Eng. trans.: Larchet, *Life after Death According to the Orthodox Tradition*, 186.

[31] Robert Ombres, "Latins and Greeks in Debate over Purgatory, 1230–1439," *Journal of Ecclesiastical History* 35 (1984): 8.

[32] Jorgenson, "The Debate over Patristic Texts on Purgatory," 326.

[33] Hofmann and Petit, *De Purgatorio disputationes*, 16–23.

[34] Ibid., 23–25.

[35] Ibid., 24. Essentially it was the same argument Photius had used centuries earlier concerning the place of Augustine—an individual father may have spoken incorrectly about a particular subject, but this did not negate his overall sanctity. Although Gregory was tainted with the Origenist heresy, it was inappropriate to apply the condemnation of a later council to an obviously saintly figure long dead and unable to defend (or amend) his views. See A. Edward Siecienski, "Avoiding the Sin of Ham: Dealing with Errors in the Works of the Fathers," in *Studia Patristica: Proceedings of the Fifteenth International Conference on Patristic Studies*, XLV (Leuven: Peeters, 2010), 175–79.

The teaching of the Latin fathers (Ambrose, Augustine, and Gregory Dialogus) on the matter were unclear and often colored by misunderstandings of Paul and the desire to overcome the errors of Origen.[36] Their language should be interpreted "mildly," for "they are not trying to teach this with authority, rather they are trying to deal with a particular circumstance" and thus we "should not imitate their expediency."[37] As for the witness of Gregory Dialogus, Bessarion wondered whether his references to purification by fire were better "understood more in the way of allegories."[38] Concerning the *ratio theologica*, Bessarion speculated that the Greeks could just as easily make a case *against* Purgatory based on God's *philanthropia* as the Latins could make a case for it based on divine justice.[39] He then concluded with a series of ten syllogisms, largely taken from Mark's original *Memorandum*, all proving the inadequacy of the Latin position.[40] The last, which came close to accusing the Latins of heresy, was perhaps the most damning.

> The doctrine of apocatastasis and the end of eternal punishment, due to Origen and accepted by some churchmen ... has nevertheless been proscribed and anathematized by the holy fifth ecumenical council as soul-destroying and encouraging laxity among the lax, who anticipate deliverance from their torment and the promised apocatastasis. For the same reason it seems that the proposed doctrine of the Divine purifying fire ought to be rejected by the church as disturbing to valiant souls diverting them from making every effort to purify themselves in this life, with the prospect of another purification.[41]

Bessarion's presentation, as the Latins were quick to note, left several important questions about the afterlife unanswered, an ambiguity perhaps explained by the Greeks' lack of unanimity on the subject,[42] the emperor's unwillingness to complicate

---

[36] Hofmann and Petit, *De Purgatorio disputationes*, 25–27.

[37] Ibid., 26; Eng. trans.: Jorgenson, "The Debate over Patristic Texts on Purgatory," 327.

[38] Hofmann and Petit, *De Purgatorio disputationes*, 26. Bessarion argued that Gregory could actual be read as an opponent of Purgatory, for he believed "that the slight faults of the just can be either compensated for in this life by good works or expiated at death by fear, or finally after death be remitted by the prayers which are offered for them." Ibid., 27; Eng. trans.: Jorgenson, "The Debate over Patristic Texts on Purgatory," 327.

[39] Hofmann and Petit, *De Purgatorio disputationes*, 28.

[40] Among the arguments were that "the slight good of the wicked should not call for a reward but only a difference in punishment and so the slight evil in the good should not call for a punishment but only a difference in blessedness.... The Gospel according to St Luke teaching about the destiny of [the rich man and Lazarus] ... did not leave a place of temporary torments between the two, but nothing save a great and impassable abyss.... The soul delivered from the body, totally incorporeal and immaterial, does not seem able to be punished by a corporeal fire.... Our holy fathers ... initiated in many places and at many times by visions, dreams, and other miracles, into the eternal punishment and lot of the impious and afflicted sinners, have never alluded to a purifying temporal fire." Ibid., 28–31; Eng. trans.: Larchet, *Life after Death According to the Orthodox Tradition*, 188–91.

[41] Hofmann and Petit, *De Purgatorio disputationes*, 31; Eng. trans.: Larchet, *Life after Death According to the Orthodox Tradition*, 191.

[42] "The Greeks had met for theological discussions before they came to Italy, and it seems that there was a kind of doctrinal committee, of which John Eugenicus (the brother of Mark) was the secretary. There is evidence, however, of lack of unanimity among the Greek delegates, which is hardly surprising given the relatively underdeveloped state of their reflections on Purgatory in comparison with the Latins." Ombres, "Latins and Greeks in Debate over Purgatory," 10. Syropoulos also recorded that there was great dissention

negotiations, and the Byzantines' general lack of interest, as there is indication in the *Acta* that they were simply "humouring the Latins by enduring these conferences."[43] The Latins, however, were taking these discussions quite seriously, and decided the time had come to press the attack.

John of Torquemada, speaking for the Latins, began his presentation on June 27,[44] almost two weeks after Bessarion's, by recognizing the common belief in "the existence of souls in the middle state, which expect help from the suffrages of the living because they are detained there ... because of some liability (to punishment) for sins (*qui aliquo reatu peccatorum detenti expectant vivorum suffragiis ad iuvari*)."[45] He then put forward a series of questions he believed had been left unanswered by the official Greek response, including whether the souls of saints enter Heaven immediately after death, just as souls with mortal sin enter Hell, or must they await the day of final judgment? Do souls in the middle state undergo punishment? And if so, what is it—simply deprivation of the beatific vision, or is there some sensible punishment? Is that sensible punishment captivity, darkness, or ignorance? Do these souls go immediately to Heaven after they are purified?[46]

Torquemada then turned to the question of purification by fire, which the Greeks had denied because they had found it neither in Scripture nor in the patristic corpus. Torquemada expressed his shock that the Greeks could discount the testimony of so many holy fathers, especially Gregory of Nyssa, whose writings they had dismissed as Origenist. This put them on a very slippery slope since "It could be asserted that all the fathers being men could [similarly err] ... and indeed the authority of the Bible itself could in that way be impugned as it had been transmitted by human agency."[47] Besides, Purgatory had nothing to do with Origenism, which Rome has

---

in the Greek ranks at this time, especially between Mark and Bessarion, and that from this time forward the two were divided despite occasional conversations. Laurent, *Les "Mémoires"*, 288–90.

[43] Gill, *The Council of Florence*, 119. "Bessarion says the same in *De Processione Spiritus Sancti ad Alexium Lascarin Philanthropinum*." Ibid.

[44] Gill noted that the *Acta Graeca* recorded another conference on the twenty-fifth but we do not have a record of it. "It would seem that there were more conferences than the number of speeches preserved in writing, both because of the long intervals that separate the few dates given by the Greek *Acts* ... and because there must have been discussions besides the reading of these papers." Ibid.

[45] Hofmann and Petit, *De Purgatorio disputationes*, 32; Eng. trans.: Bathrellos, "Love, Purification, and Forgiveness versus Justice, Punishment, and Satisfaction," 98. Bathrellos notes that "this phrase is translated into Greek as 'κηλῖσί τισι τῶν ἁμαρτιῶν διακρατηθέντες' (being detained by some stains of sins), which renders the word '*reatus*' as 'κηλίς' and thus makes the Latin view more easily palatable to the non-legalistic mentality of the Greeks." Ibid.

[46] Hofmann and Petit, *De Purgatorio disputationes*, 33–34.

[47] "Such a thing shakes the whole foundation of the faith, beginning with the Old and New Testaments which have been transmitted by men. The Latins are well aware that men, as such, can err; but in as much as they are inspired by the Spirit of God and authenticated by the Church in matters concerning the common faith, their testimony offers a total guarantee of truth. This is why the Latins can not easily accept the rejection of a man who was the brother of St Basil and of St Macrina and a friend of St Gregory the Theologian. Moreover, the Fifth Ecumenical Council was convened precisely to combat the errors of Origen; it examined the writings of Gregory of Nyssa and found them entirely beyond suspicion. As a result, Gregory rightly believed in both a temporary and an eternal fire; when the writings of Origen were being burned, those of Gregory were preserved proving that they did not contain the errors that the Greeks suppose." Hofmann and Petit, *De Purgatorio disputationes*, 35–37. English summary in Jorgenson, "The Debate over Patristic Texts on Purgatory," 328.

always detested, for the church distinguished "between the eternal fire of Hell [for grave faults] and the temporary fire of Purgatory ... [which] has been instituted for the purging only of some sins or for satisfaction by due punishments (*pro purgandis quibusdam criminibus aut satisfaciendo debitis poenis fuisset institutus*)."[48] As for encouraging laxity, the Latin experience had always been the opposite, for since the fires of Purgatory surpassed all earthly punishments (as Augustine clearly taught), people were most diligent in trying to avoid them.

Torquemada then invoked the authority of the Latin fathers, especially Augustine and Gregory,[49] and that of the Roman church, which had always followed a middle course between opposite and extreme errors (e.g., between Sabellius and Arius, Eutyches and Nestorius) and in the present question had rejected the Origenist denial of eternal punishment while affirming the reality of temporary punishments.[50] Then, to prove that Purgatory was necessary, Torquemada distinguished between the

> two aspects to every sin.... The first is the guilt (*culpa*), namely the damage or stain (*labes*) left to the soul after it has offended the Creator (*post offensionem Creatoris*). The second is the liability to punishment (*poenae reatus*). God forgives the former thanks to the sinner's contrition and renunciation of sin. However, the latter, namely the liability to punishment, remains.[51]

One normally satisfies this liability "by completing the penance ordered by the Church ... but [if, for various reasons,] penance has not been undertaken or completed ... the punishment (*poena*) must be completed in purgatorial fire."[52] This must also be what the Greeks believe, for after death "The soul can neither experience contrition nor renounce sin.... [And thus] the forgiveness and absolution, of which the Greeks also speak [taking place in the middle state], must necessarily refer to the punishment."[53] According to "the doctrine of the church, the holy fathers, and revelations shown to godly men, divine justice has ordained that purgation [i.e., the punishments due to sin] should be appropriately made by material fire (*per ignem corporeum*) ... [which] is most painful and apt to purge."[54]

John concluded by refuting the syllogisms offered by the Greeks, arguing that "when a Christian dies in charity but with small evil, namely the venial sin or liability to punishment (*parvo malo, scilicet veniali culpa aut reatu poenae*)," both "the guilt of the sin and the liability to punishment (*a culpis reatuque poenarum purgari*)" are cleansed in Purgatory since "all souls ... should be free from every guilt and liability

---

[48] Hofmann and Petit, *De Purgatorio disputationes*, 35; Eng. trans.: Bathrellos, "Love, Purification, and Forgiveness versus Justice, Punishment, and Satisfaction," 99.
[49] Augustine was not only a saint acclaimed by the universal church, but also a theologian equal to any of the Greeks. In fact, later in the presentation Torquemada expended a great deal of effort to prove that Augustine's understanding of the verb σωθήσεται in 1 Corinthians 3:15 was preferable to Chrysostom's, and that it did indeed mean "saved" rather than "preserved." Hofmann and Petit, *De Purgatorio disputationes*, 38.
[50] Hofmann and Petit, *De Purgatorio disputationes*, 38.
[51] Ibid., 39; Eng. trans.: Bathrellos, "Love, Purification, and Forgiveness versus Justice, Punishment, and Satisfaction," 100 (for this and subsequent selections).
[52] Hofmann and Petit, *De Purgatorio disputationes*, 39.
[53] Ibid.
[54] Ibid., 39–40.

[to punishment]' (*omnes animas ... ab omni culpa et reatu esse convenit liberas*)" before entering Heaven.[55] After addressing a few more Greek objections, Torquemada finished by claiming Purgatory was necessary to keep Christians from inertia and despair, for without it people will come to "believe that no sinner will ever enter heaven, given that no one is clear of minor sins (*peccatis levibus*)."[56]

As with Cesarini, Torquemada made it clear that for the Latins Purgatory was not a "place where souls are cleansed and healed in order to reach the spiritual maturity ... [but] only a place of punishment and torture for sins already forgiven."[57] And while this made perfect sense within the Latin scholastic tradition, the Greeks could not understand or accept it. Yet Torquemada had also raised some important questions about the Greeks' own views, forcing them to move beyond a mere rejection of the Latin doctrine. The task of answering them fell to Mark of Ephesus, who assured his fellow delegates that he would have "plenty to say" on the subject.

Mark's presentation is of "monumental importance" for our understanding of Orthodox eschatology because in it we find "for the first time ... a systematic exposition of the [Eastern] Church's beliefs on the afterlife."[58] He began by addressing Torquemada's question on the fate of souls after death, affirming that

> neither the righteous have as yet received the fullness of their lot and that blessed condition for which they have prepared themselves here through works, nor have sinners, after death, been led away into the eternal punishment in which they shall be tormented eternally. Rather, both the one and the other must necessarily occur after the judgment of the last day and the resurrection of all. Now, however, both the one and the other are in places proper to them: the first in absolute repose and free, are in heaven with the angels and before God himself, and already as if in the paradise from which Adam fell ... while the second in their turn, being confined in Hell remain in the lowest bit, in darkness and in the shadow of death.[59]

---

[55] Ibid., 50–51. Bathrellos notes: "The Latins had in their first text presented purgatorial fire as merely punitive. In their second text they also unambiguously argued that forgiveness in the afterlife does not refer to the *culpa* but only to the *poena*. The fire of Purgatory burns in order to punish those who have not completed the process of offering satisfaction for sins already forgiven as to the *culpa* in this life. However, in this text ... the Latins occasionally claimed that purgation in the afterlife includes also the *culpa*." Bathrellos, "Love, Purification, and Forgiveness versus Justice, Punishment, and Satisfaction," 103.

[56] For example, John argued that the reason the Parable of the Rich Man and Lazarus does not mention Purgatory is because it "refers to the *eschata*, when there will be no Purgatory" and that "the power of God [makes] it possible for an immaterial soul to burn in a material fire." Hofmann and Petit, *De Purgatorio disputationes*, 56–57; Eng. trans.: Bathrellos, "Love, Purification, and Forgiveness versus Justice, Punishment, and Satisfaction," 103.

[57] Bathrellos, "Love, Purification, and Forgiveness versus Justice, Punishment, and Satisfaction," 100.

[58] Marinis, *Death and the Afterlife in Byzantium*, 76. Mark's speech (*Oratio altera de igne purgatorio*) is in Hofmann and Petit, *De Purgatorio disputationes*, 60–103 and Petit, *Documents relatifs au concile de Florence*, 108–51. For Mark's eschatology see Nicholas Constas, "Mark Eugenikos," in Carmelo Conticello and Vassa Conticello, eds, *La théologie Byzantine et sa tradition*, vol. 2 (Turnhout: Brepols, 2002), 452–59.

[59] Hofmann and Petit, *De Purgatorio disputationes*, 61–62; Eng. trans.: Larchet, *Life after Death According to the Orthodox Tradition*, 192. "Neither have the first yet received the inheritance of the kingdom, and those good things which eye has not seen nor ear heard ... nor have the second yet been given over to eternal torments, or to burning in the unquenchable fire." Ibid.

In these "appropriate places" (προσήκοντες τόποι) Mark affirmed that the righteous "remain in every joy and gladness ... while [sinners], on the contrary, remain in total confinement and inconsolable suffering, like condemned men awaiting the judge's sentence and foreseeing their torment."[60] Mark then supported this view from Scripture and the fathers (e.g., Pseudo-Athanasius, Gregory Nazianzus, and John Chrysostom), arguing that the Latin position (i.e., that everyone gets their full reward or punishment immediately after death, but without their bodies) would make the doctrine of the Last Judgment (Mt 25:31–46) superfluous.

Concerning the type of suffering endured by souls in the middle state, Mark claimed they suffer from "sadness ... or shame and torture of conscience, or regret, or confinement, or darkness, or fear, or uncertainty for the future, or even mere postponement of the beatific vision," but not from any material fire, a concept not found anywhere in Scripture.[61] Even the texts produced by the Latins in support (e.g., 2 Mc 12:39–45, Mt 12:32) do not mention this fire, and Paul's mention of fire in 1 Corinthians 3:13–15 was to the fires of Hell, not Purgatory. It is true, Mark acknowledged, that there are references to fire in many visions of the afterlife, but he argued that these "should be taken in a figurative and allegorical sense,"[62] for "even the tortures of Hell have an allegorical meaning, signifying the torments of conscience, which makes belief in a material fire punishing [immaterial] souls after death implausible."[63]

Mark taught that "the church in the liturgy and other circumstances does not pray for just one category of souls but for all the deceased without distinction, although he acknowledged that prayers and alms for the dead were particularly beneficial for those in the middle state (οἱ μέσοι)."[64] Even the righteous, "who have still not achieved perfect blessedness according to the teaching of Saint Dionysios," benefit from the church's prayers as they continue their advance ever closer to God.[65]

Mark then addressed the Latins' shock to hear that a great saint like Gregory of Nyssa might have taught heresy.[66] After citing a number of cases where saints had

---

[60] Ibid.

[61] Hofmann and Petit, *De Purgatorio disputationes*, 70; Eng. trans.: Bathrellos, "Love, Purification, and Forgiveness versus Justice, Punishment, and Satisfaction," 106. Mark cited 2 Peter 2:4 ("For if God did not spare the angels when they sinned, but cast them into hell and committed them to chains of deepest darkness to be kept until the judgment ... ") to show that while there were chains and darkness for those awaiting the last judgment, there was no mention of a material fire. Hofmann and Petit, *De Purgatorio disputationes*, 69–70.

[62] Hofmann and Petit, *De Purgatorio disputationes,,* 70; Eng. trans.: Larchet, *Life after Death According to the Orthodox Tradition*, 193.

[63] Hofmann and Petit, *De Purgatorio disputationes,,* 82; Eng. trans.: Bathrellos, "Love, Purification, and Forgiveness versus Justice, Punishment, and Satisfaction," 108 (for this and subsequent selections).

[64] Hofmann and Petit, *De Purgatorio disputationes*, 70. This included both "sinners in Hell to gain for them, for want of a complete deliverance, at least a slight relief." In support he cited the Kneeling Prayers at Pentecost ("You who, on this most perfect and salutary feast, have been pleased to receive our intercessory prayers for those who are immured in Hell, granting us great hopes to see you grant to the departed deliverance from the pains which overwhelm them and their alleviation, hear our prayers"). Ibid., 70–71.

[65] Ibid., 73.

[66] Ibid., 74–75; Eng. trans.: Jorgenson, "The Debate over Patristic Texts on Purgatory," 330 (for this and subsequent selections). Mark taught that there was a great difference between "the assertions of the canonical Scriptures, entrusted to the Church, and the writings or the teachings of any one particular doctor. The former are doctrines revealed by God; the latter do not impose themselves on the faith and should not be received without examination. One particular doctor can err; otherwise, what is the purpose of ecumenical councils, if not to straighten out particular opinions." Jorgenson, "Debate over Patristic Texts on Purgatory," 330.

erred (e.g., Dionysius of Alexandria and Gregory Thaumaturgus), Mark asked, "What is there to prevent us from saying that Gregory of Nyssa, as a man, has erred, especially since the dogma had not yet been decided?"[67] Gregory was undoubtedly tinged with Origenism, and yet the Latins, who claim to detest Origen, cited him as a witness. This was despite the fact that

> the doctrine of Saint Gregory of Nyssa is [actually] quite different [from yours]. According to him, . . not only slight faults but *all* faults can be purified by fire, it is *all* punishment that must cease and desist since punishment is for him nothing but a purification ... which must end in the final restoration.... What is there in common between this discourse and yours on Purgatory? Without distinction, Gregory delivers all sinners and every sin to this purifying fire. You deliver there only certain sins, those of the less guilty souls.[68]

On a theological level, one of Mark's biggest problems with the Latin doctrine was the "astonishing division" between "the offense itself which is made to God (*Dei offensa*) and the punishment which follows it (*poenae reatus*).... Of these two aspects you teach the offense to God indeed can be remitted after repentance and turning away from evil, but the liability to punishment must exist in every case; so that, on the basis of this idea, it is essential that those released from sins should all the same be subject to punishment for them."[69] This made no sense to the Greeks, for if kings do not subject the guilty to more punishments after they have granted amnesty, how much more was this true of God, who "after he has forgiven [the sinner] immediately delivers him from punishment also."[70] Besides, baptism ("the first, and greatest, and most perfect remission of sins") allows for "both purification of every filth and absolution from every punishment ... so why is it necessarily the case that the forgiveness of which we talk is not able to purge" without punishment?[71]

Mark concluded his presentation by dealing with the Latins' responses to his earlier syllogisms, clarifying that the process of purgation actually begins during one's life, "either through virtue and good works, or through repentance and the punishments related to it, or through participation in rituals and Church sacraments."[72] This way of

---

[67] Hofmann and Petit, *De Purgatorio disputationes*, 77.

[68] Ibid., 80.

[69] Ibid., 82–83; Eng. trans.: Seraphim Rose, *The Soul after Death* (Platina, CA: St. Herman of Alaska Brotherhood, 2009), 212–13.

[70] Hofmann and Petit, *De Purgatorio disputationes*, 82–83. Mark argued "if forgiveness concerns the guilt, which, according to your words, is a damage left to the soul after it has offended against the Creator, what could still the punishment purge, since this damage has already been purged via forgiveness?" Hofmann and Petit, *De Purgatorio disputationes*, 84; Eng. trans.: Bathrellos, "Love, Purification, and Forgiveness versus Justice, Punishment, and Satisfaction," 108. Mark claimed that Scripture attested to this, for "the publican goes back not only absolved but justified; Manassas after being humbled is delivered from his chains and re-established on his thrones; the Ninevites, thanks to their repentance, are spared the blows that threatened them the paralytic received, along with the pardon of his sins, a rectifying of his body." Hofmann and Petit, *De Purgatorio disputationes*, 83; Eng. trans.: Larchet, *Life after Death According to the Orthodox Tradition*, 195.

[71] Hofmann and Petit, *De Purgatorio disputationes*, 84; Eng. trans.: Bathrellos, "Love, Purification, and Forgiveness versus Justice, Punishment, and Satisfaction," 108.

[72] Hofmann and Petit, *De Purgatorio disputationes*, 98; Eng. trans.: Bathrellos, "Love, Purification, and Forgiveness versus Justice, Punishment, and Satisfaction," 109–10.

living "obviously removes some filth, that is sins ... and if it proves able to erase and purge sins ... there is no longer need for any punishment."[73] However, if the process of purgation is not completed, it can continue in the world to come thanks to the prayers of the church and the *philanthropia* of God, but not come through some punitive, punishing, material fire burning in a third place (τρίτος τόπος) set aside for the satisfaction of debt.[74]

There are several important things to note about Mark's presentation. First is how similar Mark's eschatology was to Symeon of Thessalonica's, which suggests that his position here is far more traditional than previously thought. Mark is "systematiz[ing] the earlier disparate traditions," not inventing them.[75] Second, as was the case with his first memorandum, "Mark's outlook is not legalistic but medicinal and therapeutic," and thus he cannot understand why there is a need for a purely punitive punishment, if purgation has been already accomplished."[76] Third, was the conspicuous absence of the "trial of the tollgates," a tradition with which Mark was "undoubtedly familiar."[77] Its introduction at this stage might have changed the dynamics of the debate, and yet Mark never mentions it. It was, depending on one's view, either an opportunity missed or a disaster avoided.[78]

Mark's presentation left the Latins with many questions—fourteen to be precise— nine of which dealt with the state of souls before the last judgment, and five concerning the suffering that souls experienced in the middle state. In his *Response*,[79] Mark affirmed that the "souls of the saints have not yet received their proper share (οἰκεῖον κλῆρον), and their enjoyment of that blessed state is entirely incomplete and lacking (ἀτελής ἐστι πᾶσα καὶ ἐλλιπής) with respect to that restoration (ἀποκατάστασις) for which they hope."[80] This is because they themselves are "incomplete, and, as it were,

---

[73] Hofmann and Petit, *De Purgatorio disputationes*, 97.

[74] Bathrellos noted that Mark ended his speech "by suggesting in a conciliatory manner that an allegorical understanding of purgatorial fire will bring the Latins and the Greeks to agreement" (Hofmann and Petit, *De Purgatorio disputationes*, 102–3) proving that "Gill's claim that Mark 'was conciliatory [only] in the beginning' of the council is untenable." Bathrellos, "Love, Purification, and Forgiveness versus Justice, Punishment, and Satisfaction," 110.

[75] Marinis, *Death and the Afterlife in Byzantium*, 78.

[76] Bathrellos, "Love, Purification, and Forgiveness versus Justice, Punishment, and Satisfaction," 117. Here and elsewhere (e.g., *Marci Ephesii argumenta decem adversus ignem purgatorium* in Ludovico Petit, ed., *Marci Eugenici, metropolitae Ephesi, opera antiunionistica*, CF 10.2 [Rome: Pontifical Oriental Institute, 1977], 114–17) the words φάρμακον (medicine) and ἴασις (cure/remedy) are used to emphasize "the medicinal function of the purgative process," a chief "characteristic of the Greek Orthodox mentality." Demetrios Bathrellos, Email to the author.

[77] Constas, "To Sleep, Perchance to Dream," 108. Vasileios Marinis believed "that this omission is intentional. On a basic level the pious fanciful stories about balancing manuscripts of deeds and colorful demons would have been out of place in discussions that were often based on Aristotelian logic. More importantly, the notion of the passage through toll houses was dangerously close to the idea of Purgatory... [and] Mark likely thought it best to not provide his opponents with material that might support their opinion." Marinis, *Death and the Afterlife in Byzantium*, 79–80.

[78] Paul Ladouceur observed that "Toll-house theology, with its emphasis on the trial of the soul, demons, justice, judgement, and punishment, [was probably] closer to the Latin position at Ferrara than to the Orthodox position." Paul Ladouceur, "Orthodox Theologies of the Afterlife: Review of *The Departure of the Soul*," https://blogs.ancientfaith.com/orthodoxyandheterodoxy/2017/08/18/orthodox-theologies-of-the-afterlife-review-of-the-departure-of-the-soul/.

[79] Mark of Ephesus, *Responsio quibusdam quaesitis Latinis*, in Hofmann and Petit, *De Purgatorio disputationes*, 104–20.

[80] Ibid., 104; Eng. trans.: Constas, "Mark Eugenikos," 454–55 (for this and subsequent selections).

cut in half (ἀτελεῖς ὄντες καὶ οἷον ἡμίτομοι), since they lack the incorruptible body which they will receive in the Resurrection."[81] Until the Judgment Day the saints too live in "expectation" (προσδοκία) in solidarity with the entire church, and even then they will not see the essence of God, for there

> is absolutely no possibility for any created nature to see, conceive, or know the divine nature. Not even the most transcendent minds can do so. This is because whatever can be known essentially, in order to be known, must be grasped by the knower. But God is essentially incomprehensible and thus cannot be grasped.[82]

While the blessed receive the "ineffable light" and enjoy the "vision of God," albeit incomplete (ἐλλιπής),[83] those who have died in mortal sin are in Hell, where they are "tortured by the expectancy and fear of their sad lot, although the greatest pain they experience is the privation of the divine vision ... which is a pain greater than eternal fire or any other torment."[84] For those in the middle state (οἱ μέσοι), Mark maintained that the "punishments—ignorance, sadness, shame, etc.—are varied and unequal, like the faults that have merited them"[85] and that they also suffer from uncertainty about their future, not concerning "the question of *whether* they will be saved, but of *when*."[86]

Mark taught that while imperfect repentance "brings about shame and pain in one's conscience," perfect repentance brings about not only the forgiveness of sins but also the remission of the punishment.[87] Sins that went unrepented, even minor ones, required "the divine *philanthropia*" and "the prayers of the Church" in order to be forgiven, so that the sinner "may finally join the group of the saved."[88] God alone "out of love for mankind grants remission of sins, as he did when he granted paradise to the good thief" without any notion "of satisfaction based on the requirements of divine justice."[89] It was true that confessors often imposed punishments (ἐπιτίμια) upon penitents, but they did this for therapeutic reasons,[90] not as *satisfactiones*, or temporal punishments required for

---

[81] Mark of Ephesus, *Oratio altera de igne purgatorio*, in Hofmann and Petit, *De Purgatorio disputationes*, 66.

[82] Mark of Ephesus, *Responsio quibusdam quaesitis Latinis*, in Hofmann and Petit, *De Purgatorio disputationes*, 112–13.

[83] Ibid., 105–8.

[84] Ibid., 116; Eng. trans.: Larchet, *Life after Death According to the Orthodox Tradition*, 196.

[85] Bathrellos, "Love, Purification, and Forgiveness versus Justice, Punishment, and Satisfaction," 111.

[86] Mark of Ephesus, *Responsio quibusdam quaesitis Latinis*, in Hofmann and Petit, *De Purgatorio disputationes*, 116; Eng. trans.: Bathrellos, "Love, Purification, and Forgiveness versus Justice, Punishment, and Satisfaction," 111 (for this and subsequent selections).

[87] Mark of Ephesus, *Responsio quibusdam quaesitis Latinis*, in Hofmann and Petit, *De Purgatorio disputationes*, 116–17.

[88] Ibid., 118–19.

[89] Ibid., 119.

[90] "First, that they may escape the involuntary punishment of the afterlife through this voluntary ascetic suffering. Second, in order that the pleasure-loving attitude of our flesh, which leads to enmity against God and is the cause of all sin, may be cured by its opposite, namely pain. Third, in order that these ἐπιτίμια act as a bridle for the soul, so that it does not commit the same sins again. Fourth, because virtue is by nature laborious and therefore one should get used to the labours that lead to it, whereas by pleasure one falls to sin. Fifth, an ἐπιτίμια is given in order that the priest may be able to see whether the penitent will accept it,

absolution.[91] Mark noted, for example, that

> when a penitent is about to die, the Greek priests do not impose any ἐπιτίμια for they believe that repentance and sincere intention for goodness are sufficient for the forgiveness of sins. This is why the priests forgive sins—and believe that God forgives them too—along with the punishment due to them, as is shown by the fact that immediately after confession the penitent is allowed to receive Holy Communion.[92]

Mark's answers "(if they ever were presented) would assuredly have encountered opposition from the Latin theologians, [however] there is no record of any further discussion."[93] In fact, it would be almost a year (June 1439), only after the translation of the council to Florence, before discussion on Purgatory resumed, and by that time both sides were exhausted by the prolonged debate on the Filioque. However, the Latins insisted that *all* the disputed issues had to be settled before the union could be consummated, which meant that Purgatory was once again on the agenda.

While the Latins assumed the debate had largely been resolved, the Greeks still wanted to distinguish the "perfect blessedness" received after death with the "more perfect blessedness" received after the Last Judgment.[94] On June 9 the pope met with a delegation of Greek hierarchs, including the unionist leaders Bessarion and Isidore of Kyiv, to discuss the final language of the *cedula*, which had essentially repeated Cardinal Cesarini's presentation from a year earlier. Eugene, in his speech to the Greeks, went even further than the *cedula*, clarifying that there were three ranks of the dead—saints who go immediately to look upon the essence of God (*qui immediate Dei essentiam contueantur*), sinners who go immediately to Hell, and the middle group, who go to the fires of Purgatory (*in ignem abire purgatorium*) because they have not performed works of satisfaction (*nec opera satisfactionis peregerunt*).[95] The Greeks, despite all the objections they had raised a year earlier, now seemed ready to

---

which will be a reliable token that he has fully detested sin." Ibid., 119; summarized in Bathrellos, "Love, Purification, and Forgiveness versus Justice, Punishment, and Satisfaction," 112.

[91] Bathrellos disagreed with Jugie ("La Question du Purgatoire," 128) and d'Alès ("La question du Purgatoire au concile de Florence," 47) that ἐπιτίμια were imposed as "satisfaction due to God for the forgiven sin." According to him, "Gill (*Council of Florence*, 125) is closer to the truth in writing that for Mark, 'the Greek Church imposes a penance in the Sacrament of Confession for various ascetical reasons, but not in connection with any temporal punishment.' And Roncaglia (*Georges Bardanès* 48) is even closer when arguing that for the Eastern Church 'the *epitimion* is not an expiatory punishment, but a means of salvation.... It is noteworthy that [the unionist] Joseph Methones (*De Purgatorio*, 8 [PG 159:1265]), in defending the teaching of Ferrara-Florence on Purgatory, understands Purgatory as an *epitimion* that leads to the purification of the soul from the stains of sin.... This characteristically medicinal understanding of Purgatory ... brings to light his Orthodox background' despite his unionist leanings." Ibid., 112, 117.

[92] Mark of Ephesus, *Responsio quibusdam quaesitis Latinis*, in Hofmann and Petit, *De Purgatorio disputationes*, 119–20; Eng. trans.: Bathrellos, "Love, Purification, and Forgiveness versus Justice, Punishment, and Satisfaction," 113.

[93] Gill, *The Council of Florence*, 125. Gill speculated that this "was probably [due to] the plague that by the middle of July had infested Ferrara," rather than the growing realization that the two sides had made little progress in reconciling their respective positions. Ibid.

[94] de Halleux, "Problèmes de méthode," 293.

[95] *Acta Graeca*, 442–43.

accept everything, including belief in a purgatorial fire and souls seeing the very essence of God.[96]

In the days and weeks that followed Eugene continued to insist that the Byzantines include a statement on Purgatory in the union decree, while the Greek synod wanted to resolve the issue at a later time, arguing that since the doctrine was not one of the causes of the division it need not be settled prior to the union.[97] The pope could not understand their reluctance, especially after the prolonged debates at Ferrara and the alleged closeness of the Greeks' position to that of the Latins.[98] Yet there were other issues (e.g., primacy and the epiclesis debate) that demanded attention, and so discussion of Purgatory was postponed once again, only re-emerging near the end of the council (June 27) when Cardinal Cesarini was asked to summarize the state of negotiations.

Cesarini said that the subject of Purgatory had been debated at Ferrara "very seriously," so seriously, in fact, that he "almost despaired" ever reaching an agreement.[99] However, with God's help, "The Greeks now admit the truth that those who die in charity but not having satisfied the penances enjoined [on them], or in venial sin, go to Purgatory."[100] The only remaining difference concerned that fact that the Greeks believe

> that they do not see God himself, but certain lights (*certos fulgores*), and in this there was great difficulty and such as nearly upset the whole business; at length they yielded to argument and recognized that the souls of the blessed will see God, three and one, as he is but they wanted to have put into the *cedula* that some would see less and others more, and it was thought good that this should be included, since "in our father's house there are many mansions."[101]

The final statement on Purgatory, which differed little from the text Cesarini had presented at Ferrara a year earlier, stated:

> If truly penitent people die in the love of God before they have made satisfaction for acts and omissions by worthy fruits of repentance, their souls are cleansed after death by cleansing pains (*penis purgatoriis*); and the suffrages of the living faithful avail them in giving relief from such pains, that is, sacrifices of masses, prayers, almsgiving and other acts of devotion which have been customarily performed by some of the faithful for others of the faithful in accordance with the church's ordinances.
> Also, the souls of those who have incurred no stain of sin whatsoever after baptism, as well as souls who after incurring the stain of sin have been cleansed whether in their bodies or outside their bodies, as was stated above, are straightaway received

---

[96] Ibid., 443. "Secundum illud, quod de igne purgatorio dicitis, hoc etiam suscipimus, atque animas videre essentiam Dei vere admittimus."
[97] Ibid., 446. The emperor would have been happy to drop the whole subject, but the Latin cardinals were insistent that it be included in the union decree. Ibid., 448.
[98] Ibid.
[99] *Acta Latina*, 254–55; Eng. trans.: Gill, *Council of Florence*, 285.
[100] Ibid.
[101] Ibid.

into heaven (*in celum mox recipi*) and clearly behold the triune God as he is (*et intueri clare ipsum Deum trinum et unum*), yet one person more perfectly than another according to the difference of their merits.[102]

The decree, without reference to either a material fire or a "third place," actually contains a rather mild version of Purgatory, seemingly confirming the conclusion of André de Halleux that in many ways "the definition is not incompatible with the eschatology that Mark of Ephesus had proposed to Ferrara except for its teaching on the beatific vision."[103] And yet the immediacy of eternal reward and punishment, the belief that one sees God "as he is," and (perhaps most importantly) the statement's very premise—that souls must make satisfaction for the debt due to sin—are teachings that all come straight from the Latin scholastic tradition. In fact, de Halleux maintained that *Laetentur Caeli*'s language and premises are so determined by the Western mindset that a modern-day ecumenist would have to search very hard "under its Latin conceptuality, to find the traditional faith of the undivided Church."[104] The Latins had won again, or so it seemed.

The Post-Florentine Period

Mark of Ephesus, who had done so much to explicate and defend the Greeks' traditional eschatology at Ferrara, refused to sign the Florentine decree, believing it a betrayal of the Orthodox faith. As leader of the growing anti-unionist movement, Mark continued to criticize *Laetentur Caeli*'s teachings on the Filioque, azymes, and the afterlife, writing *To All Orthodox Christians on the Mainland and in the Islands* (1444):

> Neither do the saints receive the kingdom and the unutterable blessings already prepared for them, nor are sinners already sent to Hell, but both await their fate which will be received in the future age after the resurrection and judgement; while [the unionists], together with the Latins, desire immediately after death to receive according to their merits. And for those in an intermediate condition, who have died in repentance, they give a purgatorial fire (which is not identical with that of Hell) so that, as they say, having purified their souls by it after death, they also together with the righteous will enjoy the kingdom; this is contained in their Conciliar Decree.[105]

---

[102] *Laetentur Caeli*; Tanner, ed., *Decrees of the Ecumenical Councils* 1, 527–28.
[103] de Halleux, "Problèmes de méthode," 297. "Despite the attempt at irenicism, the restrained tone of the formula, it was not received by the Byzantine church when the Greek delegates, with their emperor, returned home." Nichols, *Rome and the Eastern Churches*, 253–54.
[104] de Halleux, "Problèmes de méthode," 298–99. Compare this to Jugie's assessment: "The Greeks did not then, and do not yet have, a definite doctrine on several questions relating to the end. The Latins' brilliant explanations often helped them out and suggested solutions that they had never thought of before ... [This is why] the unionists did not have too much difficulty in rallying to the doctrine expressed in the conciliar definition." Jugie, "La question du Purgatoire," 281–82.
[105] Mark of Ephesus, *Epistola encyclica contra Graeco-Latinos ac decretum synodi Florentiae*, in Petit, *Marci Eugenici, metropolitae Ephesi, opera antiunionistica*, 149–50; Eng. trans.: https://orthodoxethos.com/post/the-encyclical-letter-of-saint-mark-of-ephesus.

Mark's successor as leader of the anti-unionists was George Gennadios Scholarios (d. 1472), who wrote several treatises on the soul and one specifically on Purgatory.[106] He compared Purgatory to the tradition of the tollhouses, which was, in his opinion, like Purgatory without all the fireworks,[107] admitting that "the Church of the Orthodox has nearly the same [teaching] as the Roman, for she teaches that those who are stained by venial sin do not immediately enter into eternal life."[108] Instead, those burdened by sin ascend through a series of tollhouses, "suffer[ing] the postponement of their expected compensation and the temporary deprivation of God's glory until, through the recognition of the pardonable things … and due to the distress and sadness caused by the sins, they call out for divine mercy and, through God's benevolence, they are delivered from guilt."[109] Although he says the Latin teaching on fire is an "unnecessary notion,"[110] and that the delay is not caused "by the purification of the stain [as the Latins hold] but rather the release from some chain or impediment,"[111] with them he accepted that the suffrages of the living helped to accelerate the process by which these those in this middle state—he used the same term, οἱ μέσοι, as Mark—move toward God. Thus, as with Mark, the question for Scholarios was not "if" these souls will enter God's presence but "when," the question of exactly "how" this happens remaining somewhat mysterious since Scripture had not provided a firm guide on the matter.[112]

As the sixteenth century began, the Catholic world faced another challenge to the theology of Purgatory, this time from within, as the Protestant Reformation swept through Western Europe. Luther himself continued to affirm Purgatory even after his excommunication,[113] although by 1535 he was labeling it "a lie of the devil" invented so that "the papists may have some market days and snares for catching money."[114]

---

[106] George Gennadios Scholarios, *On Purgatory*, in Louis Petit, ed., *Oeuvres complètes de Gennade Scholarios*, vol. 1 (Paris: Maison de la Bonne Presse, 1928), 531–39. My thanks to Dr Matthew Briel for help with the Scholarios material and translations.

[107] Ibid., 533. Interestingly, it is Scholarios's efforts to liken the tollhouses to Purgatory that has made him persona non grata among modern-day apologists of the tollhouse tradition, who insist that their teaching has nothing in common with the doctrine of the Latins.

[108] Ibid.

[109] Ibid., 533–34; Eng. trans.: Marinis, *Death and the Afterlife in Byzantium*, 80.

[110] Ibid.

[111] Ibid.

[112] George Gennadios Scholarios, *On Souls after Death*, in Petit, *Oeuvres complètes*, vol. 1, 513–14; Eng. trans.: Marinis, *Death and the Afterlife in Byzantium*, 81. He wrote: "Whether the souls of the *mesoi* remain on earth and in paradise, or in the air, or in a combustible matter; and whether through sorrows in the consciousness and crushings on the earth, or through the fierceness of the fire of the combustible material, or through being retained in the toll houses in the air [these souls] are delivered from the embitterment of guilt, or they are set free of the weight, or cleansed from the dirt, or whatever one might want to call this, [namely,] the deliverance of their temporary hindrances, it makes little difference." Ibid.

[113] "The existence of a Purgatory I have never denied. I still hold that it exists, as I have written and admitted many times, though I have found no way of proving it incontrovertibly from Scripture or reason. I find in Scripture that Christ, Abraham, Jacob, Moses, Job, David, Hezekiah, and some others tasted hell in this life. This I think was Purgatory … in short, I myself have come to the conclusion that there is a Purgatory, but I cannot force anybody else to come to the same result." Martin Luther, *Defense and Explanation on All the Articles (1521)*, in George Forell, ed., *Career of the Reformer II*, *Luther's Works*, vol. 32 (Philadelphia: Fortress Press, 1958), 95.

[114] "Purgatory is the greatest falsehood because it is based on ungodliness and unbelief; for they deny that faith saves, and they maintain that satisfaction for sins is the cause of salvation. Therefore he who is in Purgatory is in hell itself; for these are his thoughts: 'I am a sinner and must render satisfaction for my sins; therefore I shall make a will and shall bequeath a definite amount of money for building churches and for

The other reformers followed suit, believing as they did that the idea of prayers and masses for the dead smacked of the "works righteousness" they so despised.[115] Particularly noisome was the claim that the "power of the keys" gave the pope the right to free souls from Purgatory when it suited him, since he had the power to draw on the church's "treasury of merit" and apply these good works to anyone, dead or alive, with an indulgence. This pretended power, they argued, was at the heart of John Tetzel's blasphemous claim that "every time a coin in the coffer rings, another soul from Purgatory springs."[116]

The Catholic Church was naturally eager to defend its teaching, especially as the logic of Purgatory had become central to the indulgence system that financed St. Peter's Basilica and the lavish lifestyle of the Renaissance popes.[117] Yet there were more than financial considerations. By the sixteenth century Purgatory was deeply ingrained in the Catholic imagination, popularized not only in art and poetry, but also in the writings of mystics (e.g., Catherine of Genoa) granted visions of the afterlife.[118] Interestingly, Catherine's famous *Treatise on Purgatory*, which did so much to inculcate a devotion to the "suffering souls," described Purgatory and its pains in terms that sounded almost "Orthodox"—that is, the fire as purificatory and the pains caused chiefly by the postponement of the beatific vision.[119]

The Council of Trent, against the Protestant attack, affirmed "that Purgatory exists, and that the souls detained there are helped by the prayers of the faithful (*suffragiis*), and most of all by the acceptable sacrifice of the altar."[120] These souls were there,

---

buying prayers and sacrifices for the dead by the monks and priests.' Such people die in a faith in works and have no knowledge of Christ. Indeed, they hate Him." Martin Luther, *Lectures on Genesis Chapters 21–25, Luther's Works*, vol. 4, ed. Jaroslav Pelikan (St. Louis: Concordia Publishing House, 1964), 424.

[115] "In attacking Purgatory, Protestantism was assaulting what was most dear to late mediaeval piety. It was a doctrine that put into practice in the most literal way the doctrine of the Communion of Saints. The dead were still among us, because prayers for their souls, which would have direct and continuing effect on their progress in the next world, went on indefinitely." John Casey, *After Lives: A Guide to Heaven, Hell, and Purgatory* (Oxford: Oxford University Press, 2009), 228.

[116] "*Sobald der Pfennig im Kasten klingt, die Selle aus dem Fegfeuer springt.*" Whether Tetzel ever said this remains a subject for debate, as none of his extant sermons contain the phrase.

[117] The Protestant critique was also seen, quite properly so, as an attack on papal power and authority, since several of Luther's *Theses* had questioned the pope's ability to remit any penalties except those imposed by the church.

[118] Le Goff described Catherine as the "pinnacle (or, if you prefer, the depths) of mystical devotion" that had begun a century earlier with Hadewijch and Mechtilde of Magdeburg, Gertrude of Hackeborn, and Gertrude the Great. Le Goff, *The Birth of Purgatory*, 357.

[119] "There is no joy save that in paradise to be compared to the joy of the souls in Purgatory. This joy increases day by day because of the way in which the love of God corresponds to that of the soul, since the impediment to that love is worn away daily. This impediment is the rust of sin. As it is consumed the soul is more and more open to God's love. Just as a covered object left out in the sun cannot be penetrated by the sun's rays, in the same way, once the covering of the soul is removed, the soul opens itself fully to the rays of the sun. The more rust of sin is consumed by fire, the more the soul responds to that love, and its joy increases. Not that all suffering disappears, but the duration of that suffering diminishes. The souls in Purgatory do not consider that punishment as suffering for, content in God's will, they are one with Him in pure charity." Catherine of Genoa, *Treatise on Purgatory*, in Serge Hughes, ed. and trans., *Catherine of Genoa: Purgation and Purgatory, The Spiritual Dialogue* (New York: Paulist Press, 1979), 72.

[120] Council of Trent, Session 25, *Decree on Purgatory*, in Tanner, ed., *Decrees of the Ecumenical Councils* 2, 774. While this "sound doctrine ... handed down by the Holy Fathers and the sacred Councils" was necessary for belief, the church also recognized that popular piety sometimes went too far, which is why the council enjoined that "difficult and subtle questions which do not make for edification and, for the most

according to the church, because even after justification "temporal punishment [due to sin] remains to be discharged, either in this world or later on in Purgatory, before entry into the kingdom of heaven can lie open."[121] These teachings were, of course, aimed chiefly at the Protestants, but as Robert Bellermine (d. 1621) later noted in his book *On Purgatory*, among those who rejected the doctrine were also the "Armenians and Greeks ... although the Greeks themselves, at the Council of Ferrara, affirmed that they do not deny Purgatory, but only the fire, and think that Purgatory is a dark place and full of labors."[122] While Purgatory *most probably* (*probabilissima*) contained a material fire, as it was the "consensus of the scholastics," Bellermine was quick to note that "such an opinion is indeed not *de fide*, because it has never been defined by the church; nay more, in the Council of Florence the Greeks professed that they do not posit a fire in Purgatory, and still in the last session a definition was made in which Purgatory was defined but with no mention of fire."[123]

The Lutherans, however, continued their attack upon the doctrine and in 1574 turned east for support, writing to Patriarch Jeremiah II (d. 1595) in an effort to convince him that the Augsburg Confession was firmly grounded in the ancient faith of the church.[124] The patriarch responded kindly, praising many of their teachings, but calling into question several others. On the subject of penances Jeremiah claimed that these were necessary "because by this voluntary affliction the penitent will be free from the involuntary punishment in the life to come."[125] At the same time, when a priest grants forgiveness of sins to one departing this life, "We believe that the punishment is also absolved, for genuine repentance depends on the intention of the sinner, but the punishment which has not been fulfilled is reserved for God's judgement," which is always tempered by his goodness and mercy.[126]

It is to the mercy of God that the church appeals when prayers are offered for the departed, for as Dionysius taught, "Prayer implores the Divine goodness to absolve the departed of all the iniquities that he committed through human weakness."[127] Gregory Nazianzus "points out that good works are a benefit even after death," and Chrysostom often asked congregants to pray for "the welfare of those who have departed ... [and] give them the proper help.... For it brings them great comfort and gain and benefit."[128] Jeremiah then chided the Lutherans for the refusal to pray for the dead, a practice contrary to both Scripture and tradition, for it was well known that

---

part, are not conducive to an increase of piety (cf. I Tim. 1:4), be excluded from the popular sermons to uneducated people.... As for those things that belong to the realm of curiosity or superstition, or smack of dishonorable gain, they should forbid them as scandalous and injurious to the faithful." Ibid.

[121] Council of Trent, Session 6, *Canons on Justification*, in Tanner, ed., *Decrees of the Ecumenical Councils* 2, 681.

[122] Robert Bellermine, *De Controversiis: On Purgatory*, trans. Ryan Grant (Post Falls, ID: Mediatrix Press, 2017), 8. In order to answer the Protestant critique that Purgatory was not found in either Scripture or the fathers, Bellermine produced many of the same prooftexts used at Ferrara over a century earlier.

[123] Ibid., 204.
[124] See chapter 5 n. 223.
[125] Mastrantonis, *Augsburg and Constantinople*, 57.
[126] Ibid., 58.
[127] Ibid., 61.
[128] Ibid.

"the prayers of the righteous ones are efficacious" (James 5:16) and there are many stories of the dead being aided by the prayers and liturgies of the living.[129]

The Tübingen theologians responded to the patriarch's criticisms by affirming that while it was a well-known "custom of the early church to impose satisfactions on those who committed sins publicly," the practice itself was unscriptural.[130] In fact, Scripture affirmed the opposite—that we can never "appease God for our sins," and that because "Christ [is] the most perfect satisfaction for the sins of the whole world ... satisfactions from us are not required."[131] Satisfactions "have no power to set us free from the sins committed against God" and cannot help us "avoid punishment after this life, which some think are imposed on those who someday will be saved. For the Holy Scriptures positively assert nothing of the kind, but know of only two places which men inherit after this life, one for the blessed, and one for the condemned."[132]

The Lutherans explained that their opposition to works righteousness and belief in justification *sola fide* led them to reject all "prayers and alms offered for the dead," for "If [the dead] have truly believed in Christ, we do not doubt that they will live with Christ enjoying the gladness in heaven ... but if they departed without true and living faith, they cannot be helped neither by prayers nor by alms."[133] And if the dead were suffering in the hereafter and in need of our prayers, why was this nowhere mentioned in Scripture?[134] The Lutheran position was clear—"As long as we are here we have good hopes. But as soon as we depart to that place, we can no longer repent or cleanse ourselves from our iniquities."[135]

In denying the efficacy of prayers for the dead, a long-standing and cherished practice of the Eastern church, the Lutherans had added to the growing list of issues (e.g., the Filioque, good works, free will, veneration of the saints, the use of icons) that separated them from Orthodoxy. Some have even speculated that this is why Jeremiah, seeing Roman Catholicism as the lesser of the two evils and fearing Muscovite hegemony over the Kyvian church, tacitly accepted the Ruthenians' efforts to begin negotiations with Rome in 1590.[136] When the Ruthenians ultimately did consummate the union in 1595, they agreed in the *Articles of Union* that they would not "enter into dispute about Purgatory" but rather "be instructed [concerning it] by the H[oly] Church," thus signaling their willingness to accept the Florentine definition without debate.[137]

---

[129] Ibid., 62.
[130] Ibid., 134.
[131] Ibid.
[132] Ibid., 134–35.
[133] Ibid., 135.
[134] It would have been "greatly inhumane" and "cruel" for "the apostles, having foreseen the future sufferings of souls and their therapy and healing, and yet never, neither to a greater nor lesser extent, made mention of such an important matter in so many letters" Ibid., 136.
[135] Ibid.
[136] "Such a possibility cannot be excluded in view of the Patriarch's own relations with Rome in earlier years, his decided opposition to Protestant propaganda which he might have considered the greatest danger for the Ruthenians, and the impression he created at the time of his first visit in the Commonwealth, in 1588, before he went to Moscow." Oscar Halecki, *From Florence to Brest (1439–1596)* (Rome: Sacrum Poloniae Millennium, 1958), 233. Halecki acknowledged as a counter to this argument that many of the Orthodox brotherhoods Jeremiah promoted had strong anti-Roman elements, but he went on to say that it was the reforming zeal of these brotherhoods that eventually made union with Rome more attractive.
[137] Articles of Union, 5; Eng. trans.: Gudziak, *Crisis and Reform*, 265.

Orthodox writers of the seventeenth and eighteenth centuries, trying to deal with Protestant and Catholic missionaries working in the East, often found themselves walking a tightrope of sorts, as they tried to balance (often unsuccessfully) their rejection of Purgatory with a defense of suffrages for the dead. Gabriel Severus (1541–1616), metropolitan of Philadelphia, was one such figure, as he contended against the Protestants on prayers and alms for the deceased, but simultaneously denied the existence of "third place" where souls went after death.[138] What is interesting is that for Severus, although there are only two places, in both there are "many different mansions or dwelling places (John 14:2)."[139] In Hell, for example, there "are many different mansions, each with its particular type of suffering, adopted to the nature of the sin to be punished—some are places of eternal punishment, from which there is no release. . [and] other mansions where less wicked souls are sent" to endure "not an everlasting, but a partial chastisement, according to the measure of their sins."[140] Severus thus accepted "places of reparation or satisfaction" (τόποι ἱκανοποιοί) after death, but since they were a part of Hell and not a separate "third place," he could, in good conscience, reject the Catholic teaching on Purgatory.[141] This was a fine line, for as Kallistos Ware observed, despite the difference in terminology "It is difficult to discover any fundamental contradiction in thought ... between him and Latin theologians," since once you accept that souls go *somewhere* to "make reparation or satisfaction" after death, "It matters very little whether we put these souls in an upper division of Hell or in the lower division of paradise or in the third place and separate place intermediate between the two."[142]

Elias Miniatis's *Rock of Offense* (1718) exhibited the same ambiguities, for while he taught that Scripture spoke only of two places (τόποι) after death, he accepted the idea of "three different states" (καταστάσεις)—the just, unrepentant mortal sinners, and "those who after sinning have repented, but because of an untimely death, or else through negligence and laziness, they have failed to perform their 'canon' here in this life ... [and thus] have not satisfied Divine Justice."[143] According to Ware, this was quibbling, for "it is meaningless to affirm three states beyond the grave and then to deny three places; for when applied to the life after death the two terms *topos* (place) and *katastasis* (state) amount to the same thing."[144]

These seemingly artificial differences remained (and to some degree remain) a constant source of frustration for Roman Catholics, who saw behind the Orthodox

---

[138] Gabriel Severus, Ἔκθεσις κατὰ τῶν ἀμαθῶς λεγόντων καὶ παρανόμως διδασκόντων, ὅτι ἡμεῖς οἱ τῆς Ἀνατολικῆς Ἐκκλησίας γνήσιοι καὶ ὀρθόδοξοι παῖδες ἐσμὲν σχισματικοί παρὰ τῆς ἁγίας καὶ καθόλου Ἐκκλησίας (London, 1625), 46–53; Eng. trans.: Ware, *Eustratios Argenti*, 145. For "God in his infinite compassion is ready to show mercy. Souls not only receive alleviation and comfort as a result of the prayers offered to God on their behalf, but also a complete release and deliverance from punishment." Ibid., 147.

[139] Severus, Ἔκθεσις, 49; Eng. trans.: Ware, *Eustratios Argenti*, 146 (for this and subsequent selections).

[140] Severus, Ἔκθεσις, 51–52. "The fire is termed temporary, not in virtue of its nature, but because of those souls who are delivered from it; yet on account of those souls who are punished there eternally, it is termed eternal." Ibid., 52.

[141] Ware, *Eustrattios Argenti*, 146.

[142] Ibid., 147. "One cannot but feel that Orthodox theologians have sometimes been over-anxious to discover differences between themselves and Rome." Ibid., 148.

[143] *Elias Miniatis, Πέτρα Σκανδάλου* (Athens, 1863), 130; Eng. trans.: Ware, *Eustratios Argenti*, 144.

[144] Ibid., 145.

protests a de facto acceptance of the Latin teaching.[145] Leo Allatios (d. 1669) argued that the Orthodox actually believed in Purgatory, because "the Greeks did have punishment of sins after death, [and since] in Hell there [was] no redemption, and in heaven no punishment," purifying punishments must take place somewhere else (i.e., in Purgatory).[146] If they "held that actions of the living aided the dead, they either had to admit the existence of Purgatory or allow the unacceptable view that these suffering souls were released from Hell."[147] According to Allatios, even though the Greeks denied the fire of Purgatory, they accepted "a fire in Hell, which by burning tortures purges souls.... [Yet] it makes little difference whether the place where the fire produces its effects be termed hell or Purgatory, so long as we agree that there is a fire, and that it punishes and purges."[148]

Purgatory continued to feature prominently in the Orthodox confessions that were written during this period, as the East tried to set forth its beliefs in terms largely defined by the churches of the West. For example, the *Confessio* (1625) of Metrophanes Kritopoulos was clear that the Protestants were wrong to deny prayer for the dead, since "It is quite clear to everyone anywhere that this tradition ... comes from the first Christians" and that "none of the holy fathers of the church fails to mention it."[149] This practice most benefits those "who do not immediately after death win actual salvation, but await this in strength and hope" while they "suffer the strokes of God's fatherly rod."[150] "In due time" they will be saved, although the when and how is not ours to know, but until then the living can still "send up prayers and requests to the Father of all on their behalf; so that either he might soon release them from the afflictions by which they are held, or at least that he would send them some relief and consolation while they remain in his prison."[151]

If, to Protestant ears, this sounded like the Catholic doctrine of Purgatory, Kritopoulos was clear that the suffering endured by the dead "is not material or physical, neither by fire, nor by any other material instrument, but by affliction and grief from their conscience. For their punishment is the result of their remembering how many wrong and sinful things they did in this world."[152] The East did "not believe in the flames of Purgatory, but in the affliction of the soul's conscience," and rejected as blasphemous the notion that "parents or children or friends may be delivered from

---

[145] According to Leo Allatios, "They acknowledge the thing and avoid the name." Leo Allatios, *De utriusque ecclesiae occidentalis atque orientalis perpetua in dogmate de Purgatorio consensione*, 219; Eng. trans.: Ware, *Eustratios Argenti*, 147.

[146] Allatios, *De Purgatorio*, 41–42; Eng. trans.: Karen Hartnup, *"On the Beliefs of the Greeks": Leo Allatios and Popular Orthodoxy* (Leiden: Brill, 2004), 207.

[147] Leo Allatios, *De Graecorum hodie quorundam opinationibus*, 157; Eng. trans.: Hartnup, *"On the beliefs of the Greeks"*, 207.

[148] Leo Allatios, *De Purgatorio*, 219; Eng. trans.: Ware, *Eustrattios Argenti*, 153. Ware pointed out that many Orthodox objections centered around purgation by means of a material fire, an idea not found in the dogmatic statements issued by Rome at Lyons, Florence, or Trent, which all affirm "that the departed suffer in Purgatory" without stating "how they suffer." Ibid., 152–53.

[149] Kritopoulos, *Confession of Faith*, in Pelikan and Hotchkiss, eds., *Creeds and Confessions* 1, 541.

[150] Ibid.

[151] Ibid.

[152] Ibid.

the fires of Purgatory ... if the relatives were to bring to the church this much or that much money."[153]

The *Confessio* of the so-called "Protestant Patriarch" Cyril Lukaris neither affirmed nor rejected prayers for the dead, but spoke about the afterlife in terms that made it difficult to see how they could be efficacious. In opposition to Mark's teaching at Ferrara-Florence, Lukaris stated that "the dead are either in blessedness or in condemnation ... for when they depart from their bodies they depart immediately either to Christ or to condemnation."[154] "The time of grace," he argued, "is the present life," which is why the church did not accept "the fiction of Purgatory," instead teaching "that each one ought to repent in the present life and seek forgiveness of sin through our Lord Jesus Christ, if he would be saved."[155]

One issue that divided the Orthodox themselves was the particular judgment, and whether a soul was judged by Christ immediately upon death. Some, like Methodios III of Constantinople (1668–71) denied it outright, as did Theophilus of Campania (d. 1795) in his book in *Treasure of Orthodoxy* (1780).[156] Theophilus wrote that the "church recognizes and teaches only one judgment for all men at the second coming of Christ; she neither knows nor accepts a particular judgment."[157] He affirmed that before the Last Judgment the righteous experienced joy (albeit incomplete) in expectation of their coming beatitude, just as sinful souls felt torment while awaiting final retribution. Because no final decisions about the soul's fate had yet been taken, the prayers, alms, and the liturgies of the church, which are made for *all* the deceased, were still capable of delivering them from torments according to the number and gravity of their sins.[158]

Other Eastern authors, such as Macarius, metropolitan of Moscow (d. 1563), defended the idea of a particular judgment with reference to the tollhouse tradition, which he called "a figurative depiction of the judgment ... which has existed in the Orthodox Church from antiquity."[159] Macarius believed that the tollhouses represent

---

[153] Ibid., 542. In fact, he taught that "if any of our priests were caught doing such a thing for money, they would be severely and harshly punished and would be in danger of expulsion from the ministry." Ibid.

[154] Cyril Lukaris, *Eastern Confession of Christian Faith*, in Pelikan and Hotchkiss, *Creeds and Confessions* 1, 555.

[155] Ibid.

[156] According to Martin Jugie, the book was quite influential, having been endorsed by Athanasius of Paros, and then recommended by the holy synod of Athens in 1860 to all the faithful, especially the clergy, "as a very useful, very edifying work, necessary for all Christians." Martin Jugie, "La doctrine des fins dernières dans l'Église gréco-russe," *Échos d'Orient* 17 (1914): 14.

[157] Theophilus of Campania, Ταμεῖον ὀρθοδοξίας (Εὐαγγελινός Μισαηλίδης, 1860), 257.

[158] Ibid., 217. Distinguishing the prayers of the Orthodox from those of the Catholics, Pérov's *Manual of Polemical Theology* affirmed: "The Church prays for the dead, but she prays for the remission of their sins, not for the remission of temporal penalties due to sin. She prays to deliver them from hell, not from Purgatory. In addition, the prayers of the church are offered for all sinners, without distinction of the sins they have committed, and therefore they extend to all kinds of sins and not only to light and venial sins." Like many, he made an exception for the sin of blasphemy against the Holy Spirit, which could not be remitted in this world or in the next. "This is why the Church excluded from her prayers only those who have willingly and stubbornly rejected the grace of Redemption." Quoted in Jugie, "La doctrine des fins dernières," 15.

[159] Macarius of Moscow, *Théologie dogmatique orthodoxe Tr. Par Un Russe*, vol. 2 (Paris, 1860), 630; Eng. trans.: St Anthony's Greek Orthodox Monastery, *The Departure of the Soul According to the Teaching of the Orthodox Church* (Florence, AZ: St Anthony's Greek Orthodox Monastery, 2017), 252 (and subsequent selections). Later in this work Macarius recognized that there is a "great resemblance between the doctrine of Purgatory and the teaching of the Orthodox church on the possibility for some sinners being released from

"the unavoidable path that each human soul, evil or good, takes during its transition from the temporal life to the eternal portion ... and is thus nothing other than the particular judgment, performed on human souls invisibly by the Lord Jesus himself through the ministry of the angels."[160]

Also affirming the particular judgment was the Metropolitan of Kyiv, Peter Mohyla in his *Orthodox Confession of the Catholic and Apostolic Eastern Church*, written by 1647,[161] which has been called "the most Latin document ever to be adopted by an official council of the Orthodox Church."[162] The *Confession* taught that there was indeed a particular judgment, and that every soul at death knows "what is to be the reward of his desserts; for as his deeds are manifest, so is the will of God concerning them also manifest."[163] This was true both of the just, who knew of their future blessedness, and the wicked, who "are immediately sensible of the torments that await them."[164] Yet neither receive "the full recompense of their deeds before the final judgment, nor are they all in one state, nor limited to one place," and "this could not be ... without some kind of (as it were) particular judgement."[165] Although the *Confession* affirmed that the departed do not all share the same degree of happiness, it explicitly denied that there was a place "in the middle between the blessed and the damned" where some

---

the bonds of hell by the prayers of [earthly] survivors." Ibid., 725. He did note some important differences, especially as it related to Rome's belief in temporal penalties imposed in order to satisfy the needs of divine justice.

[160] Ibid., 631. In Byzantine art the metaphor of the *telonies* was often joined with the use of scales, and it is not unusual to see icons of the judgment containing good angels weighing a soul's actions in the presence of the demon toll-collectors. This image is based on a text from Pseudo-Damascene: "Divinely enlightened men, affirm that at the time of the last breath the actions of men are weighed as in a scale. If the right board wins over the other, it is clear that the dying person exhales his soul into the hands of the good angels. If the two plates remain in balance, the mercy of God surely triumphs. The divinely inspired Fathers add that if the balance tilts a little to the left, even in this case the mercy of God makes up for the deficit." Pseudo-Damascene, *De his qui in fide dormiunt* (PG 95:272). Macarius recognized, however, that the tollhouse tradition contained "features which are presented more or less physically and anthropomorphically," and that it was therefore necessary, to consider them "not in a course or sensual sense, but as much as is possible for us, in a spiritual sense, and not to be tied to particulars which have been presented differently by various authors and in numerous stories of the church." Macarius of Moscow, *Théologie dogmatique orthodoxe*, 641; Eng. trans.: St Anthony's Greek Orthodox Monastery, *The Departure of the Soul*, 255–56.

[161] For Mohyla's complicated legacy in the East, especially as it pertains to his "Romanization" of the Orthodox Church, see George Florovsky, *Ways of Russian Theology, The Collected Works of George Florovsky*, vol. 5 (Belmont, MA: Nordland Publishing Company, 1979), 64–78; Ihor Ševčenko, "The Many Worlds of Peter Mohyla," in *Ukraine between East and West: Essays on Cultural History to the Early Eighteenth Century* (Edmonton: Canadian Institute of Ukrainian Studies Press, 2009), 164–86.

[162] Kallistos Ware, *The Orthodox Church* (London: Penguin Books, 2015), 93. Mohyla's original version of the confession, now lost, was thought too "Roman" because it explicitly embraced a number of Catholic doctrines, including not only the particular judgment, but also the existence of a "third place, distinct from heaven and hell, and identical with the Latin Purgatory, save that he rejected the idea of purging by fire." Ware, *Eustratios Argenti*, 11. However, it was an edited version, revised and corrected by Meletius Syrigos, that was ultimately accepted by the Synod of Jassy in 1642, endorsed by the four major patriarchates in 1643, and adopted by the Synod of Jerusalem in 1672.

[163] Peter Mohyla, *Orthodox Confession of the Catholic and Apostolic Eastern Church*, in Pelikan and Hotchkiss, *Creeds and Confessions* 1, 587.

[164] Ibid., 588.

[165] Ibid. "The souls of the righteous, although received into heaven, do not receive the full and perfect crown of glory before the last judgment, so neither did the souls of the damned feel and suffer the full measure and wake the punishments before that time." Mohyla's original *Confession* had, in fact, affirmed the opposite, that souls enter into full blessedness upon their death. Ware, *Eustratios Argenti*, 143.

souls were tortured by the fires of Purgatory.¹⁶⁶ It is true that those in Hades can be freed from their chains, not by doing some sort of postmortem penance, but rather by "the good works and alms of the living and the prayers of the church, made in their behalf."¹⁶⁷

Alongside the intra-Orthodox debate over a particular judgment, there was also the question of expiatory suffering, especially since some post-Florentine writers (e.g., Gabriel Severus and Elias Miniatis) spoke of "reparation" and "the demands of divine justice" in terms that echoed the language of the scholastics. Most significantly, the *Confession* of Dositheus of Jerusalem, accepted at the Synod of Jerusalem in 1672 (along with Mohyla's), had stated that souls

> involved in mortal sins, who have not departed in despair but while still living in the body, though without bringing forth any fruits of repentance, have repented—by pouring forth tears, by kneeling while watching in prayers, by afflicting themselves, by relieving the poor, and finally by showing forth by their works their love towards God and their neighbor, and which the Catholic Church has from the beginning rightly called satisfaction (ἱκανοποίησις)—[their souls] depart into Hades, and there endure the punishment (ποινή) due to the sins they have committed.¹⁶⁸

Scholars, both East and West, have long recognized that Dositheos's language sounds very Catholic, and its conciliar endorsement has often given the impression that Orthodoxy's teaching on satisfaction/suffering is not substantively different from Rome's.¹⁶⁹ However, before accepting this claim some important caveats should be made. First, the *Confession* of Mohyla, as revised by Meletius Syrigos and accepted at the earlier Synod of Jassy in 1642, explicitly denied expiatory suffering, demonstrating a certain lack of consistency on the issue. Second, there were many other authors, like Meletios Pigas, patriarch of Alexandria (1592–1601), who rejected the idea that one

---

¹⁶⁶ Purgatory "is nowhere talked about in the holy scriptures," and for this reason the Orthodox Church "does not admit or approve of such fables, as some men have fancied, concerning the state of souls after death, as that they are tormented in pits and waters and with sharp prongs." Peter Mohyla, *Orthodox Confession of the Catholic and Apostolic Eastern Church*, in Pelikan and Hotchkiss, *Creeds and Confessions* 1, 590.

¹⁶⁷ Ibid., 588–89. To prove the impossibility of postmortem penance Mohyla cited Theophylacht of Ohrid's commentaries on Matthew and Luke: "So long as we continue on earth we can wipe out our sins, but after we leave this earth we are no more able of ourselves to cancel our sins by our confessions. The doors are then shut. And again, on the words of Matthew ... he says: in this life we may labor and endeavor, but afterwards the active faculties of the soul are bound, nor can we any more do any atonement for our offenses. And farther, on the twenty-fifth chapter of the same gospel, he says: There is no more time for repentance and good works after this life. From all of which it is clear that after its separation the soul can no more perform penance, nor do any other work whereby it might be freed from the chains of Hades." Ibid., 589.

¹⁶⁸ Joshua Schooping, ed., *The Confession of Dositheos from the Acts and Decrees of the Synod of Jerusalem*, trans. J. N. W. B. Robertson (Olyphant, PA: St Theophan the Recluse Press, 2020), 52.

¹⁶⁹ Ware, *Eustratios Argenti*, 149. He cited the judgment of Martin Jugie, *Theologia Dogmatica Christianorum Orientalium Ab Ecclesia Catholica Dissidentium*, vol. 3 (Paris: Letouzey et Ané, 1926), 360. The *Confession* even accepted that "the souls of those who have fallen asleep are either at rest or in torment, according to how each has lived ... [having] depart[ed] immediately either to joy or to sorrow and lamentation," although he added that "it must be confessed that neither the enjoyment nor the condemnation is complete." Patriarch Dositheus, *Confession*, in Pelikan and Hotchkiss, *Creeds and Confessions* 1, 631.

can render satisfaction unto God for sins, as Christ had made "a total and full satisfaction, which excludes every secondary satisfaction provided by the sinner."[170] He argued that *epitimia* imposed by one's confessor were not punishments, "but solely pedagogical and prophylactic ... [for] after sacramental absolution, no pain of temporal satisfaction remains to burden the sinner, either in this world or the next."[171] When one dies one goes either "into the bosom of Abraham with the poor man Lazarus, or descends into hell with the wicked rich man.... There are, for souls, only two states and two abodes. Purgatory is superfluous."[172]

Finally, there is the evolving view of Dositheos himself, since his later *Manual against the Calvinist Insanity* (Ἐγχειρίδιον κατὰ καλβινικῆς φρενοβλαβείας) (1690) published an amended confession that retracted the earlier statement on purifying punishments (καθαρτικαὶ τιμωρίαι) and added some further arguments against Purgatory.[173] He denied that there was a third place or a purifying fire "separated from or close to Hell, from which souls can be delivered," for there was no "purifying fire outside of God who is rightly by himself the purifying fire working the perfect redemption, or refreshment, or remission and reconciliation of souls."[174] Moreover, Dositheos believed there was no need for punishment of venial (ἀθανάσιμα) sins after death, and that those who die with such sins are with Christ and blessed without the need for further satisfaction.[175] There was no distinction, he maintained, "between guilt (ἁμαρτία) and temporal punishment (ποινή)—if the first is forgiven, then the second is also remitted."[176] Dositheos admitted that those who have not lived an utterly sinful life (ουχ οι απεγνωσμένοι και διόλου κακοτρόπως ζήσαντες) and die before fully repenting their mortal sins (ἐλλιπὴς μετάνοια) are punished, but he taught that they go to Hell, where they suffer pains of a "moral order: sadness, regret, remorse of conscience, imprisonment, darkness, fear, and uncertainty about the future."[177] These are the souls for whom the church, following the example of the Maccabees, prays and offers suffrages, in the fervent hope that God, in his mercy, will purify and deliver them before or on the Last Day. At that time, those who, for one reason or

---

[170] Meletios Pigas, Ὀρθόδοξος διδασκαλία (Vilnius, 1596); Eng summary: Larchet, *Life after Death According to the Orthodox Tradition*, 199.

[171] Ibid.

[172] Ibid. "Between Abraham's bosom and the torments of Hades we are taught that there is a kind of chaos but no Purgatory." Meletios Pigas, Ὀρθόδοξος διδασκαλία, 31: Eng. trans.: Ware, *Eustratios Argenti*, 143.

[173] Johannes Karmiris, "Ἡ ὁμολογία τῆς ὀρθοδόξου πίστεως τοῦ Πατριάρχου Ἱεροσολύμων Δοσιθέου" Θεολογία 19 (1948): 693–707; 20 (1949): 99–119, 245–79, 457–94; 657–703. For Dositheos's evolving views see Norman Russell, "From the 'Shield of Orthodoxy' to the 'Tome of Joy': The Anti-Western Stance of Dositheos II of Jerusalem (1641–1707)," in Demacopoulos and Papanikolaou, eds., *Orthodox Constructions of the West*, 71–82. My special thanks to Rev. Dr. Demetrios Bathrellos for helping me untangle the occasionally confusing elements in Dositheos's thought.

[174] Karmiris, "Ἡ ὁμολογία τῆς ὀρθοδόξου πίστεως τοῦ Πατριάρχου Ἱεροσολύμων Δοσιθέου," 687; Eng. trans.: Larchet, *Life after Death According to the Orthodox Tradition*, 200–201.

[175] Karmiris, "Ἡ ὁμολογία τῆς ὀρθοδόξου πίστεως τοῦ Πατριάρχου Ἱεροσολύμων Δοσιθέου," 687. "These picadilloes, from which no mortal is exempt, are generously forgiven by God at the hour of death, in light of the preponderant good to be found in just souls. If this were not so, no one would ascend to heaven after death." Ibid.

[176] Ibid., 688; Eng. trans.: Ware, *Eustratios Argenti*, 151.

[177] Karmiris, "Ἡ ὁμολογία τῆς ὀρθοδόξου πίστεως τοῦ Πατριάρχου Ἱεροσολύμων Δοσιθέου," 690. However, Dositheos was clear that these punishments were not themselves purificatory.

another, remain unredeemed are given over to the eternal fire, for once the final judgment has been made all hope for them is lost.

Eustratios Argenti's *Short Treatise against the Purgatorial Fire of the Papists* was not a highly original work, employing many of the standard scriptural arguments against Purgatory while arguing that the Latins' patristic prooftexts were "obscure," or "spurious," or deeply "misunderstood."[178] Interestingly, Argenti did not deny the particular judgment and "assumes that in the life after death the souls of the departed, even before the resurrection, will be divided into different classes and assigned to different places and so, by implication, allows some kind of judgement immediately after death."[179] Like Minatis, he taught that while the "church knows of only two places" after death, Heaven and Hell, there were three states: "the saints, those in the middle, and those who are being punished."[180] It was for souls in this middle group that the church prayed,[181] yet not because they were "undergoing torment and retributive chastisement" ("since we deny [both fire and] all other expiatory punishment"), but rather to show "that their souls are alive, and have not passed into non-existence."[182] "It is not [through] our own suffering" that we are saved, but rather through "Christ the Lamb of God" who by "suffering on the cross has purged away our sins (Hebrews 1:3)."[183]

In 1838 the Constantinopolitan Synod issued an *Encyclical on Latin Innovations*, largely as a response to the rise of Eastern Catholic churches "in parts of Syria, Egypt and Palestine," where "insidious and deceiving wolves," in the guise of sheep (i.e., Orthodox priests) "have recently appeared ... sophistically teaching against our orthodox faith."[184] Among the Latin innovations they tried to introduce was the doctrine of Purgatory, which was "an evil and new-fangled invention, something altogether contrary to the gospels and opposed to God."[185] This view was repeated, albeit less polemically, in the 1895 *Reply to the Papal Encyclical of Pope Leo XIII*, which listed all

---

[178] Eustratios Argenti, Συνταγμάτιον κατὰ τοῦ Παπιστικοῦ Καθαρτηρίου Πυρός (Athens, 1939), 35; Eng. trans.: Ware, *Eustratios Argenti*, 154.

[179] Ibid., 155. That said, "He accepts the normal Orthodox view that the departed enter upon the fullness of their blessedness or torment not immediately after death, but only after their Resurrection on the last day." Ibid.

[180] Eustratios Argenti, Συνταγμάτιον, 44; Eng. trans.: Ware, *Eustratios Argenti*, 155.

[181] Eustratios Argenti, Συνταγμάτιον, 33–34; Eng. trans.: Ware, *Eustratios Argenti*, 156. Elsewhere in the treatise Argenti seems to allow that the prayers of the church do "secure release for some souls[in hell] and lightens the torments of others," although "it is not an idea to which he gives any great prominence." Ibid., 158.

[182] Eustratios Argenti, Συνταγμάτιον, 47–48, 51–52; Eng. trans.: Ware, *Eustratios Argenti*, 157.

[183] Since he "by his precious blood cleanses us from all sin" and because he "is the only satisfaction, expiation, and purgation for the sins of the faithful, when once we have repented no further act of reparation on our part is neither necessary nor possible. To affirm otherwise is to imply that Christ was crucified in vain." Eustratios Argenti, Συνταγμάτιον, 44–47; Eng. trans.: Ware, *Eustratios Argenti*, 157.

[184] Synod of Constantinople (1838), *Encyclical on Latin Innovations* in George Metallinos, *Unia: The Face and the Disguise* (Thessaloniki: Greek Orthodox Books Publications, 2015), 99. "For the unquenchable rabidity of the Papacy—which contrives in every way to deceive and proselytize—has cunningly left loose and in every manner free, all those who have embraced Papism, making allowance for them to unvaryingly perform all of the customs and mysteries of their former Church, and has considered these two things alone as enough: that is, the commemoration of the Pope's name, and the acceptance of the Pope's infallibility and sinlessness." Ibid., 97–98.

[185] Synod of Constantinople (1838), *Encyclical on Latin Innovations*; Eng. trans.: Ware, *Eustratios Argenti*, 144.

of Rome's errors since the division, including "a multitude of innovations concerning purgatorial fire, a superabundance of the virtues of the saints ... and the like, setting forth also a full reward for the just before the universal resurrection and judgment."[186]

Philaret of Moscow's *Longer Catechism of the Orthodox, Catholic, Eastern Church* (1905) did not address Purgatory directly, yet it maintained the traditional Eastern view that until the Last Judgment "the souls of the righteous are in light and rest, with a foretaste of eternal happiness [while] the souls of the wicked are in a state the reverse of this."[187] As for those souls who "have departed with faith, but without having had time to bring forth fruits worthy of repentance, ... they may be aided towards the attainment of a blessed resurrection by prayers offered in their behalf, especially such as are offered in union with the oblation of the bloodless sacrifice ... and by works of mercy done in faith for their memory."[188] Several Russian writers of the period even allowed that great sinners could be relieved and eventually delivered by the prayers of the church, exempting only those who had committed the unforgivable sin of blasphemy against the Holy Spirit.[189]

The Twentieth and Twenty-First Centuries

The beginning of the twentieth century saw little change in the position of either side, as the Orthodox continued to repeat their opposition to the doctrine, while Catholics remained just as convinced of its truth. From the Orthodox perspective Christos Androutsos's *Dogmatic Theology* (1907) was typical of the period, denying the existence of a third place, the particular judgment, expiatory punishments, and purgatorial fire, while simultaneously upholding prayers for the dead as a way of releasing souls from the non-expiatory sufferings they endured.[190] Androutsos realized that there were certain "gaps in our knowledge" about the afterlife which sometimes led "human curiosity" to construct "unnecessary distinctions," but these "served no

---

[186] Anthimos VII, *A Reply to the Papal Encyclical of Pope Leo XIII on Reunion*, in Eustathius Metallinos, ed., *Orthodox and Catholic Union* (Seattle: St. Nectarios Press, 1985), 6.

[187] Philaret of Moscow, *Longer Catechism of the Orthodox, Catholic, Eastern Church*, in R. W. Blackmore, *Doctrine of the Russian Church* (London: J. Masters, 1905), 98.

[188] Ibid., 99.

[189] "Gabriel, Metropolitan of Novgorod and Petersburg wrote in his *Explanation of the Liturgy*: 'We believe that even the souls of those who have fallen in great faults receive help from the sacrifice we offer and the prayers we address, while it is being celebrated, to the Lord of life and death.' ... Pérov's *Manual of Polemical Theology* claimed that the church 'prays for the remission of [the deceased's] sins, not for the remission of temporal penalties due to sin. She prays to deliver them from Hell, not from Purgatory. In addition, the prayers of the church are offered for all sinners, without distinction of the sins they have committed, and therefore they extend to all kinds of sins and not only to light and venial sins.' ... *The Manual of Orthodox Dogmatic Theology for Seminaries* by N. Malinovski, claimed that the church prayed for souls in Hell, especially those 'who are not hardened in evil, who can feel a deep repentance for the sins committed during the earthly life, conceive of aversion for these sins, tend with the spirit and the heart towards the good, towards which they were sometimes indifferent here below. Such souls, according to a provision of divine mercy, can be delivered from the torments of hell by the prayers of the Church, by good works, and especially by the oblation of the bloodless victim, by the intervention of the Saints of the Heavenly Church and of the Savior Himself.'" Jugie, "La doctrine des fins dernières," 15–16.

[190] Christos Androutsos, Δογματική (Athens: Τυπογραφείον του "Κράτους," 1907), 432–36. For another view see Panagiotis Trempelas, Δογματική της Ορθοδόξου Καθολικής Εκκλησίας, vol. 3 (Athens: Σωτήρ 1959–61).

spiritual ends."¹⁹¹ Among them, he argued, was the tollhouse tradition, which was based "on the isolated opinion of a few fathers and had been [erroneously] presented as a dogmatic teaching of apostolic origin."¹⁹² Androutsos argued that despite what some might claim, "the scriptural passages on which the toll-houses are based have no relation to a judgment of men by demons after death" and the few patristic texts that could be cited in its support "are not enough "to give the theory of telonies any dogmatic character."¹⁹³

Catholic manuals of theology, like Ludwig Ott's *Fundamentals of Catholic Dogma*, laid out, with the clarity one would expect of the genre, the Latin position on "the purifying fire and the expiatory character of the penal sufferings" which had been defined at both Lyons and Florence "against the schismatic Greeks whose objection was chiefly directed against a special place of purification."¹⁹⁴ After citing biblical and Latin patristic support—no Greek fathers, including Gregory of Nyssa, are enlisted—Ott distinguished between *poena damni* ("consisting in the temporary exclusion from the beatific vision") and the *poena sensus* (i.e., a physical fire), which, he admitted, had been defined at the councils as "purifying punishments (*poenae purgatoriae*)" rather than "fire" only "out of consideration for the separated Greeks, who reject the notion of a purifying fire."¹⁹⁵ Yet it is in this "purifying fire" that "the temporal punishments for sins are atoned for ... by the so-called suffering of atonement (*satispassio*), that is, by the willing bearing of the expiatory punishments imposed by God."¹⁹⁶

By the twentieth century Purgatory was so deeply ingrained in the Catholic consciousness that "prayers for the suffering souls" became a regular feature of devotional life, with Mary, in particular, seen as their chief advocate.¹⁹⁷ In Catholic art and poetry images of Purgatory were plentiful, if not always spiritually edifying. Among the most influential was John Henry Newman's "The Dream of Gerontius" (1865), a poem that detailed the twin pains of Purgatory: the delay in achieving the beatific vision and the shame one felt because of one's sins.

> And yet wilt have a longing aye to dwell
> Within the beauty of His countenance.
> And these two pains, so counter and so keen,—

---

¹⁹¹ Christos Androutsos, Δογματική, 432–36; Eng. trans.: Ware, *Eustratios Argenti*, 159.
¹⁹² Christos Androutsos, Δογματική, 415.
¹⁹³ Ibid.
¹⁹⁴ Ludwig Ott, *Fundamentals of Catholic Dogma*, trans. Patrick Lynch (Rockford, IL: Tan Books and Publishers, 1974), 483. This was, of course, only half true, since neither Lyons nor Florence had mentioned fire, as Ott later clarified.
¹⁹⁵ Ibid., 485. According to Aidan Nichols, "One beneficial effect of the debate with the Greek East was the toning down, by the Latins, of the image of purgatorial fire. Or, rather, they understood more clearly that this was an image, and not a literal reality. A contemporary theology of Purgatory, drawing on the resources of tradition at large, would wish to utilize other symbols to compliment the symbolism of fire which once so alarmed the Greeks. It will wish to make you some more models in the understanding of doctrine than simply the penal model: punishment and its performance." Nichols, *Rome and the Eastern Churches*, 257.
¹⁹⁶ Ott, *Fundamentals of Catholic Dogma*,485.
¹⁹⁷ "The suffering souls in Purgatory, who are being purified in excessive heat, and are tormented by severe punishment, assist them, in your compassion, O Mary!" *Languentibus in Purgatorio*. For more on Purgatory during this period see Guillaume Cuchet, *Le Crépuscule du Purgatoire* (Paris: Colin, 2005); Guillaume Cuchet, ed., *Le Purgatoire: Fortune Historique et Historiographique d'un Dogme* (Paris: Editions de l'Ecole des hautes études en sciences sociales, 2012).

> The longing for Him, when thou seest Him not;
> The shame of self at thought of seeing Him,—
> Will be thy veriest, sharpest Purgatory.[198]

When contact between the Catholic and Orthodox Churches was restored in the mid-twentieth century, neither side expressed great interest in renewing their earlier debates about Purgatory and the state of souls after death. Why this was so was never made clear, although the previous century's general disinterest in eschatology may be partly responsible.[199] Even when eschatology re-emerged as a subject of interest in the late twentieth century, few theologians on either side of the East-West divide wanted to put Purgatory on the list of issues to be discussed, most preferring either the primacy or the Filioque.[200] And yet, while not the subject of any ecumenical dialogues, both East and West were thinking about Purgatory, albeit for different reasons.

Among the Orthodox was Georges Florovsky, whose alleged "apologia for Purgatory" came in the form of a 1962 essay on Emil Brunner's eschatology, where he addressed the objective act of redemption and its subjective appropriation—or rejection—by the human person.[201] While Brunner had rejected Purgatory since the doctrine allegedly denied the importance of repentance in this life, Florovsky argued that the doctrine did not imply a radical overturning of a person's life-choice for/against God," but applied only to "those of good intentions, pledged to Christ, but deficient in growth and achievement."[202] Thus he allowed for an ongoing postmortem purification for those who have begun, but not completed, the "long and hard experience of asceticism, of ascetic self-examination and self-control," needed to move the will from the "nocturnal darkness of selfishness" to the union with God, "which is the essence of salvation."[203]

By the late twentieth century Orthodox theology was divided on Purgatory, some writers stubbornly maintaining that the Latin doctrine was incompatible with Eastern thought, and others seeing the differences between the two churches as largely

---

[198] John Henry Newman, "The Dream of Gerontius," in *Prayers, Verses, and Devotions* (San Francisco: Ignatius Press, 1989), 717.

[199] "An often-quoted remark of Ernst Troeltsch epitomizes that earlier situation. In surveying the eschatological thinking of that time, he commented that 'nowadays the eschatological office is closed most of the time.' (*Das eschatologische Bureau ist meist geschlossen*). In a similar vein, Karl Barth criticized Protestant theology for lulling us 'comfortably to sleep by adding at the conclusion of Christian Dogmatics a short and perfectly harmless chapter entitled—Eschatology.' In much academic theology of that era, Roman Catholic as well as Protestant, eschatology was little more than an appendix to systematic theology." Jerry Walls, "Introduction," in *Oxford Handbook of Eschatology*, 7.

[200] Even after a resurgence in eschatological studies, Purgatory itself often remained relegated to the dogmatic backwaters, especially after Vatican II, when many Catholics openly wondered whether the church still taught the doctrine. Karl Rahner admitted that "the doctrine of Purgatory does not seem particularly important today even to the devout Christian." Karl Rahner, "Purgatory," in *Theological Investigations XIX: Faith and Ministry*, trans. Edward Quinn (New York: Crossroad, 1983), 187.

[201] Nichols, *Rome and the Eastern Churches*, 258. See Georges Florovsky, "The Last Things and the Last Events," in *The Collected Works of Georges Florovsky*, vol. 3: *Creation and Redemption* (Belmont, MA: Nordland, 1976), 243–65.

[202] Nichols, *Rome and the Eastern Churches*, 262. He maintained that "it is not enough to acknowledge, by faith, the deed of the divine redemption—one has to be born anew. The whole personality must be cleansed and healed. Forgiveness must be accepted and assessed in freedom." Ibid.

[203] Ibid., 263.

exaggerated. One notable "hawk" was Jean-Claude Larchet, who in juxtaposing Catholic and Orthodox thinking on the subject argued that they have little in common except a shared belief in the efficacy of prayers for the dead.[204] Among the "doves" one might place Kallistos Ware, who believed that "Catholic and Orthodox views on the 'middle state' after death are less sharply opposed than appears at first"[205] and that the alleged differences were often inflated by "an unconscious desire on the part of some Orthodox to exaggerate their differences with Rome."[206] At the same time he was clear that "most, if not all, Orthodox theologians reject the idea of Purgatory," that the majority are "inclined to say that the faithful departed do not suffer at all," and that if there is suffering, it is "of a purificatory but not an expiatory character."[207]

Even after the Second Vatican Council,[208] the categories of expiation, punishment, and debt remained an important part of the Roman Catholic lexicon, Pope Paul VI affirming in 1967 that the doctrine of Purgatory

> clearly demonstrates that even when the guilt of sin has been taken away, punishment for it or the consequences of it may remain to be expiated or cleansed. They often are. In fact, in Purgatory the souls of those who died in the charity of God and truly resplendent, but who had not made satisfaction with adequate penance for their sins and omissions are cleansed after death with punishments designed to purge away their debt.[209]

Yet by this time a number of Catholic theologians were attempting to move beyond this language, reimagining Purgatory as a place of purification and transformation rather than satisfaction and debt. Karl Rahner, in his "On the Theology of Indulgences" (1949), had already questioned the understanding of punishment due to sin as "something which is extrinsically imposed on man by the justice of God, conceived merely as something vindictive."[210] Sin, he argued, should be understood as punishing itself, so that "wherever the connatural consequence of sin is accepted and endured to the bitter end, sin becomes of itself the temporal and medicinal punishment."[211] Punishment in this case should thus "be conceived only as a maturing process of the person, through which, though gradually, all the powers of the human being become slowly integrated into the basic decision of the free person."[212] That

---

[204] See Larchet, *Life after Death According to the Orthodox Tradition*, 202–4.
[205] Kallistos Ware, "Dare We Hope for the Salvation of All," in *The Inner Kingdom*, vol. 1 of the *Collected Works* (Crestwood, NY: St. Vladimir's Seminary Press, 2000), 205 See also Kallistos Ware, "One Body in Christ: Death and the Communion of Saints," *Sobornost* 3.2 (1981): 179–91.
[206] Ware, *Eustratios Argenti*, 153.
[207] Ware, *The Orthodox Church*, 248.
[208] At the council *Lumen Gentium* taught that "this venerable faith of our forefathers concerning the living communion with our brothers and sisters who are in heavenly glory or still being purified after their death, this holy synod accepts with great respect, and it reiterates the decrees of the sacred councils of Nicaea II, Florence, and Trent." *Lumen Gentium* 51; Eng. trans.: Tanner, *Decrees of the Ecumenical Councils* 2, 891.
[209] Pope Paul VI, Apostolic Constitution *Indulgentiarum Doctrina*, January 1, 1967.
[210] Karl Rahner, "Remarks on the Theology of Indulgences," in *Theological Investigations II: Man in the Church* (New York: Crossroad, 1963), 194.
[211] Ibid., 196. "Is it not true that whenever the will, in permanent obduracy, refuses definitively to acknowledge the most profound meaning of the attitude of sin, sin becomes of itself an eternal punishment?" Ibid.
[212] Ibid., 197. "In the conception of temporal punishment proposed for discussion above ... the remission of punishment ... would [thus] have to be conceived ... [not] as a mere abstention from punishing ... [but

does not mean that one can completely reorient one's life after one dies, but only that the "profundity of the *option fondamentale* which has been made during life" can undergo a continued maturation "in the purgatory condition of 'Purgatory.'"[213] In this way Purgatory is understood not merely a "purely passive endurance of vindictive punishments," but rather as "an integration of the whole stratified human reality into that free decision and grace ... made and won in this life."[214]

Following Rahner in the attempt to reinterpret the Catholic teaching in less juridical terms was the Dominican Robert Ombres, who defined Purgatory as

> the state or condition ... of those who have died without the guilt of mortal sin and essentially cleaving to God ... [These] souls cannot enter heaven at death because, on account of sins in this life, there is something lacking and imperfect in their response under grace to the redemption wrought by Christ. In Purgatory, aided by their continuing membership in the church, these souls complete their acceptance of God's will and are purged from all sin and its traces and transformed by the workings of God's merciful love.[215]

For Ombres Purgatory "is not to be considered literally as a place nor as holding real fire" but as a condition or state "existing before the bodily resurrection ... affecting the soul."[216] These souls are "in a state of grace and having died in charity cleave to God fundamentally. What is lacking is the total realization of this state and the needed purgation has to be undergone to bring it about."[217] How this purgation will occur after death "is not given to us to know in detail," but Ombres claimed that the images used in Scripture and tradition for sin provide us some guides.[218] He accepted that venial sins can be forgiven in this cleansing process and even suggested that "it would seem desirable, on theological as well as pastoral grounds, to abandon the vocabulary of *poena damni* as too reminiscent of damnation and hell, preferring to talk of the delay in obtaining the beatific vision, the postponement of access to the bread that will fully satisfy hunger (Saint Catherine)."[219]

As influential as Rahner and Ombres undoubtedly were, perhaps no one has done more to reshape Catholicism's understanding of Purgatory than Joseph Ratzinger, who as head of the Congregatio pro Doctrina Fidei (CDF) and then later Pope Benedict XVI had the responsibility of shaping magisterial statements on the subject.[220] For

---

as] a process of painful integration of the whole of man's stratified being into the definitive decision about his life, taken under the grace of God, happen[ing] more quickly and intensively and therefore also less painfully." Ibid., 198.

[213] Ibid., 197–98.
[214] Ibid., 198.
[215] Ombres, *Theology of Purgatory*, 52.
[216] Ibid., 62.
[217] Ibid., 67.
[218] "If sin is a stain then purgation is its removal, if missing the mark then rectification, if loss of being then fulfillment, if a blockage then its taking away, if rust then its cleansing, if admixture then separation, if false attachment to self or to passing things then reliance on God, if disorder than reordering and so forth." Ibid., 74.
[219] Ibid., 75.
[220] The 1994 *Catechism of the Catholic Church*'s section on Purgatory (CCC 1030–31) stated: "All who die in God's grace and friendship, but still imperfectly purified, are indeed assured of their eternal salvation;

Ratzinger "Purgatory is not ... some kind of supra worldly concentration camp where man is forced to undergo punishment in a more or less arbitrary fashion. Rather it is the inwardly necessary process of transformation in which a person becomes capable of Christ, capable of God and thus capable of unity with the whole communion of saints."[221] Agreeing with Gnilka's assessment that the fire of 1 Corinthians 3:13–15 is "the Lord himself," Ratzinger argued that there was no material fire, "no temporal duration involved, only eschatological encounter with the judge."[222] It is "the Lord himself as the judging fire which transforms us and conforms us to his own glorified body" whom we encounter and "whose burning flame cuts free our closed off heart, melting it, and pouring it into a new mold to make it fit for the living organism of his body."[223] He argued that "the transforming "moment" of this encounter cannot be quantified by the measurements of earthly time" and that "trying to qualify it as of "short" or "long" duration on the basis of temporal measurements ... would be [both] naive and unproductive."[224] Later, as pope, he summarized this view in his encyclical *Spe Salvi* (2007):

> Some recent theologians are of the opinion that the fire which both burns and saves is Christ himself, the Judge and Saviour. The encounter with him is the decisive act of judgement. Before his gaze all falsehood melts away. This encounter with him, as it burns us, transforms and frees us, allowing us to become truly ourselves. All that we build during our lives can prove to be mere straw, pure bluster, and it collapses. Yet in the pain of this encounter, when the impurity and sickness of our lives become evident to us, there lies salvation. His gaze, the touch of his heart heals us through an undeniably painful transformation "as through fire."[225]

Ratzinger acknowledged that this understanding of Purgatory, where each person stands before Christ to be judged and transformed, seemingly negated the need for suffrages on behalf of the dead, an ancient practice that "presupposed that Purgatory entails some kind of external punishment which can, for example, be graciously remitted through vicarious acceptance by others in a form of spiritual barter."[226] However, we must also recognize that

---

but, after death they undergo purification, so as to achieve the holiness necessary to enter the joy of Heaven. The Church gives the name Purgatory to this final purification of the elect, which is entirely different from the punishment of the damned."
[221] Ratzinger, *Eschatology*, 230.
[222] Ibid., 229.
[223] Ibid. Ratzinger held that the basic choice for God "is buried under a great deal of wood, hay and straw. Only with difficulty can it peer out from behind the latticework of an egoism we are powerless to pull down with our own hands.... Man is the recipient of the divine mercy, yet this does not exonerate him from the need to be transformed. Encounter with the Lord is this transformation. It is the fire that burns away our dross and re-forms us to be vessels of eternal joy." Ibid., 231.
[224] Ibid., 230.
[225] Benedict XVI, *Spe Salvi*, https://www.vatican.va/content/benedict-xvi/en/encyclicals/documents/hf_ben-xvi_enc_20071130_spe-salvi.html.
[226] Many have asked, "How can a third party enter into that most highly personal process of encounter with Christ, where the 'I' is transformed in the flame of his closeness? Is not this an event which so concerns the individual that all replacement or substitution must be ruled out?" Ratzinger, *Eschatology*, 231. Yet he noted that the practice "has never been in dispute as between East and West. It was the Reformation which

no man is an island, entire of itself. Our lives are involved with one another, through innumerable interactions they are linked together. No one lives alone. No one sins alone. No one is saved alone. The lives of others continually spill over into mine: in what I think, say, do and achieve. And conversely, my life spills over into that of others: for better and for worse. So my prayer for another is not something extraneous to that person, something external, not even after death. In the interconnectedness of Being, my gratitude to the other—my prayer for him—can play a small part in his purification.[227]

What is noteworthy about the work of all three Catholic authors is how "Orthodox" their views of postmortem purification are, a fact now widely recognized. N. T. Wright claimed that "by linking Purgatory to Jesus Christ himself as the eschatological fire ... [who transforms us] not during a long, drawn-out process but in the moment of final judgment ... Ratzinger [has] detached the doctrine of Purgatory from the concept of an intermediate state and broke the link that in the Middle Ages gave rise to the idea of indulgences."[228] Appreciatively, Orthodox theologian Demetrios Bathrellos wrote that the views of modern Catholic theologians are "more similar to those of Mark and the Greeks [at Florence] than to their Latin predecessors" and that the renewed mutual "emphasis on the healing transformation of the souls in the middle state and on the loving forgiveness of God—rather than on his punishing justice—is a beacon of hope for a common, and better, way forward."[229]

Before leaving, special mention should be made of two separate, and sometimes rather acrimonious, intra-Orthodox debates that have helped shape the church's stance on the state of souls after death. The first is the place of the tollhouse tradition within Orthodoxy, and whether this teaching is heresy, a *theologoumenon*, or a doctrine of the church. Supporters of the telonies argued that it was a teaching found "in the sacred works of the holy fathers ... the Holy Scriptures, the liturgical services, the writings and lives of the saints, and the iconography of the Orthodox Church."[230]

---

called it into question, and that in the face of what were in part objectionable and deformed practices. Here, then, is where the ecumenical way ahead in this matter lies, at least as between Orthodox and Catholics." Ibid., 231, 233.

[227] Benedict XVI, *Spe Salvi*. "Man is not ... a closed monad. He is related to others by love or hate," and for this reason "the encounter with Christ is an encounter with his whole body [i.e., the church]." Ratzinger, *Eschatology*, 232.

[228] N. T. Wright, *Surprised by Hope: Rethinking Heaven, the Resurrection, and the Mission of the Church* (New York: HarperCollins, 2009), 167. "This constitutes quite a radical climb-down from Aquinas, Dante, Newman, and all that went in between." Ibid.

[229] Bathrellos, "Love, Purification, and Forgiveness versus Justice, Punishment, and Satisfaction," 120–21.

[230] St Anthony's Greek Orthodox Monastery, *The Departure of the Soul*, 41. Theophan the Recluse (d. 1894), an oft-cited witness to the doctrine, responded to doubters saying, "No matter how absurd the idea of the toll-houses may seem to our 'wise men,' they will not escape passing through them." However, he did caution about taking the images used too literally: "Can one definitely suppose that everything presented in them is reality of the matter, is exactly as is depicted therein? Are they not comparative images for a more vital and full representation of a reality not contained in such images, which is being introduced here?... All of these impressionably express the reality, but, I maintain, one may not think that the reality itself is exactly such, despite the fact that it is always expressed in no other way than by means of these images." Quotation taken from the *Decisions of Synod of Bishops of the Russian Orthodox Church Outside of Russia Regarding*

Among the best-known modern-day exponents of the telonies was Seraphim Rose, who bemoaned the fact that so "many graduates of today's modernist Orthodox seminaries are inclined to dismiss the whole phenomenon as some kind of 'later addition' to Orthodox teaching, or as some kind of 'imaginary' realm without foundation in scriptural or patristic texts."[231]

In the 1980s critics of the doctrine, such as Lazar Puhalo and Michael Azkoul, authored books against the teaching—*The Soul, the Body and Death* and *The Toll-House Myth: The Neo-Gnosticism of Fr. Seraphim Rose*—arguing that it was of pagan origin, contained many gnostic elements, and tended toward Origenism.[232] Yet among their chief criticisms was its closeness to the Latin doctrine of Purgatory, for the only difference between the Purgatory myth and that of the aerial tollhouses is that the former gives God satisfaction by means of physical torment, while the latter gives him his needed satisfaction by means of physical *and* mental torture.[233] When the Synod of Bishops of the Russian Orthodox Church Outside Russia met to mediate the dispute, they censured Puhalo for his overzealousness in this regard, for by wishing to avoid "the possibility of a Western or other non-Orthodox influence, Deacon Lev Puhalo has gone to the opposite extreme … [leaving] no place for what in Orthodox dogmatic theology is referred to as the 'particular judgment,' after which the soul experiences a foretaste of the blessedness or the eternal torment which awaits it after the resurrection."[234]

The debate, however, did not end there, and in 2011 the monks of St. Anthony's Greek Orthodox Monastery published *The Departure of the Soul according to the Teaching of the Orthodox Church*, a work of over 1,100 pages in support of the tollhouse doctrine, of which some 320 pages were specifically devoted to the critiques of Puhalo and Azkoul. The authors, convinced that the telonies were a doctrine of the church, conducted an exhaustive search for texts and icons proving their point, although critics were quick to point out that "*The Departure of the Soul*, for all its thoroughness, does not cite a single conciliar statement on this subject" of the tollhouses since no such statement has ever been issued.[235] In addition to patristic texts, the authors' chief witness were "the visions, or more accurately, the *theorias* granted by God to his saints—divine revelations of the spiritual realities beyond sense perception that are beheld with the inner eyes of the soul—[which] are, after God himself, the very foundation of the doctrines of the Orthodox Church."[236]

---

the Controversy Raised by Deacon Lev. Puhalo (November 9/December 2, 1980), http://orthodoxinfo.com/death/tollhouse_debate.aspx.

[231] Rose, *The Soul after Death*, 66. The book itself "is credited with the modern revival of the toll-house teaching, even though the toll-houses are not the main focus of the book." Paul Ladouceur, "Orthodox Theologies of the Afterlife: Review of *The Departure of the Soul*," https://blogs.ancientfaith.com/orthodoxyandheterodoxy/2017/08/18/orthodox-theologies-of-the-afterlife-review-of-the-departure-of-the-soul/.

[232] For "the notion that the soul can exit the body, move about, have experiences, receive visions, revelations, wander from place to place, make progress or be examined and judged without the body, is essentially Origenistic, and is derived from the philosophies of the pagan religions of Greece and elsewhere." Lazar Puhalo, *The Soul, the Body and Death* (Dewdney, BC: Synaxis Press, 2013), 21.

[233] Ibid.

[234] *Decisions of Synod of Bishops of the Russian Orthodox Church Outside of Russia Regarding the Controversy Raised by Deacon Lev. Puhalo*.

[235] Ladouceur, "Orthodox Theologies of the Afterlife: Review of *The Departure of the Soul*."

[236] St Anthony's Greek Orthodox Monastery, *The Departure of the Soul*, 897.

Jean-Claude Larchet, perhaps more judiciously, judged that although the tollhouses had a long history and were supported by many witnesses, they were "not an article of faith, having been the object on the Church's part of no dogmatic definition. It is rather a *theolegoumenon*, a personal belief."[237] Repeating the warnings of Macarius of Moscow and Theophan the Recluse, he wrote that the images "should not be taken literally"[238] and that the "teaching should not be confused, as some have done, with the Latin conception of Purgatory."[239] If certain accounts have described the tollhouses as "torments," "This is because of the harassment of the demons and the torments their interrogations provoke in the soul."[240]

A second debate occurred after the 2019 publication of *That All Shall Be Saved: Heaven, Hell, and Universal Salvation*, a full-throated apology for universal salvation written by Orthodox theologian David Bentley Hart.[241] Hart's contention was simple: "If Christianity taken as a whole is indeed an entirely coherent and credible system of belief, then the universalist understanding of its message is the only one possible. And, quite imprudently, I say that without the least hesitation or qualification.... The *misericordes* have always been the ones who got the story right."[242] This was, to say the least, a bold claim, for while previous Protestant and Catholic authors had entertained the *hope* of universal salvation (e.g., Karl Barth and Hans Urs von Balthasar), here was an Orthodox theologian asserting it as a fact.[243]

Although, for our purposes, it is unnecessary to chronicle the book's reception or the debate it generated, it is important to note that in the book Hart voiced support for the position once rejected by the Greeks at Florence—that is, that since the punishments of the afterlife were all temporary, then the fires of Gehenna and its "remedial chastisements" would eventually come to an end.[244] Although Hart was hesitant to read into the New Testament any detailed geography of the afterlife, he seemingly "kicks down the wall that separates hell from Purgatory,"[245] by describing the biblical Gehenna in purgatorial terms, and thus appears to make an Orthodox case for Purgatory, understood here as the purification required before the inevitable entrance into the divine presence.[246]

---

[237] Larchet, *Life after Death According to the Orthodox Tradition*, 116.
[238] Ibid., 117.
[239] Ibid., 118.
[240] Ibid.
[241] David Bentley Hart, *That All Shall Be Saved: Heaven, Hell, and Universal Salvation* (New Haven, CT: Yale University Press, 2019).
[242] Ibid., 3. "I have been asked more than once in the last few years whether, if I were to become convinced that Christian adherence absolutely requires a belief in a hell of eternal torment, this would constitute in my mind proof that Christianity should be dismissed as a self-evidently morally obtuse and logically incoherent faith. And, as it happens, it would." Ibid., 208.
[243] For the history of universalism see the two-volume work by Robin Parry and Ilaria L. E. Ramelli, *A Larger Hope?* (Eugene: OR: Cascade Books, 2019).
[244] Hart, *That All Shall Be Saved*, 116.
[245] Ed Simon, "Condemned to Salvation: Considering Universalism with David Bentley Hart," *Los Angelos Review of Books*, February 15, 2020, https://lareviewofbooks.org/article/condemned-to-salvation-considering-universalism-with-david-bentley-hart/.
[246] "And if hell is to be but 'temporary' does Hart actually subscribe to the Roman doctrine of Purgatory without calling it that?" Giacomo Sanfilippo, "Review: That All Shall Be Saved: Heaven, Hell, and Universal Salvation," *Orthodoxy in Dialogue*, January 25, 2020, https://orthodoxyindialogue.com/2020/01/25/that-all-shall-be-saved-heaven-hell-and-universal-salvation-reviewed-by-giacomo-sanfilippo/.

Hart did explicitly deal with Purgatory elsewhere, affirming that like Rome "the Eastern church believes in sanctification after death" and that if this is all the doctrine of Purgatory asserted, then the difference between the two churches was not great.[247] The problem, according to Hart, was that Catholicism "has also traditionally spoken of it as 'temporal punishment,' which the pope may in whole or part remit," something the Orthodox have (in his view) rightly rejected.[248] Yet while there remained many "questions as yet unanswered" and a "genuine need for serious engagement," Hart was hopeful that East and West could eventually be "reconciled in a more than superficial way on this one issue."[249] Whether his optimism is justified or misplaced is still to be decided.

---

[247] David Bentley Hart, "The Myth of Schism," in Francesca Aran Murphy and Christopher Asprey, eds., *Ecumenism Today: The Universal Church in the 21st Century* (London: Ashgate, 2008), 103.
[248] Ibid.
[249] Ibid.

Bibliography

Abelard, Peter. *Ethical Writings: "Ethics" and "Dialogue between a Philosopher, a Jew and a Christian"*. Trans. Paul Vincent Spade. Indianapolis: Hackett, 1995.

Afentoulidou, Eirini. "Gesellschaftliche Vorstellungen in den byzantinischen Berichten von posthumen Zollstationen." *Zeitschrift für Religions- und Geistesgeschichte* 67 (2015): 17–42.

Akeliev, Evgeny. "On the History of Beard Shaving and the Introduction of 'German' Clothing in Peter the Great's Russia." *Quaestio Rossica* 1 (2013): 90–98.

Albert the Great. *On Resurrection*. Trans. Irven M. Resnick and Franklin T. Harkins. FC Medieval Continuation 20. Washington, DC: Catholic University of America Press, 2020.

Albert the Great. *On the Body of the Lord*. Trans. Albert Marie Surmanski. FC Medieval Continuation 17. Washington, DC: Catholic University of America Press, 2017.

Albright, W. F., and C. S. Mann. *Matthew*. Anchor Bible 26. New York: Doubleday, 1971.

Alexakis, Alexander. "Official and Unofficial Contacts between Rome and Constantinople before the Second Council of Lyons (1274)." *Annuarium Historiae Conciliorum* 39 (2007): 99–124.

Alger of Liège. *De sacramentis de corporis et sanguinis Dominici: Libri Tres*. London: David Nutt, 1873.

Alighieri, Dante. *The Divine Comedy*. Vol. 2: *Purgatory*. Trans. Mark Musa. New York: Penguin Books, 1985.

Allatius, Leo. *De utriusquae ecclesiae occidentalis atque orientalis perpetua in dogmate de purgatorio*. Rome: Typis Sacrae Congreg. de Propaganda Fide, 1655.

Allison, Dale, ed. *Testament of Abraham*. Berlin: Walter de Gruyter, 2003.

Allo, E. B. *Premiere Epitre aux Corinthiens*. Paris: Gabalda; Lecoffre, 1934.

Ambrose of Milan. *Commentary of Saint Ambrose on Twelve Psalms*. Trans. Íde M. Ní Riain. Dublin: Halcyon Press, 2000.

Ambrose of Milan. *Exposition on the Holy Gospel According to Saint Luke*. Trans. Theodosia Tomkinson. Etna, CA: Center for Traditionalist Orthodox Studies, 1998.

Ambrose of Milan. *Homilies of Saint Ambrose on Psalm 118 (119)*. Trans. Íde M. Ní Riain. Dublin: Halcyon Press, 1998.

Ambrose of Milan. *Letters*. Trans. Sister Mary Melchior Beyenka. FC 26. Washington, DC: Catholic University of America Press, 1954.

Ambrose of Milan. *Seven Exegetical Works*. Trans. Michael McHugh. FC 65. Washington, DC: Catholic University of America Press, 1972.

Ambrose of Milan. *Theological and Dogmatic Works*. Trans. Roy J. Deferrari. FC 44. Washington, DC: Catholic University of America Press, 1963.

Ambrosiaster. *Commentaries on Galatians-Philemon*. Trans. Gerald Lewis Bray. Downers Grove, IL: IVP Academic, 2009.

Ambrosiaster. *Commentary on Romans and 1-2 Corinthians*. Trans. Gerald Bray. Downers Grove, IL: IVP Academic, 2009.

Anderson, Gary. "Is Purgatory Biblical? The Scriptural Structure of Purgatory." *First Things*, November 2011, 39–44.

Andrea, Alfred, ed. *Contemporary Sources for the Fourth Crusade*. Medieval Mediterranean 29. London: Brill, 2000.

Andrea, Alfred. "Innocent III and the Byzantine Rite, 1198–1216." In Angeliki Laiou, ed. *Urbs Capta: The Fourth Crusade and Its Consequences (La IVe croisade et ses consequences)*. Paris: Lethielleux, 2005, 111–22.

Angelou, Athanasios. *Nicholas of Methone, Refutation of Proclus' Elements of Theology: A Critical Edition with an Introduction on Nicholas' Life and Works*. Leiden: Brill, 1984.

Angelou, Athanasios. "Nicholas of Methone: The Life and Works of a Twelfth-Century Bishop." In Margaret Mullett and Roger Scott, eds. *Byzantium and the Classical Tradition: University of Birmingham Thirteenth Spring Symposium of Byzantine Studies 1979*. Birmingham: Centre for Byzantine Studies, University of Birmingham, 1981, 143–48.

Angold, Michael. *A Byzantine Government in Exile: Government and Society under the Laskarids of Nicaea, 1204–1261*. London: Oxford University Press, 1975.

Angold, Michael. *Church and Society in Byzantium under the Comneni, 1081–1261*. Cambridge: Cambridge University Press, 1995.

Angold, Michael. *The Fourth Crusade: Event and Context*. Harlow: Longman, 2003.

Angold, Michael, ed. *Nicholas Mesarites: His Life and Works in Translation*. Liverpool: Liverpool University Press, 2018.

Annals of St-Bertin. Trans. Janet Nelson. Manchester: Manchester University Press, 1991.

Anonymous Monk of Whitby. *The Earliest Life of Gregory the Great*. Trans. Bertram Colgrave. Cambridge: Cambridge University Press, 1985.

Anrich, Gustav. "Clemens und Origenes als begründer der lehre vom Fegfeuer." In W. Nowack, et al. eds. *Theologische Abhandlungen. Eine Festgabe zum 17. Mai 1902 für H. J. Holtzmann*. Tübingen: Mohr Siebeck, 1902, 97–120.

Anselm of Havelberg. *Anticimenon: On the Unity of the Faith and the Controversies with the Greeks*. Trans. Ambrose Criste and Carol Neel. Cistercian Studies 232. Collegeville, MN: Liturgical Press, 2010.

Anthimos VII. *A Reply to the Papal Encyclical of Pope Leo XIII on Reunion*. In Eustathius Metallinos, ed. *Orthodox and Catholic Union*. Seattle: St. Nectarios Press, 1985.

Anton Michel. *Amalfi und Jerusalem im Griechischen Kirchenstreit (1054–1090): Kardinal Humbert, Laycus von Amalfi, Niketas Stethatos, Symeon II, von Jerusalem und Bruno von Segni uber die Azymen*. Rome: Pontificium Institutum Orientalium Studiorum, 1939.

Aphraates, *The Demonstrations of Aphrahat, the Persian Sage*. Trans. Adam Lehto. Piscataway, NJ: Gorgias Press, 2010.

Aquinas, Thomas. *Commentary on the Gospel of John*. Vol. 3. Trans. Fabian Larcher and James A. Weisheipl. Washington, DC: Catholic University of America Press, 2010.

Aquinas, Thomas. *Commentary on the Sentences, Book IV, Distinctions 1–13*. Trans. Beth Mortensen. Green Bay, WI: Aquinas Institute, 2017.

Aquinas, Thomas. *Commentary on the Sentences, Book IV, Distinctions 43–50*. Trans. Beth Mortensen. Green Bay, WI: Aquinas Institute, 2018.

Aquinas, Thomas. *On Evil*. Trans. Richard Regan. Oxford: Oxford University Press, 2003.

Aquinas, Thomas. *On Reasons for Our Faith against the Muslims, and a Reply to the Denial of Purgatory by Certain Greeks and Armenians to the Cantor of Antioch*. Trans. Peter Damien Fehlner. New Bedford, MA: Franciscans of the Immaculate, 2002.

Aquinas, Thomas. *The Sermon-Conferences of St Thomas Aquinas on the Apostles' Creed.* Trans. Nicholas Ayo. Notre Dame, IN: University of Notre Dame Press, 1988.

Aquinas, Thomas. *Summa contra Gentiles.* 5 vols. Trans. Charles O'Neil. Notre Dame: University of Notre Dame Press, 1975.

Aquinas, Thomas. *Summa Theologica.* 5 vols. Trans. Fathers of the English Dominican Province. Westminster: Christian Classics, 1981.

Arbel, Benjamin, Bernard Hamilton, and David Jacoby, eds. *Latins and Greeks in the Eastern Mediterranean after 1204.* London: Frank Cass, 1989.

Armstrong, Regis J. A., Wayne Hellmann, and William J. Short, eds. *Francis Trilogy: Life of Saint Francis, The Remembrance of the Desire of a Soul, The Treatise on the Miracles of Saint Francis.* Hyde Park, NY: New City Press, 2004.

Arranz, Miguel. "Circonstances et conséquences liturgiques du Concile de Ferrare-Florence." In Giuseppe Alberigo, ed. *Christian Unity: The Council of Ferrara-Florence 1438/9.* Leuven: Leuven University Press, 1991, 407–27.

Arthur, J. P., ed. *The Founders of the New Devotion.* London: Kegan Paul, Trench, Trübner, 1905.

Attridge, Harold. *The Epistle to the Hebrews: A Commentary on the Epistle to the Hebrews.* Philadelphia: Fortress Press, 1989.

Atwell, Robert. "From Augustine to Gregory the Great: An Evaluation of the Emergence of the Doctrine of Purgatory." *Journal of Ecclesiastical History* 38 (1987): 173–86.

Augustine of Hippo. *Christian Instruction; Admonition and Grace; The Christian Combat; Faith, Hope and Charity.* Trans. John Gavigan. FC 4. Washington, DC: Catholic University of America Press, 1950.

Augustine of Hippo. *The City of God Books 11–22.* Trans. William Babcock. Hyde Park, NY: New City Press, 2013.

Augustine of Hippo. *Confessions.* Trans. Vernon Bourke. FC 21. Washington, DC: Catholic University of America Press, 1953.

Augustine of Hippo. *Essential Sermons.* Trans. Edmund Hill. Hyde Park, NY: New City Press, 2007.

Augustine of Hippo. *Exposition on the Psalms.* Vol. 1. Trans. Maria Boulding. Hyde Park, NY: New City Press, 2000.

Augustine of Hippo. *Exposition on the Psalms.* Vol. 2. Trans. Maria Boulding. Hyde Park, NY: New City Press, 2000.

Augustine of Hippo. *Exposition on the Psalms.* Vol. 5. Trans. Maria Boulding. Hyde Park, NY: New City Press, 2003.

Augustine of Hippo. *Letters 156–210.* Trans. Roland Teske. Hyde Park, NY: New City Press, 2004.

Augustine of Hippo. *Letters 211–270.* Trans. Roland Teske. Hyde Park, NY: New City Press, 2005.

Augustine of Hippo. *The New Testament I and II.* Trans. Boniface Ramsey, Kim Paffenroth, and Roland Teske. Hyde Park, NY: New City Press, 2014.

Augustine of Hippo. *On Christian Belief.* Trans. Edmund Hill. Hyde Park, NY: New City Press, 2005.

Augustine of Hippo. *On Genesis.* Trans. Matthew O'Connell. Hyde Park, NY: New City Press, 2002.

Augustine of Hippo. *The Retractions.* Trans. Sister M. Inez Bogan, R.S.M. FC 60. Washington, DC: Catholic University of America Press, 1968.

Augustine of Hippo. *Sermons, Volume III/2*. Trans. Edmund Hill, O.P. Hyde Park, NY: New City Press, 1991.
Augustine of Hippo. *Sermons, Volume III/4*. Trans. Edmund Hill, O.P. Hyde Park, NY: New City Press, 1992.
Augustine of Hippo. *Sermons, Volume III/6*. Trans. Edmund Hill, O.P. Hyde Park, NY: New City Press, 1993.
Augustine of Hippo. *Sermons, Volume III/8*. Trans. Edmund Hill, O.P. Hyde Park, NY: New City Press, 1994.
Augustine of Hippo. *Teaching Christianity*. Trans. Edmund Hill. Hyde Park, NY: New City Press, 1992.
Augustine of Hippo. *Tractates on the Gospel of John 1–10*. Trans. John Rettig. FC 78. Washington, DC: Catholic University of America Press, 1988.
Augustine of Hippo. *Tractates on the Gospel of John, 55–111*. Trans. John Rettig. FC 90. Washington, DC: Catholic University of America Press, 1994.
Augustine of Hippo. *Tractates on the Gospel of John 112–24*. Trans. John Rettig. FC 92. Washington, DC: Catholic University of America Press, 1995.
Augustine of Hippo. *Treatises on Various Subjects*. Trans. Sister Mary Sarah Muldowney. FC 16. Washington, DC: Catholic University of America Press, 1952.
Aune, David. *Revelation 17–22*. Word Biblical Commentary 52C. Grand Rapids, MI: Zondervan, 1998.
Auxentios, Bishop. "St. Mark of Ephesus: His Person and Liturgical and His Theological Expertise." *Patristic and Byzantine Review* 10 (1991): 159–66.
Avvakumov, Yury P. "Anselm von Havelberg—ein Lateiner in der Auseinandersetzung mit dem Anders-Sein der Ostkirche." *Communicantes. Schriftenreihe zur Spiritualität des Prämonstratenser-ordens* 24 (2009): 51–69.
Avvakumov, Yury P. "Das Ritual: Ein unterschätzter Entfremdungs- und Verständigungsfaktor zwischen Ost und West." *Una Sancta. Zeitschrift für ökumenische Begegnung* 58 (2003): 130–38.
Avvakumov, Yury P. "Das Verhältnis zwischen Ost- und Westkirche in der mittelalterlichen Theologie." In Christian Schäfer and Martin Thurner, eds. *Mittelalterliches Denken. Debatten, Ideen und Gestalten im Kontext*. Darmstadt: Wissenschaftliche Buchgesellschaft, 2007, 89–104.
Avvakumov, Yury P. "Der Azymenstreit. Konflikte und Polemiken um eine Frage des Ritus." In Peter Bruns and Georg Gresser, eds. *Vom Schisma zu den Kreuzzügen 1054–1204*. Paderborn: Schöningh, 2005, 9–26.
Avvakumov, Yury P. "Die Beurteilung der Ostkirche im lateinischen Westen in der Zeit von Gregor VII. bis Zölestin III., 1073–1198." In Theodor Nikolaou et al., eds. *Das Schisma zwischen Ost- und Westkirche. 950 bzw. 800 Jahre danach (1054 und 1204)*. Münster: Lit Verlag, 2004, 15–28.
Avvakumov, Yury P. *Die Entstehung des Unionsgedankens. Die lateinische Theologie des Hochmittelalters in der Auseinandersetzung mit dem Ritus der Ostkirche*. Veröffentlichungen des Grabmann-Institutes 47. Berlin: Akademie-Verlag, 2002.
Avvakumov, Yury P. "Die Fragen des Ritus als Streit- und Kontroversgegenstand. Zur Typologie der Kulturkonflikte zwischen dem lateinischen Westen und dem byzantinisch-slawischen Osten im Mittelalter und in der Neuzeit." In Rainer Bendel,

ed. *Kirchen- und Kulturgeschichtsschreibung in Nordost- und Ostmitteleurop. Initiativen, Methoden, Theorien*. Münster: Lit Verlag, 2006, 191–233.

Avvakumov, Yury P. "Sacramental Ritual in Middle and Later Byzantine Theology: Ninth–Fifteenth Centuries." In Hans Boersma and Matthew Levering, eds. *The Oxford Handbook of Sacramental Theology*. Oxford University Press, 2015, 249–66.

Azkoul, Michael. *Aerial Toll-House Myth: The Neo-Gnosticism of Fr Seraphim Rose*. Synaxis Press, 2005.

Bacci, Michele. *The Many Faces of Christ: Portraying the Holy in the East and West, 300 to 1300*. London: Reaktion Books, 2014.

Bahr, Gordon J. "The Seder of Passover and the Eucharistic Words." *Novum Testamentum* 12 (1970): 181–202.

Baker, Derek, ed. *The Orthodox Churches and the West*. Studies in Church History 13. Oxford: Oxford University Press, 1976.

Baker, Derek, ed. *Relations between East and West in the Middle Ages*. Edinburgh: Edinburgh University Press, 1973.

Baker-Brian, Nicholas. "The Politics of Virtue in Julian's *Misopogon*." In Nicholas Baker-Brian and Shaun Tougher, eds. *Emperor and Author: The Writings of Julian the Apostate*. Swansea: Classical Press of Wales, 2012, 263–80.

Baldovin, John. "The Fermentum at Rome in the Fifth Century: A Reconsideration." *Worship* 79 (2005): 38–53.

Baldwin, Barry. "Physical Descriptions of Byzantine Emperors." *Byzantion* 51 (1981): 8–21.

Barker, John W. *Manuel II Palaeologos (1391-1425): A Study in Late Byzantine Statesmanship*. New Brunswick, NJ: Rutgers University Press, 1969.

Barrett, C. K. *Acts: A Shorter Commentary*. London: T&T Clark, 2002.

Barrett, C. K. *The First Epistle to the Corinthians*. New York: Harper and Row, 1968.

Barrett, C. K. *The Gospel According to St. John*. Philadelphia: Westminster Press, 1978.

Barrett, C. K. "Luke XXII.15: To Eat the Passover." *Journal of Theological Studies* 9 (1958): 305–7.

Bartlett, Robert. "Symbolic Meanings of Hair in the Middle Ages." *Transactions of the Royal Historical Society* 4 (1994): 43–60.

Bartman, Elizabeth. "Hair and the Artifice of Roman Female Adornment." *American Journal of Archaeology* 105 (2001): 1–25.

Basil of Caesarea. *Against Eunomius*. Trans. Mark DelCogliano and Andrew Radde-Gallwitz. FC 122. Washington, DC: Catholic University of America Press, 2011.

Basil of Caesarea. *Commentary on the Prophet Isaiah*. Trans. Nikolai A. Lipatov. Mandelbachtal: Edition Cicero, 2001.

Basil of Caesarea. *Exegetic Homilies*. Trans. Sister Agnes Clare Way. FC 46. Washington, DC: Catholic University of America Press, 1963.

Basil of Caesarea. *On Christian Ethics*. Trans. Jacob Van Sickle. Crestwood, NY: St. Vladimir's Seminary Press, 2014.

Bathrellos, Demetrios. "Love, Purification, and Forgiveness versus Justice, Punishment, and Satisfaction: The Debates on Purgatory and the Forgiveness of Sins at the Council of Ferrara-Florence." *Journal of Theological Studies*, NS 65 (2014): 78–121.

Bathrellos, Demetrios. *Σχεδίασμα Δογματικῆς Θεολογίας. Μέ βάση τό συγγραφικό ἔργο τοῦ Ἁγίου Συμεών Θεσσαλονίκης (†1429)*. Athens: En Plo, 2008.

Batiffol, Pierre. *L'Eucharistie: La Présence Réelle Et la transsubstantiation, études d'histoire et de théologie positive*. Vol. 2. Paris: V. Lecoffre, 1913.

Bayer, Axel. *Spaltung der Christenheit: Das sogenannte Morgenländische Schisma von 1054*. Cologne: Böhlau Vertag, 2002.

Beasley-Murray, George. *Baptism in the New Testament*. Grand Rapids, MI: William Eerdmans, 1962.

Beasley-Murray, George. *John*. Word Biblical Commentary 36. Nashville: Thomas Nelson, 2000.

Beck, Edmund, ed. *Des heiligen Ephraem des Syrers Sermones IV*. CSCO 335. Louvain: Secretariat du Corpus Scriptorum Christianorum Orientalium, 1973.

Beck, Edmund, ed. *Ephraem Syrus. Sermones in Hebdomadam Sanctam*. 2 vols. CSCO 412–13. Louvain: Secretariat du Corpus Scriptorum Christianorum Orientalium, 1979.

Beck, Hans-Georg. *Die Byzantiner und ihr Jenseits. Zur Entstehungsgeschichte einer Mentalitat*. Munich: Verlag der Bayerischen Akademie der Wissenschaften, 1979.

Beck, Hans-Georg. *Kirche und theologische Literatur im Byzantinischen Reich*. Munich: C.H. Beck, 1959.

Beck, Henry G. J. "A Ninth-Century Canonist on Purgatory." *American Ecclesiastical Review* 111.4 (1944): 250–56.

Beckwith, Roger. "The Date of the Crucifixion: The Misuse of Calendars and Astronomy to Determine the Chronology of the Passion." In R. T. Beckwith, ed. *Calendar and Chronology: Jewish and Christian. Biblical, Intertestamental, and Patristic Studies*. Leiden: Brill 2001, 276–96.

Bede. *The Ecclesiastical History of the English People*. Trans. Judith McClure and Roger Collins. Oxford: Oxford University Press, 1969.

Bede. *Homilies on the Gospels: Book One—Advent to Lent (Book 1)*. Trans. Lawrence T. Martin and David Hurst. CS 110. Kalamazoo, MI: Cistercian Publications, 1991.

Bede. *On Ezra and Nehemiah*. Trans. Scott DeGregorio. Liverpool: Liverpool University Press, 2006.

Beiting, Christopher. "The Development of the Idea of Limbo in the Middle Ages." PhD Thesis, Oxford University, 1997.

Beiting, Christopher. "The Nature and Structure of Limbo in the Works of Albertus Magnus." *New Blackfriars* 85 (2004): 492–509.

Bekker, Immanuel, ed. *Georgii Pachymeris De Michaele et Andronico Palaeologis libri tredecim*. Bonn: Weber, 1835.

Bellermine, Robert. *De Controversiis: On Purgatory*. Trans. Ryan Grant. Post Falls, ID: Mediatrix Press, 2017.

Ben-Dov, Jonathan, and Stéphane Saulnier. "Qumran Calendars: A Survey of Scholarship 1980–2007." *Currents in Biblical Research* 7 (2008): 124–68.

Benz, Ernst. *Die Ostkirche in Lichte der protestantischen Geschictsschribung von der Reformation bis zur Gegenwart*. Munich: Karl Alber, 1952.

Benz, Ernst. *Wittenburg und Byzanz: Zur Begegung und aus Einandersetzung der Reformation und der Östlich-Orthodoxen Kirche*. Marburg: Fink, 1949.

Berg, Charles. *The Unconscious Significance of Hair*. London: Allen & Unwin, 1951.

Berke, Metin. "An Annotated Edition of Euthymios Zigabenos, Panoplia Dogmatikē, Chapters 23–28." PhD diss., Queen's University Belfast, 2011.

Bernstein, Alan. "Esoteric Theology: William of Auvergne on the Fires of Hell and Purgatory." *Speculum* 57 (1982): 509–31.

Bernstein, Alan. *Hell and Its Rivals: Death and Retribution among Christians, Jews, and Muslims in the Early Middle Ages.* Ithaca, NY: Cornell University Press, 2017.

Bertrand, D. "Hypocrites selon Luc 12,1–59." *Christus* 21 (1974): 323–33.

Betz, Hans Dieter. *Galatians: A Commentary on Paul's Letter to the Churches in Galatia.* Philadelphia: Fortress Press, 1979.

Betz, Hans Dieter. *The Sermon on the Mount: A Commentary on the Sermon on the Mount, including the Sermon on the Plain (Matthew 5:3–7:27 and Luke 6:20–49).* Minneapolis, MN: Fortress Press, 1995.

Bietenhard, Hans. "Kennt das Neue Testament die Vorstellung vom Fegefeuer?" *Theologische Zeitschrift* 3 (1947): 101–22.

Bilaniuk, Petro. *Studies in Eastern Christianity.* Vol. 2. Toronto: The Ukrainian Free University, 1982.

Bird, Jessalynn, ed. *Jacques de Vitry's History of the East.* London: Routledge, 2021.

Blackmore, R. W. *Doctrine of the Russian Church.* London: J. Masters, 1905.

Blanchet, Marie-Hélène. "La question de l'union des églises (13e–15e s.): Historiographie et perspectives." *Revue dea Études Byzantines* 61 (2003): 5–48.

Blomberg, Craig. *1 Corinthians.* NIV Application Commentary. Grand Rapids, MI: Zondervan, 1994.

Bockmuehl, Markus. *This Jesus: Martyr, Lord, Messiah.* London: T&T Clark, 1994.

Boersma, Hans. *Seeing God: The Beatific Vision in Christian Tradition.* Grand Rapids, MI: Eerdmans, 2018.

Bokser, Baruch. "Unleavened Bread and Passover, Feasts of." *Anchor Bible Dictionary* 6. New Haven, CT: Yale University Press, 1992, 755–65.

Bokser, Baruch. "Was the Last Supper a Passover Seder?" *Bible Review* 3 (1987): 24–33.

Bonaventure. *Commentaria in Quatuor Libros Sententiarum Magistri Petri Lombardi.* In Collegium S. Bonaventurae, ed. *Opera Omnia*, vols. 1–4. Florence: Quaracchi, 1885.

Bonaventure. *Works of Saint Bonaventure: Breviloquium.* Trans. Dominic Monti. Bonaventure, NY: Franciscan Institute Publications, 2005.

Bonaventure. *Works of Saint Bonaventure: Commentary on the Sentences: Sacraments.* Trans. Wayne Hellmann, Timothy LeCroy, and Luke Townsend. St. Bonaventure, NY: Franciscan Institute Publications, 2016.

Bond, Helen. "Dating the Death of Jesus: Memory and the Religious Imagination." *New Testament Studies* 59 (2013): 461–75.

Borg, Marcus, and John Dominic Crossan. *The Last Week: What the Gospels Really Teach about Jesus's Final Days in Jerusalem.* New York: HarperCollins, 2006.

Borgen, Peder. "John and the Synoptics in the Passion Narrative." *New Testament Studies* 5 (1958–59): 246–59.

Borgnet, Auguste, ed. *Alberti Magni Opera Omnia.* Paris, 1894.

Borromeo, Charles. *Selected Orations, Homilies, and Writings.* Trans. John Clark and Ansgar Santogrossi. London: Bloomsbury T&T Clark, 2017.

Bossina, Luciano. "Niketas Choniates as a Theologian." In Alicia Simpson and Stephanos Efthymiades, eds. *Niketas Choniates: A Historian and a Writer.* Geneva: Pomme d'or, 2009, 166–84.

Botterweck, G. Johannes, and Helmer Ringgren, eds. *Theological Dictionary of the Old Testament*. Vol. 3. Grand Rapids: Eerdmans, 1978.

Bovon, François. *Luke 1: A Commentary on the Gospel of Luke 1:1-9:50*. Minneapolis, MN: Fortress Press, 2002.

Box, G. H. "The Jewish Antecedents of the Eucharist." *Journal of Theological Studies* 3 (1901-2): 358-60.

Brand, Charles M., ed. *Deeds of John and Manuel Comnenus by John Kinnamos*. New York: Columbia University Press, 1976.

Bredero, Adriaan. "Le Moyen Âge et le purgatoire." *Revue d'histoire ecclésiastique* 78 (1983): 429-52.

Bremmer, Jan, and István Czachesz, eds. *The Visio Pauli and the Gnostic Apocalypse of Paul*. Leuven: Peeters, 2007.

Bremmer, Jan, and Marco Formisano, eds. *Perpetua's Passions: Multidisciplinary Approaches to the Passio Perpetuae et Felicitatis*. Oxford: Oxford University Press, 2012.

Brett, Edward Tracy. *Humbert of Romans: His Life and Views of Thirteenth Century Society*. Toronto: Pontifical Institute for Medieval Studies, 1984.

Brett, Martin, Christopher Robert Cheney, Dorothy Whitelock, Frederick Maurice Powicke, Christopher Brooke, and Arthur West Hadden, eds. *Councils and Synods with other Documents relating to the English Church I (871-1204)*. Oxford: Clarendon Press, 1964.

Brightman, Frank. "The Quartodeciman Question." *Journal of Theological Studies* 25 (1923-24): 254-70.

Brock, Jared, and Aaron Alford. *Bearded Gospel Men: The Epic Quest for Manliness and Godliness*. Nashville, TN: W Publishing Group, 2017.

Brodie, Thomas. *The Gospel According to John: A Literary and Theological Commentary*. Oxford: Oxford University Press, 1993.

Bromage, R. Raikes, ed. *The Holy Catechism of Nicolas Bulgaris*. London: J. Masters, 1893.

Bromberger, Christian. "Hair: From the West to the Middle East through the Mediterranean." *Journal of American Folklore* 121.482 (2008): 379-99.

Brown, Peter. *The Body and Society: Men, Women, and Sexual Renunciation in Early Christianity*. New York: Columbia University Press, 1988.

Brown, Peter. "The Decline of the Empire of God: Amnesty, Penance, and the Afterlife from Late Antiquity to the Middle Ages." In Caroline Walker Bynum and Paul Freedman, eds. *Last Things: Death and the Apocalypse in the Middle Ages*. Philadelphia: University of Pennsylvania Press, 2000, 41-59.

Brown, Peter. "Vers la naissance du purgatoire. Amnistie et pénitence dans le christianisme occidental de l'Antiquité tardive au haut Moyen Âge." *Annales. Histoire, Sciences Sociales* 52 (1997): 1247-61.

Brown, Raymond. *The Death of the Messiah*. 2 vols. New York: Doubleday, 1993.

Brown, Raymond. *The Gospel According to John I-XII*. Anchor Bible 29. New York: Doubleday, 1970.

Brown, Raymond. *The Gospel According to John XIII-XXI*. Anchor Bible 29a. New York: Doubleday, 1970.

Brown, Raymond. *An Introduction to the New Testament*. Anchor Bible Reference Library. New York: Doubleday, 1997.

Brown, Raymond. "The Problem of Historicity in John." In Raymond Brown, ed. *New Testament Essays*. New York: Doubleday, 2010, 191–221.

Brown, T. S. "The Political Use of the Past in Norman Sicily." In Paul Magdalino, ed. *The Perception of the Past in Twelfth-Century Europe*. London: Hambledon Press, 1992, 191–210.

Brubaker, Jeff. *The Disputatio of the Latins and the Greeks 1234*. Liverpool: Liverpool University Press, 2023.

Brubaker, Jeff. "'You Are the Heretics!' Dialogue and Disputation between the Greek East and the Latin West after 1204." *Medieval Encounters* 24 (2018): 613–30.

Bruce, F. F. *The Epistle to the Hebrews*. The New International Commentary on the New Testament. Grand Rapids, MI: Eerdmans, 1990.

Buchard of Bellevaux. *Apologia de Barbis*. In R. B. C. Huygens, ed. *Apologiae duae*. Corpus Christianorum: Continuatio mediaeualis, 62. Turnholt: Brepols, 1985.

Bucossi, Alessandra, ed. *Andronicus Camaterus, Sacrum Armamentarium: Pars Prima*. CCG 75. Turnhout: Brepols, 2014.

Bucossi, Alessandra. "Dialogue and Anthologies of the *Sacred Arsenal* by Andronikos Kamateros: Sources, Arrangements, Purposes." In Peter Van Deun and Caroline Macé, eds. *Encyclopedic Trends in Byzantium? Proceedings of the International Conference Held in Leuven, 6–8 May 2009*. Leuven: Peeters, 2011, 269–84.

Bucossi, Alessandra. "New Historical Evidence for the Dating of the *Sacred Arsenal* by Andronikos Kamateros." *Revue des études byzantines* 67 (2009): 111–30.

Bucossi, Alessandra. "The *Sacred Arsenal* by Andronikos Kamateros: A Forgotten Treasure." In Antonio Rigo and Pavel Ermilov, eds. *Byzantine Theologians: The Systematization of Their Own Doctrine and Their Perception of Foreign Doctrines*. Rome: Università degli studi di Roma Tor Vergata, 2009, 33–50.

Bucossi, Alessandra, and L. D'Amelia, eds. *Nicetas Thessalonicensis, Dialogi sex de processione Spiritus Sancti*. CCG 92. Turnhout: Brepols Publishers, 2021.

Budd, Philip. *Numbers*. Word Biblical Commentary 5. Waco, TX: Word Books, 1984.

Bulbeck, W. A. "The Eucharistic Bread." *Downside Review* 13 (1894): 30–36.

Burkitt, F. C. "The Last Supper and the Paschal Meal." *Journal of Theological Studies* 17.4 (1916): 291–97.

Buse, Ivor. "St. John and the Marcan Passion Narrative." *New Testament Studies* 4 (1957–58): 215–19.

Buse, Ivor. "St. John and the Passion Narratives of St. Matthew and St. Luke." *New Testament Studies* 7 (1960–61): 65–76.

Büttner, Elmar. *Erzbischof Leon von Ohrid (1037–1056): Leben und Werk (mit den Texten seiner bisher unedierten asketischen Schrift und seiner drei Briefe an den Papst)*. Bamberg: Elmar Büttner, 2007.

Bysted, Ane. *The Crusade Indulgence: Spiritual Rewards and the Theology of the Crusades, c. 1095–1216*. Leiden: Brill, 2015.

Cabasilas, Nicholas. *Commentary on the Divine Liturgy*. Trans. J. M. Hussey and P. A. McNulty. London: SPCK, 1960.

Cadman, W. H. "The Christian Pascha and the Day of Crucifixion: Nisan 14 or 15." *Studia Patristica* 5 (1962): 8–16.

Caesarius of Arles. *Sermons, Volume II (81–186)*. Trans. Sister Mary Magdeleine Mueller. FC 47. Washington, DC: Catholic University of America Press, 1963.

Cameron, Averil. *Arguing It Out: Discussion in Twelfth-Century Byzantium.* Budapest: Central European University Press, 2016.
Cameron, Averil, and Niels Gaul, eds. *Dialogues and Debates from Late Antiquity to Late Byzantium.* London: Routledge, 2017.
Canart, Paul. "Nicéphore Blemmyde et la mémoire adressé aux envoyés de Grégoire IX (Nicée, 1234)." *Orientalia Christiana Periodica* 25 (1959): 310–25.
Canon Law Society of America. *Code of Canon Law.* Washington, DC: Canon Law Society of America, 1983.
Canon Law Society of America. *Code of Canons of the Eastern Churches.* Washington, DC: Canon Law Society of America, 1990.
Cantalamessa, Raniero. *Easter in the Early Church.* Collegeville, MN: Liturgical Press, 1993.
Carroll, M. Thomas Aquinas. "An Eighth-Century Exegete on Purgatory." *American Ecclesiastical Review* 112.1 (1945): 261–63.
Casey, John. *After Lives: A Guide to Heaven, Hell, and Purgatory.* Oxford: Oxford University Press, 2009.
Cassiodorus. *Explanations of the Psalms.* Vol. 3. Trans. P. G. Walsh. ACW 53. New York: Paulist Press, 1991.
Cassiodorus. *Institutions of Divine and Secular Learning and On the Soul.* Trans. James W. Halporn and Mark Vessey. Liverpool: Liverpool University Press, 2004.
Catherine of Genoa. *Treatise on Purgatory.* In Serge Hughes, ed. *Catherine of Genoa: Purgation and Purgatory, The Spiritual Dialogue.* New York: Paulist Press, 1979.
Cen, Esther. "The Metaphor of Leaven in 1 Corinthians 5." *Dialogismos* 3 (2019): 1–26.
Centre national de la recherche scientifique. *1274: Année charnière: Mutations et continuités.* Paris: Éditions du C.N.R.S., 1977.
Cevetello, J. F. X., and R. J. Bastian. "Purgatory." *New Catholic Encyclopedia.* 2nd ed. Vol. 11, Detroit: Gale, 2003, 824–29.
Chadwick, Henry. *East and West: The Making of the Rift in the Church: From Apostolic Times until the Council of Florence.* Oxford: Oxford University Press, 2003.
Chalendard, M. *Nicétas Stéthatos: Le Paradis spirituel et autres textes annexes.* Paris, 1944.
Charanis, Peter. "Byzantium, the West, and the Origin of the First Crusade." *Byzantion* 19 (1949): 17–36.
Charlesworth, James, ed. *The Old Testament Pseudepigrapha.* 2 vols. Garden City, NY: Doubleday, 1983–85.
Charlesworth, James, and Jolyon Pruszinski, eds. *Jesus Research: The Gospel of John in Historical Inquiry.* London: T&T Clark, 2019.
Chepey, Stuart Douglas. *Nazirites in Late Second Temple Judaism: A Survey of Ancient Jewish Writings, the New Testament, Archaeological Evidence, and Other Writings from Late Antiquity.* Leiden: Brill, 2005.
Christianson, Gerald, Thomas M. Izbicki, and Christopher M. Bellitto, eds. *The Church, the Councils, & Reform: The Legacy of the Fifteenth Century.* Washington, DC: Catholic University of America Press, 2008.
Christie, W. M. "Did Christ Eat the Passover with His Disciples?" *Expository Times* 43 (1931–32): 515–19.
Chrysostom, John. *Commentary on Saint John the Apostle and Evangelist Homilies 1–47.* Trans. Sister Thomas Aquinas Goggin. FC 33. Washington, DC: Catholic University of America Press, 1957.

Chrysostom, John. *Commentary on Saint John the Apostle and Evangelist Homilies 48–88.* Trans. Sister Thomas Aquinas Goggin. FC 41. Washington, DC: Catholic University of America Press, 1960.
Chrysostom, John. *De Laudibus Sancti Pauli.* Ed. and trans. A. Piédagnel. SC 300. Paris: Les éditions du Cerf, 1982.
Chrysostom, John. *Discourses against Judaizing Christians.* Trans. Paul Harkins. FC 68. Washington, DC: Catholic University of America Press, 1979.
Chrysostom, John. *Homilies on Genesis 18–45.* Trans. Robert C. Hill. FC 82. Washington, DC: Catholic University of America Press, 1986.
Chrysostom, John. *Homilies on Philippians.* Trans. Pauline Allen. Atlanta, GA: Society for Biblical Literature, 2013.
Chrysostom, John. *On Repentance and Almsgiving.* Trans. Gus George Christo. FC 96. Washington, DC: Catholic University of America Press, 1998.
Chrysostom, John. *On the Priesthood.* Trans. Graham Neville. Crestwood, NY: St. Vladimir's Seminary Press, 1964.
Chrysostomides, J., Jonathan Harris, Charalambos Dendrinos, and Judith Herrin, eds. *Porphyrogenita: Essays on the History and Literature of Byzantium and the Latin East in Honour of Julian Chrysostomides.* London: Ashgate, 2003.
Ciggaar, Krijnie N. *Western Travellers to Constantinople: The West and Byzantium, 962–1204: Cultural and Political Relations.* Leiden: Brill, 1996.
Cipriani, S. "Insegna 1. Cor. 3, 10–15 la dottrina del Purgatorio?" *Rivista Biblica* 7 (1959): 25–43.
Classen, Peter. "Das Konzil von Konstantinopel 1166 und die Lateiner." *Byzantinische Zeitschrift* 48 (1955): 339–68.
Clément, Olivier. "Byzance et le council de Lyon." *Klero* 7 (1975): 254–71.
Clement of Rome and Ignatius of Antioch. *The Epistles of Clement of Rome and Ignatius of Antioch.* Trans. James Kleist, SJ. ACW 1. Westminster, MD: Newman Bookshop, 1946.
Climicus, John. *Ladder of Divine Ascent.* Trans. Colm Luibheid and Norman Russell. New York: Paulist Press, 1982.
Coates, Simon. "Scissors or Sword? The Symbolism of a Medieval Haircut." *History Today* 49 (May 1999): 7–13.
Cockerill, Gareth Lee. *The Epistle to the Hebrews.* The New International Commentary on the New Testament. Grand Rapids, MI: Eerdmans, 2012.
Colish, Marcia L. "The Virtuous Pagan: Dante and the Christian Tradition." In William Caferro and Duncan G. Fisher, eds. *The Unbounded Community: Papers in Christian Ecumenism in Honor of Jaroslav Pelikan.* New York: Garland, 1996, 43–92.
Collins, Raymond. *First Corinthians.* Sacra Pagina 7. Collegeville, MN: Liturgical Press, 1999.
Concasty, M. "La fin d'un dialogue contre les Latins azymites d'après le Paris Suppl gr. 1191." In Franz Dölger and Hans-Georg Beck, eds. *Akten des xi. Internationalen Byzantinistenkongresses München, 1958.* Munich: C.H. Beck, 1060, 86–89.
Congar, Yves. *After Nine Hundred Years: The Background of the Schism between the Eastern and Western Churches.* New York: Fordham University Press, 1959.
Congar, Yves. "Le purgatoire." In *Le mystère de la mort et sa célébration.* Lex orandi, 12. Paris: Les éditions du Cerf, 1951, 279–336.
Congar, Yves. "Quatre siècles de disunion et d'affrontement. Comment les Grecs et Latins se sont apprecies reciproquement au point de vue ecclesiastique." *Istina* 13 (1968): 131–52.

Congourdeau, Marie-Hélène. "Notes sur les Dominicains de Constantinople au début du 14 siècle." *Revue des études byzantines* 45 (1987): 175–81.

Connolly, R. Hugh. *Didascalia Apostolorum: The Syriac Version Translated and Accompanied by the Verona Latin Fragments with an Introduction and Notes.* Oxford: Clarendon Press, 1929.

Constable, Giles. "Introduction on Beards in the Middle Ages." In R. B. C. Huygens, ed. *Apologiae duae*. Corpus Christianorum: Continuatio mediaeualis, 62. Turnhout: Brepols, 1985, 47–150.

Constable, Giles. *The Reformation of the Twelfth Century*. Cambridge: Cambridge University Press, 1997.

Constantelos, Demetrios. *Renewing the Church: The Significance of the Council in Trullo.* Brookline, MA: Holy Cross Press, 2007.

Constas, Nicholas. "An Apology for the Cult of Saints in Late Antiquity: Eustratius Presbyter of Constantinople, On the State of Souls after Death (CPG 7522)." *Journal of Early Christian Studies* 10 (2002): 267–85.

Constas, Nicholas. "Mark Eugenikos." In Carmelo Conticello and Vassa Conticello, eds. *La théologie Byzantine et sa tradition*. Vol. 2. Turnhout: Brepols, 2002, 411–64.

Constas, Nicholas. "To Sleep, Perchance to Dream: The Middle State of Souls in Patristic and Byzantine Literature." *Dumbarton Oaks Papers* 55 (2001): 91–124.

Conzelmann, Hans. *1 Corinthians: A Commentary on the First Epistle to the Corinthians.* Philadelphia: Fortress Press, 1975.

Conzelmann, Hans. *The Theology of St. Luke*. Trans. G. Buswell. Philadelphia: Fortress Press, 1982.

Costambeys, Marios. "Property and Ideology of the Papacy in the Early Middle Ages." *Early Modern Europe* 9 (2000): 367–96.

Coureas, Nicholas. "The Latin and Greek Churches in Former Byzantine Lands under Latin Rule." In Nickiphoros Tsougarakis and Peter Lock, eds. *A Companion to Latin Greece*. Leiden: Brill, 2015, 145–84.

Coureas, Nicholas. *The Latin Church in Cyprus, 1195–1312*. London: Routledge, 1997.

Cowdrey, H. E. J., ed. *The Epistolae vagantes of Pope Gregory VII*. Oxford Medieval Texts Oxford: Clarendon Press, 1972.

Cowdrey, H. E. J. "The Gregorian Papacy, Byzantium, and the First Crusade." *Byzantinische Forshungen* 13 (1988): 145–69.

Cowdrey, H. E. J. *The Register of Pope Gregory VII, 1073–1085: An English Translation.* New York: Oxford University Press, 2002.

Crawford, Matthew, and Nicholas Zola, eds. *The Gospel of Tatian: Exploring the Nature and Text of the Diatessaron*. London: T&T Clark, 2019.

Crawford, Paul, ed. *The Templar of Tyre: Part III of The Deeds of the Cypriote*. Crusade Texts in Translation 6. Aldershot: Ashgate, 2003.

Crockett, William. *Eucharist: Symbol of Transformation*. New York: Pueblo, 1989.

Crouzel, Henri. "L'exégèse origénienne de 1 Cor. 3, 11–15 et la Purification Eschatologique." In Jacques Fontaine and Charles Kannengiesser, eds. *Epektasis: Melanges patristiques offerts au Cardinal Jean Danielou*. Paris: Beauchesne, 1972, 272–83.

Crouzel, Henri. "L'Hadès et la Géhenne selon Origène." *Gregorianum* 59 (1978): 291–331.

Cuchet, Guillaume. *Le Crépuscule du Purgatoire*. Paris: Colin, 2005.

Cuchet, Guillaume, ed. *Le Purgatoire: Fortune Historique et Historiographique d'un Dogme*. Paris: Editions de l'Ecole des hautes études en sciences sociales, 2012.
Culpepper, R. Alan. *The Gospel and Letters of John*. Nashville: Abbington Press, 1988.
Cyprian of Carthage. *The Lapsed, The Unity of the Catholic Church*. Trans. Maurice Bévenot. ACW 25. New York: Paulist Press, 1956.
Cyprian of Carthage. *The Letters of Cyprian of Carthage*. Vol. 3. Trans. G. W. Clarke. ACW 46. New York: Newman Press, 1986.
Cyprian of Carthage. *Treatises*. Trans. Roy Deferrari et al. FC 36. Washington, DC: Catholic University of America Press, 1958.
Cyril of Alexandria. *Commentary on the Gospel of John*. Vol. 2. Trans. David Maxwell. Downers Grove, IL: IVP Academic, 2014.
Cyril of Alexandria. *Commentary on the Gospel of St. Luke*. Trans. R. Payne Smith. N.p.: Studion Publishers, 1983.
Cyril of Alexandria. *Commentary on the Twelve Prophets*. Vol. 3. Trans. Robert Charles Hill. FC 124. Washington, DC: Catholic University of America Press, 2012.
Cyril of Alexandria. *Festal Letters 1–12*. Trans. Philip Amadon, S.J. FC 118. Washington, DC: Catholic University of America Press, 2009.
Cyril of Jerusalem. *The Works of Saint Cyril of Jerusalem*. Vol. 1: *Procatechesis and Catecheses 1–12*. Trans. Leo McCauley and A. A. Stephenson. FC 61. Washington, DC: Catholic University of America Press, 1969.
Cyril of Jerusalem. *The Works of Saint Cyril of Jerusalem*. Vol. 2. Trans. Leo McCauley and A. A. Stephenson. FC 64. Washington, DC: Catholic University of America Press, 1970.
D'Agostino, Michele Giuseppe. *Il primato della sede di Roma in Leone IX (1049–1054), Studio dei testi latini nella controversia greco-romana nel periodo pregregoriano*. Cinisello Balsamo: San Paolo, 2008.
Dagron, Gilbert. "Judaïser." *Travaux et Mémoires* 11 (1991): 359–80.
Dagron, Gilbert. "La perception d'une différence: Les débuts de la querelle du purgatoire." In *Actes du XVe Congrès International d'Études Byzantines, Athènes, Septembre 1976*. Athens: Association international d'études byzantines, 1979, 84–92.
D'Alès, Adhémar. "La question du Purgatoire au concile de Florence en 1438." *Gregorianum* 3 (1922): 9–50.
Daley, Brian. "'At the Hour of Our Death': Mary's Dormition and Christian Dying in Late Patristic and Early Byzantine Literature." *Dumbarton Oaks Papers* 55 (2001): 71–89.
Daley, Brian. *The Hope of the Early Church: A Handbook of Patristic Eschatology*. Peabody, MA: Hendrickson Publishers, 2003.
Damian, Peter. *Book of Gomorrah: An Eleventh-Century Treatise against Clerical Homosexual Practices*. Trans. Pierre J. Payer. Waterloo, ON: Wilfrid Laurier University Press, 1982.
Damian, Peter. *Letters 31–60*. Trans. Owen Blum. FC Medieval Continuation 2. Washington, DC: Catholic University of America Press, 1990.
Damian, Peter. *Letters 91–120*. Trans. Owen Blum, O.F.M. FC Medieval Continuation 3. Washington, DC: Catholic University of America Press, 1998.
Daniel-Hughes, Carly. *The Salvation of the Flesh in Tertullian of Carthage: Dressing for the Resurrection*. New York: Palgrave Macmillan, 2011.
Daniélou, Jean. "L'apocatastase Chez Saint Grégoire de Nysse." *Recherches de Science Religieuse* 30 (1940): 328–47.

Darrouzès, Jean. "Le mémoire de Constantin Stilbès contre les Latins." *Revue des études byzantines* 2 (1963): 50–100.
Darrouzès, Jean. "Les documents byzantins du XIIe siècle sur la primaute romaine." *Revue des études byzantines* 23 (1965): 42–88.
Darrouzès, Jean. "Les réponses canoniques de Jean de Kitros." *Revue des Etudes Byzantines* 31 (1973): 319–34.
Darrouzès, Jean, ed. *Nicétas Stéthatos Opuscules et lettres.* SC 81. Paris: Les éditions du Cerf, 1961.
Darrouzès, Jean. "Nicolas d'Andida et les Azymes." *Revue des études byzantines* 32 (1974): 199–210.
Darrouzès, Jean. "Trois documents de la controverse gréco-arménienne." *Revue des Etudes Byzantines* 48 (1990): 89–92.
Darrouzès, Jean. "Un faux περὶ τῶν ἀζύμων de Michel Cérulaire." *Revue des Etudes Byzantines* 25 (1967): 288–91.
Davey, Colin. *Pioneer for Unity: Metrophanes Kritopoulos, 1589–1639, and Relations between the Orthodox, Roman Catholic and Reformed Churches.* London: British Council of Churches, 1987.
Davies, William, and Dale Allison. *A Critical and Exegetical Commentary on the Gospel according to Saint Matthew.* 3 vols. Edinburgh: T&T Clark, 1991–97.
Dawes, Elizabeth, and Norman H. Baynes. *Three Byzantine Saints: Contemporary Biographies of St. Daniel the Stylite, St. Theodore of Sykeon, and St. John the Almsgiver.* Oxford: Blackwell, 1948.
Dawkins, Richard McGillivray. *Monks of Athos: Life and Legends of the Holy Mountain.* London: G. Allen & Unwin, 1936.
de Halleux, André. "Problèmes de méthode dans les discussions sur l'eschatologie au Concile de Ferrare et de Florence." In Giuseppe Alberigo, ed. *Christian Unity: The Council of Ferrara-Florence 1438/9.* Leuven: Leuven University Press, 1991, 251–301.
de la Casa, Carlos, and Elena de la Casa. "La idea del Purgatorio y Bernardo de Claraval." *Revista Cistercium* 223 (April–June 2001): 343–56.
de Voragine, Jacobus. *The Golden Legend: Readings on the Saints.* Trans. William Granger Ryan. Princeton, NJ: Princeton University Press, 1993.
Deferrari, Roy, ed. *Sources of Catholic Dogma.* St. Louis: Herder, 1955.
Delacroix-Besnier, Claudine. *Les dominicains et la chrétienté grecque aux XIVe et XVe siècle.* Rome: Ecole française de Rome, 1997.
Delacroix-Besnier, Claudine. "Mendicant Friars between Byzantium and Rome: Legates, Missionaries and Polemists (XIIIth–XVth Centuries)." In Falko Daim, Christian Gastgeber, Dominik Heher, and Claudia Rapp, eds. *Menschen, Bilder, Sprache, Dinge Wege der Kommunikation zwischen Byzanz und dem Westen 2: Menschen und Worte.* Mainz: Verlag des Römisch-Germanischen Zentralmuseums, 2018, 277–90.
Delobel, J. "1 Cor 11:2–16: Towards a Coherent Explanation." In Albert Vanhoye, ed. *L'apôtre Paul: Personalité, style et conception du ministère.* Leuven: Leuven University Press, 1986, 369–89.
Demacopoulos, George. "The Popular Reception of the Council of Florence in Constantinople (1439–1453)." *St. Vladimir's Theological Quarterly* 43 (1999): 37–53.
Demetracopoulos, Andronicus. *Ἐκκλησιαστικὴ Βιβλιοθήκη.* Vol. 1. Leipzig, 1866.

Demetracopoulos, John, and Charalambos Dendrinos, eds. *When East met West: The Reception of Latin Theological and Philosophical Thought in Late Byzantium—Acts of the Institute of Classical Studies International Byzantine Colloquium (London, 11-12 June 2012)*. Bari: Istituto di Teologia ecumenico-patristica, 2013.

Demurger, Alain. "The Beard and the Habit in the Templars' Trial: Membership, Rupture, Resistance." In Helen Nicholson and Jochen Burgtorf, eds. *Templars, the Hospitallers and the Crusades: Essays in Homage to Alan J. Forey*. London: Routledge, 2020, 129-37.

Derrett, J. Duncan M. "Religious Hair." *Man*, NS 8 (1973): 100-103.

Dewick, E. C. *Primitive Christian Eschatology*. Cambridge: Cambridge University Press, 1912.

Dibelius, Martin, and Hans Conzelmann. *The Pastoral Epistles: A Commentary on the Pastoral Epistles*. Philadelphia: Fortress Press, 1972.

Diekamp, F. "Johannes von Damaskus 'Über die im Glauben Entschlafenen.'" *Römische Quartalschrift* 17 (1903): 371-82.

Dienes, Mary. "Eastern Missions of the Hungarian Dominicans in the First Half of the Thirteenth Century." In James Ryan, ed. *The Spiritual Expansion of Medieval Latin Christendom: The Asian Missions*. London: Routledge, 2016.

Dio Chrysostom. *Discourses*. Vol. 3. Trans. J. W. Cohoon. Cambridge, MA: Harvard University Press, 1995.

Dischner, Margit. *Humbert von Silva Candida: Werk und Wirkung des lothringischen Reformmönches*. Neuried: Ars Una, 1996.

Dix, Gregory. *The Shape of the Liturgy*. London: Dacre Press, 1945.

Dockx, Stanislas. *Chronologies néotestamentaires et vie de l'église primitive: Recherches exégétiques*. Paris-Gembloux, Duculot, 1976.

Dodd, C. H. *Historical Tradition in the Fourth Gospel*. New York: Cambridge University Press, 1963.

Dodd, C. H. *The Parables of the Kingdom*. New York: Scribners, 1961.

Donahue, John, and Daniel J. Harrington. *The Gospel of Mark*. Sacra Pagina 2. Collegeville, MN: Liturgical Press, 2002.

Dondaine, Antoine. "Contra Graecos: Premiers écrits polémiques des dominicains d'Orient." *Archivum Fratrum Praedicatorum* 21 (1951): 320-446.

Dondaine, Antoine. "Hugues Éthérien et Léon Toscan." *Archives d'histoire doctrinale et littéraire du Moyen Âge* 19 (1952): 67-134.

Dondaine, Antoine. "Nicolas de Cotrone et la sources du *Contra errores Graecorum* de Saint Thomas." *Divus Thomas* 29 (1950): 313-40.

Doran, Robert. *2 Maccabees*. Minneapolis, MN: Fortress Press, 2012.

Doukas. *Decline and Fall of Byzantium to the Ottoman Turks (Historia Turco-Byzantina)*. Trans. Harry Magoulias. Detroit: Wayne State University Press, 1975.

Drummond, James. "The Fourth Gospel and the Quartodecimans." *American Journal of Theology* 1.3 (1897): 601-57.

Du Cange, Charles, et al., eds. *Glossarium mediae et infimae latinitatis, Tomos sextus*. Niort: Favre, 1886.

Dugauquier, Jean-Albert, ed. *Summa De Sacramentis et Animae Consiliis*. Louvain: Louvain University Press, 1957.

Dugmore, Clifford. "A Note on the Quartodecimans." *Studia Patristica* 4 (1961): 411-21.

Dunn, Geoffrey, ed. *Tertullian*. Early Church Fathers. London: Routledge, 2004.
Dunn, James D. G. *Jesus Remembered: Christianity in the Making*. Vol. 1. Grand Rapids, MI: Eerdmans, 2003.
Dunn, James D. G. *Unity and Diversity in the New Testament: An Inquiry into the Character of Earliest Christianity*. London: SCM, 1977.
Dunn, James D. G. "The Washing of Disciples' Feet in John 13:1–20." *Zeitschrift für die Neutestamentliche Wissenschaft* 61 (1970): 247–52.
Dunn, Marilyn. "Gregory the Great, the Vision of Fursey, and the Origins of Purgatory." *Peritia* 14 (2000): 238–54.
Dupuy, Bernard. "Le dialogue Rutki-Moghila en vue de l'union des Ruthènes (1624–1647)." *Istina* 35 (1990): 50–75.
Durandus, Guillaume. *Rationale Divinorum Officiorum*. Vol. 2. Trans. Janet Gentles. Bedford: Paschal Light, 2019.
Dutton, Paul Edward. "Charlemagne's Mustache." In *Charlemagne's Mustache and Other Cultural Clusters of a Dark Age*. New York: Palgrave Macmillan, 2004, 3–42.
Dvornik, Francis. *Byzantium and the Roman Primacy*. New York: Fordham University Press, 1966.
Dvornik, Francis. *L'affaire de Photios dans la littérature latine du Moyen Age*. Prague: Institut Kondakov, 1938.
Dvornik, Francis. *Photian and Byzantine Ecclesiastical Studies*. London: Variorum Reprints, 1974.
Dvornik, Francis. *The Photian Schism: History and Legend*. Cambridge: Cambridge University Press, 1948.
Dykmans, Marc. *Les Sermons de Jean XXII sur la vision béatifique*. Miscellanea Historiae Pontificiae 34. Rome: Presses de l'Université Grégorienne, 1973.
Edsall, Benjamin. "Greco-Roman Costume and Paul's Fraught Argument in 1 Corinthians 11.2–16." *Journal of Greco-Roman Christianity and Judaism* 9 (2013): 132–46.
Edwards, Graham Robert. "Purgatory: Birth or Evolution." *Journal of Ecclesiastical History* 36 (1985): 634–46.
Egan, M. F. "The Two Theories or Purgatory." *Irish Theological Quarterly* 17 (1951): 24–34.
Elliot, J. K., ed. *The Apocryphal New Testament: A Collection of Apocryphal Christian Literature in English Translation*. Oxford: Oxford University Press, 2005.
Elliott, Charles. "The Schism and Its Elimination in Humbert of Rome's *Opusculum Tripartitum*." *Greek Orthodox Theological Review* 34 (1989): 71–83.
Elliott, John. *1 Peter*. Anchor Bible 37b. New Haven, CT: Yale University Press, 2000.
Ellis, G. M., and Peter Munz, trans. and eds. *Boso's Life of Alexander III*. Oxford: Blackwell, 1973.
Elsner, Jaś. *Imperial Rome and Christian Triumph: The Art of the Roman Empire, AD 100–450*. Oxford: Oxford University Press, 1998.
Emerton, Ephraim, ed. *The Correspondence of Pope Gregory VII: Selected Letters from the Registrum*. New York: Columbia University Press, 1990.
Emminghaus, Johannes. *The Eucharist: Essence, Form, Celebration*. Trans. Matthew O'Connell. Collegeville, MN: Liturgical Press, 1978.
English, Adam. "Mediated, Mediation, Unmediated: 1 Corinthians 15:29: The History of Interpretation, and the Current State of Biblical Studies." *Review & Expositor* 99 (2002): 419–28.

Eno, Robert. "The Fathers and the Cleansing Fire." *Irish Theological Quarterly* 53 (1987): 184–202.

Ephrem the Syrian. *Commentary on Tatian's Diatessaron: An English Translation of Chester Beatty Syriac MS 709*. Trans. Carmel McCarthy. Oxford: Oxford University Press, 1993.

Ephrem the Syrian. *Hymns*. Trans. Kathleen McVey. New York: Paulist Press, 1989.

Ephrem the Syrian. *Hymns on Paradise*. Trans. Sebastian Brock. Crestwood, NY: St. Vladimir's Seminary Press, 1990.

Ephrem the Syrian. *Hymns on the Unleavened Bread*. Trans. J. Edward Walters. Piscataway, NJ: Gorgias Press, 2012.

Epiphanius of Salamis. *Ancoratus*. Trans. Young Richard Kim. FC 128. Washington, DC: Catholic University of America Press, 2014.

Epiphanius of Salamis. *Panarion of Epiphanius of Salamis, Book I (Sects 1–46)*. 2nd ed. Trans. Frank Williams. Leiden: Brill, 2009.

Epiphanius of Salamis. *Panarion of Epiphanius of Salamis, Book II and III (Sects 47–80, De Fide)*. 2nd ed. Trans. Frank Williams. Leiden: Brill, 2013.

Erickson, John. "Leavened and Unleavened: Some Theological Implications of the Schism of 1054." In John Erickson, ed. *The Challenge of Our Past*. Crestwood, NY: St. Vladimir's Seminary Press, 1991, 133–55.

Ernst, Joseph. *Die Lehre des hl. Paschasius Radbertus von der Eucharistie: Mit besonderer berücksichtigung der Stellung des hl. Rhabanus Maurus und des Ratramnus zu derselben*. Freiburg: Herder, 1896.

Eusebius of Caesarea. *De sollemnitate Paschali*. In Angelo Mai, ed. *Novae Patrum Bibliotheca* 4. Rome, 1847, 209–16.

Eustathios of Thessaloniki. *The Capture of Thessaloniki: A Translation with Introduction and Commentary*. Trans. John R. Melville-Jones. Canberra: Australian Association for Byzantine Studies, 1988.

Evangelatou, Maria. "Krater of Nectar and Altar of the Bread of Life: The Theotokos as Provider of the Eucharist in Byzantine Culture." In Thomas Arentzen and Mary Cunningham, eds. *The Reception of the Virgin in Byzantium: Marian Narratives in Texts and Images*. Cambridge: Cambridge University Press, 2019, 77–119.

Evans, Craig. *Mark 8:27–16:20*. Word Biblical Commentary 34b. Nashville: Thomas Nelson, 2001.

Every, George. "Peter Lombard and II Lyons." *Eastern Churches Review* 9 (1977): 85–90.

Every, George. "Toll Gates on the Air Way." *Eastern Churches Review* 8 (1976): 139–50.

Fearns, James. "Peter von Bruis und die religiöse Bewegung des 12. Jahrhunderts." *Archiv für Kulturgeschichte* 48 (1966): 311–35.

Fedalto, Giorgio. *La Chiesa Latina in Oriente*. Verona: Mazziana, 2006.

Festugière, André-Jean. *Vie de Théodore de Sykéon*. Subsidia hagiographica 48. Brussels: Société des Bollandistes, 1970.

Finegan, Jack. *Die Überlieferung der Leidens- und Auferstehungsgeschichte Jesu*. Giessen: A. Töpelmann, 1934.

Finney, Mark. "Honour, Head-Coverings and Headship: 1 Corinthians 11:2–16 in Its Social Context." *Journal for the Study of the New Testament* 33 (2010): 31–58.

Firey, Abigail. *A New History of Penance*. Leiden: Brill, 2008.

Fischer, Joseph. *Studien zum Todesgedanken in der alten Kirche*. Munich: Hueber, 1954.

Fitzmeyr, Joseph. *Acts of the Apostles*. Anchor Bible 31. New York: Doubleday, 1998.

Fitzmeyr, Joseph. *First Corinthians*. Anchor Bible 32. New Haven, CT: Yale University Press, 2008.

Fitzmeyr, Joseph. *The Gospel According to Luke I–IX*. Anchor Bible 28. New York: Doubleday, 1981.

Fitzmeyr, Joseph. *The Gospel According to Luke X–XXIV*. Anchor Bible 28a. New York: Doubleday, 1985.

Flavius Josephus. *The New Complete Works of Josephus*. Trans. William Whiston. Grand Rapids, MI: Kregel Publications, 1999.

Florovsky, Georges. "The Last Things and the Last Events." In Georges Florovsky, ed. *The Collected Works of Georges Florovsky*. Vol. 3: *Creation and Redemption*. Belmont, MA: Nordland, 1976, 243–65.

Foot, Sarah. "Anglo-Saxon 'Purgatory.'" *Studies in Church History* 45 (2009): 87–96.

Fornasari, Massimo, ed. *Collectio Canonum in V Libris*. CCCM 6. Turnholt: Brepols, 1970.

Fortescue, Adrian. *The Mass: A Study of the Roman Liturgy*. New York: Longmans, Green, 1922.

Fortescue, Adrian. *The Orthodox Eastern Church*. London: Catholic Truth Society, 1908.

Foschini, Bernard M. *"Those Who Are Baptized for the Dead," 1 Cor. 15:29: An Exegetical Historical Dissertation*. Worcester, MA: Heffernan, 1951.

France, R. T. *The Gospel of Matthew*. New International Commentary on the New Testament. Grand Rapids, MI: Eerdmans, 2007.

Franchi, Antonio, ed. *Il Concilio II di Lione (1274) secondo la ordinatio concilii generalis Lugdunensis*. Studi e Testi Francescani 33. Rome: Edizioni Francescane, 1965.

Frayer-Griggs, Daniel. "Jesus and the Last Supper." *Reviews in Religion & Theology* 23 (April 2016): 161.

Frayer-Griggs, Daniel. *Saved through Fire: The Fiery Ordeal in New Testament Eschatology*. Eugene, OR: Pickwick Publications, 2016.

Frazee, Charles. "The Christian Church in Cilician Armenia: Its Relations with Rome and Constantinople to 1198." *Church History* 45 (1976): 166–84.

Funk, Robert. "Beyond Criticism in Quest of Literacy: The Parable of the Leaven." *Interpretation* 25 (1971): 149–70.

Gadenz, Pablo. *The Gospel of Luke*. Catholic Commentary on Sacred Scripture. Grand Rapids, MI: Baker Academic, 2018.

Gahbauer, Reinhard, ed. *Gegen den Primat des Papstes: Studien zu Niketas Seides*. Munich: Verlag Uni-Druck, 1975.

Galavaris, George. *Bread and the Liturgy. The Symbolism of Early Christian and Byzantine Bread Stamps*. Madison: University of Wisconsin Press, 1970.

Gallagher, Clarence. *Church Law and Church Order in Rome and Byzantium: A Comparative Study*. Birmingham Byzantine and Ottoman Studies 8. Aldershot: Ashgate, 2002.

Galtier, Paul. "La Date de la Didascalie des Apôtres." *Revue d'histoire ecclésiastique* 42 (1947): 315–51.

Gardner, Paul. *1 Corinthians*. Zondervan Exegetical Commentary on the New Testament. Grand Rapids, MI: Zondervan, 2018.

Gautier, Paul. "Jean V l'Oxite, patriarche d'Antioche: Notice biographique." *Revue des études byzantines* 22 (1964): 132–35.

Gautier, Paul, ed. *Théophylacte d'Achrida: Discours, traités, poésies. Introduction, texte, traduction et notes*. Thessaloniki: Association de Recherches Byzantines, 1980.

Gaventa, Beverly. *The Acts of the Apostles*. Nashville, TN: Abingdon Press, 2003.
Gavin, F. "The Sleep of the Soul in the Early Syriac Church." *Journal of the American Oriental Society* 40 (1920): 103–20.
Gay, Jules. *D'Italie méridionale et l'empire Byzantin 867–1071*. Paris: Frontemoing, 1904.
Gay, Jules. *Les Registres de Nicolas III*. Paris: Bibliothèque des Ecoles Françaises d'Athènes et de Rome, 1904.
Geanakoplos, Deno John. *Byzantium: Church, Society and Civilization Seen through Contemporary Eyes*. Chicago: University of Chicago Press, 1984.
Geanakoplos, Deno John. *Byzantine East and Latin West*. New York: Harper and Row, 1966.
Geanakoplos, Deno John. *Constantinople and the West*. Madison: University of Wisconsin Press, 1989.
Geanakoplos, Deno John. "The Council of Florence (1438–1439) and the Problem of Union between the Greek and Latin Churches." *Church History* 24 (1955): 324–46.
Geanakoplos, Deno John. *Emperor Michael Palaeologus and the West*. Cambridge, MA: Harvard University Press, 1959.
Geanakoplos, Deno John. *Interaction of the Sibling Byzantine and Western Cultures in the Middle Ages and Italian Renaissance (330–1600)*. New Haven, CT: Yale University Press, 1976.
Geanakoplos, Deno John. "Michael VIII Palaeologus and the Union of Lyons (1274)." *Harvard Theological Review* 46 (1953): 79–90.
Geanakoplos, Deno John. "An Orthodox View of the Councils of Basel (1431–49) and Florence (1438–39) as Paradigm for the Study of Modern Ecumenical Councils." *Greek Orthodox Theological Review* 30 (1985): 311–34.
Geffert, Bryn, and Theofanis Stavrou, eds. *Eastern Orthodox Christianity: The Essential Texts*. New Haven, CT: Yale University Press, 2016.
Gemeinhardt, Peter. "Joachim the Theologian: Trinitarian Speculation and Doctrinal Debate." In Matthias Riedl, ed. *A Companion to Joachim of Fiore*. Leiden: Brill, 2018, 41–87.
Geoffrey de Villehardouin. "Chronicles of the Fourth Crusade and the Conquest of Constantinople." In Margaret Shaw, ed. *Chronicles of the Crusades*. New York: Penguin, 1972, 1–136.
Germanus of Constantinople. *On the Divine Liturgy*. Trans. Paul Meyendorff. Crestwood, NY: St. Vladimir's Seminary Press, 1984.
Giannoni, Carl. *Paulinus II, Patriarch von Aquileia: Ein Beitrag zur Kirchengeschichte Österreichs im Zeitalter Karls des Grossen*. Vienna, 1896.
Gibbon, Edward. *The Decline and Fall of the Roman Empire*. Vol. 3. New York: Modern Library, 1995.
Gigalski, Bernhard. *Bruno, Bischof von Segni, Abt von Monte-Cassino (1049–1123): Sein Leben und seine Schriften*. Münster: Verlag von Heinrich Schöningh, 1898.
Gill, David W. J. "The Importance of Roman Portraiture for Head-Coverings in 1 Corinthians 11:2–16." *Tyndale Bulletin* 41 (1990): 245–60.
Gill, Joseph. *Byzantium and the Papacy, 1198–1400*. New Brunswick, NJ: Rutgers University Press, 1979.
Gill, Joseph. *Church Union: Rome and Byzantium, 1204–1453*. London: Variorum Reprints, 1979.

Gill, Joseph. "The Church Union of the Council of Lyons (1274) Portrayed in Greek Documents." *Orientalia Christiana Periodica* 40 (1974): 5–45.
Gill, Joseph. *Constance et Bâle-Florence*. Paris: Éditions de l'Orante, 1965.
Gill, Joseph. *The Council of Florence*. Cambridge: Cambridge University Press, 1959.
Gill, Joseph. "Eleven Emperors of Byzantium Seek Union with the Church of Rome." *Eastern Churches Review* 9 (1977): 72–84.
Gill, Joseph. *Eugene IV: Pope of Christian Unity*. Westminster: Newman Press, 1961.
Gill, Joseph. "Franks, Venetians, and Pope Innocent III." *Studi Veneziani* 3 (1970): 85–106.
Gill, Joseph. "John Beccus, Patriarch of Constantinople." *Byzantina* 7 (1975): 251–66.
Gill, Joseph. *Personalities of the Council of Florence*. Oxford: Basil Blackwell, 1964.
Gill, Joseph, ed. *Quae supersunt Actorum Graecorum Concilii Florentini: Res Ferrariae gestae*. CF 5.1.1. Rome: Pontifical Oriental Institute, 1953.
Gill, Joseph, ed. *Quae supersunt Actorum Graecorum Concilii Florentini: Res Florentinae gestae*. CF 5.2.2. Rome: Pontifical Oriental Institute, 1953.
Gill, Joseph. "An Unpublished Letter of Germanos, Patriarch of Constantinople." *Byzantion* 44 (1974): 138–51.
Glaber, Rodulfus. *The Five Books of the Histories*. John France and Neithard Bulst, eds. and trans. Oxford: Clarendon Press, 1990.
Glorieux, Paul. "Les Deflorationes de Werner de Saint-Blaise." In *Mélanges Joseph de Ghellinek*. Vol. 2. Gembloux: J. Duculot, 1951, 699–721.
Glykas, Michael. Εἰς τὰς ἀπορίας τῆς Θείας Γραφῆς κεφάλαια. In S. Eustratiadis, ed. Athens and Alexandria, 1906 and 1912.
Gnilka, Joachim. *Ist 1 Kor 3, 10–15 ein Schriftzeugnis für das Fegfeuer? Eine exegetisch-historische Untersuchung*. Düsseldorf: Triltsch, 1955.
Gnilka, Joachim. *Jesus of Nazareth*. Trans. Siegfried Schatzmann. Peabody, MA: Hendrickson, 1997.
Goldstein, Jonathan. *II Maccabees*. Anchor Bible 41a. New Haven, CT: Yale University Press, 1983.
Golubovich, Girolamo. "Cenni storici su Fra Giovanni Parastron." *Bessarione* 10 (1906): 295–304.
Golubovich, Girolamo. "Disputatio Latinorum et Graecorum seu Relatio Apocrisariorum Gregorii IX de gestis Nicaeae in Bithynia et Nymphaeae in Lydia 1234." *Archivum Franciscanum Historicum* 12 (1919): 418–70.
Gonzalez, Eliezer. *The Fate of the Dead in Early Third Century North African Christianity: The Passion of Perpetua and Felicitas and Tertullian*. Tübingen: Mohr Siebeck, 2014.
Goodacre, Mark. "Does Περιβόλαιον Mean 'Testicle' in 1 Corinthians 11:15?" *Journal of Biblical Literature* 130 (2011): 391–96.
Gowing, Thomas. *The Philosophy of Beards*. London: British Library, 2014.
Graber, Andre. *Christian Iconography: A Study of Its Origins*. Princeton, NJ: Princeton University Press, 1968.
Gray, George. *A Critical and Exegetical Commentary of Numbers*. International Critical Commentary. New York: Charles Scribner's Sons, 1906.
Greenblatt, Stephen. *Hamlet in Purgatory*. Princeton, NJ: Princeton University Press, 2013.
Gregory of Nazianzus. *Festal Orations*. Trans. Nonna Verna Harrison. Crestwood, NY: St. Vladimir's Seminary Press, 2008.

Gregory of Nazianzus and Ambrose of Milan. *Funeral Orations*. Trans. Leo McCauley, John Sullivan, Martin McGuire, and Roy Deferrari. FC 22. Washington, DC: Catholic University of America Press, 1953.
Gregory of Nyssa. *Ascetical Works*. Trans. Virginia Woods Callahan. FC 58. Washington, DC: Catholic University of America, 1967.
Gregory of Nyssa. *Catechetical Discourse: A Handbook for Catechesis*. Trans. Ignatius Green. Crestwood, NY: St. Vladimir's Seminary Press, 2019.
Gregory of Tours. *The Glory of the Martyrs*. Trans. Raymond Van Dam. Liverpool: Liverpool University Press, 1988.
Gregory of Tours. *History of the Franks*. Trans. Lewis Thorpe. New York: Penguin, 1976.
Gregory the Great. *The Book of Pastoral Rule*. Trans. George Demacopoulos. Crestwood, NY: St. Vladimir's Seminary Press, 2007.
Gregory the Great. *Dialogues*. Trans. Odo John Zimmerman. FC 39. Washington, DC: Catholic University of America Press, 1959.
Gregory the Great. *Forty Gospel Homilies*. Trans. Dom David Hurst. CS 123. Kalamazoo, MI: Cistercian Publications, 1990.
Gregory the Great. *The Letters of Gregory the Great: Books 1–4*. Trans. John R. C. Martyn. Toronto: Pontifical Institute of Medieval Studies, 2004.
Gregory the Great. *The Letters of Gregory the Great: Books 5–9*. Trans. John R. C. Martyn. Toronto: Pontifical Institute of Medieval Studies, 2004.
Gregory the Great. *Moral Reflections on the Book of Job*. Vol. 2 (Books 6–10). Trans. Brian Kerns. Collegeville, MN: Liturgical Press, 2015.
Gregory the Great. *Morals on the Book of Job*. Vol. 1. Trans. Edward Pusey, John Keble, and John Henry Newman. Jackson, MI: Ex Fontibus, 2012.
Greshake, Gisbert, ed. *Ungewisses Jenseits? Himmel, Hölle, Fegefeuer*. Düsseldorf: Patmos, 1986.
Grimlaicus. *Rules for Solitaries*. Trans. Andrew Thornton. CS 200. Kalamazoo, MI: Cistercian Publications, 2011.
Grosse, Jeremiah. "Abbot Baldwin of Ford on the Sacrament of the Altar." *Downside Review* 127 (2009): 269–78.
Grossi, Vittorino. "La Pasqua quartodecimana e il significato della croce nel II secolo." *Augustinianum* 16 (1976): 557–71.
Grumel, V. "Autour de voyage de Pierre Grossolanus, archevêque de Milan, à Constantinople en 1112." *Echos d'Orient* 32 (1933): 22–33.
Grumel, V. "Les Préliminarires du schism de Michel Cérulaire ou la question romaine avant 1054." *Revue des études byzantines* 10 (1953): 5–23.
Grumett, David. *Material Eucharist*. Oxford: Oxford University Press, 2016.
Gudziak, Borys. *Crisis and Reform: The Kyivan Metropolitanate, the Patriarchate of Constantinople, and the Genesis of the Union of Brest*. Cambridge, MA: Harvard University Press, 1998.
Guelich, Robert. *Mark 1–8:26*. Word Biblical Commentary 34a. Dallas, TX: Word Book Publishers, 1989.
Guibert of Nogent. *The Deeds of God through the Franks: A Translation of Guibert de Nogent's Gesta Dei per Francos*. Trans. Robert Levine. Woodbridge, Suffolk: Boydell Press, 1997.

Guido of Monte Rochen. *Handbook for Curates: A Late Medieval Manual for Pastoral Ministry*. Trans. Anne Thayer. Washington, DC: Catholic University of America Press, 2011.

Guillaume de Tyr. *L'Estoire de Eracles, empereur, et la conqueste de la Terre d'Outre-Mer, c'est la continuation de "l'Estoire" de Guillaume, arcevesque de Sur.—Continuation de Guillaume de Tyr, de 1229 à 1261.* Vol. 2. Paris: Académie des inscriptions et belles-lettres, 1859.

Gunther of Pairis. *The Capture of Constantinople: The Hystoria Constantinopolitana of Gunther of Pairis*. Trans. Alfred Andrea. Philadelphia: University of Pennsylvania Press, 1997.

Haenchen, Ernst. *Acts of the Apostles: A Commentary*. Trans. Bernard Noble and Gerald Shinn. Philadelphia, PA: Westminster Press, 1971.

Haenchen, Ernst. *John 1: A Commentary on the Gospel of John Chapters 1-6*. Trans. Robert W. Funk. Philadelphia: Fortress Press, 1984.

Haenchen, Ernst. *John 2: A Commentary on the Gospel of John Chapters 7-21*. Trans. Robert W. Funk. Philadelphia: Fortress Press, 1984.

Hagner, Donald. *Matthew 1-13*. Word Biblical Commentary 33a. Dallas, TX: Word Books, 1993.

Hagner, Donald. *Matthew 14-28*. Word Biblical Commentary 33b. Waco, TX: Word Books, 1995.

Hallpike, Christopher. "Social Hair." *Man* 4 (1969): 256-64.

Halučynskyj, Theodosius, and Meletius M. Wojnar, eds. *Acta Alexandri PP VI (1254-1261)*. Rome: Pontificia Università Gregoriana, 1966.

Hamilton, Bernard. *The Latin Church in the Crusader States*. London: Routledge, 2016.

Hamilton, John. "The Chronology of the Crucifixion and the Passover." *Churchman* 106 (1992): 323-38.

Hammond, C. E. *The Saint James Liturgy*. Piscataway, NJ: Gorgias Press, 2009.

Harrington, Daniel. *The Gospel of Matthew*. Sacra Pagina 1. Collegeville, MN: Liturgical Press, 1991.

Harrington, Wilfrid. *Revelation*. Sacra Pagina 16. Collegeville, MN: Liturgical Press, 1993.

Harris, Jonathan. *Byzantium and the Crusades*. New York: Palgrave, 2003.

Hart, David Bentley. "The Myth of Schism." In Francesca Aran Murphy and Christopher Asprey, eds. *Ecumenism Today: The Universal Church in the 21st Century*. London: Ashgate, 2008, 95-106.

Hart, David Bentley. "Saint Origen." *First Things* (October 2015): 72.

Hart, David Bentley. *That All Shall Be Saved: Heaven, Hell, and Universal Salvation*. New Haven, CT: Yale University Press, 2019.

Hartley, John. *Leviticus*. Word Biblical Commentary 4. Dallas, TX: Word Books, 1992.

Hartmann, Wilfred, and Kenneth Pennington. *The History of Byzantine and Eastern Canon Law to 1500*. Washington, DC: Catholic University of America Press, 2012.

Hartnup, Karen. *"On the Beliefs of the Greeks": Leo Allatios and Popular Orthodoxy*. Leiden: Brill, 2004.

Haskins, Charles. "Leo Tuscus." *English Historical Review* 33 (1918): 492-96.

Hatzaki, Myrto. *Beauty and the Male Body in Byzantium Perceptions and Representations in Art and Text*. New York: Palgrave Macmillan, 2009.

Hayes, Zachary. *Four Views on Hell*. Grand Rapids, MI: Zondervan, 1996.

Head, Constance. "Physical Descriptions of the Emperors in Byzantine Historical Writing." *Byzantion* 50 (1980): 226–40.
Heffernan, Thomas J., ed. *The Passion of Perpetua and Felicity*. Oxford: Oxford University Press, 2012.
Heisenberg, August, ed. *Georgii Acropolitae Opera*. Vol. 2. Lipsiae: Teubner, 1903.
Heisenberg, August, ed. *Neue Quellen zur Geschichte des lateinischen Kaisertums und der Kirchenunion 1: Der Epitaphios des Nikolaos Mesarites auf seinen Bruder Johannes*. Munich: Verlag der bayer. Akad. der Wissenschaften, 1922.
Heisenberg, August, ed. *Neue Quellen zur Geschichte des lateinischen Kaisertums und der Kirchenunion 2: Die Unionsverhandlungen vom 30. August 1206*. Munich: Verlag der bayer. Akad. der Wissenschaften, 1923.
Heisenberg, August, ed. *Neue Quellen zur Geschichte des lateinischen Kaisertums und der Kirchenunion 3: Der Bericht des Nikolaos Mesarites über die politischen und kirchlichen Ereignisse des Jahres 1214*. Munich: Verlag der bayer. Akad. der Wissenschaften, 1923.
Heiser, Lothar. *Die Responsa ad consulta Bulgarorum des Papstes Nikolaus I. (858–867): Ein Zeugnis päpstlicher Hirtensorge und ein Dokument unterschiedlicher Entwicklungen in den Kirchen von Rom und Konstantinopel*. Trier: Paulinus-Verlag, 1979.
Henderson, Ernest, ed. *Select Historical Documents of the Middle Ages*. London: George Bell and Sons, 1910.
Hengel, Martin. *Acts and the History of Earliest Christianity*. Philadelphia: Fortress Press, 1980.
Hengel, Martin. *Studies in the Gospel of Mark*. Trans. J. Bowden. Philadelphia: Fortress Press, 1985.
Hengel, Martin, and Anna Marie Schwemer. *Jesus und das Judentum*. Tübingen: Mohr Siebeck, 2007.
Hergenröther, Joseph, ed. *Monumenta graeca ad Photium eiusque Historiam Pertinentia*. Ratisbon, 1869.
Hergenröther, Joseph. *Photius, Patriarch von Constantinopel: Sein Leben, seine Schriften und das griechische Schisma* 1. Regensburg: Manz, 1867.
Herman, Emil. "I legati inviati da Leoni IX nel 1054 a Constantinopoli." *Orientalia Christiana Periodica* 8 (1942): 209–18.
Herodotus. *Histories Books 3–4*. Trans. A. D. Godley. New York: G.P. Putnam's Sons, 1928.
Hershman, Paul. "Hair, Sex and Dirt." *Man* 9 (1974): 274–98.
Herter, Hans. "Effeminatus." *Reallexikon für Antike und Christentum* 4 (1959): 620–50.
Higgitt, John. "The Iconography of St Peter in Anglo-Saxon England and St Cuthbert's Coffin." In Gerald Bonner, D. W. Rollason, and Clare Stancliffe, eds. *St. Cuthbert, His Cult and His Community: To AD 1200*. Woodbridge, Suffolk: Boydell Press, 1989, 267–86.
Hilary of Poitiers. *Commentary on Matthew*. Trans. D. H. Williams. FC 125. Washington, DC: Catholic University of America Press, 2012.
Hilary of Poitiers. *The Trinity*. Trans. Stephen McKenna. FC 25. Washington, DC: Catholic University of America Press, 1954.
Hildegard of Bingen. *The Book of the Rewards of Life: Liber Vitae Meritorum*. Trans. Bruce Hozeski. Oxford: Oxford University Press, 1997.
Hilferty, Mary Cesilia. "The *liber adversus Waldensium sectam* of Bernard, Abbot of Fontcaude: A Translation with Critical Introduction." MA thesis, Catholic University of America, 1963.

Hinterberger, Martin, and Christopher Schabel. "Andreas Chrysoberges' Dialogue against Mark Eugenikos." In Alison Frazier and Patrick Nold, eds. *Essays in Renaissance Thought and Letters: In Honor of John Monfasani*. Leiden: Brill, 2015, 492–545.

Hinterberger, Martin, and Christopher Schabel, eds. *Greeks, Latins, and Intellectual History 1204–1500*. Leuven: Peeters, 2011.

Hobart, Michelle, ed. *Companion to Sardinian History, 500–1500*. Leiden: Brill, 2017.

Hoeck, Johannes M., and Raimund J. Loenertz. *Nikolaos-Nektarios von Otranto Abt von Casole: Beiträge zur Geschichte der ost-westlichen Beziehungen unter Innozenz III. und Friedrich II*. Ettal: Buch-Kunstverlag, 1965.

Hoehner, Harold. *Chronological Aspects of the Life of Christ*. Grand Rapids, MI: Zondervan, 1977.

Hoffmann, R. Joseph. *Porphyry's "Against the Christians": The Literary Remains*. Amherst, NY: Prometheus Books, 1994.

Hofmann, Georg, ed. *Andreas de Santacroce, advocatus consistorialis, Acta Latina Concilii Florentini*. CF 6. Rome: Pontifical Oriental Institute, 1955.

Hofmann, Georg. *Griechische Patriarchen und Römische Päpste: Untersuchungen und texte*. Rome: Pont. Institutum Orientalium Studiorum, 1932.

Hofmann, Georg. "Papst Gregor VII und der christliche Osten." *Studi Gregoriani* 1 (1947): 169–81.

Hofmann, Georg. "Papst und Patrirach unter Kaiser Manuel I Komnenos." *Epeteris Etaireias Byzantinon Spoudon* 23 (1953): 74–82.

Hofmann, Georg. "Patriarch von Nikaia Manuel II an Papst Innozenz IV." *Orientalia Christiana Periodica* 19 (1953): 59–70.

Hofmann, Georg. "Wiedervereinigung der Ruthenen." *Orientalia Christiana* 3 (1925): 139–42.

Hofmann, Georg, and Ludovico Petit, eds. *De Purgatorio disputationes in Concilio Florentino habitae*. CF 8.2. Rome: Pontifical Oriental Institute, 1969.

Hofmeister, Philipp. "Der Streit um des Priesters Bart." *Zeitschrift für Kirchengeschichte*, ser. 3.42 (1943–44): 72–94.

Holl, Karl. "Ein Bruchstück aus Einem Bisher Unbekannten Brief des Epiphanius." In Rudolf Bultmann, ed. *Festgabe für Adolf Jülicher*. Tübingen: J.C.B. Mohr, 1927, 159–89.

Holtzman, Walther. "Die Unionsverhandlungen zwischen Kaiser Alexios I und Papst Urban II im Jahre 1089." *Byzantinische Zeitschrift* 28 (1928): 38–67.

Hopkins, Jasper, and Herbert Richardson, eds. *Complete Philosophical and Theological Treatises of Anselm of Canterbury*. Minneapolis, MN: Arthur J. Banning Press, 2000.

Horn, Hans-Jürgen. "Ignis aeternus: Une interprétation morale du feu éternel chez Origène." *Revue des Études Grecques* 82 (1969): 76–88.

Hossfeld, Frank Lothar, and Erich Zenger. *Psalms 2: A Commentary on Psalms 51–100*. Trans. L. M. Maloney. Minneapolis, MN: Fortress Press, 2005.

Houben, Hubert. *Roger II of Sicily: A Ruler between East and West*. Cambridge: Cambridge University Press, 2002.

Houghton, H. A. G. "The Biblical Text of Jerome's Commentary on Galatians." *Journal of Theological Studies* 65 (2014): 1–24.

Howard, J. K. "Baptism for the Dead: A Study of 1 Corinthians 15:29." *Evangelical Quarterly* 37 (1965): 137–41.

Huber, Wolfgang. *Passah und Ostern: Untersuchungen zur Osterfeier der alten Kirche.* Beihefte zur Zeitschrift für die neutestamentliche Wissenschaft 35. Berlin: Töpelmann, 1969.

Hughes, Lindsey. "A Beard Is a Necessary Burden: Peter I's Laws on Shaving and Their Roots in Early Russia." In Roger Bartlett and Lindsey Hughes, eds. *Russian Society and Culture and the Long Eighteenth Century.* Münster: Verlag, 2004, 21–34.

Hull, Michael F. *Baptism on Account of the Dead (1 Cor 15:29): An Act of Faith in the Resurrection.* Atlanta: Society of Biblical Literature, 2005.

Humbert of Romans. *Opusculum tripartitum.* In *Fasciculum rerum expetendarum et fugiendarum* 2. Ed. Ortuin Gratius. London, 1690, 185–229.

Humphreys, Colin. *The Mystery of the Last Supper: Reconstructing the Final Days of Jesus.* Cambridge: Cambridge University Press, 2011.

Hussey, J. M. *The Orthodox Church in the Byzantine Empire.* Oxford History of the Christian Church. Oxford: Clarendon Press, 1986.

Hyland, William. "John-Jerome of Prague (1368–1440) and the *Errores Graecorum*: Anatomy of a Polemic against Greek Christians." *Journal of Religious History* 21 (1997): 249–67.

Ignatius of Antioch and Clement of Rome. *The Epistles of St. Clement of Rome and St. Ignatius of Antioch.* Trans. James Kleist. ACW 1. Westminster, MD: Newman Bookshop, 1946.

Inglessis, Emilios. *Maximos IV: L'Orient conteste l'Occident.* Paris: Les éditions du Cerf, 1969.

Instone-Brewer, David. "Jesus' Last Passover: The Synoptics and John." *Expository Times* 112 (2001): 122–23.

Irenaeus of Lyons. *Against the Heresies Book 1.* Trans. Dominic J. Unger. ACW 55. New York: Newman Press, 1992.

Irenaeus of Lyons. *Against the Heresies Book 2.* Trans. Dominic J. Unger. ACW 65. New York: Newman Press, 2012.

Irenaeus of Lyons. *Against the Heresies Book 3.* Trans. Dominic J. Unger and M. C. Steenberg. ACW 64. New York: Newman Press, 2012.

Isidore of Seville. *De Ecclesiasticis Officiis.* Trans. Thomas Knoebel. ACW 61. New York: Newman Press, 2008.

Izbicki, Thomas. *The Eucharist in Medieval Canon Law.* Cambridge: Cambridge University Press, 2015.

Jaeger, Werner, et al. *Gregorii Nysseni Opera Online.* Leiden: Brill, 1992.

James, Edward. "Bede and the Tonsure Question." *Peritia* 3 (1984): 85–98.

Janssens, D. Laurent. "La question des azymes." *Revue bénédictine* 6 (1889): 485–99.

Jaubert, Annie. *The Date of the Last Supper.* Trans. Isaac Rafferty. Staten Island, NY: Alba House, 1965.

Jaubert, Annie. "La date de la derniere Cène." *Revue de l'Histoire des Religions* 146 (1954): 140–73.

Jaubert, Annie. "Le calendrier des Jubilés et les jour liturgiques de la semaine." *Vetus Testamentum* 7 (1957): 35–61.

Jay, Pierre. "Saint Augustin et la doctrine du purgatoire." *Recherches de théologie ancienne et médiévale* 36 (1969): 17–30.

Jay, Pierre. "Saint Cyprien et la doctrine du purgatoire." *Recherches de théologie* 27 (1960): 133–36.
Jefford, Clayton, ed. *The Didache in Context: Essays on Its Text, History, and Transmission*. Leiden: Brill, 1995.
Jensen, Robin. *Face to Face: Portraits of the Divine in Early Christianity*. Minneapolis, MN: Augsburg Fortress, 2004.
Jensen, Robin. "The Two Faces of Jesus." *Bible Review* 18 (2002): 42–50.
Jensen, Robin. *Understanding Early Christian Art*. London: Routledge, 2000.
Jeremias, Joachim. *The Eucharistic Words of Jesus*. Trans. Norman Perrin. New York: Charles Scribner's Sons, 1966.
Jeremias, Joachim. *The Parables of Jesus*. Trans. S. H. Hooke. New York: Scribner's, 1963.
Jeremias, Joachim. "The Last Supper." *Journal of Theological Studies* 50 (1949): 1–10.
Jerome. *Commentary on Ezekiel*. Trans. Thomas Scheck. ACW 71. New York: Newman Press, 2017.
Jerome. *Commentary on Matthew*. Trans. Thomas P. Scheck. FC 117. Washington, DC: Catholic University of America Press, 2008.
Jerome. *The Homilies of Saint Jerome*. Vol. 2: *Homilies 60–96*. Trans. Marie Liguori Ewald. FC 57. Washington, DC: Catholic University of America Press, 1966.
Jerome. *The Letters of St. Jerome*. Vol. 1. Trans. Thomas Comerford Lawler. ACW 33. New York: Newman Press, 1963.
Jerome. *Select Letters of Saint Jerome*. Trans. F. A. Wright. New York: G.P. Putnam's Sons, 1933.
Jiroušková, Lenka. *Die Visio Pauli: Wege und Wandlungen einer orientalischen Apokryphe im lateinischen Mittelalter unter Einschluß der alttschechischen und deutschsprachigen Textzeugen*. Leiden: Brill, 2006.
John of Damascus. *Writings*. Trans. Frederic Chase. FC 37. Washington, DC: Catholic University of America Press, 1958.
Johnson, Luke Timothy. *Acts of the Apostles*. Sacra Pagina 5. Collegeville MN: Michael Glazier, 1992.
Johnson, Luke Timothy. *The Gospel of Luke*. Sacra Pagina 3. Collegeville, MN: Michael Glazier, 1991.
Johnson, Maxwell, ed. *Issues in Eucharistic Praying in East and West*. Collegeville, MN: Liturgical Press, 2010.
Jordan, Mark. "Theological Exegesis and Aquinas' Treatise 'Against the Greeks.'" *Church History* 56 (1987): 445–56.
Jorgenson, James. "The Debate over Patristic Texts on Purgatory at the Council of Ferrara-Florence." *St. Vladimir's Theological Quarterly* 30 (1986): 309–34.
Jotischky, Andrew. "Greek Orthodox and Latin Monasticism around Mar Saba during Crusader Rule." In Joseph Patrich, ed. *The Sabaite Heritage in the Orthodox Church from the Fifth Century to the Present*. Leuven: Peeters, 2001, 85–96.
Joy, John. "Ratzinger and Aquinas on the Dating of the Last Supper: In Defense of the Synoptic Chronology." *New Blackfriars* 94 (2013): 324–39.
Jugie, Martin. "La doctrine des fins dernières dans l'Église gréco-russe." *Échos d'Orient* 17 (1914): 5–22.
Jugie, Martin. "La question du Purgatoire au Concile de Ferrare-Florence." *Échos d'Orient* 20 (1921): 269–82.

Jugie, Martin. *Le Schisme Byzantin*. Paris: P. Lethielleux, 1941.
Jugie, Martin. *Theologia Dogmatica Christianorum Orientalium Ab Ecclesia Catholica Dissidentium*. Vol. 3. Paris: Letouzey et Ané, 1926.
Julian the Apostate. *The Works of the Emperor Julian II*. Trans. Wilmer Cave Wright. Cambridge, MA: Harvard University Press, 1913.
Jungmann, Joseph. *The Mass of the Roman Rite*. 2 vols. Westminster, MD: Christian Classics, 1986.
Justin Martyr. *The First and Second Apologies*. Trans. Leslie William Barnard. ACW 56. New York: Paulist Press, 1997.
Justin Martyr. *Writings of Saint Justin Martyr*. Trans. Thomas Falls. FC 6. Washington, DC: Catholic University of America Press, 1948.
Kaffa, Elena. *The Greek Church of Cyprus, the Morea and Constantinople during the Frankish Era (1196-1303): A New Perspective*. Newcastle, UK: Cambridge Scholars Publishing, 2014.
Kaldellēs, Antōnios. *Hellenism in Byzantium: The Transformations of Greek Identity and the Reception of the Classical Tradition*. Cambridge: Cambridge University Press, 2011.
Kalomiros, Alexander. *Against False Union*. Trans. George Gabriel. Seattle, WA: St. Nectarios Press, 1967.
Kappes, Christiaan. *The Epiclesis Debate at the Council of Florence*. Notre Dame, IN: University of Note Dame Press, 2019.
Kappes, Christiaan. *The Immaculate Conception: Why Thomas Aquinas Denied, While John Duns Scotus, Gregory Palamas, & Mark Eugenicus Professed the Absolute Immaculate Existence of Mary*. New Bedford, MA: Academy of the Immaculate, 2014.
Kappes, Christiaan. "A Latin's Defense of Mark of Ephesus at the Council of Ferrara-Florence (1438-1439)." *Greek Orthodox Theological Review* 59 (2014): 161-230.
Karmiris, Johannes. "Ἡ ὁμολογία τῆς ὀρθοδόξου πίστεως τοῦ Πατριάρχου Ἱεροσολύμων Δοσιθέου." *Θεολογία* 19 (1948): 693-707; 20 (1949): 99-119, 245-79, 457-94; 657-703.
Kavanagh, Joseph. "The Date of the Last Supper." *Philippine Studies* 6 (1958): 105-14.
Kazhdan, A. P., and Ann Wharton Epstein. *Change in Byzantine Culture in the Eleventh and Twelfth Centuries*. Berkeley: University of California Press, 1985.
Keener, Craig. *The Historical Jesus of the Gospels*. Grand Rapids, MI: Eerdmans, 2009.
Kennedy, Archibald. "Leaven." In Thomas Kelly Cheyne and John Sutherland Black, eds. *Encyclopedia Biblica*. London: Adam and Charles Black, 1902, 2752-54.
Kiapidou, Eirini-Sophia. "Chapters, Epistolary Essays and Epistles. The Case of Michael Glykas' Collection of Ninety-Five Texts in the 12th Century." *Parekbolai* 3 (2013): 45-64.
Kilchör, Benjamin. "Passah und Mazzot: Ein Überblick über Die Forschung Seit Dem 19. Jahrhundert." *Biblica* 94 (2013): 340-67.
Kittel, Gerhard, and Gerhard Friedrich, eds. *Theological Dictionary of the New Testament*. Trans. and abridged by Geoffrey W. Bromiley. Grand Rapids, MI: Eerdmans, 1985.
Klawans, Jonathan. "Was Jesus' Last Supper a Seder?" *Bible Review* 17 (October 2001): 24-33.
Kodell, Jerome. *The Eucharist in the New Testament*. Collegeville, MN: Liturgical Press, 1991.
Koester, Craig. *Revelation*. Anchor Bible 38A. New Haven, CT: Yale University Press, 2014.
Kolbaba, Tia. "1054 Revisited: Response to Ryder." *Byzantine and Modern Greek Studies* 35 (2011): 38-44.

Kolbaba, Tia. *The Byzantine Lists: Errors of the Latins*. Urbana: University of Illinois Press, 2000.

Kolbaba, Tia. "Byzantine Perceptions of Latin Religious 'Errors': Themes and Changes from 850 to 1350." In Angeliki Laiou and Roy Parviz Mottahedeh, eds. *The Crusades from the Perspective of Byzantium and the Muslim World*. Washington, DC: Dumbarton Oaks, 2001, 117–43.

Kolbaba, Tia. "Byzantines, Armenians, and Latins: Unleavened Bread and Heresy in the Tenth Century." In George Demacopoulos and Aristotle Papanikolaou, eds. *Orthodox Constructions of the West*. New York: Fordham University Press, 2013, 45–57.

Kolbaba, Tia. *Inventing Latin Heretics: Byzantines and the Filioque in the Ninth Century*. Kalamazoo, MI: Medieval Institute Publications, 2008.

Kolbaba, Tia. "Meletios Homologetes: On the Customs of the Italians." *Revue des études byzantines* 55 (1997): 137–68.

Kolbaba, Tia. "On the Closing of the Churches and the Rebaptism of Latins: Greek Perfidy or Latin Slander?" *Byzantine and Modern Greek Studies* 29 (2005): 39–51.

Kolbaba, Tia. "The Orthodoxy of the Latins in the Twelfth Century." In Andrew Louth and Augustine Casiday, eds. *Byzantine Orthodoxies: Papers from the Thirty-Sixth Spring Symposium of Byzantine Studies, University of Durham, 23–25 March 2002*. Aldershot: Ashgate, 2006, 199–214.

Kolbaba, Tia. "Theological Debates with the West, 1054–1300." In Anthony Kaldellis and Niketas Siniossoglou, eds. *The Cambridge Intellectual History of Byzantium*. Cambridge: Cambridge University Press, 2017, 479–93.

Kolbaba, Tia. "The Virtues and Faults of the Latin Christians." In Paul Stephenson, ed. *The Byzantine World*. New York: Routledge, 2010, 114–30.

Kolditz, Sebastian. *Johannes VIII. Palaiologos und das Konzil von Ferrara-Florenz (1438/39)*. 2 vols. Stuttgart: Anton Hiersemann Verlag, 2013–14.

Komnene, Anna. *Alexiad*. Trans. E. R. A. Sewter. London: Penguin Classics, 2003.

Köstenberger, Andreas J. "Was the Last Supper a Passover Meal?" In Thomas R. Schreiner and Matthew R. Crawford, eds. *The Lord's Supper: Remembering and Proclaiming Christ until He Comes*. NAC Studies in Bible and Theology 10. Nashville: B&H Publishing Group, 2010, 6–30.

Kovacs, Judith, ed. *1 Corinthians: Interpreted by Early Christian Commentators*, The Church's Bible. Grand Rapids, MI: Eerdmans, 2005.

Krause, Hans-Georg. "Das Constitutum Constantini im Schisma von 1054." In Hubert Mordek, ed. *Aus Kirche und Reich: Festschrift für Friedrich Kempf*. Sigmaringen: Thorbecke, 1983, 131–58.

Krausmüller, Dirk. "What Is Mortal in the Soul? Nicetas Stethatos, John Italos and the Controversy about the Care of the Dead." *Mukaddime* 6 (2015): 1–17.

Krsmanović, Bojana, and Milanović, Ljubomir. "Beards That Matter: Visual Representations of Patriarch Ignatios in Byzantine Art." *Zograf* 41 (2017): 25–36.

Kucharski, Janek, and Marciniak, Przemysław, "The Beard and Its Philosopher: Theodore Prodromos on the Philosopher's Beard in Byzantium." *Byzantine and Modern Greek Studies* 41 (2017): 45–54.

Kyriacou, Chrysovalantis. *Orthodox Cyprus under the Latins, 1191–1571: Society, Spirituality, and Identities*. Lanham, MD: Lexington Books, 2018.

La chiesa greca in Italia dall'viii al xvi secolo: Atti del convegno storico interecclesiale (Bari, 30 Apr.–4. Magg. 1969). 3 vols. Padua: Editrice Antenore, 1972–73.

La Verdiere, Eugene. *The Breaking of the Bread: The Development of the Eucharist According to the Acts of the Apostles*. Chicago: Liturgy Training Publications, 1998.

La Verdiere, Eugene. *Dining in the Kingdom of God: The Origins of the Eucharist According to Luke*. Chicago: Liturgy Training Publications, 1994.

La Verdiere, Eugene. *The Eucharist in the New Testament and the Early Church*. Collegeville, MN: Liturgical Press, 1996.

Lactantius. *The Divine Institutes, Books I–VII*. Trans. Sister Mary Francis McDonald. FC 49. Washington, DC: Catholic University of America Press, 1964.

Ladouceur, Paul. "Orthodox Theologies of the Afterlife: Review of *The Departure of the Soul*." (2017) https://blogs.ancientfaith.com/orthodoxyandheterodoxy/2017/08/18/orthodox-theologies-of-the-afterlife-review-of-the-departure-of-the-soul/.

Lambert, John C. "The Passover and the Lord's Supper." *Journal of Theological Studies* 4.14 (1903): 184–93.

Lane, William. *Hebrews 9–13*. Word Biblical Commentary 47b. Grand Rapids, MI: Zondervan, 1991.

Lanne, Emmanuel. "L'enseignement de l'Église catholique sur le purgatoire." *Irénikon* 64 (1991): 205–29.

Laourdas, Vasileios, and Leendert Gerrit Westerink, eds. *Epistulae et amphilochia*. Vol. 1. Leipzig: Teubner, 1983.

Larchet, Jean-Claude. *Life after Death According to the Orthodox Tradition*. Trans. G. John Champoux. Rollingsford, NH: Orthodox Research Institute, 2012.

Larson, Atria. *Master of Penance: Gratian and the Development of Penitential Thought and Law in the Twelfth Century*. Washington, DC: Catholic University of America Press, 2014.

Latimer, Hugh. *Sermons by Hugh Latimer, Sometime Bishop of Worcester*. London: J.M. Dent, 1906.

Laurent, Vitalien. "La croisade et la question d'Orient sous le pontificat de Grégoire X." *Revue historique du Sud-Est européen* 22 (1945): 105–37.

Laurent, Vitalien. "Le schisme de Michel Cérulaire." *Echos d'Orient* 31 (1932): 97–110.

Laurent, Vitalien, ed. *Les "Mémoires" du Grand Ecclésiarque de l'Église de Constantinople Sylvestre Syropoulos sur le Concile de Florence (1438–1439)*. CF 9. Rome: Pontifical Oriental Institute, 1971.

Laurent, Vitalien, ed. *Les Regestes des Actes du Patriarcat de Constantinople 4: Les Regestes de 1208 à 1309*. Paris: Institut français d'études byzantines, 1971.

Laurent, Vitalien. "Rome et Byzance sous le Pontificat de Célestin III." *Echo d'Orient* 39 (1940): 26–58.

Laurent, Vitalien, and Jean Darrouzès, eds. *Dossier Grec de l'Union de Lyon 1273–1277*. Paris: Institut français d'études byzantines, 1976.

Lauxtermann, Marc, and Mark Whittow, eds. *Byzantium in the Eleventh Century: Being in Between*. London: Routledge, 2017.

Le Goff, Jacques. *The Birth of Purgatory*. Trans. Arthur Goldhammer. Chicago: University of Chicago Press, 1984.

Leach, Edmund. "Magical Hair." *Journal of the Royal Anthropological Institute* 88 (1958): 147–68.

Leaney, A. R. C. "What Was the Lord's Supper?" *Theology* 70 (1967): 51–62.

Lebreton, M.-M. "Recherches sur les manuscrits contenant des sermons de Pierre le Mangeur." *Bulletin d'information de l'Institut de Recherche et d'Histoire des Textes* 2 (1953): 25–44.

Leclercq, Jean, John Morson, and E. de Solms, eds. *Le Sacrement de l'autel*. Vols. 1 and 2. SC 93 and 94. Paris: Les éditions du Cerf, 1963.

Lees, Jay. *Deeds into Words in the Twelfth Century*. Leiden: Brill, 1997.

Legassie, Shayne. *The Medieval Invention of Travel*. Chicago: University of Chicago Press, 2017.

Leib, Bernard. *Deux inédits byzantins sur les azymes au début du XIIe siècle*. Contribution à l'histoire des discussions theologiques entre grecs et latins. Rome: Pontificio Instituto Orientale, 1924.

Leib, Bernard. *Rome, Kiev, et Byzance à la Fin du XIe siècle. Rapports religieux des Latins et des Gréco-Russes sous le pontificat d'Urbain II (1088–1099)*. Paris: Auguste Picard, 1924.

Lemerle, P. "L'Orthodoxie byzantine et loecumenisme medieval: Les origins du schism des Eglises." *Bulletin de l'Association Guillaume Bude* 2 (1965): 228–46.

Leo the Great. *Letters*. Trans. Edmund Hunt. FC 34. Washington, DC: Catholic University of America Press, 1957.

Leo the Great. *Sermons*. Trans. Jane Patricia Freeland and Agnes Josephine Conway. FC 93. Washington, DC: Catholic University of America Press, 1996.

Lessing, Hans. *Die Abendmahlsprobleme im Lichte der neutestamentlichen Forschung seit 1900*. Bonn: Bouvier, 1953.

Levine, Baruch. *Numbers 1–20*. Anchor Bible 4A. New York: Doubleday, 1993.

Levine, Molly. "The Gendered Grammar of Ancient Mediterranean Hair." In Howard Eilberg-Schwartz and Wendy Doniger, eds. *Off with Her Head! The Denial of Women's Identity in Myth, Religion, and Culture*. Berkeley: University of California Press, 1995, 76–130.

Levy-Rubin, Milka. "'The Errors of the Franks' by Nikon of the Black Mountain: Between Religious and Ethno-cultural Conflict." *Byzantion* 71 (2001): 422–37.

Liber Pontificalis: The Book of Pontiffs. Trans. Raymond Davis. Liverpool: Liverpool University Press, 1989.

Lidov, Aleksej. "Byzantine Church Decoration and the Great Schism of 1054." *Byzantion* 68 (1998): 381–405.

Lietzmann, Hans. *An die Korinther I/II*. Tübingen: Mohr Siebeck, 1949.

Lietzmann, Hans. *Mass and Lord's Supper*. Leiden: Brill, 1979.

Likoudis, James. *Eastern Orthodoxy and the See of Peter: A Journey towards Full Communion*. Waite Park, MN: Park Press, 2006.

Likoudis, James. *Ending the Byzantine Greek Schism*. New Rochelle: Catholics United for the Faith, 1992.

Lilie, Ralph-Johannes. *Byzantium and the Crusader States, 1096–1204*. Trans. J. C. Morris and Jean Ridings. Oxford: Clarendon Press, 1993.

Liutprand of Cremona. *The Complete Works of Liutprand of Cremona*. Trans. Paolo Squatriti. Washington, DC: Catholic University of America Press, 2007.

Loenertz, Raymond-Joseph. "Ambassadeurs grec auprès du pape Clément VI (1348)." *Orientalia Christiana Periodica* 19 (1953): 178–96.

Loenertz, Raymond-Joseph. "L'epitre de Theorien le Philosophe aux pretres d'Oreine." In Institut français d'études byzantines, ed. *Memorial Louis Petit: Melanges d'histoire et d'archeologie byzantines*. Bucharest, 1948, 317–35.

Loenertz, Raymond-Joseph. "Les dominicains byzantins Théodore et André Chrysobergès et les négociations pour l'union des Eglises grecque et latine de 1415–1430." *Archivum Fratrum Praedicatorum* 9 (1939): 5–61.

Loenertz, Raymond-Joseph. "Les établissements dominicains de Péra-Constantinople." *Échos d'Orient* 34 (1935): 332–49.

Lohfink, Gerhard. *Jesus of Nazareth: What He Wanted, Who He Was*. Trans. Lina Maloney. Collegeville, MN: Liturgical Press, 2012.

Lohmeyer, Ernst. "Die Fusswaschung." *Zeitschrift für die Neutestamentliche Wissenschaft* 38 (1939): 74–94.

Lohse, Bernhard. *Das Passafest der Quartadecimaner*. Beiträge zur Förderung christlicher Theologie 54. Gütersloh: Bertelsmann, 1953.

Lombard, Peter. *The Sentences, Book 4: On the Doctrine of Signs*. Trans. Guilio Silano. Toronto: Pontifical Institute of Medieval Studies, 2010.

Longere, Jean, ed. *Alan of Lille: Liber poenitentialis*. Vol. 2. Louvain: Editions Nauwelaerts, 1965.

Loud, G. A. *The Latin Church in Norman Italy*. Cambridge: Cambridge University Press, 2007.

Louth, Andrew. "Eastern Orthodox Eschatology." In Jerry Walls, ed. *Oxford Handbook of Eschatology*. Oxford: Oxford University Press, 2007, 233–47.

Louth, Andrew. *Greek East and Latin West: The Church, AD 681–1071*. The Church in History 3. Crestwood, NY: St. Vladimir's Seminary Press, 2007.

Lowden, John. *Early Christian and Byzantine Art*. London: Phaidon, 1997.

Lucian. *On the Syrian Goddess*. Trans. J. L. Lightfoot. Oxford: Oxford University Press, 2003.

Ludlow, Morwenna. *Universal Salvation: Eschatology in the Thought of Gregory of Nyssa and Karl Rahner*. Oxford: Oxford University Press, 2000.

Luz, Ulrich. *Matthew: A Commentary 8–20*. Hermeneia. Minneapolis, MN: Augsburg, 2001.

Luz, Ulrich. *Matthew: A Commentary 21–28*, Hermeneia. Minneapolis, MN: Augsburg, 2005.

MacCulloch, Diarmaid. *The Reformation: A History*. New York: Viking, 2004.

MacGregor, Kirk. "Is 1 Corinthians 11:2–16 a Prohibition of Homosexuality?" *Bibliotheca Sacra* 166 (2009): 201–16.

Madden, Thomas. *The Fourth Crusade: Event, Aftermath, and Perceptions*. London: Ashgate, 2008.

Maddox, Robert. *The Purpose of Luke-Acts*. Göttingen: Vandenhoeck & Ruprecht, 1982.

Magdalino, Paul. *The Empire of Manuel I Komnenos, 1142–1180*. Cambridge: Cambridge University Press, 1993.

Magoulis, Harry. *Byzantine Christianity: Emperor, Church, and the West*. Detroit: Wayne State University Press, 1970.

Mai, Angelo, ed. *Novae Patrum Bibliothecae, Tomos Quintus: Sancti Nicephori Patriarchae Constantinopolitani Opera Adversus Iconomachos. Sancti Theodori Studitae scripta varia quae in Sirmondi editione desunt*. Rome, 1849.

Maier, Christopher, ed. *Crusade Propaganda and Ideology: Model Sermons for the Preaching of the Cross*. Cambridge: Cambridge University Press, 2000.

Malaterra, Geoffrey. *The Deeds of Count Roger of Calabria and Sicily and of His Brother Duke Robert Guiscard*. Trans. Kenneth Baxter Wolf. Ann Arbor: University of Michigan Press, 2005.

Maloney, George, ed. *Pseudo-Macarius: The Fifty Spiritual Homilies and the Great Letter*. New York: Paulist Press, 1992.

Mandeville, John. *The Travels of Sir John Mandeville*. Trans. C. W. R. D. Moseley. London: Penguin Books, 1983.

Mango, Cyril. *The Homilies of Photius of Constantinople: English Translation, Introduction, and Commentary*. Cambridge, MA: Harvard University Press, 1958.

Manselli, Raoul. "Il monaco Enrico e la sua eresia." *Bolletino dell' Istituto Storico Italiano per il medio evo e Archivo Muratoriano* 65 (1953): 44–62.

Manselli, Raoul. *Studi sulle eresie del secolo XII*. Studi Storici 5. Rome: Istituto storico italiano per il medio evo, 1953.

Marcus, Joel. *Mark 1–8*. Anchor Bible 27. New York: Doubleday, 2000.

Marcus, Joel. "Passover and Last Supper Revisited." *New Testament Studies* 59 (2013): 303–24.

Marinis, Vasileios. *Death and the Afterlife in Byzantium: The Fate of the Soul in Theology, Liturgy, and Art*. Cambridge: Cambridge University Press, 2017.

Marius Victorinus. *Commentary on Galatians*. Trans. Stephen Adam Cooper. Oxford: Oxford University Press, 2005.

Mark of Ephesus. *Encyclical Letter to All Orthodox Christians on the Mainland and in the Islands*. Boston, MA: Romiosyne, 2013.

Marshall, I. Howard. *Last Supper and Lord's Supper*. Grand Rapids, MI: Eerdmans, 1980.

Martimort, A. G., ed. *The Church at Prayer*. 4 vols. Trans. Matthew O'Connell. Collegeville, MN: Liturgical Press, 1987.

Martin, Jean-Marie. "Petri Diaconi Altercatio pro Romana Ecclesia contra Graecum quendam (1137) Édition, traduction et commentaire." In Olivier Delouis, Sophie Métivier, and Paule Pagès, eds. *Le saint, le moine et le paysan: Mélanges d'histoire byzantine offerts à Michel Kaplan*. Paris: Éditions de la Sorbonne, 2016, 407–56.

Martin, Troy W. "Paul's Argument from Nature for the Veil in 1 Corinthians 11:13–15: A Testicle Instead of a Head Covering." *Journal of Biblical Literature* 123 (2004): 75–84.

Martyn, James Louis. *Galatians*. Anchor Bible 33a. New York: Doubleday, 1998.

Martyn, James Louis. *Gospel of John in Christian History*. New York: Paulist Press, 1978.

Massey, Preston T. "Long Hair as a Glory and as a Covering: Removing an Ambiguity from 1 Cor 11:15." *Novum Testamentum* 53 (2011): 52–72.

Massey, Preston T. "The Meaning of κατακαλύπτω and κατὰ κεφαλῆς ἔχων in 1 Corinthians 11.2–16." *New Testament Studies* 53 (2007): 502–23.

Massey, Preston T. "Veiling among Men in Roman Corinth: 1 Corinthians 11:4 and the Potential Problem of East Meeting West." *Journal of Biblical Literature* 137 (2018): 501–17.

Mastrantonis, George, ed. *Augsburg and Constantinople: The Correspondence between the Tübingen Theologians and Patriarch Jeremiah II of Constantinople on the Augsburg Confession*. Brookline, MA: Holy Cross Orthodox Press, 1982.

Mathews, Thomas, and Eugenio Russo, *Scontro di dei: Una reinterptretazione dell'arte paleocristiana*. Milan: Jaca Books, 2018.
Matson, Mark. "The Historical Plausibility of John's Passion Chronology: A Reconsideration." In Paul N. Anderson, Felix Just, and Tom Thatcher, eds. *John, Jesus, and History*. Vol. 2. Atlanta, GA: SBL Press, 2007–16, 291–312.
Matthews, Thomas. *The Clash of Gods: A Reinterpretation of Early Christian Art*. Princeton, NJ: Princeton University Press, 1993.
Maximus of Turin. *The Sermons of Maximus of Turin*. Trans. Boniface Ramsey. ACW 50. New York: Newman Press, 1989.
Mayer, Wendy, and Pauline Allen, eds. *John Chrysostom*. New York: Routledge, 2000.
Mayne, Richard. "East and West in 1054." *Cambridge Historical Journal* 11 (1954): 133–48.
Mazza, Enrico. *The Celebration of the Eucharist*. Trans. Matthew J. O'Connell. Collegeville, MN: Pueblo Books, 1999.
McConville, J. Gordon. "Deuteronomy's Unification of Passover and Maṣṣôt: A Response to Bernard M. Levinson." *Journal of Biblical Literature* 119 (2000): 47–58.
McEleney, Neil. "1–2 Maccabees." In Raymond Brown, Joseph Fitzmyer, and Roland Murphy, eds. *New Jerome Biblical Commentary*. Englewood Cliffs, NJ: Prentice Hall, 1990, 421–46.
McGuire, Brian Patrick. "Purgatory, the Communion of Saints, and Medieval Change." *Viator* 20 (1989): 61–84.
McKenna, John. *The Eucharistic Epiclesis: A Detailed History from the Patristic to the Modern Era*. Chicago: Hildebrand Books, 2009.
Meens, Rob. *Penance in Medieval Europe, 600–1200*. Cambridge: Cambridge University Press, 2014.
Meier, John. *A Marginal Jew: Rethinking the Historical Jesus*. Vol. 3. Anchor Bible Reference Library. New Haven, CT: Yale University Press, 2001.
Meinardus, Otto. "The Beardless Patriarch: St. Germanos." Μακεδονικά 13 (1973): 178–86.
Mercati, Giovanni. *Notizie di Procoro e Demetrio Cidone Manuele Caleca e Teodoro Meleniota ed altri appunti per la storia della teologia e della letteratura bizantina del secolo XIV*. Studi e testi 56. Rome: Biblioteca Apostolica Vaticana, 1931.
Merkt, Andreas. *Das Fegefeur: Enstehung und Funktion einer Idee*. Darmstadt: Wissenschaftliche Buchgesellschaft, 2005.
Metallinos, George. *Unia: The Face and the Disguise*. Thessaloniki: Greek Orthodox Books Publications, 2015.
Metochites, George. *Historia dogmatica*. Mai, Angelo and Joseph Cozza-Luzi, eds. Rome, 1871.
Metzger, Marcel. *Les Constitutions Apostoliques 1–3*. SC 320, 329, 336. Paris: Les éditions du Cerf, 1985–87.
Mews, Constant, and Claire Renkin. "The Legacy of Gregory the Great in the Latin West." In Bronwen Neil and Matthew Dal Santo, eds. *A Companion to Gregory the Great*. Leiden: Brill, 2013, 315–42.
Meyendorff, John. *Byzantine Theology: Historical Trends and Doctrinal Themes*. New York: Fordham University Press, 1974.
Meyendorff, John. *Imperial Unity and Christian Divisions: The Church, 450–680 AD*. The Church in History 2. Crestwood, NY: St. Vladimir's Seminary Press, 1989.
Meyendorff, John. "Les causes directes du schism." *Le Messager Orthodoxe* 7 (1959): 4–9.

Meyendorff, John. *Living Tradition*. Crestwood, NY: St. Vladimir's Seminary Press, 1978.
Meyer, Harding, and Lukas Vischer, eds. *Growth in Agreement: Reports and Agreed Statements of Ecumenical Conversations on a World Level*. New York: Paulist Press, 1994.
Michel, Albert. "Origène et le dogme du purgatoire." *Questions ecclésiastiques*. Lille, 1913, 407–32.
Michel, Albert. "Purgatoire." In Alfred Vacant, Eugène Mangenot, and Émile Amann, eds. *Dictionnaire de théologie catholique, fasc CXVI–CXXI*. Paris: Letouzey, 1936, 1163–326.
Michel, Karl. *Das Opus Tripartitum des Humbertus de Romanis, o.p.: Ein Beitrag zur Geschichte der Kreuzzugsidee und der kirchlichen Unionsbewegungen*. Graz: Styria, 1926.
Michel, Anton. "Die vier Schriften des Niketas Stethatos über die Azymen." *Byzantinische Zeitschrift* 35 (1935): 308–36.
Michel, Anton, ed. *Humbert und Kerularios: Quellen und Studien zum Schisma des XI. Jahrhunderts*. 2 vols. Paderborn: Schöningh, 1924.
Michl, Johannes. "Der Sinn der Fusswaschung." *Biblica* 40 (1959): 697–708.
Michl, Johannes. "Gerichtsfeuer und Purgatorium, zu I Kor 3,12–15." In *Studiorum Paulinorum Congressus Internationalis Catholicus*. Vol. 1. Rome: Pontificio Istituto Biblico, 1963, 395–401.
Miladinova, Nadia. *The Panoplia Dogmatike by Euthymios Zygadenos: A Study on the First Edition Published in Greek in 1710*. Texts and Studies in Eastern Christianity. Leiden: Brill, 2014.
Milavec, Aaron. "The Birth of Purgatory: Evidence of the Didache." In Terrance Callan, ed. *Proceedings of the Eastern Great Lakes Biblical Society 12*. Cincinnati: Eastern Great Lakes and Midwest Bible Societies, 1992, 91–104.
Milgrom, Jacob. *Leviticus 17–22*. Anchor Bible 3A. New York: Doubleday, 2000.
Mills, Robert. "The Signification of the Tonsure." In Patricia Cullum and Katherine Lewis, eds. *Holiness and Masculinity in the Middle Ages*. Toronto: University of Toronto Press, 2005, 109–26.
Mîrşanu, Dragaş-Gabriel. "Dawning Awareness of the Theology of Purgatory in the East: A Review of the Thirteenth Century." *Studii Teologice* 4 (2008): 179–93.
Mitchell, Nathan. *Cult and Controversy: The Worship of Eucharist Outside Mass*. Collegeville, MN: Liturgical Press, 1990.
Mitton, C. Leslie. "New Wine in Old Wine Skins: IV: Leaven." *Expository Times* 84 (1973): 339–43.
Moloney, Francis. *The Gospel of John*. Sacra Pagina 4. Collegeville, MN: Liturgical Press, 2005.
Moorhead, John, ed. *Gregory the Great*. The Early Church Fathers. New York: Routledge, 2005.
Moreira, Isabel. *Heaven's Purge: Purgatory in Late Antiquity*. Oxford: Oxford University Press, 2010.
Morris, Rosemary. *Monks and Laymen in Byzantium, 843–1118*. Cambridge: Cambridge University Press, 1995.
Mouhanna, A. "La Conception du Salut Universel selon Saint Grégoire de Nysse." In Adel-Theodor Khoury and Margot Wiegels, eds. *Weg in Die Zukunft: Festschrift für Prof. DDr. Anton Antweiler Zu Seinem 75. Geburtstag*. Leiden: Brill, 1975, 135–54.
Mounce, Robert. *The Book of Revelation*. New International Commentary on the New Testament. Grand Rapids, MI: Eerdmans, 1998.

Mühlen, H. "Das Konzil von Florenz (1439) als vorlaufigen Modell eines kommenden Unionskonzils." *Theologie und Glaube* 63 (1973): 184–97.
Mullett, Margaret. *Theophylact of Ochrid: Reading the Letters of a Byzantine Archbishop*. Birmingham Byzantine and Ottoman Monographs 2. London: Variorum, 1997.
Munier, Charles. *Le Statuta ecclesiae antiqua*. Bibliothèque de l'Institut de droit canonique de l'Université de Strasbourg, 5. Paris, 1960.
Munitiz, Joseph, ed. *Nikephoros Blemmydes: A Partial Account*. Leuven: Spicilegium Sacrum Lovaniense, 1988.
Munitiz, Joseph. "A Reappraisal of Blemmydes First Discussion with the Latins." *Byzantinoslavica* 51 (1990): 20–26.
Munro, Dana. "Did the Emperor Alexius I. Ask for Aid to the Council of Piacenza, 1095?" *American Historical Review* 27 (1922): 731–33.
Murphy-O'Connor, Jerome. "1 Corinthians 11:2–16 Once Again." *Catholic Biblical Quarterly* 50 (1988): 265–74.
Murphy-O'Connor, Jerome. "Baptized for the Dead (1 Cor., XV, 29): A Corinthian Slogan?" *Revue Biblique* 4 (1981): 532–43.
Murphy-O'Connor, Jerome. "Sex and Logic in 1 Corinthians 11:2–16." *Catholic Biblical Quarterly* 42 (1980): 482–500.
Myerowitz Levine, Molly. "The Gendered Grammar of Ancient Mediterranean Hair." In Howard Eilberg-Schwartz and Wendy Doniger, eds. *Off with Her Head! The Denial of Women's Identity in Myth, Religion, and Culture*. Berkeley: University of California Press, 1995, 76–130.
Myllykoski, Matti. *Die Letzen Tage Jesu: Markus und Johannes, ihre Traditionen und die historische Frage*. 2 vols. Helsinki: Suomalainen Tiedeakatemia, 1991–94.
Naxidou, Eleonora. "The Archbishop of Ohrid Leo and the Ecclesiastical Dispute between Constantinople and Rome in the Mid-11th Century." *Cyrillomethodianum* 21 (2016): 7–19.
Naxidou, Eleonora. "The Latin West in the Eyes of the Orthodox East: The Paradigm of the Archbishop of Ohrid Demetrios Chomatenos." *Church Studies* 15 (2018): 329–41.
Neale, John Mason. *A History of the Holy Eastern Church*. London: Joseph Masters, 1847.
Nedungatt, George, and Michael Featherstone, eds. *The Council in Trullo Revisited*. Rome: Pontifical Oriental Institute, 1995.
Negoiţă, Athanase, and Constantin Daniel. "L'énigme du levain: Ad Mc. VIII 15; Mt. XVI 6; et Lc. XII 1." *Novum Testamentum* 9 (1967): 306–14.
Neil, Bronwen, ed. *Leo the Great*. Early Church Fathers. London: Routledge, 2009.
Neocleous, Savvas. *Heretics, Schismatics, or Catholics? Latin Attitudes to the Greeks in the Long Twelfth Century*. Toronto: Pontifical Institute of Medieval Studies, 2019.
Neuner, Josef, and Jacques Dupuis, eds. *The Christian Faith*. New York: Alba Houe, 1982.
Newman, Barbara. "Hildegard of Bingen and the 'Birth of Purgatory.'" *Mystics Quarterly* 19.3 (1993): 90–97.
Newman, John Henry. *Prayers, Verses, and Devotions*. San Francisco: Ignatius Press, 1989.
Nicholas I Patriarch of Constantinople. *Letters*. Trans. R. J. H. Jenkins and R. G. Westerink. Washington, DC: Dumbarton Oaks Center for Byzantine Studies, 1973.
Nichols, Aidan. *Rome and the Eastern Churches*. 2nd ed. San Francisco: Ignatius Press, 2010.
Nicodemus the Hagorite, *The Rudder or Pedalion*. Trans. Denver Cummings. Chicago: Orthodox Christian Educational Society; New York: Luna Printing, 1957.

Nicol, Donald. *Byzantium: Its Ecclesiastical History and Relations with the Western World*. London: Variorum, 1972.

Nicol, Donald. "The Byzantine Reaction to the Second Council of Lyons, 1274." In G. J. Cuming and Derek Baker, eds. *Councils and Assemblies: Papers Read at the Eighth Summer Meeting and the Ninth Winter Meeting of the Ecclesiastical History Society*. Cambridge: Cambridge University Press, 1971, 113–46.

Nicol, Donald. "Byzantine Requests for an Oecumenical Council in the Fourteenth Century." *Annuarium Historiae Conciliorum* 1 (1969): 69–95.

Nicol, Donald. "Byzantium and the Papacy in the Eleventh Century." *Journal of Ecclesiastical History* 13 (1962): 1–20.

Nicol, Donald. "The Fourth Crusade and the Greek and Latin Empires, 1204–1261." In J. M. Hussey, ed. *The Cambridge Medieval History IV: The Byzantine Empire Part 1: Byzantium and Its Neighbors*. Cambridge: Cambridge University Press, 1966, 275–330.

Nicol, Donald. "Greeks and the Union of the Churches: The Preliminaries to the Second Council of Lyons, 1261–1274." In John Watt, John Morrall, and Francis X. Martin, eds. *Medieval Studies Presented to Aubrey Gwynn*. Dublin: Lochlainn, 1961, 454–80.

Niditch, Susan. *"My Brother Esau Is a Hairy Man": Hair and Identity in Ancient Israel*. Oxford: Oxford University Press, 2008.

Niederwimmer, Kurt, and Harold Attridge. *The Didache: A Commentary*. Minneapolis, MN: Fortress Press, 1998.

Niketas Choniates. *O City of Byzantium, Annals of Niketas Chroniates*. Trans. Harry Magoulias. Detroit: Wayne State University Press, 1984.

Nikolov, Angel. "'A Useful Tale About the Latins': An Old Bulgarian Translation of a Lost Byzantine Anti-Latin Text of the End of 11th–Early 12th Century." *Scripta & E-Scripta* 1 (2003): 99–119.

Nikolov, Angel. "Mediaeval Slavonic Anti-Catholic Texts from the Manuscript Collection of the Romanian Academy." In Irina Vainovski-Mihai, ed. *New Europe College Regional Program, 2003–2004, 2004–2005*. Bucharest: New Europe College, 2007, 261–90.

Nodet, Étienne. "On Jesus' Last Supper." *Biblica* 91 (2010): 348–69.

Nolland, John. *Luke 1–9:20*. Word Biblical Commentary 35a. Dallas, TX: Thomas Nelson, 1989.

Nolland, John. *Luke 9:21–18:34*. Word Biblical Commentary 35b. Dallas, TX: Thomas Nelson, 1993.

Norwich, John Julian. *Byzantium: The Early Centuries, History of Byzantium* 1. London: Viking, 1988.

Nothaft, C. Philipp. *Dating the Passion: The Life of Jesus and the Emergence of Scientific Chronology (200–1600)*. Leiden: Brill, 2012.

Nothaft, C. Philipp. *Medieval Latin Christian Texts on the Jewish Calendar: A Study with Five Editions and Translations*. Leiden: Brill, 2014.

Nothaft, C. Philipp. "A Tool for Many Purposes: Hermann Zoest and the Medieval Christian Appropriation of the Jewish Calendar." *Journal of Jewish Studies* 65 (2014): 148–68.

Nothaft, C. Philipp, and Chris Schabel. *The Cistercian Hermann Zoest's Treatise on Leavened and Unleavened Bread: De fermento et azimo. Oecumenism, Exegesis, and Science at the Council of Basel*. Recherches de Théologie et Philosophie médiévales–Bibliotheca, 21. Leuven: Peeters, 2022.

Ntedika, Joseph. *L'évolution de la doctrine du purgatoire chez Saint Augustin*. Paris: Études augustiniennes, 1966.
Oberhelman, Steven. *Dreambooks in Byzantium: Six Oneirocritica in Translation, with Commentary and Introduction*. Aldershot: Ashgate, 2008.
Obeyesekere, Gananath. *Medusa's Hair: An Essay on Personal Symbols and Religious Experience*. Chicago: University of Chicago Press, 1981.
Obolensky, Dimitri. *Six Byzantine Portraits*. Oxford: Clarendon Press, 1988.
O'Brien, Elmer. "Scriptural Proof for the Existence of Purgatory from 2 Maccabees 12:43-45." *Sciences Ecclesiastiques* 2 (1949): 80-108.
O'Callaghan, Paul. *Christ Our Hope: An Introduction to Eschatology*. Washington, DC: Catholic University of America Press, 2011.
Odo of Deuil. *De Profectione Ludovici VII in Orientem: The Journey of Louis VII to the East*. Trans. Virginia Berry. New York: Columbia University Press, 1948.
Odom, R. L. "The Sabbath in the Great Schism of A.D. 1054." *Andrews University Seminary Studies* 1 (1963): 74-80.
Ogg, George. "The Chronology of the Last Supper." In Dennis Nineham, ed. *Historicity and Chronology in the New Testament*. London: SPCK, 1965, 75-96.
Ogg, George. *The Chronology of the Public Ministry of Jesus*. Cambridge: Cambridge University Press, 1940.
Ohgme, O. H. "Das Concilium Quinisextum. Neue Einsichten zu einem umstrittenen Konzil." *Orientalia Christiana Periodica* 56 (1992): 367-400.
Oldfather, W. A. *Epictetus: Discourses* I. Cambridge, MA: Harvard University Press, 1967.
Oldstone-Moore, Christopher. *Of Beards and Men: The Revealing History of Facial Hair*. Chicago: University of Chicago Press, 2016.
Olyan, Saul M. "What Do Shaving Rites Accomplish and What Do They Signal in Biblical Ritual Contexts?" *Journal of Biblical Literature* 117 (1998): 611-22.
Ombres, Robert. "The Doctrine of Purgatory According to St. Thomas Aquinas." *Downside Review* 99 (1981): 279-87.
Ombres, Robert. "Latins and Greeks in Debate over Purgatory, 1230-1439." *Journal of Ecclesiastical History* 35 (1984): 1-14.
Ombres, Robert. *The Theology of Purgatory*. Butler, WI: Clergy Book Service, 1978.
Orderic Vitalis. *The Ecclesiastical History of Orderic Vitalis*. Vol. 4: Books 7-8. Trans. Marjorie Chibnall. Oxford: Clarendon Press, 1973.
Orderic Vitalis. *The Ecclesiastical History of Orderic Vitalis*. Vol. 6: Books 11, 12, and 13. Trans. Marjorie Chibnall. Oxford: Clarendon Press, 1978.
Origen. *The Commentary of Origen on the Gospel of St Matthew*. 2 vols. Trans. Ronald Heine. Oxford: Oxford University Press, 2018.
Origen. *Commentary on the Gospel According to John Books 1-10*. Trans. Ronald Heine. FC 80. Washington, DC: Catholic University of America Press, 1989.
Origen. *Contra Celsum*. Trans. Henry Chadwick. Cambridge: Cambridge University Press, 1953.
Origen. *Homilies 1-14 on Ezekiel*. Trans. Thomas Scheck. ACW 62. New York: Newman Press, 2010.
Origen. *Homilies on Genesis and Exodus*. Trans. Ronald E. Heine. FC 71. Washington, DC: Catholic University of America Press, 1982.

Origen. *Homilies on Jeremiah and Homily on 1 Kings 28*. Trans. John Clark Smith. FC 97. Washington, DC: Catholic University of America Press, 1998.
Origen. *Homilies on Luke*. Trans. Joseph Lienhard. FC 94. Washington, DC: Catholic University of America Press, 1996.
Origen. *On First Principles*. 2 vols. Trans. John Behr. Oxford: Oxford University Press, 2017.
Orr, William, and James Arthur Walther, *1 Corinthians*. Anchor Bible 32. New York: Doubleday, 1976.
Osiek, Carolyn. *The Shepherd of Hermas: A Commentary*. Minneapolis, MN: Fortress Press, 1999.
Ostroumoff, Ivan. *The History of the Council of Florence*. Trans. Basil Popoff. Boston: Holy Transfiguration Monastery, 1971.
Ott, Ludwig. *Fundamentals of Catholic Dogma*. Trans. Patrick Lynch. Rockford, IL: Tan Books and Publishers, 1974.
Pachymeres, George. *De Michaele et Andronico Palaeologis libri tredecim* 1. Bonn: Corpus Scriptorum Historiae Byzantinae, 1835.
Pahlitzsch, Johannes. "Die Bedeutung der Azymenfrage für die Beziehungen zwischen griechisch- orthodoxer und lateinischer Kirche in den Kreuzfahrerstaaten." In Walter Beltz, ed. *Die Folgen der Kreuzzuge fur die orientalischen Religionsgemeinschaften*. Hallesche Beiträge zur Orientwissenschaft 22. Halle: Martin-Luther-Universität, Institut für Orientalistik, 1996, 75–93.
Pahlitzsch, Johannes. *Graeci und Suriani im Palästina der Kreuzfahrerzeit. Beiträge und Quellen zur Geschichte des griechisch-orthodoxen Patriarchats von Jerusalem*. Berliner historische Studien 33. Berlin: Duncker and Humblot, 2001.
Palaiologos, Konstantinos. "An Annotated Edition of the Refutation of the Errors of the Latins by Matthaios Blastares." PhD thesis, University of London, 2011.
Palau, Annaclara Cataldi. "L'Arsenale Sacro di Andronico Camatero. Il proemio ed il dialogo dell' imperatore con i cardinali latini: Originale, imitazioni, arrangiamenti." *Revue des études byzantines* 51 (1993): 5–62.
Palladius. *Lausiac History*. Trans. Robert Meyer. ACW 34. New York: Newman Press, 1964.
Palmer, William. *Dissertations on Subjects Relating to the "Orthodox" or "Eastern-Catholic" Communion*. London: Joseph Masters, 1853.
Papadakis, Aristeides. "Byzantine Perceptions of the Latin West." *Greek Orthodox Theological Review* 36 (1991): 231–42.
Papadakis, Aristeides. *The Christian East and the Rise of the Papacy*. Crestwood, NY: St. Vladimir's Seminary Press, 1994.
Papadakis, Aristeides. "Ecumenism in the 13th Century: The Byzantine Case." *St. Vladimir's Theological Quarterly* 27 (1983): 207–17.
Papadakis, Aristeides. "Late Thirteenth Century Byzantine Theology and Gregory II of Cyprus." In N. M. Vaporis, ed. *Byzantine Ecclesiastical Personalities*. Brookline:, MA Holy Cross Orthodox Press, 1975, 57–72.
Papadakis, Aristeides, and Alice Mary Talbot, eds. "John X Camaterus Confronts Innocent III: An Unpublished Correspondence." *Byzantinoslavica* 33 (1972): 26–41.
Papademetriou, Athanasia. *Presbytera: The Life, Mission, and Service of the Priest's Wife*. Boston: Somerset Hall Press, 2004.
Papadogiannakis, Yannis. "Michael Glykas and the Afterlife in Twelfth-Century Byzantium." *Studies in Church History* 45 (2009): 130–42.

Papadopoulos, Chrysostomos. *Rome: A Reply to the Encyclical* Lux Veritatis *of Pius XI*. London: Faith Press, 1933.

Parry, Robin, and Ilaria L. E. Ramelli. *A Larger Hope?* Eugene, OR: Cascade Books, 2019.

Patrick, James E. "Living Rewards for Dead Apostles: 'Baptized for the Dead' in 1 Corinthians 15.29." *New Testament Studies* 52 (2006): 71–85.

Paulinus of Nola. *The Poems of St Paulinus of Nola*. Trans. P. G. Walsh. ACW 40. New York: Newman Press, 1975.

Paulis, Giulio. *Lingua e cultura nella Sardegna bizantina: Testimonianze linguistiche dell'influsso Greco*. Sassari: Asfodelo, 1983.

Pavlov, Andrei. *Kriticheskie opyty po istorii drevneishei greko-russkoi polemiki protiv latinian*. Saint Petersburg: Imperatorskaia akademiia nauk, 1878.

Paxton, Nicholas. "The Eucharistic Bread: Breaking and Commingling in Early Christian Rome." *Downside Review* 122.427 (April 2004): 79–93.

Payne, Philip Barton. *Man and Woman, One in Christ: An Exegetical and Theological Study of Paul's Letters*. Grand Rapids, MI: Zondervan, 2015.

Pechler, Gloys. *Geschichte des Protestantisme in der orientischen Kirche im XVII Jahrhundert order der Patriarch Cyrill Lukaris und seine Zeit*. Munich, 1862.

Pelikan, Jaroslav, and Valerie Hotchkiss, eds. *Creeds and Confessions of Faith in the Christian Tradition*. 3 vols. New Haven, CT: Yale University Press, 2003.

Peri, Vittorio. *Ricerche sull'editio princeps degli atti greci del Concilio di Firenze*. Vatican City: Biblioteca Apostolica Vaticana, 1975.

Pesch, Rudolf. *Das Abendmahl und Jesu Todesverständnis*. Freiberg: Herder, 1978.

Pesch, Rudolf. *Das Markusevangelium*. Herders Theologischer Kommentar zum Neuen Testament 2/1. Freiburg: Herder, 1977.

Pesch, Rudolf. *Die Apostelgeschichte*. Evangelisch-Katholischer Kommentar zum Neuen Testament. Zurich: Benzinger Verlag, 1986.

Peters, Edward, ed. *The 1917 or Pio-Benedictine Code of Canon Law in English Translation*. San Francisco: Ignatius Press, 2001.

Peterson, David. *Hebrews and Perfection: An Examination of the Concept of Perfection in the "Epistle to the Hebrews"*. Cambridge: Cambridge University Press, 1982.

Peterson, William. *Tatian's Diatessaron: Its Creation, Dissemination, Significance, and History in Scholarship*. Leiden: Brill, 1994.

Petit, Ludovico, ed. *Documents relatifs au Concile de Florence: La question du purgatoire à Ferrare, Documents I–VI*. Paris: Firmin-Didot, 1921.

Petit, Ludovico, ed. *Marci Eugenici, metropolitae Ephesi, opera antiunionistica*, CF 10.2. Rome: Pontifical Oriental Institute, 1977.

Phillips, Jonathan. *The Fourth Crusade and the Sack of Constantinople*. New York: Penguin, 2005.

Phillips, Jonathan. "Odo of Deuil's *De profectione Ludovici VII in Orientem* as a Source for the Second Crusade." In Marcus Bull, Norman Housley, Peter Edbury, and Jonathan Phillips, eds. *The Experience of Crusading*. Vol. 1. Cambridge: Cambridge University Press, 2003, 80–95.

Philo. *Works*. Vol. 7: *On the Decalogue. On the Special Laws, Books 1–3*. Trans. F. H. Colson. Cambridge, MA: Harvard University Press, 1937.

Piatti, Pierantonio, ed. *The Fourth Crusade Revisited: Atti della conferenza internazionale nell'ottavo centenario della IV crociata, 1204–2004: Andros, Grecia, 27–30 maggio 2004*.

Atti e documenti (Pontificio Comitato di sscienze storiche) 25. Rome: Libreria editrice vaticana, 2008.

Picard, Jean-Michel, ed. *Saint Patrick's Purgatory: A Twelfth Century Tale of a Journey to the Other World*. Dublin: Four Courts Press, 1985.

Pitra, Joannes Baptista. *Analecta Sacra et Classica Spicilegio Solesmensi. Juris Ecclesiastici Graecorum VI*. Rome, 1891.

Pitra, Joannes Baptista, ed. *Questiones Magistri Odonis Suessionis, Analecta novissima Spicilegii Solesmensis. Continuatio altera* 2. Paris and Frascati, 1888.

Pitre, Brant. *Jesus and the Last Supper*. Grand Rapids, MI: Eerdmans, 2015.

Pius V. *Catechism of the Council of Trent*. Trans. John McHugh and Charles Callan. Rockford, IL: Tan Books, 1982.

Pixner, Bargil. *Paths of the Messiah: Messianic Sites in Galilee and Jerusalem*. San Francisco, CA: Ignatius Press, 2010.

Plank, Peter. "Patriarch Symeon II. von Jerusalem und der erste Kreuzzug." *Ostkirchliche Studien* 43 (1994): 277–327.

Pliny the Elder. *The Natural History*. Trans. H. Rackham. Cambridge MA: Harvard University Press, 1942.

Plutarch. *Moralia*. Vol. 4. Trans. Frank Cole Babbitt. Cambridge, MA. Harvard University Press, 1936.

Podolak, Pietro, and Anna Zago, eds. *Hvgonis Eteriani Epistolae, De sancto et immortali Deo, Compendiosa expositio, fragmenta Graeca, qvae extant*. CCCM 298. Turnhout: Brepols Publishers, 2020.

Podskalsky, G. *Theologie und Philosophie in Byzanz*. Munich: C.H. Beck, 1977.

Poppe, André. "Le traité des azymes Λεοντος μητροπολιτου της εν Ῥωσιαι Πρεσθλαβας: Quand, où et par qui a-t-il été écrit?" *Byzantion* 35 (1965): 504–27.

Power, David. *The Eucharistic Mystery: Revitalizing the Tradition*. New York: Crossroads, 1993.

Preisker, Herbert. "Die Vikariatstaufe 1 Cor 15:29—ein eschatologischer—nicht sakramentaler Brauch." *Zeitschrift für die neutestamentliche Wissenschaft* 23 (1924): 298–304.

Pringle, Denys, ed. *Pilgrimage to Jerusalem and the Holy Land, 1187–1291*. London: Routledge, 2012.

Psellos, Michael. *De omnifaria doctrina: A Critical Text and Introduction*. Ed. Leendert Gerrit. Nijmegen: Centrale Drukkerij, 1948.

Psellos, Michael. *Un discours inédit de Psellos: Accusation du patriarche Michel Cérulaire devant le synode (1059)*. Ed. Louis Bréhier. Paris: E. Leroux, 1904.

Pseudo-Dionysius. *The Complete Works*. Trans. Com Luibheid. Mahwah, NJ: Paulist Press, 1987.

Puhalo, Lazar. *The Soul, the Body and Death*. Dewdney, BC: Synaxis Press, 2013.

Puhalo, Lazar. *The Tale of Elder Basil "The New" and the Theodora Myth: Study of a Gnostic Document and a General Survey of Gnosticism*. Dewdney, BC: Synaxis Press, 1999.

Quasten, Johannes. *Patrology*. Vol. 1: *The Beginnings of Patristic Literature*. Westminster, MD: Christian Classics, 1986.

Queller, Donald, and Thomas Madden. *The Fourth Crusade: The Conquest of Constantinople*. Philadelphia: University of Pennsylvania Press, 1997.

Rabin, Andrew. "Bede, Dryhthelm, and the Witness to the Other World: Testimony and Conversion in the Historia Ecclesiastica." *Modern Philology* 106 (2009): 375–98.

Raeder, Maria. "Vikariatstaufe in 1 Cor 15:29." *Zeitschrift für die neutestamentliche Wissenschaft* 46 (1955): 258–61.

Rahner, Karl. "The Penitential Teaching of the Shepherd of Hermas." In *Theological Investigations 15: Penance in the Early Church*. Trans. Lionel Swain. New York: Crossroad, 1982, 57–113.

Rahner, Karl. "Purgatory." In *Theological Investigations XIX: Faith and Ministry*. Trans. Edward Quinn. New York: Crossroad, 1983, 181–93.

Rahner, Karl. "Remarks on the Theology of Indulgences." In *Theological Investigations II: Man in the Church*. Trans. Karl-H. Kruger. New York: Crossroad, 1963, 175–201.

Ralles, G. A., and M. Potles, eds. *Syntagma ton theion kai hieron kanonon*. Vol. 2. Athens: Charophylakos, 1852–59.

Ramelli, Ilaria L. E. "Christian Soteriology and Christian Platonism: Origen, Gregory of Nyssa, and the Biblical and Philosophical Basis of the Doctrine of Apokatastasis." *Vigiliae Christianae* 61 (2007): 313–56.

Ramelli, Ilaria L. E. "Origen in Augustine: A Paradoxical Reception." *Numen* 60 (2013): 280–307.

Ratzinger, Joseph (Benedict XVI). *Eschatology: Death and Eternal Life*. Trans. Michael Waldstein. Washington, DC: Catholic University of America Press, 1988.

Ratzinger, Joseph (Benedict XVI). *Jesus of Nazareth: Holy Week: From the Entrance into Jerusalem to the Resurrection*. San Francisco: Ignatius Press, 2011.

Ratzinger, Joseph (Benedict XVI). *Principles of Catholic Theology: Building Stones for a Fundamental Theology*. San Francisco, CA: Ignatius Press, 1987.

Ratzinger, Joseph (Benedict XVI). *Spe Salvi*. Rome: Libreria Editrice Vaticana, 2007. https://www.vatican.va/content/benedict-xvi/en/encyclicals/documents/hf_ben-xvi_enc_20071130_spe-salvi.html.

Reaume, John D. "Another Look at 1 Corinthians 15:29, 'Baptized for the Dead.'" *Bibliotheca Sacra* 152 (1995): 457–75.

Reeves, Marjorie. "The Originality and Influence of Joachim of Fiore." *Traditio* 36 (1980): 269–316.

Reinach, Sacha. "L'Origine des prières pour les morts." *Revue des études juives* 41 (1900): 161–73.

Reuss, Joseph. *Matthäus-Kommentare aus der griechischen Kirche*. Berlin: Akademie-Verlag, 1957.

Reynolds, Reginald. *Beards: An Omnium Gatherum*. London: George Allen & Unwin, 1950.

Reynolds, Roger. "Christ's Money: Eucharistic Azyme Hosts in the Ninth Century According to Bishop Eldefonsus of Spain: Observations on the Origin, Meaning, and Context of a Mysterious Revelation." *Peregrinations: Journal of Medieval Art and Architecture* 4.2 (2013): 1–69.

Ribaillier, Jean, ed. *Magistri Guillelmi Altissiodorensis Summa aurea*. Vol. 4. Spicilegium Bonaventurianum 19. Paris: Editions du Centre National de la Recherche Scientifique, 1980–87.

Richard, Marcel, and Joseph A. Munitiz, eds. *Anastasii Sinaitae: Quaestiones et responsiones*. Turnhout: Brepols, 2006.

Richardson, Cyril. "The Quartodecimans and the Synoptic Chronology." *Harvard Theological Review* 33 (1940): 177–90.

Richter, Georg. "Die Fusswaschung: Joh 13,1–20." *Münchener theologische Zeitschrift* 16 (1965): 13–26.

Richter, Georg. *Die Fusswaschung im Johannesevangelium: Geschichte ihrer Deutung.* Regensburg: F. Pustet, 1967.

Ridlehoover, Charles Nathan. *The Lord's Prayer and the Sermon on the Mount in Matthew's Gospel.* New York: T&T Clark, 2019.

Riedl, Andrea. "Das Purgatorium im 13. Jahrhundert: Schlaglichter auf ein Novum der ost-westlichen Kontroverstheologie am Vorabend des II. Konzils von Lyon (1274)." *Annuarium Historiae Conciliorum* 46.1 (2014; erschienen 2016): 355–70.

Riedl, Andrea. *Kirchenbild und Kircheneinheit: Der dominikanische "Tractatus contra Graecos" (1252) in seinem theologischen und historischen Kontext.* Berlin: de Gruyter, 2020.

Riedl, Andrea. "Polemik im Kontext literarisch-theologischer Auseinandersetzung zwischen Ost- und Westkirche im 13. Jahrhundert." In Svorad Zavarský, Lucy Nicholas, and Andrea Riedl, eds. *Themes of Polemical Theology across Early Modern Literary Genres.* Newcastle upon Tyne: Cambridge Scholars Publishing, 2016, 129–42.

Riedl, Andrea, ed. *Tractatus contra Graecos (1252).* CCCM 303. Turnhout: Brepols Publishers, 2020.

Riesner, Rainer. *Essener und Urgemeinde in Jerusalem: Neue Funde und Quellen.* Gießen: Brunnen-Verlag, 1998.

Riesner, Rainer. "Jesus, the Primitive Community, and the Essene Quarter of Jerusalem." In James Charlesworth, ed. *Jesus and the Dead Sea Scrolls.* New Haven, CT: Yale University Press, 1992, 198–234.

Riesner, Rainer. "Josephus 'Gate of the Essenes' in Modern Discussion." *Zeitschrift des Deutschen Palästina-Vereins* 105 (1989): 105–9.

Rietbergen, Peter. *Europe: A Cultural History.* New York: Routledge, 1998.

Rissi, Mathias. *Die Taufe für die Toten: Ein Beitrag zur paulinischen Tauflehre.* Zurich: Zwingli, 1962.

Roberg, Burkhard. *Das Zweite Konzil von Lyon.* Paderborn: Ferdinand Schöningh, 1990.

Roberg, Burkhard. *Die Union zwischen der griechischen und der lateinischen Kirche auf dem II Konzil von Lyon.* Bonner historische Forschungen 24. Bonn: L. Röhrscheid, 1964.

Robert of Clari. *The Conquest of Constantinople.* Trans. Edgar Holmes McNeal. New York: Columbia University Press, 2005.

Robertson, J. N. W. B. *The Acts and Decrees of the Synod of Jerusalem.* New York: AMS Press, 1969.

Robinson, Ian, ed. *The Papal Reform of the Eleventh Century: Lives of Pope Leo IX and Pope Gregory VII.* Manchester Medieval Sources. Manchester: Manchester University Press, 2004.

Robinson, James, ed. *The Nag Hammadi Library in English.* New York: HarperCollins, 1990.

Robinson, James Harvey, ed. *Readings in European History* 2. Boston: Athenaeum Press, 1906.

Robinson, James Harvey, ed. *Translations and Reprints from the Original Sources of European History.* Philadelphia: University of Pennsylvania Press, 1912.

Robinson, John A. T. "The Significance of the Foot-Washing." In Amos Wilder et al., eds. *Neotestamentica et patristica: Eine Freundesgabe für O. Cullmann*. Leiden: Brill, 1962, 144–47.
Rolfe, J. C. *The Lives of the Caesars*. 2 vols. Cambridge, MA: Harvard University. Press, 1979.
Romanides, John. *An Outline of Orthodox Patristic Dogmatics*. Trans. George Dragas. Rollinsford: Orthodox Research Institute, 2004.
Roncaglia, Martiniano Pellegrino. *Les discussions sur le purgatoire entre Georges Bardanès, Métropolite de Corfou, et frère Bartélemy, franciscain (15 oct.–17 nov. 1231): Étude critique avec texte inédit*. Studi e testi francescani 4. Rome: Scuola tipografica italo-orientale, 1953.
Roncaglia, Martiniano Pellegrino. *Les frères mineurs et l'église grecque orthodoxe au XIII siècle (1231–1274)*. Le Caire: Centre d'Etudes Orientales de la Custodie Franciscaine de Terre-Sainte, 1954.
Rooijakkers, Christina Thérèse. "The Luscious Locks of Lust: Hair and the Construction of Gender in Egypt from Clement to the Fāṭimids." *Al-Masāq* 30 (2018): 26–55.
Rose, Paula. *A Commentary on Augustine's De cura pro mortuis gerenda: Rhetoric in Practice*. Leiden: Brill, 2013.
Rose, Seraphim. *The Soul after Death*. Platina, CA: St. Herman of Alaska Brotherhood, 2009.
Rosemann, Philipp. *Peter Lombard*. Oxford: Oxford University Press, 2004.
Rosik, Mariusz. "The Dispute over the Date of the Last Supper: Its Chronology Revisited." *Verbum Vitae* 38 (2020): 179–98.
Rothschild, Clare. *Luke-Acts and the Rhetoric of History: An Investigation of Early Christian Historiography*. Tübingen: Mohr Siebeck, 2004.
Routledge, Robin. "Passover and Last Supper." *Tyndale Bulletin* 53 (2002): 203–21.
Rouwhorst, Gerard. "The Quartodeciman Passover and the Jewish Pesach." *Les Questions Liturgiques: Revue Trimestrielle* 77 (1996): 152–73.
Royel, Mar Awa. "The Sacrament of the Holy Leaven (Malkā) in the Assyrian Church of the East." In Cesare Giraudo, ed. *The Anaphoral Genesis of the Institution Narrative in Light of the Anaphora of Addai and Mari: Acts of the International Liturgy Congress Rome 25–26 October 2011*. Rome: Edizioni Orientalia Christiana, 2013, 363–86.
Rubin, Jonathan. *Learning in a Crusader City: Intellectual Activity and Intercultural Exchanges in Acre, 1191–1291*. Cambridge: Cambridge University Press, 2018.
Ruckstuhl, Eugen. *Chronology of the Last Days of Jesus. A Critical Study*. Trans. Victor Drapela. New York: Desclée 1965.
Rufinius. *A Commentary on the Apostles' Creed*. Trans. J. N. D. Kelly. ACW 20. Westminster, MD: Newman Press, 1955.
Rufinius. *Inquiry about the Monks in Egypt*. Trans. Andrew Cain. FC 139. Washington, DC: Catholic University of America Press, 2019.
Rufus, Musonius. *Lectures & Sayings*. Trans. Cynthia King. Scotts Valley, CA: CreateSpace Independent Publishing, 2011.
Runciman, Steven. *The Eastern Schism: A Study of the Papacy and the Eastern Churches during the XIth and XIIth Centuries*. London: Oxford University Press, 1955.
Rupert of Deutz. *Liber de divinis officiis*. Rhaban Haacke, ed. CCM 7. Turnhout: Brepols, 1967.
Russell, Norman. "Anselm of Havelberg and the Union of the Churches." *Sobornorst* 1 (1979): 19–41.

Russell, Norman. "From the 'Shield of Orthodoxy' to the 'Tome of Joy': The Anti-Western Stance of Dositheos II of Jerusalem (1641–1707)." In George Demacopoulos and Aristotle Papanikolaou, eds. *Orthodox Constructions of the West*. New York: Fordham University Press, 2013, 71–82.

Russell, Norman, ed. *Lives of the Desert Fathers*. CS 34. Trappist, KY: Cistercian Publications, 1980.

Ryan, J. Joseph. "Cardinal Humbert De s. Romana ecclesia: Relics of Roman-Byzantine Relations 1053/54." *Medieval Studies* 20 (1958): 206–38.

Ryder, Judith. "Byzantium and the West in the 1360's: The Kydones Version." In Jonathan Harris, Catherine Holmes, and Eugenia Russel, eds. *Byzantines, Latins, and Turks in the Eastern Mediterranean World after 1150*. Oxford: Oxford University Press, 2012, 345–66.

Ryder, Judith. "Changing Perspectives on 1054." *Byzantine and Modern Greek Studies* 35 (2011): 20–37.

Sachs, John. "Apocatastasis in Patristic Theology." *Theological Studies* 54 (1993): 617–40.

Safran, Linda. *The Medieval Salento: Art and Identity in Southern Italy*. Philadelphia: University of Pennsylvania Press, 2014.

Salza, John. *The Biblical Basis for Purgatory*. Charlotte, NC: Saint Benedict Press, 2009.

Sand, Alexa. "Religion and Ritualized Belief." In Roberta Milliken, ed. *A Cultural History of Hair*. Vol. 2. London: Bloomsbury Academic, 2019, 19–36.

Sanders, E. P. *The Historical Figure of Jesus*. London: Penguin, 1993.

Sanfilippo, Giacomo. "Review: That All Shall Be Saved: Heaven, Hell, and Universal Salvation." *Orthodoxy in Dialogue*, January 25, 2020. https://orthodoxyindialogue.com/2020/01/25/that-all-shall-be-saved-heaven-hell-and-universal-salvation-reviewed-by-giacomo-sanfilippo/

Sarbak, Gábor, and Lorenz Weinrich, eds. *Sicardi Cremonensis episcopi Mitralis de officiis*. CCCM 228. Turnhout: Brepols, 2008.

Saulnier, Stéphane. *Calendrical Variations in Second Temple Judaism: New Perspectives on the "Date of the Last Supper" Debate*. Leiden: Brill, 2012.

Schabel, Christopher. "*Ab hac hora in antea*: Oaths to the Roman Church in Frankish Cyprus (and Greece)." In M. Sinibaldi, K. J. Lewis, B. Major, and J. A. Thompson, eds. *Crusader Landscapes in the Medieval Levant: The Archaeology and History of the Latin East*. Cardiff: University of Wales Press, 2016, 361–72.

Schabel, Christopher. "Martyrs and Heretics, Intolerance of Intolerance: The Execution of Thirteen Monks in Cyprus in 1231." In Christopher Schabel, ed. *Greeks, Latins, and the Church in Early Frankish Cyprus*. London: Routledge, 2010, 1–33.

Schabel, Christopher. "Religion." In Angel Nicolaou-Konnari and Christopher Schabel, eds. *Cyprus: Society and Culture, 1191–1374*. Leiden: Brill, 2005, 157–218.

Schabel, Christopher. *The Synodicum Nicosiense and Other Documents of the Latin Church of Cyprus, 1196–1373*. Nicosia: Cyprus Research Center, 2001.

Schabel, Christopher, and Alexander Beihammer. "Two Small Texts on the Wider Context of the Martyrdom of the Thirteen Monks of Kantara in Cyprus, 1231." In Encarnatió Motos Guirao and Morfakidis Filactós, eds. *Polypthychon: Homenaje al Profesor Ioannis Hassiotis*. Granada: Centro de Estudios Bizantinos, 2008, 69–81.

Schabel, Christopher, Fritz Pedersen, and Russell Friedman. "Matthew of Aquasparta and the Greeks." In Kent Emery, Russell Friedman, and Andreas Speer, eds. *Philosophy and*

Theology in the Long Middle Ages: A Tribute to Stephen F. Brown. Leiden: Brill, 2011, 813–53.

Schäfer, Peter. *Jesus in the Talmud*. Princeton, NJ: Princeton University Press, 2007.

Scheibelberger, Friederic. *Gerhohi Reichersbergensis praepositi: Opera hactenus inedita. Tomus I. Libri III De investigatione Antichristi, unacum tractatu adversus Graecos*. Lincii: M. Quirein, 1875.

Schiano, Claudio. "Nicholas-Nektarios of Otranto: A Greek Monk under Roman Obedience." In Barbara Crostini and Ines Angeli Murzaku, eds. *Greek Monasticism in Southern Italy: The Life of Neilos in Context*. London: Routledge, 2018, 208–25.

Schiano, Claudio. "Omnes civitates nostre obedient venerationi: Nicola di Otranto e le fonti latine." *Rudiae. Ricerche sul mondo classico*, NS 3 (2017): 151–90.

Schmemann, Alexander. *For the Life of the World*. Crestwood, NY: St. Vladimir's Seminary Press, 1995.

Schmemann, Alexander. "St. Mark of Ephesus and the Theological Conflicts in Byzantium." *St. Vladimir's Seminary Quarterly* 1 (1957): 11–24.

Schmidt, Carl, ed. *Pistis Sophia*. Trans. Violet MacDermot. Nag Hammadi Studies 9. Leiden: Brill, 1978.

Schmidt, Josef, ed. *Des Basilius aus Achrida, Erzbischofs von Thessalonich, bisher unedierte Dialog: Ein Beitrag zur Geschichte des griechischen Schismas*. Munich: J. J. Lentner, 1901.

Schnackenburg, Rudolf. *Baptism in the Thought of St Paul*. Trans. G. R. Beasley-Murray. Oxford: Basil Blackwell, 1964.

Schnackenburg, Rudolf. *The Gospel According to St. John*. 3 vols. New York: Crossroad, 1982.

Schnackenburg, Rudolf. *The Gospel of Matthew*. Trans. Robert Barr. Grand Rapids, MI: Eerdmans, 2002.

Schnackenburg, Rudolf. *The Passion of Jesus in the Gospel of John*. Collegeville, MN: Liturgical Press, 1991.

Scholarius, George. *Oeuvres completes*. 7 vols. Ed. Ludovico Petit and Martin Jugie. Paris: Bonne Presse, 1928–36.

Schooping, Joshua, ed. *The Confession of Dositheos from the Acts and Decrees of the Synod of Jerusalem*. Olyphant, PA: St Theophan the Recluse Press, 2020.

Schröter, Jens. *Das Abendmahl: Frühchristliche Deutungen und Impulse für die Gegenwart*. Stuttgarter Bibelstudien 210. Stuttgart: Katholisches Bibelwerk, 2006.

Schultz, Hans-Joachim. *The Byzantine Liturgy: Symbolic Structure and Faith Expression*. Trans. Matthew O'Connell. New York: Pueblo, 1980.

Schultze, Bernard, ed. *Libellus de ordine generalium conciliorum et unione Florentina*. CF 2. Rome: Pontifical Oriental Institute, 1944.

Schwartz, Daniel. *2 Maccabees*. Commentaries on Early Jewish Literature. Berlin: de Gruyter, 2008.

Schweinburg, K. "Die Textgeschichte des Gesprächs mit den Franken von Niketas Stethatos." *Byzantinische Zetischrift* 34 (1934): 313–47.

Scott, Bernard Brandon. *Hear Then the Parable: A Commentary on the Parables of Jesus*. Minneapolis, MN: Fortress Press, 1989.

Scourtis-Gaddis, Constantina. The Failure of Reconciliation: The Byzantine Experience at the Council of Ferrara-Florence (1438—39). PhD dissertation, UCLA, 2004.

Scriptores Historiae Augustae I. Trans. David Magie. Cambridge, MA: Harvard University Press, 1921.

Searby, Denis, ed. *Never the Twain Shall Meet? Latins and Greeks Learning from Each Other in Byzantium*. Berlin: de Gruyter, 2018.

Seghers, Charles. "The Practice of Shaving in the Latin Church." *American Catholic Quarterly Review* 7 (1882): 278–310.

Sels, Lara. "Lawless, Forbidden and Abominable Customs: О Латинѣхъ сирѣчь Фроугохъ, a Slavonic List of Latin Errors." In Michel De Dobbeleer and Stijn Vervaet, eds. *(Mis)understanding the Balkans: Essays in Honour of Raymond Detrez*. Ghent, Belgium: Academia Press, 2013, 271–88.

Senior, Donald. *Matthew*. Abbington New Testament Commentaries. Nashville: Abbington Press, 1998.

Setton, Kenneth. *The Papacy and the Levant, 1204–1571*. 3 vols. Philadelphia: American Philosophical Society, 1976.

Ševčenko, Ihor. "Intellectual Repercussions of the Council of Florence." *Church History* 24 (1955): 291–323.

Ševčenko, Ihor. "The Many Worlds of Peter Mohyla." In Ihor Ševčenko, ed. *Ukraine between East and West: Essays on Cultural History to the Early Eighteenth Century*. Edmonton: Canadian Institute of Ukrainian Studies Press, 2009, 164–86.

Sharp, Daniel. "Vicarious Baptism for the Dead: 1 Corinthians 15:29." *Studies in the Bible and Antiquity* 6 (2014): 36–66.

Shepard, Jonathan. "Aspects of Byzantine Attitudes and Policy towards the West in the Tenth and Eleventh Centuries." *Byzantinische Forshungen* 13 (1988): 67–118.

Shepard, Jonathan. "Cross Purposes: Alexios Comnenus and the First Crusade." In Jonathan Phillips, ed. *The First Crusade: Origin and Impact*. Manchester: Manchester University Press, 1997, 107–29.

Shepard, Jonathan. "Hard on Heretics, Light on Latins: The Balancing-Act of Alexios I Komnenos." In D. Renault, ed. *Mélanges Cécile Morrisson*. Travaux et Mémoires 16. Paris: Association des Amis du Centre d'Histoire et Civilisation de Byzance, 2010, 765–77.

Shepherd, Massey H. "Are Both the Synoptics and John Correct about the Date of Jesus' Death?" *Journal of Biblical Literature* 80 (1961): 123–32.

Shirazi, Faegheh. "Men's Facial Hair in Islam: A Matter of Interpretation." In Geraldine Biddle-Perry and Sarah Cheang, eds. *Hair: Styling, Culture and Fashion*. Oxford: Berg, 2008, 111–22.

Sieben, Herman Josef. *Die Konzilsidee des lateinischen Mittelalters 847–1378*. Paderborn: Schoningh, 1984.

Siecienski, A. Edward. "Avoiding the Sin of Ham: Dealing with Errors in the Works of the Fathers." In *Studia Patristica: Proceedings of the Fifteenth International Conference on Patristic Studies XLV*. Leuven: Peeters, 2010, 175–79.

Siecienski, A. Edward. "Byzantium and Papacy from the Fifth to Fifteenth Centuries: The Three Stage Response." In Alessandra Bucossi and Anna Calia, eds. *Contra Latinos et Adversus Graecos: The Separation between Rome and Constantinople from the Ninth to the Fifteenth Century*. Leuven: Peeters, 2020, 1–30.

Siecienski, A. Edward. *The Filioque: History of a Doctrinal Controversy*. Oxford: Oxford University Press, 2010.

Siecienski, A. Edward. "Holy Hair: Beards in the Patristic Tradition." *St. Vladimir's Theological Quarterly* 58 (2014): 41–67.

Siecienski, A. Edward. *The Papacy and the Orthodox: Sources and History of a Debate.* Oxford: Oxford University Press, 2017.

Siecienski, A. Edward. "(Re)defining the Boundaries of Orthodoxy: The Rule of Faith and the 20th Century Rehabilitation of Origen." In Ronnie Rombs and Alex Hwang, eds. *Tradition and the Rule of Faith in the Early Church: Festschrift for Joseph Lienhard.* Washington, DC: Catholic University of America Press, 2010, 286–307.

Sigler, Sebastian. *Anselm von Havelberg: Beiträge zum Lebensbild eines Politikers, Theologen und königlichen Gesandten im 12. Jahrhundert.* Aachen: Shaker, 2005.

Silvano, Luigi. "'How, Why and When the Italians Were Separated from the Orthodox Christians': A Mid-Byzantine Account of the Origins of the Schism and Its Reception in the 13th–16th Centuries." In Marie-Hélène Blanchet and Frédéric Gabriel, eds. *Réduire le schisme? Ecclésiologies et politiques de l'Union entre Orient et Occident (XIIIe–XVIIIe siècle.* Paris: Centre de recherche d'histoire et civilisation de Byzance, 2013, 117–50.

Silverstein, Theodore. *Visio Sancti Pauli: The History of the Apocalypse in Latin together with Nine Texts.* London: Christophers, 1935.

Simon, Ed. "Condemned to Salvation: Considering Universalism with David Bentley Hart." *Los Angelos Review of Books*, February 15, 2020. https://lareviewofbooks.org/article/condemned-to-salvation-considering-universalism-with-david-bentley-hart/.

Simonetti, Manlio, ed. *Matthew 14–28.* Ancient Christian Commentary on Scripture Ib. Downers Grove, IL: InterVarsity Press, 2002.

Skehan, Patrick. "The Date of the Last Supper." *Catholic Biblical Quarterly* 20 (1958): 192–99.

Skotnicki, Andrew. "God's Prisoners: Penal Confinement and the Creation of Purgatory." *Modern Theology* 22 (2006): 85–110.

Skylitzes, John. *A Synopsis of Byzantine History.* Trans. John Wortley. Cambridge: Cambridge University Press, 2010.

Smith, Barry. "The Chronology of the Last Supper." *Westminster Theological Journal* 53 (1991): 29–45.

Smith, D. Moody. *Johannine Christianity: Essays on Its Setting, Sources, and Theology.* Columbia: University of South Carolina Press, 1989.

Smith, Dennis. *From Symposium to Eucharist: The Banquet in the Early Christian World.* Minneapolis, MN: Fortress Press, 2003.

Smith, Mahlon. *And Taking Bread ... Cerularius and the Azymite Controversy of 1054.* Théologie Historique 47. Paris: Beauchesne, 1978.

Smyth, Marina. "The Origins of Purgatory through the Lens of Seventh-Century Irish Eschatology." *Traditio* 58 (2003): 91–132.

Snodgrass, Klyne. *Stories with Intent: A Comprehensive Guide to the Parables of Jesus.* Grand Rapids, MI: Eerdmans, 2018.

Sorensen, Clifford Teunis Gerritt. "The Elucidarium of Honorius Augustodunensis: Translation and Selected Annotations." MA thesis, Brigham Young University, 1979.

Souarn, Romulad. "Tentatives d'union avec Rome: Un patriarche grec catholique au XIIIe siècle." *Echos d'Orient* 3 (1899–1900): 229–37, 351–70.

Speck, Paul. "Die griechischen Quellen zur Bekehrung der Bulgaren und die zwei ersten Briefe des Photios." In Cordula Scholz and Georgios Makris, eds. *Polupleuros Nous. Miscellanea für Peter Schreiner zu Seinem 60. Geburtstag.* Munich: K.G. Saur, 2005, 342–59.

Spier, Jeffrey, ed. *Picturing the Bible: The Earliest Christian Art*. New Haven, CT: Yale University Press, 2009.

Spingou, Foteini. "John IX Patriarch of Jerusalem in Exile." *Byzantinische Zeitschrift* 109 (2016): 179–206.

Spiteris, Jannis. *La Critica Bizantina del Primato Romano nel secolo XII*. Orientalia Christiana Analecta 208. Rome: Pontificium Institutum Orientalium Studiorum, 1979.

St Anthony's Greek Orthodox Monastery. *The Departure of the Soul According to the Teaching of the Orthodox Church*. Florence, AZ: St Anthony's Greek Orthodox Monastery, 2017.

Stafford, Pauline. "The Meaning of Hair in the Anglo-Norman World: Masculinity, Reform, and National Identity." In Mathilde van Dijk and Renee Nip, eds. *Saints, Scholars, and Politicians: Gender as a Tool in Medieval Studies*. Turnhout: Brepols, 2005, 153–71.

Stanley, David Michael. "The Passion According to St. John." *Worship* 33 (March 1959): 210–30.

Stegmüller, Friedrich. "Bonacursius Contra Graecos: Ein Beitrag zur Kontroverstheologie." In *Vitae et Veritati: Festgabe für Karl Adam*. Düsseldorf: Patmos-Verlag, 1958, 57–82.

Stern, Sacha. *Calendar and Community: A History of the Jewish Calendar, 2nd Century BCE–10th Century CE*. Oxford: Oxford University Press, 2001.

Stewart-Sykes, Alistair, ed. *The Didascalia apostolorum: An English Version with Introduction and Annotation*. Turnhout: Brepols, 2009.

Stone, M. E. *Fourth Ezra: A Commentary on the Book of Fourth Ezra*. Minneapolis, MN: Fortress Press, 1990.

Stopka, Krzysztof. *Armenia Christiana: Armenian Religious Identity and the Churches of Constantinople and Rome (4th–15th century)*. Trans. Teresa Baluk-Ulewiczowa. Crakow: Jagiellonian University Press, 2016.

Story, Cullen I. K. "The Bearing of Old Testament Terminology on the Johannine Chronology of the Final Passover of Jesus." *Novum Testamentum* 31 (1989): 316–24.

Strack, Hermann Leberecht, and Paul Billerbeck, eds. *Kommentar zum Neuen Testament aus Talmud und Midrasch*. Vol. 4/2: *Exkurse zu einzelnen Stellen des NT*. Munich: C.H. Becksche Verlagsbuchhandlung, 1928.

Strack, Hermann Leberecht, and Paul Billerbeck, eds. *Kommentar zum Neuen Testament aus Talmud und Midrasch*. Vol. 2. Munich: C.H. Becksche Verlagsbuchhandlung, 1924.

Strong, James. *The New Strong's Expanded Exhaustive Concordance of the Bible*. Peabody, MA: Hendrickson, 1996.

Sturgeon, Johnna. "Cares at the Curia: Andreas de Escobar and Ecclesiastical Controversies at the Time of the Fifteenth-Century Councils." PhD diss., Northwestern University, 2017.

Sullivan, Denis F., Alice-Mary Talbot, and Stamatina McGrath, eds. *The Life of Saint Basil the Younger: Critical Edition and Annotated Translation of the Moscow Version*. Washington, DC: Dumbarton Oaks Research Library and Collection, 2014.

Sveshnikov, Sergei. *Break the Bread Master: A Theology of Communion Bread*. San Francisco: Booksurge, 2009.

Sykes, Catherine Philippa. *Latin Christians in the Literary Landscape of Early Rus, c. 988–1330*. PhD dissertation, Newnham College, University of Cambridge, 2017.

Symeon of Thessalonika. *The Liturgical Commentaries*. Trans. Steven Hawkes-Teeples. Toronto: Pontifical Institute of Medieval Studies, 2011.

Synnott, Anthony. "Shame and Glory: A Sociology of Hair." *British Journal of Sociology* 38 (1987): 381–413.

Taft, Robert. *Beyond East and West: Problems in Liturgical Understanding*. Rome: Edizioni Orientalia Christiana, 1997.

Tafur, Pero. *Travels and Adventures (1435–1439)*. Trans. Malcolm Letts. New York: George Routledge and Sons, 1926.

Tallmadge, Margaret, ed. *Galen on the Usefulness of the Parts of the Body*. 2 vols. Ithaca, NY: Cornell University Press, 1968.

Tanner, Norman. *Decrees of the Ecumenical Councils*. 2 vols. Washington, DC: Georgetown University Press, 1990.

Tăutu, Aloysius L., ed. *Acta Honorii III (1216–1227) et Gregorii IX (1227–1241)*. Rome: Typis Polyglottis Vaticanis, 1950.

Tăutu, Aloysius L., ed. *Acta Urbani IV, Clementis IV, Gregorii X (1261–1276)*. Rome: Typis Polyglottis Vaticanis, 1953.

Tăutu, Aloysius L., ed. *Acta Urbani PP. V (1362–1370)*. Rome: Typis Pontificiae Universitatis Gregorianae, 1964.

Taylor, Barry. "Late Medieval Travellers in the East: Clavijo, Tafur, Encina, and Tarifa." In Rosamund Allen, ed. *Eastward Bound: Travel and Travellers, 1050– 1550*. Manchester: Manchester University Press, 2004, 221–34.

Taylor, Vincent. *The Gospel According to St. Mark*. London: Macmillan, 1952.

Teilenbach, Gerd. *The Church in Western Europe from the Tenth to the Early Twelfth Century*. Trans. Timothy Reuter. Cambridge: Cambridge University Press, 1993.

Tertullian. *Apologetical Works and Minucius Felix Octavius*. Trans. Rudolph Arbesmann, Sister Emily Joseph Daly, and Edwin A. Quain. FC 10. Washington, DC: Catholic University of America Press, 1950.

Tertullian. *Disciplinary, Moral, and Ascetical Works*. Trans. Rudolph Arbesmann, O.S.A., Sr. Emily Joseph Daly, C.S.J., and Edwin A. Quain, S.J. FC 40. Washington, DC: Catholic University of America Press, 1959.

Tertullian. *Treatises on Marriage and Remarriage: To His Wife, An Exhortation to Chastity, Monogamy*. Trans. William Le Saint. ACW 13. New York: Newman Press, 1951.

Thatcher, Oliver, and Edgar Holmes McNeal, eds. *A Source Book for Medieval History*. New York: Scribners, 1905.

Theiner, Augustino, and Francisco Miklosich, eds. *Monumenta spectantia ad unionem Ecclesiarum græcæ et romanæ*. Vienna, 1872.

Theodore of Mopsuestia. *Commentary on the Gospel of John*. Trans. Marco Conti. Downers Grove, IL: IVP Academic, 2010.

Theodoret of Cyrus. *Commentaries on Ezekiel*. Trans. Robert Charles Hill. Brookline, MA: Holy Cross Orthodox Press, 2006.

Theodoret of Cyrus. *Commentary on the Letters of St. Paul*. Vol. 1. Trans. Robert Charles Hill. Brookline, MA: Holy Cross Orthodox Press, 2001.

Theophanes. *The Chronicle of Theophanes*. Trans. Harry Turtledove. Philadelphia: University of Pennsylvania Press, 1982.

Theophylact of Ohrid. *The Explanation of Blessed Theophylact Archbishop of Ochrid and Bulgaria of the Holy Gospel According to Saint John*. Trans. Christopher Stade. House Springs, MO: Chrysostom Press, 2007.

Theophylact of Ohrid. *The Explanation of Blessed Theophylact Archbishop of Ochrid and Bulgaria of the Holy Gospel According to Saint Luke*. Trans. Christopher Stade. House Springs, MO: Chrysostom Press, 2004.

Theophylact of Ohrid. *The Explanation of Blessed Theophylact Archbishop of Ochrid and Bulgaria of the Holy Gospel According to Saint Mark*. Trans. Christopher Stade. House Springs, MO: Chrysostom Press, 2008.

Theophylact of Ohrid. *The Explanation by Blessed Theophylact Archbishop of Ochrid and Bulgaria of the Holy Gospel According to Saint Matthew*. Trans. Christopher Stade. House Springs, MO: Chrysostom Press, 2006.

Thibodeaux, Jennifer D. *The Manly Priest: Clerical Celibacy, Masculinity, and Reform in England and Normandy, 1066–1300*. Philadelphia: University of Pennsylvania Press, 2015.

Thiselton, Anthony. *The First Epistle to the Corinthians: A Commentary on the Greek Text*. Grand Rapids, MI: Eerdmans, 2000.

Thompson, Cynthia L. "Hairstyles, Head-Coverings, and St. Paul: Portraits from Roman Corinth." *Biblical Archaeologist* 51 (1988): 99–115.

Thorpe, Lewis, ed. and trans. *Einhard and Notker: Two Lives of Charlemagne*. London: Penguin, 1969.

Tibber, Peter Harris. "The Origins of the Scholastic Sermon, c. 1130–c. 1210." DPhil thesis, Oxford University, 1984.

Tinnefeld, Franz. "Michael I. Kerullarios, Patriarch von Konstantinopel (1043–1058): Kritische Überlegungen zu einer Biographie." *Jahrbuch der österreichischen Byzantinistik* 39 (1989): 95–127.

Torrey, Charles Cutler. "In the Fourth Gospel the Last Supper Was the Passover Meal." *Jewish Quarterly Review* 42 (1951–52): 237–50.

Torrey, Charles Cutler. "The Date of the Crucifixion according to the Fourth Gospel." *Journal of Biblical Literature* 50 (1931): 227–441.

Tougher, Shaun. "Bearding Byzantium: Masculinity, Eunuchs and the Byzantine Life Course." In Bronwen Neil and Lynda Garland, eds. *Questions of Gender in Byzantine Society*. London: Routledge, 2013, 153–66.

Tougher, Shaun. "Byzantine Eunuchs with Special Reference to Their Creation and Origin." In Liz James, ed. *Women, Men, and Eunuchs: Gender in Byzantium*. New York: Routledge, 1997, 168–84.

Townsend, John. "1 Cor 3:15 and the School of Shammai." *Harvard Theological Review* 61 (1968): 500–504.

Trapp, Erich. "Die Quellen von Zigabenos' Panoplia, Tit. 23 (Gegen die Armenier)." *Jahrbuch der Österreichischen Byzantinistik* 29 (1980): 159–64.

Trichet, Louis. *La tonsure*. Paris: Les Éditions du Cerf, 1990.

Trocmé, Etienne. *The Formation of the Gospel According to Mark*. Philadelphia: Westminster Press, 1975.

Trofimov, Denys. "I dibattiti sul fuoco purgatorio al Concilio di Ferrara-Firenze (1438–1439) come culmine della controversia sulla sorte dei defunti tra Oriente e Occidente." PhD thesis, Gregorian University, 2015.

Trottmann, Christian. *La Vision béatifique des disputes scolastiques à sa définition par Benoît XII*. Bibliothèque des écoles françaises d'Athènes et de Rome 289. Rome: École française de Rome, 1995.

Trumbower, Jeffrey. *Rescue for the Dead: The Posthumous Salvation of Non-Christians in Early Christianity*. Oxford: Oxford University Press, 2001.

Tsirpanlis, Constantine. *Mark Eugenicus and the Council of Florence: An Historical Reevaluation of His Personality*. New York: Kentron Buzantinwn Ereunwn, 1979.
Tsougarakis, Nickiphoros. "Perceptions of the Greek Clergy and Rite in Late Medieval Pilgrimage Accounts to the Holy Land." In Nikolaos G. Chrissis, Athina Kolia-Dermitzaki, and Angeliki Papageorgiou, eds. *Byzantium and the West: Perception and Reality (11th–15th C.)*. London: Routledge, 2019, 230–42.
Tuilier, André. "Michel VII et le pape Grégoire VII: Byzance et la réforme grégorienne." *XV Congrès international des Études Byzantines*. Athens: Association international d'études byzantines, 1980, 350–64.
Turner, Jack. "Was Photios an Anti-Latin? Heresy and Liturgical Variation in the *Encyclical to the Eastern Patriarchs*." *Journal of Religious History* 40 (2016): 475–89.
Ullmann, Walter. "Cardinal Humbert and the Ecclesia Romana." *Studi Gregoriani* 4 (1952): 111–27.
Ullmann, Walter. *The Origins of the Great Schism: A Study in Fourteenth Century Ecclesiastical History*. Hamden, CT: Archon Books, 1967.
Upson-Saia, Kristi. "Hairiness and Holiness in the Early Christian Desert." In Kristi Upson-Saia, Carly Daniel-Hughes, and Alicia J. Batten, eds. *Dressing Judeans and Christians in Antiquity*, Aldershot: Ashgate, 2014, 155–72.
Upton-Ward, Judith M. ed. *The Rule of the Templars: The French Text of the Rule of the Order of the Knights Templar*. Woodbridge, Suffolk: Boydell Press, 2005.
Van Engen, John. *Rupert of Deutz*. Berkeley: University of California Press, 1983.
van Goudoever, J. *Biblical Calendars*. Leiden: Brill, 1961.
van Liere, F. A. "Johannes XXII en het conflict over de visio beatifica." *Nederlands Theologisch Tijdschrif* 44 (1990): 208–22.
Van Tricht, Filip. *The Horoscope of Emperor Baldwin II: Political and Sociocultural Dynamics in Latin-Byzantine Constantinople*. Leiden: Brill, 2019.
van Unnik, W. C. "The 'Wise Fire' in a Gnostic Eschatological Vision." In Patrick Granfield and Josef Jungmann, eds. *Kyriakon: Festschrift Johannes Quasten*. Vol. 1. Munster Westfalen: Verlag Aschendorf, 1970, 277–88.
VanderKam, James. *Calendars in the Dead Sea Scrolls: Measuring Time*. London: Routledge, 1998.
VanderKam, James. *Jubilees 1: A Commentary on the Book of Jubilees Chapters 1–21*. Minneapolis, MN: Fortress Press, 2018.
VanderKam, James and Peter Flint. *The Meaning of the Dead Sea Scrolls: Their Significance for Understanding the Bible, Judaism, Jesus, and Christianity*. San Francisco, CA: Harper San Francisco, 2002.
Vasiliev, A. "Pero Tafur: A Spanish Traveler of the Fifteenth Century and His Visit to Constantinople, Trebizond, and Italy." *Byzantion* 7 (1932): 75–122.
Vause, Corinee, and Frank C. Gardiner, trans. *Innocent III: Between God and Man: Six Sermons on the Priestly Office*. Medieval Texts in Translation. Washington, DC: Catholic University of America Press, 2004.
Velikonja, Mitja. *Religious Separation and Political Intolerance in Bosnia-Herzegovina*. Trans. Rang'ichi Ng'inja. College Station: Texas A&M University Press, 2003.
Velykyj, Atanasij Hryhorij, ed. *Documenta Unionis Berestensis eiusque auctorum (1590–1600)*. Rome: Basiliani, 1970.
Vernadsky, George, ed. *A Source Book for Russian History from Early Times to 1917*. Vol. 2. New Haven, CT: Yale University Press, 1972.

Viller, Marcel. "La question de l'union des Eglises entre Grecs et Latins depuis le Concile de Lyon jusqu'à celui de Florence (1274–1438)." *Revue d' histoire ecclésiastique* 17 and 18 (1921 and 1922): 260–305, 20–60.

Viscuso, Patrick Demetrios, ed. *Guide for a Church under Islam: The Sixty-Six Canonical Questions Attributed to Theodoros Balsamon*. Brookline, MA: Holy Cross Orthodox Press, 2014.

Von Balthasar, Hans Urs. *Dare We Hope That All Men Be Saved*. Trans. David Kipp and Lothar Krauth. San Francisco: Ignatius Press, 1988.

Vooght, Paul. *Les pouvoirs du concile et l'autorité du pape au concile de Constance*. Unam Sanctam 58. Paris: Les éditions du Cerf, 1965.

Walker, William. "1 Corinthians 15:29–34 as a Non-Pauline Interpolation." *Catholic Biblical Quarterly* 69 (2007): 84–103.

Walls, Jerry. *Purgatory: The Logic of Total Transformation*. Oxford: Oxford University Press, 2012.

Walters, J. Edward. "Sleep of the Soul and Resurrection of the Body: Aphrahat's Anthropology in Context." *Hugoye: Journal of Syriac Studies* 22 (2019): 433–65.

Ward, Benedicta, ed. *Sayings of the Desert Fathers: The Alphabetical Collection*. CS 59. Kalamazoo, MI: Cistercian Publications, 1975.

Ware, Kallistos. "Christian Theology in the East: 600–1453." In Hubert Cunliffe-Jones, ed. *A History of Christian Doctrine*. London: T&T Clark, 1978, 181–225.

Ware, Kallistos. "Dare We Hope for the Salvation of All." In Kallistos Ware, ed. *The Inner Kingdom*. Vol. 1 of *The Collected Works of Kallistos Ware*. Crestwood, NY: St. Vladimir's Seminary Press, 2001, 193–215.

Ware, Kallistos. *Eustratios Argenti: A Study of the Greek Church under Turkish Rule*. Oxford: Clarendon Press, 1964.

Ware, Kallistos. "One Body in Christ: Death and the Communion of Saints." *Sobornost* 3.2 (1981): 179–91.

Ware, Kallistos. "Orthodox and Catholics in the Seventeenth Century: Schism or Intercommunion?" In Derek Baker, ed. *Schism, Heresy and Religious Protest*. Studies in Church History 9. Cambridge: Cambridge University Press, 1972, 259–76.

Ware, Kallistos. *The Orthodox Church*. London: Penguin Press, 2015.

Weakland, John. "Pope John XXII and the Beatific Vision Controversy." *Annuale Mediaevale* 9 (1968): 76–84.

Weeden, Theodore. *Mark: Traditions in Conflict*. Philadelphia: Fortress Press, 1971.

Wegman, Herman. *Christian Worship in East and West: A Study Guide to Liturgical History*. Trans. Gordon Lathrop. New York: Pueblo, 1985.

Weiss, Herold. "Foot Washing in the Johannine Community." *Novum Testamentum* 21 (1979): 298–325.

Weisweiler, Heinrich, ed. *Maitre Simon et son groupe De sacramentis*. Spicilegium sacrum Lovaniense 17. Louvain: Spicilegium sacrum lovaniense bureau, 1937.

Wellhausen, Julius. "Ἄρτον ἔκλασεν, Mc 14,22." *Zeitschrift für die Neutestamentliche Wissenschaft* 7 (1906): 182.

Wendebourg, Dorthea. *Reformation und Orthodoxie: Der ökumenische Briefwechsel zwischen der Leitung der Württembergischen Kirche und Patriarch Jeremias II. von Konstantinopel in den Jahren 1573–1581*. Göttingen: Vandenhoeck & Ruprecht, 1986.

Wenham, Gordon. *The Book of Leviticus*. Grand Rapids, MI: Eerdmans, 1979.

Whalen, Brett. *Dominion of God: Christendom and Apocalypse in the Middle Ages.* Cambridge, MA: Harvard University Press, 2009.

Whalen, Brett. "Rethinking the Schism of 1054: Authority, Heresy, and the Latin Rite." *Traditio* 62 (2007): 1–24.

Whatley, Gordon. "The Uses of Hagiography: The Legend of Pope Gregory and the Emperor Trajan in the Middle Ages." *Viator* 15 (1984): 25–64.

White, Andrew Walker. "The Artifice of Eternity: A Study of Liturgical and Theatrical Practices in Byzantium." PhD diss., University of Maryland, 2006.

White, Joel R. "'Baptized on Account of the Dead': The Meaning of 1 Corinthians 15:29 in Its Context." *Journal of Biblical Literature* 116 (1997): 487–99.

Will, Cornelius, ed. *Acta et Scripta quae de controversiis ecclesiae graecae et latinae saeculo undecimo composite extant.* Leipzig, 1861.

William of Tyre. *A History of Deeds Done beyond the Sea.* 2 vols. Trans. E. Babcock and A. C. Krey. New York: Columbia University Press, 1943.

Williams, J. "Use of Sources in the Canons of the Council in Trullo." *Byzantion* 66 (1996): 470–88.

Wilmart, André. "Les sermons d'Hildebert." *Revue Bénédictine* 47 (1935): 12–51.

Wilson, Walter. *The Sentences of Pseudo-Phocylides.* Berlin: de Gruyter, 2005.

Winslow, Donald. *Dynamics of Salvation: A Study in Gregory of Nazianzus.* Cambridge, MA: Philadelphia Patristic Foundation, 1979.

Witherington, Ben. *The Acts of the Apostles a Social Rhetorical Commentary.* Grand Rapids, MI: Eerdmans, 1998.

Wolff, Robert Lee. "The Latin Empire of Constantinople and the Franciscans." *Traditio* 2 (1944): 213–37.

Wolter, Hans, and Henri Holstein. *Lyon I et Lyon II.* Paris: Editions de l'Orante, 1966.

Wood, Ian. "Hair and Beards in the Early Medieval West." *Al-Masāq Journal of the Medieval Mediterranean* 30 (2018): 107–16.

Wooley, Reginald. *The Bread of the Eucharist.* London: Mowbray, 1913.

Wright, N. T. *Jesus and the Victory of God.* Minneapolis, MN: Fortress Press, 1996.

Wright, N. T. *Surprised by Hope: Rethinking Heaven, the Resurrection, and the Mission of the Church.* New York: HarperCollins, 2009.

Yost, Charles. "Neither Greek nor Latin, but Catholic: Aspects of the Theology of Union of John Plousiadenos." *Journal of Orthodox Christian Studies* 1 (2018): 43–59.

Zeitlin, Solomon. "The Date of the Crucifixion According to the Fourth Gospel." *Journal of Biblical Literature* 51 (1932): 263–71.

Zeitlin, Solomon. "The Last Supper as an Ordinary Meal in the Fourth Gospel." *Jewish Quarterly Review* 42 (1952): 251–60.

Zernov, Nikolay. "Eusebius and the Paschal Controversy at the End of the Second Century." *Church Quarterly Review* 116 (1933): 24–41.

Zmijewski, Josef. *Die Apostelgeschichte.* Regensburger Neues Testament. Verlag Friedrich Pustet, 1994.

Zola, Nicholas. "Tatian's Diatessaron and the Passion Chronology." PhD diss., Abilene Christian University, 2009.

Zucker, Mark. "Raphael and the Beard of Pope Julius II." *Art Bulletin* 59 (1977): 524–33.

Index

For the benefit of digital users, indexed terms that span two pages (e.g., 52–53) may, on occasion, appear on only one of those pages.

Acts of Paul and Thecla, 204–5
Aeneas of Paris, 43–44
Akropolites, George, 264–65, 264n.223
Alan of Lille, 239–40
Albert the Great, 167
Alexander of Hale, 162n.70, 241
Alexios I Komnenos, Emperor, 51, 51n.94
Alger of Liège, 144
Allatios, Leo, 296–97
All Souls Day, 234
Ambrose of Milan, 86–87, 110, 222–23, 222n.212, 222n.213, 222n.218
Ambrosiaster, 88–89, 223
Andreas Chrysoberges, Archbishop of Rhodes, 179–80
Androutsos, Christos, 303–4
Anselm of Canterbury, 142–43
Anselm of Havelberg, 144–46
Antioch, Peter III of, 49–50
Apocalypse of Paul, 218–19, 218n.188
Apologia de Barbis (Buchard), 57–58
Apology in Favor of Priestly Beards, An (Valeriano), 70–71
Apostolic Constitutions, 27, 205–6
Argenti, Eustratios, 183–84, 184n.235, 302
Argyros, 118–19, 118n.13
Augsburg Confession, 294
Augustine of Hippo, 29–30, 87, 92n.78, 105n.160, 111, 111n.196
  as theologian, 283n.49
  and tradition of purgatory, 223–28, 224n.231, 224n.233, 224n.234, 224–25n.236, 225–26nn.237–42, 226–27nn.246–54
Avvakumov, Yury P., 117, 129, 129n.89
azyme debate, and martyrdom of monks on Cyprus, 168–69
azyme debate, and mid-twelfth century, 144–50, 148n.225
  Anselm of Havelberg, 144–46

Baldwin of Forde, 149
Innocent III, Pope, 149–50
Niketas of Nicomedia, 144–46
Peter the Deacon, 146–47
Tractatus contra Graecos, 160–61
azyme debate, and the First Crusade, 135–44
  Alger of Liège, 144
  Anselm of Canterbury, 142–43
  Barsalibi, Dionysius, 140–41, 140n.166
  Guibert of Nogent, 141–42, 142n.176
  Malaterra, Geoffreddo, 141
  Rupert of Deutz, 143–44
  Symeon II, Patriarch of Jerusalem, 136–38
  Urban II, Pope, 141
azyme debate, and the Fourth Crusade, 151–69
  Albert the Great, 167
  Bonacursius of Bologna, 161–62
  Bonaventure, 164–65
  Chomatenos, Demetrios, 154, 154n.22
  conquest of Constantinople, 152–53
  Cyprus, martyrdom of monks on, 157–59, 157–58nn.45–48, 158n.51, 160–61
  Eucharist, debates regarding matter and form, 162–64
  Greek and Latin religious debates, 155–57, 159–61, 159n.55, 159n.57, 159n.59
  Greek and Latin religious kinship, 153–54, 153n.15
  Guerric of Saint-Quentin, 163
  Matthew of Aquasparta, 163–65
  Niketas Choniates, 152–53, 153n.11
  Thomas Aquinas, 165–67, 166–67n.105
  Tractatus contra Graecos, 160–61
azyme debate, and the Second Council of Lyons, 169–75
azyme debate, eleventh century, 116–18, 116n.2, 117n.4
  Argyros, 118–19, 118n.13

azyme debate, eleventh century (*cont.*)
  crumbs, and breaking of the bread, 125
  Gregory VII, Pope, 133–34
  Humbert, Cardinal, 122n.41, 123n.44, 123n.47, 122–26, 127–30, 128n.79, 128n.80, 130n.95
  issues in contention, 124n.53
  Keroularios, Patriarch Michael, 121, 122, 131–33
  Leo IX, Pope, 121, 121n.31
  Leo of Ohrid, 119–22
  Peter III of Antioch, 125–27, 126n.63, 126n.64, 127n.74, 132–33
  Stethatos, Niketas, 127–31
  Theophylact of Ohrid, 134, 135n.128, 135n.129
azyme debate, into modern era, 183–86
azymes
  Council of Ferrara-Florence, discussion at, 3–5
  and early Christian practices, 7–8

Baldwin of Forde, 149
baptism, rites for the dead, 200n.73
Barcelona, First Council of, 33–34
Bardanes, George, 249–51
Barsalibi, Dionysius, 140–41, 140n.166
Basil of Ohrid, 146n.213
Bathrellos, Demetrios, 284n.55, 309
Bearded Gospel Men, evangelical Christian movement, 75–76, 75n.262, 75–76n.263
beardlessness, perceptions of, 24–27
  eunuchs, 40–41, 41n.11, 61–62
  feminization, 61–62, 62n.172
  as Judaic practice, 61–62
beards
  in early Christian literature, 5–7
  Greek and Latin customs, 1–3
  and portraits of Christ in early Christian era, 23–24, 23n.46, 23n.47, 24n.53
  and spiritual strength, 56
beards, in biblical tradition, 15–24, 36–37
  and hair styling, 21–23, 22n.37
  New Testament, 20–23, 20n.26, 20n.28, 28–29
  in Old Testament, 16–19, 30, 30n.100
  origin of practices, 19
beards, in East-West polemic, 38–40, 38n.1, 69–74
  Aeneas of Paris, 43–44

Apology in Favor of Priestly Beards, An (Valeriano), 70–71
  attitudes in United States, 74, 74n.252, 74n.253
  beardlessness as Judaic practice, 61–62
  Borromeo, Charles, 71
  Buchard of Bellevaux, 57–58, 57n.135
  Byzantine practices, 40–41, 40n.10
  Choniates, Niketas, 61
  Constantinople, conquest of, 60–61, 60n.160
  and cultural differences, 39, 39n.3, 52–53
  Dialogue of Panagiotes with an Azymite, 65–66
  dwindling emphasis on beards, 66–69
  eleventh century, 46–51
  Encyclical to the Eastern Patriarchs, 42–44
  Eustathios of Thessaloniki, 59–60
  fourteenth and fifteenth centuries, 66–69
  Gregory VII, Pope, 50–51
  Humbert, Cardinal, 48–49
  and Islam, 53
  Joachim of Fiore, 58–59, 59n.153
  Keroularios, Patriarch Michael, 48–49
  Knights Templar, 58
  and mandatory tonsure, 47, 62–63
  Nicholas I, Pope, 41–43, 42n.24
  ninth century, 40–45
  in northern Europe, 54–55
  Peter, Saint, legend of tonsure, 45, 49–50
  Photios, Patriarch of Constantinople, 41–42, 43n.27
  Protestant Reformation, attitudes toward beards, 72
  Ratramnus of Corbie, 44–45
  seventeenth century, 72, 73, 73n.246
  Sicard of Cremona, 55–56
  sixteenth century, 70
  and spiritual strength, 56
  Symeon of Thessalonika, 67
  Tafur, Pero, 67–68
  Thessaloniki, sacking of, 59–60, 60n.159
  thirteenth century, 60–66
  twelfth century, 52–60
  twentieth and twenty-first centuries, 74–76
beards, in patristic tradition, 15–16, 25–37
  and Christian modesty, 31–32, 37
  Epiphanius, 27–28
  and Leviticus, 28
  and monastic tradition, 32–33, 46–47

perceptions of beardlessness, 25–27
Peter, Saint, legend of tonsure, 35–36, 49–50
Bessarion, 279–81, 280n.35, 281n.38
Blastares, Matthew, 171–72
Bonacursius of Bologna, 161–62, 267–69
Bonaventure, 164–65, 256–58
Boniface VIII, Pope, 270–71
Book on the Divine Offices, The (Rupert of Deutz), 143–44
Borromeo, Charles, 1–2, 71
bread
 chief objections to unleavened, 165–66
 Council of Ferrara-Florence, discussion at, 3–5
 and early Christian practices, 7–8
 and East-West polemic, 113n.208, 168
bread and leaven, in biblical tradition
 and contaminants in leaven, 81–85, 83n.28
 issues in contention, 79–80, 124n.53, 127
 Last Supper, disputed chronology of, 90–101
 scriptural references, 80–85, 80n.6
 spurious texts regarding, 114–15, 115n.217, 115n.218
bread and leaven, in patristic tradition
 Ambrose of Milan, 86–87
 Ambrosiaster, 88–89
 Augustine of Hippo, 87
 Chrysostom, John, 85–86, 85n.42, 88
 Cyril of Alexandria, 87
 and Eucharist in the early church, 108–14, 108n.181, 110n.194
 Irenaeus of Lyons, 86, 86n.44
 issues in contention, 79–80, 127
 Judaism, tradition of unleavened bread in, 89–90
 Last Supper, disputed chronology of, 90–101
 leaven, symbolic connotations of, 87–90, 87n.54
 leaven and the fathers of the church, 85–90
 Origen, 88n.61
 parable of the leaven, 86n.44
 spurious texts regarding, 114–15, 115n.217, 115n.218
 See also Last Supper, in patristic tradition
bread of the Eucharist, in the early church, 108–14, 108n.181

Bread of the Eucharist, The (Wooley), 112–13n.204
Break the Holy Bread, Master (Sveshnikov), 186
Breviloquium (Bonaventure), 256
Brown, Raymond, 94–95
Bruno of Segni, 56
Buchard of Bellevaux, 57–58, 57n.135

calendars, and disputed chronology of Last Supper, 92–93
Catherine of Genoa, 293, 293n.119
celibacy, as prerequisite for ordination, 46n.59
Cesarini, Cardinal, 277–78, 290–91
Chalcedon, Canon of, 130, 130n.94
Charlemagne, Roman style and dress, 40
Charles the Great. *See* Charlemagne, Roman style and dress
Chesterton, G. K., 74–75, 74–75n.256
Chomatenos, Demetrios, 154, 154n.22
Choniates, Michael, 61–62
Choniates, Niketas, 61
Chrysostom, John, 31–32, 85–86, 85n.42, 88, 104–5, 111
 intercessory prayers for the dead, 206, 206n.115
 purification by fire, 212–13, 213n.155
City of God (Augustine of Hippo), 227
Clement of Alexandria, 25–27, 25n.61, 25n.62, 105–6, 208–9
clerical beards
 in early Christian literature, 5–7
 Greek and Latin customs, 1–3
Collins, Raymond, 193, 193n.27
Comester, Peter, 238–39
Commentary on Galatians (Victorinus), 87–88
Commentary on the Gospel of John (Thomas Aquinas), 166–67n.105
Commentary on the Sentences (Bonaventure), 164–65
Commentary on the Sentences (Matthew of Aquasparta), 163–65
"Concerning Those Who Have Fallen Asleep in the Faith," 216–17
Confessio (Kritopoulos), 297–98
Confessio (Lukaris), 298
Constantinople, conquest of, 60–61, 60n.160, 152–53

Constantinopolitan synod, *Encyclical on Latin Innovations* (1838), 302–3
Contra Errores Graecorum (Thomas Aquinas), 166–67
Conzelmann, Hans, 193–94n.29
crumbs, and breaking of the bread, 125
crusader indulgence, 234–35, 235n.12
cultural differences, in East-West polemic, 39, 39n.3
Cyprian of Carthage, 31, 110–11, 220–21
Cyprus
  martyrdom of monks on, 157–59, 157–58nn.45–48, 158n.51, 160–61, 168–69
  and tensions over purgatory, 253
Cyril of Alexandria, 87
Cyril of Jerusalem, 205–6

Daley, Brian, 220n.204, 223n.224
Damian, Peter, 125–26, 125n.59
Dante Alighieri, 269–70
Date of the Last Supper, The (Jaubert), 91–94
Day of the Dead, 234
debt, as metaphor for sin, 194–96, 195n.44, 278
De Erroribus Graecorum (John-Jerome of Prague), 173–74
De Fabrica Mundi, 103
Dialogue of Panagiotes with an Azymite, 65–66, 170–71, 267
Didache, 207–8
Didascalia Apostolorum, 101–3, 103n.144
Divina Commedia (Dante Alighieri), 269–70
Dogmatic Theology (Androutsos), 303–4
Dominic of Grado, 125–26
Dondaine, Antoine, 115n.218
Dositheus of Jerusalem, 300–2
"Dream of Gerontius, The," 304–5
Durandus, Guillaume, 56n.124

Encyclical on Latin Innovations (1838), 302–3, 302n.184
Encyclical to the Eastern Patriarchs, 42–44
Epictetus, 15n.6, 21n.32
Epiphanius, 27–28, 102–3
Essene hypothesis, and disputed date of Last Supper, 91–94, 92n.78
Eucharist, debates regarding matter and form, 162–64, 173, 177–78, 181, 181n.214
Eucharist, in the early church, 108–14, 108n.181, 110n.194

Ambrose of Milan, 110
Augustine of Hippo, 111, 111n.196
Chrysostom, John, 111
Cyprian of Carthage, 110–11
Irenaeus of Lyons, 110
Eucharist Words of Jesus (Jeremias), 98
eunuchs, and beardlessness, 40–41, 41n.11
Eusebius, 105, 105n.161
Eustathios of Thessaloniki, 59–60
Exposition on the Psalms (Augustine of Hippo), 29–30

Fantinus Vallaresso, 179
Ferrara-Florence, Council of, 2–5, 175–86, 269–74
  aftermath, 178–79, 178n.192
  Andreas Chrysoberges, Archbishop of Rhodes, 179–80
  Eucharist, debates regarding matter and form, 177–78
  Fantinus Vallaresso, 179
  John of Torquemada, 176, 282–84, 282n.47
  Kritopoulos, Metrophanes, 181–83, 182n.221
  Mark of Ephesus, 178–80, 284–89
  Plousiadenos, John, 178–79, 178n.197
  preparation of delegates, 281–82n.42
  and purgatory, 276–91
  repentance, perfect *vs.* imperfect, 288–89, 288–89n.90
  and subsequent ecumenical dialogue, 10–12, 10n.43
Filioque, and Council of Ferrara-Florence, 2–5, 5n.24
First Crusade, azyme debate and, 135–44
  Alger of Liège, 144
  Anselm of Canterbury, 142–43
  Barsalibi, Dionysius, 140–41, 140n.166
  Guibert of Nogent, 141–42, 142n.176
  Malaterra, Geoffredo, 141
  Rupert of Deutz, 143–44
  Symeon II, Patriarch of Jerusalem, 136–38
  Urban II, Pope, 141
Florovsky, Georges, 305
Fourth Lateran Council, 156–57
Francis of Assisi, 68–69, 68n.214
Fundamentals of Catholic Dogma (Ott), 304

Germanos II, Patriarch, 251
Gesta Dei per Francos, 141–42

INDEX 371

Glykas, Michael, 241–43, 245–47
Gnilka, Joachim, 192–94
Gregory IX, Pope, 158, 158–59n.54
Gregory of Nazianzus, 214, 214nn.163–67
Gregory of Nyssa, 215–16, 215nn.171–72
Gregory the Great, and tradition of purgatory, 228–30
Gregory VII, Pope, 50–51, 133–34
Grimlaicus, 33
Guerric of Saint-Quentin, 163
Guibert of Nogent, 141–42, 142n.176
Guido de Monte Rochen, 168–69

Handbook for Curates (Guido de Monte Rochen), 168–69
Hart, David Bentley, 311–12, 311n.242
Heresies of the Franks and Their Neighbors, The, 171
Hilary of Poitiers, 89, 221
Hildegard of Bingen, 237
Homilies for Advent (Venerable Bede), 231
Humbert, Cardinal, 48–49, 121, 122–26
 and Keroularios, Patriarch Michael, 131–33
 and Niketas Stethatos, 127–31, 128n.79, 128n.80, 130n.95

indulgences
 challenge of Protestant Reformation, 292–93
 introduction of, 234–35
 to pilgrims, 270–71
Inferno (Dante Alighieri), 269–70
Innocent III, Pope, 60–61, 60–61n.162, 149–50
 on Greek and Latin religious debates, 156–57, 156n.38
Innocent IV, Pope, 253–54, 253n.141
Irenaeus of Lyons, 86, 86n.44, 104, 110
Islam, and beards in East-West polemic, 53
Ist 1 Kor 3, 10–15 ein Schriftzeugnis für das Fegfeuer? (Gnilka), 192–94

Jaubert, Annie, 91–94
Jeremias, Joachim, 96–98
Jerome, 31–32, 89
Joachim of Fiore, 58–59, 59n.153
Johannine hypothesis, and disputed date of Last Supper, 91, 94–97, 95n.94
John IV, Patriarch of Antioch, 135–37

John-Jerome of Prague, 173–74, 174n.164
John of Torquemada, 176, 282–84, 282n.47
John XI Bekkos, Patriarch of Constantinople, 65
Josephus, Flavius, 93–94, 93n.85
Judaism, tradition of unleavened bread in, 89–90, 142–43
 See also Last Supper, disputed chronology of
Julian the Apostate, 24, 24n.56

Keroularios, Patriarch Michael, 48–49, 49n.78, 121, 122, 131–33
Klawans, Jonathan, 98
Knights Templar, 58
Kolbaba, Tia, 119n.14, 119n.19
Kritopoulos, Metrophanes, 181–83, 182n.221, 297–98

Lactantius, 221
La date de la cène (Jaubert), 91–94
Laetentur Caeli, 177, 177n.183
Larchet, Jean-Claude, 243, 305–6, 311
Last Supper, disputed chronology of, 90–101, 107–8, 163–65, 164n.82, 164n.85, 166–67n.105
 Essene hypothesis, 91–94, 92n.78, 92–93n.80, 93n.85
 Johannine hypothesis, 91, 94–97, 95n.94, 95n.97
 Passover hypothesis, 91, 99–101, 99n.124, 99n.127
 postponements of Passover, 174–75, 175n.168, 182n.223
 solar *vs.* lunar calendars, 92–93
 Synoptic hypothesis, 91, 97–98, 97n.115
 See also Judaism, tradition of unleavened bread in
Last Supper, in patristic tradition, 101–8, 113–14n.211
 Augustine of Hippo, 92n.78, 105n.160
 Chrysostom, John, 104–5
 Clement of Alexandria, 105–6
 Didascalia Apostolorum, 101–3, 103n.144
 Eusebius, 105, 105n.161
 Irenaeus of Lyons, 104
 Peter of Alexandria, 106–7
leaven and bread, in biblical tradition
 and contaminants in leaven, 81–85, 83n.28
 Irenaeus of Lyons, 86n.44

leaven and bread, in biblical tradition (*cont.*)
  issues in contention, 79–80, 124n.53, 127
  Last Supper, disputed chronology of, 90–101
  scriptural references, 80–85, 80n.6
  spurious texts regarding, 114–15, 115n.217, 115n.218
leaven and bread, in patristic tradition
  Ambrose of Milan, 86–87
  Ambrosiaster, 88–89
  Augustine of Hippo, 87
  Chrysostom, John, 85–86, 85n.42, 88
  Cyril of Alexandria, 87
  Eucharist in the early church, 108–14, 108n.181, 110n.194
  Irenaeus of Lyons, 86
  issues in contention, 79–80, 127
  Judaism, tradition of unleavened bread in, 89–90
  Last Supper, disputed chronology of, 90–101
  leaven, symbolic connotations of, 87–90, 87n.54
  leaven and the fathers of the church, 85–90
  Origen, 88n.61
  parable of the leaven, 86n.44
  spurious texts regarding, 114–15, 115n.217, 115n.218
  See also Last Supper, in patristic tradition
Leo IX, Pope, 121, 121n.31
Leo of Ohrid, 119–22, 119n.17, 120n.22
Leo XIII, Pope, 185–86
Letter to All Christians (Pseudo-Athanasios), 171
Letter to Antonianus (Cyprian of Carthage), 220
Letter to Eustochium (Jerome), 31–32
Leviticus, and beards in biblical tradition, 18–19, 18n.15, 19n.18, 28
limbo, described, 252n.127
Limoges, Council of, 48
Longer Catechism of the Orthodox, Catholic, Eastern Church (1905), 303
Lukaris, Cyril, 298
Luther, Martin, 292–93, 292n.113, 292–93n.114, 294–95
  on beards, 1–2, 1n.6
  purgatory as theological issue, 11
Luz, Ulrich, 106n.168
Lyons, Second Council of, 169–75
  and aftermath, 262–69–263nn.213–17, 264–264–65nn.218–25
  Blastares, Matthew, 171–72
  Dialogue of Panagiotes with an Azymite, 170–71
  Eucharist, debates regarding matter and form, 173
  John-Jerome of Prague, 173–74, 174n.164
  Michael VIII, Emperor, 169–70
  Zoest, Hermann, 174–75

Macarius, metropolitan of Moscow, 298–99, 298–99n.159
Magnus, Albert, 254–57
Malaterra, Geofreddo, 141
Manual against the Calvinist Insanity (Dositheos), 301–2
Manual of Polemical Theology (Pérov), 298n.158
Mark of Ephesus, 178–80, 278–79, 278n.18, 278n.20, 279n.23
  and Council of Ferrara-Florence, 284–89, 285n.66
  in post-Florentine period, 291–92
Matthew of Aquasparta, 163–65
Meier, John, 95n.97, 96n.102
Michael VIII, Emperor, 169–70, 262–69, 265n.229
Michael VIII Palaeologos, 64–65, 64n.188
Miniatis, Elias, 296
modesty, and beards in patristic tradition, 31–32, 37
Mohyla, Peter, 299–300, 299–300nn.165–67
monastic tradition, beards and, 32–33, 46–47
Moreira, Isabel, 191–92
Morosini, Thomas, 60–61, 60–61n.162
Mystical Catechesis, 205–6

Nazirite vow, and beards in biblical tradition, 17–18, 17–18n.12
Newman, John Henry, 304–5
Nicholas I, Pope, 41–43, 42n.24
Nicholas of Otranto, 62–63
Nicodemus the Hagorite, 32
Nikephoros the Hesychast, 265–67, 267n.244
Niketas Choniates, 152–53, 153n.11
Niketas of Nicomedia, 144–46
Nothaft, C. Philipp, 124–25
Numbers, and beards in biblical tradition, 18

Ombres, Robert, 307
On the Apparel of Women (Tertullian), 31
On the Customs of the Italians
 (Homologetes), 171
On the Errors of the Latins
 (Theophylact), 52–53
On the Soul (Stethatos), 245–46, 246n.84,
 246n.85
"On the Theology of Indulgences"
 (Rahner), 306–7
Opusculum contra Francos, 58–59, 138
Origen, 88n.61, 89
Origen of Alexandria, 209–14, 210n.142,
 210–11n.143, 211n.144, 211n.146,
 211n.149, 212n.151
Orthodox Confession of the Catholic and
 Apostolic Eastern Church (Mohyla),
 299–300, 299–300nn.165–67
Ott, Ludwig, 304
Owein, 236

Panagiotes, 170–71, 171n.135
Panarion, The (Epiphanius), 27–28
Parastron, John, 263, 263n.216
Passion of Perpetua and Felicity, 217–18
Passover, three ways of understanding, 164n.88
Passover hypothesis, and disputed date
 of Last Supper, 91, 99–101, 99n.124,
 99n.127
Paul, Apostle, 189–90, 190n.6
Paulinus of Nola, 221
Paul VI, Pope, 306
penitential system, 234–35
Peter, Saint, legend of tonsure, 35–36,
 45, 49–50
Peter III of Antioch, 49–50, 125–27, 126n.63,
 126n.64, 127n.74, 132–33
Peter of Alexandria, 106–7
Peter the Deacon, 146–47
Philaret of Moscow, 303
Photios, Patriarch of Constantinople, 41–
 43, 43n.27
Pierre d'Ailly, 162–63
Pistis Sophia, 206–7, 207n.119, 207n.120
Pitre, Brant, 95–96, 99–101, 100n.130
Pius IX, Pope, 185, 185n.243
Plousiadenos, John, 178–79, 178n.197
Protestant Reformation, 292–96, 293n.115,
 293n.117, 295n.134
 attitudes toward beards, 72

form and matter of Eucharist, 180–81,
 181n.216
Pseudo-Athanasius, 245, 245n.78
Purgatorio (Dante Alighieri), 269–70
purgatory
 Council of Ferrara-Florence, discussion at,
 3–5, 4n.16, 9–10
 and early Christian tradition, 9–10
purgatory, and classifications of people, 235–
 36, 235–36n.13
purgatory, from Ferrara-Florence to modern
 times, 275–76, 275n.2
 Bessarion, 279–81, 280n.35, 281n.38
 Catherine of Genoa, 293, 293n.119
 Cesarini, Cardinal, 277–78, 290–91
 Constantinopolitan synod, *Encyclical on*
 Latin Innovations (1838), 302–3,
 302n.184
 The Council of Ferrara-Florence, 276–91
 debt, as metaphor for sin, 278
 Dositheus of Jerusalem, 300–2
 indulgences, 292–93
 intercessory prayers and alms, 285,
 285n.64, 295–96
 John of Torquemada, 282–84, 282n.47
 Kritopoulos, Metrophanes, 297–98
 Longer Catechism of the Orthodox,
 Catholic, Eastern Church (1905), 303
 Lukaris, Cyril, 298
 Luther, Martin, 292–93, 292n.113, 292–
 93n.114, 294–95
 Macarius, metropolitan of Moscow, 298–
 99, 298–99n.159
 Mark of Ephesus, 278–79, 278n.18,
 278n.20, 279n.23, 284–89
 Mark of Ephesus, in post-Florentine
 period, 291–92
 Mohyla, Peter, 299–300,
 299–300nn.165–67
 post-Florentine period, 291–303
 Protestant Reformation, 292–96, 293n.115,
 293n.117, 295n.134
 and punishment after death, 301–2
 purgative fire, 296–98
 repentance, perfect *vs.* imperfect, 288–89,
 288–89n.90
 Scholarios, George Gennadios, 292,
 292n.112
 Theophilus of Campania, 298, 298n.156
 tollhouse tradition, 298–99

purgatory, in biblical tradition, 189–203, 191n.13
  biblical ideals, 194–95, 194n.38, 194n.39
  debt as metaphor for sin, 194–96, 195n.44
  postmortem purification, 201–2, 202n.88
  prayers of intersession on behalf of the dead, 197–200, 197nn.58–59, 197–98n.60
  punishments after death, 196
  and purity of God, 200–1
  scriptural images, 191–92
  scriptural text, 192–94, 192n.20, 193n.23, 202–3
purgatory, in Eastern patristic tradition, 189–91, 203–17
  intercessory prayers and alms, 204–6, 204n.105, 205n.112
  postmortem fate of souls, 203–4, 204n.99
  purgative fire, 215–16
  purification by fire, 206–9, 214–16
purgatory, in thirteenth and fourteenth centuries, 233–34
  Alexander of Hale, 241
  Bardanes, George, 249–51
  beginnings of dispute, 249–62
  Byzantine background, 241–48
  Day of the Dead, 234
  Ferrara-Florence, Council of, 269–74
  Glykas, Michael, 241–43, 245–47
  and Hildegard of Bingen, 237
  Innocent IV, Pope, 253–54, 253n.141
  intercessory prayers and alms, 247–48, 248n.100
  introduction of proper noun, 238–40, 238n.25, 240n.41
  Latin background, 234–41
  limbo, described, 252n.127
  Michael VIII, Emperor, 262–69
  penitential system and indulgences, 234–35, 270–71
  Pseudo-Athanasius, 245, 245n.78
  punishments after death, 271–73
  purgatory, and classifications of people, 235–36, 235–36n.13
  purification by fire, 237–39
  and Second Council of Lyons, 262–69
  St. Patrick, 236, 236n.18
  Stethatos, Niketas, 245–46, 246n.84, 246n.85
  tollhouse tradition, 243n.61, 244n.70
  tollhouse tradition, and purgatory, 243–45
  William of Auvergne, 240–41
purgatory, in Western patristic tradition, 189–91, 217–32
  Ambrose of Milan, 222–23, 222n.212, 222n.213, 222n.218
  Ambrosiaster, 223
  Augustine of Hippo, 223–28, 224n.231, 224n.233, 224n.234, 224–25n.236–225–26nn.237–42, 226–226–27nn.246–54
  Cyprian of Carthage, 220–21
  geography of afterlife, 230
  Hilary of Poitiers, 221
  Lactantius, 221
  Paulinus of Nola, 221
  Pope Gregory the Great, 228–30
  postmortem fate of souls, 219–20
  Tertullian, 219–20, 219nn.194–95
purgatory, twentieth and twenty-first centuries, 303–12
  Androutsos, Christos, 303–4
  Catholic reimaginings, 306–9
  Hart, David Bentley, 311–12
  internal Orthodox divisions, 305–6, 309–11
  Newman, John Henry, 304–5
  and punishment after death, 303–4
  purgative fire, 304, 304n.195
  and universal salvation in Orthodox theology, 311–12

Quinisext Council, 32, 32n.113

Rahner, Karl, 306–7
Ratramnus of Corbie, 44–45
Ratzinger, Cardinal Joseph (Benedict XVI, Pope), 307–9, 308n.223
Refutation of the Errors of the Latins (Blastares), 171–72
repentance, perfect *vs.* imperfect, 288–89, 288–89n.90
Rock of Offense (Miniatis), 296
Rules for Solitaires (Grimlaicus), 33
Rupert of Deutz, 143–44
Ruthenians, 295

Sacrifice of Leavened and Unleavened Bread, The (Anselm of Canterbury), 142–43
Samson, and beards in biblical tradition, 17

Samuel, and beards in biblical tradition, 17–18
Sardinia and Sardinian Church, 50–51
Scholarios, George Gennadios, 292, 292n.112
Severus, Gabriel, 296
Shepherd of Hermas, 207–8, 207n.124, 208n.125
Short Treatise against the Purgatorial Fire of the Papists (Argenti), 302
Sicard of Cremona, 55–56
Smith, Mahlon, 116
spiritual strength, beards and, 56
St. Patrick, 236, 236n.18
Stethatos, Niketas, 127–31, 129n.90, 130n.95, 245–46, 246n.84, 246n.85
Stilbes, Konstantinos, 61–62
Story about How Rome Fell from the Orthodox Faith, A, 66n.197
Symeon II, Patriarch of Jerusalem, 136–38
Symeon of Thessalonika, 67, 173, 273–74, 274n.297
Synoptic hypothesis, and disputed date of Last Supper, 91, 97–98, 97n.115, 98n.117

Tafur, Pero, 67–68
Tertullian, 31, 219, 219nn.194–95
That All Shall Be Saved (Hart), 311–12
Theophilus of Campania, 298, 298n.156
Theophylact of Ohrid, 52–53, 135n.128, 135n.129
Theorianos, 147–48
Thessaloniki, sacking of, 59–60, 60n.159
Thomas Aquinas
  intercessory prayer and alms, 261nn.200–3
  and Nikephoros the Hesychast, 265–67, 267n.244
  pains of purgatory, 261n.199, 262n.205, 262n.208
  and proper matter for Eucharist, 165–67, 166–67n.105
  on purgatory, 258–62, 258nn.180–82, 259nn.183–87, 260n.192, 260nn.194–95, 260–61n.198
Thomas of Strassburg, 115n.217
tollhouse tradition
  and internal Orthodox divisions, 309–11
  and purgatory, 243–45, 243n.61, 244n.70, 298–99, 303–4
Tractatus contra Graecos, 160–61, 251–53
Treasure of Orthodoxy (Theophilus of Campania), 298, 298n.156
Treatise against Unleavened Bread (Argenti), 183–84, 184n.235
Treatise on Purgatory (Catherine of Genoa), 293
Trent, Council of, 293–94, 293–94n.120

universal salvation, and Orthodox theology, 311–12
Urban II, Pope, 141

Valeriano, Pierio, 70–71
Venerable Bede, 112–13, 112n.203, 231
Victorinus, Marius, 87–88
Victorinus of Petau, 103
Vision of Dryhthelm, 230, 230n.275
Visio Sancti Pauli, 218–19, 218n.188

William of Auvergne, 163, 163n.78, 240–41
William of Meliton, 162–63
Wooley, Reginald, 112–13n.204

Zoest, Hermann, 174–75